American Immigrant Cultures

Editorial Board

EDITORS IN CHIEF

David Levinson
Berkshire Reference Works, Great Barrington, MA

Melvin Ember
Human Relations Area Files, New Haven, CT

ADVISORY EDITORS

Nancy Foner
State University of New York, Purchase

Steven J. Gold
Michigan State University

Faye V. Harrison
University of Tennessee

Arthur W. Helweg
Western Michigan University

Harry H. L. Kitano
University of California, Los Angeles

Rubén G. Rumbaut
Michigan State University

Marcelo M. Suárez-Orozco
Harvard University

Robert Theodoratus
Colorado State University

AMERICAN IMMIGRANT CULTURES

Builders of a Nation

Edited by

DAVID LEVINSON
MELVIN EMBER

Volume 1

BLOOMINGTON, ILLINOIS PUBLIC LIBRARY

MACMILLAN REFERENCE USA
Simon & Schuster Macmillan
NEW YORK

Simon & Schuster and Prentice Hall International
London   Mexico City   New Delhi   Singapore   Sydney   Toronto

R
305.8
AME
V. 1

American Immigrant Cultures was prepared under the auspices and with the support of the Human Relations Area Files at Yale University. HRAF, the foremost international research organization in the field of cultural anthropology, is a not-for-profit consortium of twenty-three sponsoring members and three hundred participating member institutions in twenty-five countries. The HRAF archive, established in 1949, contains nearly one million pages of information on the cultures of the world.

Copyright © 1997 by Simon & Schuster Macmillan

All rights reserved. No part of this book may be reproduced or transmitted in any form or by any means, electronic or mechanical, including photocopying, recording, or by any information storage and retrieval system, without permission in writing from the Publisher.

Simon & Schuster Macmillan
1633 Broadway
New York, NY 10019

Printed in the United States of America

Printing Number
1 2 3 4 5 6 7 8 9 10

Library of Congress Cataloging-in-Publication Data

American immigrant cultures: builders of a nation / David Levinson
    and Melvin Ember, editors in chief.
        p.   cm.
    Includes bibliographical references and index.
    ISBN 0-02-897214-7 (vol. 1: alk. paper) — ISBN 0-02-897213-9
(vol. 2: alk. paper) — ISBN 0-02-897208-2 (set: alk. paper).
    1. Minorities–United States.   2. Ethnicity–United States.
3. Immigrants–United States.   4. United States–Ethnic relations.
I. Levinson, David.   II. Ember, Melvin.
E184.A1A63448   1997
305.8′00973–dc21   97-17477
                                                                                      CIP

This paper meets the requirements of ANSI-NISO Z39.48-1992 (Permanence of Paper).

CONTENTS

Preface   vii

List of Articles   xi

List of Contributors   xvii

American Immigrant Cultures   **1**

Appendix   959

Index   1019

Editorial and Production Staff

Brian Kinsey
Project Editor

William D. Drennan
Copy Editor

Helen Wallace
Proofreader

Robert J. Sullivan
Cartographer

Doyle Graphics
Compositor

Katharyn Dunham
Indexer

Paul Wells
Production Manager

MACMILLAN REFERENCE
Elly Dickason, *Publisher*
Paul Bernabeo, *Editor in Chief*

PREFACE

The United States is a nation of immigrants. Since the Declaration of Independence, but especially since the mid-nineteenth century, the United States has received an enormous number of immigrants from all over the world. This transfer of population has produced perhaps the most ethnically diverse country in the world (India being the closest rival). People from every nation in the world and from many distinct cultural groups within those nations now live in the United States. Although people from some nations or groups are few in number and do not form large or visible ethnic communities in the United States, many do. Americans vary in their evaluations of this diversity; some are proud of it, and some reject it. President Bill Clinton addressed this ambivalence in his 1997 State of the Union speech:

> We must never believe that diversity is a weakness—it is our greatest strength. Americans speak every language, know every country. People on every continent can look to us and see the reflection of their own greatness, as long as we give all of our citizens, whatever their background, an opportunity to achieve their greatness. We are not there yet. We still see evidence of abiding bigotry and intolerance, in ugly words and awful violence, in burned churches and bombed buildings. We must fight against this in our country and in our hearts.

Despite the ambivalence about immigration, despite government policies that have at times restricted the flow of immigrants or certain categories of immigrants such as Asians or southern Europeans, and despite other policies that have discriminated against groups such as African Americans, the United States continues to be a nation of immigrants, more so now in some ways than ever before. Immigrants arrive every day, in large numbers, from many countries, and the immigration of some groups has accelerated in the 1990s. Indeed, it is probably accurate to say that, given the opportunity, many millions of people all over the world would move to the United States tomorrow.

But even if most immigrants have sought or would seek assimilation into American culture and society, not all groups have assimilated to the same degree, and even the most assimilated may retain some beliefs and customs of their homelands. *American Immigrant Cultures* is about this ethnic diversity. It is an up-to-date, comprehensive, and authoritative compendium of knowledge about the nonindigenous cultural groups of the United States. By "nonindigenous" we mean groups who arrived and stayed in the United States after Native Americans were already there. This includes groups such as the English, Scots, Dutch, French, and Spanish who were the first to arrive in what was to become the United States, the many other European and Asian groups who began arriving in the nineteenth century, and the groups who arrived after the Immigration Act of 1965 was enacted. This work does not cover the indigenous peoples of the United States—American Indians, Eskimo peoples, Aleutian Islanders, and native Hawaiians. These groups are, however, covered in the *Encyclopedia of World Cultures*, previously published by Macmillan.

In these volumes, we provide descriptive profiles of 161 groups, commonly labeled ethnic groups. Two key tasks in developing this project were deciding what is an ethnic group and what groups to cover in this work. We took a broad and pragmatic approach to resolving these issues. We decided to define a group as an ethnic group if members of the group or members of other groups consider it to be a distinct cultural entity. The basis of that distinctiveness is most commonly place of birth, place of ancestors' birth, physical features (race), religion, and language, as well as various combinations of these factors. Thus, the Irish are considered an ethnic group because of their or their ancestors' place of birth, Mexicans because of place of birth and language, African Americans because of their skin color and ancestors' homelands, Jews mainly because of their religion, and so on.

While social scientists continue to debate what ethnic identification means and how it may change, we have proceeded from the perspective that ethnic group identity is mainly a cultural phenomenon—people assign and are assigned ethnic identities. As a cultural phenomenon, ethnic identity is not fixed in place or time. Thus a group may stress its identity or downplay it at different points in time or from one situation to another. Similarly, any individual may be defined differently by others at different times or in different social situations. For example, Jamaicans in the United States see themselves as a distinct ethnic group, based to a large extent on place of birth (Jamaica), language (Jamaican English), and sharing the basic elements of Jamaican culture. However, other Americans of African ancestry but not Caribbean birth may define Jamaicans as West Indians and thereby lump them with other people of African ancestry from the Caribbean, such as Barbadians. White Americans might go even further and lump all Americans of African ancestry into one ethnic group (African American) without any finer distinctions. This variation in ethnic identity also operates at the individual level. The historically strong assimilation pressures in American society require that people act "American" when interacting with other Americans while these same individuals may act more "ethnic" when with co-ethnics. For example, a person of Italian or Jewish ancestry might speak only in English in business, but with family and friends or other Italians or Jews that individual might also use Italian or

Yiddish sayings that communicate culturally meaningful information that cannot be readily communicated in English. Use of the ethnic language, as well as adherence to ethnic customs, also tends to reinforce group identity and helps define who is "us" and who is "them."

As with the concept of ethnic identity, we have also taken a broad view as to what groups to cover in this work. In this regard we have taken a broader and more inclusive approach than other surveys of U.S. ethnic groups that tend to focus mainly on nationality (country of origin) or region of origin. Many nations in the world have ethnically heterogeneous populations, and we want to reflect that diversity in this survey of immigrant groups in the United States. Thus we have not limited our coverage to nationalities, such as Asian Indians or Lebanese, because to do so would mask significant cultural variation that often continues to be expressed in the United States. We do not treat Asian Indians as a group because they are not a single ethnic group. Instead, we cover the major ethnic groups from India in separate articles: Bengalis, Biharis, Gujaratis, Jains, Maharashtrians, Malayalam Speakers, Punjabis, Sikhs, Tamils, and Telugus. To assist readers who may not be aware of these distinctions, we include "See" entries; for example, there is an entry for Asian Indians, but it merely includes cross-references to the separate articles on the different groups from India. Similarly, we include separate articles on groups from one nation, even though they may be culturally similar in some ways, if they have adapted differently to life in the United States. For example, we cover Mexicans in four articles—Mexicans (the recent immigrants), Mexicans of the Southwest, Californios, and Punjabi Mexicans—with "See also" cross-references provided to guide the reader to the other related articles. This approach to the development of the project plan produced the list of 161 groups covered in these two volumes.

Of course, coverage of all groups is not equal, although we have tried to see that the same basic information is provided for all groups. Coverage is not equal for a number of reasons. First, the kinds of information on which these articles are based—historical, sociological, and anthropological studies of the groups—vary in quantity, depth of coverage, breadth of coverage, and timeliness across the groups. Some groups such as Mexicans, Japanese, Poles, and Italians are described in enormously rich literatures. Others are barely covered at all. And some are so poorly documented that the authors of the articles in this reference work had to conduct original research to complete their assignments.

The information we have assembled for each group includes

1. Name of the group, alternative names, and names of major subgroups.
2. Defining features of the group that cause group members and/or outsiders to define the group as unique in American society.
3. Patterns of cultural variation within the group, both over time and place.
4. Immigration and settlement history, including some basic information about the nations of origin.
5. Demographic facts, including population and composition, changes in population, and current distribution in the United States. (To some extent the authors have relied on census data for this information, but other sources have been used for groups not counted separately in the census, and additional information has been provided when experts consider the census data to be less than adequate.)
6. Languages spoken on arrival in the United States and subsequent changes in language use.
7. Cultural characteristics of the group, including but not limited to economic patterns, housing, religion, worldview, marriage and family, kinship, interpersonal relationships, the arts, health and illness, social organization, and political organization. (Attention is given to variation within the group as well as general or overall patterns.)
8. Extent of assimilation or cultural persistence, including degree and types of discrimination, relations with other groups, changes over time and place, pan-ethnic ties, and transnational ties.
9. Bibliographic citations with an emphasis on articles and books available to the general reader.

This detailed research by the authors has, in many instances, been augmented with photographic illustrations. Additional information designed to serve as a companion to that provided by the authors in relation to their particular ethnic groups is located in the appendix section of this publication. A series of world maps has been designed to provide the reader with a clear idea concerning the geographical origins of the various groups. Tables in the appendix provide state-by-state statistical breakdowns of the ethnic populations as reported in the 1990 U.S. Census. The cultural information provided by the individual authors is also augmented with a list of the major holidays that continue to be celebrated by many of these ethnic groups after their immigration to the United States.

While we have tried to provide this basic information for all groups, the purpose of *American Immigrant Cultures* is not just to provide basic descriptive and historical information. It is meant to provide profiles of each group that give the reader a sense of what the key cultural features of the group are, along with the key issues or problems it faces in American society.

The creation of *American Immigrant Cultures* has been a group effort, and there are many people to acknowledge and thank. First, we want to thank the eight editorial advisors: Nancy Foner, Steven Gold, Faye Harrison, Arthur Helweg, Harry Kitano, Rubén Rumbaut, Marcelo Suárez-Orozco, and Robert Theodoratus. They were most helpful in developing the list of groups to cover and in recommending experts to write the articles. Arthur Helweg and Robert Theodoratus deserve special thanks for their efforts to locate experts who have recently studied the ethnic groups firsthand. In addition, although not on the advisory board, Nabeel Abraham, Paul Hockings, Abraham Rosman, Paula Rubel, and Adrian (Josh) DeWind also helped with these matters. Second, we wish to thank the people at Macmillan Library Reference, particularly Elly Dickason, the publisher, and Brian Kinsey, the project manager, for their sup-port and careful supervision of this work. Most of all, we thank our contributors. Without their knowledge and commitment, this work would not have been possible.

DAVID LEVINSON
MELVIN EMBER

LIST OF ARTICLES

A

Acadians and Cajuns
Carl A. Brasseaux

Afghans
Patricia A. Omidian
Juliene G. Lipson

African Americans
Lewis Walker
Benjamin C. Wilson

African Muslims
Sulayman S. Nyang

Albanians
Dennis L. Nagi

Amish
Gertrude Enders Huntington

Argentineans
Judith Freidenberg
Edit Masuelli

Armenians
Anny Bakalian

Austrians
Oliver Rathkolb

B

Bangladeshis
Michael S. Harris

Barbadians
Susan Makiesky Barrow

Basques
William A. Douglass

Belarusans
Vitaut Kipel

Belgians
William G. Laatsch

Bengalis
Naheed Islam

Biharis
R. S. Khare

Bosnian Muslims
Daniel Cetinich

Brazilians
Maxine L. Margolis

Buddhists
Thomas A. Tweed

Bulgarians
Katia McClain

Burmese
Michael W. Charney

C

Californios
James Diego Vigil

Cambodians
Rubén G. Rumbaut

Canadians
Arthur W. Helweg

Cape Verdeans
Marilyn Halter

Carpatho-Rusyns
Paul Robert Magocsi

Cham
    Eric Crystal

Chileans
    Carlos U. López

Chinese
    Bernard P. Wong

Chinese-Vietnamese
    Steven J. Gold

Circassians
    John Colarusso

Colombians
    Maria Dolores Espino

Cornish
    Shirley Ewart

Croatians
    Daniel Cetinich

Cubans
    Guillermo J. Grenier
    Lisandro Perez

Cypriots
    Stavros T. Constantinou

Czechs
    Zdenek Salzmann

D

Danes
    Marion T. Marzolf

Dominicans
    Eugenia Georges

Druze
    Rula Abisaab

Dutch
    Larry ten Harmsel

E

Ecuadorians
    Lauris McKee

Egyptian Copts
    Hany N. Takla
    Maged S. Mikhail
    Mark R. Moussa

Egyptian Muslims
    Walter Armbrust

English
    Arthur W. Helweg

Estonians
    M. Ann Walko

Ethiopians and Eritreans
    Tekle Mariam Woldemikael

F

Filipinos
    Cristina Szanton Blanc

Finns
    A. William Hoglund

French
    André J. M. Prévos

French Canadians
    Jean Lamarre

Frisians
    Philip E. Webber

G

Garifuna
    Catherine L. Macklin

Georgians
    Stephen Jones

Germans
    Jeremy W. Kilar

Germans from Russia
    Timothy J. Kloberdanz

Ghanaians
    Enid Schildkrout
    Ama B. Boakyewa

Greeks
Charles Moskos

Grenadians
Paula Aymer

Guamanians
Larry W. Mayo

Guatemalan Maya
Allan F. Burns

Gujaratis
Padma Rangaswamy

Guyanese
Susan Makiesky Barrow

Gypsies
Matt T. Salo

H

Haitians
Nina Glick Schiller
Carolle Charles

Hmong
Ray Hutchison

Hondurans
Sarah England
Walter L. Krochmal

Hungarians
Éva Veronika Huseby-Darvas

Hutterites
Jack Glazier

I

Icelanders
Playford V. Thorson

Igbo
Ifi Amadiume

Indo-Caribbeans
Parsram Sri Thakur

Indonesians
Clark E. Cunningham

Indos
Greta Kwik

Iranians
Mehdi Bozorgmehr

Iraqi Chaldeans
Mary C. Sengstock

Iraqi Muslims
Wanda E. Carlile

Irish
JoEllen McNergney Vinyard

Ismailis
Nizar A. Motani

Italians
Diane C. Vecchio

J

Jains
Holly A. Seeling

Jamaicans
Nancy Foner

Japanese
Mitchell T. Maki

Jews, European
Jack Glazier

Jews, Hasidic
Janet S. Belcove-Shalin

Jews, Israeli
Steven J. Gold

Jews, Middle Eastern
Marc D. Angel

Jews, Soviet
Steven J. Gold

Jordanians
Hani Fakhouri

K

Kalmyks
Arash Bormanshinov

Kashubians
Jan L. Perkowski

Khmu
Frank Proschan

Koreans
Pyong Gap Min

L

Lao
Frank Proschan

Latvians
Arnold Sildegs

Lebanese Christians
Linda S. Walbridge

Lebanese Muslims
Linda S. Walbridge

Lithuanians
Aleksandras Gedmintas

M

Macedonians
Peter Vasiliadis

Maharashtrians
Mahadev Apte

Malayalam Speakers
N. Prabha Unnithan

Mennonites
Jeffrey L. Longhofer

Mexicans
Leo R. Chavez

Mexicans of the Southwest
Carlos G. Vélez-Ibáñez

Mien
Eric Crystal

Montenegrins
Christopher Boehm

N

Nepalese
Ramesh K. Dhungel

Nicaraguans
Guillermo J. Grenier

Norwegians
Kaarin Lillehei-Bakhtiar

O

Okinawans
Mitsugu Sakihara

P

Pacific Islanders in Hawaii
Paul R. Spickard

Pakistanis
Salahuddin Malik

Palestinians
Rosina Hassoun

Panamanians
Roy S. Bryce-Laporte

Peruvians
Sarah J. Mahler
Alejandro F. Loarte

Poles
Andris Skreija

Portuguese
Bela Feldman-Bianco
James MacDonald

Puerto Ricans
Arlene Torres

Punjabi Mexicans
Karen Isaksen Leonard

Punjabis
Arthur W. Helweg

R

Romanians
G. James Patterson

Russian Molokans
Richard A. Morris
Serafima E. Nikitina

Russian Old Believers
Richard A. Morris

Russians
Eugene A. Alexandrov

S

Salvadorans
Sarah J. Mahler

Samoans
Robert W. Franco

Sardinians
Diane C. Vecchio

Scotch-Irish
John B. Rehder

Scots
John B. Rehder

Sea Islanders
Patricia Guthrie

Serbs
Andrei Simić
Joel M. Halpern

Sicilians
Diane C. Vecchio

Sikhs
Gurinder Singh Mann

Sindhis
Carol Kohn Sheikh

Sinhalese
H. L. Seneviratne

Slovaks
M. Mark Stolarik

Slovenes
Irene Portis-Winner

Sorbs
George R. Nielsen

South Asian Christians
Raymond Brady Williams

Spaniards
Oriol Pi-Sunyer
Susan M. DiGiacomo

Sri Lankans
H. L. Seneviratne

Swede-Finns
Robert Jarvenpa

Swedes
H. Arnold Barton

Swiss
Ervan G. Garrison

Syrians
Caesar E. Farah

T

Taiwanese
Shu-min Huang

Tamils
Vasudha Narayanan

Telugus
Rajagopal Vakulabharanam

Thai
Nantawan Boonprasat Lewis

Tibetans
Frank J. Korom

Tongans
Tamar Gordon

Travelers
Matt T. Salo

Trinidadians
Mahin Gosine

Turks
Barbara Bilgé

U

Ukrainians
Robert B. Klymasz

V

Vietnamese
Lucy Nguyen-Hong-Nhiem
Joel M. Halpern

Vlachs
Emil Vrabie

W

Welsh
D. Douglas Caulkins

Y

Yemenis
Jonathan Friedlander

Yoruba
George Brandon

Z

Zoroastrians
Janet Kestenberg Amighi
Afruz Sharron Amighi

LIST OF CONTRIBUTORS

Rula Abisaab
Yale University
Druze

Eugene A. Alexandrov
Queens College, Flushing, NY (emeritus)
Russians

Ifi Amadiume
Dartmouth College
Igbo

Afruz Sharron Amighi
Bryn Mawr College
Zoroastrians

Janet Kestenberg Amighi
Bryn Mawr College
Zoroastrians

Marc D. Angel
Congregation Shearith Israel, New York City
Jews, Middle Eastern

Mahadev Apte
Duke University
Maharashtrians

Walter Armbrust
University of Pennsylvania
Egyptian Muslims

Paula Aymer
Tufts University
Grenadians

Anny Bakalian
College of Notre Dame of Maryland
Armenians

H. Arnold Barton
Southern Illinois University, Carbondale
Swedes

Janet S. Belcove-Shalin
The National Conference,
Southern Nevada Region, Las Vegas
Jews, Hasidic

Barbara Bilgé
Eastern Michigan University
Turks

Ama B. Boakyewa
African Burial Ground, New York City
Ghanaians

Christopher Boehm
University of Southern California
Montenegrins

Arash Bormanshinov
Lanham-Seabrook, MD
Kalmyks

Mehdi Bozorgmehr
City College of the City University of New York
Iranians

George Brandon
City University of New York Medical School
Yoruba

Carl A. Brasseaux
University of Southwestern Louisiana
Acadians and Cajuns

Roy S. Bryce-Laporte
Colgate University
Panamanians

Allan F. Burns
University of Florida
Guatemalan Maya

Wanda E. Carlile
Center for Cultural Dynamics, Littleton, CO
Iraqi Muslims

D. Douglas Caulkins
Grinnell College
Welsh

Daniel Cetinich
City College of San Francisco
Bosnian Muslims
Croatians

Carolle Charles
Baruch College, City University of New York
Haitians

Michael W. Charney
University of Michigan
Burmese

Leo R. Chavez
University of California, Irvine
Mexicans

John Colarusso
McMaster University, Canada
Circassians

Stavros T. Constantinou
Ohio State University, Mansfield Campus
Cypriots

Eric Crystal
University of California, Berkeley
Cham
Mien

Clark E. Cunningham
University of Illinois, Urbana-Champaign
Indonesians

Ramesh K. Dhungel
Tribhuvan University, Nepal, and
Columbia University
Nepalese

Susan M. DiGiacomo
University of Massachusetts, Amherst
Spaniards

William A. Douglass
University of Nevada, Reno
Basques

Sarah England
University of California, Davis
Hondurans

Maria Dolores Espino
Florida International University
Colombians

Shirley Ewart
Portland Community College
Cornish

Hani Fakhouri
University of Michigan, Flint
Jordanians

Caesar E. Farah
University of Minnesota
Syrians

Bela Feldman-Bianco
Universidade Estadual de Campinas, Brazil
Portuguese

Nancy Foner
State University of New York, Purchase
Jamaicans

Robert W. Franco
Kapiolani Community College
Samoans

Judith Freidenberg
University of Maryland, College Park
Argentineans

Jonathan Friedlander
University of California, Los Angeles
Yemenis

Ervan G. Garrison
University of Georgia
Swiss

Aleksandras Gedmintas
State University of New York, Delhi
Lithuanians

Eugenia Georges
Rice University
Dominicans

Jack Glazier
Oberlin College
Hutterites
Jews, European

Nina Glick Schiller
  University of New Hampshire
    Haitians

Steven J. Gold
  Michigan State University
    Chinese-Vietnamese
    Jews, Israeli
    Jews, Soviet

Tamar Gordon
  Rensselaer Polytechnic Institute
    Tongans

Mahin Gosine
  State University of New York,
    Suffolk County Community College
    Trinidadians

Guillermo J. Grenier
  Florida International University
    Cubans
    Nicaraguans

Patricia Guthrie
  California State University, Hayward
    Sea Islanders

Joel M. Halpern
  University of Massachusetts, Amherst (emeritus)
    Serbs
    Vietnamese

Marilyn Halter
  Boston University
    Cape Verdeans

Larry ten Harmsel
  Western Michigan University
    Dutch

Michael S. Harris
  Florida Atlantic University
    Bangladeshis

Rosina Hassoun
  University of Michigan, Ann Arbor
    Palestinians

Arthur W. Helweg
  Western Michigan University
    Canadians
    English
    Punjabis

A. William Hoglund
  University of Connecticut
    Finns

Shu-min Huang
  Iowa State University
    Taiwanese

Gertrude Enders Huntington
  University of Michigan, Ann Arbor
    Amish

Éva Veronika Huseby-Darvas
  University of Michigan, Dearborn and Ann Arbor
    Hungarians

Ray Hutchison
  University of Wisconsin, Green Bay
    Hmong

Naheed Islam
  University of California, Berkeley
    Bengalis

Robert Jarvenpa
  State University of New York, Albany
    Swede-Finns

Stephen Jones
  Mount Holyoke College
    Georgians

R. S. Khare
  University of Virginia
    Biharis

Jeremy W. Kilar
  Delta College
    Germans

Vitaut Kipel
  Belarusan Institute of Arts and Sciences, Inc.,
    Rutherford, NJ
    Belarusans

Timothy J. Kloberdanz
  North Dakota State University
    Germans from Russia

Robert B. Klymasz
  Canadian Museum of Civilization, Hull
    Ukrainians

Carol Kohn Sheikh
Florida International University
Sindhis

Frank J. Korom
Museum of International Folk Art, Santa Fe, NM
Tibetans

Walter L. Krochmal
Federation of Honduran Organizations in New York
Hondurans

Greta Kwik
Los Angeles
Indos

William G. Laatsch
University of Wisconsin, Green Bay
Belgians

Jean Lamarre
Royal Military College of Canada
French Canadians

Karen Isaksen Leonard
University of California, Irvine
Punjabi Mexicans

Nantawan Boonprasat Lewis
Metropolitan State University
Thai

Kaarin Lillehei-Bakhtiar
Washington, DC
Norwegians

Juliene G. Lipson
University of California, San Francisco
Afghans

Alejandro F. Loarte
Queens, NY
Peruvians

Jeffrey L. Longhofer
University of Missouri, Kansas City
Mennonites

Carlos U. López
Menlo College
Chileans

James MacDonald
Washington, DC
Portuguese

Catherine L. Macklin
Institute for the Study of Social Change,
University of California, Berkeley
Garifuna

Paul Robert Magocsi
University of Toronto
Carpatho-Rusyns

Sarah J. Mahler
University of Vermont
Peruvians
Salvadorans

Mitchell T. Maki
University of California, Los Angeles
Japanese

Susan Makiesky Barrow
New York State Psychiatric Institute, New York City
Barbadians
Guyanese

Salahuddin Malik
State University of New York, Brockport
Pakistanis

Gurinder Singh Mann
Columbia University
Sikhs

Maxine L. Margolis
University of Florida
Brazilians

Marion T. Marzolf
University of Michigan, Ann Arbor (emeritus)
Danes

Edit Masuelli
Montclair University
Argentineans

Larry W. Mayo
DePaul University
Guamanians

Katia McClain
University of California, Santa Barbara
Bulgarians

Lauris McKee
Franklin and Marshall College
Ecuadorians

JoEllen McNergney Vinyard
Eastern Michigan University
Irish

Maged S. Mikhail
St. Shenouda, Archimandrite Coptic Society
Egyptian Copts

Pyong Gap Min
Queens College, City University of New York
Koreans

Richard A. Morris
University of Oregon, Eugene
Russian Molokans
Russian Old Believers

Charles Moskos
Northwestern University
Greeks

Nizar A. Motani
Atlanta, GA
Ismailis

Mark R. Moussa
St. Shenouda, Archimandrite Coptic Society
Egyptian Copts

Dennis L. Nagi
Hudson Valley Community College, Troy, NY
Albanians

Vasudha Narayanan
University of Florida
Tamils

Lucy Nguyen-Hong-Nhiem
University of Massachusetts, Amherst
Vietnamese

George R. Nielsen
Concordia University
Sorbs

Serafima E. Nikitina
Russian Academy of Sciences, Moscow
Russian Molokans

Sulayman S. Nyang
Howard University
African Muslims

Patricia A. Omidian
California State University, Hayward
Afghans

G. James Patterson
Eastern Oregon State College
Romanians

Lisandro Perez
Florida International University
Cubans

Jan L. Perkowski
University of Virginia
Kashubians

Oriol Pi-Sunyer
University of Massachusetts, Amherst
Spaniards

Irene Portis-Winner
Harvard University
Slovenes

André J. M. Prévos
Pennsylvania State University,
Worthington-Scranton Campus
French

Frank Proschan
Indiana University
Khmu
Lao

Padma Rangaswamy
University of Illinois, Chicago
Gujaratis

Oliver Rathkolb
Ludwig Boltzmann Institute for
History and Society, Vienna
Austrians

John B. Rehder
University of Tennessee
Scotch-Irish
Scots

Rubén G. Rumbaut
Michigan State University
Cambodians

Mitsugu Sakihara
Hawaii International College
Okinawans

Matt T. Salo
U.S. Bureau of the Census, Washington, DC
Gypsies
Travelers

Zdenek Salzmann
Northern Arizona University
Czechs

Enid Schildkrout
American Museum of Natural History, New York City
Ghanaians

Holly A. Seeling
Harvard University
Jains

H. L. Seneviratne
University of Virginia
Sinhalese
Sri Lankans

Mary C. Sengstock
Wayne State University
Iraqi Chaldeans

Arnold Sildegs
Kalamazoo, MI
Latvians

Andrei Simić
University of Southern California
Serbs

Andris Skreija
University of Nebraska, Omaha
Poles

Paul R. Spickard
Brigham Young University, Hawaii
Pacific Islanders in Hawaii

M. Mark Stolarik
University of Ottawa, Canada
Slovaks

Cristina Szanton Blanc
Columbia University
Filipinos

Hany N. Takla
St. Shenouda, Archimandrite Coptic Society
Egyptian Copts

Parsram Sri Thakur
Community College of Rhode Island
Indo-Caribbeans

Playford V. Thorson
University of North Dakota (emeritus)
Icelanders

Arlene Torres
University of Illinois
Puerto Ricans

Thomas A. Tweed
University of North Carolina, Chapel Hill
Buddhists

N. Prabha Unnithan
Colorado State University
Malayalam Speakers

Rajagopal Vakulabharanam
University of Wisconsin, Madison
Telugus

Peter Vasiliadis
Toronto, Canada
Macedonians

Diane C. Vecchio
Furman University
Italians
Sardinians
Sicilians

Carlos G. Vélez-Ibáñez
University of California, Riverside
Mexicans of the Southwest

James Diego Vigil
University of California, Los Angeles
Californios

Emil Vrabie
Florida Atlantic University
Vlachs

Linda S. Walbridge
Indiana University, Purdue University, Indianapolis
Lebanese Christians
Lebanese Muslims

Lewis Walker
Western Michigan University
African Americans

M. Ann Walko
Kean College of New Jersey
Estonians

Philip E. Webber
Central College
Frisians

Raymond Brady Williams
Wabash College
South Asian Christians

Benjamin C. Wilson
Western Michigan University
African Americans

Tekle Mariam Woldemikael
University of Redlands
Ethiopians and Eritreans

Bernard P. Wong
San Francisco State University
Chinese

ACADIANS AND CAJUNS

Portrayals of Louisiana Cajuns, descendants of the Acadians who settled along the Bay of Fundy in the early seventeenth century, by the popular media in the late twentieth century are symptomatic of the widespread popular confusion about this enigmatic people. The confusion results from the creation and persistence of conflicting (complimentary and uncomplimentary) stereotypes by generations of American writers. For a small minority of these writers, Cajuns embodied all the virtues envisioned by Thomas Jefferson for the nation's agricultural proletariat. This vision of the Cajuns is based primarily on Henry Wadsworth Longfellow's *Evangeline* (1847), an epic poem about two Acadian lovers—Evangeline and Gabriel—who are separated by the Acadian dispersal on the eve of their wedding and spend the remainder of their lives searching for each other, only to have Evangeline eventually find Gabriel on his deathbed in Philadelphia, where he dies in her arms. The far more numerous Cajun detractors, on the other hand, have invariably portrayed the Cajuns in terms that are shockingly intemperate in this age of political correctness. These critics usually char-acterize Cajuns as poor, ignorant, hedonistic, lazy, unambitious, inbred, xenophobic, and violent swamp denizens.

These conflicting and equally flawed judgments belie the limited vision and experience of their creators. Preoccupied with the Cajun community's "exotic" characteristics, journalists and popular writers consistently fail to note the society's complexity. Indeed, Louisiana's Cajun community is among the most complex in North America, with a highly stratified and heavily urbanized society living in highly diverse economic and topographical environments.

Subregional differences, however, among Louisiana's Acadian communities were initially superficial, masking the shared values and basic lifestyle that bound the group together. Cohesiveness within individual New Acadia settlements was bolstered by an extensive network of blood relationships and by persistent friction between the exiles and neighboring groups.

The group's enduring cultural integrity is seen in the persistence of the community's core values. The typical predispersal Acadian cherished land, family, and self-dignity above all else. Having emigrated from France prior to the rise of capitalism, they were not materialistic in the modern sense of

1

the term. Predispersal Acadians generally sought only a comfortable existence, producing small agricultural surpluses to acquire European manufactured goods to ameliorate the often harsh existence, but never for conspicuous consumption.

These common values were perpetuated by the increasingly common endogamous (intragroup) marriages in seventeenth-century Acadian society. Group boundaries coincided with extended families, and as the Acadian settlements were peopled primarily by the intermarried descendants of French colonial Acadia's remarkably prolific 1632 immigrants, the Acadian community did, in fact, constitute one large clan. This complex network of human relationships quickly became so tightly interwoven that by 1700 the Acadians had become the first European immigrant group to consider itself a distinctive people.

Dispersal and the Exiles

The Acadian community's cultural homogeneity permitted them to endure the trauma of the 1755 diaspora, known to historians as the *Grand Dérangement*. The dispersal resulted from the Acadian refusal to become party to the almost continuous Anglo-French imperial wars in North America. The Nova Scotian government interpreted Acadian intransigence as disaffection, and the acting colonial governor determined to resolve the festering Acadian problem by means of "ethnic cleansing." The British military disarmed the Acadians and, after hundreds of Acadian men were taken hostage to foil any attempt at resistance, six thousand of the approximately eighteen thousand Acadians were crammed aboard small merchantmen and subsequently scattered throughout the British Atlantic Seaboard colonies. Most of the remaining Acadians fled into the wilderness that is present-day New Brunswick, where thousands fell victim to malnutrition, disease, and exposure.

The Acadians sent into exile in the thirteen British Atlantic Seaboard colonies shared many of these hardships, which were compounded by the virulent francophobia directed against the exiles by their reluctant English colonial hosts. The exiles

consequently sought to relocate when permitted to do so by the Treaty of Paris of 1763 and to seek out a new homeland in which their Acadian society could be reassembled. The largest contingent of Acadians ultimately congregated in the Louisiana bayou country, which they dubbed New Acadia.

The Acadian exiles' cohesiveness permitted them to weather the rigors of adapting to semitropical Louisiana. The Acadian exiles who had been engaged in ranching in predispersal Nova Scotia found themselves established in Louisiana's prairie country for the purpose of raising cattle for the New Orleans market. The Acadian exiles from Grand Pré, the former Nova Scotian breadbasket, were established on some of the world's best farmland along the Mississippi River above New

A man cooks a pot of gumbo during the Cajun Mardi Gras in Mamou, Louisiana. (Philip Gould/Corbis)

Orleans. Because the various waves of Acadian immigrants were providentially placed on lands not dissimilar to those of their Nova Scotian settlements, adaptation was amazingly rapid. Most Acadians attained their predispersal standard of living within a decade of their arrival in Louisiana.

Continued accumulation of wealth over several decades by industrious Acadians, however, threatened the community with cultural disintegration. Economic stratification had existed in Acadia, but wealth had not automatically conferred social status. In Louisiana's emerging plantation society, however, ownership of slaves automatically conferred social status.

First-generation Acadian immigrants exhibited little interest in their social standing and, although some exiles acquired African field hands and wet nurses in the 1770s and 1780s, the Acadians' simple, pastoral existence remained basically unaltered. But prosperous second- and third-generation Acadians clearly envied the prestige enjoyed by their white Creole neighbors, and they consciously emulated their social "betters."

Such cultural apostasy was atypical. Most Acadians preferred the less ostentatious existence of their forebears. A small minority of Acadians owned slaves outside of the plantation areas, and most landholders engaged in small-scale farming and ranching. These yeomen were the result of an early nineteenth-century exodus of poor Acadians from the parishes along the Mississippi River and the Teche and Lafourche bayous. Acadians departing Bayou Teche migrated into the prairie region extending to the Texas border. Acadians leaving the banks of the Mississippi River were forced into the swamps along the fringes of the Atchafalaya Basin (North America's largest waterbottom swamp) or into the coastal marshlands along the lower reaches of Bayou Lafourche. Poor Acadians who remained behind became socially and culturally isolated. Successful Acadians were absorbed into the local elite, while landless Acadians found ready employment in the sugar industry as overseers, artisans, and laborers, but, having lost their economic independence, these workers became the first casualties of Americanization.

Further erosion of traditional Acadian life was accelerated by the outbreak of the Civil War. Acadians were generally unaffected by the outbreak of hostilities, though many scions of Acadian planter families quickly volunteered for service in the Confederate army. As the South's military fortunes declined in 1862, many yeoman farmers became victims of Confederate conscription. Acadian conscripts deserted their Confederate units whenever the rebel army periodically retreated through South Louisiana. Free from their effective bondage in the army, the deserters greeted the invaders as liberators, but their cheers were soon replaced by grumbling as the men in blue proved more oppressive than the Confederates.

Faced with the ever-present threat of destruction by combatants and the possibility of arrest and execution for desertion, Acadians again found themselves in a crossfire between rival powers. Once again, Acadians were victimized by a cause they generally did not espouse, and once again, their homeland lay in ashes.

Cajun Transformation

The task of rebuilding was complicated not only by the political turbulence that plagued Louisiana between 1865 and 1877 but also by the significant social and economic changes that accelerated the transformation of the Acadians into Cajuns. Class distinctions, which had emerged in the antebellum period, became more pronounced as the community's educated elite turned its back on its cultural heritage. These cultural apostates increasingly wished to avoid the onerous social stigma borne by the poor French-speakers now universally identified as "Cajuns" (an Anglo corruption of "Acadians") in the postbellum period.

Abandoned by the group's natural leadership element and under mounting pressure to conform to the Anglo-American norm, many Acadians found themselves ill equipped to meet the challenges before them. Economically ruined by the war, some Acadians were forced to abandon their traditional agricultural pursuits and to seek their livelihood as cypress lumberjacks, fishermen, trappers in the Atchafalaya Basin and in the coastal marshes. Many more were reduced to tenantry by the 1880s. They would generally remain mired in tenantry until the industrialization of Texas's "Golden Triangle" area (the region bounded by Beaumont, Port Arthur, and Orange) in the first two decades of the twentieth century provided well-paying jobs to thousands of these people. Throughout the late nineteenth and early twentieth centuries, the tenants' reduced circumstances forced them to interact daily with black fellow tenants—despite mounting pressure for segregation—and the resulting cultural interchanges helped produce both modern Cajun music and Cajun cuisine (as well as zydeco music in the black Creole community).

Such interchanges also helped to blur, at least in the eyes of outside observers, the long-standing cultural cleavages between the Acadians and their white Creole neighbors to the north. By 1900, these poor prairie Creoles, who, like the Acadians, had been abandoned by their own ethnic leadership, gravitated economically and politically toward their southern, French-speaking neighbors, with whom they shared an increasingly common lifestyle. Indeed, the traditional prairie Creole settlement was designated Evangeline Parish in 1910 in honor of its officially recognized but appropriately mythical Acadian heritage. Poor Creoles east of the Atchafalaya River, and particularly in the Lafourche Basin, also adopted the Cajun identity as they became acculturated through intermarriage.

As with the lower strata of Acadian society, many members of the up-and-coming antebellum gentry were profoundly affected by the Civil War and its aftermath. The war itself claimed most of its prominent young politicians. Not until the turn of the twentieth century would the Acadian gentry begin to reassert a modicum of its notable antebellum influence at the regional and state levels.

Loss of political influence reflected the Cajun community's corresponding loss of economic power. Most severely affected were those planters' children who grew to manhood just before, or during, the conflict. Unable to find a niche in

agriculture, many of these young Acadians migrated to southern Louisiana's farming villages, where they emerged as a new professional class.

This movement into the professional class held profound social and cultural ramifications for the Cajun elite; in postbellum Louisiana, the language of business was English, and the Acadian social climbers who had formerly aspired to the social heights of Creole society now moved rapidly into the Anglo-American mainstream. Because of the social stigma now associated with poor Acadians, the Acadian gentry made every effort to disassociate itself from its heritage, initially wrapping itself instead in the ennobling mantle of the Evangeline legend.

Americanization Movements

The children of acculturated Acadians were in the vanguard of the early twentieth-century movement to Americanize the Acadians. Focusing on public education as the best means of bringing the state's illiterate French-speakers into the national mainstream, the movement was propelled by the Compulsory Education Act of 1916 and by the compulsory English educational provisions of the 1921 state constitution. Though the authors of the foregoing laws were Anglos, many of the teachers who ruthlessly implemented the English instructional program were drawn from the Acadian gentry.

The frontal assault on Cajun French by the state's educational establishment was complemented by technological, social, and economic developments that more effectively undermined the language by discouraging its use at home. The appearance of movies, radio, and other popular new forms of entertainment, all of which were available exclusively in English, encouraged monolingual French Cajuns to become fully bilingual. Meanwhile, Louisiana's burgeoning oil industry, run by English-speaking Texans and Oklahomans, provided unprecedented employment opportunities in Acadiana (a twenty-two parish region established by the Louisiana legislature as a means of officially recognizing the French-speaking area of

A young woman teaches French to Cajun children in Avery Island, Louisiana. (Philip Gould/Corbis)

the state), but only for those Cajuns with at least a moderate degree of fluency in English. To provide their children with the opportunity for a better standard of living than they themselves had enjoyed, many working-class Cajun parents began to use English exclusively when conversing with their children.

The threatened demise of the French language jeopardized numerous cultural institutions, including Cajun music, which, in the 1940s, saw the introduction of bluegrass and country music styles and the increasing use of English. Louisiana's Cajuns had embarked upon a seemingly irreversible march into the American mainstream. The mainstream offered promise of the good life, and those elements of their cultural baggage popularly associated with their heritage were denigrated as archaic, crude ("low class"), or absurd. By the late 1950s, the very term "Cajun," for example, came to be viewed as the supreme insult to persons of French descent.

Survival in the American mainstream, however, required a broad range of educational and

occupational skills that the blue-collar parents themselves could not provide. Having gained an appreciation for education through their participation in the Civilian Conservation Corps (CCC) camps or in military service during World War II, these parents stressed education as the key to economic success in the 1950s and 1960s. Cajun children were pressured to attend college, and the student populations at South Louisiana universities doubled in size during this period. The resulting wave of Cajun college graduates tended to congregate in the college towns, where they came to constitute a notable segment of the white-collar population.

Unlike their counterparts of the preceding century, however, these upwardly mobile, urban Cajuns did not abandon their parents' culture entirely. By the late 1960s, these Cajun urbanites came to resent the fact that they had ever been made to feel ashamed of their heritage.

In 1968, the resulting backlash contributed to the establishment of the Council for the Development of French in Louisiana (CODOFIL). By the early 1970s placards in business places throughout South Louisiana proclaimed, for the first time since World War II, *"Ici on parle français"* (French spoken here).

Though centered in Lafayette, the self-proclaimed cultural capital of Acadiana and home of the largest urban Cajun community, this ethnic revival was by no means an urban, white-collar phenomenon. By the early 1970s, the movement enjoyed the unspoken popular endorsement of blue-collar groups that had traditionally been the main guardians of the culture. Blue-collar Cajun attitudes are particularly significant because of the group's tremendous growth—relative to the other segments of the Cajun population—in the 1970s and early 1980s, as thousands of Cajuns left high school for the oil fields.

Though the short-term benefits of oil-field employment were high, the long-term costs to the Cajun community were also great. The global oil crisis of 1985–1990 left most of the Cajun blue-collar work force without employment, and the presence of a large reservoir of poorly educated workers has discouraged desirable industries from moving into southern Louisiana.

Faced with bleak prospects of short-term improvement in the local economy and burdened with straitened personal finances, many unemployed Cajuns began, in 1986, to relocate in Tennessee, Georgia, and Florida, where jobs were more abundant. The actual number of migrants was estimated at tens of thousands. This diaspora, reminiscent of the Cajun migration to southeastern Texas earlier in the twentieth century, will undoubtedly result in the wholesale induction of the migrants into the American mainstream.

Conclusion

Most of Louisiana's Cajuns have remained in Acadiana, and like their Acadian immigrant ancestors, they face major economic, cultural, and linguistic challenges. Despite the introduction of French immersion programs in several southern Louisiana parishes, Cajun French is particularly threatened, as is the community's traditional adherence to Roman Catholicism. Cajun anticlericalism, coupled with a strong backlash against post–Vatican II changes and the church's unpopular stands on divorce and birth control, have propelled thousands of Cajun Catholics out of the church. Many Cajuns have transferred to fundamentalist churches that have enjoyed a regional growth rate approximately twenty times that of the natural increase in the local population.

Other facets of Cajun culture, however, have remained vibrant. Nuclear family cohesiveness remains strong, and the extended family, while not the force it once was in Acadian society, remains the mortar that holds the Cajun community together. Cajun cuisine and Cajun music—the latter on the verge of disappearing around World War II—are now subjects of national fascination and will endure for some time, if only for economic reasons. The Cajun proclivity for getting the most out of life—a trait grossly distorted by the popular media—remains a necessary counterbalance to their traditional fatalism and the monotony of their long and arduous workweeks. Cajuns also have

maintained not only a strong appreciation for their natural surroundings but also a deep-seated attachment to their Louisiana homeland. Though modern economic realities have forced them to surrender their traditional self-sufficiency, they have nevertheless maintained their spirit of independence and irreverence toward all forms of authority.

See also: CANADIANS; FRENCH; FRENCH CANADIANS

Bibliography

Ancelet, B. J. (1988). *"Capitaine, voyage ton flag": The Traditional Cajun Country Mardi Gras*. Lafayette, LA: Center for Louisiana Studies.

Ancelet, B. J. (1989). *Cajun Music: Its Origins and Development*. Lafayette, LA: Center for Louisiana Studies.

Ancelet, B. J., Edwards, J. D., and Pitre, G. (1991). *Cajun Country: Folklife in the South Series*. Jackson: University Press of Mississippi.

Ancelet, B. J., and Morgan, E., Jr. (1984). *The Makers of Cajun Music/Musiciens Cadiens et Creoles*. Austin: University of Texas Press.

Arceneaux, W. (1972). *Acadian General: Alfred Mouton and the Civil War*. Lafayette, LA: Center for Louisiana Studies.

Brasseaux, C. A. (1987). *The Founding of New Acadia: Beginnings of Acadian Life in Louisiana, 1765–1803*. Baton Rouge: Louisiana State University Press.

Brasseaux, C. A. (1988). *In Search of Evangeline: Birth and Evolution of the Evangeline Myth*. Thibodaux, LA: Blue Heron Press.

Brasseaux, C. A. (1991). *"Scattered to the Wind": Dispersal and Wanderings of the Acadians, 1755–1809*. Lafayette, LA: Center for Louisiana Studies.

Brasseaux, C. A. (1992). *Acadian: Transformation of a People*. Jackson: University Press of Mississippi.

Brasseaux, C. A.; Garcia, E. F.; and Voorhies, J. K., trans. and eds. (1989). *Quest for the Promised Land: Official Correspondence Relating to the First Acadian Migration to Louisiana, 1764–1769*. Lafayette, LA: Center for Louisiana Studies.

Brasseaux, L. (1990). *Where Yesterday Meets Tomorrow: An Illustrated History*. Chatsworth, CA: Windsor Publications.

Comeaux, M. (1972). *Atchafalaya Swamp Life: Settle-*

ment and Folk Occupations. Baton Rouge: Louisiana State University Press.

Conrad, G. R., ed. (1978). *The Cajuns: Essays on Their History and Culture.* Lafayette, LA: Center for Louisiana Studies.

Delahoussaye, S. (1983). *Pouponne and Balthazar/ Pouponne et Balthazar,* trans. J. J. Perret. Critical edition by M. Waggoner. Lafayette, LA: Center for Louisiana Studies.

Dormon, J. H. (1983). *The People Called Cajuns: An Introduction to an Ethnohistory.* Lafayette, LA: Center for Louisiana Studies.

Edmonds, D. C. (1979). *Yankee Autumn in Acadiana: A Narrative of the Great Texas Overland Expedition Through Southwest Louisiana, October–December 1863.* Lafayette, LA: Acadiana Press.

Estaville, L. E., Jr. (1987). "Changeless Cajuns: Nineteenth-Century Reality or Myth?" *Louisiana History* 28: 117–140.

Hebert, T. (1994). *Acadian-Cajun Genealogy: Step-by-Step.* Lafayette, LA: Center for Louisiana Studies.

Jean Lafitte National Park. (1987). *The Cajuns: Their History and Culture,* 5 vols. Opelousas, LA: Hamilton & Associates.

Leistner, C. (1986). "French and Acadian Influences Upon the Cajun Cuisine of Southwest Louisiana." M.A. thesis, University of Southwestern Louisiana.

Orso, E. G. (1992). *Louisiana Live Oak Lore.* Lafayette, LA: Center for Louisiana Studies.

Post, L. C. (1962). *Cajun Sketches: From the Prairies of Southwest Louisiana.* Baton Rouge: Louisiana State University Press.

Read, W. A. (1963). *Louisiana French,* revised edition. Baton Rouge: Louisiana State University Press.

Uzee, P. D. (1985). *The Lafourche Country: The People and the Land.* Lafayette, LA: Center for Louisiana Studies.

Winzerling, O. (1955). *Acadian Odyssey.* Baton Rouge: Louisiana State University Press.

CARL A. BRASSEAUX

AFGHANS

Afghanistan, a landlocked country in the Middle East about the size of Texas, is surrounded by Pakistan, Iran, Turkmenistan, Uzbekistan, Tajikistan, and China. In 1979, the population was about fifteen million, with 85 percent living in rural and nomadic settings, and the literacy rate was less than 10 percent. One of the world's poorest countries, Afghanistan's infrastructure has been destroyed by years of continuous war.

Refugees are people who flee their countries and are afraid to return because of persecution based on race, religion, nationality, social group, or political opinion. During the war between Afghanistan and the Soviet Union, Afghans comprised the world's single largest refugee group. The war in Afghanistan started in 1978 with a Soviet-backed coup d'etat, followed by an invasion by the former Soviet Union. From 1979 to 1989 the Communist-backed government fought the U.S.-backed mujahedeen (freedom-fighters). During this decade, nearly seven million Afghans lived in refugee camps and cities in Pakistan, Iran, and India or fled to Western countries such as Germany, Canada, and the United States. Millions more left their villages for the relative peace of Kabul, the capital of Afghanistan.

The Soviet withdrawal of forces from Afghanistan in 1989 was followed by a bitter civil war between rival political groups. This war continues to result in civilian deaths and food and energy shortages. Even though tens of thousands have returned to Afghanistan from Pakistan and Iran, several hundreds of thousands are still being displaced, many fleeing to new refugee camps near Jalalabad.

Life in the United States

Afghan refugees began arriving in the United States in 1980 as refugees, political asylees, through the family reunification program, or by illegal entry. By 1985, more than forty thousand Afghan refugees had been relocated to the United States and Canada, with the largest concentrations in San Francisco, New York, Washington, D.C., and Toronto. Initially families resettled throughout the United States, but most chose to relocate later to be near family members or other Afghans. Local communities, which vary in size and level of integration, allow people to maintain Afghan culture. California communities have local mosques, Afghan grocery stores and restaurants, and television and radio programs in Dari and/or Pashto (the two dominant languages of Afghanistan).

These refugees call themselves Afghans, although many non-Afghans, including some Farsi-speaking interpreters, inappropriately call them "Afghanis." Afghans are generally too polite to correct people who call them "Afghani," which is the unit of money in Afghanistan. Afghans generally speak either Dari (a dialect of Farsi or Persian) or Pashto, but many Afghans speak four or five languages from among the following: Dari, Pashto, Urdu, Hindi, German, and English. Many educated Afghans also speak Russian. Afghan children are expected to speak Dari or Pashto, but the younger children learn English and become more Americanized; many speak their parents' language poorly. However, part of what defines a good Afghan child is the ability to converse with one's elders.

English-language fluency varies by age at time of arrival in the United States, gender, education level, and opportunity. The first arrivals were highly educated professionals and the elite, many of whom worked with Americans or were educated in the United States. Later arrivals had less education, fewer experiences with Americans, and fewer opportunities to learn English. Elderly men and women, and women who were married with children when they arrived in the United States, are less likely to speak English. Many Afghan women are illiterate in their own language and have difficulty with ESL (English as a second language) classes. Those who suffer from post-traumatic stress disorder find learning a new language much more difficult.

Afghanistan is a country with very pronounced ethnic divisions. The largest ethnic group is the Pashtun (Pashto-speakers), which comprise about 50 percent of the total population and include many of those in positions of power. The former Shah was Pashtun. The other dominant group is

Farsi-speaking Tajiks (Persians). Other groups include Hazara, Uzbek, and Turkmen, each speaking their own languages and dialects. These ethnic divisions are reflected in the politics of Afghanistan, as well as in the communities of the diaspora. Ethnic divisions in U.S. communities play out in local politics, often interfering with the development of community service programs that would serve all groups.

Afghans in the United States maintain ties with family members still living in Afghanistan or other countries of the diaspora and help to support them financially. Relatives in other countries often attend weddings in the United States, and parents may look to families living in another country to find a spouse for a son or daughter. These arrangements cement relationships between extended families and stretch notions of community across national borders.

Integration

Afghan refugees of all ages suffer from the trauma of war, death of close family members, dislocation, and relocation. Because of their relatively short time in the United States, they are still becoming settled. Elderly men must cope with status loss and role ambiguity at a time in life when they expected to retire and live in respect, as guides to their children and grandchildren. Grandmothers are lonely, isolated from family members and friends. Parents and youths contend with social service, education, and health-care systems that only partially provide for their families' needs yet force them to seek help outside of their family system. Each generation's efforts to keep extended families intact is undermined by the fast pace of American life and generational differences.

Islamic history, traditions, and identity permeate Afghan beliefs and behavior and underlie many conflicts with American society. Muslims avoid pork products and alcohol, and many participate in Ramadan, the month of fasting. During Ramadan, no food, drink, cigarettes, or sexual activity are allowed between sunrise and sunset. Families gather to eat and socialize during the evening and often continue on into the night. People who are ill or on medication (and are therefore exempt from the rules of fasting) often fast anyway, merely reversing their day and night activities. For instance a diabetic or pregnant woman may try to sleep most of the day and take medications at night with meals interspersed between prayer times.

Muslims discourage their children from marrying outside the religion. If a son marries a non-Afghan, the bride is expected to convert to Islam and raise the children as Muslims. A daughter, on the other hand, may be ostracized from her family if she marries a non-Muslim because she is perceived to have turned her back on her religion and culture. Afghan refugees struggle to maintain their cultural values and heritage, including their religion, and in-group marriage is one way to ensure cultural continuity. This is most difficult for the young people, who live in two worlds.

The most important social unit for Afghans is the family. Being an individual is seen as less important than being a member of a family, with obligations to both nuclear and extended families. Afghans have strong family ties and family obligations, and no one, man or women, is expected to stand alone as an individual. Although women's power may vary according to social class, education, and family, women, the elderly, and unmarried children are generally expected to seek guidance from and obey the father, who is the head of the family. This practice is changing to some extent because of residence patterns and economic pressures, but most Afghans still follow the tradition.

Economic issues are prominent in the Afghan community. Most families experienced an extreme loss of status when they arrived in the United States. Professionals, such as physicians or teachers, are often unable to obtain licenses in the United States and may become taxi drivers, cooks, or babysitters. They may also participate in the underground economy of flea markets and garage sales. However, because families stay together and try to pool their resources, many have become more economically stable. For example, in California it is common for the mother to work as a hairdresser while the husband buys and fixes things for sale at local flea markets or repairs cars and the children work in retail or computer component companies. After a few years, a family may buy a convenience store or pizza restaurant. When the children graduate from high school, many prepare for professional careers and move into their own apartments, living like most other Americans after marriage.

Conclusion

Afghan refugees have been in the United States only since the early 1980s. They struggle to maintain their cultural identity as Afghans regardless of age at time of arrival or length of stay in the United States. The communities are still insular, striving to remain separate from other ethnic groups, partly because Afghans did not immigrate to the United States by choice but fled their homeland because of war. Their original goal was to maintain their culture through their children and return to Afghanistan when peace was established. Many, however, have been forced to come to terms with the notion that they may never be able to return to Afghanistan because of the continued fighting. Although many of these individuals have become U.S. citizens, being Afghan (demonstrated by the maintenance of strong family relationships, the language, cultural traditions, and Islamic identity), is still vitally important in how they perceive themselves.

Bibliography

Anderson, E. W., and Dupree, N. H. (1990). *The Cultural Basis of Afghan Nationalism*. New York: Pinter Publishers.

Canfield, R. L. (1989). "Afghanistan: The Trajectory of Internal Alignments." *Middle East Journal* 43(4): 635–648.

Dupree, L. (1980). *Afghanistan*. Princeton, NJ: Princeton University Press.

Lipson, J. G., and Omidian, P. A. (1992). "Health Issues

of Afghan Refugees in California." *Western Journal of Medicine* 157:271–275.

Noorzoy, M. S. (1988). "Long-Term Soviet Economic Interests and Politics in Afghanistan." In *Afghanistan: The Great Game Revisited,* edited by R. Klass. Boston: Freedom House.

Omidian, P. A. (1996). *Aging and Family in an Afghan Refugee Community.* New York: Garland.

Omidian, P. A., and Lipson, J. G. (1992). "Elderly Afghan Refugees: Traditions and Transitions in Northern California." In *Selected Papers on Refugee Issues 1992,* edited by P. A. De Voe. Washington, DC: American Anthropological Association.

Rahmany, K. (1992). "A Long Journey: The Psychological Adjustment of the Afghan Refugees in the United States." Ph.D. diss., Rosebridge Graduate School of Integrative Psychology, Concord, CA.

Rais, R. B. (1994). *War Without Winners: Afghanistan's Uncertain Transition After the Cold War.* New York: Oxford University Press.

Reeve, C. (1987). "Remnants of an Invasion." *Chicago Tribune Magazine,* July 5, Section 10.

PATRICIA A. OMIDIAN
JULIENE G. LIPSON

AFRICAN AMERICANS

A common slave history, dating back to the fifteenth and sixteenth centuries, is shared by African Americans throughout the United States. The work of Johann Blumenbach, an eighteenth-century German anatomist who divided the human race into five racial categories (Caucasian, Mongolian, Ethiopian, American, and Malay) greatly influenced how Europeans used the concepts of race and ethnicity. Tersely, they came to view people of color as biologically inferior beings. It is also in this context that the notion emerged that any known trace of African ancestry makes one a "Negro." W. E. B. Du Bois, a noted black scholar, argued that the word "Negro," a creation of whites, was used for the first time to conjoin race, color,

and "blackness of slavery and degradation." The "one drop of Negro blood" concept is an interesting phenomenon in the United States, because that same amount of African ancestry in many other societies would perhaps place that person in some racial category other than black.

Forced Immigration

A Dutch man-of-war, though not the first ship to carry blacks to America (e.g., Pedro Alonzo, captain of the Nina, was with Christopher Columbus), dropped anchor at Jamestown in 1619 with twenty Africans on board. They were indentured servants, but the Africans who followed were slaves, and their numbers would grow into millions before the end of the nineteenth century. They came from many tribes and villages of Africa, including Angolans, Akans, Igbos, Mendes, Kongos, Krus, Tivs, Fullahs, Fantis, Yorubas, and Ibibios, among many other groups. The Dutch, French, Danish, Portuguese, and British brought them from such kingdoms as Dahomey and Benin, and from numerous sites on the western coast of Africa such as Goree, Cape Verde, the Gold Coast (El Mina), and the Ivory Coast. In addition to the U.S. colonies, African slaves were taken to the Bahamas, Barbados, Brazil, Cuba, Guadeloupe, Haiti, Jamaica, Martinique, St. Thomas, and other places.

By 1860, there were 1,982,625 male slaves and 1,971,135 female slaves in the United States, and many were owned by some of the wealthiest and most powerful white families in the country, including George Washington and Thomas Jefferson. They could be found in the Piedmont Plateau of Virginia and South Carolina, in the Tidewater areas of Virginia and Maryland, in the Delta regions and Black Bottom areas of Mississippi and Alabama, and elsewhere. In those areas, rice, tobacco, sugar cane, indigo, and cotton were grown on large plantations. Not all blacks in America were slaves; there were nearly half a million freed blacks, who resided largely in urban areas in 1860.

The post–Civil War years were a time of transition for both whites and blacks in the South.

During the Reconstruction era a negligible number of blacks experienced some socioeconomic and political progress, but for many it was an era of uncertainty and instability. Though slavery had been abolished, it was very evident that white dominance was still pervasive, and the notion of black inferiority had not diminished among whites, either in their attitude to or treatment of blacks. Jim Crowism (segregation) had quickly become a way of life in the South, affecting virtually all aspects of black-white relations with respect to schools, housing, theaters, parks, buses, trains, restaurants, hotels, drinking fountains, waiting rooms, bars, and other public places. Most Southern states also had antimiscegenation laws, which disallowed interracial dating and marriage.

Where does one go with one's newly found freedom? How does one survive in a country hostile to the recently emancipated blacks? These and many other questions plagued them. Many blacks, not unlike some of the poor whites, became tenant farmers and/or sharecroppers, and many opted to migrate from rural regions to urban environments in both the South and North.

The large northern cities, for example, became magnets and terminals of the "great black trek." By 1910, of a total population of roughly 465,766 in Detroit, African Americans numbered 5,741. Chicago had an estimated population of 2,185,283, and 44,103 were blacks. By 1920, of the 993,678 people in Detroit, African Americans numbered 40,838. In Chicago, where the total count was 4,549,008, African Americans numbered 84,459. In Philadelphia in 1910 and 1920, the total numbers were 1,549,008 and 1,823,779, while the numbers of blacks were 34,229 and 84,459, respectively. For New York, the total population was 4,766,883 and 5,620,048 for the same two periods; the black population there was 91,709 in 1910 and 152,467 in 1920.

In the South, Birmingham in 1910 had a black population of 52,305, which grew to 70,230 ten years later; Atlanta's black population went from 51,902 in 1910 to 62,796 in 1920. The black population in Memphis rose from 52,441 to 61,181 during the same period.

Faced with labor shortages, northern capitalists hired labor recruiters to canvas the agricultural fields of the South to lure a cheap work force. Blacks, on the other hand, desperate for a better social life, better housing, better jobs, and a way to escape the South's Jim Crowism, were highly motivated to move North.

The North, however, was not pristine in its treatment of blacks. It was not uncommon for blacks to be barred from membership in unions, red-lined by the banks, denied employment, denied housing in certain neighborhoods, and discriminated against in other ways. Blacks were terrorized by race riots, which erupted in several cities from time to time during the early part of the twentieth century. In the 1930s and 1940s, for example, New York City had race riots. The Ku Klux Klan, a powerful group that was formed in the nineteenth century and deeply rooted in the South, was one of several groups that played on the fears of whites and that was instrumental in much of the hatred and hostility directed against blacks in the North.

The 1950s and 1960s

Attempts to overcome the numerous Jim Crow laws in the South and the de facto practices of discrimination in the North gave rise to the civil rights movement of the 1950s, 1960s, and 1970s. The National Association for the Advancement of Colored People (NAACP), the Congress of Racial Equality (CORE), the Student Nonviolent Coordinating Committee (SNCC), and the Southern Christian Leadership Conference (SCLC) were among the leading groups in the fight for a more just society for black people. These groups, as part of the civil rights movement, were successful in getting important U.S. Supreme Court decisions and major laws enacted by Congress. Among them were the Civil Rights Acts of 1964, 1965, and 1968, which dealt with voting rights and prohibited discrimination in housing and other areas.

With new laws on the books, African Americans have made some dramatic gains in a number

REV. S.T. BYRD AND FAMILY

The church was the "Rock of Ages" in the African-American community because it was the singular institution that provided the spiritual awareness and motivation for African Americans to persevere in their daily struggles. (Benjamin C. Wilson)

of areas. For example, black mayors have been elected in some major U.S. cities: Detroit, Cleveland, Washington, D.C., Atlanta, Birmingham, Richmond, Los Angeles, and Chicago among them. More than eight thousand blacks have been elected to office since the passage of the Civil Rights Acts of 1964 (at which time there were perhaps 170 elected black officials). Many view these political changes as necessary steps toward ameliorating some of the racist aspects of U.S. society.

In the 1960s, dozens of cities (Chicago, Philadelphia, Detroit, Los Angeles, and Washington, D.C., among them) had black uprisings. The riots had profound impact on the way blacks and whites related to one another. For instance, the riots accel-erated "white flight" to the suburbs, a pattern already begun during the 1950s. As of the mid-1990s, significantly fewer whites reside in central cities of the United States than did two decades earlier. Racial isolation, an erosion of the tax base of the central city, a markedly changed employment picture, and strained municipal services are some of the consequences of this white flight.

Controversy over U.S. involvment in the Vietnam War and the assassination of key leaders (Malcolm X, Martin Luther King Jr., Robert F. Kennedy, and Medgar Evers, among others) brought into question the direction of the civil rights movement and its impact on integration.

The melting-pot theory came under closer scrutiny and severe criticism, especially as the clamorous voices of women, Mexican Americans, Native Americans, gays and lesbians, and other groups cried out for social change. One of the outcomes was a resurgence of ethnicity and a renewed emphasis on cultural pluralism, not assimilation or integration.

Once African Americans challenged the well-established notion that all immigrant groups were expected in time to assimilate and integrate into one common culture, other ethnic groups quickly joined them in that challenge. These groups began to revisit their cultural histories and their influence on the development of their contemporary ethnic identities. For African Americans there were numerous attempts to cast off the yoke of "whiteness" in the face of their newly found "black is beautiful" cultural emphasis. Dashiki clothes, the "big" Afro hairdo, the black power handshake, black pride, and so on were some of the more readily recognizable changes as the black community unashamedly challenged white Anglo-Saxon Protestant patterns as the only viable cultural option in the United States.

Institutions

Throughout their history in the United States, African Americans have made enormous contributions in virtually every field of endeavor. Their industry is seen in science, government, medicine, manufacturing, inventions, business, and the arts. In the arts they have distinguished themselves in literature, sculpture, painting, dance, and music. They have given the world unique musical expressions in the form of jazz, gospel, the blues, and rap.

Though numerous black organizations and societies (e.g., burial associations and secret societies and orders) exist in the black community, the black church continues to be its premier institution. It has been the most reliable change agent because it does not depend on white society for its existence. Some of the most charismatic and dynamic black leaders have been pastors of black churches. In addition to supporting orphanages, small business, and attending to the needs of the poor and the sick, the black churches continue to play a powerful role in higher education by financing black colleges and universities such as Morris Brown, Philander Smith, Wilberforce, Clark, and Payne Theological Seminary.

Social Class and Important Social Factors

Historically, though there has never been a black upper class comparable to what is known as the white upper class, there has been a small number of black families who occupied the most coveted (or elitist) position in their neighborhood. "White blood," the more the better, was an index of the quality of the family. Belonging to the right churches (e.g., Episcopal, Congregational, or Presbyterian), clubs, and organizations, along with conspicuous patterns in dress, automobiles, and houses, were extremely important to those in this elite status. Their leisure time activities, planned vacations, travel, occupations, and education differentiated the "*café au lait* society" from the rest of black America. By the 1920s, a noticeable number of black Americans could lay claim to this elite status. Their contemporary counterparts are found among the extremely wealthy families of sports figures, movie stars, celebrities, a few business entrepreneurs, and politicians.

In the social structure of black America, there are also blacks who have achieved a middle-class status. The size of that class doubled from 1970 to 1990. The civil rights movement opened up numerous opportunities for mobility, and today many stable middle-class black communities are found throughout the country. For many, however, being in the middle class does not mean being comfortable; just the opposite. It is a precarious existence exacerbated by racism. It often means fighting many of the same battles but on a different level and on a different front. There is the constant fear that life circumstances can change so dramatically and drastically that fate can return them to a life they struggled to escape: the central city ghetto.

According to the 1990 U.S. Census, while 83.7 percent of African Americans lived in metropolitan areas, compared to 76.4 percent for whites, the major difference is in the percent of blacks versus whites who live in suburbs. Because of the rapid increase in the black middle class, the incidence of blacks living in suburbs increased from 16.1 percent in 1970 to 27.0 percent in 1990. During the same time, white suburbanization skyrocketed from 16.1 percent to 50.2 percent. The percent of both blacks and whites living in central cities was identical (58.2%) in 1970, but two decades later the picture had changed dramatically: Only 25.2 percent of whites were in central cities, compared to 56.7 percent of blacks.

While there may be some doubt about the size of the elite black group in the United States, there is little or no doubt that its lower class is the largest segment in black America. Of the nearly six million blacks living in poverty, at least one-third of them have been identified as being in the underclass. (It is claimed that African Americans make up more than 50 percent of those in this position.) Those in the underclass are said to endure an unending cycle of poverty. They are members of multiple-problem families and the homeless. They are among those who are victimized by crime and violence as well as institutional racism.

Unemployment Problems. Of the 36.9 million (14.7%) Americans living in poverty in 1992, according to the U.S. Bureau of the Census, the poverty rate for African Americans stood at a staggering 33 percent. This rather alarming trend started in the 1970s and continued into the 1990s, a time when the unemployment rate for African Americans was about 23.4 percent.

The employment picture is even bleaker for many African Americans who find themselves in the economically depressed areas of U.S. inner cities. For black youths age sixteen to nineteen, the unemployment outlook is even more ominous

Four members of the Knights Templar, a social organization (where light complexion was valued and membership was often determined by skin color) that displayed the importance of class and color among African Americans before the "Black is Beautiful" era. (Benjamin C. Wilson)

because their unemployment rate has reached more than 50 percent in some areas. Today's unemployed youth is likely to become tomorrow's unemployed adult.

Income, Occupations, and Education. Blacks earn about fifty-six cents to every dollar earned by whites, and the median family income differential between white and black families has widened over the decades. In 1950, the median family income of blacks as a percent of white income was 54.3 percent; in 1990, it has increased to only 58 percent. The tremendous disparity between the two races is also noted in the fact that the median net worth of black households is approximately ten times less than that of white households.

Slight gains have occurred in some fields. There has been an increase, for example, in the number of black female lawyers and psychologists. Both black males and females, however, continue to be vastly underrepresented in such fields as medicine and dentistry and in top managerial/administrative positions. About 70 to 75 percent of blacks are employed either in production or service-related jobs. Many from the remaining percentage can be found in education, civil service positions, counseling, or certain middle-management positions in industry.

When compared to whites, blacks have made some dramatic changes since 1950. Blacks closed the gap in median years of schooling from several years in 1950 to only a few months in 1989. The dropout rate among black youths went from 21.6 percent in 1968 to 12 percent in 1986. However, the percentages of blacks who either enter or complete college continues to lag substantially behind the percentages of whites entering or completing college. This pattern has some serious implications for African-American communities. Without an adequate education, the prospects are indeed poor that African-American youths will find the kinds of jobs that will lift them out of poverty.

Marriage and the Family. The number of African-American families headed by a married couple has dramatically declined since 1960. Of the more than ten million black households, the number of households with a married couple is less than 50 percent and rapidly declining. That 70 percent of black births are to unwed mothers does not bode well for the future of African-American children nor for the stability of the black family. Regarding single parents, the rate at which the African-American female is becoming the sole head of the household is another factor that contributes enormously to the changing patterns of the family. The rate is alarming because half of all African-American families with children are headed by females and because a significant percent of those families are only able to eke out an existence at the poverty level.

The plight facing black males — an "endangered species" — in the United States is most frightening. Many live in an environment where the unemployment rate is inordinately high; the arrest and imprisonment rates are very high; and the death rate is high because black young men are killing other black young men. This situation is exacerbated by the high drop out rate, drug and alcohol addiction, and problematic relationships in the family — young men who are not viable parents, single-parent teenagers, and more.

Many of the traditional differences in socialization are no longer accepted, and in many instances this trend has exacerbated the relationships between black men and women, young and old alike. The complexity of these issues involving self-identity, male-female relationships, and more is confounded by factors of race, sex, and social class. For example, the socialization of black females and males in the lower class is occurring primarily within the context of a single-parent family (primarily headed by a female), where there is heavy influence by the mass media, peers, and an inadequate school system.

A consequence of this is that black boys are socialized in this social class to view themselves primarily in terms of the "masculine mystique." The masculine mystique speaks to both the facts and the fancy of young black men, especially those who are involved in sexual athleticism, bravadoism, hustlerism, and ghetto suvivalism. These "isms" define who is a "real man," and they are

Prior to the dramatic decline in two-parent households, the traditional African-American family was represented by a large number of children, their parents, and their grandparents, all of whom either lived together or in close proximity. (Benjamin C. Wilson)

often very detrimental to both the young men themselves and their communities. These are the young who are in the highest-risk category: They are less educated, have children out of wedlock, are unemployed, spend time in jails and prisons, and are more often victims of a violent death at an early age.

On the other hand, the socialization processes tend to be less damning for many of the young black females who reside in the lower class. Though an alarming number have children out of wedlock, they are better educated and seen to be headed in a more positive direction than their male counterparts. Many of these young women feel that, even without a husband or a permanent male partner in their lives, legitimate options are available to them. They do not perceive of their success as being restricted to those illegitimate venues too commonly pursued by too many young black males, especially those unemployed youths who are recruited as drug marketers. Options for these women include being a success in the service

industry, the allied health professions, education, and other areas of legitimate employment. The situation for young women socialized in the middle class is even brighter; their aspirations and achievements include being lawyers, physicians, research scientists, and business entrepreneurs.

The above comments about gender differences and socialization barely scratch the surface of a very complex area of the black experience that should include the ongoing changes and problems associated with black feminism, sexism, and racism. Socialization of black boys and girls differs more significantly in the 1990s than two or three decades earlier. For example, there is more emphasis on egalitarianism and the elimination of all forms of sexism. That the black male should be more sensitive to the changing roles and needs of the black female, and vice versa, is an aspect of this emphasis.

Health and Illness. Because millions of families are not covered by either private or public health insurance, and because of federal cutbacks in Medicaid, health care is grossly inadequate for many black children and adults. In the fifteen years following Medicaid's enactment in 1965, black infant mortality fell 49 percent. Between 1976 and 1986, however, the percentage of poor families covered by Medicaid fell from 65 percent to 46 percent, and now one in every four African-American children is completely uninsured.

Poverty has always fallen disproportionately on black families and their children, and it breeds infant and maternal death and childhood sickness and disease. For example, black children in the United States face far greater health risks than white children. A black infant is twice as likely as a white infant to die or be born at low birthweight and less likely to be born to a mother who received early prenatal care. Moreover, the majority of children infected by the AIDS virus will be those from economically disadvantaged homes.

Changes in Intergroup Relations

Not unlike other racial/ethnic groups in the United States, blacks also were influenced by the prevailing notion that America was a melting pot and out of the crucible would come the "true America." The dominant motif was one of Anglo-conformity (i.e., all groups had to exchange their languages and ways of life for white, Anglo-Protestant ideas, values, and practices).

Historically, coercive acculturation—an aspect of assimilation—was commonly found throughout slavery. This institution exercised practices that systematically stripped slaves of their African heritage. For example, slaves were punished for speaking their native language and were forced to acquire a taste for whites' food, religion, clothing, and values—in short, whites'

Protesters assert their demand for civil rights as they march past a blockade of National Guardsmen on Beale Street in Memphis, Tennessee, in 1968. (UPI/Corbis-Bettmann)

culture. This so-called seasoning process was part of the apparatus to tame the "dangerous domestic enemy" from within, to root out their language, culture, and any sense of a historical identification.

That blacks today have not achieved the same level of assimilation as other immigrant or ethnic groups is due primarily to structural barriers designed to limit their rate of absorption into mainstream America. These barriers were, and still are, based on notions that blacks are racially inferior to whites. Consequently, most blacks still live in segregated neighborhoods and send their children to segregated schools. An argument can be made that African Americans, regardless of socioeconomic circumstances, experience some form of personal, group, or institutional discrimination in housing, employment, recreation, religion, health care, the arts, education, and more. However, a certain amount of cultural amalgamation occurs at the same time that black cultural practices continue to flourish. A consequence of this duality is that many in the black community began to see assimilation as dysfunctional and counterproductive to the aspirations of black Americans.

Though difficult to define in precise terms, there is an African-American culture embraced by virtually every person in the black community. Some scholars have argued that one must look to the southern black experience as the source of the core of black culture. It was during the southern experience that African Americans fashioned their unique values, beliefs, and norms as well as their emergent social institutions, many of which have come to form the core of the African-American culture. For example, it was the emergent black church that defined the type of spirituality and music found in contemporary churches throughout black America. That one is expected to make "a joyful noise unto the Lord" is very much alive in the singing, shouting, and speaking-in-tongues worship services.

Though in rather modified form, the black society also includes the "African extended family" concept and the belief that children are sacred and should be the objects of family adoration, love, and affection. Moreover, the values of communal economic and social support continue as part of a unique belief structure of many African Americans, especially those who view self-help programs as a viable option to white handouts and who subscribe to the notion that "it takes a village to raise a child." These are only a few of the many beliefs and patterns that emerged out of the southern black experience and contributed enormously to the unique cultural life that is associated with African Americans.

Like other immigrant cultures, the African-American culture is composed of many different things: cuisine, style of worship, gospel music, blues, jazz, intrapersonal relationships, popular culture with unique forms of creativity in dance and song, and more. Much of what is taken as an aspect of African-American culture was influenced over time by the culture of the larger society. For African Americans, slavery and its aftermath had a profound effect on their beliefs, moods, myths, facts, and fancies—in sum, their culture, both then and now.

Relations with Other Black Groups

From 1970 to 1990, the number of Jamaicans and Haitians entering the United States increased significantly. Though entry has not always been easy for Haitians, especially the so-called boat people, they have made their presence known in southern Florida and New York City. Jamaicans also are noticeable on the East Coast. Both groups have some misgivings when it comes to associating with other peoples of African ancestry (i.e., black Americans). The same holds true for Barbadians and others from the Caribbean. Haitians appear more inclined to hold tenaciously to their own ethnic cultural forms and identities. Jamaicans, on the other hand, seem to have more in common with black Americans, at least linguistically, and appear more willing to associate with them.

From 1960 to 1995, a total of 1.6 million people from Africa and the Caribbean have immigrated to the United States. In general they tend to be better off economically and educationally than black Americans and thus the source of some intergroup tension. A wide cultural gulf exists between those who call themselves African American and the African immigrants. On college and university campuses, for example, it is not uncommon for each group to have its own separate organizations and to self-segregate from other groups.

Government sources revealed, in the 1989 annual report of the U.S. Immigration and Naturalization Service, that the number of African immigrants to the United States increased dramatically since the 1960s, when 28,954 entered the country. However, more than 131,000 entered the country between 1981 and 1988, with Nigeria, South Africa, and Ethiopia contributing vastly more immigrants than other African countries (21,304, 11,849, and 19,489, respectively). But regardless of their country of origin, many of them desire to be known as Africans and not to be identified as black Americans. Most whites, however, do not perceive any significant racial differences among the various black groups and thus treat them alike for the most part.

Panethnic and Transnational Ties

With few exceptions, panethnic and transnational ties are weak or nonexistent among and between the various ethnic groups and African Americans. There might be some consciousness-raising in higher education but very little is occurring among the rank and file at the community level. Simply put, there is little interaction between African Americans and other people of color. In fact, intergroup tension has increased in some communities between African Americans and Korean Americans, Vietnamese Americans, and Hispanics. The same is also true regarding certain white ethnic groups. For example, the relationship between Jewish Americans and black Americans is not as amiable as it was during the days of the civil rights movement.

Parenthetically, blacks historically were generally sympathetic to and supportive of newcomers into their neighborhoods, especially those who were objects of discrimination. Events in the 1990s, however, suggest that the black communities view nonblacks as interlopers and exploiters. That Asian-American businesses in Los Angeles were targeted in the 1992 riot is indicative of this trend. Though themselves once the victims of discrimination, they are now seen as perpetrators of it. These developments make it very difficult to develop and sustain panethnic ties.

That African-American transnational ties are either weak or nonexistent does not bode well for a group with a population of more than thirty million people. The absence of a strong transnational voice means that African Americans will not be part of the economic calculus in such countries as Japan, West Germany, and South Africa. U.S. multinationals already have relocated many of their manufacturing jobs away from the black community and into other parts of the world. (In the 1960s manufacturing jobs were easily accessible to those in central cities.) Such economic decisions are made on the grounds that labor costs are significantly lower and regulations less stringent in other countries. The end result for many African Americans, especially those in large metropolitan areas, is high unemployment and underemployment rates.

Conclusion

Relationships between and among the races and ethnic groups have worsened in the United States, where racial hatred and hostility point to a serious breakdown in the racial dialogue. The so-called racial divide has widened, and many whites tend to be fixated on the amount of black progress, while many blacks tend to be fixated on the lack of progress. Such views only exacerbate the situation and make it extremely difficult for the two groups to reason together about the future of race and ethnic relations in the United States.

If there is a worldview in black America, it is an ever-increasing one of multiculturalism and Afrocentrism, which, as a potential unifying factor, speaks to a need for the United States to develop a greater appreciation of the richness of diversity. It is also a view that seeks to correct the miseducation and misperceptions about African Americans and other people of color, with an eye to the ultimate elimination of exploitation, oppression, sexism, and racism in the United States, if not the world.

See also: AFRICAN MUSLIMS; BARBADIANS; CAPE VERDEANS; GHANAIANS; GRENADIANS; HAITIANS; IGBO; JAMAICANS; SEA ISLANDERS; TRINIDADIANS; YORUBA

Bibliography

Asante, M. K. (1980). Afrocentricity: *The Theory of Social Change.* Buffalo, NY: Amulefi.

Cruse, H. (1968). *Rebellion or Revolution?* New York: William Morrow.

Farley, R., and Allen, W. R. (1987). *The Color Line and the Quality of Life in America.* New York: Russell Sage Foundation.

Feagin, J. R., and Sikes, M. P. (1994). *Living with Racism: The Black Middle Class Experience.* Boston: Beacon Press.

Hacker, A. (1992). *Two Nations: Black and White, Separate, Hostile, and Unequal.* New York: Scribner.

King, M. L., Jr. (1958). *Stride Toward Freedom: The Montgomery Story.* New York: Harper & Row.

King, M. L., Jr. (1968). *Where Do We Go From Here: Chaos or Community?* New York: Harper & Row.

Kozol, J. (1991). *Savage Inequality: Children in America's Schools.* New York: Crown.

Morris, A. D. (1984). *The Origins of the Civil Rights Movement.* New York: Free Press.

Pickney, A. (1987). *Black Americans.* Englewood Cliffs, NJ: Prentice Hall.

Rose, P. I. (1990). *They and We: Racial and Ethnic Relations in the United States.* New York: McGraw-Hill.

Spear, A. H. (1967). *Black Chicago: The Making of a Negro Ghetto, 1890–1920.* Chicago: University of Chicago Press.

Wilson, W. J. (1987). *The Truly Disadvantaged.* Chicago: University of Chicago Press.

Woodward, C. V. (1966). *The Strange Career of Jim Crow.* New York: Oxford University Press.

LEWIS WALKER
BENJAMIN C. WILSON

AFRICAN MUSLIMS

African Muslims have a long history in the United States; they certainly existed on U.S. soil during the antebellum period. These individuals were mainly slaves taken from those regions of the African continent where Islam was known. Today the term "African Muslims" refers specifically to those Africans who entered the United States after World War II. They are called African Muslims in contradistinction to the African-American Muslims. The majority of African Muslims come from the following locations: the Maghrebian states (Morocco, Algeria, and Tunisia), Libya, Egypt, Sudan, Nigeria, Senegambia (Senegal and the Gambia), Guinea-Bissau, Sierra Leone, Togo, Ghana, Mali, Uganda, Chad, Guinea, Ivory Coast, Kenya, Tanzania, Sudan, South Africa, Liberia, Somalia, Zanzibar, Eritrea, and Ethiopia.

Immigration to the United States

The arrival of African Muslims in the United States was largely due to three important developments: (1) the Cold War, which pitted the United States against the Soviet Union; (2) the independence of African countries from colonial rule during the 1960s and 1970s, with the establishment of African diplomatic and consular missions in Washington, D.C., and at the United Nations headquarters in New York City; and (3) the fascination with America that developed with the arrival of U.S. Peace Corps volunteers and the wider dissemination of American cultural wares in various parts of Muslim Africa. These three developments had significant effects on Muslims in Africa. As a result of their greater exposure to American people and products, many African Muslims from Francophone Africa, who previously went to France for education and shopping, now looked to the United States. The increase in the traffic flow from Dakar, Senegal, to New York by way of Air Afrique, and by other available means, has led to the emergence of African Muslim communities in several metropolitan centers of the United States.

Cold War. During the Cold War, the United States employed a strategy of recruiting young African students to attend American colleges and universities. As a result of this pattern of recruitment, many students entered the United States during the 1960s to pursue further studies. This effort at reaching out to the young Africans of the postcolonial generation brought to the United States thousands of students from all former colonies in Africa. Most of these graduates later went back home to work in their countries of origin. However, because of the political climate in their countries, many again returned to the United States under different circumstances. Among these returnees were many African political refugees who were at the upper reaches of their countries. Fleeing from repressive regimes and forced to reexamine their life chances and careers, many of these men and women opted to live permanently in the United States. Their decisions made them a part of the Muslim community in the United States.

African Independence. The emergence of African Muslim communities also involves the commercial and trade ties that developed after the arrival of independence and the establishment of African embassies and consulates in the United States. Because of the growing familiarity with things American, and as a result of the change in the taste and appetite of the African leadership and the well-to-do in their societies, many African Muslims immigrated to America for business reasons. Evidence of this can be gleaned from the pages of the *New York Times*, the *Wall Street Journal*, and *Forbes Magazine*, all three of which have reported on the activities of African entrepreneurs and peddlers in New York. Although there are no precise statistics that tell how many of the Africans engaged in businesses in New York are Muslims, an estimate would be that 60 to 80 percent of the persons involved are Muslims. The parties in this zone of enterprise are self-selected, and they are linked to organizations and institutions that have an extensive history in long-distance trade and commerce in West Africa. Some of these men and women are independent agents from groups like the Serahulis (or Marakas) from Senegambia or neighboring areas. Others are members of religious Sufi orders from West Africa, particularly from Mali, Guinea, Nigeria, and the Senegambia region, where the Tijaniyya, Qadiriyya, and Muridiyya brotherhoods exercised a great deal of influence among a community of interethnic elements driven both by the profit motive and by the quest for spiritual benefits in this life and the next. As a result of these emerging patterns of trade and commerce between the United States and West African states, one now sees a small but growing number of African wares entering the United States market.

Dissemination Flow. The emergence of African Muslim communities in certain eastern U.S. cities and in a small part of the American Midwest involves the transaction flow between African Americans and the Muslims in West Africa and beyond. This factor is related to African independence in that the number of African Americans coming into contact with African Muslims of West Africa has increased since the 1960s. This growth in the number of contacts and the greater exposure of African Americans to Islam in Africa have somehow created opportunities for some Muslims of these parts of Africa to immigrate to the United States to teach and do *dawah* (propagation) among the blacks of American society. This state of affairs is a result of the increasing trade activities of the African immigrant population and the greater desire to study and understand the Islamic chapter of black history. This provides a good example of Islam spreading through commercial means.

Other Influence. Another factor that is partly responsible for the emigration of African Muslims into the United States lies in the fact that the Islamic revivalist movement in many parts of the Muslim world has created a new opening for young men and women from Africa to journey to the Middle East, South Asia, and Southeast Asia. Those who made this journey to parts of the Muslim world unknown to others back home have somehow joined new fraternities and sororities of Islam. By coming into contact with new faces and new brothers and sisters, these African Muslims have come to meet and establish friendships with their counterparts among American Muslims. Some of these young Muslims have been recruited to work with independent Muslim centers and *masajid* (mosques) across the country. Some of the ones who established such contacts, which are very rare indeed, have become fairly well established within the Sunni Muslim community. Invariably they are recruited as imams or teachers in the Muslim schools of the different Muslim communities. Their attractiveness largely depends on their command of the Arabic language and their better grounding in Islamic studies. It should be noted that African services are more widely sought by African-American Muslims running independent masajid than by members of the various successors of the old Nation of Islam. Two reasons can be given for this differential attitude toward the African Muslim *dai* (proselytizer). First of all, Africans who are well-grounded in Arabic and Islamic studies receive attention from Sunni immigrant communities because they are usually identified with this segment of the American Muslim community. The second reason lies in the fact that most of those who aspire to the position of

imam (leader of prayer), *khatib* (deliverer of sermons), *muezzin* (caller to prayer), or *alim* (teacher in the Muslim school) received their education and training in the Arab world. Because of this cultural exposure and experience within the Arab Muslim world they have the much needed psychological and sociological wherewithal to survive the socialization process within the predominantly Arab Muslim centers and masajid. There are, however, other African Muslim immigrants who work closely with members of the old Nation of Islam. Prominent among these African Muslims are West African graduates of Arab/Islamic universities in the Middle East. There are a few others, who developed ties with Louis Farrakhan, especially after the establishment of an office of the Nation of Islam in Accra, Ghana.

Demography

In describing the African Muslim immigrants to the United States, one must also focus on the demographic facts about these groups and subgroups of Africans. First of all, the overwhelming majority of these African Muslims are literate. This includes both the men and the women. Such statistics are certainly a major departure from the ones for those Muslims who immigrated to the United States early in the twentieth century. Another fact about this community is the disproportionate number of adults among them. Drawn almost entirely from persons between the ages of eighteen and forty-five, this group of African immigrants is just beginning to raise a second or third generation. Unlike the waves of Muslim émigrés who arrived in the early 1900s, this more recent group is not completely denied access to African-born women eligible for marriage. Many African Muslim women have joined the waves of emigration out of Africa. However, due to the paucity of these women in relation to the male population living in the United States, many of the African Muslim men have settled for American brides.

Many African Muslims are caught in the web of transatlantic marriages. This situation has in-

Students in a Chicago Muslim School are instructed by their teacher. (Hulton Deutsch Collection/Corbis)

variably caused divorces between separated couples, but it has also led many, if not most, of the parties to such marriages to entertain the "myth of return." That is, many of these parties to long-distance marriages tell themselves that their stay in the United States is for a brief period; once they strike it rich, they will take the next plane home. For many African Muslims, this optimistic plan is never fulfilled. As a response to this social and psychological predicament, many African Muslims, especially among the taxi drivers, peddlers, and itinerant traders in the New York–New Jersey area and elsewhere along the Eastern Seaboard, have resorted to circular and return migration; some of these immigrants, legal or illegal, return to their countries of origin after several years in the United States. The main reason for this circular and return migration is the question of familial pressures and the inability to adjust fully to the demands and realities of American life.

Language and Assimilation

The African Muslim immigrants can be divided linguistically into three broad categories. The first group consists of those who can be classified as perfectly or almost perfectly acculturated. These are the highly educated who had earlier immigrated to the West for higher university education and went home, only to return later to the United States. These individuals do not have the problem of articulation or the problem of cultural adjustment in U.S. society. The second group consists of those who are known in the literature as the *Arabisant*. Trained in Arabic/Islamic institutions of higher learning after many years in African Koranic schools, these immigrants, usually with few exceptions, are more fluent in Arabic and African languages than in English or French. Their command of the Arabic language almost always casts them in the role of community religious leaders. The third category consists of those who are not fluent in English, French, or Arabic. However, because of their exposure to the colonial or postcolonial education system, they have acquired some degree of mastery of the colonial language. These imperfectly acculturated immigrants constitute the majority of the African Muslims in the United States. Because of their limited command of American English and their desire to strike it rich and go back home, many of these individuals have opted for one or the other of two responses to the American experience. The first response is to embrace the "American Dream" and to assimilate as much as possible. Those who choose this position are called "cultural Muslims," individuals who do not practice the faith in their daily lives but do culturally identify themselves with the Muslim community. The other category of Muslims consists of those who try to maintain their Islamic identities by creating a cultural boundary between themselves and the larger society. Within this category are several subcategories, including the selective assimilationists and the rigid advocates of Islamic orthodoxy.

The selective assimilationists are individuals who share many things in common with the cultural Muslims in that both of them wish to be accepted in some way by the larger society. Whereas the cultural Muslims are willing to be involved in the secular culture without any inhibition, the selective assimilationists are willing to embrace the American secular culture, but only in those areas where their Islamic identity is not threatened. Here these Muslims are similar to the Christian fundamentalists and Orthodox Jews in the larger society. The rigid advocates of Islamic orthodoxy, however, do not approve of such a close relationship with the secular humanism of the larger society. Frightened by the possible effects of being involved with the secular humanists, these rigid advocates of Islamic orthodoxy have decided to avoid the entanglements of American secular humanism completely. This is most obvious in their isolationist lifestyle, in their circles of friends, and in the hijab culture of the women (veiling of the face and covering of the head).

Organizations

Because of the embryonic nature of the African Muslim community, social, religious, and political institutions are still in their formative period. Socially speaking, each of the countries represented in the United States has one or more organizations trying to give unity and coherence to the collective needs and interests of their membership. In most instances these Muslims are members of ethnically or regionally based organizations, even though most if not all of their members come from Muslim backgrounds. The persistence of ethnicity has affected the manner in which African Muslims, like other Africans in the United States, organized themselves for collective self-development. This tendency is most evident among the Nigerians and Sierra Leoneans. In these two African Muslim communities, individuals still budget their psychological and emotional energies in such a way that some amount goes to the ethnic group and some other amount goes to the religious community. In the case of the Senegambians, ethnicity does not have that impact, but, especially among Senegalese, sectarian allegiance does play an important part in the definition and maintenance of one's loyalty. In other African Muslim communities, individuals are usually polarized along political and ideological lines. This is most evident among Maghrebians and sub-Saharans. The ongoing conflict between the Islamic revivalists and their secular opponents in Algeria and elsewhere in North Africa have led to this polarization, which is also evident among Sudanese and Muslims from East Africa, Zanzibar, the Horn of Africa, and South Africa. Somalis and Ethiopian Muslims have manifested this tendency in the United States. During the Mohamed Siad Barre regime many Somalis supported his administration and its policies. Similarly, a growing number of Somalis who fled to the United States became vocally opposed to his rule. The dividing lines were drawn by clan, political, and ideological lines. In the case of the Hararis of Ethiopia, there were some, though definitely a minority, who supported the Dergue under Mengistu Haile Mariam and others who were aligned with the groups fighting for Eritrean liberation. In Zanzibar, this political and ideological divide goes back to the early days of the union with the mainland of Tanganyika. It has continued to the present, and the small number of Zanzibaris have replicated such splits in the United States.

The same kind of polarization is evident among the East African Muslims. Some of the Muslims from Uganda, Tanzania, and Kenya now living in the United States at one time supported Idi Amin, Arap Moi, or Julius Nyerere; but because of changing times and circumstances, they have changed loyalties and are now opposed to the status quo. Many are now in the United States either because of political differences with one faction or the other or because of economic realities back home. In the case of the Muslims from southern Africa, there are those who fled South Africa during the times of apartheid. Composed mainly of persons of Indo-Pakistani origin, a sizeable number now live in southern California.

Because of the African Muslim communities' diversity and dynamism, there are forces inside and outside of the communities that would like to affect the course of community development. The advocates of pan-Islamism and their nationalist and ethnic rivals are beginning to compete for mental space in communities. Faced with the challenge of rearranging their mental stances, and increasingly confident with new social and political realities in American society, many African Muslims are beginning to establish religious societies and masajid. There are various arrangements evident in the African Muslim community; there are those who try to replicate their Maliki, Ismaili, Wahabi, or Salafi Islamic school of thought, and there are others who are seeking ways to build up structures for their *tarigian* (sufi order) chapters in the United States. These efforts, like those of earlier generations of immigrants, are designed to assure cultural and religious continuity within the African Muslim communities. For this and other related reasons, one can argue that today almost every Muslim *madhab* (legal school of thought) and sufi order existing in the African Muslim world is represented in American religious life. Sufi orders range from the Tijaniyya and Muridiyya of the Senegambia region of West Africa, through the Ansars and Mirghaniyya orders

The Fruit of Islam, the bodyguards of the Nation of Islam, attempt crowd control outside a rally in New York City for Louis Farrakhan, the group's leader. (David Wells/Corbis)

of the Republic of Sudan, to the various brotherhoods of Egypt, Somalia, and eastern Africa.

The followers of the Aga Khan, more widely known as the Ismailis, are among the most Westernized of the African Muslims living in the United States. Their small population within the larger Muslim community belies their influence and access to the larger American society. They and the followers of the Ahmadiyya Movement in Islam are usually identified as minorities by members of other Muslim groups, who considered themselves to be living within the mainstream of Shi'a and Sunni Islam in America.

Publications

Like other American religious communities, African Muslims also have their own publications to project and defend their identity within the American society. There are three kinds of publications in the community: (1) pan-Islamic publications (both national and international) in which African Muslims are occasionally or frequently featured; (2) publications that are generated by individual religious orders or national groups, often specializing in matters affecting members of a particular country; and (3) secular publications that address the needs of immigrants from individual Muslim countries.

Among the international Muslim publications, *Impact* from London and *Crescent* from Toronto are among the most widely read. There are several Arabic, French, and English publications that also circulate among the African Muslims. All of these cater to a specialized sectarian audience, and they usually have an ideological tinge about them. Those that address the needs and interests of American Muslims are *Minaret* from the Islamic

Center of Southern California; *Message International,* from the Jamaat Islami of Mawlana Maududi's followers; *The Muslim Journal,* from the followers of Imam W. D. Mohammed; *Islamic Horizon* from the Islamic Society of North America; *Ismaili American,* for the followers of the Aga Khan in the United States and Canada; *New Trend* from the Jamaat al-Muslimeen; *Muslim World Monitor,* a bi-weekly American Muslim paper controlled by Arab Muslims; and the *Ahmadiyya Gazette,* a publication of the controversial Ahmadiyya Movement.

Besides the international and national publications catering to the needs of the African Muslims in the United States, there are several newsletters published in Arabic, English, and French. There is, for example the *African Voice* from Washington, D.C. Not necessarily a religious paper, it covers issues affecting African Muslims. At the height of the Somali crisis, the *African Voice* provided several relevant analyses. There are a few newsletters put out by groups such as the Ethiopian Muslim community and the Nigerian Muslim Association. Coverage of African Muslims in the United States can also be gleaned from the secular-oriented African magazines and newspapers published in the United States. Many of these secular-oriented news sources have a very short lifespan, but they do provide information while they are publishing. Examples include *Profiles International, African Mirror, African Times, Africa News Weekly, Ethiopian Review, Gaffat Ethiopia, Jaliba* (from the Senegambian community), and *Somalia Today.*

Conclusion

African Muslims have a long relationship with the Western Hemisphere. Without necessarily embracing the Afrocentric perspective of pre-Columbian African presence in the Americas, one can still argue that African Muslims were present in the United States during the time of slavery. This historical connection with early America constitutes an important chapter in the assimilation of early Muslim immigrants to the United States.

More secure about their identity in a democratic, republican America and determined to succeed by means of hard work and seriousness of purpose, many of these Muslims can join hands with men and women of other faiths as Americans.

The diversity and dynamism of the African Muslim communities can be either positive or negative, depending on the activities and leadership of the Muslim communities in general and the African Muslim communities in particular. The homogenizing effects of Americanization could cement the bonds of these diverse African groups and help create a new American Muslim consciousness. Such a development could certainly change the course of events in Africa and the United States.

As the African Muslim communities become more and more organized, and as they establish structures to perpetuate their families and communities, they will become more responsive to the challenges of American life and culture. With a greater degree of institutionalization, chances are that African Muslims will be able to deploy their resources in concert with members of the Muslim and non-Muslim communities living in their neighborhood. One can also conclude that African Muslims will be successful in the American experience only when they convince the larger society that they are willing to internalize American values that reinforce their *din* (religion) and strengthen their religious identity, taking full advantage of the Second Amendment to the U.S. Constitution.

See also: AFRICAN AMERICANS; EGYPTIAN MUSLIMS; ETHIOPIANS AND ERITREANS; GHANAIANS; YORUBA

Bibliography

Austin, A. D., ed. (1984). *African Muslims in Antebellum America: A Sourcebook.* New York: Garland.

Brenner, L., ed. (1993). *Muslim Identity and Social Change in Sub-Saharan Africa.* Bloomington: Indiana University Press.

Charles, N., and Speer, T. (1995). "Closing the Door." *Emerge* 6(9):34–40.

Egan, T. (1994). "An Ancient Ritual and a Mother's Asylum Plea." *New York Times*, March 4, p. A25.

Hicks, J. P. (1994). "Vendors' Ouster and Boycott Divide Harlem." *New York Times*, October 23, p. 1.

Lewis, I. M. (1980). *Islam in Tropical Africa*, 2nd edition. Bloomington: Indiana University Press.

Loose, C. (1995). "Wedded to Tradition: For the Extended Family of Sierra Leone Natives." *Washington Post*, July 20, p. DC1.

McCall, D. F., and Bennett, N. R., eds. (1971). *Aspects of West African Islam*. Boston: African Studies Department, Boston University.

McCloud, A. B. (1995). *African-American Islam*. New York: Routledge.

Millman, J. (1994). "From Dakar to Detroit." *Forbes* 154(7):86–90.

Numan, F. H. (1992). *The Muslim Population in the United States: A Brief Statement*. Washington, DC: American Muslim Council.

Speer, T. (1994). "The Newest African Americans Aren't Black." *American Demographics* 16(1):9–10.

Stein, C. B. (1994). *African Art in Transit*. New York: Cambridge University Press.

Takougang, J. (1995). "Recent African Immigrants to the United States: An Historical Perspective." *Western Journal of Black Studies* 19(1):50–57.

SULAYMAN S. NYANG

AFRICANS

See AFRICAN AMERICANS; AFRICAN MUSLIMS; BAR-BADIANS; CAPE VERDEANS; ETHIOPIANS AND ERI-TREANS; GHANAIANS; HAITIANS; IGBO; JAMAICANS; SEA ISLANDERS; TRINIDADIANS; YORUBA

ALBANIANS

Albania covers an area of approximately 11,100 square miles ffand runs halfway down the western coast of the Balkan Peninsula. It is bounded on the north by Yugoslavia, on the south and southwest by Greece, and on the east by Macedonia. It faces Italy across the Strait of Otranto, with the Adriatic Sea to the north and the Ionian Sea to the south. Like most of the Balkans, Albania has always been a poor, rugged, isolated, mountainous country. Although scholars are still debating the origins of present-day Albanians, there is general agreement that they are probably descendants of the old Illyrian tribes. The ancient Albanians and their descendants called their country Shqipni or Shqiperi and themselves Shqipter, which translates as "Sons of the Eagle." The name "Albania" in common usage in the Western world is of much more recent origin. Robert Guiscard, the Norman Crusader who in the eleventh century had invaded central Albania, is said to be responsible for its adoption. When he and his followers established themselves in the town of Elbasan, they found the name hard to pronounce and corrupted it to Albania. Through many years of its history, the Albanian people were divided into two main groups, known as the Ghegs of the north and the Tosks of the south. The Ghegs were more isolated and the Tosks were more worldly due to their proximity to Greece. Linguistically, each group spoke its own distinct dialect.

For much of its history, Albania has also been divided religiously into three groups: Catholic to the north (approximately 15%), Eastern Orthodox to the south (15%), and Muslim throughout the country (70%). Prior to World War I, the southern Tosks supplied the largest number of immigrants to the United States. The largest numbers of these early immigrants proved to be sojourners because their primary intent was to go to America, earn money, and return to their homeland to purchase land, buy tools, or gain enough capital to start a business. However, like many sojourners who originally immigrated to America to work and return home, many Albanians ended up staying in their newfound homeland. Today it is estimated that approximately seventy-five thousand Albanians and their descendants live in America. Their relatively small number has always been one of their chief characteristics. This number has remained fairly constant until the late 1980s. Albanian immigration to America was cut off in 1939 as a result of World War II and the subsequent takeover of the Albanian government by Communist forces in 1944. The fact that immigration was severed resulted in creating an American ethnic group that could no longer receive cultural transfusions from waves of new immigrants. However, in the late 1980s, with the collapse of the Communist government of Albania, small numbers of Albanians once again began to arrive in America.

Early Immigration and Settlement

In general, pre–World War I immigration to America was composed of those who immigrated to America to increase their economic position and those who immigrated as political refugees, motivated by the civil wars in Albania between 1904 and 1914. Whatever their differing reasons for immigrating to America, they were all originally united by their desire to return someday to their native land. This explains why the immigrants were predominantly young males. Fiak Konitza, former Albanian ambassador to the United States, estimated that in 1919, out of every one hundred men, only fifteen had wives in America, and of the approximately thirty thousand Albanians in America, only one thousand were women. After World War I, many of the Albanian Tosks who arrived in America intended to stay and either brought their families or married in America. After World War II a different group of Albanians immigrated to America. Many were political exiles from Communist-ruled Albania or Yugoslavia. Most of this group were Ghegs, who were Muslim or Roman Catholic.

It is assumed that the first Albanian who immigrated to America was Koli Kristofer, who arrived between 1884 and 1886. By 1900, there were probably no more than forty Albanians in America. They had chosen Boston as their primary city of residence. As years passed, the Albanian population of Boston continued to grow. In 1907,

the earliest recorded unofficial census of Albanians in Massachusetts was conducted by Sotir Petsi, editor of the Albanian newspaper *Kombi* (The Nation). This census indicated that seven hundred Albanians lived in Boston, four hundred in Worcester and Southbridge, Massachusetts, and two hundred in Natick, Massachusetts.

As Boston emerged as the center of Albanian immigration, several Albanian institutions began to develop. One such institution was the *konak* (dog kennel) or tenement dwelling where Albanian immigrants chose to live. Ten to fifteen men would share a flat as well as all the living expenses. These tenements were usually in close proximity to transportation and employment. A common profession for these early immigrants was as pushcart peddlers selling either vegetables or fish throughout the streets of Boston. As immigration continued, Albanians established colonies throughout Massachusetts wherever work could be found. However, Boston and Worcester continued to attract the largest numbers, since work was plentiful. Because many of these immigrants were unskilled and illiterate, they had no choice but to join the masses of unskilled labor toiling in the factories of industrial America. As the years passed, Albanian immigrants followed work to other areas including New York City; Detroit; Philadelphia; Bridgeport, Connecticut; Jamestown, Albany, and Rochester, New York, as well as to other cities, such as Manchester, New Hampshire; Biddeford-Saco, Maine; Cleveland; Chicago; and as far west as St. Louis. Since later immigrants were drawn to these same cities, the population distribution of Albanian Americans remains fairly similar to that in the early years of immigration. Wherever they settled, Albanian immigrants maintained their konaks as well as other Albanian customs and institutions. Another such institution that developed was the *kafane* (coffeehouse or small restaurant), where Albanians congregated during their off hours. They reminisced about the homeland and discussed new job openings and their favorite topic: politics. Societies were also formed to aid villages in the homeland to provide funding to build schools, roads, and hospitals. The well-being of the homeland continued to be foremost on their minds. As years passed, more and more Albanians went into business. The three most common business enterprises were fruit stores, restaurants, and grocery stores. By 1925, the Albanians of Greater Boston could claim more than three hundred grocery and food stores. Also of significance is that after World War I a number of the Albanian immigrants who arrived in America were intellectuals, professionals, and political leaders. This acted to bring greater diversity to the Albanian-American community. When Albanian immigration to America resumed in the 1980s, Albanian immigrants still found it necessary to begin work in menial occupations. Such is the case of many recently arrived Albanians who have settled in and around the Bronx in New York City.

Regardless of when they arrived in the United States, Albanians have tended to remain clannish and have attempted to maintain many aspects of their cultural identity.

Religion

The most important institution in America that has served to trigger and maintain Albanian religious, cultural, and national identity has proved to be the Albanian Orthodox Church. In southern Albania, where Orthodox Christians prevailed, the Greek Orthodox Church exercised significant influence and control over Orthodox Christians. They also attempted to extend this control over Albanian Americans through the Greek Orthodox churches in America. However, in America a series of clashes between Albanians and the Greek Orthodox Church led Albanians to establish their own independent Albanian Orthodox Church in America. This historic event occurred in Boston in 1908. A key figure in this development was Fan S. Noli. A Harvard-educated writer, composer, and politician, Noli first arrived in America in 1908 with the express purpose of organizing immigrants to work for the Albanian national cause. Having received training as a chanter in the Orthodox Church, he was selected as the first Albanian Orthodox priest in America

and ordained at the Russian Orthodox Cathedral in New York City. Eventually he rose to the position of metropolitan of the church and served as the prime mover in establishing thirteen Albanian Orthodox parishes in the United States. Noli championed the cause of Albanian religious, cultural, and national identity until his death in 1965.

In 1971, the Albanian Orthodox Church in America approved affiliation with the Orthodox Church in America. The Orthodox Church in America, with a membership reported at more than one million, came into being in 1970 when the Russian Orthodox Church in the then Soviet Union granted independence to the former Russian Orthodox Church in America. Many of the smaller Orthodox denominations in America have also affiliated with the Orthodox Church in America. This affiliation has allowed these smaller groups, such as the Albanians, to have the advantage of belonging to a larger, organized, recognized body and, at the same time to maintain their own identity and jurisdictions. In recent years, numerous Albanian Orthodox communities have undertaken major building projects. In 1982, the community of Worcester, Massachusetts, completed a new religious center, providing a new house of worship along with a church school, offices, and a fellowship hall. Two senior citizen residences have since been added to this complex. Similar building activities have occurred in the Albanian Orthodox Community of Farmington Hills, Michigan, and Trumbull, Connecticut. Undertakings of this magnitude would not be happening if Albanian religious and cultural identity were declining. They clearly demonstrate overt manifestations of Albanian ethnic and religious identity and the desire to preserve these identities.

Albanian-American Muslims founded their first society in America in 1915 in Biddeford, Maine. A common meetinghouse for them was an Albanian coffeehouse in Bidderford, where they apparently conducted religious services in a back room. An Albanian-American Muslim society was founded in Detroit in 1949, and other Albanian-Muslim societies have developed in Waterbury, Connecticut; Chicago; and Brooklyn, New York.

The Bektashi Muslim sect built a monastery in Detroit in 1954.

Albanian Catholics, who tend to be more recent arrivals, have established churches in the Bronx and Detroit. In 1969, the Albanian Catholic Center began serving the needs of more than thirty-five hundred Albanian Catholics throughout the New York City area.

Social and Family Life

Without question, the early Albanian immigrants as well as those who arrived in later periods made every effort to keep the Albanian language, culture, and their respective religions alive in America. The family was and still is an important element in the lives of most Albanians regardless of their generation. Albanian families in America just as in Albania tended to be male dominated, with the husband as the prime authority figure. Of course, with the passage of time and the coming of new generations, family structure has undergone numerous changes. Many elements of the American family have also become part of the Albanian family, much to the regret of the elderly. In the past, marriage outside the group was viewed as an evil to be avoided. However, Albanians have had to face the fact that because of their extremely small numbers in America, intermarriage was inevitable. With the passage from one generation to the next, intermarriage has become a way of life for most Albanian families. This is not to say that Albanian ethnic identity and commitment are automatically decreasing. In certain areas with large Albanian populations, many activities continue to maintain ethnic identity. Besides Albanian religious services, many Albanian communities still sponsor Albanian picnics and bazaars. In recent years Albanian festivals have proved very successful in attracting Albanians as well as non-Albanians. The Albanian Festival in Worcester is a well-recognized and well-attended event. At many of these events, traditional Albanian foods continue to be served to young and old alike, both Albanian and non-Albanian. These traditional foods include barbecued roast lamb; spinach; leek-

or squash-filled pies (lakror); and pastries such as kurabie, brushtull, and baklava. In addition, many Albanian religious centers offer courses in the Albanian language, history, literature, and folklore.

Although relatively small, an Albanian press has existed in the United States since the early 1900s. The efforts of these early publications were to inform Albanian Americans of events in the homeland, to keep them abreast of developments in America, and to support specific political views. Currently, each of the Albanian religious communities has its own publication. Several of the cities supporting large Albanian populations also have radio broadcasts in Albanian. They usually air once a week for an hour. The oldest such program, *Zeri i Shqiperise* (Voice of Albania), was founded in Boston in 1938.

Several national Albanian organizations that began their existence supporting particular political views have graduated into organizations seeking to support Albanian cultural life. Two such organizations are Vatra and the Free Albanian Organization; each has a newspaper circulated to its members. In 1946, a group of young Albanian Americans in the New York City area established the Albanian-American National Organization (AANO). Its original aim was to help its members adjust better to the realities of life in America. It now has chapters in various cities with sizable enough Albanian populations to support its activities. AANO is best recognized for its cultural affairs, which bring its members together. Every year in early August, a national convention is held in a major city where a chapter exists. This three-day affair brings Albanians together from across America. While originally identified with Orthodox Christians, efforts were undertaken to encourage membership regardless of religious persuasion. This effort has paid off, resulting in an increased membership whose only concern is Albanian ancestry.

In 1981, an extensive research project was undertaken to assess the contemporary levels of ethnic commitment and identity among Albanian Americans. This effort centered on the Albanian community in Boston, which was chosen because of its large Albanian population and because it is often viewed as the center of Albanian life in America. Several areas were investigated, including the level of Albanian ethnic identity by generation, the level of Albanian ethnic identity by social class, the extent of outward residential movement of Boston's Albanian Americans, and the level of generational occupational mobility. Results indicated that generational-occupational mobility has increased significantly among second- and third-generation Albanians, outward residential movement from traditional Albanian neighborhoods has been extensive, and old Albanian neighborhoods have all but ceased to exist. In terms of ethnic commitment and identity, the two variables of class and generation did not significantly decrease. This is not to say that assimilation has not occurred. However, the general conclusion was that Albanian ethnic identity and commitment continue to be important in the lives of many Albanian Americans in Boston. Evidence also suggests that these findings may be generalized to other sizable Albanian communities in America.

Bibliography

Chekrezi, C. (1971). *Albania Past and Present*. New York: Arno Press.

Federal Writers Research Project. (1939). *The Albanian Struggle in the Old World and the New*. Boston: The Writer, Inc.

Handlin, O. (1959). *Boston's Immigrants*. New York: George Braziller.

Hoberman, B. (1980). "New Albania." *The Boston Journal* 4(6):33–38.

Nagi, D. (1989). *The Albanian American Odyssey*. New York: AMS Press.

DENNIS L. NAGI

AMISH

The Amish are a socioreligious, ethnic minority living only in North America. Identified by their horses and buggies, broad-brimmed hats, and bonnets, they are the most visible of the so-called Pennsylvania Dutch.

The Amish descend from Anabaptists, a radical sect of the Reformation, originating among the followers of Zwingli, in Zurich, Switzerland, in 1525. Beliefs that set them apart from other reformers were (1) adult baptism, (2) separation of church and state, (3) nonresistance, (4) not swearing oaths, and (5) personal accountability to one another within the community of believers. Anabaptists rejected infant baptism and instigated believer's baptism. To receive a believer's baptism an individual must be mature enough to distinguish right from wrong and must have heard the word preached, believed in the message, and confessed the faith. This sequence negated infant baptism and threatened the power of the state by rejecting the state's right to dictate the religious affiliation of its subjects, thereby creating a separation of church and state and, ipso facto, freedom of religion. Nonresistance, which demanded refusal to serve in any military activity, and the refusal to swear an oath also threatened the power of the central government. In spite of severe persecution this nonviolent Swiss Brethren segment of the Anabaptists attracted many converts, who gradually became known as Mennonites after Menno Simons, a sixteenth-century writer and leader of the nonresistant Dutch Anabaptists. A rift developed in 1693 among the Swiss Mennonites who had taken up residence in Alsace and the Palatinate after being driven out of Switzerland. Jacob Ammann, a Mennonite bishop, preached strict church discipline, demanding avoidance of disobedient church members in all social interactions. Excommunicated individuals were barred from the family dinner table as well as from the communion table. Ammann added foot-washing to the communion service, which was to be held twice a year instead of only once; favored a distinctive dress code; and severely restricted interaction with those outside the religious fellowship. Congregations that followed Ammann became known as Amish. Amish still practice foot-washing, celebrate communion twice a year, and will not eat or participate in social activities with a person who is under the ban. Individuals who are under the ban have been ritually removed from church membership until they repent their wrong doing, which they illustrate by their everyday actions and in a formal confession in front of the members of their own church district.

During the third quarter of the nineteenth century, those Amish who wished to retain the old ways of strict shunning, conservative dress, and limited use of technology withdrew from fellowship with the "change-minded" Amish Mennonite churches. The Old Order Amish encompass numerous subdivisions, characterized by minor variations in church regulations. The New Order Amish separated from the Old Order during the 1960s. The New Order Amish maintain the distinctive dress and drive the horse and buggy but are more tolerant in church discipline and in the use of technology. The Beachy Amish, named after Moses M. Beachy, separated from the Old Order in 1927. The Beachy Amish dress somewhat like the traditional Amish but are permitted car ownership. Other conservative Mennonite groups, such as the Conservative Amish Mennonites and the Egly Amish, called themselves Amish until they became assimilated into American society. In 1996, the single term "Amish" included both the Old Order and the New Order Amish but generally not the Beachy Amish. In this entry the term "Amish" will be used to include those people who identify themselves as Amish, reject car ownership, and drive a horse and buggy to church services.

Immigration and Demographics

Approximately five hundred Amish immigrated to the Pennsylvania colony during the eighteenth century. Emigrating from Switzerland and the Palatinate, the first Amish arrived between 1727 and 1732, with the heaviest immigration between 1737 and 1754. More Amish immigrants arrived after the turbulent years of the French and Indian Wars and the Revolutionary War. About three thousand emigrated from Alsace, Lorraine, Montbeliard, Bavaria, Hesse, Waldeck, and the

Palatinate between 1804 and 1860, establishing Amish settlements in Ohio, Indiana, Illinois, Ontario, Iowa, and New York. Only about fifty Amish families immigrated to America after the Civil War. None of the immigrants returned to Europe, and by 1870, there were probably fewer than two thousand Amish scattered in small congregations in Alsace, Lorraine, France, Luxembourg, Switzerland, Hesse, and Bavaria. The last European Amish church, Ixheim, merged with neighboring Mennonites in 1937. There are no longer any Amish in Europe.

The Amish population in North America increased slowly during the second half of the eighteenth century, never spreading beyond Pennsylvania. Nineteenth-century immigrant Amish founded fifteen settlements scattered across the Midwest, New York, and Ontario. However, by 1890, due to secularization and loss of congregation to the change-minded or meeting house Amish Mennonites, there were only twenty-two Old Order Amish church districts, with an estimated population of thirty-three hundred. Since the mid-twentieth century, the Amish have experienced rapid growth. The average size of a completed Amish family is between six and seven living children, and the loss of individuals from the faith is about 22 percent, so although there are very few converts, there is substantial biological growth. By 1996, the Amish population had reached about 155,000, with more than a thousand church districts located in twenty-two states and the province of Ontario. The largest settlements of Amish are in Holmes and adjoining counties in Ohio, in eastern Lancaster County in Pennsylvania, and in Elkhart and LaGrange counties in Indiana. Seventy-five percent of the Amish live in these three states.

The Amish are a young population and a rural people. The age of marriage has remained relatively stable over time. The medium age for men at first marriage is slightly over twenty-three years and for women is just under twenty-two years. The rate of childlessness is 4.4 percent compared to 7.5 percent for the United States as a whole. Artificial contraception and abortion are forbidden. Amish use of modern as well as traditional medicine probably contributed to an increase in fecundity and family size during the twentieth century and to their relatively low death-rate. Inbreeding among the Amish makes a minor contribution toward reducing length of life. The average age of death from natural causes is seventy-one years for males and seventy-two years for females.

Community Characteristics

Amish culture is viable only when individuals and families are part of an Amish community. The basic unit of the Amish community is the church district. A mature church district is composed of up to thirty families living in the immediate geo-

An Amish farmer in Pennsylvania works in his field with a team of horses. (Dave Bartruff/Corbis)

graphical area and a bishop, two ministers, and a deacon chosen from within the local congregation by the casting of lots. Ordination is for life, and if a minister moves to another communing church district, he will continue to preach. Worship services are held every other Sunday, rotating among the homes of the members of that church district. In addition to a functioning church, Amish settlements need a school in which the children learn the languages of "the English" (the dominant U.S. culture) and how to function as Amish individuals within the dominant culture. All teaching in the Amish community schools is in English, except for German-language lessons taught as a distinct course. In older Amish settlements some children attend the public school, but most of the newer communities have established their own private schools.

The Amish use three languages: English for business and interaction with outsiders (non-Amish), Pennsylvania German within the home and the community, and High German when reading the Luther Bible and their prayer books and hymnbooks. Pennsylvania German (Pennsylvania "Dutch") or in dialect Pennsylvania Deitsh (Pennsylfawnisch Deitsch, Pennsilfaanisch Deitsch), is a modification of various South German dialects incorporating some Swiss German and many English words. This intimate discourse is considered to be an unwritten language although there is a small literature in Pennsylvania Deitsh. The New Testament is available in the Ohio Amish Pennsylvania Deitsh dialect, with the Deitsh translation of the Luther Bible and the English King James Bible printed in parallel columns. Amish children do not learn English until they start school at age six or seven. Those who attend Amish schools are taught to read High German. Even within the family and the community, most of the written communication is in English, with a sprinkling of Pennsylvania "Dutch" words.

As the Amish population increased and daughter communities were founded, the need for more formal written communication became evident. The first national publication to serve the Amish was the weekly *Budget*, which is also the

An Amish woman works on quilts at her sewing machine in Berlin, Ohio. (Clay Perry/Corbis)

Mennonites. The content of *Die Botschaft*, including the advertising, is supervised by a board of Amish deacons. Both these papers have a national circulation. Several of the larger Amish communities publish local newsletters giving location of church services, weddings, funerals, accidents, and other news of local interest: *Die Blatt*, LaGrange County, Indiana; *Die Gemeinde Register*, Holmes County, Ohio; *Echo*, Arthur, Illinois; and *Gemeinde Brief*, Geauga County, Ohio. *The Diary*, Lancaster County, Pennsylvania, publishes, in addition to community columns from across North America, lists of births, baptisms, marriages, ordinations, migrations, and obituaries and has various other specialty sections. These publications are written in English, using German and Pennsylvania "Dutch" words and phrases.

Raber's Calendar (Baltic, Ohio) has been published in a German edition (1930) as *Der Neue Amerikanische Calender* and in English (1970) as *The New American Almanac*. It is used throughout the various Amish settlements and contains suggested Scripture readings and hymns for use on a specific Sunday, a place to record where church was held and who preached, zodiac and inspirational material, and a list of Amish ministers with their addresses. Since 1915, Raber — first John and then his son Ben — has printed and sold books in German and now also in English of interest to the Amish. During the late 1950s, the Gordonville Print Shop in Pennsylvania began printing genealogies, tracts business cards, funeral cards, and minutes of various Amish meetings and reprinting books, workbooks, and other materials needed by Amish schools.

Pathway Publishers in Aylmer, Ontario (1964), publishes three periodicals, with a combined national circulation of about fifty-eight thousand: *Blackboard Bulletin*, *Young Companion* (formerly *Ambassador of Peace*) and *Family Life*. In addition to reprinting the traditional German religious literature, Pathway publishes more than one hundred different books and workbooks authored by Amish and Old Order Mennonites. Although most of the material from these presses is in English,

local paper for Sugarcreek, Ohio. This paper has never been owned or managed by the Amish, but since July 1890 it has published letters from Amish "scribes" who send in news from their own settlements. In 1941, there were twenty scribes who had been writing for the *Budget* for fifty years. A typical issue of the *Budget* in 1996 printed letters from 230 Amish church districts and one hundred non-Amish writers. The *Budget* publishes articles from a variety of correspondents, including individuals who have left the Amish and must be avoided by the strict Amish churches. In 1974, concerned about undesirable articles in the *Budget*, a group of Amish started a more conservative weekly paper, *Die Botschaft*, published in Lancaster, Pennsylvania, which prints only letters from horse-and-buggy church districts, Amish and Old Order

they are ethnic presses in that they are owned and managed by Amish and they print material specifically for the Amish. Associated with Pathway Publishers, the Heritage Historical Library, founded in 1972, houses a large collection of written material and artifacts.

Conflicts with the State

In an effort to maintain their basic religious tenets, to keep their traditional way of life, and to remain separate from the dominant culture (or, as they put it, to remain "separate from the world"), the Amish have frequently come into conflict with the state. The Amish do not vote in national elections. They refuse to participate in the military. Any Amish individual who serves in the military is removed from the church and is by definition no longer Amish. During the Vietnam War most drafted Amishmen performed alternative service, but some were jailed for refusal to work in a non-farm, nonrural assignment that required wearing non-Amish clothing.

Education has been an area of tension. The Amish responded to public school consolidation by establishing their own community schools managed by a school board of lay churchmen and taught by church members who each have eight years of formal schooling supplemented by training within the community and occasionally by correspondence courses. Problems with the state have arisen over building and safety requirements, teacher certification, curriculum, and length of the school year. Concern about number of years of schooling was largely resolved in 1972 when the U.S. Supreme Court ruled in *Wisconsin v. Yoder* that Amish children do not have to attend high school because they received sufficient supplementary education within the family and community. One- and two-room rural community schools prepare the children well for Amish adulthood.

Another area of conflict was over Social Security, which the Amish view as a form of insurance, indicating a lack of trust in God and the church. Therefore they are forbidden to participate in the Social Security program, neither paying the self-employed tax nor accepting Social Security and Medicare benefits. Seizure of Amish property for nonpayment did not induce cooperation, and in 1965 the law was amended to excuse self-employed Amish from paying the Social Security tax. Those Amish who hire non-Amish pay the Social Security tax for their non-Amish workers and those Amish who work in small factories and for non-Amish employers pay the tax but generally their church forbids their accepting any Social Security or health-care benefits. Amish pay all local, property, and income taxes.

Although the Amish use conventional medicine, there have been misunderstandings in the area of health care, especially when Amish parents have refused approved medical treatment for sick children. Amish individuals have been charged with practicing medicine (generally alternative medicine) without a license. A few church districts discourage immunization, but most Amish cooperate when approached by sympathetic health professionals.

The Amish pay for their own schools, and help those individuals who would normally receive Social Security, Medicare, or payments from commercial insurance companies. Individuals and families faced with catastrophic medical bills, death of a breadwinner, or similar loss are provided for by the Amish community without recourse to money from the state or commercial insurance. The Amish barn-raising is a well-known example of "the sharing of one another's burdens" — a basic value of the Amish.

Horse-drawn transportation has led to disagreement over the type of buggy wheels or horse shoes used, the problem of horse manure, licensing of buggies, and safety markings on buggies and wagons. Some of the plainest subdivisions of the Amish seriously object to the use of the orange slow-moving vehicle triangle, feeling that it is a worldly symbol in a forbidden, brilliant color and that using it implies trust in the symbols of man rather than in the protection of God. The Amish are willing to use lanterns or flashing red lights at night and to use reflector tape to mark their horse-drawn equipment.

Zoning laws sometimes pose problems. May horses be kept on the property? Is an outhouse legal? May a small shop be housed in part of the barn? Is adapting tractor-drawn equipment to horse use an industry? Must one have a permit to erect a building on one's own farm?

Regulations pertaining to agricultural production have caused some Amish to change their occupation or move to another locality—specifically, regulation of milk production that requires the use of electricity, bulk milk tanks, or collecting milk on Sunday. In Lancaster, there have been problems with nitrogen-rich runoff from Amish dairy farms.

The Amish Lifestyle in America

The Amish are known for their self-imposed limitation of technology. They may not own or drive an automobile, though they can hire a car and driver. They may not use high-line electricity in the home, primarily because it brings with it modern appliances. However, they may modify machinery to run by gasoline or diesel engines, and they use air-powered equipment and batteries. The Old Order Amish may not have a telephone in their home, lightning rods on their barns, tractor-drawn field equipment, or central heating. The windmill and hand pump are still widely used, although all except the strictest Amish now allow indoor plumbing.

For centuries diversified farming has been the preferred occupation for the Amish. Their growing population and the increasing difficulty of obtaining farms are forcing many Amish into specialized farming and into nonfarming occupations. A major reason for establishing new settlements is to obtain land suitable for farming. As the discrepancy between Amish lifestyles and those of their American neighbors increased, Amish entered occupations that supported their way of life: blacksmithing, buggy-making, harness construction, adapting equipment to horsepower, and adapting electrical machinery for use with gasoline engines or pressurized air. Amish established specialized shops such as dry goods stores

that sell only plain cloth for clothes and quilts, hardware stores that carry nonelectrical tools and furnishings, furniture and cabinet shops, greenhouses, and bookstores. Amish make products to sell inside and outside the community: pallets, gazebos, birdhouses, hickory rockers, baked goods, and quilts. They sell farm produce and handicrafts to tourists from roadside stands. Amish women as well as Amish men are successful entrepreneurs. Some Amish work in small factories making recreation vehicles, wooden cabinets, bricks, and aluminum products. These factories are operated by executives who have learned that Amish are skilled, intelligent, responsible employees who do not join labor unions. In the older, larger Amish communities and in many of the newer communities, fewer than half of the family heads are farmers.

An Amish buggy in Nappanee, Indiana, displays the triangular caution indicator on the back. (Joseph Sohm/ ChromoSohm Inc./Corbis)

During their first two centuries in North America, the Amish were largely ignored. With the advent of rural electrification, paving of country roads, consolidation of schools, and New Deal programs in agriculture, the Amish were actively disliked as people who impeded progress. Their refusal to serve in the armed forces during World War I and World War II contributed further to their negative image. Beginning in the 1950s and increasing during the 1960s, 1970s, and 1980s, a tourist industry developed, built on a fascination with people who reject many of the amenities most Americans consider essential and on whom was projected a nostalgic image. For the Amish, tourism is an inconvenience and a trial, but it may be a limited source of income, and in a perverse manner tourism strenghtens the boundary between Amish and others. When the Amish have public support, their informal bargaining power with the state increases. In some counties tourist interest in the Amish has brought great financial rewards to non-Amish promoters. In the late 1980s, five million tourists spent more than $400 million annually while visiting Lancaster County. There were some 350 tourists for each Amish individual, and these tourists spent $29,000 per Amish person—far more than the average Amish income.

The Amish are neither a rigid, fossilized culture, a peasant remnant, nor a frozen segment of American history. To retain their traditional values and maintain their distinct culture, the Amish must adapt to the rapidly changing life around them. Their flexibility and willingness to change specific, less important aspects of their culture has enabled them to maintain their basic values and perpetuate a viable way of life that is distinct from the dominant culture yet integrated with it. However, the Amish are challenged by a fast-growing population, a decrease in the availability of farmland, an increase in governmental regulations, and a breakdown of barriers between their society and the larger society. If the Amish can continue to be the primary acculturating agents for their children and can continue to build strong, supportive communities that exclude those who do not share their view of the world, and if

they can continue to buffer their own people from disasters and from inroads of the dominant culture, then they should be able to adapt to the changes and remain a self-identified subculture that enriches American society.

See also: GERMANS; HUTTERITES; MENNONITES; SWISS

Bibliography

Beiler, J. F. (1982). "Ordnung." *Mennonite Quarterly Review* 56:382–384.

Bender, H. S., ed. (1955–1959). *The Mennonite Encyclopedia: A Comprehensive Reference Work on the Anabaptist-Mennonite Movement*, Vols 1–4. Hillsboro, KS: Mennonite Brethren Publishing House.

Dyck, C. J., and Martin, D. D., eds. (1990). *The Mennonite Encyclopedia: A Comprehensive Reference Work on the Anabaptist-Mennonite Movement*, Vol. 5. Scottdale, PA: Herald Press.

Hostetler, J. A. (1993). *Amish Society*. 4th edition. Baltimore, MD: Johns Hopkins University Press.

Hostetler, J. A., and Huntington, G. E. (1992). *Amish Children: Education in the Family, School, and Community*, 2nd edition. Fort Worth, TX: Harcourt Brace Jovanovich.

Huntington, G. E. (1988). "The Amish Family." In *Ethnic Families in America: Patterns and Variations*, 3rd edition, edited by C. H. Mindel, R. W. Habenstein, and R. Wright Jr. New York: Elsevier.

King, T. M. (1994). "Survival Analysis of Familial Data: A Study of the Aggregation of Length of Life." Ph.D. diss., Johns Hopkins University.

Kraybill, D. B. (1989). *The Riddle of Amish Culture*. Baltimore, MD: Johns Hopkins University Press.

Kraybill, D. B., ed. (1993). *The Amish and the State*. Baltimore, MD: Johns Hopkins University Press.

Kraybill, D. B., and Olshan, M. A., eds. (1994). *The Amish Struggle with Modernity*. Hanover, NH: University Press of New England.

Luthy, D. (1986). *The Amish in America: Settlements That Failed, 1840–1960*. Aylmer, ON: Pathway Publishers.

Nolt, S. M. (1992). *A History of the Amish*. Intercourse, PA: Good Books.

Scott, S. E., and Pellman, K. (1990). *Living Without Electricity*. Intercourse, PA: Good Books.

Stoll, J. (1975). "Who Shall Educate Our Children?" In *Compulsory Education and the Amish: The Right Not to Be Modern,* edited by A. N. Keim. Boston: Beacon Press.

Zook, L. J. (1993). "Slow-Moving Vehicles." In *The Amish and the State,* edited by D. B. Kraybill. Baltimore: Johns Hopkins University Press.

GERTRUDE ENDERS HUNTINGTON

ARABS

See EGYPTIAN MUSLIMS; IRAQI MUSLIMS; JORDANIANS; LEBANESE CHRISTIANS; LEBANESE MUSLIMS; PALESTINIANS; SYRIANS; YEMENIS

ARGENTINEANS

While the Argentinean immigrant population shares a history with those Argentineans who did not emigrate, the immigrants differ in that they are rooted in two sociocultural contexts: origin and destination.

During the nineteenth century Argentina declared political independence from Spain, conquered or colonized its relatively small Native Argentinean population, and increased its foreign-born stock by about three million from 1880 to 1900. This transatlantic immigration, primarily European, modified the existing ethnic stock of the country: mestizos (result of Spanish and Native Argentinean breeding), Spaniards, and Native Argentineans, with a very small proportion of blacks. Most contemporary Argentineans trace their descent to either a mix of the native populations with the Spaniards who settled in South America since the sixteenth century or the large contingents of European immigrants arriving during the late nineteenth and early twentieth centuries.

By the beginning of World War I, 43 percent of the country's population had been born abroad. The largest contingents of transatlantic immigrants admitted to Argentina mainly between 1880 and 1930 originated in West European countries, particularly Italy and Spain, with smaller but sizable proportions from East European and Middle Eastern countries. These international contingents, attracted to Argentina by the prospects of a better life, also responded to the political projects of the local elites: to increase manual labor necessary for the development of an export-oriented, agriculturally based economy; and to promote civilization, equated with whiteness and European stock in the ideology of immigration policies.

During the second half of the twentieth century three major trends characterized Argentinean immigration history. First, large population displacements to major urban centers responded to incipient industrialization and labor wage and regulation policies. Second, the origin and direction of international immigration changed: While transatlantic immigration virtually stopped, with the exception of southern Italians at the end of World War II, and small contingents from Southeast Asia, primarily Korea, immigration to Argentina originated in neighboring countries, primarily Bolivia and Paraguay. Third, for the first time in Argentina's history, there was emigration. Until the 1950s, Argentina was primarily a destination for international immigrants, particularly manual laborers. Since the second half of the 1950s, the process has been reversed: Neighboring countries provide manual labor, while skilled labor has immigrated to development poles such as the United States. Despite the fact that immigration will continue to outweight emigration, Argentina's role of exporter of human resources is a new phenomenon.

Social History of Argentinean Emigration

Although personal motivations vary, several structural factors in the society of origin can be linked to the immigration of Argentineans to the United States since the 1960s. These are: (1) recurrent shifts of power between military and constitutional regimes, often resulting in political repression or merely ostracism of large sectors of the population, (2) frequent booms and busts in economic development that translate to economic uncertainty and unpredictability of career paths, and (3) the absence of long-term policies providing institutional support to the career advancement of scientists, technicians, professionals, artists, and civil servants, thus deepening the already existing imbalance between the labor market demand and the oversupply of a highly educated labor force with high expectations.

In the society of destination, two major factors account for the entry of Argentineans: (1) immigration policies that favor the entry of highly skilled personnel and/or family reunification and (2) the psychosocial halo effect of those who had already emigrated and attracted their own networks to follow on the same path.

Available information on this immigration is limited and not always reliable. The three major sources documenting demographic trends for immigrants in the United States—the annual *Statistical Yearbook of the Immigration and Naturalization Service*, the annual *Statistical Abstract of the United States*, and the decennial U.S. Census—compile information differently, thus making comparisons more difficult. There are other obstacles for sociodemographic descriptions and comparative analyses as well. Until 1960, Argentineans were included in the totals for other South Americans; total population size is often computed on the basis of country of past residence, thus failing to include those who underwent stepmigrations; and foreign stock (which includes the children born in the United States of Argentinean parents) and foreign birth are often not discriminated in total population size. For purposes of clarity and comparability, this entry will restrict the population size of U.S. Argentineans to Argentinean birth, regardless of country of last residence. Finally, there are no hard data or reliable estimates of the size of the undocumented population. Despite these drawbacks, it is possible to identify the impact of structural factors on the cohorts of Argentineans residing in the United States from 1960 to 1990.

At the time of the 1960 U.S. Census, there were an estimated thirteen thousand Argentineans in the United States, including large percentages of medical doctors and scientists. Since the 1950s, the occupational profile of Argentinean immigrants to the United States has not changed considerably: a comparatively highly skilled pool of specialized labor, a large proportion holding degrees in higher education or experienced at management levels in industry, and a high proportion of highly skilled manual labor.

By 1970, according to the U.S. Census, the number of Argentineans in the United States had risen to forty-five thousand, three-quarters of whom were born in Argentina and were listed as white. This represents 0.2 percent of the total foreign-born population in the United States. Since the 1960s, the group receiving most attention by analysts are those with a high level of educational attainment, what the literature refers to as the "brain drain." During the 1960s, the U.S. demand for skilled labor in specified fields, especially medicine and science, far exceeded the existing supply. According to U.S. Immigration and Naturalization Service records, 8,080 professionals and technicians were admitted from 1950 to 1970, representing 17 percent of the total number of Argentineans reported by this agency. Important changes in U.S. immigrant legislation in 1965 favored the entry of family members, political exiles, and those in occupational categories in demand at the time. However, the composition has been diversified to include manual workers, who constitute about 50 percent of the Argentineans admitted to the United States since the 1960s.

From 1970 to 1980, the Argentinean population in the United States increased by twenty-four thousand, according to the U.S. Census. During this period changes in the political economy in Argentina motivated emigration and exile: For more than a decade Argentina was in one of the worst periods of political turmoil in its history, and profound economic instability altered the structure of opportunity for many occupational sectors. During this period the education levels of the general population in Argentina continued to increase, yet only the most educated exhibited a greater tendency to emigrate. While educational attainment was always an important selective factor in the immigration of Argentineans to the United States, the educational levels for this group increased during the 1970s. At the same time, the U.S. demand for those categories subsided due to an increase in its own supply of skilled labor. A sizable component among the self-employed immigrated with some capital that allowed them to start their own businesses. The median annual household income of Argentinean immigrants to the United States was then $18,892.

Population Profile

According to the U.S. Bureau of the Census, there were seventy-eight thousand Argentineans in the United States by 1990, a number that, in the estimate of the Argentinean government and recognized scholars, does not reflect the real size of this population. Major population sectors are not counted by the U.S. Census methodology; this includes primarily the undocumented and those caught up in circular migratory paths.

Argentineans reside predominantly in large urban or suburban areas. Although Argentineans are dispersed throughout the United States, the largest group lives in California (almost 31% of the total), followed by New York (17%), Florida (13%), and New Jersey (8.5%).

According to the 1990 U.S. Census, the Argentinean population in the United States is equally distributed by gender, with a slight preponderance of males (39,823 males to 38,163 females). Even though the heavy concentration in the working-age categories is expected, the birth rate has decreased, while the population has aged (22.7% over age forty-five in 1970 compared to 39.1% in 1990). With the general aging of the population, the proportion of widowers and divorced individuals has increased considerably, a trend that also reflects changes in social organization in both Argentina and the United States.

Family life is important to Argentineans. Nuclear units, usually two to four people, spend major holidays together, yet relationships with extended family networks tend to exist with relatives residing in Argentina. Studies comparing the mental health of Argentinean immigrants by gender confirm that immigration is more stressful for women than for men. Women who experienced changes in their work patterns, marital status, family structure, and lifestyle upon immigration were more demoralized than men, regardless of social class background or mobility patterns.

Although the immigration of Argentineans, as distinguished from most immigrations of Latinos, has a predominant middle-class flavor, there is heterogeneity in the social class background of the immigrants and in their insertion into existing labor markets. Consequently, a discussion of the educational, occupational, and income structure—as proxies of social class—is in order.

According to the 1990 U.S. Census, 52.1 percent of the Argentinean population in the United States has had some higher education. The high levels of skill and training exhibited by the Argentinean immigrants had a positive effect on their occupational distribution, which reflects the urban character of settlement as well as the educational levels.

While 49 percent of householders owned their house in 1990, 75 percent had arrived in the United States before 1980. More than half of the more recent immigrants cannot, however, afford home ownership and primarily rent their living space. Households, ranging from two to four persons, have a median income of $39,000 (mean income was $50,690). The heterogeneity in social class standing of Argentineans in the United States accounts for the 7.8 percent households that fell below the poverty level.

Cultural Characteristics

A minority among Spanish-speaking populations, Argentineans in the United States self-report by either birth or descent from Argentinean ancestors. The institutional sector also classifies Argentineans as South Americans, Hispanic, or Latino. "Argentinean" and "Argentine" are terms often used as synonyms by the immigrants themselves. Within-group distinctions emphasize locality of origin; to cite two examples, those from Buenos Aires (the capital city) are called *porteño* (referring to the *puerto*, or harbor), and those from the Cuyo region are called *cuyano*. Although they share a national culture, there are wide variations in cultural traits, depending on social class background and mobility patterns in the United States. Numerous organizations of Argentineans, for example, reflect the occupational distribution of Argentineans in the United States. There are organizations catering exclusively to physicians, such as the Argentina American Medical Society, and others that extend membership to all professionals, such as the Argentine-North American Association for the Advancement of Science, Technology, and Culture. Established in 1985 by Argentinean professionals residing in the United States to support the return of democratic government in Argentina, this latter association continues to promote cultural, scientific, and artistic exchanges between Argentina and the United States. Other social organizations of more localized populations represent the gamut of the occupational spectrum. Some examples are ethnic associations, carrying names such as Argentine Center in New Jersey or Argentina Center in Washington, among others; literary clubs; folklore organizations; Catholic organizations, such as the Association of the Virgin of Luján; Jewish organizations; and others that can be found in each state with a sizable Argentinean population.

An example of Argentinean national culture maintained in the United States is the tango, a dance that emerged from Buenos Aires but stands out as a strong symbol of Argentinean national identity. The tango is a language that still speaks of a national culture that is translated and backtranslated as Argentineans make sense of their complex webs of identity. There are tango organizations in most states where Argentineans reside, such as the Association of Friends of Tango in New York, and Capital Tangueros in Washington.

A national culture could hardly survive without a native language, however, and for Ar-

gentineans language plays an important role as an identity marker. Spanish, the national language of Argentina, is a distinctly Argentinean Spanish, characterized by expressions and pronunciations that have evolved over more than 350 years of fusion of Castilian Spanish with the languages spoken by the people who constituted the major international immigrations to Argentina. In the United States, Argentinean schools were established in cities with high concentrations of Argentineans (e.g., New York, Washington, D.C., and Los Angeles), where children are taught Argentine language, history, and culture. This institutional drive to enhance language and cultural maintenance is reflected at the household level, where spoken Spanish is encouraged. This interest does not detract from linguistic assimilation to an English-speaking country; in fact, as noted in the 1990 U.S. Census, 68 percent of the population reported fluency in English, with a third of these living in linguistically isolated households where only English was spoken.

The extent to which the assimilation of Argentineans is related to the fact that they look more white European than other groups of immigrant Latinos is open to question. Still, it is true that Argentineans do not face the overt discrimination suffered by other Latino groups. Conversely, those other groups often single Argentineans out as "non-Latino," given their physical appearance, the predominantly Castilian Spanish they speak, the different music and dances, and, in many cases, their non-Spanish last names.

In addition to activities organized by grassroots organizations, the representations of the Argentinean government in the United States—namely, the six consulates and one embassy—organize cultural and social events and invite Argentineans to join in celebrating major national occasions such as Independence Day (July 9). The Argentinean government also encourages Argentineans in the United States, 60 percent of whom are not U.S. citizens, to register to vote in Argentinean elections.

As they are different from other Latino populations—perhaps a function of their diversity in social class backgrounds—Argentineans do not tend to gather in "ethnic communities."

Most Argentineans in the United States also create and re-create a distinct ethnic identity by maintaining transnational links with their country of origin. These links, established among social network members via the exchange of goods and services, range from money remittances and financial investments to periodic visits. For many, this has the effect of depoliticization of identity; while typically they fail to vote in Argentine elections, they also typically fail to vote in U.S. elections.

See also: SPANIARDS

Bibliography

Baron, A.; Del Carril, M.; and Gómez, A. (1995). *Why They Left: Testimonies from Argentines Abroad* (in Spanish). Buenos Aires: EMECE.

Freidenberg, J. (1985). "Middle-Class Hispanic Women in the United States: 'One Migrant History.'" Working Paper 100, Women International Development, Michigan State University.

Freidenberg, J. (1989). "The Argentinean Migration to the United States: The Case of Ana." *Estudios Migratorios Latinoamericanos* 11:111–134.

Freidenberg, J.; Imperiale, G.; and Skovron, M. L. (1988). "Migrant Careers and Well-Being of Women." *International Migration Review* 22(2):208–225.

Lattes, A. E., ed. (1986). *Argentine Migratory Dynamic (1955–1984): Democratization and Return of Exiled* (in Spanish). Buenos Aires: Centro Editor de América Latina.

Marshall, A. (1985). *The Argentine Migration* (in Spanish). Buenos Aires: Flacso.

Oteiza, E. (1971). "Emigration of the Argentine Professionals, Technicians, and Skilled Workers to the United States: An Analysis of the Fluctuations of Emigration as a Whole, July 1950 to June 1970." *Desarrollo Económico* 10(39–40):429–454.

Reddy, M. A., ed. (1993). *Statistical Record of Hispanic Americans*. Detroit: Gale.

U.S. Bureau of the Census. (1970, 1981, 1994). *Statistical Abstract of the United States*. Washington, DC: U.S. Government Printing Office.

U.S. Bureau of the Census. (1970, 1980, 1990). *U.S. Census of Population and Housing: Persons of Hispanic Origin in the United States*. Washington, DC: U.S. Government Printing Office.

U.S. Department of Justice. (1984, 1991). *Statistical Yearbook of the Immigration and Naturalization Service*. Washington, DC: U.S. Government Printing Office.

JUDITH FREIDENBERG
EDIT MASUELLI

ARMENIANS

Armenian immigrants arrived in the United States with the knowledge that they were an ancient people who were proud of their Christian faith, which they had kept against all odds since the fourth century. Initially, Armenian immigrants sought refuge from the events that culminated in the 1915 Genocide by the Turkish government. The *spiurk* (diaspora) remained the main source of Armenian emigration until the 1980s, when Soviet Armenians were allowed to leave. Like some groups, the Armenian-American community has grown in size and complexity, and many of its members have prospered and made significant contributions to American society. Unlike others, however, the Turkish denial of the Genocide and transformations within the diaspora and historical Armenia have defined Armenian issues and shaped their social and political relations with each other.

Ethnicity

Armenians trace their origins as a distinct people and culture to the Kingdom of Urartu, the landlocked, mountainous region of eastern Anatolia and Transcaucasia, starting in the ninth century B.C.E. Historians dispute the circumstances of the immigration of these Indo-European people to this area and the extent of their assimilation with local Caucasian-speaking tribes. In any case, by the sixth century B.C.E. their powerful Greek and Persian neighbors were calling them "Armenian." On the other hand, Armenians identify themselves as Hay and their country as Hayastan, after Hayk, one of their legendary heroes.

One of the most significant events in Armenian history is the conversion of the Armenian king Trdat III to Christianity through the efforts of St. Gregory the Illuminator. In becoming the first Christian nation in the world (in 301 or 314 C.E.), Armenia created a distinct identity and culture. An equally crucial development was the invention of the Armenian alphabet (initially thirty-six letters, now thirty-eight) by the learned monk Mesrop Mashtotz between 400 and 405 C.E. The Armenian Apostolic Church, with its distinct theology and rituals, has maintained a central role in Armenian life since its inception.

Modern-day political borders place Historic Armenia in eastern Turkey, northwestern Iran, the Republic of Armenia, and adjacent territories in the republics of Georgia and Azerbaijan. Due to Armenia's geographic location at the crossroads of East and West, and its nearly three thousand years of history, its boundaries have waxed and waned with the fate of both domestic dynasties and alien conquerors. Moreover, after the late fourteenth century, the Armenian culture survived, and at times thrived, in Europe, Russia, Iran, India, and Southeast Asia, where Armenians established a diaspora. Between 1918 and 1920, a small fraction of Historic Armenia declared independence but soon came under Soviet rule. In 1991, the people of the Armenian Soviet Socialist Republic voted to form the independent Republic of Armenia.

To set the stage for the immigration of Armenian people to America at the turn of the twentieth century and the creation of the *nor spiurk* (new diaspora), it is necessary to understand their situation in the decaying and strife-ridden Ottoman Empire. By the end of the eighteenth century, as a non-Muslim minority group, the Armenians were organized into the self-governing Ermeni Millet (Turkish for "Armenian people") headed by the Armenian patriarch in Constantinople. Even though the patriarch administered the community's schools and hospitals, recorded

marriages and baptisms, and issued travel documents within and outside the empire, his authority was often superseded by the small but powerful Amira (Arabic for "prince") class, Armenian moneylenders to the sultans and others.

On the Anatolian plateau, where the bulk of the population lived, peasants and small-town craftsmen and shopkeepers were considered *raya* (flock) and *giavur* (infidel). They were heavily taxed, their sons were taken away and raised as Muslim to serve in the army or administration, they were required to provide winter shelter and pasture to nomadic tribes, and they had to bribe corrupt officials for government services and to prevent harassment. The Armenian leaders in the capital, Constantinople, were uninterested or unable to alter the situation of the peasantry, who were left in dire neglect, poverty-stricken, and prone to ravages of drought, locusts, and diseases such as cholera.

During the 1800s, competition forced the Ottoman rulers to open the doors of the empire to Western industrial products and advisers. Soon after, Orientalism became fashionable, and European travelers, scholars, and artists flocked to the Middle East. Catholic and Protestant missionaries were not far behind. Unable to convert the Muslims, European and American missionaries directed their attention to the Armenians and other Christians in the area. They opened schools, hospitals, colleges, and orphanges. Though a small proportion of Armenians converted, most took advantage of these educational institutions and imbibed the progressive ideals of the Enlightenment and the French Revolution.

During the second half of the nineteenth century, the Armenian people witnessed an awakening. The Armenian economic elite in the diaspora financed the establishment of schools, hospitals, and printing presses; a new generation of mostly Western-educated intellectuals fueled a cultural and literary revival that shook the Armenian people out of its centuries-old slumber.

The socioeconomic circumstances of those living in western Armenia, however, did not improve. The reforms of the nineteenth century threatened the local Turkish elite, who retaliated against Armenians. A number of uprisings in various Armenian localities between 1862 and 1878 was followed with the establishment of self-protection societies, a precursor to the political parties. Increased natonalistic consciousness and political mobilizations frightened the already weak and disintegrating Ottoman regime. In 1895–1896, between 100,000 and 200,000 Armenians were killed, and more than 500,000 were left homeless. The ever-present threat of forced conversion, rape, and looting instilled a deep sense of insecurity in the Armenians, and the urgency to emigate increased.

During the evening of April 24, 1915, more than two hundred Armenian intellectuals and community leaders were taken from their homes, and they were never seen again. All able-bodied men were conscripted into the army and put in labor battalions. Women, children, and old men left in the towns and villages were then deported. Forming "death caravans," they were marched into the Syrian desert, where they faced starvation, rape, torture, destitution, and death. More than 1.5 million Armenians—more than half the Armenian population of Ottoman Turkey—perished. Later Turkish governments have denied the Genocide. Except for a small community in Constantinople (modern Istanbul), few Armenians live in modern Turkey.

Immigration History

The earliest known Armenian to set foot in America was "Martin the Armenian," who, according to the *British State Colonial Papers*, the *Court Book* of the Virginia Company of London, and Peter Force's *Historical Tracts*, landed in Jamestown in 1618 or 1619. Most likely he was a servant of the Virginia governor, George Yeardley. In 1653, two other Armenians, probably from Smyrna, arrived to produce silk for Virginia planter Edward Diggs. Diggs's father was the English ambassador to Russia, where he might have heard of the reputation of Armenians for growing silk.

Historian Robert Mirak divides the Armenian immigration to North America at the turn of the twentieth century into three phases. The first phase consisted of the pioneers who arrived between the 1830s and 1890. They were mostly young, male, and relatively few in number. The earliest arrivals were students or clergymen, followed by merchants, many of whom started the Oriental rug trade. After the 1870s they were joined by larger numbers from the peasant and crafts classes.

During the second phase, 1890 to 1899, their numbers grew exponentially and included women, children, and a wider age and socioeconomic distribution. The third phase, between 1900 and 1914, was characterized by mass emigration. Though the majority of Armenians were fleeing the massacres and political and economic insecurity in Turkey, some also emigrated from Russia. By the beginning of World War I, more than sixty thousand Armenians had settled in America.

After the war, immigration first escalated, then plummeted in 1924, when the "quota laws" went into effect. Survivors of the Genocide, mostly women and children who had regrouped in orphanages and refugee camps in the Middle East, sought the safety of distant relatives, and young women became "picture brides." Between 1920 and 1924, more than thirty thousand Armenians landed in America.

Even though the quota system drastically restricted Armenian immigration to the United States, it was possible to circumvent the law. Between the two world wars, some entered with "Nansen passports," papers provided to refugees by the League of Nations. Immediately following World War II, about forty-five hundred Armenians labeled "displaced persons," mostly from the Soviet Union, were waiting for homes in refugee camps across Europe. The American National Committee for Homeless Armenians (ANCHA) came to their rescue. ANCHA was founded by George Mardikian, owner of the famous Omar Khayyám restaurant in San Francisco, and other notable Armenians in 1947, to assist Armenian refugees. In the 1960s and 1970s, ANCHA also sponsored more than twenty-five thousand Armenians from Communist bloc countries (mainly Romania and Bulgaria) as well as the socialist regimes of Egypt, Syria, and Iraq.

The repeal of the quota laws in 1965 made possible another wave of Armenian mass immigration to the United States, nearly doubling the size of the Armenian-American population. The timing was opportune for those fleeing the Lebanese Civil War after 1975 and the Islamic Revolution in Iran after 1978. Armenians with Turkish passports also immigrated during this period. Between 1971 and 1988, approximately forty-seven thousand Soviet Armenians were allowed to exit. In the 1990s, the collapse of the Soviet Union, the war in Karabagh, the pogroms in Baku and Sumgait in Azerbaijan, and the economic blockade of the Republic of Armenia by Turkey brought more Armenians to the United States.

The Armenian immigrants of the late nineteenth century compared favorably to their contemporaries: Most were literate, one in three was a skilled craftsman, and a few were entrepreneurs and professionals. They settled in industrial cities such as New York; Providence, Rhode Island; Worcester, Massachusetts; and Boston, where they found factory jobs or opened small businesses. Some ventured farther to Chicago; Detroit; Racine, Wisconsin; and Waukegan, Illinois, for better prospects. The Armenian community of Fresno, California, was an exception. Farming was their main livelihood. In spite of virulent discrimination, Armenians prospered and came to dominate the raisin industry. This community, which dates from the early 1880s, has managed to survive over the course of the twentieth century without the influx of many immigrants. Fresno's early Armenians are immortalized in the American stories of its native son William Saroyan.

The aim of the firstcomers from Ottoman Turkey was to amass enough money to return home, but the deteriorating conditions in Asia Minor precluded the realization of their wishes. Most lived frugally in overcrowded boardinghouses to finance the immigration of their relatives. After World War I many bachelors married; others were joined by their families. With the addition of more immigrants, the Armenian-American community started to establish roots in earnest. Soon the number of churches, charitable societies, language schools, newspapers, and other associations multiplied. Self-employment was a goal that many achieved over time. Armenian Americans also shared a strong belief in the basic value of education. Thus a large number of the second generation attended college. When the U.S. economy expanded after World War II, Armenians were able to move comfortably into suburbia and the middle class.

Subsequent immigrants have generally settled in areas where an Armenian community already exists. There are sizable concentrations of Armenians in New York, New Jersey, Boston, Philadelphia, Washington, D.C., Chicago, Detroit, and California. Los Angeles has been the favorite destination of the post-1965 immigration, where the bulk of the émigrés from Lebanon, Iran, Turkey, and Soviet Armenia have made their home. Some 200,000 to 300,000 Armenians reside in Los Angeles, which boasts thirteen Armenian day schools, including four high schools, twenty-eight churches, a large network of clubs and associations, and an Armenian telephone directory listing more than forty thousand households and businesses. In downtown Hollywood and Glendale, Armenian-owned shops, restaurants, and businesses prominently display their ethnic affiliation on their store fronts through Armenian alphabet signs. Unlike any other place in North America, it is not surprising to hear Armenian spoken in public places in these areas.

The post–World War II immigrants can be distinguished from the turn-of-the twentieth-century pioneers in a number of ways. First, most of the later immigrants have no direct experience of the Genocide or of Historic Armenia. Second, they have more resources. They tend to be cosmopolitan in their worldview, fluent in several languages, and proficient in English. A significant proportion are college-educated, many have professional or graduate degrees, and a few have arrived with sizable bank accounts. Third, the

An Armenian husband and wife who operated a vegetable farm in West Andover, Massachusetts, in the 1940s. (Library of Congress/Corbis)

reception that each wave of immigration received in the United States has been drastically different. Whereas xenophobia characterized the early 1900s, a more tolerant atmosphere prevailed after the so-called resurgence of ethnicity in the 1970s. Ethnic festivals and cuisine became popular, and academia and the mass media paid lip service to multiculturalism. Finally, the post–World War II immigrants were fortunate to have a ready-made community they could join on arrival. After the late 1970s, Armenian social service agencies were set up in New York and Los Angeles to help the arriving flood of refugees with their basic needs.

The reception of Armenian immigrants in the United States has been marked with indifference, vagueness, and near anonymity. For a number of reasons, including their small size and the con-

fusion over their origins (e.g., is one a Lebanese or an Armenian?), few of the immigrants' neighbors or coworkers seemed to know about the existence of the Armenian people or where Historic Armenia was located. The exceptions were those who could recall being told as children in the first half of the twentieth century that they should finish the food on their plate because of those "starving Armenians." In Fresno, however, Armenians were overtly discriminated against until World War II. They were classified as "Asiatic" and thus prevented from buying land and from becoming members of social clubs, professional societies, and even Protestant churches.

Although an ideology of an eventual return to the ancestral homeland dominates the collective consciousness of the communal institutions,

Armenians are in America to stay. In the late 1940s the Armenian Soviet Socialist Republic opened its doors for "repatriation," but few from the United States chose to go. Since the creation of the independent Republic of Armenia, many Armenian Americans have visited and many more plan to, but hardly any express the intention of settling there permanently. There is some traffic within the diaspora. For example, a few of the Lebanese Armenians who had fled the civil war in Lebanon have returned, and there are Armenians from Latin America who have moved to the United States.

Demographic Characteristics

There are approximately six million Armenians in the world, half of whom live in the Republic of Armenia. In the diaspora, the Armenian community in America is the largest, and the most affluent and powerful. There are an estimated 800,000 people of Armenian descent in the United States.; however, only 308,096 of them wrote in their Armenian ancestry in the 1990 U.S. Census. Statistical data on Armenian Americans are in short supply because of their small numbers, nonminority status, and lack of funding.

A mail survey conducted in metropolitan New York and New Jersey in 1986 and believed to be representative of Armenian Americans found that 37.5 percent of the sample of 584 people were foreign-born, 46.6 percent were born in the United States of foreign-born parents, and the rest were third- or fourth-generation Armenian Americans. This sample underrepresented newcomers from the Soviet Union and Iran. The ratio of foreign-born to American-born Armenians is roughly 40 to 60. The first generation, from different waves of immigration, and their children's generation tend to dominate the formally organized Armenian-American community.

For the most part, Armenian Americans are solid members of the middle class, with a significant segment being in the upper middle class. The metropolitan New York–New Jersey survey and one conducted of a sample of one hundred people in Los Angeles in 1987 concur that about 47 percent of Armenian Americans have a college degree and/or graduate degree. About 24 percent are business owners, and another 22 percent are in traditional professions such as medicine, law, and engineering. More than 45 percent of those surveyed had an income greater than $50,000 per year. Small business ownership continues to be a cultural goal for Armenian Americans in their quest of the American Dream.

In terms of family characteristics, Armenians tend to be conservative. Many believe that family comes before individual needs. Most maintain close ties with kin. However, only 20 percent of the first generation and 14 percent of the second generation live in extended households. With assimilation, parents begrudgingly accept the *odar* (foreign) spouses of their children and their divorces, both of which are increasing. The birthrate is low—the average number of children per family is two. As traditional Armenian culture is steeped in patriarchy, feminists have begun to critique the inherent sexism within the community. At the same time, women, in large numbers, continue to cook Armenian dishes, assemble relatives and friends for the holidays, and recount folktales to and educate the young, instilling in them a strong sense of Armenian identity. In other words, the women do the work that keeps Armenianness alive in the United States.

Language Maintenance

Speaking or not speaking the Armenian language is a divisive factor. In general, immigrants are more likely to speak Armenian at home and advocate ethnic schooling. The metropolitan New York–New Jersey survey discovered that 97 percent of the first generation speak, while 78 percent of them read and write, Armenian. In the second generation, the numbers are 74 percent and 19 percent, respectively. However, the matter is not simple. First there are differences in dialect. The vast majority of those who have emigrated from Ottoman Turkey and their descendants, including those who settled in the Middle East before relocating to the United States, speak Western Armenian. Iranian Armenians and those from the Russian diaspora and the Republic of Armenia speak Eastern Armenian. This leads to the question of which language should be taught in ethnic schools. Second, diasporan Armenians adopted colloquialisms from their host societies that are not readily understood by other Armenians. Third, many Armenians in Ottoman Turkey spoke Turkish, and some of those who emigrated from Turkey after 1965, especially older women, speak Turkish. Finally, the children of mixed marriages are far less likely to speak Armenian.

Even though the earliest immigrants had established language schools for their children, their efforts were short-lived. After 1965, with the influx of Middle Eastern Armenians, a variety of schools were sponsored by church committees, charitable organizations, and political parties. In the 1990s, there were twenty-four all-day Armenian schools and sixty-eight Saturday or part-time schools in the United States. Unless the all-day school has an excellent academic reputation, American-born parents usually consider ethnic schools too parochial and un-American. Fueling the concerns of community leaders regarding assimilation, studies have shown that even when students attend Armenian high school they are more likely to speak English with their friends and siblings. They reserve the Armenian language to communicate with their grandparents and parents.

Spread across the United States, people of Armenian descent are kept informed of news on people and things Armenian by the ethnic press. Nineteen newspapers, four academic journals, a couple of literary magazines, and scores of newsletters are published in the United States and distributed through the mail. Of the six papers in the Armenian language, five are subsidized by Armenian political parties. Not surprisingly, the weeklies with the widest circulation are published in English. The *Hairenik Weekly*, founded in 1899 in Watertown, Massachusetts, and the *Asbarez Armenian Daily*, founded in 1908 in Fresno, are the oldest. In the 1990s twenty-two radio programs and three Los Angeles television stations broadcast Armenian music, shows, and news in English and Armenian.

Religion, Politics, and Community Life

For centuries the Armenian Apostolic Church (the "mother church") was the undisputed religious institution of the Armenian people. The proselytizing efforts of Catholic missionaries starting in the sixteenth century and more earnestly in the eighteenth century, and of Protestant missionaries in the nineteenth century, created the Eastern Rite Armenian Catholic Church and the Armenian Evangelical Church, respectively. The metropolitan New York–New Jersey survey found that 64 percent of the respondents were affiliated with the Armenian Apostolic Church, 10 percent attended Armenian Protestant churches, 4 percent belonged to the Armenian Catholic Church, 16 percent were members of mainline Protestant denominations or the Roman Catholic Church, and 6 percent declared "no religion."

Communal life among the immigrants in the United States centered around the church. First they met in rented halls or churches; then, as soon as they could afford to buy or build their own traditional domed edifice, they did so. Having a church in any given locality meant having a collective existence as a people. The adjoining large hall and kitchen was as important as the sanctuary. Social gatherings such as dinner dances, lectures, and theatrical productions as well as weddings and christenings were made affordable and accessible. The Armenian Congregational Church of the Martyrs was founded in Worcester as early as 1881. Ten years later, the first Apostolic church was established in Worcester. At the end of the twentieth century, Armenian churches in the United States number 152, including thirty-eight Protestant and seven Catholic churches.

It is impossible to talk about the Armenian Apostolic Church without mentioning ethnic politics. The three Armenian political parties that the immigrants brought with them to the New World—the Dashnak, Ramgavar, and Hnchak parties—played a pivotal role in forging the character of the Armenian community in America. All three parties developed out of the social and political circumstances and the Armenian cultural awakening in Ottoman Turkey and Russia during the last decades of the nineteenth century.

The Dashnaktsutiun (Armenian Revolutionary Federation—ARF) was founded in 1890 to liberate the Armenian people from political domination and bring about social and economic change. Its socialist and nationalist agenda was popular with the masses and radical intellectuals, especially because it eventually endorsed aggressive tactics in self-defense. The Ramgavar party (Armenian Democratic Liberal party—ADL), first formed in Egypt in 1908, advocated the interests of the bourgeoisie. The oldest party, the Social Democratic Hnchakian party, was never able to attract a large following because of its dogmatic Marxist tenets. The major points of contention among these parties involve the fate of the first Armenian republic (1918–1920) and its subsequent Sovietization. The Dashnaks, who played a prominent role in the government of the short-lived republic, were at odds with the Armenian SSR and mistrusted the catholicos (supreme head of the Armenian Church) in Etchmiadzin, Armenia, for being allegedly under the influence of the Soviets. The party maintained the goal of a free and independent Armenia.

The conflict between the Dashnaks and the anti-Dashnaks—a loose coalition of Ramgavar, Hnchak, and Chezok (neutral) individuals who opposed the militant Dashnak style—escalated in the United States and ended in a schism within the Apostolic Church. On December 24, 1933, Archbishop Levon Tourian (a representative of the See of Etchmiadzin in Soviet Armenia) was stabbed to death while celebrating Divine Liturgy in Holy Cross Church in upper Manhattan. Although the Dashnak party denied any connection with the murder, nine of their members were convicted of the crime.

The Armenian Apostolic Church in North America has since been administered by two theologically identical but separate bureaucracies: the Diocese, whose members are mostly anti-Dashnak and who follow the orders of the catholicos in Etchmiadzin, and the Prelacy, whose members are Dashnak sympathizers and are under the jurisdiction of the see of Cilicia in Antelias, Lebanon. The split was responsible for the doubling of almost every Armenian institution or club and has been the subject of much debate and headache for Armenian Americans.

With the end of the Cold War and the election of Karekin II, the former catholicos of Cilicia, to the "mother see," the see of Etchmiadzin in 1995, it was hoped that the Apostolic Church would end the schism. This has not yet come about. Polls indicate that more than 93 percent of Armenian Americans favor unity, and the overwhelming majority of youths are totally disinterested in Armenian political parties. In the 1990s, young people raised in either the Diocese or Prelacy churches flock to Armenian sports weekends and dances totally oblivious of the "side" of the organization sponsoring the event.

Many college-educated Americanized Armenians support the work of the Armenian Assembly of America, an organization that advocates greater involvement in American politics. Since its founding in 1972, the assembly has worked for the recognition of the Armenian Genocide by the U.S. government and run a successful summer internship program for college students. It also served as a conduit for information and resources between the Republic of Armenian and the West after the earthquake in Armenia in 1988.

The Armenian General Benevolent Union (AGBU), founded by Boghos Nubar in Cairo in 1906 to assist Armenian refugees, is a charitable institution that has significant resources and continues to play a powerful role in the Armenian world. For decades, it financed schools, distributed scholarships, and sponsored cultural activities such as plays and art exhibits. Since the independence of Armenia, it has invested heavily in the educational and economic development of that country. In 1990, AGBU had twenty-two thousand members worldwide, most of them in the United States. Members tend to be affluent and anti-Dashnak in their Armenian political ideologies.

Armenian-American organizations sponsor a wide range of events that keep the social calendars of many of those in the first and second generations filled. Typical activities are dinner dances, lectures, concerts, bazaars, and picnics. Since the 1980s, new associations have emerged that address the professional and lifestyle needs of college-educated young men and women more satisfactorily. A successful example is the Armenian Network of America, Inc., which organizes seminars and mixers for young professionals. There are also associations for those in specific disciplines, such as physicians, lawyers, and social scientists.

Assimilation and Symbolic Armenianness

Ever since the earliest Armenian immigrants landed in America, they have feared assimilation, the "white massacre." In the more than one hundred years of their presence in the United States, their traditional culture and their communal structures have witnessed significant changes. Although the metropolitan New York–New Jersey survey found widespread cultural and structural assimilation, 8.4 percent of the 584 respondents identified themselves as "American"; the rest said they were Armenian or gave hyphenated labels. The overwhelming majority — 96 percent — of the respondents felt very proud of their Armenian background. It has been argued that with the passage of time in the United States, Armenianness changes in its form and function. The first generation is characterized with a taken-for-granted way of "being" Armenian. Immigrants' behavior tends to be consistent with the cultural baggage they import from abroad. They are more likely to be users of the Armenian language, and participants in church services and communal activities.

In contrast, American-born descendants "feel" Armenian. Even though they consciously choose to identify with their Armenian heritage and are very proud of it, they become symbolic Armenians. They demonstrate their Armenianness by refusing to change the "ian" ending of their family name;

by wearing jewelry with Armenian lettering; by generously financing Armenian charities; and by supporting the establishment of museums, libraries, and the publication of books on Armenian subjects. The fundamental connection of the American-born to their Armenian ancestry remains the family. Family gatherings connote love, generosity, stories, and, of course, food. Armenian Americans do not need to speak Armenian or know the history or be aware of the political divisions to appreciate a deep sense of roots and the knowledge of having a specially rich and enduring cultural heritage.

Armenian Americans have been fortunate in many ways. They have taken advantage of the numerous opportunities that the United States could offer them: in education, in freedom of thought and expression, in exposure to a wide array of other cultures and peoples, and in pursuit of the American Dream. Armenian Americans boast many sons and daughters who have excelled in the arts, in the sciences, in the business world, and in politics. They have done so by bridging the two worlds they claimed as their own: the Armenian and the American.

The Genocide remains a common denominator that unites all people of Armenian descent. Armenian Americans are outraged at the denial of the Genocide by Turkish governments and revisionist historians. April 24 is commemorated every year with requiems and public gatherings like the one in Times Square in New York City that attracts American politicians and the news media. Developments in the Republic of Armenia have created new opportunities for strengthening the ties of symbolic Armenians in the United States. Exchanges between professionals and technological experts are being established, and many Armenian Americans have offered their skills and know-how to their brothers and sisters in Armenia. The Land and Culture organization has taken teenagers and college students to rebuild old churches in Armenia during the summer. Such visits, long or short, for whatever purpose, foster affinity and encourage allegiance. In spite of visits and keen interest in the future of the Republic of

Armenia, most American men and women of Armenian descent are likely to remain symbolic Armenians.

See also: IRANIANS; TURKS

Bibliography

Adalian, R. (1991). "The Armenian Genocide: Context and Legacy." *Social Education* 55(22):99–105.

Armenian Assembly of America. (1987). *Armenians in America—Celebrating the First Century on the Occasion of the National Tribute for Governor George Deukmejian, October 10, 1987.* Washington DC: Armenian Assembly of America.

Avakian, A. S. (1977). *The Armenians in America.* Minneapolis: Lerner.

Bakalian, A. (1993). *Armenian-Americans: From Being to Feeling Armenian.* New Brunswick, NJ: Transaction.

Bournoutian, A. G. (1993). *A History of the Armenian People*, Vol. 1: *Pre-History to 1500 A.D.* Costa Mesa, CA: Mazda.

Bournoutian, A. G. (1994). *A History of the Armenian People*, Vol. 2: *1500 A.D. to the Present.* Costa Mesa, CA: Mazda.

Hovannisian, R. G., ed. (1986). *The Armenian Genocide in Perspective.* New Brunswick, NJ: Transaction.

Hovannisian, R. G., ed. (1992). *The Armenian Genocide: History, Politics, Ethics.* New York: St. Martin's Press.

Kassabian, L. (1993). "Like Grains of Sand Swept Up in the Wind: The Relative Contribution of Displacement Status and Ethnic Identity to Psychological Well-Being." Ph.D. diss., Columbia University.

Miller, D. E., and Miller, L. T. (1993). *Survivors: An Oral History of the Armenian Genocide.* Berkeley: University of California Press.

Mirak, R. (1983). *Torn Between Two Lands: Armenians in America 1890 to World War I.* Cambridge, MA: Harvard University Press.

Vassilian, H. B., ed. (1995). *Armenian America Almanac*, 3rd edition. Glendale, CA: Armenian Reference Books.

Waldstreicher, D. (1989). *The Armenian Americans.* New York: Chelsea House.

Walker, C. J. (1980). *Armenia: The Survival of a Nation.* New York: St. Martin's Press.

ANNY BAKALIAN

ASIAN INDIANS

See BENGALIS; BIHARIS; GUJARATIS; JAINS; MAHARASHTRIANS: MALAYALAM SPEAKERS; PUNJABIS; SIKHS; TAMILS; TELUGUS

AUSTRIANS

It seems to be extremely difficult to define Austrians as an ethnic entity due to historical and statistical confusion and a large variety of perceptions by the immigrants themselves. In the context of this entry "Austrians" means Austrian citizens within the borders of small Austria in 1918 and today. Especially for the period before 1914, therefore, "Austrian" would include provincial national identities, too, which in most cases became even stronger in America. Many immigrants saw themselves as Burgenlaender, Lower or Upper Austrians (Nieder- oder Oberösterreicher), Styrians (Steirer), Carinthians (Kärtner), Salzburger, Tyroleans (Tiroler), Vorarlberger, or Viennese (Wiener). In the nineteenth century and the first half of the twentieth century some of the immigrants from the territory of today's Austria saw themselves as German Austrians (Deutsch-Oesterreicher). After 1938, the refugees from Vienna who fled Nazi racist terror and genocide identified themselves under a provincial label (e.g., Viennese) or as Jews.

Early Immigration History

Austrian pioneers and Roman Catholic missionaries before 1819 are excluded from statistical research. Even after emigration data are available the numbers are extremely low and do not contain information on the ethnic composition of the immigration. From 1821 to 1830, a total of 14,255 subjects of the Hapsburg empire left for overseas (with most of them going to North America). From 1851 to 1860, overseas emigration increased to

27,045, falling back to a total of 14,693 for the period from 1861 to 1866.

Before the nineteenth century, larger groups emigrated from Austria only because of severe religious purges—in Salzburg in 1731 against Protestants by the Roman Catholic authorities; allegedly thirty thousand left for German lands. Some fifty Salzburg families were able to immigrate to America, where they settled in Ebenezer, Georgia. Eighty other Salzburgers followed in the winter of 1735–1736.

The reasons for emigration were partly political. After the defeat of the democratic revolution of 1848 some of the Austrian revolutionaries escaped persecution by immigrating to America, but the numbers were small: two groups totaling sixty-six men and two women. Religious pressure during these years led to a second wave of emigration by Protestants from Upper Austria, the Tyrol, and Carinthia. On the other hand, Austrian Roman Catholic missionaries contributed to the development of the Roman Catholic Church in America.

Austrians were scattered around the United States during the early nineteenth century, but they did not form ethnic communities. Individual immigrants, such as those who arrived after the 1848 revolution, tended to settle in cities such as New York, Cincinnati, St. Louis, and Milwaukee. The 1848 immigrants established an elite network. Negative political (absolute monarchy and police state) and religious (Roman Catholic dominance) perceptions in America resulted in a strong trend within the small immigrant group not to see themselves as Austrians, former subjects of the Hapsburg empire. The small group of peasants (e.g., from Vorarlberg, 1850–1870) who tried to take over new land came from families with many children and belonged to the lower rural class. Islands of the Vorarlberg immigration corresponded with hometown chain migration and concentrated from the beginning in Dubuque, Iowa; Fremont, Ohio; Erie, Pennsylvania; Akron, Ohio; and St. Louis. After 1870, individual homesteaders from Austria could be found in the Dakotas, Nebraska, Colorado, and Idaho and later in California, Oregon, and Washington State.

Jerusalem Lutheran Church, which was built in 1769 by the early settlers of Ebenezer, Georgia. (Lee Snider/ Photo Images/Corbis)

Austro-Hungarian Immigration

Between 1867, when the right to emigrate from the Austro-Hungarian Empire was proclaimed, and 1910, a total of 1,531,382 inhabitants of the Austrian half of the empire immigrated to the United States. A total of 1,422,205 left the Hungarian part of the empire for the United States during the same period. At least for 1901–1910, figures for the Austrian and Hungarian halves can be given along ethnic lines. With 11.8 percent the Germans were strongly underrepresented, which means that the core Austrians were even more marginal. Most of the immigrants were Poles (18.6%); Serbs, Croats, and Slovenes (16.1%); Slovaks (15.4%); Hungarians (14.7%); or Jews (7.1%). They came primarily from Galicia and the Bukovina, the Slovakian-speaking parts of Hungary, central and eastern Hungary, as well Croatia, Slovenia, and Bosnia.

From this 1901–1910 sample of U.S. immigration from the empire, it can be seen that the original predominance of farm labor (for 1876–1910, 45.4%) declined (to 19.5%), whereas the total for craftsmen and trademen rose (to 15.9%). During the high peak of immigration from the Hapsburg lands, two-thirds of the immigrants were men, and 82 percent were fourteen to forty-five years old.

Return immigration differed among ethnic groups. From 1908 to 1913, the percentage of return immigration was about 38.7 percent (460,000 people), an indication that for some, this labor move was planned in advance as a temporary one. The highest rates of return migration were with Poles, the lowest with German Austrians. The German-Austrian, Czech, and Jewish groups were characterized by family immigration, whereas others, such as the Poles, Romanians, Serbs, Croats, and Carpatho-Rusyns were typically individuals.

The push factors for large scale emigration from parts of the empire to the United States at the turn of the twentieth century were consequences of the growing pressures of industrialization in rural areas, affecting many unskilled workers. Tobacco workers could earn three times as much in the United States as they did in Austria; the same is well documented for farm labor. From 1908 to 1911, however, a decline in the low-skilled labor market, as a result of economic problems in the United States, resulted in a decline in immigration. In total, the inner migration into the urban centers of Vienna, Budapest, and Prague was considerably higher than the emigration overseas. Especially in the core Austrian provinces the pull factors played an important role, too; for example, many "Burgenlaenders" and people from Vorarlberg followed the pattern of chain migration. They were lured by the personal experiences in the United States of Austrian pioneers from their hometown.

Immigration to the United States from the empire — both the Austrian and the Hungarian halves — affected U.S. society substantially, especially from 1900 to 1910, when nearly as many people immigrated from Austria-Hungary as from Italy, and considerably more than from Germany or Russia. U.S. immigration statistics show that from 1821 to 1911 more than 3.3 million people immigrated from Austria-Hungary, compared to 3.27 million Italians and 2.67 million Russians; only England (7.9 million) and Germany (5.4 million) show higher numbers. This large Austro-Hungarian group, however, consisted of at least twelve different ethnic entities that became independent in Europe after 1918 and that already differed from each other among the immigrants. Even in the central European immigration archives at the University of Minnesota in Minneapolis the Austrians are excluded as a group, despite the fact that many of them settled in Minnesota.

The German-speaking group in return was quickly absorbed by the Germans from Germany, and only very few groups of Austrians born on the territory that constitutes Austria today continued to function as local, small Austrian communities in America, such as the Burgenlaender, as well as people from Styria, the Tyrol, and Vorarlberg. More than 1,500 people from Vorarlberg immigrated from 1890 to 1925 to the textile industry area in New Jersey along the "Bergen line" from Jersey City to West New York, Union City, Guttenberg, North Bergen, and Fairview.

Immigration from "Little Austria"

The quota system introduced by the United States after World War I hindered a broader Austrian immigration. From 1921 to 1924, only 7,342 people were accepted under a 3 percent quota system (according to the 1890 U.S. Census). From 1924 to 1929, only 785 people per year were accepted, and from 1929 to 1939, the immigration quota was limited to 1,413 people per year. Five thousand Austria citizens were preregistered in 1931 for immigration to the United States. Despite the economic and social disaster in Austria following the collapse of the Hapsburg monarchy, causing extremely high unemployment in the 1920s and especially in the 1930s, immigration did not seem to solve Austria's social problems. The United States, too, was confronted with major economic and social problems. Within the non-quota system the U.S. government tried to foster self-generating immigration, which meant that ethnic groups with functioning economic and social networks such as the Burgenlaender could continue bringing their friends and family members into the United States. These communities were originally organized partly as Landsmannschaften, community structures based on religious terms or the regional origins of the immigrants (e.g., Jewish groups from the empire as well as groups from Austrian provinces such as Styria, the Tyrol, Vorarlberg, and Vienna).

Before 1914, thirty-three thousand people immigrated from the later Burgenland (then German West Hungary). This group functioned as a relatively closed community, and more than 60.7 percent married within their ethnic network (e.g., in New York), compared with 37.2 percent for other German-speaking groups from Austria. After World War I and the establishment of the province of Burgenland, this ethnic group even increased their inner coherence and founded in 1922 a newspaper in German, *Eintracht*, with a circulation of four thousand copies. This newspaper was considered to be the "independent voice of Austrians, Burgenlaender, and German Hungarians in North America." In total, 24,300 Burgenlaender left for North America between 1920 and 1938; 14.4 percent, however, returned to Europe.

Another Austrian group that formed ethnic local communities are the Vorarlberger — six thousand have immigrated to the United States since the late nineteenth century. From 1919 to 1937, according to Austrian sources, 34,014 Austrians left for the United States. In general, Austrian overseas migration became more diversified than before, and South America nearly reached the U.S. quota (15,341 went to Brazil and 11,260 to Argentina). In addition, 5,423 migrated from Austria to Canada.

Cultural Exodus and "Brain Drain"

A deep impact on the intellectual and cultural development of U.S. society resulted from persecution, expulsion, and extermination of Austrians of Jewish origin by the Nazi regime after 1938. More than 30,000 — according to some sources even 40,000 — émigrés found shelter in the United States, despite severe restrictions within the quota system. Approximately 150,000 went into exile to eighty different countries; more than 60,000 of these Austrian Jews were killed by the Nazis. This exodus affected Austrian society in a negative way, since large segments of the elite were expelled and then integrated into their new host societies. Compared with previous immigration waves into the United States, this group was the best educated, with high intellectual and artistic capabilities.

From the point of view of cultural history, the United States gained a tremendous amount from those who had to flee the Nazi regime and were granted exile in America. But some of them were too old or too deeply rooted in Austrian society to assimilate.

A number of the refugees were able to resume their careers, especially in academia, and even continue research in Austrian economic theory, the social sciences (here especially successful in psychoanalysis and empirical social research), and music. In cultural affairs, the impact was strongest within the music and film business (even considering previous individual immigration before 1938). In total, the cultural exodus contained five thousand individuals from different professions, of whom up to 40 percent immigrated to the United States.

The immigrants were grateful that the United States granted them shelter, but still exile was different from the homeland they had been forced to leave. Anthony Heilbut documented in his book *Exiled in Paradise* (1983) the complexity of this "double" problem of uprootedness (as Jew and Austrian) and adjustment in a new world. Although America could have admitted more refugees from Europe than it did, a good deal of resistance to the absorption of immigrants complicated the situation of the primarily Jewish refugees, with their own perception of American society and civilization as "superficial, materialistic, and vulgar." Many artists gratefully grasped the chance to enter the United States, but under considerable emotional pressure.

This middle-class German and Austrian refugee group tended to settle first in large cities, especially New York, although there was a group of twenty-two thousand former Austrian citizens in California in 1953. Within two years the necessary command of English was obtained, and by 1948, 95 percent of these Austrian refugees had become U.S. citizens, but only 37 percent of the group stated that they were financially secure. Nevertheless, the post–World War II return migration rate was low—in the academic field about 7 percent.

There was also a non-Jewish exile group in this period, a few hundred people mostly from pre-1938 authoritarian regimes as well as a few former Social Democrats and some groups that supported the former House of Hapsburg (within the latter two groups many were of Jewish origin). For some years they tried to influence the Roosevelt administration by persistent but unsuccessful lobbying. They produced more than twenty-five newspapers and formed numerous short-lived exile organizations.

Post–World War II Immigration

Between 1945 and 1950, Austrian immigration reached the interwar quotas, with a 11,460 total. During this period women among the Austrian-born in the United States began to outnumber males (by 1952, 63% were women). The 1960 U.S. Census shows 300,000 Austrians born in the

A group of children sit at the milkbar at Children's Colony, a school for refugee children in New York City in the 1940s. (Library of Congress/Corbis)

United States, with one-third of them living in New York, 20,000 in Chicago, 12,000 in Los Angeles, and 37,000 in Pennsylvania.

The yearly immigration quota went down to 1,400 per year, less than the Swiss figure. From 1945 to 1988, 62,713 Austrians (among them 8% from Burgenland) immigrated to the United States. Especially in the 1950s, the percentage of well-trained immigrants in research was relatively higher due to the lack of development in this field in Austria. Return migration increased after the economic situation in Austria reached a break-even point in the mid-1960s and continued toward prosperity and a broad social network. Within the Burgenlaender group more than twenty thousand returned due to better housing and living conditions (40%), private reasons (36%), or professional changes (11.5%).

The trend toward complete assimilation is extremely strong among the post-1945 immigrants. Their children are not interested in speaking German anymore, whereas in the interwar period they learned German first from their grandparents and then studied English at school. Various Burgenlaender organizations in large cities such as New York and Chicago underlined this coherence up to the 1990s, focusing on cultural festivities and regular contacts with their Austrian province, Burgenland. In 1955, an umbrella organization with headquarters in Austria was founded, Burgenlaendische Gemeinschaft (Burgenlaender Community), to coordinate the various groups in New York, Chicago, Pennsylvania, and New Jersey. Functioning ethnic networks still can be traced in Pennsylvania, such as in Allentown, Coplay, Lehigh, Northampton, and Nazareth, but these are limited to musical activities. Organizations that were founded in the 1920s for financial assistance in case of illness were closed in the 1970s. The original-residence communities have been diversified, and the flow of immigration from Austria has virtually ended.

See also: CARPATHO-RUSYNS; CROATIANS; GERMANS; HUNGARIANS; JEWS, EUROPEAN; POLES; ROMANIANS; SERBS; SLOVAKS; SLOVENES

Bibliography

Fassmann, H. (1994). "Emigration, Immigration, and Internal Migration." In *Roots of the Transplanted,* Vol. 1, edited by D. Hoerder and I. Blank. New York: Columbia University Press.

Hödl, K. (1991). *Vom Shtetl an die Lower East Side: Galizische Juden in New York.* Vienna: Böhlau Verlag.

Hölbling, W., and Wagnleitner, R., eds. (1992). *The European Emigrant Experience in the U.S.A.* Tübingen: Gunter Narr Verlag.

Horvath, G. (1994). "Burgenländerinnen und Burgenländer in den USA." Ph.D. diss., University of Vienna.

Horvath, T., and Neyer, G., eds. (1996). *Auswanderung aus Österreich.* Vienna: Böhlau Verlag.

John, M. (1996). "Push and Pull Factors for Overseas Migrants from Austria-Hungary in the 19th and 20th Centuries." In *Austrian Immigration to Canada,* edited by F. Szabo, F. Engelmann, and M. Prokop. Ottawa: Carleton University Press.

Spaulding, E. W. (1968). *The Quiet Invaders: The Story of the Austrian Impact upon America.* Vienna: Österreichischer Bundesverlag.

Stadler, F., and Weibl, P., eds. (1995). *Cultural Exodus from Austria,* 2nd revised edition. Vienna: Springer Verlag.

OLIVER RATHKOLB

BANGLADESHIS

"Bangladeshi" is the term by which those persons born in Bangladesh, the former country of East Pakistan, or former province of East Bengal, refer to themselves. The present-day country of Bangladesh straddles the Bay of Bengal in South Asia. To the west is India, while to the east are Burma and the beginnings of Southeast Asia. Thus the people from Bangladesh are from an area that is a bridge between two subcontinents and two major cultural areas.

Ecology and Population of Bangladesh

The country of Bangladesh is characterized by a low-lying floodplain in which major river systems empty into the Bay of Bengal. The great Ganges and Brahmaputra river systems meet in Bangladesh, and that vast deltaic plain, in conjunction with a monsoon climate, leads to annual flooding of large portions of the country. This annual flooding, while hazardous in some years, is the reason for Bangladesh's excellent agricultural system of wet rice production. The flooding of the rivers deposits nutrient-laden silt onto paddy fields annually and allows two to three rice crops per year from most fields.

The great agricultural productivity has made possible population growth to an extent rarely seen in rural countries. Bangladesh is 55,598 square miles in size, yet has more than 130 million inhabitants as of 1996 estimates. Thus the country is one of the most densely populated rural nations, with a population density of more than 2,300 persons per square mile. The great number of people in such a small area is the primary cause for migration to other countries.

Historical Framework

The twentieth-century person from this region of the world may have begun life as something other than a Bangladeshi. Prior to 1947, Bangladesh was part of British India's East Bengal Province. At the partition of India in 1947, East Bengal became East Pakistan. Pakistan was created from two sections of British-controlled India that were predominaly Muslim, along both its western and its eastern borders. The country of Pakistan, composed of eastern and western wings, was separated by more than one thousand miles of intervening Indian territory. West Pakistan stood on the northwestern side of India, and East Pakistan was along India's southeastern border. The creation of Pakistan was an attempt to create a Muslim state, yet the power of religious commonality ultimately was not enough to bind the two wings together. There were important differences between the east and the west, notably language, culture, and economic systems. From the beginning, constant struggles for political control between the two wings were commonplace, and these conflicts finally came to a head during the early 1970s. The most insoluble political difficulty consisted in the fact that political parties remained localized within the respective wings. National politics was never able to transcend the cultural differences between the two populations.

In 1971, the country of Bangladesh was created in a war of liberation from the western wing of Pakistan. The birth of this new nation was recognition of significant cultural, linguistic, economic, and political differences with the western wing. More than anything else, the creation of Bangladesh was a statement of a distinctive Bangladeshi culture.

Language and Culture

Bangladeshis, then, are the people of Bangladesh. One of their primary means of identification is their language, Bengali, which they refer to as Bangla. Bengali is one of the most commonly spoken languages in the world. Speakers of Bengali stretch from the east in Bangladesh to the West Bengal region of India, which includes the city of Calcutta. To the Bangladeshi, Bengali is a source of pride. The language is derived from Sanskrit and has been well established in the Bengal region for at least one thousand years. Bangladeshis believe Bengali to be a poetic, expressive means for communication, and many people point to Nobel Prize winner Rabindranath Tagore's poems, songs, and stories as evidence. To the Bangladeshi, Bengali is more than a language; it is the framework for a thriving and meaningful cultural identity. During the East Pakistan years, from 1947 to 1971, this symbolic attachment was strengthened as Bengali-

speakers fought off West Pakistani attempts to install Urdu as the national language.

Culturally, the Bangladeshis are those Bengalis, or Bengali-speakers, from Bangladesh. Bengali, however, is also a term used to refer to people from both East and West Bengal. This region crosses the international border of India and Bangladesh. Bengalis of both countries share at the very least a common language, economic organization, social and village life, and kinship system. The largest difference between East and West Bengali culture is in religion.

In 1947, when India was partitioned, large groups of Muslim and Hindu populations were uprooted in Bengal. Many Hindus moved from the East to the West Bengal region, into predominantly Hindu India, while West Bengali Muslims moved east into what is today Bangladesh. Although many families did move at this time, many also remained. In the early 1960s and during Bangladesh's war of liberation, further population exchanges occurred as Hindus moved into West Bengal and Muslims moved into East Bengal. As of 1995, about 83 percent of Bangladeshis were Muslim, 16 percent were Hindu, with the remainder spread among Buddhist, Christian, and other faiths.

Immigration to the United States

Official counts of the Bangladeshi population in the United States are unsatisfactory. The U.S. Immigration and Naturalization Service legally admitted as immigrants 28,850 Bangladeshis between 1982 and 1992. However, the actual numbers traveling to the United States and residing there are much greater. For example, it has been estimated that in the early 1990s more than 50,000 Bangladeshis were living in the New York City area alone. And this may represent an undercount of the population. Estimates from persons familiar with Bangladeshi organizations suggest that in 1995 between 100,000 and 150,000 Bangladeshis were living in the United States, although all sources admit that there is no means to validate this number.

A Bangladeshi brother and sister relax at home. (Mukul Roy)

Emigration from Bangladesh historically has been the domain of young men. Most of those immigrating to the United States come as university students and are from the two largest cities in Bangladesh—the capital, Dhaka, and the port of Chittagong. A secondary route of migration has been by way of such Middle Eastern countries as Saudi Arabia, Oman, Dubai, and Kuwait. During the oil boom of the 1970s, many Middle Eastern countries actively recruited Bangladeshis as construction workers, maintenance workers, and domestic helpers. Some Bangladeshis acquired skills and familiarity with American companies while in the Middle East, and this facilitated their secondary migration to the United States.

Bangladeshis have come to the United States for a variety of reasons. Many enter the country as students at American universities and then, upon graduation, find jobs in the U.S. economy. Others immigrate in search of better economic opportunities than those available at home. The young men who enter the United States are generally well educated, having completed at least fourteen years of schooling in Bangladesh. The majority of the Bangladeshis in the United States are professionals such as economists, university professors, computer engineers, architects, and physicians. From the mid-1980s to the mid-1990s, Bangladeshi immigration to the United States increased. This new wave of immigrants and visa lottery winners has begun to occupy the types of occupations common to new immigrants. In New York City in 1996, for example, many Bangladeshis were driving cabs. In the stretch of cities from Miami to West Palm Beach in Florida, Bangladeshis work in convenience stores. The largest concentrations of Bangladeshis in 1996 were in major U.S. urban centers such as New York City, Los Angeles, Atlanta, and Miami.

These primary places of residence are also the loci for Bangladeshi cultural organizations. Such organizations tend to provide a platform for presenting Bangladeshi cultural heritage to Bangladeshis in the United States and often include performances featuring Bangladeshi dance, song, drama, and poetry. In those cities in which the Bangladeshi population is high enough, there may be more than one cultural organization that represents differing regions of Bangladesh, most commonly the cities of Dhaka and Chittagong. There are also a number of Bangladeshi newspapers published in the United States. Many of these are published in New York City, including the *Probashi*, *Weekly Thikana*, *Porichoy*, *Bangali*, and *Shongbad*.

Cultural Identity

Marriage. Retaining a Bangladeshi cultural identity in the United States is important to most of the immigrants, but some difficulties exist in maintaining these cultural roots. Foremost is the problem of finding a mate. Since male migrants vastly outnumber their female counterparts, marriage partners must be located in Bangladesh rather than in the United States. This is not as difficult as might be imagined since traditional marriage customs in Bangladesh favor arranged matches.

Bangladeshis most often marry others from their country. Arranged marriage is the most common method for finding a partner, and a young Bangladeshi person in the United States is likely to fly back to Bangladesh for the marriage. Decisions regarding marriage are usually initiated by a young person's parents. For example, the parents of a man twenty-five to thirty years of age often begin to mention marriage to their son. When he gives his assent to their wish, the parents set out to find a young woman of a background comparable to that of their own. The parents of a marriageable girl begin to look for a son-in-law when the girl is between sixteen and twenty years of age. Thus marriages match a groom at least ten years older than the bride. Most often considered in the choice of a mate are factors beyond the characters of the potential bride and groom. The marriage is viewed as a family matter in which the two families examine each other's standing in society as well as the characteristics of the potential newlyweds. The couple and their families should be matched in educational level, economic status, familial stability, and religious piety. If the groom lives in the United States, this fact will also be taken into account by the bride's family. Her family is likely to view such a son-in-law as a benefit because his future economic position will be better than it could be if he remained in Bangladesh. The two families consult with their respective members about the suitability of the match, and the young people may be given a range of potential spouses who have met with familial approval. The young couple today may speak to each other on the telephone to determine compatibility, and they may exchange photos. Traditionally, however, the couple did not see each other prior to the actual wedding ceremony. The marriage takes place in Bangladesh. Afterward the couple relocates to the home base of the partner living in the United States.

Religion. Most Bangladeshis are members of the Islamic faith. For Bangladeshi Muslims the core of their beliefs are framed by the belief in one God, Allah, and the strictures and words of his prophet Muhammad, as laid out in the Koran.

Distinctive religious beliefs include praying five times a day while facing Mecca, covering the head while in prayer, the giving of alms to the poor, and a ban on eating pork and drinking alcohol. One of the major calendrical events of the Muslim year is the lunar month of Ramadan (in Bengali, Ramzan), during which the devout are expected to refrain from food, drink, and cigarettes from sunrise to sunset. Many men will try to visit a mosque if possible on every Friday at 1:00 P.M., although this is often hard to accomplish in the United States. Women are expected to pray in the home and are not allowed to pray in the mosque.

There are about twenty million Hindus in Bangladesh. The tenets of Hinduism include a belief in gods and goddesses; a belief in an endless cycle of birth, death, and rebirth; and a system of hereditary occupation and position within society, called *jati*, or caste. Major religious festivals, called *pujas*, honor the different gods and goddesses. Villages with a Hindu population may have a couple of small temples at which offerings of flowers, leaves, milk, and grains may be left.

While there have been problems between Muslims and Hindus over the years in Bangladesh, for the great majority of the time, people live together there peacefully. A common settlement pattern in the country is Muslim agricultural villages with small Hindu satellite neighborhoods of craftsmen producing pottery, baskets, tanned hides, and cloth. Thus the two communities exist in economic complementary niches.

While their overarching Islamic and Hindu religious beliefs are a powerful and pervasive aspect of Bangladeshis' worldview, the Bengali cultural pattern is foremost—that is, whether Hindu or Muslim, the Bengali cultural heritage forms the basic foundation of the Bangladeshi.

Gender Roles. Bengali gender roles are an example of how the cultural pattern forms a foundation for differences in religious expression. In both Muslim and Hindu Bengali culture, men and women live in divided worlds. Men work outside the household, while women work in the home. Primary child-care responsibilities fall to women. The ideal Bengali woman is to be giving, loving to family, respectful of her husband and his relatives, subservient of her husband, demure, and shy in front of strangers. Men are to be the breadwinners and leaders of their families. These fundamental gender-role requirements inform the dynamics of all Bangladeshi families and exist in both Hindu and Muslim families.

Islam further defines these separations. In an Islamic family, a woman should not leave her home without her head being covered. In Bangladesh some women may wear a *burkha*, a garment that covers them from head to toe, when outside the household. In the United States, however, rarely does a Bangladeshi woman wear the burkha. Rather, she is most likely to wear the *sawar-chamise*, a colorful, loose pants long-shirt combination. In the home and on special occasions with other Bangladeshi families, she is likely to wear the traditional sari. In the United States it is rare for the Bangladeshi woman to cover her head or face or to wear the sari in public.

Kinship and Interpersonal Relations. The kinship system of Bangladesh is complex, having unique terms for a vast number of kin. For example, there are different terms for types of "uncle": father's brother (*chacha*), mother's brother (*mama*), father's sister's husband (*phupha*), and mother's sister's husband (*kalu*). Most interpersonal relations assume kinship dimensions in an individual's life. Typically, Bangladeshis recognize relative age and gender as important kinship principles that influence personal interactions. For example, in this patrilineal system, one should always show deference to those older than oneself. Even if not truly related, one who is elder should be referred to by a kinship term such as paternal uncle (*chacha*), aunt (*chachi/kaki*), grandfather (*dada*), or grandmother (*dadi*). Persons younger can be referred to by name. Persons of the same generation may be referred to as brother (*bhai*), sister (*bon/apa*), or brother's wife (*bhabi*). In most interactions, people are referred to by their kinship category, and a Bangladeshi is likely to feel some hesitation and discomfort with using many people's individual names in the new culture of the United States.

In the Bangladeshi family, this kinship framework assumes a behavioral component. Father (*abba*) and mother (*amma*) should not be disputed and must always be shown respect. Further, mother is idealized as all-loving, indulgent, and caring. Older brothers must be shown respect, and reticence must be displayed in their presence. Older brothers' commands and advice, like the father's, must be heeded. Sisters, on the other hand, are a relaxed, joking, and tender category of kin. Similar behavioral components color other relations, such as the many different categories of uncles and aunts.

The complexity of the kinship system points to the fact that Bangladeshis view themselves primarily as parts of family systems, rather than as individuals making their way alone in the world. A person sees himself or herself as intimately bound within a web of kinship and family ties that are ever present and vital, even if most of the family still resides in Bangladesh. The ideal of the American who strives to move out of his or her parents' house by age eighteen is confusing to the Bangladeshis, who like to live with their natal, and often extended, family. In Bangladesh the newly married couple lives with the groom's family. A typical household in Bangladesh is the parental couple with their grown sons, the sons' wives, and grandchildren. In the United States this residence pattern is modified toward the common American nuclear family household pattern; unmarried adults reside with their parents until marriage, and then they take up their own residence.

See also: BENGALIS; PAKISTANIS

Bibliography

Arens, J., and Beurden, J. van. (1977). *Jhagrapur: Poor Peasants in a Village in Bangladesh.* Amsterdam: Third World Publications.

Bardhan, K. (1990). *Of Women, Outcastes, Peasants, and Rebels: A Selection of Bengali Short Stories.* Berkeley: University of California Press.

Baxter, C. (1984). *Bangladesh: A New Nation in an Old Setting.* Boulder, CO: Westview Press.

Harris, M. S. (1991). "Diversity in a Bangladeshi Village: Landholding Structure, Economic Differentiation, and Occupational Specialization of Moslems and Hindus." *Research in Economic Anthropology* 13:143–160.

Hartmann, B., and Boyce, J. K. (1983). *A Quiet Violence: View from a Bangladesh Village*. London: Zed Press.

Islam, A. K. M. A. (1974). *A Bangladesh Village: Political Conflict and Cohesion*. Prospect Heights, IL: Waveland Press.

Jannuzi, F. T., and Peach, J. T. (1980). *The Agrarian Structure of Bangladesh*. Boulder, CO: Westview Press.

Khan, A. R. (1972). *The Economy of Bangladesh*. London: Macmillan.

Maloney, C. (1986). *Behavior and Poverty in Bangladesh*. Dhaka: University Press.

Mascarenhas, A. (1986). *Bangladesh: A Legacy of Blood*. London: Hodder & Stoughton.

Novak, J. J. (1993). *Bangladesh: Reflections on the Water*. Bloomington: Indiana University Press.

O'Donnel, C. P. (1984). *Bangladesh: Biography of a Muslim Nation*. Boulder, CO: Westview Press.

Sisson, R., and Rose, L. E. (1990). *War and Secession: Pakistan, India, and the Creation of Bangladesh*. Berkeley: University of California Press.

Wennergren, E. B.; Antholt, C. J.; and Whitaker, M. D. (1984). *Agricultural Development in Bangladesh*. Boulder, CO: Westview Press.

MICHAEL S. HARRIS

BARBADIANS

Barbadians have immigrated to the United States from the island nation of Barbados, located near the southern end of the island chain that stretches across the Caribbean Sea between Florida and Venezuela. Only 166 square miles in area, Barbados is small in size but regionally prominent. Moreover, with more than a quarter of a million residents, it is the most densely populated country in the Western Hemisphere.

Colonialism, sugar cultivation, and slavery shaped Barbadian society. English settlers first arrived on the island in 1627, and for the next 340 years Barbados remained a British colony with an economy based on sugar production and export. Plantation slavery and its aftermath produced a bipolar social order dominated by a small white "plantocracy" that exercised economic and political control over the lives of enslaved Africans and their descendants. With the introduction of universal suffrage in the 1950s, Afro-Barbadians assumed control of the government and led the island to independence in 1966. Subsequent economic development, centered mainly on tourism, diminished sugar's importance but increased the influence of foreign capital, creating a fragile prosperity dependent on global economic forces over which Barbados has little control.

Barbadians are known for an island chauvinism often satirized in the West Indies and even among islanders themselves, and their self-identification as "Bajans" overshadows more inclusive regional identities. Although Barbadians in the United States maintain strong ties with the island and see themselves as a distinct immigrant ethnic group, white Americans have categorized them in racial rather than ethnic terms. Since the 1980s, the growth of the West Indian immigrant population and an emerging public discourse on pluralism and multiculturalism have given an ethnic visibility to Barbadians and other Afro-Caribbean groups.

Immigration and Settlement History

Large-scale Barbadian immigration to the United States is a twentieth-century phenomenon, but emigration from the island has a much longer history. The earliest emigrants from Barbados to North America were white settlers and indentured laborers displaced by the sugar economy's expansion after 1650. Successful planters and merchants followed later in the seventeenth century, investing their wealth in the Carolinas and other North American colonies. The continuing search for investment opportunities, education, and social credentials has propelled an ongoing circulation of white Barbadians between the island, North America, and England.

Black Barbadian emigration only began after emancipation in 1838. But since the 1860s, when Barbadians were recruited to work in Guyana and Trinidad, emigration has been a significant livelihood strategy for the working class. In the late nineteenth and early twentieth century, Barbadians sought economic opportunities throughout the Caribbean and Latin America, most notably in Panama, where more than forty thousand worked on construction of the canal.

The first large-scale Barbadian immigration to the United States began around 1900 and continued until 1924, when new U.S. policies severely curtailed admission of nonwhite immigrants. By this time, West Indian communities were well established in New York and other northeastern cities, but immigration quotas, nativist sentiment, and the depression economy of the 1930s discouraged newcomers. During World War II, Barbadians were among forty-one thousand West Indians recruited to replace American workers, but most came on brief contracts, returning home after the war. In 1952, new discriminatory restrictions further reduced admissions, and for the next decade, Barbadian emigration was redirected to England. But after 1965, with changes in U.S. policies, a second large wave of Barbadians and other West Indians arrived in the United States.

New York City is the major center of Barbadian settlement in the United States. Early immigrants settled in Harlem and Brooklyn, with smaller numbers going to Boston, Hartford, and other northeastern cities. Later immigrants continued to settle in the Northeast. In 1970, 73 percent of West Indians in the United States lived in New York City, with half living in Brooklyn. In the 1980s, Barbadians began to move to other boroughs and to suburban or more distant urban areas.

The Barbadian tradition of mobility is both a safety valve for a society unable to meet its population's subsistence expectations and a flexible livelihood strategy families use to augment their resources with savings and remittances from work abroad. Barbadians usually plan to remain overseas only long enough to accumulate resources to enhance their standard of living at home. Although social scientists contrast this "myth of return" with the fact that most remain, some observers detected an increase in return immigration to the island in the 1990s.

Demographic Facts

Close to 100,000 West Indians immigrated to the United States between 1900 and 1924. The first Barbadians who arrived during this period came from middle-class backgrounds—teachers, clerks, professionals. But as writer Paule Marshall (1992) notes in describing Barbadian immigrants of her parents' generation, "Panama money" (the savings and remittances from those who went to Panama to work on the canal) allowed the children of artisans, estate workers, and small landholders to join the movement to New York. A majority of the immigrants were men, although women comprised a significant minority.

In the immigration stream that began in the 1960s, working-class Barbadians predominated. A total of 16,413 Barbadians arrived between 1967 and 1976. Of the 9,733 who were employed, 17 percent worked in professional, technical, and managerial positions; 14 percent were clerical and sales workers; 27 percent were craftsmen, foremen, operatives, and other skilled workers; 39 percent were private household and other service workers; and 3 percent were laborers.

The 1990 U.S. Census enumerated 33,178 persons of Barbadian ancestry, including 24,735 (74.6%) who were born on the island. Their median age was 37.4 years, and 74 percent were older than twenty-four years of age. Women comprised 55 percent of the population. In the twenty-five years since the second wave of Barbadian immigration began, Barbadians experienced considerable occupational mobility: 59 percent held managerial, professional, administrative, technical, or sales positions; 17 percent worked in production, crafts, and repair, or as operators, fabricators, or laborers; and 25 percent were service workers.

Language

Barbados remained under British rule throughout its colonial history, and English has no rivals as the island's language. A standard "metropolitan" English generally spoken by the middle and upper classes is taught in school and used in formal settings. It coexists with a local creolized form, known as Bajan, that emerged from the linguistic encounter of Africans and English colonists. Islanders of all classes appreciate the rich expressive qualities of Bajan but describe it as "broken English" and associate it with low status and lack of education. Most Barbadians switch easily between Bajan and "proper English," and in the United States, their command of English gives them an employment advantage over non-English-speaking immigrants in fields requiring communication skills.

Cultural Characteristics

Economic Activity. Barbadians immigrate to the United States to improve their economic circumstances. Both the skills and education they bring and the structuring of opportunities in the U.S. economy affect their success. Although early Barbadian immigrants came from middle-class and skilled working-class backgrounds, the jobs available to them in New York's racially segregated economy were low-paying unskilled positions as porters, elevator operators, and household workers. Despite a reputation for business acumen, relatively few Barbadians were self-employed, but by pursuing education and professional training, many became prominent among Harlem's professional elite.

Barbadians immigrating after 1965 arrived in a period of significant economic change in the United States. Middle- and upper-middle class women were entering the labor force in unprecedented numbers, creating a demand for household and child-care workers that Barbadian and other West Indian women filled. As the service sector expanded, Barbadians found employment in health care, transportation, security, and communications industries as service workers, technicians, and clerical and administrative staff. In 1990, 20 percent of Barbadians in the United States held municipal, state, or federal government jobs.

Housing. Although early Barbadian immigrants lived in crowded conditions within New York's black communities, they avidly pursued home ownership, a powerful symbol of autonomy and status. Marshall's novel of Barbadian life in Brooklyn, *Brown Girl, Brownstones* (1959), describes the preoccupation with "buying house" that motivated Barbadians laboring long hours at menial jobs. Through frugality, pooling of family resources, and use of rotating credit associations, many eventually succeeded in purchasing homes.

Following passage of civil rights and open housing legislation in the 1960s, and the subsequent growth of New York's West Indian population, identifiable Caribbean neighborhoods emerged in Brooklyn, the Bronx, and Queens. In the 1980s, communities of Barbadian and other West Indian homeowners contributed to revitalizing areas of the city abandoned by former landlords and created businesses catering to island tastes and needs. The Caribbean ambiance of the commercial strips in these neighborhoods has heightened West Indian visibility in the city.

Religion. Anglicanism is the dominant religion in Barbados, and for Barbadian immigrants, Episcopalian congregations provide continuity with the island's religious traditions. Barbadians also join other major Protestant denominations, but in the United States, as on the island, day-to-day religious life centers on small churches—some independent, others affiliated with groups with large national memberships. Pentecostal, Apostolic, Ethiopian Orthodox, Jehovah's Witnesses, and numerous independent churches have drawn adherents from the immigrant community, and church-related activities constitute a particularly important domain of social life for women.

Worldview. The history of Barbados as a slave plantation colony produced a deeply divided society in which the differential values and meanings ascribed to folk and elite cultural practices upheld the structures of race and class privilege. The black

Barbadian culture that developed in this context entails not only distinctive language, religious, and family practices but what W. E. B. Du Bois identified among African Americans as "double consciousness"—an awareness of the dominant perspective that disvalues black cultural forms, coexisting with an alternative view that inverts these negative valuations of black folk culture. The dual perspective persists among Barbadians in the United States, although the hegemonic definitions of cultural value increasingly reflect the North American rather than the English or white Barbadian premises.

Family and Social Life. Among West Indians, the family is a resilient and creative institution. Barbadian families consist of networks of bilateral extended kin with highly elastic boundaries. Ideology and practices of mutual support link family members within and across households, communities, and nations. Unlike dominant Euro-American family forms centered on co-residential conjugal couples, Barbadian family networks are built on diverse ties including marriage, nonmarital unions, and consanguineal links within and across generations. Their expansive boundaries and non-localized character permit a flexible distribution of responsibilities for economic support, child care, and other family tasks, enabling families to respond to shifting economic opportunities on the island or abroad.

Family networks structure the flow of immigrants to the United States. New immigrants usually stay with relatives who preceded them, and once employed and settled, they often "send for" other family members. Young children may remain in Barbados, where "child fostering" within the family network has long supported livelihood strategies that entail high rates of female labor force participation and the emigration of adults. Frequent communication and travel between the United States and Barbados sustain immigrants' involvement with kin and friends at home. Through remittances and savings, they support children and other relatives on the island, bring family members to visit the United States, and purchase land and housing in Barbados.

Since the 1970s, the growing Barbadian immigrant community in the United States has provided an increasingly encompassing context for social life. While Bajans interact with other groups in the workplace, schools, and other public settings, they live in increasingly West Indian neighborhoods, and many socialize primarily with kin and compatriots—at parties, social clubs, churches, and in one another's homes. Many immigrants whose experience of the United States is limited to the New York area, have visited or hosted kin living in Toronto, London, or other points to which Barbadian transnational networks extend.

Arts. West Indian writers, musicians, and intellectuals have played prominent roles in U.S. cultural life since the Harlem Renaissance of the early twentieth century. Barbadian contributions to literature have been particularly noteworthy. Island-born writers George Lamming and Edward Kamau Brathwaite have received international critical recognition. The fiction of second-generation Barbadian Paule Marshall has given visibility to the experiences of black immigrants, bringing feminist and Afro-Caribbean perspectives to the forefront of contemporary developments in literature. In journalism, Barbadian Tony Best, as editor of the *New York Carib News*, has contributed to the emergence of a U.S.-based Caribbean press that provides a forum for information and debate on Caribbean, African, and North American political and social issues affecting the immigrant community.

West Indian musical traditions have significantly influenced popular culture in the United States. Calypso has long been recognized in the United States as a folk musical form, but West Indian music entered mainstream American culture when Jamaican reggae infused the popular music scene throughout North America and much of the rest of the world. West Indians were also formative participants in the development of rap music and hip hop culture. Barbadians take part in New York's West Indian American Day Festival, an annual public celebration of Afro-Caribbean arts that showcases calypso and soco musical forms, which remain the most popular rhythms at Barbadian parties and social gatherings in the United States. Barbadian youths in the United States participate in an increasingly global musical culture that incorporates the diverse musical styles produced in the African diaspora.

Health and Illness. Barbadians' experience with Western biomedical traditions informs their approach to health and illness. The health-care sector employs significant numbers of Barbadian immigrants, often in professional and technical capacities, and Barbadians use biomedical treatment as the primary recourse in the face of serious illness. However, they often supplement biomedical approaches with both traditional remedies (e.g., herbal "bush teas") and various newly popular alternative medical therapies (holistic, homeopathic, herbal) that are consistent with folk philosophies of the nature of the body.

Social and Political Organizations. Voluntary associations and mutual aid societies have a long history among West Indians in the United States. The Sons and Daughters of Barbados has assisted immigrants since the early twentieth century, providing sick and death benefits and sponsoring educational, charitable, and social events. Groups like the "old boys" and "old girls" associations of island secondary schools and the Barbadian Ex-Policemen's Association not only sustain ties formed at home but reaffirm statuses threatened by the downward social mobility new immigrants commonly experience. Occupational groups, such as the Barbadian Nurses Association, focus on common professional interests in the United States, while sports and social clubs promote recreational and social activities within the immigrant community. An umbrella group, the Council of Barbadian Organizations, links the diverse associations and reinforces a home-country focus for the community.

Through most of the twentieth century, islanders who became active in U.S. politics—both within and outside the dominant party structures—did so as members of the larger black community. Barbadian Richard B. Moore was prominent among the activists who, in the

1920s, turned Harlem's street corners into an alternative political forum where illustrious West Indian and African-American orators—including Jamaican Marcus Garvey and Florida-born A. Philip Randolph—held forth on socialism, anticolonialism, tenant and labor organizing, African cultural achievements, and racial pride. The crowds they drew included both African Americans and Caribbean immigrants.

Within the major political parties, Barbadians joined in the struggle for black recognition and representation. Adolph Howell, the first black immigrant to seek election to the New York State Assembly, and Herbert Bruce, elected in the 1930s as Harlem's first Democratic district leader, were members of Barbadian associations but also participated in fraternal orders that linked Caribbean and native-born blacks. Second-generation Barbadian Shirley Chisholm, who in 1968 became Brooklyn's first black congressional representative and subsequently declared her candidacy for the U.S. presidency, achieved prominence as a black political leader rather than as a Barbadian or West Indian.

Although West Indians were active in the civil rights struggles of the 1960s, African-American leaders who emerged during this period subsequently eclipsed West Indian politicians in party leadership and elected positions. In the 1970s and 1980s, however, new pan-Caribbean organizations became involved in local politics, increasing West Indian political visibility. In New York City, where the pluralistic image of the ethnic mosaic has long been salient, visible ethnic culture legitimizes claims for political recognition. A primarily Caribbean constituency elected Jamaican Una Clarke to New York's City Council in 1991, and candidates are increasingly expected to be responsive to Caribbean agendas. West Indians have challenged both white and African-American representation of Caribbean constituencies in local contests, but immigrants and native-born blacks have maintained solidarity in broader arenas of U.S. politics. Similarly, West Indian and other women of color in the United States have contested how Euro-

American women have represented their interests, while building alliances around issues of common concern.

Assimilation and Transnationalism

The deep racial division between blacks and whites in the United States historically rendered West Indian immigrants invisible to the white majority, and the system of racial ascription offered Barbadians little incentive to embrace new "American" identities. Expectations of returning home—however often deferred—allowed immigrants to distance themselves somewhat from the harshness of racism in the United States, but among second-generation West Indians, a more encompassing racial identity prevailed over ethnic allegiances.

For Barbadians arriving after the 1970s, eruptions of racial tensions, including several highly publicized incidents of white violence against blacks, again underscored the overriding role of race in the United States. Moreover, in the 1990s, growing U.S. nativist sentiment prompted legislation withdrawing long-established rights of legal immigrants. Despite Barbadians' economic achievements, a restructuring U.S. economy offers them fewer jobs with economic security.

Barbadians and other West Indians have responded to these marginalizing processes with efforts to protect the gains they have made in the United States, while safeguarding their transnational options. They express on the one hand an increased racial consciousness and solidarity with African Americans, a new interest in acquiring U.S. citizenship, and a growing political activism. But at the same time, a transnational orientation informs their engagement in U.S. social and political arenas, giving racial solidarity a diasporic dimension and introducing a Caribbean perspective on local and national political issues. Thus, as Barbadians increase their involvement in U.S. society, they also strengthen the transnational social field within which they pursue their livelihood and construct their identities.

See also: AFRICAN AMERICANS

Bibliography

Basch, L.; Glick Schiller, N.; and Szanton Blanc, C. (1994). *Nations Unbound: Transnational Projects, Postcolonial Predicaments, and Deterritorialized Nation States.* Langhorne, PA: Gordon and Breach.

Chisholm, S. (1970). *Shirley Chisholm: Unbought and Unbossed.* New York: Avon Books.

Colen, S. (1990). "'Housekeeping' for the Green Card: West Indian Household Workers, the State, and Stratified Reproduction in New York." In *At Work in Homes: Household Workers in World Perspective,* edited by R. Sanjek and S. Colen. Washington, DC: American Anthropological Association.

Conway, D., and Cooke, T. J. (1996). "New York City: Caribbean Immigration and Residential Segregation in a Restructured Global City." In *Social Polarization in Post Industrial Metropolises,* edited by J. O'Loughlin and J. Friedrichs. Berlin: Walter de Gruyter.

Gmelch, G. (1992). *Double Passage: The Lives of Caribbean Migrants Abroad and Back Home.* Ann Arbor: University of Michigan Press.

Hebdige, D. (1987). *Cut 'N' Mix: Culture, Identity, and Caribbean Music.* London: Routledge.

Kasinitz, P. (1992). *Caribbean New York: Black Immigrants and the Politics of Race.* Ithaca, NY: Cornell University Press.

Marshall, P. (1959). *Brown Girl, Brownstones.* New York: Avon Books.

Marshall, P. (1992). "Black Immigrant Women in *Brown Girl, Brownstones.*" In *Caribbean Life in New York City: Sociocultural Dimensions,* edited by C. R. Sutton and E. M. Chaney. New York: Center for Migration Studies.

Palmer, R. W. (1995). *Pilgrims from the Sun: West Indian Migration to America.* New York: Twayne.

Sutton, C. R., and Makiesky, S. (1992). "Migration and West Indian Racial and Political Consciousness." In *Caribbean Life In New York City: Sociocultural Dimensions,* edited by C. R. Sutton and E. M. Chaney. New York: Center for Migration Studies.

Watkins-Owens, I. (1996). *Blood Relations: Caribbean Immigrants and the Harlem Community, 1900–1930.* Bloomington: Indiana University Press.

SUSAN MAKIESKY BARROW

BASQUES

The homeland of the Basques, or Euskaldunak in their own language, is in north-central Spain and southwestern France, where the western ridges of the Pyrenees meet the Cantabrian seacoast. While at least a few persons of Basque descent reside in every one of the fifty states of the United States, the largest concentrations are in California, Idaho, and Nevada. Beginning in the mid-nineteenth century, Basque immigrants began entering the American West and quickly emerged as the region's sheepherders. The "Bascos" (stemming from the Spanish term *vascos*), as they are called in western slang, are still closely associated with the sheep industry within the ethnic stereotyping of the region.

Division of their European homeland between Spain and France gives rise to distinction in the American West between "French Basques" and "Spanish Basques." The former settled mainly in California and northern Nevada, with small concentrations in Arizona, Colorado, Wyoming, and Montana. Spanish Basques, particularly those from the region of Bizkaia, also setted in parts of California and northern Nevada and predominate in eastern Oregon and southern Idaho. So in terms of distribution there are actually two Basque colonies in the American West, with only slight overlap and, until the 1960s, minimal mutual awareness.

Ethnic Origins

Basques sometimes are referred to as the "mystery people of Europe," reference being to the enigma regarding their origins. Most of the Continent's ethnic groups descend directly from the invasions of Indo-European-speaking peoples out of western Asia during the second millennium B.C.E. Prehistorians agree that the Basques have occupied their Pyrenean territory since at least 3000 B.C.E. Some suggest that they may represent the remnants of a proto-European population once much more widely distributed throughout the

southwestern part of the Continent—possibly descended from the Cro-Magnon population and the famed cave painters of the Upper Magdalenian Period (12,000 B.C.E.).

Serological and linguistic evidence support the view that the Basques are ethnically distinct from the surrounding European populations. Basques have the highest percentage of any European group of blood type O and the lowest of blood type B. They also have the highest incidence in the world of the Rh negative factor (27.5%), prompting many geneticists to believe that this genetic marker originated in the Basque population. Thus serological evidence suggests that Basques have maintained a considerable degree of physical isolation with respect to other Europeans.

The Basque language constitutes the sole entry under its own "family" in the *World Linguistic Atlas*. Despite efforts by linguists and philologists to discover links between Basque and other languages throughout the world, to date there are no definitive ones. Basque remains, so far as we know, a unique language unrelated to any other.

Basques have a keen awareness of their ethnic uniqueness. The self-notion that they differ from the Spaniards and the French sustains an ethnonationalist challenge to Spanish and, to a much lesser degree, French hegemony over the Basque country. At present the Spanish Basque provinces of Araba, Bizkaia, and Gipuzkoa constitute an autonomous community (with its own presidency and parliament) within Spain, as does the fourth province of Navarra. This political arrangement, however, does not satisfy the more intransigent nationalists, who demand sovereignty for an independent Basque state. The clash between Spanish and Basque nationalists has, since the 1960s, caused more than eight hundred fatalities. Therefore the Basque conflict ranks only behind that of Northern Ireland as Western Europe's most virulent and violent political confrontation. However, in contrast to the Irish-American case, the ethnonationalist conflict in their European homeland fails to mobilize Basque-American public opinion and support to a significant degree.

Immigration History

The Basque presence in the New World corresponds to the beginnings of the European involvement. There is even speculation that Basque whalers may have been active in the Terranovan waters of the eastern Canadian seaboard prior to the first voyage of Columbus. In any event, the Basques, as Iberia's quintessential mariners, were well represented in Columbus's crews and in Spain's earliest voyages of discovery. Sebastian Elcano, the first man to circumnavigate the globe, was from the Basque seacost village of Getaria.

Basques were prominent among Spain's missionaries, soldiers, and administrators. In these capacities they often played key roles in the Spanish administration of its borderland regions with the United States. For example, during both the Spanish and Mexican periods of its history most of California's governors were Basque, as were many of its missionaries.

The present border between Mexico and the United States crystallized in the mid-nineteenth century, bringing California and the American Southwest under U.S. control. This created a watershed between older Basque immigration, characterized by a European colonial elite within the framework of the Spanish imperial enterprise, and the new immigration of European Basques of largely modest circumstances fleeing Old World political and economic oppression in search of New World freedom and opportunity. The discovery of gold in California was a critical catalyst.

Several hundred Basques entered California among the fortune-seeking argonauts. However, many came not from Europe but from southern South America, where, during the first decades of the postcolonial era of Argentine and Uruguayan history, or by the 1840s, Basque immigrants had made their mark within the expanding sheep industry of the pampas. Like most of the gold-seekers, the majority of California's Gold Rush Basque immigrants failed to find their El Dorado and turned to other activities. In the vast, open ranges of California some recognized a new opportunity to engage in sheep husbandry on an expanding frontier.

The aspiring Basque sheepman required little capital, since most of the range remained open on a first-come basis. Under the region's generally arid conditions it was necessary to practice transhumance—that is, the sheep bands were summered in pastures in the higher mountain ranges and wintered in the adjacent valleys. All that a sheepherder required was a bedroll and camp gear, a pack animal (and possibly a mount), and a trusty sheepdog. He could spend the entire year with his sheep band in the endless, nomadic search for adequate feed and water.

Thus, by the late 1850s, there was a discernible pattern of itinerant Basque sheepmen established in southern California. By the 1860s, they were expanding into the Central Valley and had penetrated the Great Basin by the 1870s. By the end of the century, nomadic Basque sheepmen—"tramps" to their detractors—were present in all thirteen western states. By then Basques also had a reputation as the best herders and were in demand as guardians of non-Basque sheep outfits as well.

The activities of the itinerant Basque sheepmen produced considerable conflict. Settled ranchers, primarily though not exclusively cattlemen, contested control of the land. While legally no more entitled than the Basque itinerants to the public range, they depicted the Basques as swarthy usurpers of American resources who were bent upon making their fortune before going back to Europe to spend it. The ranchers employed harassing tactics such as legislation that excluded the itinerants (later deemed unconstitutional) and outright violence.

Of more lasting effect, however, was the legislation during the last decade of the nineteenth century and the first of the twentieth that created the national parks and the national forests. The parks legislation excluded all livestock interest from the reserves, but the considerably more extensive national forests affected the Basques in particular. Indeed, the region's newspaper trumpeted the settled Anglo ranchers' victories with headlines such as "Basques Excluded from the Reserves," a reference to rules that allocated grazing permits in the national forests exclusively to American citizens with ranchland in private ownership. The new order placed much of the traditional range off-limits to itinerant Basque sheepmen.

While the new restrictions were a death knell for some Basque sheepmen, the rules had the unintended effect of concentrating the surviving ones on the more marginal range as yet free from much federal control. Overgrazing became a serious issue. In 1934, with passage of the Taylor Grazing Act, all of the remaining western range was brought under direct federal control, signaling the end of the era of the itinerants. Some managed to acquire their own ranch property, others went to work for established ranchers, and many simply sold their sheep and went back to Europe.

By this time, or beginning in the 1920s, Basque immigration into the United States had been se-verely curtailed by an increasingly restrictive U.S. immigration policy. The national origins quota approach was particularly detrimental to Spanish Basques. Under the new system only 121 Spanish nationals were to be admitted annually. The quota for French nationals was much higher, but France's Basque population was only one-tenth of Europe's Basques.

By the 1940s, there was a serious shortage of sheepherders in the American West, exacerbated by the mobilization of manpower during World War II. Several hundred Basques managed to enter the United States illegally and make their way to the American West, where they found eager employers. Western representatives began introducing legislation to normalize the status of individual Basque illegal aliens. These "sheepherder laws" were obviously inefficient, and in 1950, the U.S. Congress passed the first of several laws that exempted intending Basque herders from the Spanish nationals' quota. Under the provisions of these

A Basque herder and his dog trail a band of sheep in the mountains of southern Idaho. (Richard Lane)

laws, over the next three decades several thousand herders were recruited in Spain, primarily in its Basque region, by the Western Range Association (a sheep ranchers' organization founded solely for this purpose).

Initially, the recruits were required to sign three-year herder contracts, which forced them to leave the country after their termination. Subsequently the contracts were modified to allow the ex-herder to remain in the United States as a permanent resident, so the contract herder program provided an avenue for Basque immigration into the United States. For a while it was the means whereby the aging Basque-American colony was renewed.

However, by the mid-1970s, the economic recovery of the Basque economy made the low-paying sheepherder jobs unattractive, and the Western Range Association shifted its recruiting efforts from Europe to Latin America. Whereas in 1970, there were about fifteen hundred Basque sheepherders in the American West, by the mid-1990s, they numbered a few dozen at most. From the mid-1970s to the mid-1990s, there was minimal Basque immigration into the United States. The recent immigrant is likely to be a student, a professional, or a person effecting a family reunion in America.

The Basque-American Population

Until the 1980 U.S. Census, Basques in the United States were counted as French or Spanish nationals and were aggregated with considerably larger non-Basque immigrant populations. It is therefore impossible to provide a comprehensive historical demographic profile of the Basque-American community. In the 1990 U.S. Census, 47,956 persons self-identified as being of at least partial Basque descent. More than half resided in the states of California (19,122), Idaho (5,587), and Nevada (4,840). The remainder were scattered primarily throughout the remaining western states. New York (1,300) has a port-of-entry colony dating from the latter third of the nineteenth century, when most Basque immigrants disembarked in

New York, spent a few days in a Basque hotel on Cherry Street, and then were put on a train by the hotelier with the name of their destination pinned to their lapel, to advise the conductor where to put them off. Connecticut (319) has a small but growing Basque colony, which consists largely of jai alai (a Basque game) players who have married U.S. citizens or otherwise managed to obtain permanent residency. Florida (1,189) has its Basque jai alai dimension as well, augmented by a contingent of Basques among refugees from Fidel Castro's Cuba.

The majority of Basque immigrants in the United States from 1850 to the present have been young, single males. Most were the products of chain migration whereby established Basque sheepmen brought their kinsmen and fellow villagers to work for them or their neighbors as sheepherders. Few entered the United States with the intention of remaining (Basques intending permanent immigration preferred a Latin American destination, where their knowledge of Spanish and the Hispanic culture made them far more functional than in the United States). Most Basques planned to work for their sponsors, possibly taking their wages in ewes, spend a few years as an itinerant sheepman, and then sell out to return to Europe. Consequently, if several hundred Basque immigrants entered the country annually, they were largely replacing those departing for their European homeland.

Some, of course, changed their mind and became committed to a New World future. Of these, most became upwardly mobile within the sheep industry—a possible career path being herder to camp tender to foreman to ranch owner. Others settled in the small towns and cities of the open range districts of the American West (e.g., Stockton, Fresno, Bakersfield, Chino, Reno, Elko, Winnemucca, Jordan Valley, Boise, Mountain Home, Shoshone, Buffalo, and Glasgow). Although an ex-herder might become a miner, gardener, baker, milker, or construction worker, one particular occupation constituted, after herding, the second Basque-American occupational marker: hotelkeeper.

By the late nineteenth century, there was an established network of Basque hotels throughout the American West. Sheepherding was seasonal for many, since in the autumn, once the year's lambs had been sent to market, two bands were combined into one under the care of a single herder until the next spring's lambing season. Consequently, nearly half of the work force was laid off for several months. The unemployed congregated in boardinghouses to await the next season.

The Basque hotel became the most important social institution for the largely single-male Basque population of the American West. By its nature sheepherding insulated the young immigrant from American culture, and it was common for the immigrant to spend years in the United States without learning more than a few words of English. Thus, the hotel was an ethnic haven and home for the herder when in town. It provided him with an address, a place to store his town clothes when on the range and his rifle, saddle, and bedroll when in town or on a return visit to Europe. The hotelkeeper was his confidant, banker, and translator on a shopping excursion or a visit to a doctor or dentist. For the Basque Americans born in the United States, the hotel was a place to recharge their ethnic batteries, practice their halting Basque, and acquire knowledge (albeit fragmentary) of the Old World. For the aged bachelor herder with insufficient funds or interest to return to Europe, the Basque hotel served as a retirement home.

Most important, the hotel was the prime catalyst in the formation of an enduring Basque-American community. Each required domestic help, and it was common for the hotelkeeper to send back to the Basque country for single women willing to work as cooks, waitresses, and maids. Few remained single for long once they arrived in the American West. It also became common for the hotels to sponsor weekly dances attended by the area's first-generation, American-born Basque women. Many ex-herder met his future bride in this fashion. The Basque hotel offered additional services to the new established family. If the young couple lived on a ranch, the wife might move into the hotel as her pregnancy neared term and give birth there. The christening would likely be celebrated at the hotel. Once the children reached school age they might become its semipermanent boarders during the school year, going home to the ranch only on weekends and holidays. Many a wedding was celebrated and funeral observed in the Basque hotel.

Over time the Basque hotel became the ethnic group's primary mechanism for projecting its image and identity to the wider American society. They became famed for their inexpensive, hearty boardinghouse cuisine served family-style at long tables. Particularly since 1970, when the era of the Basque sheepherder was all but over, the hotels have evolved into ethnic restaurants in which the food is likely served by waitresses in Basque folk costume while photographs, paintings, wall hangings, and implements drawn from both Old World Basque peasant life and the herding legacy create an ethnic atmosphere. It is here, while sipping a Picon Punch, that the visitor can pose to the bartender the oft-repeated question, "Who are the Basques?"

Old Basques and New

Basque immigrants in the United States were few in number and scattered over a vast area. Consequently, Basque Americans did not possess the critical mass that would create the ethnic neighborhood and ethnic merchant and professional classes that characterized and perpetuated the collective life of some immigrant groups within the American experience. Nor, for the most part, did Basque Americans possess an ethnic intelligentsia that might create a Basque church or a Basque-American press. Rather, to the extent that their Roman Catholicism was given a Basque flavor, it was expressed in the perambulations of the lone Basque chaplain assigned the entire American West as his "parish." Similarly, excepting the short-lived attempts to found *Escualdun Gazeta* (Basque Gazette) in 1885; *California'ko Eskual Herria* (California Basque Land), 1893–1898, in Los Angeles; and *Voice of the Basques*, 1974–1977, in

Boise, Basque Americans have lacked an ethnic press.

Prior to World War II, Basques maintained an extremely low ethnic profile. Their close identification with sheepherding, a lowly position in the region's occupational scale, and the controversy over the "tramp" itinerant sheepman gave Basques a negative image. At that time the hotels were no-nonsense establishments whose precincts were largely off-limits to non-Basques. Basque children recall playground slights and even fights over ethnic epithets. However, Basques, like other minorities and hyphenated Americans, were influenced by such postwar developments as the countercultural and civil rights movements, as well as the search for roots that prompted people to explore their genealogies and display their ethnic heritage.

In 1949, Boise Basques organized a production called *Song of the Basques*, which was performed with great success before a citywide audience. That same year they incorporated the social club Euskaldunak, Inc., and began construction on the Boise Basque Center. In 1960, a group of Boise youngsters traveled to the Basque country for a summer's visit. They became fast friends with a professional Basque dance group called Oinkari. The Basque Americans picked up some of the dances and upon their return to Boise formed their own Oinkari, which quickly emerged as the premier Basque dance group in the United States. In 1962, they performed at the Century 21 Exposition in Seattle and represented Idaho at the 1964 New York World's Fair.

Meanwhile, in 1957, Robert Laxalt, son of a French Basque sheepman, published his book *Sweet Promised Land*, the story of his father's life in the American West and return visit to Europe. It was a huge success, establishing Laxalt as the literary spokesman of the Basque-American community while relating their group experience to the wider, non-Basque reading public. In 1959, in part trading on the reputation and interest created by Laxalt's book, the First National Basque Festival was held in Sparks, Nevada. For the first time several thousand persons gathered together to en-

joy Basque folk costumes and dances and witness such Basque sporting events as woodchopping and stonelifting competitions.

The festival was a defining event in many regards. Western Nevada is a crossroads for the two broad Basque colonies of the American West, and through the festival they were brought in contact. The event was itself an "invention," combining Old World Basque cultural elements without much regard for the European regional distinctions that would have made such commingling unthinkable in the homeland. The festival also embraced such New World features as the town dance, the public barbecue, and sheephooking and sheepdog trials. Unbeknownst to its organizers, they were establishing a Basque festival model unique to the American West that continues to flourish. In the aftermath of the festival, in more than a dozen communities Basque clubs were established whose main purposes were to found a local dance group for the children and to sponsor an annual festival. Today the "national" festival is held each Fourth of July weekend in Elko, Nevada, while on several weekends throughout the summer the local clubs hold their own Basque festival.

Another development during the 1960s that was stimulated by the growing public awareness of Basques was the decision by the University of Nevada system to create a Basque Studies program. Founded in 1967, the program edits a Basque Book Series for the University of Nevada Press, offers courses on Basque culture and language at the Reno campus, and organizes study-abroad programs in Europe. Hundreds of Basque Americans have attended the European courses and have returned to their communities with more profound knowledge and heightened enthusiasm for their culture, which has inspired them to seek leadership roles within the local Basque scene.

In 1973, representatives of several Basque clubs met in Reno and created NABO (North American Basque Organizations, Inc.) to foster cultural contacts among the clubs while facilitating relations with the Basque country and with other colonies throughout the Basque emigrant diaspora (primarily in several countries of Latin America and in Australia). NABO sponsors an annual music camp at which Basque-American children are taught dance and the intricacies of playing the *txistu* (flute) and drum. NABO sometimes brings Basque performing artists from Europe to tour in the United States. It also holds regional championships for *pelota* (handball) and *mus* (a card game somewhat similar to poker) and sends its representative team to international competitions.

The Future

At present, several of the Basque clubs have their own clubhouse. In 1983, San Francisco Basques built their Basque Cultural Center, an impressive structure complete with meeting rooms, restaurant, and ball court. In 1987, Boise Basques celebrated their first *jaialdi*, a major cultural event that included elements of the Basque festival as well as university lectures, contemporary films, and art exhibits. Jaialdi was attended by thirty thousand persons. Boise Basques have also established a Basque museum adjacent to their Basque Center. NABO now has more than twenty constituent clubs, more than at any time in its history. The courses held for American students in the Basque country are oversubscribed. In short, there has never been as much public expression in the United States of Basque culture. To the casual observer the Basque-American scene might seem particularly robust.

Indeed, there is a sense in which Basques have an ancient tradition of maintaining their cultural distinctiveness in the face of considerable assimilatory pressures, even in their homeland. Certainly, in the American West Basque Americans are regarded as one of the region's most unique ethnic groups—frequent object of museum exhibits, documentary films, and journalistic stories—that is seemingly impervious to assimilation. However, there are several reasons to regard the future with apprehension (assuming, of course, that the persistence of a recognizable Basque-American community is deemed desirable). In Europe preservation of the Basque language is at the center of the Basques' struggle for cultural

A Zenbat Gara dance group poses before the National Monument to the Basque Sheepherder in Reno, Nevada. (Zenbat Gara Basque Cultural Association)

survival; in the American West that battle has been all but lost. While a few Basque Americans make the effort to learn the language, the payoff is more at the level of personal satisfaction. Basque, which was once the vernacular of the sheep outfits and hotels, is now a casualty of the decline of the open-range sheep industry in general and Basque involvement within it in particular.

With the cessation of immigration of Old Word Basque herders, the Basque-American community no longer receives an infusion of "new blood." It is aging in both a chronological and generational sense. During the sheepherding era the Basque-American population was characterized by a high degree of endogamy. Whether formed by the union of two Old World-born persons or that of an ex-herder and an American woman of Basque descent, the Basque-American family was its own little ethnic enclave. This is no longer the case, since today's eligible Basque-American adult is unlikely to marry within the ethnic group.

Nor does the future seem propitious when viewed in terms of the outside forces affecting Basque-American identity. Since the demise of Basque involvement in the sheep industry there is no longer a particular economic raison d'être underpinning the Basque-American reality and its expression. Attendance at the festivals is generally waning, and at least one has been suspended for lack of interest. While some Basque Americans avail themselves of the educational opportunities to learn about their heritage that were simply unavailable to previous generations, it is equally true that for the majority of young people their Basque ethnicity is a highly compartmentalized part of their overall persona. For most it is virtually impossible to lead a daily "Basque" existence, since in no community of the American West are Basques in a majority or even residentially concentrated. Nor, since the days of the tramp sheepmen, have Basques felt discrimination. Indeed, the opposite is true, since Basques now are generally highly regarded as hardworking and honest citizens. There is no identification, for example, of Basques with the Hispanic or Latino community by either the Basque Americans themselves or the wider society. In short, the Basque Americans simply lack the incentives for creating an ethnic solidarity as a defense against perceived prejudice that holds some other groups together. For Basque Americans ethnic pride far outweighs any sense of a collective siege mentality.

On August 27, 1989, twenty-five hundred Basque Americans and Basque politicians from Europe gathered on a hillside near Reno to dedicate the National Monument to the Basque Sheepherder. In doing so they commemorated the passing of an era; only time will tell if they were also celebrating the strength and vitality of Basque-American culture or signaling its demise.

See also: SPANIARDS

Bibliography

Bieter, P. (1957). "Reluctant Shepherds: The Basques in Idaho." *Idaho Yesterdays* 1(2):10–15.

Decroos, J. F. (1983). *The Long Journey: Social Integration and Ethnicity Maintenance Among Urban Basques in the San Francisco Bay Region*. Reno: Basque Studies Program, University of Nevada.

Douglass, W. A. (1980a). "Inventing an Ethnic Identity: The First Basque Festival." *Halcyon* 2:115–130.

Douglass, W. A. (1980b). "The Vanishing Basque Sheepherder." *The American West* 17(4):30–31, 59–61.

Douglass, W. A., and Bilbao, J. (1975). *Amerikanuak: Basques in the New World*. Reno: University of Nevada Press.

Echeverria, J. (1988). "California-Ko-Ostatuak: A History of California's Basque Hotels." Ph.D. diss., North Texas State University.

Gaiser, J. H. (1944). "The Basques of the Jordan Valley Area: A Study in Social Process and Social Change." Ph.D. diss., University of Southern California.

Lane, R. H. (1985). *Basque Sheepherders of the American West: A Photographic Documentary*, text by William A. Douglass. Reno: University of Nevada Press.

Laxalt, R. (1957). *Sweet Promised Land*. New York: Harper & Row.

Laxalt, R. (1989). *The Basque Hotel*. Reno: University of Nevada Press.

McCall, G. E. (1973). *Basque-Americans and a Sequential Theory of Migration and Adaptation*. San Francisco: R&E Research Associates.

Paris, B. (1979). *Beltran, Basque Sheepman of the American West*, as told to William A. Douglass. Reno: University of Nevada Press.

Urza, M. (1993). *The Deep Blue Memory*. Reno: University of Nevada Press.

WILLIAM A. DOUGLASS

BELARUSANS

The Republic of Belarus is a newly independent country located almost in the center of Europe. It is situated between Poland on the west and Russia on the east, between Ukraine on the south and the republics of Latvia and Lithuania to the north and northwest. Belarus was known prior to August 25, 1991, as the Byelorussian Soviet Socialist Republic and formed part of the former Soviet Union. The Byelorussian Soviet Socialist Republic was one of the founding members of the United Nations in 1945.

The population of Belarus is slightly more than ten million, of whom about 80 percent are Belarusans (also known as Belarusians, Bielarusians, Byelorussians, White Russians, and Whiteruthenians); the remaining 20 percent are Russians, Ukrainians, Poles, Jews, or others. More than two million Belarusans live in other parts of the former Soviet Union; about 500,000 Belarusans live in their ethnic territory in Poland (Bielastok region), and about 700,000 Belarusans reside elsewhere.

Minsk, the capital of Belarus, has a population of two million. Other major cities of Belarus are Brest, Gomel, Grodno, Mogilev, Polotsk, Vitebsk, and Slutsk. About 80 percent of Belarusans profess the Eastern Orthodox faith, and about 15 percent are Roman Catholics; the remainder are Old Believers, Protestants, Muslims, or Jews. Until the 1950s, Belarus was exclusively an agricultural country; flax, lumber, potatoes, and other agricultural commodities were the main items of export. Belarus is now an industrial nation with diversified industries. The major areas of specialization are electronics, chemicals, and machine-building.

Since 1986, Belarusan territory and the nation have been associated with the tragedy of Chernobyl, which is located only a few miles south of the country's border; about one-fifth of Belarusan agricultural lands were contaminated by radioactivity.

Belarusans belong to the family of Slavic nations, part of the eastern branch of this group, which also includes Ukrainians and Russians.

Historical Roots

Historical sources reveal three major Belarusan principalities on their ethnic territory during the ninth to eleventh centuries: Smolensk, on the Dnieper River; Polack-Vitebsk, on the Dvina and the Upper Neman rivers; and Turau-Pinsk, on the Pripyat River. During the thirteenth century Belarusan principalities formed the core of a newly emerging state, the Grand Duchy of Lithuania, with its capital in the city of Navahradak, now in west-central Belarus. Because Belarusan lands served as the birthplace of the Grand Duchy of Lithuania, it was natural that the Belarusan language became the official language of the grand duchy, and Belarusan culture flourished. The fourteenth and fifteenth centuries witnessed the territorial and political growth of the grand duchy, which became a hugh multinational state, with a multitude of diverse problems. Gradually this state came under the strong religious and cultural influence of Poland, reinforced by several treaties of political union. The upper social strata of the population became Roman Catholic, accepted some elements of Polish culture, and became distant from the broader masses of the population. This weakened the Grand Duchy of Lithuania socially, politically, and militarily. This internal destabilization presented an opportunity for a new state to the east, Muscovy (which later became known as Russia), to begin a westward expansion.

Gradually all Belarusan territory fell under the dominion of Muscovy/Russia during the seventeenth and eighteenth centuries. Russian policies toward Belarus were very precise: to Russify this land by all means necessary and make it part of Russia. Belarus was denied a specific national name and labeled by the czars as the Northwestern Territory of the Empire. The Belarusan language was outlawed, and all other signs of Belarusan separateness were suppressed. Belarusan newspapers, theater, and other cultural outlets were banned. Russia imported thousands of new administrators, teachers, and Orthodox priests. Schools, governmental administration, and the Orthodox religion became the most important tools of Russification. Economically, Belarus was also reduced to colonial status, with no significant capital investment. It was a region serving the central government in the provision of raw agricultural materials, wood products, and cheap labor.

The idea of Russification of Belarus as formulated by the czars remained vigorous through the decades of the Soviet regime.

Belarusan Survival

Although the Russian administration exerted enormous pressure to uproot any characteristics of Belarusan separateness, political, cultural, and ethnic awareness among Belarusans began to emerge toward the second half of the nineteenth century. An uprising in Belarus in 1863–1864, led by a national hero, Kaustus Kalinouski, and his publication of a newspaper in the Belarusan language, were the first signs of a national awakening. A revealing fact emerged after the 1897 Russian Census, in which about 5,880,000 persons were listed as Belarusans.

The beginning of the twenty century witnessed the formation of numerous Belarusan political parties and organizations, including the publication of the newspaper *Nasa Niva* (Vilna, 1906–1915), which played a particularly important role in national determination.

The Establishment of the Republic

The wave of national activities prior to World War I achieved their highest point at the All-Belarusan Congress in December 1917 in Minsk, and the consequent proclamation on March 25, 1918, of the Belarusan Democratic Rupublic. This new democratic state was short-lived, as Bolshevik forces overran it, but the idea of establishing a Belarusan state did not die. To assuage Belarusan national aspirations, the Bolsheviks proclaimed their own Belarusan state, the Byelorussian Soviet Socialist Republic, in the city of Smolensk on January 1, 1919.

Belarus Between the World Wars

According to the Treaty of Riga (1921), Belarusan territory was split among many nations. About two-thirds of Belarusan ethnic territory was occupied by a newly emerging state, the Soviet Union. Part of Belarus's territory was ceded to Poland, and small portions went to Lithuania and Latvia. The Russian Federation appropriated the

A Belarusan youth dance group performs at the 1976 Garden State Arts Center Festival in Edison, New Jersey. (Vitaut Kipel)

most eastern portion of Belarus, including the city of Smolensk.

Belarusan activities achieved considerable success in Poland and in the Soviet Union during the 1920s: Belarusan schools opened in significant numbers, the administration was in Belarusan, and daily Belurasan newspapers numbered in the hundreds. Unfortunately, the Belarusan national revival was crushed toward the end of the 1920s. Belarusan activities were restricted to Poland from 1925 to 1928 and totally suppressed after 1930. In Soviet Belarus, Belarusans suffered several waves of purges in 1930, 1933, and 1937. For a politically emergent nation, the years 1931–1941 were an enormous traumatic blow—by the outbreak of World War II, the Belarusan nation had lost all of its national cadres and leadership. Killing grounds discovered in Kuropaty, near Minsk, in 1988 are proof of a holocaust in Belarus prior to World War II.

World War II

World War II devastated Belarus. Approximately nine thousand villages and towns were wiped out, and more than two hundred cities were burned to the ground. The loss of population amounted to close to six million souls. It took Belarus several decades to heal the material loss resulting from the war; unfortunately, the demographic loss was never renewed.

The post–World War II decades in Soviet Belarus were characterized by almost unprecedented Russification and Sovietization. Belarusan schools were closed, programs Russified, and the Belarusan language pushed out of daily use. The goal of Soviet policies in Belarus was to produce a psychological loss of ethnic esteem among Belarusians, while elevating Russian ethnic identity. Such policies worked. Belarus is the most Russified country of the former Soviet republics.

New Beginning

A strong revival process began after 1985. Belarusan educational programs began to be introduced, and schools were Belarusianized. This revival contributed to the development of a political climate in which a democratic opposition was established in the parliament and political debates began. Finally, on August 25, 1991, the independence of the Republic of Belarus was declared.

Unfortunately, economic hardship continues to prevail in Belarus, and democracy is still developing, although the elections of 1994 proved that the country is trying to maintain a democratic form of government. Obviously many obstacles will face the development of a truly democratic state in Belarus, but the hope lies in the younger generation, more nationally conscious, educated, and technologically literate, with a clear determination that only through the creation of an independent national state can higher standards of living be achieved, human rights preserved, and the country become a member of world society.

Emigration and Resettlement

The main cause for emigration was the economic and political situation of Belarus as a colonial region of the Russian Empire. By the end of the nineteenth century, Belarusan territory became a major source of emigration from eastern Europe. The first emigrants from Belarus were Jews; in fact, those American Jews who called themselves "Litvaks" came from Belarusan territory. Belarusans emigrated first to Siberia (close to one million) and major industrial cities in Poland, Ukraine, and Russia. However, during the last decade of the nineteenth century, emigration en masse began from Belarus to the United States.

It is possible that the earliest Belarusan immigrants inhabited the colony of Virginia. Captain John Smith, who became the first governor of Virginia in 1608, had visited Belarus only five years earlier. He recalls the event in his book *True Travels*, first published in 1629. Thus it would not be surprising if Captain Smith brought Belarusans with him to Virginia.

During the eighteenth and nineteenth centuries, individual Belarusans immigrated to America and made significant contributions in many fields.

For example, Aleksander Curtius, originally from the Belarusan city of Polack, contributed to education in New York during the second half of the seventeenth century. Many Americans know that Thaddeus Kosciusko played an important role in the Battle of Saratoga and the fortification of West Point during the American Revolution, but few are aware of his biological roots in Belarus. Reverend Francishak Dzeruzynski, who was born in the town of Orsha and studied in Polack (both in northeastern Belarus), contributed to the nineteenth-century spread of Roman Catholic education in the United States. However, prior to the end of the nineteenth century only individual Belarusans immigrated to American shores.

Mass emigration from Belarus began during the last decade of the nineteenth century and reached its peak during the years 1910–1913. Slightly more than one million Belarusans arrived in America, but only about 600,000 to 650,000 settled permanently. The next significant wave of Belarusan immigrants arrived after World War II. From 1948 to the mid-1950s, about 50,000 to 75,000 Belarusans entered the United States.

Unfortunately for Belarusans, their ethnicity was not properly registered at their time of arrival. The majority were recorded as "Russians," having imperial passports and being of the Eastern Orthodox religion, or as Poles, if they were Roman Catholic. Thus, because of bureaucratic inertia, an entire group was mislabeled and misidentified. This situation lasted until 1980, when after a long struggle by Belarusan-American groups, the rubric "Belarusans" was introduced into census data.

Belarusan-American Life

The most visible and expressive form of Belarusan character is the national costume. Red, white, and black colors are predominant, with embroidery in distinctive symmetrical and geometrical patterns. The man's costume consists of linen trousers, an embroidered shirt, and a hand-woven belt. The woman's dress includes a white linen blouse, always ornamented with embroidery; an apron; a long pleated skirt; and a vest buttoned in the front, often with slits from the waist down. Examples of Belarusan national costume are preserved, and worn, in Belarusan-American communities on special occasions.

Belarusan surnames are rather difficult to differentiate among other Slavic names, but names such as Kalosha, Sienka, Savionak, Barsuk, and Burbiel are typical, as are names with geographical symbolism, such as Slutski, Minskii, and Homielski, all of which are widespread.

Predominant crafts include weaving, embroidery, rugs, table covers, and bedspreads. Of particular significance are towels, which are used on numerous occasions, such as for weddings, christenings, and to honor icons. Each Belarusan-American family has numerous towels and is proud of exhibiting them. Pottery, straw incrustations, and woodcarving also are old Belarusan crafts often found in the United States. Egg painting is a significant feature of Belarusan-America art during the Easter season. Belarusan painted eggs are ornamented with simple geometric designs and are decorated in red, white, and black.

Belarus is located in the forest, grain, and potato belt of eastern Europe, and Belarusan cookery reflects a wide variety of grains, a diversity of mushrooms, animal meats, and an abundance of fish and vegetables. There are many dishes that Belarusans have in common with their neighbors, such as *halubcy* (stuffed cabbage) and *kaubasa* (kielbasa). But the most famous food of Belarus is potatoes. There are close to one hundred dishes based on the potato, specific to various occasions. Belarusan Americans preserve their ethnic cuisine, especially during holidays.

Belarusan music is very old, its origins tracing back to pagan times. Belarusan communities usually have their own bands, and combine old and new music in their festivities. The most commonly used instruments are the violin, accordion, cymbals, pipe, and often tambourine. Belarusans sing on all occasions: birth and death, marriage and military service, work and leisure, in happiness and in grief. Thousands of songs reflect seasonal changes. The custom of singing is well preserved in the communities, and each has its

A Belarusan youth soccer team in New York in 1953. (Vitaut Kipel)

own choir. The lullaby also is very popular in Belarusan-American families; generations of children grew up with lyrics in Belarusan sung to them by their mothers and grandmothers. Belarusan folk dancing has a very long tradition and has been transplanted to America. Belarusan folk dancing is characterized by a diversity of compositions, simple movements, and a small number of rapid steps. Dances often are accompanied by songs. The most popular folk dance among Belarusan Americans is "Lavonicha," which usually commences all weddings and soirees. Belarusans have always cherished drama. From pre-Christian times, religious rites and ceremonies were dramatized. The Christian era provided new material for dramatization. Folk theater is for the most part associated with the activities of supplementary schools, and folk tales constitute a very rich reservoir for shows and plays.

Characteristic of Belarusan customs is the interweaving of natural, pagan, and Christian elements. For the most part, customs are associated with religious seasons. Christmas is one of the most celebrated. It begins with a *kuccia*, a very solemn and elaborate supper on Christmas Eve; caroling accompanies the entire Christmas period, which lasts for more than two weeks. Easter season also is an occasion for many customs. Other religious-pagan customs include the celebration of Kupalle (end of spring, beginning of summer); Dziady, the feast commemorating the departed, which is celebrated four times a year; and the custom of honoring army recruits, usually done in the parish hall, where traditional draftee songs are sung. Celebrated in the fall is Dazhynki, the harvest feast, which is a joyous event marked by a community dinner. Family traditions surrounding births, marriages, and christenings also are observed.

The most frequently observed saint days are those of St. Euphrosynia of Polack (May 23) and St. Cyril of Turau (April 28). The Mother of Zyrovicy is the patron of many Belarusan churches; her day is marked on May 20. Other religious observances are held to commemorate the Smalensk Adyhitria (August 10) and the Feast of All Saints of Belarus (the third Sunday after Pentecost). Roman Catholic Belarusians observe the day of Our Lady of Vostraja Brama in Vilna (November 16) and St. Mary of Budslau (July 2).

Language Preservation

The community makes an effort to teach the Belarusan language to Belarusan Americans through a variety of programs: Sunday schools, plays, customs, and musical activities. Youngsters who passed through these programs understand the language without difficulty and have a command of conversational Belarusan.

Generational differences are obvious; the first generation understands and speaks Belarusan better than the second and third generations. However, what improves linguistic skills tremendously are visits of American-born youths to the country of their grandparents. Contact with people there force young Americans to speak Belarusan, which helps them to master the language. In recent times this is happening far more often than in the years under the Soviets.

Belarusan Organizations

Very simple criteria controlled the distribution of Belarusan immigrants: the availability of non-skilled jobs, proximity to their landsmen, and the decision of the agent where to direct the immigrant. Thus Belarusans settled all over the country, although the majority settled in the states between New York and Illinois, with concentrations in industrial cities and mining towns. The largest Belarusan groups live in Illinois, Ohio, Pennsylvania, New York, New Jersey, and California. A very distinctive trait of Belarusan pioneers was that they did not stay on their first jobs too long — they quickly learned the basic skill of upward mobility. About 75 percent of the children of these first immigrants received technical schooling or a college education.

Belarusan-American organizations began to be established during the 1920s. The first organization, the White Ruthenian Committee, was formed in New York City in 1921. Then followed Belarusan organizations in Illinois, Indiana, and New Jersey. The first Belarusan newspaper in the United States was published in Chicago in 1926. The post–World War II period witnessed the formation of numerous new organizations, which during the 1950s assembled under the umbrella of two major groups: the Belarusan American Association and the Belarusan American Congress Committee. The activities carried out by these two organizations are very diversified but primarily involve cultural projects, political representation, and the expression of the political views of Belarusan Americans. The major goal of these two groups is to help restore the modern democratic independent Belarusan state (i.e., the Belarusan Democratic Republic) that was originally proclaimed on March 25, 1918.

The Belarusan Institute of Arts and Sciences, established in 1951, is the major Belarusan intellectual organization and publishes most Belarusan books in the United States. *Belarus* is a monthly Belarusan-language newspaper, and the *Belarusan Review* is an English-language quarterly.

In addition to these major organizations, Belarusan Americans have smaller groups with varied objectives: choirs, dance groups, theatrical ensembles, youth hiking groups and other sports clubs.

Religious Structures

The majority of Belarusans in the United States are of the Eastern Orthodox faith. They have numerous parishes within two jurisdictions: the Belarusan Autocephalous Orthodox Church, and the Belarusan Parishes Council, within the jurisdiction of the Ecumenical Patriarchate. Belarusan Orthodox parishes exist in New York City (Brooklyn and Queens), New Jersey (South River, Highland Park, Dorothy), Detroit, Chicago, and Cleveland. Belarusans of the Catholic faith have one parish (Uniate, a mix of Roman Catholic and Eastern Orthodoxy instituted in Belarus in 1596) in Chicago. The majority of Belarusan Christians in the United States use Belarusan in their religious services.

Conclusion

Contacts with the home country were almost nonexistent when Belarus was Soviet-dominated. However, after Belarus proclaimed independence in 1991, contacts expanded quickly. All generations of Belarusan Americans have reestablished either familial or organizational relationships with Belarus. The new state has been very receptive to this initiative, organizing a world convention of Belarusans in 1993, attended by a sizable contingent from the United States. Without doubt, contacts will continue in the future with increased intensity, if Belarus will remain within the democratic family of nations. There are signs that this will be the case.

See also: JEWS, SOVIET; POLES; RUSSIAN OLD BELIEVERS; RUSSIANS; UKRAINIANS

Bibliography

Carter, M., and Christensen, M. (1993). *Children of Chernobyl*. Minneapolis: Augsburg.

Kasiak, I. (1989). *Byelorussia: Historical Outline*. London: Byelorussian Central Council.

Kipel, V. (1977). "Byelorussians in New Jersey." In *The New Jersey Ethnic Experience*, edited by B. Cunningham. Union City, NJ: William H. Wise.

Kipel, V. (1982). *Byelorussian Americans and Their Communities of Cleveland*. Cleveland: Cleveland State University.

Kipel, V. (1985). "Byelorussia Under Russian Occupation: Past, Present, Future." In *Russian Empire: Some Aspects of Tsarist and Soviet Colonial Practices*, edited by M. Pap. Cleveland: Institute for Soviet and East European Studies, John Carroll University.

Kipel, V. (1989). "Byelorussians in the United States." *Ethnic Forum* 9(1–2):75–90.

Kipel, V., and Kipel, Z. (1983). "Byelorussian-American Theatre." In *Ethnic Theatre in the United States*, edited by M. S. Seller. Westport, CT: Greenwood Press.

Kipel, V., and Kipel, Z. (1988). *Byelorussian Statehood*. New York: Belarusan Institute of Arts and Sciences.

Kipel, Z. (1978). "Captain John Smith in Byelorussia." *Zapisy* 16:119–128.

Kipel, Z. (1992). "Byelorussian Art Literature Collections." *Art Libraries Journal* 17(2):16.

Kipel, Z., trans. (1988). *The Byelorussian Tristan*. New York: Garland.

Lubachka, I. (1972). *Belorussia Under Stalin Rule: 1917–1957*. Lexington: University Press of Kentucky.

Rodgers, M., Streissguth, T., and Sexton, C., eds. (1993). *Belarus: Then and Now*. Minneapolis: Lerner.

Unbegaun, B. (1972). *Russian Surnames*. Oxford, Eng.: Clarendon Press.

Zaprudnik, J. (1993). *Belarus at a Crossroads in History*. Boulder, CO: Westview Press.

VITAUT KIPEL

BELGIANS

Since 1830, perhaps only 250,000 Belgians have immigrated to the United States. The Belgians include two ethnic groups: the Flemish, Dutch-speakers from the northern Provinces bordering on the North Sea and the Netherlands; and the Walloons, from the southern provinces, who speak the French patois of Walloon. Flemish immigrants before 1900 tended to be drawn to the East Coast and to be absorbed into the industrial-urban centers. Walloons, with more rural traditions, were pulled to growing midwestern states around the upper Great Lakes and Iowa.

A well-established and distinctive ethnic island of Walloon-speaking Belgians is found in northeastern Wisconsin's Door Peninsula, which is composed of Door, northwestern Kewaunee, and northeastern Brown counties. The Belgian immigrants were attracted to this area between 1853 and 1857 from their homes in the south-central provinces of Brabant, Hanaut, and Namur. Crop failures, the decline of local industries, and population growth encouraged people to emigrate. Wisconsin, achieving statehood in 1848, was an attractive destination, with land selling at $1.25 an acre. The immigration was encouraged by aggressive Antwerp shipowners and agents who advocated Wisconsin as an attractive place to settle. However, the mass immigration was sharply curtailed in 1857 by the Belgian government because of sharply falling land values and rapidly increasing labor costs. In addition, letters from previous emigrants were discouraging, with details of hardships suffered on the passage and the difficulties faced in their new homeland. By a combination of water and overland travel the Belgian pioneers initially settled near the city of Sheboygan, fifty miles north of Milwaukee. This area became increasingly unattractive to the Walloon-speakers because of the predominance of Dutch and German spoken by the locals. Through a chance encounter with a Walloon-speaking Belgian priest, the band of Belgians moved to the vicinity of his parish on the Door Peninsula a few miles northeast of the city of Green Bay. At the village of Champion, the Belgians first acquired land.

By 1860, there were 3,812 foreign-born Belgians in the three-county area. Within this area 80 percent of the farmland was owned by Belgians, or approximately 150 square miles, with a population estimated at 10,000 to 15,000 persons.

Cultural Elements

A variety of nonmaterial and material cultural elements are employed to define the Belgian community. Distinctive elements are surnames, place names, language, diet, and various celebrations, especially the Kermiss. Material cultural distinctiveness can be seen in house types and ancillary buildings.

Place names include the villages of Brussels, Thiry Daems, Namur, and Duvall. The Belgian influences can be seen in other names as well:

Vaness Road, Depeau Road, Dhuey Hill, Renard Creek, and St. Hubert's Cemetery.

Belgian English has some distinctive grammatical features that have made their way from Walloon into English. The most common is "ain'so" (pronounced enso), which is probably from *n'est-ce pas.* Other common language elements that reflect the French patois of Walloon are the use of a plural, hairs for hair. and the troublesome "th" sound, thousands comes out "tousands" and three is pronounced "tree."

A diet that has a high proportion of pork is a distinctive element, along with jutt (cabbage simmered with pork and potatoes), tripp (a sausage made with pork and cabbage), booyah (a chicken stew with vegetables), and Belgian pie (a one-crust pie with either prune, raisin, rice, apple, or cherry filling and covered with white cheese). All of these foods would be available at the Kermiss, a harvest and thanksgiving festival that takes place on nine consecutive weekends from late August through late October. Originally a religious celebration, it is now held in the local tavern, usually adjacent to the Roman Catholic church, and in homes.

Distinctive Belgian Structures

The earliest structures constructed by the Belgians were destroyed, with very few exceptions, by a wildfire that swept the area in October 1871. More than two hundred lives were lost, along with innumerable farm animals, crops, and buildings. The exceptions are houses that were constructed in the late 1860s from locally quarried dolomite. These houses are modest in scale, with appropriate proportions, and generally without windows on the gable ends. The early settlers expected to follow their European traditions and employ connecting masonry architecture, with a series of barns and sheds attached linearly, but connecting architecture never assumed its European popularity. Wood was available in quantities unknown in Europe, and connecting architecture with wood buildings presented a dangerous fire hazard. Connecting architecture conserved space, which was

A typical Belgian farmhouse of brick over log with a bull's-eye window and decorative use of contrasting brick. (William G. Laatsch)

not an issue in the New World. However, a few of the buff-colored irregular stone houses did survive the fire.

Common, and providing an unmistakable index to the Belgian cultural island, are the structures built in the decade after the fire. The winter of 1871–1872 was one of timber harvest. Many of the trees, though stripped of their foliage and badly charred, were left standing. Harvested and trimmed before the wood could rot or become infested, the salvaged logs were used for building. The resulting vernacular houses date from the late 1870s to the early 1880s. These modest-size houses, their dimensions relative to the size logs from which they were constructed, are similar in form, material, scale, and detail. Much of the

logwork is rough, especially when compared to that of Finns, Scandinavians, and other northern Europeans. After the laying up of the logs, most of the houses were eventually covered with a red brick veneer or with clapboards. Residents explain that the veneer made the structures more weather-resistant and that the brick was a fire retardant. Of broader and more subtle importance may have been the desire of the Belgians to adopt the building material common to their homeland, where brick and stone structures prevailed.

These simple utilitarian structures do have some decorative elements. A "bull's-eye" window just under the gable facing the road is a common builder's trademark. Contrasting white or cream-colored brick is used to highlight windows, doors, and house corners. Some structures have more elaborate decoration, employing a Flemish bond rather than a monotonous course of stretchers.

Barns have tended to reflect economic necessity rather than ethnic tradition. However, while brick barns, sheds, smokehouses, pigsties—and even brick privies—do exist, they cannot be said to characterize the region.

Two structures, in addition to the house, that can be used as an index to the Belgian cultural region are the outdoor bake oven and the roadside chapel. The bake oven is distinctive because of its attachment to the rear of the relic summer kitchen rather than being incorporated into the interior of the house or kitchen. In the past the oven was used year-round with greater use during holidays, especially Kermiss, and harvest time, when additional workers would be present on the farm. The Wisconsin oven clearly had its origins in Belgium. However, in Belgium the oven was communal and, as such, was freestanding and located under a roof that covered the oven and work area as well.

The votive chapel also has its roots in Belgium. These structures are small, accommodating only one or two individuals, and are equipped with a simple kneeler facing a two- or three-tier altar. The altar is often filled with religious artifacts and the walls adorned with appropriate art and certificates of baptism, first communion, marriage, and death. Those certificates from before 1920 are usually in French.

These are votive chapels built by devout Catholics and dedicated to, and in honor of, a saint or the Blessed Virgin, in gratitude for favors sought or received through prayer. They may be used now for general purposes, such as family devotion, or as sites where people gather on special occasions to recite the rosary. Their primary function is as a place of prayer for those who seek relief from types of distress similar to those that caused the chapels to be built initially.

Cultural Persistence

The persistence of the Belgian cultural island is remarkable. In the 1880s, as families grew, the

farm could not support the additional population. Fortunately, the industries of the nearby cities of Green Bay, Sturgeon Bay, Algoma, and Kewaunee were expanding and able to absorb the excess regional population. Thus, young people could easily maintain their ties to the home, parish, and community, even if they moved to one of these cities, which are only ten to twenty miles distant. By the 1960s, change was obvious. Churches, cheese factories, general stores, and mills closed in the hamlets in favor of more centralized functions in larger villages and cities. In addition, rural nonfarm residences have become common in the area and tend to dilute the character of the ethnic landscape. These dwellings emerge from three distinct groups. Scattered widely in the area are the new ranch-style homes of locals who have retired

A characteristic Belgian roadside chapel. (William G. Laatsch)

from the farm or younger couples who live on a corner of the family farm and are employed elsewhere. The new construction on the southern margins of the region house individuals who work in Green Bay and commute to their jobs from the pastoral countryside. The third type of rural non-farm residence is encroaching from the north. As land values increase in northern Door County's "vacation land," individuals are seeking the southern portion of the peninsula to build their vacation or retirement homes.

Finally, marriage patterns are changing. In the 1950s and 1960s, it was unusual for individuals to marry outside the Belgian community. By the 1990s, the pattern had changed, with the records of one church revealing that three-quarters of the Belgian women were marrying non-Belgian men.

The continuance and preservation of the culture is the goal of the Peninsula Belgian-American Club, which sponsors and participates in ethnic events, exchanges visits with friends and relatives abroad, supports scholarships, promotes research and genealogical investigation, and acquires valuable archival material. Much of the archival material is deposited in the Area Research Center, University of Wisconsin at Green Bay, which houses an important research collection documenting the Belgian community. A major annual event is Belgian Days, held in Brussels each July. This celebration of Belgian culture attracts thousands and is often attended by the Belgian ambassador to the United States as well as by many European Belgians. Green Bay's Heritage Hill State Park continues to develop a Belgian farmstead, circa 1890. The ensemble includes a log-brick house, a number of barns, a summer kitchen with attached oven, and a chapel, all accurately restored and interpreted. The farmstead is enthusiastically supported by the devoted Belgian community and has appeal to Belgians and non-Belgians alike.

Bibliography

Ellis, W. S. (1969). "Wisconsin's Door Peninsula: A Kingdom So Delicious." *National Geoqraphic Magazine* 135:347–371.

Holand, H. (1933). *Wisconsin's Belgian Community.* Sturgeon Bay, WI: Door County Historical Society.

Holmes, F. L. (1948). *Old World Wisconsin: Around Europe in the Badger State.* Eau Claire, WI: E. M. Hale.

Laatsch, W. G., and Calkins, C. (1992). "Belgians in Wisconsin." In *To Build in a New Land: Ethnic Landscapes in North America*, edited by A. G. Noble. Baltimore, MD: Johns Hopkins University Press.

Larmouth, D. W. (1990). "Belgian English in Wisconsin's Door Peninsula." *Kansas Quarterly* 22:135–141.

WILLIAM G. LAATSCH

BENGALIS

Bengalis are from South Asia and share a common language and history. Bangla is the language spoken by the peoples of Bangladesh and in the Indian states of Bengal and parts of Assam. The commonly used Anglicized name for the language and people is Bengali. Two hundred million people speak Bengali, making it one of the most widely spoken languages in the world. One must examine the history of Bengal to understand Bengali immigration and community formation in the United States.

History

Bengal is a region that has been divided many times by conquerors and internal politics. The first partition came when British viceroy George Curzon divided Bengal in 1905 into East and West Bengal. Unified Bengal was seen as a threat. An independence movement was brewing against British rule in India, and Bengal was a center of resistance. Bengali students staged protests, but unfortunately this partition had only set the stage for further division. In 1947, the British were forced to withdraw from the region, and West and East Bengal became part of the newly created nation states of India and Pakistan, respectively.

Local politicians negotiated the partition based on religion. India was to be predominantly Hindu; Pakistan was to be predominantly Muslim. Bloodshed accompanied separation, particularly in Bengal. As Muslims from West Bengal fled into East Bengal and Hindus from East Bengal fled into West Bengal, communalists from each side murdered thousands of migrants. This event left a permanent mark in the collective memories of both sides.

There was to be one further critical development in the history of East Bengal: It became East Pakistan for twenty-four years. While Pakistan had been a nation built on religious commonality, it was separated geographically and culturally. East and West Pakistan were 1,125 miles apart and did not share a common language or history. East Pakistan sought independence from economic, political, and linguistic domination by West Pakistan. Thousands of East Pakistanis fled to the Indian state of Bengal to escape the subsequent civil war. The Indian government gave critical military and civil aid to the independence movement, renewing ties between the two nations. In 1971, after the bloody civil war, East Pakistan became Bangladesh.

The common language shared across national borders and family ties created overlaps in culture and affiliation between Bangladesh and Bengal. Bengalis share a rich literary tradition that goes back to the tenth century. Two famous Bengali writers are Rabindranath Tagore and Kazi Nazrul Islam. Both were authors of plays, songs, and poems that tried to draw on the commonalities between Hindu and Muslim Bengalis. Tagore received the Nobel Prize for Literature in 1913.

Early Immigration

Bengali immigration to the United States and community formation are closely tied to changes in Bengal. Bengali immigrants between 1887 and 1925 were male, dissident students. Bengali students in San Francisco, Oregon, and Washington State were involved in the movement for independence from Britain. Taraknath Das was a Bengali student at the University of Washington. He helped publish the *Free Hindustan* newspaper from 1908 to 1910. Das joined hands with Punjabi activist Har Dayal and formed the Gadar (Mutiny) Party. Bengali students organized, published newspapers, and tried to build alliances with other anticolonial movements. They contacted the *Gaelic American* to ally themselves with the Irish community. They sent copies of the paper to students in Calcutta to inform them about the common struggles for independence. Another activist, Kumar Goshal, represented a different faction of this immigrant group. Goshal was a journalist, actor, and director. He formed alliances with leftist and black groups in the United States and worked with such notable black leaders as Paul Robeson and W. E. B. Du Bois. Due to this rise in activism the British government persuaded the U.S. State Department to curtail Indian immigration.

Another group to immigrate between 1887 and 1925 were merchant marines working on British ships. They arrived in San Francisco, Los Angeles, or New York ports and stayed ashore. These men immigrated to escape poverty, but they could not own land and had restricted access to jobs in the United States. Most men in California worked in agriculture, hotels, restaurants, or as extras in Hollywood films. Those who went to New York worked in hotels, restaurants, and construction. A few created alternative employment in Los Angeles. For example, one man sold makeup to black women, one taught and performed Indian dance in Hollywood, and yet another became a teacher of Eastern mysticism in a black community. Bengalis married black, Mexican, or mixed-race women; antimiscegenation laws barred them from marrying white women. These Bengalis formed communities with blacks, Mexican Americans, and other ethnic Indians.

Battle Over Citizenship

Bengali immigration was a trickle between 1887 and 1965. Bengalis and other Indians had to fight for citizenship and rights during this period. They share a common history of discrimination with other Asians. In 1790, the U.S. Congress had decided that only whites could be naturalized citizens of the United States. This racial clause was used to deny naturalization to those Asians who were already in the United States. In 1906, the U.S. attorney general specifically ordered exclusion of Japanese immigrants from gaining citizenship. In 1917, immigration laws were modified to deny further entry of Asian immigrants. A "barred zone," including India, was created. During this period the courts and states were not always uniform in their decisions about immigration and naturalization laws. From 1860 to 1925, there is evidence of random approval and denial of citizenship to Asians. Asian Indians posed a special problem within this scenario. Indians had been categorized as Caucasians by anthropological literature. Therefore they fought for citizenship based on their Caucasian race. There was a great deal of confusion and contestation among the federal government, the states, the courts, and the clerks who handled initial applications about who was white/Caucasian. The landmark cases of *In Re Akhay Kumar Mazumdar* and *United States v. Bhagat Singh Thind* document the struggle of Indians for citizenship.

In 1913, Mazumdar, a Bengali, was granted citizenship in Washington State. The Bengali student activist Taraknath Das was initially denied his application because the clerk was unclear about his racial classification. A court in Seattle gave Das his citizenship in 1914. Between 1908 and 1922, sixty-nine Indians were granted citizenship. In 1923, the U.S. Supreme Court decided that Indians may be Caucasian but they were not white. Therefore they were not eligible for citizenship based on race. The exclusionary Immigration Act of 1924 further restricted citizenship and rights of "non-white" immigrants. After the exclusion act, immigration from India was almost stagnant. But the

A Bengali family gathers together for a birthday celebration. (Mukul Roy)

court battles continued, and Congress passed a bill in 1946 granting naturalization to Indians. A quota was set for one hundred immigrants per year. In 1965, a revised immigration law allowed Indians and Pakistanis status equal to that of other nationalities.

Post-1965 Immigration

After 1965, a large group of students and professionals from India and Pakistan immigrated to the United States. Since 1980, there has been an increase in immigration from all socioeconomic backgrounds. There are no accurate statistics available about the number of Bengali immigrants to the United States due to the complicated formations of this group. The U.S. Immigration and Naturalization Service (INS) documents immigration based on nationality, and Bengalis have been part of different nations.

There have been INS records of immigration from Bangladesh since 1971. More than 26,000 Bangladeshis have been granted immigration to the United States. Between 1988 and 1993, a total of 6,000 Bangladeshis won the OP-1 lottery for immigrant visas. There is also a large number of undocumented immigrants within the community. According to New York– and Los Angeles–based community estimates, more than 55,000 Bangladeshis live in New York and 10,000 Bangladeshis live in California.

Since 1985, Bengali immigrants have been concentrated in New York, California, and Texas. Bengalis in New York live primarily in Astoria and Flushing. Areas in and around downtown Los Angeles have Bangladeshi enclaves. In Los Angeles there are numerous store and restaurant signs in Bengali. Bengalis are becoming a visible community in the United States. The New York State Department of Education has created a bilingual program for Bengalis. In 1994, David Letterman's *Late Show* made salespersons Shirajul Islam and Mujibur Rahman the most famous Bangladeshis in the media. Bengalis have their own newspaper and radio shows. *Thikana* and *Banga Barta* are Bangladeshi newspapers published from New York

and Los Angeles, respectively. *Probashi* is an Indian Bengali newspaper from New York. Los Angeles also has a weekly radio program called *Voice of Bangladesh*.

The growth in the Bengali community has been accompanied by diversity. Bengalis do not always immigrate from India or Bangladesh. There are many Bengalis who were working in the Middle East, Africa, England, or Australia before immigrating to the United States. They bring different histories, experiences, and cultural backgrounds. Bangladeshis from Chittagong, Sylhet, Shondip, and other regions have local organizations in New York. These immigrants from northern and southern Bangladesh speak their own dialect and form subgroups within the larger Bengali community. The Hill Peoples of Chittagong are also distinct in their culture, religion, and language. They are escaping political repression in Bangladesh and form alliances with Southeast Asian Buddhist communities in the United States.

The contours of the Bengali community in the United States have changed with the shifts in national boundaries. Between 1900 and 1947, Bengali Hindus and Muslims formed a common community. They were a small group and saw undivided India as their extended community. The fabric of Bengali immigrant life was first torn in 1947 when immigrants were forced to confront the division of India. Bloody battles between Hindus and Muslims in India marred the communities in the United States. They formed new alliances based on these divisions. The Pakistani civil war in 1971 once again rearranged these alliances. There are individual relationships between Hindus and Muslims, Bangladeshis and Indian Bengalis. But there also has been a slow move toward separate communities based on religion and the new national boundaries. This separation was solidified with the increase in the number of immigrants from each region and religion.

There are ogranizations and conventions that provide a forum for the diverse Bengali communities to come together. The Federation of Bangladesh Associations in North America (FOBANA) was formed in 1986 to bring together Bangladeshi

A Bengali dancer performs a folk dance in Chicago. (Mukul Roy)

centration of Bengali and Indian immigrants. There are some business owners in Los Angeles and New York. A few Bengalis have also achieved prominent positions in academic and cultural areas. Architect Fazlur R. Khan designed the Sears Tower and the John Hancock Building in Chicago. Gayatri Chakravarti Spivak is a Bengali professor at Columbia University. She teaches cultural studies and is renowned for her theoretical contributions in her field. Muhammad Yunus is another prominent Bengali. He is an example of a small but significant return migration of Bengalis. He received his doctorate in economics from Vanderbilt University, lived and taught in the United States for seven years, and then returned to Bangladesh. He has revolutionized the concept of banking. His model is being replicated in Malaysia, Malawi, Africa, South America, and North America. Among other notable Bengalis, classical musician Ali Akbar Khan and Kathak dancer Chitresh Das live in California. Khan and Das have schools of music and dance in San Rafael and San Francisco, respectively.

Not all Bengalis are in such prominent positions in the United States. There is a growing class division within the Bengali community. Most Bengalis work in the service industry as cabdrivers, gas station attendants, convenience store clerks, and parking attendants. Many street vendors in New York City are Bengalis. This part of the community is growing rapidly and shaping community life. These immigrants are between ages twenty-one and thirty-five, mostly male, and single. Bengali businesses such as restaurants, travel agencies, and grocery stores have sprung up to meet their needs. Large cultural programs are also organized to provide entertainment for the community. Popular singers and dancers from India and Bangladesh are invited to perform, forming a concert circuit of American cities. Bengali Buddhists, Christians, Hindus, and Muslims celebrate their own religious festivals, such as Buddha Purnima, Christmas, Puja, and Id, respectively. Buddha Purima is the celebration of the birth of Buddha. Puja means "to worship"; Durga Puja, a tribute to the goddess Durga, is the biggest such celebration. There are

organizations around the nation. FOBANA holds an annual convention known as the Bangladesh Shommelan. In 1994, this organization split into two factions carrying the same name and have been holding separate conferences. The North American Bengali Convention, also known as Banga Shommelan, is held every year. Indian Bengalis are the majority and control the umbrella organization. Organizations such as the Bangladesh American Friendship Society try to link their community with the mainstream American society.

The common perception of Bengalis is that they are professionals. South Asians in general are known to be concentrated in engineering, computer science, medicine, and university teaching positions. Professionals usually immigrate with their immediate family. Silicon Valley has a con-

two Id celebrations; one celebrates the end of Ramadan (the month of fasting), and the other celebrates Abraham's sacrifice of his son. These religious and cultural practices are integral parts of immigrant life. Immigrants also send remittances back to families in Bangladesh and India, affecting national economies and politics.

Bengalis are a linguistic group whose history in the United States can be traced to the early 1900s. They are a diverse group of people with a complex history. Multiple national identities and religious differences differentiate them as a common language ties them together. In the United States, those differences and commonalities give shape to the formation of the immigrant community.

See also: BANGLADESHIS

Bibliography

Chandras, K. V. (1977) *Arab, Armenian, Syrian, Lebanese, East Indian, Pakistani, and Bangladeshi Americans: A Study and Guide Source Book.* San Francisco: R & E Research Associates.

Clarke, C.; Peach, C.; and Vertovec, S. (1990). *South Asians Overseas: Migration and Ethnicity.* Cambridge, Eng.: Cambridge University Press.

Fisher, M. (1980) *The Indians of New York City: A Study of Indians from New York.* Columbia, MO: South Asia Books.

Gagai, L. A. (1972). *The East Indians and the Pakistanis in America.* Minneapolis: Lerner.

Gordon, L. A. (1989). "Bridging India and America: The Art and Politics of Kumar Goshal." *Amerasia* 15(2):68–88.

Jensen, J. M. (1988). *Passages from India: Asian Indian Immigrants in North America.* New Haven, CT: Yale University Press.

Melendy, H. B. (1977). *Asians in America: Filipinos, Koreans, and East Indians.* New York: Twayne.

Spector, R. (1980). "The Vermont Education of Taraknath Das: An Episode in British-American Indian Relations." *Vermont History* 48(Spring): 89–95.

Tinker, H. (1977). *The Banyan Tree: Overseas Emigration from India, Pakistan, and Bangladesh.* New York: Oxford University Press.

NAHEED ISLAM

BIHARIS

The term "Bihari" (literally, the resident of Bihar) refers to a regional cultural group of the Indo-Gangetic plains of the Republic of India comprised of divergent castes and communities, predominantly Hindu, Muslim, and tribal. To know the Bihari immigrants better, it is essential to know about their geographic, historical, and cultural background. Known in India since the early Vedic period (1500 B.C.E.), several kingdoms existed in the Bihar plains, including the Magadha Empire (475 B.C.E.), with its ancient capital Pataliputra (modern Patna), under the reign of Emperor Ashoka (c. 272–232 B.C.E.) and the Guptas (c. 319–510 C.E.) until the late fifth century. The region became a fertile meeting ground for the Aryan and local autochthonous (indigenous) cultures, shaping the early Indian civilization. The region was given the new name Bihar at the end of the twelfth century by Turkish Muslim conquerors who mistook the numerous distinctive Buddhist monasteries (*viharas*) for forts.

The British administrative reorganization of 1911, however, produced the modern state of Bihar, with Nepal to its north, and the Indian states of West Bengal to the east, Orissa to the south, and Uttar Pradesh and Madhya Pradesh to the west. About 67,134 square miles in area, Bihar has a population of more than sixty million and is divided by the Ganges River into northern and southern (populous) regions. About 87 percent of the population live in villages, and 75 percent depend on agriculture. Bihar is about 83 percent Hindu (and Sikh) and 14 percent Muslim, the rest are Christians and tribals confined largely to the Chota Nagpur region.

Most Biharis speak Indo-European languages (Hindi, Urdu, and the dialects Bhojpuri, Maithili and Magahi), while the tribes have Austro-Asiatic (Mundari, Santhali, and Ho) and Dravidian (Oraon) languages. Bihar's cultural and linguistic profiles closely overlap. Maithili, for instance, which has a distinct script and a literary history, is found in the Mithila region, where the orthodox upper-caste ways of life dominate. Bhojpuri and Magahi, found in the Bihar plains, on the other hand, have considerable folk and oral traditions of their own, while tribal religions dominate the Chota Nagpur region.

The economy is based on agriculture, mining, and industry, showing significant gains in mining and manufacturing, but not without the mounting pressure of large population, divisive politics, and poverty. Though rice is Bihar's dominant crop, corn, wheat, barley, gram, oilseeds, and legumes are also raised. The Chota Nagpur plateau is rich in mineral resources, and the industrial plants at Ranchi, Bokaro, and Jamshedpur (India's largest) showcase the region's industrial progress. But still this large state, electorally crucial, remains one of the poorest in the Indian Union. It is prone to draughts, famines, and festering social conflicts that caste divisions, feudal politics, and glaring economic inequalities create.

The Bihari diaspora, still unstudied, generally follows the preceding economic, religious, and linguistic profile. The British colonial period, for example, saw Biharis immigrating to such parts of the world as Southeast Asia, Eastern Africa, Fiji, and the Caribbean islands, including Trinidad and (British) Guyana. During the partition of India in 1947, a large number of Bihari Muslims immigrated to Pakistan.

Immigration and Demographics

America received Biharis from both India and Pakistan, mostly during the 1960s and 1970s, when the United States relaxed its immigration laws and allowed the immigrants to bring in their relatives. These immigrants, not unlike most other Asian Indians of the period, often identify themselves by their local and regional cultural loyalties on the one hand and by their advanced modern education and successful professional careers on the other. The majority of the early immigrants entered the United States either as students or as professionals qualified to occupy positions in science, medicine, engineering, and university-level instruction. But the subsequent arrivals had fewer professional qualifications, thus diluting the group's occupational profile.

Biharis in America cleave to their regional and Asian Indian cultural heritage. They are proud of the central role Bihar has played from ancient times in the formation of the major religions in India, such as Hinduism, Buddhism, and Jainism, and in shaping the social organization, polity, and fine arts of India. In modern times, the Biharis recall Mahatma Gandhi's peasant reform movement in the state, alongside other national leaders such as Dr. Rajendra Prasad (the first president of the Indian Republic, 1950–1962), and Jaya Prakash Narayan (freedom fighter and influential socialist leader). To preserve and pass on such cultural heritage, Biharis in the United States formed the Bihar Association of North America (BANA) in September 1975. BANA aims to provide "a common forum to the people of Bihar" by organizing social and cultural activities, community entertainment programs, and receptions for dignitaries and by assisting those needing medical and educational help. The younger generation is encouraged to learn the culture of Bihar and India.

Though no systematic survey is available, Biharis are known to be numerically fewer (and less organized) than, for example, Gujaratis and Punjabis in the United States. Biharis tend to cluster around major cities in New York, New Jersey, Illinois, Texas, and California. There is also a large concentration of Biharis in Washington, D.C. Because of the lack of statistical data on the Bihari community, the following sketch of the social issues that recurrently engage the community was obtained from interviews conducted with Bihari families settled between New York and Virginia and with Ranvir Sinha of BANA.

Family Dynamics

The Bihari family in America most often measures its success by education, professional advancement, annual income, home ownership, and such possessions as a healthy bank balance, new cars, electronic gadgets, gold ornaments, and household goods. Yet all is considered hollow if there is no happy family life. A Bihari family rests on a marriage that is status appropriate, culturally compatible, and personally satisfying. Such a family is believed to raise bright and obedient sons and daughters. Admiring social notices from one's relatives and local community members complete the first generation Bihari's "American Dream." Not unlike other Indian Americans, Biharis closely track personal achievements and those of their children. Periodic nostalgic visits to India are made for the sake of remaining in touch with their rich cultural heritage.

Biharis (male and female, old and young), know well that higher education is their best bet for social progress in America. Children's schooling is therefore of paramount concern, though not without a subtle but clear traditional social bias for sons over daughters. Biharis are extremely watchful of their daughters as they grow and form friendships, particularly when they approach the dating age. In response, Bihari youths, increasingly born and raised in America, selectively accept or reject such parental controls as they grow through schools and colleges and often force their parents to recognize the reality of American social forces. When the children satisfy their ambitious parents with excellent grades, they often insist on enjoying the school life, just as their American peers do. They slowly cultivate self-centered American individualism in place of that self-sacrificing, duty-bound family behavior of Asian Indians.

But the parents do not give up easily. While committing themselves to paying for their children's education at prestigious schools and colleges, they often insist on their right to "supervise" their sons and daughters until they "settle down" (i.e., have a job and marry). The parents begin to discipline their young children early against undesirable social company, language, and behavior, and college students are closely watched for mediocrity and for wrong steps taken in life. Hairstyle, clothing, disobedience, cursing, dating, and sex become the most closely watched issues for providing flags of warning. Heated arguments occur when adolescents bring home the American cul-

ture of their peers, questioning and rebelling against their parents' authority and control. Each side complains that the other side does not understand. Marriage invariably becomes the crux of the matter. Most America-resident Asian Indian parents, though mentally "enlightened" against the vices of the caste system, still strongly wish that their children marry a Bihari or an Asian Indian of similar caste, someone who shares the same social ways, religion, and language.

Today, Bihari youths, normally living either with the parents or under parental supervision, face a range of choices for a suitable spouse. It could be either a person of shared caste, region, and religion from India (the option most preferred by parents); an America-resident Asian Indian who is educationally and socially compatible; an American-born Asian Indian of the same religion; or a compatible American who is not of Asian Indian origin (the last option). Some individuals believe that many Asian Indians in America are already too liberal with regard to their children's marriages.

As with other Asian Indian immigrants, Biharis still raise their daughters more strictly than their sons. The daughters who receive formal education are still closely supervised by their mothers and have at least some domestic training, including social and religious observances. Though American-born girls increasingly rebel against such social restrictions, most parents still insist on their daughters marrying grooms with Asian Indian origin and background. Only after many heated family discussions, when they are totally helpless, will parents possibly give a daughter their grudging consent to marry her own choice. In fact, such marriages are no longer unknown in the Bihari community. Among twenty families studied, for example, three reported that their son or daughter, after prolonged family arguments, had married an American who was not of Asian Indian origin. The parents in such cases saw both advantages and disadvantages. On the positive side, they thought that the traditional caste, dowry, and religious and cultural prejudices declined and hard work, punctuality, and efficiency increased in such couples. However, they also feared marital instability and a quick loss of the Asian Indian and Bihari culture. After one such marriage, the bride's mother felt "a sense of great personal failure, emptiness, and loss." She felt that she had failed in the most cherished moral duty of an Indian parent. An Orthodox Hindu mother, in another case, refused to accommodate an American bride. The groom's father, on the other hand, took a "distinctly liberal view" and Americanized his food habits (except eating beef), leisure activities, and personal hobbies. The bride reciprocated by participating in major family festivals and rituals. The family expected the mother to come around because she had grudgingly recognized love marriages in the past while still in India. In spite of his support, the father worried that such marriages are unstable; they rest on personal independence and selfishness, the children receive lower priority, and there is also the potential for religious and racial discord.

The highly educated first generation Bihari immigrants thus spend their lives centered on family matters, with much devotion given to their children's education, career, and married life. They organize their social life around the immigrant Asian Indians who share (or are nearer to) their language, regional culture, foodways, and religious beliefs and practices. Local Asian Indian community organizations often reflect such clusters based on regional cultural sharing, with Biharis congregating with other Biharis and individuals from northern India. In community activities, Asian Indian movies, dance, drama, and music play a distinct role. They provide entertainment and bring to the immigrant the popular Asian Indian cultural ethos and aesthetics, thereby socializing the younger generation in Asian Indian cultural ways.

Cultural Persistence

The young Biharis, particularly teenagers, sometimes confront their parents with their betwixt-and-between cultural life, forcing them to address many unresolved moral and social conflicts. The unquestioned Indian parental status and authority are often challenged, as are many family customs involving age, gender, caste, and religion. Still, not unlike most other Asian Indian Americans, the immigrant Bihari world—and its worldview—firmly remains grounded in the Asian Indian ways, where religion, caste, and regionalism coexist with ambition for advanced education and a successful personal career and marriage.

First-generation Bihari immigrants argue that such goals demand hard work, self-discipline, and a stable family life from the second generation; a young couple has to learn to sacrifice their personal comfort and convenience as they become parents and raise their children, and this responsibility ends only when their children successfully settle in life. To shoulder such a responsibility, in one couple's words, "We both had to sacrifice, by turn, our early career goals. But we raised our children well prepared to compete and succeed in today's America.... This society has little to offer to the incompetent and the misfit. There are no relatives here to shelter or support the unsuccessful. It is not India. Our [American-born] children should also realize that without a happy family life, American society is extremely lonely. Any amount of [psychological or psychiatric] counselling is no substitute." The same couple thought that the Indian family, based on the parent-arranged marriage, survived the stress of modern life much better "because most couples are customarily inclined to adjust and compromise rather than opt for separation, bitter child custody disputes, and financially ruinous divorce." In another Bihari couple's view, however, the traditional marriages faced increasing difficulties in America and were fast declining with the younger generation, along with much of the Asian Indian family's ethos and culture.

The first-generation Bihari immigrants in America, though successful in their chosen professions or businesses, often are ambivalent toward the changes that they themselves and their children face within today's America. Finding America to be distinctly conservative and less hospitable to a small immigrant group, they find that they have to be honest with themselves and their children. If they know from their experience that America is a land of opportunities, then they also know that they face "glass ceilings," social marginalization, and racial discrimination in life. Many mid-career professionals face either sudden retrenchment or a "disappearing level field" (reappearing discrimination) and declining job satisfaction.

The greying first-generation immigrant, simultaneously, faces increasing social loneliness and isolation. As with other such Americans, they are worried about their retirement and health-care problems. With their children Americanized, one Bihari couple openly worried about their life in old age. "There is little left of the emotional closeness so characteristic of the Indian family," they remarked, particularly since their children were "increasingly selfish, disrespectful, and self-absorbed." Other immigrants, however, blame themselves for making their problems worse. They find their social isolation to be the main culprit. Once it decreases, a more positive view of social life will reinforce itself.

In practice, Biharis convince their children that the American society rewards the meritorious, offers new opportunities, and allows one to pursue one's own dream. Most Biharis live a comfortable and rewarding life in America, contributing to both the cultures and countries they love—America and India.

Bibliography

Agehananda Bharati, S. (1972). *The Asians in East Africa: Jayhind and Uhuru.* Chicago: Nelson-Hall.

Das, A. (1992). *The Republic of Bihar.* New York: Penguin.

Klass, M. (1961). *East Indians in Trinidad.* New York: Columbia University Press.

Sewak, R. (1985). *History of Bihar Between the Two World Wars, 1919–1939.* New Delhi: Inter-India Publications.

Whitaker, B.; Guest, I.; and Ennais, D. (1982). *The Biharis in Bangladesh.* London: Minority Rights Group.

R. S. KHARE

BOSNIAN MUSLIMS

Bosnian Muslims represent one of the South Slavic peoples who comprised 44 percent of the population of Bosnia-Herzegovina, 9 percent of Serbia, and 4 percent of Montenegro before the 1992 war. They speak the same South Slavic language as is spoken in Croatia and Serbia but with the addition of vocabulary of Turkish origin. Prior to their 1971 recognition as a separate national group, Bosnian Muslims increasingly saw themselves as a distinct people because of their religion, referring to themselves as Muslims even if they were not practicing. During the more than four hundred years of Ottoman rule, the people in Bosnia were simply Bosnians; but in the nineteenth century, Serbs and Croats began to employ so-called ethnic labels. Even after the 1992 war, there are people from all the ethnic groups, especially those living in urban areas, who prefer to be called *Bosanci* or *Bosnjaci* (Bosnians).

The earliest Bosnian Muslim immigrants were a few hundred Herzegovinians who settled in large urban areas in the Midwest at the beginning of the twentieth century. They were followed in 1908—when Austria-Hungary annexed Bosnia—by several thousand who probably emigrated illegally, since the provincial records in Sarajevo reveal that only a few hundred emigrated from 1905 to 1914. Another group emigrated after the 1919 land reform, when the kingdom of the Serbs, Croats, and Slovenes expropriated land from Muslim landowners.

Several thousand Muslims from urban and rural areas of Bosnia immigrated after World War II; they represented the entire spectrum of Bosnian society. When these new immigrants arrived in Chicago, most of the earlier immigrants had died or their descendants had moved West, particularly to the Los Angeles area. The World War II refugees, because of their education, had little in common with the early settlers, and there was little compatibility. The new refugees flooded the old neighborhoods and were much more active, resulting in the old pioneers taking a subordinate place. The World War II immigrants began moving out to the northern suburbs of Chicago by the mid-1950s.

A third group, largely uneducated, emigrated mainly from the Bosnian countryside after Josip Broz Tito allowed a large number of Yugoslavs to immigrate to the West in 1965. Quite a few originated from the western Bosnian town of Gracanica and the Montenegrin town of Bar, on the Adriatic coast.

The number of Bosnian Muslim refugees who have arrived in the United States since the beginning of the 1992 war is about forty thousand, a figure that will increase. Chicago has received the largest percentage of any city in the United States, followed by Detroit.

History

Slavic and Celtic tribes migrated into Bosnia in the late sixth and early seventh centuries. In the second quarter of the seventh century, the Croats took over northwestern Bosnia, while the Serbs conquered the southern and eastern portions. Both Croats and Serbs were probably Iranians who were assimilated into the large Celtic and Slavic populations they ruled; all of them eventually became simply Bosnians. For most of the early Middle Ages Bosnia was under various foreign rulers, but it maintained a distinct culture and society.

During the fourteenth century, the Bosnian state coalesced into an important power in the Balkans under King Stjepan Kotromanic (1318–1353) and King Tvrtko Kotromanic (1353–1391) and comprised parts of contemporary Croatia and Serbia. The Ottoman Turks conquered the kingdom of Bosnia in 1463 and the duchy of Herzegovina in 1482. They held Bosnia for more than four hundred years, and great number of Bosnians adopted Sunni Islam—not in mass conversions, as is generally believed, but over a long period of time. The borders of the ancient kingdom were preserved, and there was a land-based hereditary nobility that made Bosnia a legitimate entity among all the Ottoman provinces. Austria-Hungary administered Bosnia beginning in 1878 until annexing it in 1908. After World War I it became part of Serbia in the creation of the kingdom of the Serbs, Croats, and Slovenes. Between the world wars, nationalistic Serbs and Croats laid claim to the Muslims as members of their respective groups; the majority of Muslims, however, refused to associate with either. Bosnia-Herzegovina became one of the six republics of Yugoslavia in 1946, and in the 1971 census President Tito recognized Bosnian Muslims as a nationality due to their culture and religion.

In a 1992 referendum, Bosnia declared its independence from Yugoslavia. At the start of the war in April 1992, 750,000 Bosnian Muslims had been killed or forced from their homes. It is only with the Dayton Peace Accords of 1995 that the conflict in Bosnia ceased, but with the country ethnically divided.

Settlement

Most of the early Bosnian Muslim immigrants to the United States settled in Chicago's near North Side around 1900 after the political protests against Austrian rule in 1899. The majority—primarily from the towns of Gacko and Trebinje—were peasants from Herzegovina, the poorest and most barren area of Bosnia. They were mostly young bachelors who planned to return to Bosnia after amassing an amount of money. They established a number of cafes that evolved into social centers for men from their respective towns. These cafes originated from the Karaethane in Mostar, Herzegovina, which was known as the Muslim Reading and Benevolent Society and was a coffeehouse where men could read newspapers, attend lectures, and help students and artisans financially.

Another large influx of Bosnians arrived in America after World War II. They were political refugees who had to flee Yugoslavia because of their voluntary or forced involvement with the fascist Croation Ustasha regime or the monarchist Serbian Chetniks. They were a diverse and educated group who emigrated with their families from towns and rural areas throughout Bosnia and represented the entire spectrum of Muslim society, including rich landowners whose property had been seized by the Communist government in the 1950s.

A third group immigrated to the United States to improve its economic future when Yugoslavia, because of pressing unemployment, allowed its citizens to emigrate in 1965. In the late 1960s and early 1970s, a large number of less educated single men and families emigrated from the countryside.

A fourth wave of immigration occurred after the 1992 war began in Bosnia. These refugees formed part of the two million who were forced to flee during the war. An estimated fifty to fifty-two thousand Bosnian Muslims now reside in the United States. Seventy-five percent of all Bosnian-Muslims in the United States live in Chicago (the largest population), Milwaukee, and Gary, Indiana. In Detroit, Bosnian Muslims have found asylum in the Polish neighborhood of Hamtramck, or in Dearborn or Madison Heights. Cleveland, New York, San Francisco, and Los Angeles have opened their doors as well. The San Francisco Bay Area has one of the ten largest Bosnian refugee settlements in the United States. The cities of San Francisco, San Jose, and Santa Clara have accepted a large number of Bosnian refugees, most of them Muslims. In the Los Angeles area there is a sizable Muslim refugee community from the Bihac, Banja Luka, Sarajevo, and Mostar regions.

Economy

In Chicago, many of the Bosnian Muslims who immigrated around 1900 worked on the constuction of the subway system and other building projects. Chain migration took a number to large industrial cities such as Gary, Indiana, where they got jobs in the steel mills. Others from Chicago moved to Butte, Montana, worked in the copper mines, and then returned to Chicago. Fewer than one hundred ever worked in Butte at one time, but it was not a town of permanent employment for them. They laid no roots there, and the Bosnian Muslim community has completely disappeared.

The World War II Bosnian immigrants were professionals and well educated. They obtained white-collar jobs and have done quite well for themselves. The refugees who arrived in the late 1960s and 1970s, although less educated than the World War II immigrants, have been employed in semiskilled and skilled trades because of the good training they received in Yugoslavia. They have become janitors, apartment building managers (some later buying apartment buildings themselves in working-class areas), metalworkers, machinists, or carpenters. A small number, especially those from rural areas, have gone into businesses of their own and done very well. The refugees from the 1992 war have found it difficult to find jobs equal to what they had in the former Yugoslavia because of their lack of English, thus forcing them into low-paying, entry-level jobs.

Organizations and Politics

The Bosnian Muslims from Herzegovina who settled in Chicago during the early 1900s first began to meet in cafes in the near North Side: Those from Gacko met in their own cafes, and the men from Trebinje had their cafes to go to. These became their social centers where they exchanged news and handled business. They did not have enough members to build a mosque, so they gathered at each other's homes for Friday night prayers.

In 1906, the first Dzemijetul Hajrije (Benevolent Society) lodge was established in Chicago. It was a mutual-aid association, but its main purpose was to offer medical insurance to its members. They also founded two Muslin cemeteries, one for married couples and the other for the many bachelors.

The Bosnian immigrants in Gary became members of the Chicago lodge, but branches of the Benevolent Society spread to other cities. The lodge in Detroit was still going strong in 1939 at a cafe on East Fort Street, where it served the thirty Bosnian Muslim men who congregated there before World War II.

After World War II, the Bosnian Muslim communities in Chicago, Milwaukee, Cleveland, Detroit, and New York were reinvigorated by the settlement of the dynamic and educated refugees from the internecine fighting caused by the war in Bosnia. Most of the earlier immigrants had died or their descendants had moved West, causing the Dzemijetul Hajrije to lose members. The post–World War II émigrés in Chicago revitalized the community so that they were able to open the Moslem Religious and Cultural Home. In 1955, this organization became the Bosnian American Cultural Association. With members in other midwestern cities, it is now the most important Bosnian Muslim organization in the United States. The same year they opened a mosque, cultural center, and school in Chicago's near North Side, the same neighborhood where the first group of Bosnian Muslims settled in 1900. A few years later they launched the *Glasnik Muslimana* (Muslim Herald), which lasted until the early 1960s. In 1976, after selling the property they owned in Chicago, the Bosnian Muslim community built an impressive Islamic center and school in the Chicago suburb of Northbrook, with sizable donations from Saudi Arabia and Kuwait. Muslims from other communities share the facility, controlling 40 percent.

The Bosnian Muslims who arrived in the early 1900s had experienced the nationalist stirrings that had spread among the Serbs and Croats in Bosnia in the nineteenth century, but it was not strong. It was only after the bloodshed of World War II that most of the Bosnian Muslims who immigrated to the United States designated themselves as Muslim Croats, and only a minority labeled themselves Bosnian Serbs.

The 1992 war has seen the creation of more organizations, such as the Bosnian-Herzegovinian Society of Northern California, whose three hundred members accept Bosnian Muslims, Croats, and Serbs. Bosnian Muslims have relations with other groups of South Slavs, depending on what level of education they have in common. The most important factor to consider, however, is how strongly the Bosnian Muslim immigrant or refugee clings to the interethnic rivalries that existed in Bosnia-Herzegovina. Individual Bosnian Muslims may accept Serbs or Croats and reject the ethnic intolerance that has swept Bosnia since the outbreak of the 1992 war. Interethnic tolerance in the areas of settlement in the United States depends on the kind of socialization that the immigrant received within the communities of the former Yugoslavia. Refugees from rural villages tend to internalize nationalist rhetoric, whereas those from the larger cities accept the tolerant pluralism that was encouraged by the Yugoslav regime. This attitude has been aided by the urban rates of intermarriage, which were 30 to 40 percent in large cities such as Sarajevo.

Family and Religion

The early Bosnian Muslim immigrants to the United States were on the whole young bachelors who brought more secular and cosmopolitan attitudes with them when they arrived in the early 1900s. They maintained adherence to their cultural roots by observing all or some Muslim customs, such as the Ramadan *bajram*, a three-day celebration marking the end of the month-long fast where people visit and congratulate each other and proffer gifts of sweets or delicacies to relatives and close friends. This gave them a certain cultural identity and distinguished them from Serbs and Croats. The Bosnian Muslims were a supportive and tightly-knit community, even when they later married Turks or other Muslims. A form of fictive kinship among Bosnian Muslims exists in which the godparents sponsor the cutting of the dried umbilical cord five to seven days after the child's birth and the first cutting of the male child's hair; these acts foster relations with Serbs and Croats as well as strengthen bonds among Muslim kin. The bonds of religion were weakened, however, when they married Christian Croats or people from other Slavic groups.

After Bosnian Muslims gradually converted to Islam following the Ottoman conquest of 1463, they evolved a more lax attitude toward their religion, since they were so far from the centers of Islam and Istanbul. In the twentieth century, Bosnian Muslims have become more secular as the country has modernized. Polygamy was always rare, and religious belief has been a matter of personal choice and symbolism rather than adherence to dogma. Fifty years of communism further weakened the already thin strands of belief as government repression eroded mosque attendance and traditional Islamic beliefs. Bosnian Muslims in the United States, however, especially those who fled the 1992 war, have experienced a strengthening of ties with Muslims from throughout the world as they worship together.

Culture

Among the older generation, and even the youth since the 1992 war, traditional music has been the main link to Bosnian traditions and culture. Bosnian Muslim secular music revolves around the romantic ballad called *sevdalinka* (from the Turkish word *sevdah*, "passion"), which is sung to the accompaniment of accordions, violin, and bass guitar. It fosters intimacy and reflection and is a Bosnian's connection not only with his or her homeland but with Turkish culture as well. Turkish melodic modes influenced both religious chant and the sevdalinka. For the Bosnian Muslim immigrant this music also symbolizes his or her cultural identity, which is Islamic.

See also: CROATIANS; SERBS; SLOVENES

Bibliography

Andric, I. (1977). *The Bridge on the Drina*. Chicago: University of Chicago Press.

Balic, S. (1970). "Cultural Achievements of Bosnian and Hercegovinian Muslims." In *Croatia: Land, People, Culture*, Vol. 2, edited by F. H. Eterovich and C. Spalatin. Toronto: University of Toronto Press.

Bringa, T. (1995). *Being Muslim in the Bosnian Way: Identity and Community in a Central Bosnian Village*. Princeton, NJ: Princeton University Press.

Cohen, R. (1995). "A War in the Family." *The New York Times Magazine*, August 6, pp. 32–39, 44–45, 60.

Friedman, F. (1996). *The Bosnian Muslims: Denial of a Nation*. Boulder, CO: Westview Press.

"Ibrahim Alickovic: Prisoner in Bosnia, Poet in the City." (1997). *The San Francisco Examiner and Chronicle*, February 9, pp. W8, W27.

Lockwood, W. (1975). *European Muslims: Economy and Ethnicity in Western Bosnia*. New York: Academic Press.

Malcolm, N. (1994). *Bosnia: A Short History*. New York: New York University Press.

Olszewski, L. (1995). "The Newest Refugees." *The San Francisco Examiner and Chronicle*, October 1, pp. 1, 6.

Weekes, R., ed. (1984). *Muslim People: A World Ethnographic Survey*, 2nd edition. Westport, CT: Greenwood Press.

DANIEL CETINICH

BRAZILIANS

Brazilians in the United States are sometimes called Brazucas, a colloquial term in Portuguese meaning "Brazilian immigrants in the United States." The term is used both in Brazil and in Brazilian immigrant communities in North America.

Many Brazilians in the United State have the unusual and, for them, uncomfortable status of being a minority within a minority. They are in this odd situation because they are often classified as "Hispanics." But "Hispanic" refers to Spanish-speakers or those of Spanish-speaking descent and, because Brazilians speak Portuguese, this term is a misnomer when applied to them. The murky ethnicity of Brazilians in the United States results from the fact that most Americans simply do not realize that Brazil is distinct linguistically and culturally from the rest of Latin America. Even many educated Americans think that Spanish is the language of Brazil and that Portuguese is spoken only in Portugal.

Brazilian immigrants are also confused with Hispanics because they often live in parts of New York, Miami, and other American cities where Spanish is commonly spoken. Brazilians sometimes express frustration and occasional anger about the ambiguity surrounding their ethnic identity in the United States. Some make a point of telling Americans that they do *not* speak Spanish.

The effort of Brazilians to distinguish themselves linguistically from other Latin American groups in the United States is rooted not only in their sense of cultural pride, the distinctiveness of their "race," as they call it, but also in considerations of ethnic discrimination. Brazilians sometimes claim that they encounter discrimination because Americans *think* they are Hispanics, making them victims of negative Hispanic stereotypes. Brazilians maintain they receive better treatment when they make it clear that they are *not* Hispanic.

Despite the growing numbers of Brazilians, their confused ethnicity has made them invisible as a distinct immigrant group in some American cities. In New York, for example, few New Yorkers seem to know that there are Brazilians in their midst, and Brazilians are not mentioned in the media or in popular or academic works dealing with the city's diverse ethnic mélange. Similarly, the only journalistic reference to San Francisco's Brazilian community was during the 1994 World Cup finals, when local Brazilians noisily celebrated their nation's triumph in city streets. In Boston, on the other hand, Brazilians have more visibility because they are grouped with the city's sizable Portuguese-speaking community from Cape Verde, the Azores, and Portugal rather then with the resident Hispanic population. Similarly, large numbers of Brazilians make their distinctive presence felt in such small Massachusetts communities as Sommerville, Framingham, and Marlboro, where they account for 10 to 20 percent of the local population.

History and Numbers

Brazilian immigration to the United States is relatively recent. Although there have long been scattered pockets of Brazilians, evidence suggests that the number of Brazilians in the United States has risen dramatically since the mid-1980s. The rate of immigration increased slowly but steadily through the 1970s and early 1980s and then took off between 1984 and 1987. The 1980 U.S. Census counted only some forty-four thousand Brazilian Americans who were born in Brazil, more than 60

percent of whom lived in New York, New Jersey, Connecticut, Massachusetts, Florida, and California. These states remain the primary areas of Brazilian residence and are home to perhaps two-thirds of the Brazilians living in the United States. Smaller Brazilian enclaves can be found in Chicago; Philadelphia; Washington, D.C.; Roanoke, Virginia; and Austin and Houston, Texas.

The New York metropolitan area may have the largest concentration of Brazilians in the United States. New York City itself has no distinct Brazilian residential neighborhood, although most Brazilians live in Queens, particularly in Astoria and adjacent Long Island City. There is one commercial street in the heart of Manhattan (West 46th Street, between Fifth Avenue and Sixth Avenue), known as "Little Brazil," that has restaurants, stores, and services that cater to Brazilians. Brazilian nuclei also dot the New York suburbs, with Brazilian enclaves on Long Island and in Westchester County. Newark and several small cities in New Jersey also have sizable Brazilian communities.

New England is another region of major Brazilian settlement. Danbury, Waterbury, and Bridgeport, Connecticut, all have their share of brazucas. But probably nowhere in the United States outside of New York is there as large a concentration of Brazilians as in Boston, its suburbs, and communities south and west of the city.

Central and southern Florida, especially Palm Beach, Broward, and Dade counties, are also nuclei of Brazilian settlement, and some call the small community of Pompano Beach the "Brazilian immigrant capital of South Florida." Finally, California is home to untold numbers of Brazilian immigrants, with significant populations in San Francisco, Los Angeles, and San Diego.

It is uncertain where Brazil's pioneer immigrants to the United States first settled, but as far back as the mid- and late 1960s there were small enclaves of Brazilians in New York City, the Catskill Mountains region of New York State, Newark, and Boston. Some of the first Brazilian immigrants to arrive in the United States came from Governador Valadares, a city of some 230,000 in the

Brazilian state of Minas Gerais. Even today, Val-adarenses — as natives of the city are known — constitute a major segment of the Brazilian population in Greater Boston, Newark, Danbury, and in some towns in South Florida. In fact, immigrants from various parts of Minas Gerais are well represented in Brazilian communities throughout the United States. A significant number of Brazilians living in the United States also come from Rio de Janeiro, São Paulo, and other cities in south-central and southern Brazil.

As with many other immigrants to the United States, the majority of Brazilians initially viewed their stay as temporary, and perhaps most still do. From their perspective, immigration was not to make a new life in the United States but to make a new life in Brazil. Indeed, a significant but unknown percentage of Brazilians have returned home. Others have adopted a pattern of "yo-yo immigration," in which they return to Brazil "for good," only to find that they cannot adjust to their homeland and reimmigrate to the United States. Nevertheless, the ideology of return continues to exert a powerful pull on many Brazilian immigrants despite their increasingly lengthy stays in the United States, and many say they will eventually retire in Brazil.

There are no dependable data on the actual size of Brazilian immigration to the United States. The figures on legal immigration are modest. Between 1966 and 1994, only about seventy thousand Brazilians immigrated legally to the United States, a very small number considering the size of the Brazilian population (about 160 million in 1996) as well as the magnitude of total legal immigration to the United States during the period. Still, legal emigration from Brazil is only part of the picture, and a small part at that. Most Brazilian immigrants arrive in the United States as tourists, overstay their visas, and thus become undocumented. Although some later become legalized, it is impossible to determine the size of the total Brazilian population in the United States because so many Brazilians remain undocumented.

The 1990 U.S. Census counted 94,023 foreign-born Brazilians living in the United States. Without doubt this figure is far too low, the only question being the magnitude of the undercount. Although estimates of Brazilians in the United States have ranged up to 600,000 the Brazilian newsweekly *Veja* puts the number at a far more modest 330,000. If population estimates from the regions of greatest Brazilian concentration in the United States are added up, the total may well reach 350,000 to 400,000.

Why Immigrate to the United States?

A central question concerns what draws Brazilians to the United States. Until very recently Brazil was a nation lacking any history or tradition of immigration. There are several related reasons for this growing flight. Brazilians in the United States often describe themselves as "economic refugees" or "economic prospectors" — immigrants fleeing Brazil's endemic economic problems of low wages, underemployment, a high cost of living, and general economic uncertainty. Moreover, Brazilians are very precise about what attracted them to the United States: Jobs in the United States, in contrast to those in Brazil, pay high enough wages to allow immigrants to save a considerable sum of money. Brazilian immigrants say that even after working twenty years in Brazil, buying a house is still out of reach for most people. But in the United States the wages saved from only one or two years' labor can translate into a down payment on a house or an apartment or a nest egg to begin a small business in Brazil.

What sorts of jobs do Brazilian immigrants have in the United States? In New York, Newark, Boston, South Florida, and undoubtedly other cities with large Brazilian enclaves, most Brazilian immigrants hold low-wage, service sector positions. In New York City, Brazilians are employed as maids, nannies, baby-sitters, dishwashers, busboys, and street vendors. They drive radio cabs and limousines and work as parking lot attendants. Shining shoes (for men) and go-go dancing (for women) are two specialized Brazilian job niches. In New York's suburbs, Brazilian immigrants are gardeners and have unskilled renovation and construction jobs. Jobs in construction and demolition are also major sources of employment for Brazilians in Newark.

As in New York, restaurants in Boston seem to be the largest employers of Brazilian men; for women, it is domestic service. Boston's brazucas also clean offices for janitorial companies, bag groceries in supermarkets, work in beauty salons, deliver pizzas, and have jobs as chambermaids in the region's hotels and motels. Not surprisingly, restaurants and hotels are also major employers of Brazilian immigrants in South Florida.

Then, too, virtually all towns and cities in the United States with significant concentrations of Brazilians have small businesses—usually owned by Brazilians—that cater to their compatriots. These include travel and remittance agencies, restaurants, food stores, and shops selling imported goods from Brazil, including magazines, newspapers, tapes, compact discs, and videos. These businesses also employ immigrants.

A Profile of Brazilian Immigrants

In three important respects—social class, race, and education—Brazilian immigrants in the United States do not mirror the Brazilian population of South America. In Brazil the working class and the poor account for about 60 percent of the population, but in the United States no more than 10 percent of the immigrant population comes from these bottom social strata. Brazilians in the United States are overwhelmingly middle and lower-middle class and generally are better educated than their compatriots in Brazil.

The racial makeup of Brazilian immigrant communities is also skewed toward the lighter end of the color spectrum. In New York City, for example, more than 80 percent of Brazilians are white. Thus blacks and other "people of color," to use the Brazilian term, account for less than one-fifth of New York's Brazilian community, a fraction of the 45 percent reported in the 1990 Brazilian Census.

Brazilian Americans participate in a Brazilian street parade in New York City. (Maxine L. Margolis and J. T. Milanich)

The social class and educational level of Brazilian immigrants varies by place of residence in the United States and place or origin in Brazil. Immigrants in New York City and parts of Boston are mostly middle and lower-middle class, and many have some university education. The majority of immigrants in these two cities come from large Brazilian cities, primarily Belo Horizonte, Rio de Janeiro, and São Paulo. However, in Framingham, other enclaves in Massachusetts, Danbury, and Newark, there are pockets of poorer, lower-middle, or even working-class Brazilians who generally have not been educated beyond high school. They, in turn, tend to come disproportionately from Governador Valadares and nearby towns in the state of Minas Gerais. At the other end of the social spectrum are members of the Brazilian elite who live in New York, Boston, Los Angeles, and especially Miami where, in recent years, many wealthy Brazilians have invested in homes and businesses.

Other than race and class, how might the Brazilian immigrant population in the United States be characterized? Research in New York City and Boston suggests that Brazilians are about evenly divided in terms of gender, although there is evidence that during the first years of Brazilian immigration it was predominantly male. This is also a rather young population; the majority of brazucas are in their twenties and thirties, and not many are over fifty. During the first years of immigration there were few children in this population because many immigrants were single when they arrived in the United States. As this immigration stream aged and more immigrants married (typically with other Brazilians), the number of children increased. In addition, whereas in the past some immigrants who had children left them behind with relatives in Brazil, more Brazilians are now immigrating to the United States with their families as a unit.

These immigration patterns, however, seem to vary according to chosen place of residence in the United States, in addition to time period. In New York City the vast majority of married Brazilians emigrated from Brazil together, but in some smaller Brazilian communities in Massachusetts, the typical Brazilian immigrant is still a young unmarried male, or, if married, one whose family has stayed behind in Brazil.

The religious affiliations of Brazilian immigrants are similar to those of their fellow citizens back in Brazil. In New York City, about three-quarters of the Brazilian immigrants are Catholic and about equal numbers of the remainder are Protestant, espouse other beliefs (including Spiritism), or are unaffiliated. Attendance at evangelical Protestant churches has skyrocketed in Brazilian communities in New York, Boston, and southern Florida, just as it has in Brazil.

Community Institutions

The majority of Brazilian immigrants immigrate to the United States to work and, at least initially, to earn as much money as quickly as possible for the return to Brazil. As such, many immigrants hold two or even three jobs and have little time or inclination to spend in social clubs or other community-based organizations. The paucity of community structures among Brazilians is also linked to their common expressions of impermanence. Most Brazilians deny their immigrant status; they say they are mere sojourners in the United States. Their intention of being "here today and gone tomorrow" and their ongoing ties to the homeland make many Brazilian immigrants reluctant to invest in community-building. As a result, one notable characteristic of the Brazilian immigrant communities in Boston and New York is the paucity of community institutions. The lone exception are the ethnic churches around which members coalesce for both religious and social activities.

Brazilian immigrants themselves complain of the lack of community ethos, and many say that their compatriots in the United States behave badly toward one another. They claim that once in the United States Brazilians "change," they become interested only in making money and "don't help each other out." Contradicting this stream of complaints is the reality that Brazilians could hardly survive the immigrant experience without one another. When they first arrive in the United States, Brazilian immigrants get help from Brazilian friends and relatives in finding a place to live and a job. In fact, in many Brazilian immigrant communities, earlier arrivals provide funds to help siblings, parents, other relatives, and friends move to the United States. What little leisure time Brazilian immigrants have is spent with their own countrymen and countrywomen. Informal gatherings, parties, nights out at a restaurant or club, and sports events are usually all-Brazilian affairs.

Most Brazilian immigrants lack proficiency in English, especially when they first arrive in the United States, and this contributes to feelings of isolation from American society and increases their dependence on other Brazilians. Although many Brazilians take classes in English after they arrive in the United States, Portuguese remains the language of choice within the community. Consequently, as the number of Brazilian immigrants with children increases, demand grows for bilingual instruction, particularly in cities such as Boston that already have sizable Portuguese-speaking populations.

The Future

Transnationalism is central to the lives of Brazilians in the United States. It is a process through which international immigrants maintain ties to the home country—despite its geographical distance—while living in the country of settlement. Brazilians, like other transmigrants, preserve familial, economic, and cultural ties across international borders. They read Brazilian magazines and newspapers, keep up-to-date with Brazil's famed *telenovelas* (television soap operas) via imported videotapes, and know the latest exchange rate between Brazilian and U.S. currencies. Moreover, because of frequent contact with friends and relatives in Brazil, many Brazilian immigrants say that their "head is in two worlds." Some immigrants return to Brazil for visits with family and friends, or they maintain close contact with them through frequent (and costly) telephone calls. Transna-

tional links are also maintained by Brazilian immigrants who send money to relatives in Brazil.

Transnational elements in the lives of Brazilians in the United States are particularly marked because the majority of immigrants see themselves as sojourners in the United States, not as permanent residents. "The Brazilian is not an immigrant," they often say. Still, if the economic forces that originally propelled Brazilians to immigrate to the United States continue, further delaying the return home, it is likely that "Brazilian American" will become a common term in the ethnic lexicon.

See also: PORTUGUESE

Bibliography

Barrow, A. (1988). "Generations of Persistence: Kinship Amidst Urban Poverty in São Paulo and New York." *Urban Anthropology* 17:193–228.

"Brazil and the United States, Stay Away." (1994) *The Economist*, October 29, pp. 48–50.

Goza, F. (1994). "Brazilian Immigration to North America." *International Migration Review* 28:136–152.

Margolis, M. L. (1989). "A New Ingredient in the 'Melting Pot': Brazilians in New York City." *City & Society* 3:179–187.

Margolis, M. L. (1990). "From Mistress to Servant: Downward Mobility Among Brazilian Immigrants in New York City." *Urban Anthropology* 19:1–17.

Margolis, M. L. (1994). *Little Brazil: An Ethnography of Brazilian Immigrants in New York City.* Princeton, NJ: Princeton University Press.

Margolis, M. L. (1995a). "Brazilians and the 1990 United States Census: Immigrants, Ethnicity, and the Undercount." *Human Organization* 54:52–59.

Margolis, M. L. (1995b). "Transnationalism and Popular Culture: The Case of Brazilian Immigrants in the United States." *Journal of Popular Culture* 29:29–41.

MAXINE L. MARGOLIS

BUDDHISTS

Religion has shaped immigrant cultures in the United States, as many of the newly arrived have turned to religious beliefs and practices to make sense of their new lives in their adopted land. Those beliefs and practices have been as varied as the immigrants themselves. Most immigrants in the United States have been Christians, but others have arrived as Muslims, Jews, Hindus, Jains, Sikhs, and Zoroastrians. Many immigrants from Asia have practiced Buddhism, a religion that originated in India about 500 B.C.E.

Buddhism

Buddhists agree to trust—or "take refuge in"—the "Three Jewels": the founder Siddhartha Gautama (563–483 B.C.E.), whom followers revere as the "Awakened One" (*buddha*); his exemplary teachings and experience (*dharma*); and the religious community he founded (*sangha*). According to Buddhist tradition, the Buddha offered some of his most important teachings in his first sermon at Deer Park in India. There he talked about the Four

A family offers prayers at the Kong Chow Buddhist Temple in San Francisco's Chinatown. (Phil Schermeister/Corbis)

Noble Truths: the truth of suffering, the truth of the origin of suffering, the truth of the ending of suffering, and the truth of the path that leads to elimination of suffering. He taught that all humans suffer, and they do so because they desire. They desire, in turn, because they fail to understand the nature of reality. But there is a way out, a path to *nirvana*, the elimination of suffering and release from the endless cycles of rebirth. Buddhists can follow the "noble eightfold path." In simplest terms, that path to liberation involves morality, wisdom, and concentration.

If Buddhists have agreed to revere the Three Jewels—Buddha, his teachings, and his community—they also have disagreed among themselves in important ways. Those divisions began as early as one hundred years after the Buddha's death. Eventually Buddhists came to identify three major forms of the religion, or three Buddhist "vehicles": Hinayana, Mahayana, and Vajrayana.

Opponents named the first form, calling it Hinayana (the small vehicle). It is not surprising, then, that this name offends many followers and scholars, who prefer other labels. It might be called Nikaya Buddhism (sectarian Buddhism), alluding to the eighteen early Buddhist schools or sects, although most refer to it by the name of the one surviving Hinayana sect, Theravada (Teachings of the Elders). This Theravada Buddhism describes a gradual path of individual religious striving. The original Buddhist community was made up of monks who renounced the world, with lay supporters of various degrees of dedication offering contributions. Following that early model, lay Theravada Buddhists (those who are not monks) adhere to the moral and religious teachings of the Buddha, but they do not engage in the same renunciations that lead more directly to nirvana. However, they do gain "merit" by supporting the monks and nuns (e.g., by providing food and clothing). That merit, lay Theravadin Buddhists believe, might help them achieve a better rebirth in the next life. This form of Buddhism is influential in Southeast Asian countries such as Sri Lanka, Myanmar (Burma), Thailand, Laos, and Kampuchea (Cambodia).

Mahayana Buddhists were those who dismissed their opponents as the "lesser" vehicle. Their "great" vehicle emphasized the active virtue of compassion as well as the reflective virtue of wisdom, which had been so highly valued by Theravadins. The ideal for Theravada Buddhists had been the *arhat*, one who is free from all impurities through the realization of nirvana and therefore free from all subsequent rebirth. Mahayanists, however, preferred the ideal of the *bodhisattva*, a superhuman being and future Buddha who has compassion as well as wisdom. This emphasis on the compassionate bodhisattva distinguishes the Mahayana sects that predominate in East Asian nations such as China, Korea, and Japan.

A third Buddhist way to find religious fulfillment, Vajrayana (the Diamond Vehicle), emphasized that the religious path could be briefer, even in this lifetime. They suggested that this world of rebirth and suffering (*samsara*) is ultimately identical to the final state of liberation and bliss (*nirvana*), at least for those spiritually advanced persons who could see reality as it really is. Vajrayanists reconceived the religious goal in texts called *tantras*, and in their practices followers used sacred syllables (*mantras*) and cosmic paintings (*mandalas*). As with the other two forms of Buddhism, this Vajrayana or Tantric tradition had Indian roots, but it predominated in Tibet and Mongolia.

The Three Vehicles in America

By the 1970s, almost the full range of Buddhist traditions had found a place in the American religious landscape, both among converts and immigrants. Whereas in Asia one Buddhist vehicle or another tended to predominate in a region, a wide range of Buddhist traditions have been brought together in the United States. Vajrayana Buddhism was represented among the 1,970 Tibetans living in the United States in 1995 and the more numerous Euro-American and African-American converts to Tibetan forms of Buddhism, but few Asian Americans have arrived from nations where Vaj-

rayana predominates. Theravada and Mahayana Buddhism have had much greater influence among immigrants. Southeast Asians who arrived in significant numbers during and after the 1960s have transplanted forms of Theravada Buddhism. East Asian immigrants from China and Japan have brought forms of Mahayana, especially Zen Buddhism, Nichiren Buddhism, and Pure Land Buddhism. Zen originated in China (where it is called *Chan*), as Taoism and Buddhism blended into a tradition that emphasizes meditation and the study of *koan* (religious riddles). Nichiren founded a sect of Buddhism in thirteenth-century Japan that focused attention on one Buddhist sacred text, the Lotus Sutra. The heart of the sect's religious practice involves chanting "hail to the wonderful law of the lotus" before the *gohonzon* (a scroll depicting Nichiren's sacred calligraphy). Other immigrants from East Asia have been Pure Land Buddhists. They focus their devotion on Amida Buddha, the Buddha who presides over the Western Paradise and brings his faithful devotees to that "pure land." Although rebirth there does not constitute nirvana, it is much easier to achieve nirvana from that Western Paradise.

A History of Asian-American Buddhism

The first period in immigrant Buddhist history began in 1848 when the Gold Rush attracted Chinese to California. A few years later, in the 1850s and 1860s, immigrants from China landed in Hawaii to work on sugar plantations. Buddhism was a part of the religious life of many of these Chinese immigrants. It is difficult to say how many Buddhists there were at that time since they did not keep clear records, establish vigorous organizations, or have strong religious leadership. Further, Buddhist beliefs and practices blended with Taoism, Confucianism, and folk traditions in Chinese-American homes and temples. The Chinese built the first temple in America in 1853, in San Francisco's Chinatown. By the 1860s, tens of thousands of Chinese immigrants had some allegiance to Buddhism. By the 1890s, there were fifteen Chinese temples in San Francisco alone, with Buddhist as well as Taoist images in them. Although fully reliable figures were not available, officials from the U.S. Bureau of the Census reported in 1906 that there were sixty-two Chinese temples and 141 shrines in twelve states. Many of these temples and shrines were located in California.

The Japanese were the next Buddhists to arrive in America. They began to travel to Hawaii in significant numbers during the 1860s, and a priest of the True Pure Land Buddhist Sect, Soryu Kagahi, was nurturing Buddhist field workers there by 1889. In the 1890s, thousands of Japanese immigrants arrived in the United States. Almost from the start, the Japanese Buddhists were more organized than the Chinese. Religious leaders traveled from the homeland, and they formed religious institutions to support Buddhist practice. On September 2, 1899, the True Pure Land Buddhist organization in Kyoto, Japan, sent two missionaries to the United States. By 1906, Japanese Pure Land Buddhists reported twelve organizations, seven temples, and fourteen priests. They also reported 3,165 members, although many more Japanese would have been loosely affiliated with the religion. Meanwhile, Buddhism continued to flourish among the Japanese in the Hawaiian Islands, which had become a U.S. possession in 1898. Chinese and Koreans on the islands also practiced Buddhism in this early period. For example, at least half of the 7,200 Koreans who moved to Hawaii to labor on sugar plantations between 1903 and 1905 were Buddhists.

However, as they would soon find out, these pioneer Asian immigrants were not welcomed by all other Americans. They were, as some scholars have suggested, the ultimate aliens. Not only were they legally unable to become naturalized citizens, but they also were racially, linguistically, culturally, and religiously distinct from their neighbors. If their Buddhist religious tradition provided a source of identity and comfort, it also was another feature that set them apart in a predominantly Christian nation. U.S. lawmakers targeted first the Chinese and later the Japanese. The Chinese Exclusion Act of 1882 set the tone, and by

the time legislators had passed the Immigration Act of 1924, which in practical terms excluded Asian immigrants, the pattern was clear for the next period in Buddhist immigrant history, a period that lasted from 1925 to 1965.

During the four decades after the passage of the Immigration Act of 1924, legal restrictions changed the character of Buddhist life among the Chinese, Koreans, and Japanese since they did not enjoy the same freedoms as other groups to immigrate, settle, and worship. One of the most extreme instances of constraint and hostility was the U.S. internment of more than 110,000 Japanese—the majority of them Buddhists—in camps during World War II. Although many of the Japanese Americans in the camps continued to practice Buddhism as the conditions allowed, the horrors of that period delayed the emergence of a self-confidently distinctive religious tradition among Pure Land Buddhists. In fact, many seem to have left the camps more determined than ever to conform to an imagined American and Christian norm.

The Immigration Act of 1965 altered the cultural landscape of the United States in important ways. The act increased the volume of immigration by ending the national quotas that the 1924 law had established, and in particular it allowed a dramatic rise in the number of Asian immigrants. Asians accounted for 37 percent of the total immigration between 1960 and 1989, and the Asian-origin population doubled during the 1980s, rising to more than 7.2 million.

The Immigration Act of 1965 also changed Asian-American Buddhist history. The post-1965 immigrants have come from a variety of nations and practiced a range of religions. For example, Hindus have arrived from India, and Muslims have arrived from Pakistan. Approximately half of the Asian immigrants have been Christians: most Filipinos are Catholics, and most Koreans are Protestants. (Even though Buddhists make up a greater proportion of the Korean population in the homeland, Protestants are disproportionately represented among Koreans in the United States.) Some of the post-1965 Asian immigrants have been Buddhists, however (e.g., Mahayana Buddhists

A child in Hilo, Hawaii, pours tea over a statue of the Buddha as part of the flower festival in celebration of the Buddha's birthday. (Michael S. Yamashita/Corbis)

from Vietnam and China and Theravadins from Thailand and Sri Lanka). The descendants of those who entered with the first wave of Buddhist immigrants did not disappear, of course. In 1997, the Japanese-American dominated Buddhist Churches of America reported 16,902 members in sixty temples, while some others in the Japanese-American population of more than 850,000 had an official affiliation or a loose connection with one or another form of Mahayana Buddhism. Chinese Buddhists, with new immigrants from China and Taiwan adding to their numbers, were probably better organized in the 1990s than they were in the 1890s. They boasted flourishing temples in many regions of the United States, especially along the West Coast and the East Coast. What changed most dramatically in the post-1965 period was that Buddhist immigrants from many other nations also

arrived, expanding and invigorating Buddhist communities in the United States. The Asian-American Buddhist presence continued to be strongest along the Pacific Rim—in Hawaii, California, and the western states. However, post-1965 immigrants established Buddhist temples—both modest split-level homes and elaborate Asian-styled structures —in all regions of the United States. Vietnamese Buddhist temples were located in Oklahoma City, Oklahoma, as well as San Jose, California; Thai Buddhists constructed temples in Miami and Los Angeles; and Laotian Buddhists could visit temples in Milwaukee, Wisconsin, and Portland, Oregon.

In spite of all the changes in the "built" environment of American cities and all the widely noticed shifts in the post-1965 population, few studies of Buddhist immigrants have appeared. For that reason—and because the U.S. Census no longer records religious affiliation—it is not certain how many Buddhists live in the United States, and the estimates vary widely (from 400,000 to 4,000,000). On the low end, the National Survey of Religious Identification (NSRI), a telephone survey that was conducted by the Graduate School of the City University of New York in 1990, counted 401,000 Buddhists in the United States, converts and immigrants together. Some scholars think that estimate is low. Consider, for example, that the 1990 U.S. Census identified 404,847 residents from Theravada Buddhist nations (Laos, Kampuchea, Thailand, Sri Lanka, and Myanmar). A majority of those, although not all, would have been Buddhists. To gain some sense of the proportion of Buddhists among these Southeast Asian immigrants, which cannot be quantified precisely, consider the results of one study that found that two-thirds of the Cambodian residents in one major urban area, San Diego County, identified themselves as Buddhist. Another scholar has estimated that there probably were at least 500,000 to 750,000 Theravada Buddhists in the United States in 1990. Consider also that between 60 and 80 percent of the 593,213 Vietnamese in the United States in that year were Mahayana Buddhists. Assuming the lower proportion, that would mean at least 360,000 more Buddhists to add to the working total. And this does not include other Mahayana Buddhists of Chinese, Korean, and Japanese heritage or the Euro-American and African-American Buddhist converts. It seems probable, then, that there were considerably more than 401,000 Buddhists in the United States in 1990. But if the number of American Buddhists seems higher, how much higher? The highest estimate comes from the American Buddhist Congress (ABC), a Buddhist organization based in southern California. That group estimates that in 1997 there were fifteen hundred Buddhist centers and approximately four million Buddhists in the United States. Religious groups routinely inflate estimates of affiliation and membership, and this count does seem a bit high. If the NSRI figures are low and the ABC numbers seem inflated, a conservative esti-

mate of the total number of American residents who identified themselves as Buddhists in the 1990s, converts and immigrants, might be approximately one million, although it could be as high as two million or more depending on how Buddhist identity is defined. Even if Euro-American and African-American converts are an important presence in the Buddhist community, the vast majority of American Buddhists are Asian immigrants or their descendants. And as long as transnational emigration from Asia continues, the U.S. Buddhist population should continue to grow.

All this indicates that Asian-American Buddhists are an important and growing segment of the American population, but it reveals little about how ordinary followers turn to religious beliefs and practices to make sense of themselves and their lives. A fuller account of that will require more studies of contemporary immigrant communities. Scholars do know something about Buddhist immigrant life, however. Although many of the post-1965 Asian immigrants come from higher economic and social spheres in their homeland than did the nineteenth-century immigrants, many still worry about finances, illness, and other matters of daily life, sometimes turning to their religion in times of need. Like almost all religions everywhere, Asian-American Buddhism also ritually marks transitions in the life cycle such as birth, marriage, and death. As in their homelands, Buddhists' religious life includes public celebrations of annual festivals. However, it is centered as much in the home as in the temple, involving chanting, meditating, or offering homage at a domestic altar to the Buddha in the bedroom or living room.

Key Issues for Asian-American Buddhists

Although some of the practices might seem distinctive, in many ways the religious life of Asian-American Buddhists resembles that of other immigrant religious communities—Catholic, Protestant, Muslim, and Jewish. Three issues in particular that have been prominent in Asian-

American Buddhist communities in the United States also have arisen in other immigrant religious groups: How can followers establish religious organizations? How can the generational lines be crossed? How should the community respond to American culture?

Most Asian-American Buddhist communities have faced the task of organizing groups, raising funds, attracting leaders, and building temples. In the first generation these activities usually have involved adapting former homes or Christian churches for use. The Japanese Pure Land Buddhists in San Francisco around the turn of the century first used Victorian homes in the area for gatherings. Only later did they build independent temples that resembled the religious architecture in the homeland. Post-1965 Asian refugees and immigrants have followed the same pattern. For example, although large Asian-styled structures had appeared in many American cities by the 1990s (for example in San Jose), many Vietnamese Americans continued to worship in refurbished home temples in residential areas (such as the Chua Van Hanh Pagoda in Raleigh, North Carolina). Even if the immigrant community has managed to organize, the problem of finding religious leadership often remains. Although some Buddhist temples have several monks in residence, other smaller ones have difficulty attracting religious leaders for their emerging communities. As with Catholic and Jewish immigrants in the nineteenth century, Asian-American Buddhists first have had to go through their "brick and mortar" phase, as historians of American Catholicism have called it, a time when forming stable religious institutions is a high priority.

A Vietnamese Buddhist temple, Chua Van Hanh, in Raleigh, North Carolina. In 1988, members of the North Carolina Buddhist Association converted a home into this building of worship. (Thomas A. Tweed)

As with other immigrants, Asian-American Buddhists have wanted to purchase, rent, or construct religious buildings in order to nurture the younger generation. Of course, adult children establish temples for themselves and their aged parents, but Asian-American Buddhist groups share a desire to pass on the religious tradition. With that in mind, many of the larger temples sponsor religious education for the children, which might include language instruction as well. The concern for crossing generational boundaries is also evident in Buddhist publications. These include manuals for parents about how to train their young children to be faithful Buddhists and periodicals aimed at Buddhist youths. As in other immigrant religious groups, the second-generation Buddhists usually have less devotion than the first, despite the best efforts of the parents. That, in turn, has caused some intergenerational tensions.

Finally, like other immigrant religious communities, Asian-American Buddhists have had to confront dominant American values, beliefs, and practices—in the schools, the courts, the legislatures, hospitals, the workplace, and even their own homes. Some of the intergenerational tensions among these immigrant groups arise in family disputes about how much children ought to accommodate U.S. cultural patterns in dress, food, language, dating, and entertainment. However painful these intergenerational domestic disputes have been, some of the most important interactions with others have occurred in the public arena. Anti-Asian and anti-immigrant legislation blocked or slowed attempts to establish effective religious Buddhist organizations among many of the earlier Buddhist immigrants, but even in the post-1965 period Asians have faced hostility. For example, well-publicized local disputes about zoning laws have been repeated in every region of the United States as non-Asian residents have challenged Buddhists' attempts to convert homes to temples or construct new buildings for worship. Sometimes those disputes have involved rock-throwing and name-calling. Tensions have also surfaced elsewhere in the public arena as Buddhists struggled with a legal system that used the

Bible as guarantor of truth-telling, a public school system whose textbooks subtly privileged Christianity, and a political system with a full-blown civil religion that uncritically celebrated a Judeo-Christian creator God, thereby ignoring the nontheistic Buddhists. By the 1990s, there had been some changes. Asian-American Buddhist leaders had joined local interreligious organizations all across America, the U.S. military officially had recognized Buddhist chaplains, and the more than fifteen hundred Buddhist centers had established a Buddhist presence in the American cultural landscape. Still, Asian-American Buddhists continued to find religious meaning and negotiate collective identity—as Buddhists and as Americans—in a cultural context that was sometimes friendly and sometimes not.

See also: BURMESE; CAMBODIANS; CHINESE; CHINESE-VIETNAMESE; JAPANESE; KOREANS; LAO; NEPALESE; SINHALESE; SRI LANKANS; TAIWANESE; THAI; TIBETANS; VIETNAMESE

Bibliography

Buddhist Churches of America. (1974). *Buddhist Churches of America: Seventy-Five Year History, 1899–1974.* Chicago: Nobart.

Eckel, M. D. (1994). "Buddhism in the World and in America." In *World Religions in America: An Introduction,* edited by J. Neusner. Louisville, KY: Westminster/John Knox Press.

Harvey, P. B. (1990). *Introduction to Buddhism.* Cambridge, Eng.: Cambridge University Press.

Hunter, L. H. (1971). *Buddhism in Hawaii: Its Impact on a Yankee Community.* Honolulu: University of Hawaii Press.

Kashima, T. (1977). *Buddhism in America: The Social Organization of an Ethnic Religious Organization.* Westport, CT: Greenwood.

Kivisto, P. (1993). "Religion and the New Immigrants." In *A Future for Religion? New Paradigms for Social Analysis,* edited by W. H. Swatos Jr. Newbury Park, CA: Sage Publications.

Numrich, P. D. (1996). *Old Wisdom in the New World: Americanization in Two Theravada Buddhist Temples.* Knoxville: University of Tennessee Press.

Prebish, C. S. (1979). *American Buddhism*. North Scituate, MA: Duxbury Press.

Robinson, R. H., and Johnson, W. (1982). *The Buddhist Religion*, 3rd edition. Belmont, CA: Wadsworth Publishing.

Rutledge, P. J. (1985). *The Role of Religion in Ethnic Self-Identity: A Vietnamese Community*. Lanham, MD: University Press of America.

Tweed, T. A. (1992). *The American Encounter with Buddhism, 1844–1912: Victorian Culture and the Limits of Dissent*. Bloomington: Indiana University Press.

Tweed, T. A. (1997). "Asian Religions in America: Reflections on an Emerging Subfield." In *Religious Diversity and American Religious History: Studies in Traditions and Cultures*, edited by W. Conser and S. Twiss. Athens: University of Georgia Press.

THOMAS A. TWEED

BULGARIANS

The Bulgarians are one of the smallest European immigrant groups in North America and one of the groups least known to the general public. The term "Bulgarians" refers to immigrants coming from the Balkan country of Bulgaria. Bulgaria was part of the Ottoman Empire from 1378 to 1878, a parliamentary monarchy from 1878 to 1944 (its political borders were changed several times due to various wars and peace conferences), a socialist state from 1944 to 1989, and a parliamentary democracy after 1989. Eighty-seven percent of the Bulgarian citizens consider themselves to be Eastern Orthodox. However, there are substantial minority populations that speak different languages and embrace different religions. These minority groups include Turks, Roma (Gypsies), and Pomaks (Bulgarian Slavic Muslims), as well as smaller populations of Armenians, Jews, and others.

Immigrants from the majority population of Bulgaria self-identify as Bulgarians. Well-established immigrants may also identify themselves as Bulgarian Americans. Members of minority groups may self-identify as Bulgarians or as members of the relevant minority group: Macedonians, Jews, Armenians, Turks, Roma, and others. The term "Macedonia" refers to territory that—in a complicated geographic reshuffling related to the break-up of the Ottoman Empire, the Balkan Wars, World War I and World War II—was divided between southwestern Bulgaria, northern Greece, and the Yugoslav Republic of Macedonia. (After 1978 and during World War II, some parts of Macedonia, now part of the Republic of Macedonia, were temporarily within the political boundaries of Bulgaria). Some Macedonians living within Bulgaria may self-identify as Macedonians only, some as Bulgarians only, and some as both Macedonian and Bulgarian. When they immigrate to the United States, if they self-identify as Macedonians, they may group themselves with the Macedonians from the Republic of Macedonia. If they self-identify as Bulgarians, they may group themselves with other Bulgarians. A small portion of immigrants to the United States from areas of Macedonia that became part of Greece or Yugoslavia, especially those who arrived in the United States in the early part of the twentieth century, self-identified as Macedono-Bulgarians. Although Bulgarian and Macedonian immigrants in the post–World War II period have separate standard languages, separate cultural identities, and separate histories, their immigration patterns, especially before 1920, are often very similar.

Immigration History and Demographics

Bulgarian immigrants to North America have come from all regions of Bulgaria, but there was very little immigration to North America before the twentieth century. The few pre-twentieth-century immigrants were young men sent (by Protestant missionaries working in Bulgaria) to North America in the 1880s for higher education. The largest wave of immigration to North America arrived between 1903 and 1908 and was spurred by the poor economic conditions in Bulgaria. Many immigrants did not truly settle in one place, but followed the seasonal work, such as laying railroad tracks. However, by 1908, there were about twenty settlements of Bulgarians. Although many new immigrants had planned to return to Bulgaria once they had achieved financial success, many never returned. New immigrants continued to arrive during the 1910s, 1920s, and 1930s. By the early 1930s, there were more than seven hundred settlements. Some of the places of initial settlements in the United States include Cleveland, Ohio (1903), Steelton, Pennsylvania (1903), Granite City, Illinois (1904), Toledo, Ohio (1906), and Detroit, Michigan (1910). In Canada, many Bulgarians settled in Ontario, especially in and around Toronto. Immigration slowed to a trickle after the 1930s.

Official estimates of the Bulgarian population in the United States are very low. For example, according to the 1990 U.S. Census, the population of people with Bulgarian ancestry in the United States was only 20,894, while there were more than two million people with Russian ancestry and more than six million people of Polish ancestry. Newer figures from U.S. Immigration and Naturalization Service show that the trend continues. In 1993, for example, only 1,029 Bulgarians were admitted to the United States as immigrants, while there were 58,575 immigrants admitted from the Soviet Union and 27,846 from Poland. Nikolay Altankov, author of *The Bulgarian Americans*, suggests that the official figures of around twenty thousand underestimate the actual number of Bulgarians; he offers instead the figure of seventy thousand based on various surveys made of ethnic communities. Statistics from 1971 reporting membership in Bulgarian Eastern Orthodox churches (eighty-six thousand members) would support the higher figures. However, the figures reported for 1992 (eleven hundred members) tend to suggest a lower number.

The young male emigrants from Bulgaria in the early 1900s were continuing a long Bulgarian tradition of seeking seasonal work in other parts of Europe, but as the word spread about the opportunities available in the Americas, they soon changed their destination. Most came from the villages and rural areas of Bulgaria but the majority ended up working in heavy labor—mining, steel mills, and the building of railroads—and lived together in crowded boarding houses. Although some immigrants did return to Bulgaria, many did not. Once these men decided not to return to Bulgaria, they often sent for their wives and children or asked their families in Bulgaria to find brides from their original village or local area. In the post–World War II era, the majority of Bulgarians were political refugees. Again, many of these were young unmarried people, although there were some families. Most postwar immigrants came from urban areas and were better educated than the earlier immigrants. After 1989, most Bulgarian immigrants were again economic immigrants, including many professionals and well-educated people from urban areas. More immigrants arrived with their families. Immigrants in the 1980s and 1990s gravitated toward well-known urban centers. These include New York, Chicago, and Los Angeles in the United States and Toronto in Canada. The older population centers of Pittsburgh and Granite City still have substantial numbers of Bulgarians. A sense of the change in the Bulgarian immigrant community, its integration into the greater American community, can be seen in the advertisements listed in the 1996 edition of the *Directory of the Bulgarian American Chamber of Commerce*, published in Los Angeles. These include advertisements from Bulgarian doctors, dentists, lawyers, brokers, accountants, and photographers.

Language

Bulgarian is a South Slavic language. The standard literary language emerged during the middle of the nineteenth century and was officially codified by the ministry of education in 1899. First-generation Bulgarian immigrants to North America maintain their language abilities, even as they quickly strive to learn English. Second-generation Bulgarian Americans from the first wave of immigration tended to maintain their fluency in Bulgarian when communities based around churches with their accompanying schools still existed.

However, in the post–World War II period, most second-generation Bulgarian Americans, especially those without a community base, have low language maintenance. Only the largest communities (Granite City, Steelton, Detroit, New York) still maintain the church-related schools. Some of the immigrant children rediscover the Bulgarian language when they attend universities that offer instruction in the Bulgarian language. However, language maintenance is not necessarily a component in maintaining ethnic identity.

Immigrants coming from the minority groups may be bilingual, in Bulgarian and the language of the minority group—Turkish, Armenian, Romany (spoken by the Roma), Ladino (spoken by the Jews, who belong to the Sephardic tradition), and others. Their maintenance of Bulgarian in the United States is tied to whether they maintain an identity as Bulgarians or as a member of another group. Bulgarian Jews, for example, may group with other Sephardic non-Bulgarian Jews, with Ladino seen as an important measure of cultural identity.

Cultural Characteristics

The Arts. Bulgarians have a rich tradition of folk music and dance that was originally an integral part of the agrarian calendar cycle and life cycle rituals, especially weddings. Much of this tradition was brought to North America with the immigrants, although the original contexts were sometimes lost. Holiday celebrations and weddings at churches and community centers typically included some type of Bulgarian music played by an orchestra. Often traditional instruments were replaced by the accordion (as was the case in Bulgaria itself). Children in Bulgarian schools learned to sing folk songs. Some children of immigrants joined folk ensembles like the Duquesne Tamburitzans in Pittsburgh. From the 1960s on, many non-Bulgarians became interested in Bulgarian music and dance. They began to study the dance and music both of the immigrant community in North America and of Bulgaria itself. These non-Bulgarians also formed folk groups and, in many cases, now participate in events sponsored by the Bulgarian community. In the late 1980s, Bulgarian music even reached mainstream communities in America, Canada, and Europe with the promotion of records and concerts by female Bulgarian folk singers billed as *Le Mystère des Voix Bulgares.*

Religion. The majority of Bulgarians immigrating to North America belong to the Eastern Orthodox religion. Important religious holidays, including Christmas and Easter, continue to be celebrated by the immigrants. Bulgarians everywhere also celebrate Saints Cyril and Methodius day, May 24, honoring the two brothers for bringing literacy to the Slavs in the ninth century. The first Bulgarian Orthodox church in North America was founded in Granite City in 1909. The church, with its attendant social organizations, was the main source of Bulgarian immigrant identity in the larger immigrant communities. Bulgarian Protestant immigrants (converted by missionaries in the late nineteenth century) arrived in the United States in significant numbers only up to the 1920s. There have been many fewer immigrants from other religions in Bulgaria, such as Islam and Judaism.

Health. Bulgarians, even with the strong urbanization of the post–World War II period, are still closely tied to the land. Most urban Bulgarians still have family living in the country and return to their villages frequently to work in their gardens. Many Bulgarians combine a belief in Western medicine with a belief in the efficacy of traditional remedies. This practice holds true with the immigrant community in North America. Bulgarians will recommend herbal teas for headaches, stomach ailments, and colds. The traditional Bulgarian diet is hearty, but healthy, quite similar to that of the Greeks and Turks. However, except for yogurt, with its famous *lactobacillus bulgaricus,* Bulgarian food remains largely unknown to the general American public.

Assimilation and Cultural Persistence

The extent to which Bulgarians have assimilated into the American mainstream may be gauged by the fact that they are generally unknown to the American public. Although successfully assimilated, Bulgarians often maintain many aspects of their culture in the home. The Bulgarian church in larger communities also helps immigrants maintain their identity with community events and Bulgarian schools.

Bulgarians have not experienced the type of blatant discrimination experienced by some immigrant groups. Bulgarians in the 1910s and 1920s experienced the generalized hostility directed at the entire wave of immigrants from southern Europe, but they were not singled out as Bulgarians. The only exceptions came during World War I and World War II, when the Bulgarian government allied itself with Germany, resulting in some hostility directed specifically at Bulgarian Americans.

See also: ARMENIANS; GYPSIES; JEWS, MIDDLE EASTERN; MACEDONIANS

Bibliography

Altankov, N. (1979). *The Bulgarian-Americans.* Palo Alto, CA: Ragusan Press.

Boneva, B. (1995). "Ethnic Identities in the Making: The Case of Bulgaria." *Cultural Survival Quarterly* 19(2):76–78.

Carlson, C., and Allen, D. (1990). *The Bulgarian Americans.* New York: Chelsea House.

Chary, F. B. (1972). *The Bulgarian Jews and the Final Solution, 1940–1944.* Pittsburgh: University of Pittsburgh Press.

Christowe, S. (1976). *The Eagle and the Stork.* New York: Harper's Magazine Press.

Friedman, V. (1993). "Macedonian." In *The Slavonic Languages,* edited by B. Comrie and C. G. Corbet. London: Routledge.

Iordanova, D. (1995). "Media Coverage of Bulgaria in the West and Its Domestic Use." In *Communication in Eastern Europe,* edited by F. L. Casmir. Mahwah, NJ: Lawrence Erlbaum.

Kramer, C. (1993). "Language in Exile: The Macedonians in Toronto, Canada." In *Language Contact–Language Conflict,* edited by E. Fraenkel and C. Kramer. New York: Peter Lang.

Paprikoff, G. (1985). *Works of Bulgarian Emigrants: An Annotated Bibliography.* Chicago: Author.

Petroff, L. (1995). *Sojourners and Settlers: The Macedonian Community in Toronto to 1940.* Toronto: University of Toronto Press.

Rice, T. (1994). *May it Fill Your Soul: Experiencing Bulgarian Music.* Chicago: University of Chicago Press.

Rudin, C., and Eminov, A. (1993). "Bulgarian Nationalism and Turkish Language in Bulgaria." In *Language Contact–Language Conflict,* edited by E. Fraenkel and C. Kramer. New York: Peter Lang.

Scatton, E. A. (1993). "Bulgarian." In *The Slavonic Languages,* edited by B. Comrie and C. G. Corbet. London: Routledge.

Yankoff, P. D. (1928). *Peter Menikoff: The Story of a Bulgarian Boy in the Great Melting Pot.* Nashville: Cokesbury Press.

KATIA MCCLAIN

BURMESE

"Burmese" is a loose category encompassing a myriad of ethnic identities (more than 125 separate ethnic groups are found among the Burmese) whose origins within the boundaries of old British Burma gave them their name. Further, the terms "Burma" and "Burmese" are disputed due to political allegiances involving the various political factions struggling to overthrow Myanmar's military regime (known as the State Law and Order Restoration Council or simply by the acronym SLORC).

Traditionally, the majority ethnic group in Myanmar, from which the Burmese derive their name, referred to themselves as Myanma. In colonial times, however, the British misinterpreted the pronunication of Myanma as "Burma," and then called all the ethnic groups within the political boundaries of Myanmar "Burmese." The current military regime changed the official spelling of these names back to near precolonial pronunciations, with Myanmar (or Myanmars) as the correct English pronunciation and spelling of their name. The matter was further confused when political opponents of the military regime called on the rest of the world to refuse to revert to the precolonial and current military government spellings and to continue to use Burman (for the majority ethnic group) and Burmese (as the blanket appellation for all groups living within the political boundaries of Myanmar). For simplicity, this entry will use Burmans or Burmese to refer to the relative ethnic groups and Myanmar to refer to the military-ruled country.

While Burmans form the majority of the population of Myanmar, other ethnic groups brought under the name Burmese are also numerous and well represented among immigrants from Myanmar to the United States. The main ethnic groups in this category are Arakanese, Karens, Mons, Shans, and Nagas. The Arakanese, however, are often indistinguishable from the Burmans, as they form a branch of the main ethnic group that migrated in the tenth century over the Arakan Yoma mountain range from Myanmar (establishing an independent kingdom lasting until its incorporation into Myanmar in 1784) but that maintained Burman culture, language, and, like the Burmans, converted to Theravada Buddhism. Other groups were introduced into the Burmese population by British colonial rule and in the postwar period. These include South Asians and Chinese, who consider themselves to be Burmese but who often are not regarded as such by either the Burmans or by other indigenous members of the Burmese group. This has been especially true since large-scale immigration of Chinese into Upper Myanmar in the 1990s led to resentment in Myanmar by the Burmese, and this resentment has carried over into the Burmese-American community.

Another important ingredient of self-definition by the Burmese has been religious identification. Burmans are generally Theravada Buddhist and often do not include Burmese of other religious affiliations within their self-defined group. This has led to discrimination against non-Buddhist religious minorities in Myanmar, which has been carried over into the Burmese-American community.

This is especially true of the Arakanese Muslims, who are known as Rohengyas.

Immigration History

The immigration of Burmese into the United States is largely a post-1962 phenomenon. After military rule was established in Myanmar in 1962, political refugees, many of them academics, began the immigration of Burmese to countries including the United States and Australia. After Myanmar's military government began to suppress the pro-democracy movement and, later, when it shut down Myanmar's universities, Burmese students became a major group among the émigrés. In addition, economic opportunities brought many doctors and other professionals to the United States.

A significant number of the older generation of Burmese within the United States regard it as a temporary home and either return to Myanmar or plan to do so. Among the younger generation, however, the United States is considered to be their permanent home, and they are quick to affirm that they never plan to return to Myanmar.

On the whole, the Burmese population of the United States remains small. Figures from the early 1990s suggest that they number about 7,000, most of these being first-generation immigrants. The U.S. Bureau of the Census does not enumerate the Burmese as a separate category and lumps the Burmese, and their statistics, under the general term "other Asian," which makes reliable statistical generalization of this immigrant group problematic. Further, the small size of the Burmese community in the United States has meant that almost no literature has been published concerning them, in great contrast to the plethora of works related to Chinese Americans or Japanese Americans. Similarly, while there are various newsletters published in English for academic audiences, there are no American newspapers or other periodicals published in Burmese.

The most significant centers of settlement of the Burmese in the United States are in major cities such as Chicago, New York, Los Angeles, and

A Burmese refugee sits with her child at a medical clinic in the early 1990s. (Alison Wright/Corbis)

Washington, D.C. In regional terms, the Burmese are concentrated in the Northeast, the Midwest, and California. In fact, after Tokyo, Southern California is one of the largest centers of Burmese residing outside of Myanmar. Maryland is also an important center on the East Coast.

Cultural Traditions

Due to their British colonial heritage and a modern education system that requires general instruction in both the English and Burmese languages, adult immigrants from Myanmar are usually bilingual, and at most social gatherings of Burmese Americans, the Burmese language is the chief medium of communication. Due to the im-

portance of Buddhism in the daily life of many Burmese, some Burmese immigrants are also competent in Pali, the language of Theravada Buddhism. Those of the younger generation who were born in the United States or who arrived when they were very young do not know the Burmese language, and there are little or no Burmese community projects to instruct them in the Burmese language. Further, Burmese is usually taught at only four sites in the United States: Northern Illinois University in DeKalb; Cornell University in Ithaca, New York; the Southeast Asian Studies Summer Institute (SEASSI) summer language program, which is hosted by a different United States university every two summers; and the Foreign Service Institute (FSI). Thus there are few other opportunities for young Burmese to learn their parents' language.

Due to their small number and the variety of religious and cultural identities within this group, the Burmese in the United States generally do not settle in groups, but maintain community ties from a geographical distance. Often many will travel several hours to locations of ethnic gatherings. A common meeting place is the *pongyi-gyaun*, the Burmese term for a Theravada Buddhist monastery. There are at least seven pongyi-gyauns in the United States, and they are primarily located in California (which has three pongyi-gyauns), as well as in several other areas of the country, especially Illinois and Maryland. At such locations, traditional Burmese holidays are celebrated, and often such events as the water festival take place. Christian Burmese, however, avoid such gatherings and choose to identify with local church communities outside of their ethnic community. The Burma-America Buddhist Association is located in Silver Springs, Maryland, and provides support for a variety of Burmese Buddhist religious holidays, as well as the celebration of the Burmese New Year's Day.

Burmese cooking is another part of Burmese culture that persists among Burmese living in the United States. Burmese cooking owes much to the curries and spices of India and is quite distinct from the East Asian foods typically associated with

Asian cooking by Americans. In the home, Burmese in the United States, regardless of their generational identification, maintain their cooking traditions, although few Burmese restaurants can be found. Burmese food can be eaten with Western utensils; chipsticks; or, in the traditional Burmese style of eating, with one's hands, keeping the food above the first joint and literally popping the food into one's mouth.

Community Characteristics

The Burmese in the United States who are employed tend to be white-collar professionals, although there are blue-collar workers as well. There are almost no Burmese immigrants engaged in farming, forestry, or fishing. Typical occupations include medicine, academia, business, and technical work. Among the younger generation, a large proportion go to college. Most Burmese immigrants can be characterized as middle class. Among the Burmese in the United States, the family is held as an important value, and strong superfamilial bonds are considered important as well.

Another important characteristic of the Burmese immigrant community is the strong participation of many Burmese in the political activities of Myanmar. Many contribute time, energy, and money to political organizations seeking the end of military rule there. Among these Burmese, the pro-democracy movement's leader, Aung San Suu Kyi, is an important figure and is highly venerated. There is, however, a vocal minority of Burmese in the United States who do not share this view. As this sometimes causes friction and animosity among Burmese Americans, political topics are often avoided at community gatherings.

Conclusion

The older generations of the Burmese immigrant community maintain a strong attachment to Myanmar and identify closely with political, religious, and social movements within their former home. The younger generations, however, tend to identify less closely with Myanmar and identify most closely along common generational lines with their peers in mainstream American society.

See also: BUDDHISTS

Bibliography

Aung Aung Taik. (1993). *Under the Golden Pagoda: The Best of Burmese Cooking.* San Francisco: Chronicle Books.

Aung San Suu Kyi. (1991). *Freedom from Fear and Other Writings,* edited by M. Aris. New York: Penguin Books.

Backus, K., and Furtaw, J. C., eds. (1992). *Asian-Americans Information Directory.* Detroit: Gale.

Haseltine, P., comp. (1989). *East and Southeast Asian Material Culture in North America: Collections, Historical Sites, and Festivals.* New York: Greenwood Press.

Kitano, H. H. L., and Daniels, R. (1988). *Asian Americans: Emerging Minorities.* Englewood Cliffs, NJ: Prentice Hall.

Lintner, B. (1990). "Homing Instincts." *Far Eastern Economic Review* 150:63.

Mi Mi Khaing. (1984). *The World of Burmese Women.* London: Zed Books.

Swan, J. (1993). "Utilization of Mental Health Services Among the Myanmar Americans." Ph.D. diss., California School of Professional Psychology, Los Angeles.

MICHAEL W. CHARNEY

CAJUNS

See ACADIANS AND CAJUNS

CALIFORNIOS

"Californios" is a label first applied to the group of the earliest settlers who came from Mexico to the West Coast of the present-day United States. They arrived starting in 1769, during the Spanish Colonial period in the late eighteenth century. In time, the settlers consisted of Indian, black, and mestizo (racially mixed) farmers and artisans, as well as a small proportion of Spanish missionaries and soldiers. Over the last years of the century they established themselves from present-day San Diego far into northern California.

The name "Californios" actually stems from Calafia, a fictional leader of Amazonian tribeswomen in the sixteenth-century novel *Las Sergas de Esplandian* (The Labors of the Very Brave Knight Esplandian) by Garci Rodriguez de Montalvo. Spanish seafaring explorers thought the indigenous population resembled, with their long hair and dark skin tones, Calafia and her people. Through common use the name became popular for the region and for the newcomers there, especially after independence from Spain in 1821, when other regional names, such as Tejas and Nuevo Mexico, also came into popular use. It was applied to subsequent immigrants from Mexico, Europe, and, later, the eastern United States, especially those who through intermarriage became part of the landed gentry.

Present-day descendants of these original settlers are so varied and submerged in the general California population that competing social organizations based on class and racial differences have emerged to claim this early heritage. Californianos, Californios, Los Soldaderos (soldiers), and Los Pobladores (settlers) are the names of four groups that represent this diffused ethnic tradition. Some of the claimants have very light complexions and definitely are more northern European in appearance, belying their Spanish or mestizo roots, but nevertheless revel in the "Spanish Days" celebrations that are commonplace in California, especially, for example, in Santa Barbara. Others are mestizo Mexican in appearance and bear a strong resemblance to many of the recent Mexican immigrants in the state.

Basic Social Structure

The label "Californios" came to mean principally the owners and operators of the cattle ranches that spread all over California, including some *vaqueros* (cowboys), craftsmen, and small landowners. This industry flourished in the terrain and climate of southern and central California. These ranches and the social and cultural life inspired by cattle industries, including horse culture—vaqueros, lassos, rodeos, branding, range life, and the like—evolved into an economic system with international implications. The extensive trade that developed might be considered a portent of a global economy.

A number of ranches were patterned along the lines of the hacienda in Mexico, with mestizo Californios supervising hundreds of workers, mostly Indians and darker-hued mestizos and *cholos* (racial and cultural marginals). The ranch economy was a separate entity from the mission system, which also controlled tens of thousands of California Indians. Initially the landed gentry and the religious clerics maintained a working relationship. Church fathers ministered to family needs and religious events (birth, marriage, death), to the social life of the community, and helped commemorate the round of yearly economic activities in the cattle industry. All this changed with independence from Spain in 1821, slowly at first but soon very rapidly. Almost from the beginning the Californios, because of their distance from the capital of New Spain in Mexico City, had exercised considerable autonomy. This tendency toward local control became more marked under the Mexican government as the Californios gained in power. The church in general, in California as in all Mexico, came under attack, especially its exalted privileges and vast landholding estates; these challenges led to the secularization of mission property. Californios seized and incorporated these holdings into their own properties.

Many of the ranches were quite large, some bordering on the size of a modern-day county in Southern California. The Yorba family estate, for example, spanned acreage from Newport Beach to Riverside (about fifty miles inland from the coast). The last parcel of the Yorba estate was sold in the 1960s; the remainder had earlier been taken over by the Irvine family. Other family names identified with these *latifundia* (large landed estates) were the Alvarados, Verdugos, Sepúlvedas, Vallejos, and Carrillos, among many others; streets and other landmarks bear testimony throughout the state to their early presence. Smaller plots were ranchitos or minifundias operated largely by well-to-do vaqueros and assimilated Indians from Mexico, some of whom were allowed into the Californio circle. Size of the ranchitos varied from a few hundred acres to thousands of acres, with the largest approaching the dimensions of a small town, such as Los Nietos, near Whittier.

Arrival of the Yankees

When American entrepreneurs from New England established contact, circling Cape Horn in South America to launch the clipper ship trade in hides and tallow. A lucrative economic transaction gradually developed into cultural interactions and exchanges. Many of these Yankees became captivated by the land and people; some stayed and became Californios by marriage and acculturation. Learning Spanish and adapting to the land and lifestyle led them to become champions of their adopted people when wholesale Anglo immigration occurred in the aftermath of the Mexican-American War (1846–1848), especially in the Gold Rush shortly after.

Counting these assimilated Yankees, there were only four thousand Californios in the 1850s. By this time a lifestyle and seasonal ritual had become entrenched as the cattle industry now catered to the hundreds of thousands of newcomers from the eastern United States and other regions of the world. The affluence and routine cycle of the Californios was characterized by swings of intensive work during *rodeo* (roundup) to celebratory fiestas ending such activities. Celebrations for religious events, weddings, baptisms, and so on, as well as community affairs ending a cycle of work, could last for days, even weeks.

Intermarriage among the Californio families, and occasionally a socially mobile lower-status mestizo or Indian, was something that the *gente de razón* (people of reason, a label often applied to Californios of purer Spanish and mestizo heritage, and more generally to all non-Indian settlers) would take seriously. Although women's public roles were quite restricted, female rights to a portion of their families' land under community property and inheritance customs provided them with significant status and an important, if not highly visible, position. Passing land ownership to the next generation was conducted bilaterally, and many Californio women married Yankee newcomers to start a new ranch and also add a new dimension to the *mestizaje* (racial and cultural blending) heritage that is so much a part of Mexico.

As part of the communal nature of their existence in a harsh environment in a land peopled mostly with native Indians, the celebrations of the Californios gave credence to the fiesta syndrome popularized by Yankees upon their return to the East Coast. Everyone from miles around was invited to these affairs, including many of the workers and servants, and were expected to stay for the duration, often lasting several days. The rancheros and their families, of course, remained in the main house while the lower-status visitors shared accommodations in the smaller, simpler one-room adobe dwellings of the resident workers. Food and drink were plentiful, as the beef from the cattle and wine from the vineyards, supplemented with other culinary products from the citrus fields and cornfields, were more than enough to sate the appetites and quench the thirsts of the multitudes.

Early U.S. Domination

In the early years of California history under U.S. domination, the Californios enjoyed a prominence never before or since reached by a Hispanic group in the state. Landownership reflected one's economic and social standing and translated into political power and influence. In the state legislature formed just before California was admitted to the Union, the Californios wielded control over many of the state's future plans. At their insistence, laws and statutes were written in Spanish as well as English; the 1850 state constitution was bilingual, and shifted into monolingual English only after the decline of the Californios in the 1870s. This occurred when landownership fell into the hands of Anglos, a transfer that resulted from a combination of natural catastrophes (droughts and floods that brought financial ruin) and legal chicanery (lawyers and courts that swindled the Californios). Loss of land decreased the status and influence of Californios until they were only a shadow of their former selves.

The early economic exchanges and ties with the United States also influenced material and cultural transformations. Most obvious were the exchange of California "banknotes" (cattle hides) and tallow for Yankee goods, furniture, lamps, textiles, metal products, and so on. As noted, some of the Yankee traders and seamen adopted California and the lifestyle that prevailed there, but in addition they introduced new architectural and building habits. Residences in the early years of settlement in a rather sparse desert habitat were somewhat primitive. Houses were made of adobe bricks, a mixture of clay soil and straw or grass, and had flat roofs made from small tree branches covered by a mixture of thatch grass and *brea* (tar). When the population became more fully rooted and trade goods from Mexico more abundant, domiciles improved and many household furnishings were added.

Life After Statehood

Statehood for California changed matters in several ways. Not least was the importance with which Yankee maritime interests came to view the natural California harbors as gateways to the Pacific and Asia. Trade with the Eastern Seaboard was mutually beneficial, as more goods exchanged meant more money, and buying power escalated. Home life and its material surroundings improved for Californios. Soon, simply constructed structures made from local products were embellished with Yankee products, techniques, and ingenuity. Two-story adobes became more common, and many were further adorned with the New England style of second-story covered balconies. Manufactured goods such as iron tools made the construction of new buildings and other productive undertakings easier. Generally, a syncretic way of life (blended from aspects of the local and Eastern Seaboard cultures) was emerging; however, a strong emphasis on the Mexican side was retained.

When Anglo-American newcomers wrested control of the economy and political apparatus from the Californios, all this changed. For example, the Californios were accustomed to measuring the land simply by establishing boundaries with natural landmarks, such as a big oak tree or a rocky ledge. The Anglos introduced precise and legally binding land survey practices and a more fixed way of delineating private property, further disrupting the less formal nature of the Californio system. Such revampments caused a great deal of havoc among residents and are most glaringly evident in another cultural replacement: the introduction of procedures to control and allocate water. Californio customs often allowed anyone in need to partake of the water on their land with little fear or accusation of trespassing, even though there were occasional conflicts. With the gradual application of practices that placed greater emphasis on individual property rights and permanent boundary lines, water and range conflicts became more commonplace. The California courts eventually clarified and corrected the water rights laws to bring peace to the area. (Similar developments based on contrasting and often conflicting cultural traditions occurred throughout the Southwest.)

Today the Californios are rather difficult to identify with any accuracy. Some of the descendants of early Californios proclaim their status through membership in ethnic social organizations. However, most of the descendants are integrated into and hidden among the general population. Thus their present number and characteristics cannot be clearly stated. Many prominent "public" Californios are very light in skin color and highly assimilated, often taking pains to draw attention away from their humble ancestry and any link to more recent immigrants. Nevertheless, they maintain a sense of pride in and nostalgia for their roots. When historic occasions bring about a celebratory moment, these Californios appear. A visit by King Juan Carlos of Spain in the early 1990s to the old Mexican center of Los Angeles, for example, was hosted by light-skinned Californios dressed as Spanish dons. Interestingly, they were surrounded by robust Mexican women dressed in traditional servant garb attending to the king and his dons.

See also: MEXICANS; SPANIARDS

Bibliography

Bancroft, H. H. (1888). *California Pastoral, 1769–1848.* San Francisco: History Company.

Camarillo, A. (1979). *Chicanos in a Changing Society: From Mexican Pueblos to American Barrios in Santa Barbara and Southern California, 1848–1930.* Cambridge, MA: Harvard University Press.

Cleland, R. G. (1951). *The Cattle on a Thousand Hills: Southern California, 1850–1880.* San Marino, CA: Huntington Library.

Cleland, R. G. (1952). *The Irvine Ranch of Orange County, 1810–1950.* San Marino, CA: Huntington Library.

Dakin, S. B. (1939). *A Scotch Paisano: Hugo Reid's Life in California, 1832–1852.* Berkeley: University of California Press.

Dana, R. H. (1840). *Two Years Before the Mast.* New York: Harper & Brothers.

Hass, L. (1995). *Conquests and Historical Identities in California, 1769–1936.* Berkeley: University of California Press.

Hittel, T. H. (1898). *History of California,* Vol. 3. San Francisco: Stone.

Hundley, N. (1992). *The Great Thirst: Californians and Water, 1770s–1990s.* Berkeley: University of California Press.

Hutchinson, C. A. (1969). *Frontier Settlement in Mexican California.* New Haven, CT: Yale University Press.

McWilliams, C. (1946). *Southern California: An Island on the Land.* New York: Duell, Sloan, and Pearce.

Monroy, D. (1990). *Thrown Among Strangers: The Making of Mexican Culture in Frontier California.* Berkeley: University of California Press.

Pitt, L. (1966). *The Decline of the Californios.* Los Angeles: University of California Press.

Robinson, A. (1846). *Life in California.* New York: Wylie & Putnam.

Weber, D. (1982). *The Mexican Frontier, 1821–1846: The American Southwest Under Mexico.* Albuquerque: University of New Mexico Press.

Woolsey, R. C. (1996). *Migrants West: Toward the Southern California Frontier.* Sebastopol, CA: Grizzly Bear Publishing.

JAMES DIEGO VIGIL

CAMBODIANS

More than one million refugees from Cambodia, Laos, and Vietnam were resettled in the United States after the end of the Indochina War in 1975. They arrived as part of the largest refugee resettlement program in U.S. history, peaking in 1980 and continuing into the mid-1990s. Because they arrived as refugees rather than as immigrants, their story differs fundamentally from that of other Asian-origin ethnic groups. But even among the Indochinese refugees the story of the Cambodians, most of them survivors of the holocaust that came to be known as the "killing fields" of the late 1970s, stands out in distinct ways.

As refugees from three countries devastated by war and internecine conflicts, the Cambodians, Laotians, and Vietnamese experienced far more traumatic events than other newcomers in modern American history, while having no realistic prospects of return to their homelands. Unlike so-called brain-drain immigrant flows characterized by large proportions of professionals and managers, the Indochinese were characterized by much larger proportions of rural-origin and less-educated peoples than any other Asian immigrant group. Unlike regular immigrants, however, their refugee status facilitated access to public assistance programs on the same means-tested basis as U.S. citizens. The Indochinese also comprise the youngest populations in the United States, partly a reflection of high levels of fertility. All of these particular characteristics and contexts of exit and reception have shaped their adaptation to the American economy and society.

While as refugees of the Indochina War they generally share a common history and experiences that distinguish them from Asian American groups, the various Indochinese ethnic groups— the Cambodians (predominantly Khmer), Vietnamese, lowland Lao, Hmong, Mien, and other Laotian highlanders, along with ethnic Chinese from Cambodia, Vietnam, and Laos—also differ from each other in fundamental ways. They have different social backgrounds, languages, cultures, and often adversarial histories, and they reflect different patterns of settlement and adaptation in America. Even within each of these ethnic groups there are major differences based on social class, age, and gender.

The Refugee Exodus

The Indochinese refugees are a product of the longest war in modern history—thirty years of warfare in Southeast Asia—the thirty-year warfare that began in Vietnam and was extended into Laos and Cambodia in the 1960s and early 1970s. The war created a massive refugee population for whom the United States assumed a historic responsibility. The circumstances of the U.S. withdrawal from the region provided added moral and political justification for significantly expanded domestic refugee programs, which totaled some $5 billion in cash, medical assistance, and social services to primarily Indochinese refugees between 1975 and 1985 alone.

If the war divided America, it devastated Vietnam, Laos, and Cambodia, shattering the region's economy and traditional society. A tragedy of staggering proportions, the "war that nobody won" left these three countries among the poorest in the world. Indeed, in an economic ranking of 211 countries in the mid-1980s, Cambodia was ranked last — the world's poorest with a per capita national annual income of roughly $50.

In the years after the end of the warfare in 1975, more than two million refugees fled Vietnam, Laos, and Cambodia in a series of distinct waves. The refugee exodus was shaped by complex political and economic factors. As is true of refugee movements elsewhere, the first waves of Indochinese refugees were disproportionately comprised of elites who left because of political opposition to the new regimes, while later waves included masses of people of more modest backgrounds fleeing continuing regional conflicts and deteriorating economic conditions. Unlike Vietnamese professionals and former notables who were greatly overrepresented among those who

A Cambodian musician plays a "troh" instrument in Oakland, California. (Eric Crystal)

were evacuated to American bases in Guam and the Phillippines during the fall of Saigon in 1975, Cambodian elites who managed to escape were much more likely to have gone to France (the former colonial power in Indochina, where French-speaking Indochinese communities, particularly in Paris, had developed during the previous half century).

In Cambodia, when the government backed by the United States fell to Khmer Rouge forces in 1975, the cities were deurbanized as the population was forced into labor camps in the countryside; the capital of Phnom Penh became a ghost town practically overnight. As many as two million people — a quarter of Cambodia's population — may have died during the Pol Pot regime that ensued. A massive increase in Cambodian refugees beginning in late 1978 was triggered by the Vietnamese invasion of Cambodia, which quickly ended three years of Khmer Rouge rule, and a new guerilla war in the Cambodian countryside, already wracked by famine and the destruction of the country's infrastructure. Hundreds of thousands of Cambodian survivors of the Pol Pot labor camps fled to the Thai border. These events, occurring alongside a flood of Vietnamese "boat people," led to an international resettlement crisis when "first asylum" countries such as Thailand refused to accept more refugees into their already swollen camps — often forcing land refugees at gunpoint back to Cambodia across border mine fields. In response, under agreements reached at the Geneva Conference in July 1979, Western countries began to absorb significant numbers of the refugee camp population in Southeast Asia.

The resettlement of Cambodians in the United States took place almost entirely during the 1980s. The flows of refugees from Cambodia to the United States were virtually terminated after 1990; the focus then shifted to the voluntary repatriation of refugees still in camps in Thailand and elsewhere. The end of the Cold War in 1989, the collapse of the former Soviet Union in 1991, elections (supervised by the United Nations) in Cambodia in 1993 that sought to end its long-running civil war, and the end of the U.S. trade embargo against Vietnam in February 1994 were but the most remarkable events of a compressed period of rapid and fundamental changes in international relations that transformed the nature of Indochinese refugee resettlement in the United States.

Immigration History and Population Size

Among Asian Americans, the Cambodians constitute one of the most recently formed ethnic groups. According to the U.S. Immigration and Naturalization Service, the first Cambodian immigrant arrived in 1953; by 1970, only slightly more than one hundred Cambodians had immigrated to the United States. In the early 1970s the number of these pioneer immigrants increased by less than three hundred. Thus, when Phnom Penh fell in 1975, the number of Cambodians already in America was miniscule.

About 130,000 Indochinese refugees were resettled in the United States in 1975, nearly all of them from South Vietnam, with fewer than 5,000 from Cambodia. A small number arrived between 1976 and 1978 (bottoming out in 1977), but a massive new inflow began in late 1978 in the context of the international refugee crisis. About 450,000 Indochinese refugees arrived between 1979 and 1982, peaking in 1980 (the record year in U.S. refugee resettlement history), when 167,000 were admitted. Compared to the 1975 "first wave," this new wave of refugees was much more numerous than the 1975 wave, and it was also much more heterogeneous; the new refugees included the boat people from Vietnam, the lowland Lao, the highland Hmong, and the survivors of the Pol Pot period in Cambodia. Many of them came from rural backgrounds; had little education, knowledge of English, or transferable occupational skills; and had endured prolonged stays in refugee camps. What is more, the timing and context of their entry into the United States further complicated their reception; the peak year of their arrival (1980) coincided both with the crisis of the tens of thousands of Mariel Cubans and Haitians arriving in Florida in small boats and with the highest

domestic inflation rates in memory, followed during 1981–1982 by the most severe economic recession since the Great Depression in the 1930s. The confluence of these events in turn contributed to an accompanying political climate of intensifying nativism, racism, xenophobia, and "compassion fatigue."

Nonetheless, the resettlement process continued, and by 1990, according to the U.S. Office of Refugee Resettlement, total Indochinese refugee arrivals had reached almost one million, of whom 147,000 were from Cambodia (another 600,000 from Vietnam, and more than 200,000 from Laos). Of the Cambodians, less than 10 percent (only 13,330) arrived in the 1975–1979 period; fully two-thirds (99,400) arrived during the 1981–1985 period, making the early 1980s the critical period of ethnic group formation in the short history of Cambodians in America. After 1985 the number of admissions dropped precipitately and then virtually ended after 1990 (even though Vietnamese and Laotian admissions continued at substantial rates into the mid-1990s). These government figures tally only persons officially admitted as refugees from abroad and do not take into account the sizable number of children born to Cambodian parents in the United States or mortality after arrival.

The 1990 U.S. Census, which should provide a fuller estimate of population size, enumerated a total Cambodian population of just under 150,000, of whom 118,000 were foreign-born (a figure well below the number of Cambodians brought as refugees to the United States through 1990). Of these foreign-born, 14,000 indicated they had arrived before 1980 (a figure that matches the refugee admissions data for the 1975–1979 period), while 104,000 said they had arrived between 1980 and 1990. It appears that sizable numbers of ethnic Chinese from Cambodia indicated their ethnicity as Chinese in the census responses. Earlier research had estimated that ethnic Chinese comprised up to 15 percent of Cambodian arrivals, especially among those arriving after 1980; applying that proportion to the 1990 U.S. Census figures would yield an additional 20,000 from

Cambodia and bring the numbers closer to the data on refugee admissions. After 1990, in any case, the Cambodian population in the United States has grown almost entirely as a result of natural increase, since the number of refugees has not exceeded more than a few hundred annually during the 1990s.

Patterns of Settlement

The first waves of Cambodian and other Indochinese refugees could not be resettled into coethnic communities previously established by earlier immigration, since they were virtually nonexistent prior to 1975; instead, in the resettlement process the refugees were more likely to be dispersed throughout the country than were other large immigrant groups. Despite this general pattern of dispersal—shaped by deliberate government policy, the availability of sponsorships, and the relative absence of family ties and previously established ethnic communities in the United States—areas of Indochinese concentration nonetheless began to emerge, particularly in California, and to grow rapidly as a result of secondary migration from other states.

As the much larger waves of Indochinese refugees began to arrive in the late 1970s and especially during the 1980s, their patterns of settlement continued to be shaped by various factors, but they were increasingly influenced by the social networks of family and friends that were becoming consolidated over time. Government policies and programs (such as the Khmer Guided Placement Project, dubbed the "Khmer Refrigerator Project" by Cambodians because of its Frostbelt locations) sought the dispersal of refugees without family ties away from high-impact areas, while most others were reunited with family members already residing in areas of high concentration. Remarkably, by the early 1980s, about a third of arriving refugees already had close relatives in the United States who could serve as sponsors, and another third had more distant relatives, leaving only the remaining third without kinship ties subject to the dispersal policy.

The 1990 U.S. Census showed that, while California is home for 12 percent of the total U.S. population, almost half (46.3%) of all Cambodians (about 70,000) were concentrated there. After California, the largest Cambodian populations are located bi-coastally in Massachusetts (14,000) and Washington (11,000), with other sizable communities in Texas and Pennsylvania (about 6,000 in each state). Despite their comparatively small numbers (almost 4,000), Cambodians are the largest Asian-origin group in Rhode Island.

Within states, different localities of concentration have emerged for the different ethnic groups, with by far the largest Cambodian community developing in the Long Beach area of Los Angeles County. With almost thirty thousand Cambodians residing there in 1990, Long Beach is the capital of Cambodian America, accounting for close to half of California's Cambodian population. Nearly ten thousand more reside just to the south, in the Santa Ana and San Diego areas. In northern California sizable communities have developed as well, including the city of Stockton, site of the 1989 massacre of Cambodian children at the Cleveland Elementary School by Patrick Purdy, a racist drifter who fired more than a hundred rounds from an AK-47 assault rifle into a crowd of children before shooting himself—an incident that severely shook an already traumatized community.

Social and Economic Characteristics

A detailed socioeconomic portrait of the Cambodian population in the United States is sketched in Table 1, drawn from the 1990 U.S. Census, comparing the Cambodians to the total United States and Asian-origin populations. These data in particular underscore the significant differences between the Cambodians and other Asian Americans. While only 8 percent of all Americans in 1990 were foreign-born, two-thirds of all Asian Americans consisted of immigrants. Despite their recent arrival, already one fifth of all Cambodians were born in the United States, reflecting much higher levels of fertility. American women average just under two children ever born per woman aged

TABLE 1 Social and Economic Characteristics of Cambodians in the United States, Compared to the U.S. Population and the Asian-Origin Population, 1990

	Total U.S.	Total Asian	Cambodian
Total Persons	248,709,873	6,876,394	149,047
Nativity and Immigration			
% Born in the United States	92.1	34.4	20.9
% Immigrated pre-1980	4.5	27.9	9.4
% Immigrated 1980–1990	3.5	37.8	69.6
Age			
Median age	33.0	29.2	19.7
Median age (U.S.-born only)	32.5	14.7	4.7
Family Contexts			
Fertility (children per woman)[a]	2.0	1.9	3.4
% Female householder	16.0	11.5	25.4
% with own children under 18 years	48.2	59.2	83.8
% children living with two parents	73.0	84.6	71.0
English (persons over 5)			
% Speak English only	86.2	24.6	4.0
% Does not speak "very well"	6.1	39.8	70.0
% Linguistically isolated[b]	3.5	25.1	54.7
Education (persons over 25)			
% Less than fifth grade	2.7	7.1	40.7
% High school graduate	75.2	77.6	34.9
% College graduate	20.3	37.7	5.7
Employment (persons over 16)			
% In labor force	65.3	67.4	46.5
% Unemployed	6.3	5.2	10.3
Of Those Employed			
% Professionals, managers	26.4	31.2	9.8
% Clerical, sales	31.7	33.3	23.3
% Repair, craft	11.4	7.8	17.2
% Operators, fabricators, laborers	14.9	11.9	30.0
Income			
Median family income ($)	35,225	41,583	18,126
Per capita income ($)	14,420	13,806	5,121
% Below poverty line	13.1	14.0	42.6
% Receives public assistance	7.5	9.8	51.1
% Own home	64.2	48.3	19.7

Source: U.S. Bureau of the Census, *1990 Census of Population: Asians and Pacific Islanders in the United States,* CP-3-5 (1993).

[a]Fertility: children ever born per woman aged 35–44.

[b]Linguistically isolated: a household in which no person age 14 or older speaks English only or very well.

thirty five to forty four (an approximate measure of completed fertility), compared to 3.5 children per woman for the Cambodians. The median age for Cambodians as a whole is less than twenty years, compared to twenty-nine for all Asian Americans and thirty-three for the total U.S. population.

These indicators vividly demonstrate the dynamics of new ethnic group formation through immigration and rapid natural increase, as well as the socioeconomic importance among the Cambodians of families with a high proportion of dependent children. While less than half of all American households have children under age eighteen, more than four-fifths of Cambodian households consist of families with minor children. The structure of their families is a key social context shaping the adaptation of these recently resettled refugees—including their efforts at collective pooling or "patchworking" of economic resources amid constant tension over changing gender roles and intergenerational conflicts. Asian Americans generally exhibit a smaller proportion of single-parent female-headed households than the U.S. norm; the Cambodians' higher level of marital disruption (25%) reflects not divorce but rather the disproportionate presence of many widows whose husbands were killed during the Pol Pot period; one study in San Diego found that more than 20 percent of Cambodian women were widowed.

The socioeconomic disadvantages of the Cambodians are underscored by the census data. Most Cambodians (70%) did not yet speak English "very well"; in fact, more than half of all Cambodian households were classified by the 1990 U.S. Census as "linguistically isolated" (that is, households in which no person age fourteen or older speaks English only or very well). However, children pick up the new language very quickly and without an accent; in one well-known case in Chattanooga, Tennessee, a twelve-year-old Cambodian girl, Linn Yann, placed second in a 1983 regional spelling bee (she missed on "enchilada"); her story was made into a Disney movie for television: "The Girl Who Spelled Freedom."

While 38 percent of all Asian American adults were college graduates—almost double the respective level of attainment of the U.S. adult population (20%)—the Cambodians are much less educated on average. According to the 1990 U.S. Census, only one in twenty had a college degree, only a third were high school graduates, and 40 percent had less than a fifth-grade education, reflecting their rural origins and modest backgrounds. A high level of prior education among the adults, it turns out, is the strongest predictor of good English ability, followed by a young age and a long length of residence in the United States. Still, significant strides are being made by Cambodian students. Despite initial language handicaps, the academic grade point average of Cambodian high school students has significantly exceeded that of majority white students in Cali-

A Cambodian woman in Santa Rosa, California, prepares the spices necessary for cooking a meal. (Eric Crystal)

fornia; increasing numbers are enrolling in college; and organizations such as the United Cambodian Students of America, founded at California State University at Long Beach, have over the years developed an impressive national-level reach, focusing on educational and community development activities and networks.

Relative to the U.S. population in the 1990 U.S. Census, Asian Americans as a whole showed higher rates of labor force participation, lower unemployment, and a greater percentage of professionals and managers among those employed. But as Table 1 shows, the profile for the Cambodians was precisely the opposite in each of these indicators; less than half were in the labor force (with

51 percent receiving public assistance), unemployment rates were twice as high, and employed Cambodians were twice as likely to have unskilled or semiskilled jobs as operators, fabricators, and laborers. While their level of self-employment remains significantly below those for other Asian Americans and the U.S. population, Cambodian entrepreneurs (who tend to be of Chinese ancestry) have carved out, like other immigrants before them, special niches in the economy. Doughnuts are the most notable example; by the mid-1990s Cambodians ran more than 80 percent of California's doughnut shops.

Family and per capita incomes and rates of homeownership among the Cambodians, as detailed in Table 1, ranked among the lowest in the United States. The poverty rate for Cambodians was more than three times higher than for the general population, and the disparity in welfare dependency rates was even greater (both of these are among the highest rates in the country). Concern over medical-care coverage is often a decisive consideration for large refugee families who continue to remain on public assistance (including Medicaid); although it keeps them below the poverty line, the situation is preferable to the risk of low-wage jobs that provide no health-care insurance at all. Cambodian refugees interviewed in San Diego in the 1980s, for example, referred to their MediCal stickers (as Medicaid is called in California) as being "more valuable than gold." By comparison, poverty rates for the total U.S. and Asian American populations were about the same (13 to 14%), with fewer than a tenth of households relying on public assistance. The diversity of these socioeconomic profiles underlines the widely different social origins, age and family composition, and modes of incorporation of Asian-origin immigrants and refugees, as well as the inaccuracy of "model minority" stereotypes.

Mental Health and the Refugee Experience

Census data, while valuable, are limited in the kind of information they can provide. Table 2 presents other evidence to illuminate aspects of the Cambodian experience that are missing from census and other official data, such as the refugees' educational, occupational, and religious backgrounds in their country of origin, along with their migration experiences and mental health status. The data are drawn from a large-scale study in the San Diego metropolitan area, one of the principal places of settlement for Indochinese refugee groups. The respondents, a representative sample of men and women ranging in age from eighteen to seventy one, were interviewed at length in their native languages in the mid-1980s.

A distinction often made between refugees and other classes of immigrants revolves around their different motives for migration and the traumatic nature of their flight experiences. Refugees are said to be motivated to flee by fear of persecution ("political" motives), while immigrants are defined by their aspirations for better material opportunities and self-advancement ("economic" motives). However, when the Indochinese refugees in the San Diego study were asked to state all of their motives for leaving the homeland, more than fifty different reasons were given, ranging from fear of repression or imprisonment in reeducation camps, to past associations with the former regime and ideological opposition to communism, to desires for family reunification, better education for their children, and an improved standard of living. The reasons reported by the Cambodians reflected their life-threatening experiences during the holocaust of the late 1970s.

Some of the extraordinarily stressful exit experiences of the refugees are detailed in Table 2. Most feared they would be killed during their escape. The Cambodians suffered the greatest number of family loss and violence events, followed by the Hmong and the Vietnamese. Once they reached a country of first asylum, the Hmong stayed in refugee camps far longer than any other group before being resettled in the United States (almost three years on average), followed by the Cambodians (more than two years on average), and then the Chinese and the Vietnamese (less than a year on average). Taken together, such

Table 2 Social Background and Migration Experiences of Cambodians and Other Southeast Asian Refugee Groups in San Diego County

	Ethnic Group			
	Cambodian	Hmong	Vietnamese	Chinese
Educational Background				
% High school graduate	13.3	2.8	47.1	19.3
% Never attended school	23.3	67.9	1.9	12.3
% Knew some English	5.8	1.8	39.5	13.2
% Rural background	55.0	89.9	5.1	4.4
Occupational Background				
% Professional/Managerial	5.3	3.0	25.6	11.2
% Military	15.9	31.3	25.6	6.1
% Sales	14.2	2.0	18.8	38.8
% Blue Collar	8.0	2.0	10.5	27.6
% Farming, Fishing	54.0	59.6	10.5	14.3
Religion				
% Buddhist	66.7	4.6	49.0	56.1
% Ancestor Worship	0.8	46.8	12.1	20.2
% Catholic	4.2	10.1	23.6	0.9
% Christian, other	15.8	16.5	2.5	4.4
% No religion	4.2	8.3	10.8	14.0
Migration Events				
% Fled without family	29.2	19.3	13.4	11.4
% Gave bribes to exit	19.3	21.3	32.7	71.7
% Feared would be killed	80.7	92.7	73.2	73.7
% Assaulted in escape	25.2	25.7	30.6	36.8
% Cannot contact family (whereabouts unknown)	61.7	12.8	3.8	12.3
# Violence events in exit	3.1	2.5	2.1	1.9
# Years in refugee camps	2.1	2.9	0.6	0.9
Health and Mental Health				
% Poor or fair health	49.2	26.6	32.5	30.7
% Sleep problems	55.8	61.5	21.7	23.9
% Appetite problems	42.5	22.0	14.6	11.4
% Positive well-being	15.0	35.5	50.6	31.0
% Demoralization, moderate	46.7	34.6	28.8	43.4
% Demoralization, severe	38.2	29.9	20.5	25.7

Source: Rubén G. Rumbaut. (1989). "Portraits, Patterns, and Predictors of the Refugee Adaptation Process." In *Refugees as Immigrants: Cambodians, Laotians, and Vietnamese in America*, edited by D. W. Haines. Totowa, NJ: Rowman & Littlefield.

differences in the migration events experienced by these refugee groups help explain why the Cambodians and the Hmong had a significantly higher number of chronic health problems (physical symptoms lasting six months or longer) whose onset occurred between their exit from their homeland and their arrival in the United States.

The measure of mental health status reported in Table 2 was used by the National Center for Health Statistics in a major national survey of the general American adult population. It found that 74 percent of Americans scored in the "positive well-being" range, 16 percent in the "moderate demoralization" range, and 9.6 percent in the "severe demoralization" range (indicative of "clinically significant distress"). But the respective prevalence rates for the Indochinese refugees were 34 percent for "positive well-being," 38 percent for "moderate demoralization," and 28 percent for "severe demoralization." That latter figure was three times the level of severe distress found for the general American population. The demoralization rates were highest for the Cambodians—who had experienced the most traumatic contexts of exit—followed by the Hmong, Chinese, and Vietnamese. Other studies throughout the United States confirm that Cambodian refugees have exhibited higher prevalence rates of depressive symptomatology than have been found for other American ethnic groups and that Cambodian refugees have had to confront chronic mental health problems, such as posttraumatic stress disorder, flashbacks, and recurrent nightmares.

The process of psychological adaptation is temporally patterned. The first several months after arrival in the United States tend to be a relatively hopeful and even euphoric period, but during the second year, a period of "exile shock," depressive symptoms reach their highest levels, followed by a phase of psychological recovery after the third year. The general pattern was described succinctly by an elderly Cambodian widow:

> I was feeling great the first few months. But then, after that, I started to face all kinds of worries and sadness. I started to see the real thing of the United States, and I missed home more and more. I missed everything about our country: people, family, relatives and friends, way of life, everything. Then, my spirit started to go down; I lost sleep; my physical health weakened; and there started the stressful and depressing times. But now [almost three years after arrival] I feel kind of better, a lot better! Knowing my sons are in school as their father would have wanted, and doing well, makes me feel more secure. [Rumbaut, 1995, p. 260].

The San Diego study found that, over time, the effect of pre-arrival stressors receded, and current difficulties (primarily being unemployed) emerged as stronger predictors of depressive symptoms. Past losses and events seemed to heal with time and recede in importance as present demands and challenges grew in psychological significance. Over time, as their frames of reference change, the "refugees" generally become more like "immigrants."

See also: CHAM; LAO; VIETNAMESE

Bibliography

Becker, E. (1986). *When the War Was Over: Cambodia's Revolution and the Voices of Its People*. New York: Simon & Schuster.

Haines, D. W., ed. (1989). *Refugees as Immigrants: Cambodians, Laotians, and Vietnamese in America*. Totowa, NJ: Rowman & Littlefield.

Hein, J. (1995). *From Vietnam, Laos, and Cambodia: A Refugee Experience in the United States*. New York: Twayne.

Isaacs, A. R. (1983). *Without Honor: Defeat in Vietnam and Cambodia*. Baltimore, MD: Johns Hopkins University Press.

Ngor, H., with Warner, R. (1987). *A Cambodian Odyssey*. New York: Macmillan.

Portes, A., and Rumbaut, R. G. (1996). *Immigrant America: A Portrait*, 2nd edition. Berkeley: University of California Press.

Rumbaut, R. G. (1989). "The Structure of Refuge: Southeast Asian Refugees in the United States, 1975–1985." *International Review of Comparative Public Policy* 1:97–129.

Rumbaut, R. G. (1991). "The Agony of Exile: A Study of Indochinese Refugee Adults and Children." In *Refugee Children: Theory, Research, and Services*, edited by F. L. Ahearn Jr. and J. L. Athey. Baltimore, MD: Johns Hopkins University Press.

Rumbaut, R. G. (1994). "The Crucible Within: Ethnic Identity, Self-Esteem, and Segmented Assimilation Among Children of Immigrants." *International Migration Review* 28(4):748–794.

Rumbaut, R. G. (1995). "Vietnamese, Laotian, and Cambodian Americans." In *Asian Americans: Contemporary Trends and Issues*, edited by P. G. Min. Thousand Oaks, CA: Sage Publications.

Rumbaut, R. G., and Ima, K. (1988). *The Adaptation of Southeast Asian Refugee Youth: A Comparative Study*. Washington, DC: U.S. Office of Refugee Resettlement.

Rumbaut, R. G., and Weeks, J. R. (1989). "Infant Health Among Indochinese Refugees: Patterns of Infant Mortality, Birthweight, and Prenatal Care in Comparative Perspective." *Research in the Sociology of Health Care* 8:137–196.

Shawcross, W. (1977). *Sideshow: Kissinger, Nixon, and the Destruction of Cambodia*. New York: Pocket Books.

Shawcross, W. (1984). *The Quality of Mercy: Cambodia, Holocaust, and Modern Conscience.* New York: Simon & Schuster.

Weleratna, U. (1993). *Beyong the Killing Fields: Voices of Nine Cambodian Survivors in America.* Stanford, CA: Stanford University Press.

RUBÉN G. RUMBAUT

CANADIANS

To define a Canadian is not only complicated but also has changed in recent years. Before 1776, Canadian identity was like that of the United States, determined by the principle of land. Residing in Canadian territory and swearing allegiance to the Canadian government was the basis of claiming Canadian identity. However, with pressure from the Thirteen Colonies and as a result of the American Revolution, concessions were made to keep Quebec in the British Empire. The result was the creation of two groups of Canadians: French Canadians and British Canadians. However, the overall trend in Canada up to 1971 was one of conformity to Anglo culture and society.

Due to immigration, however, other ethnic communities have become more prominent numerically, so that by the mid-1960s a "third force" had developed in Canadian politics, composed of aboriginals as well as Asian and European ethnic communities. They demanded rights and recognition for their contribution to Canadian society. As a result, the Liberal Party, under Prime Minister Pierre Elliott Trudeau, unveiled a policy of multiculturalism in 1971 whereby the participation of all ethnic communities was advocated. Ethnic diversity was promoted to allow each individual to choose his or her cultural preference while respecting the rights of others. In other words, a pluralistic society was advocated where the central government promoted and provided financial support for ethnic communities to promote their distinctive cultural heritage, including language maintenance. Canada embarked on a policy that rejected the idea of a cultural monolith or a melting pot framework and opted for a pluralistic society where the patchwork quilt analogy would be the guiding principle.

The result is that Canadian identity is becoming a compound entity wherein an individual is a Chinese Canadian or a Ukrainian Canadian. Thus Canadian identity is not a monolith based on land or genetic ancestry. Canadian identity encompasses a variety of cultures based on both land and genetic ancestry, all under a unifying ideology of mutual respect and tolerance. One caveat, however, is that the British and French are still considered more Canadian than the other groups. In the 1980 and 1990 U.S. Censuses, Canada is the third largest supplier of immigrants to the United States; yet those claiming Canadian ancestry in the 1990 U.S. Census are not even ranked in the top thirty-three, except for French Canadians, who rank seventeenth.

In spite of the facts that Canadians tend to identify with their provinces over the central government and that more than a third of the Canadian population is neither French nor British, descriptions of Canadian culture focus primarily on British Canadians. Thus, works such as Seymour Lipset's *Continental Divide* describe Canadian culture in general as being in the middle of a hypothetical continuum with Britain at one extreme and the United States at the other. More specifically, Canadians are less suspicious of centralized government than are the people of the United States. Whereas people of the United States emphasize the concepts of "life, liberty, and the pursuit of happiness," Canadians focus on "peace, order, and good government." The people of the United States reject church establishment in their government; Canadians do not. Along with these differences, there is a strong animosity among people in Canada toward the influence and penetration of U.S. economic and cultural influence.

Immigration and Settlement History

Between 1820 and 1860, European immigration to North America was extensive — five million entered the United States, and additional millions went to Australia, Latin America, Africa, and Canada. During this time and later, Canada was not only a receiving nation but a sending one as well, for many entrants would leave it for the United States. Thus, there were and still are two types of emigrants from Canada: those born in Canada and who immigrated to the United States, and those who immigrated to Canada and then emigrated from Canada to the United States, the later process termed "second immigration."

During most of the nineteenth century, Western Europe experienced radical economic downturns. People emigrated because leaving for a new land was their only viable option. The British government encouraged British immigration to Canada—Britain wanted to counter French influence with immigrants from Britain. Thus low fares were inducements to encourage Britishers to immigrate to Canada. However, some, such as the Irish, were distrustful of the British government and moved on to the United States. Thus, in the early years, Canada was not only a stepping-stone to the United States, it also was the cheapest way for Britishers, and some others, to enter the United States, because crossing the St. Lawrence River to the United States was free.

When U.S. laws in 1924 restricted immigration, exceptions were made for the Americas; thus no restrictions were placed on Canadians immigrating to the United States. As a result, Canada remained a stepping-stone for immigration to the United States.

There were no reliable statistics kept before the 1910 U.S. Census and the 1911 Canadian Census. However, it is known now that emigration from Canada to the United States has been seasonal—older Canadians go to Florida or Arizona for the winter. To support this view, the 1990 U.S. Census revealed that 30 percent of the Canadians in the United States were sixty-five or older. Movement between the two countries was relatively unrestricted until changes in U.S. immigration laws in 1965 and changes in the Canadian legislation in 1976. In the early twentieth century, 1.2 million Canadians entered the United States,

which was four times the number of people moving from the United States to Canada. The year 1920 was a record one, with almost a million Canadians entering the United States. In 1930, the Canadian population in the United States peaked at 1.3 million. Due to the Depression and World War II, emigration from Canada declined, but it increased in the 1950s and early 1960s. Tightened U.S. immigration laws implemented in the 1960s and 1970s caused Canadian immigration to drop by 60 percent—a decline that continued through the 1980s.

Demography

According to the 1990 U.S. Census, a little over 500,000, or 0.2 percent of the U.S. population, claim Canadian ancestry—a definition that excludes Newfoundland, Nova Scotia, and French Canadians. The highest concentration is in the northeastern United States, but the state with the highest single-state number is California, with 86,341. Massachusetts ranks second, with 66,007, and New York is third, with 45,274. In general, those who immigrated before 1960 live in northern states, while those who arrived later live farther south.

Language

Since Canada instituted its policy of multiculturalism, the central government has encouraged different ethnic communities to have language classes and keep their linguistic heritage alive in Canada. However, French and English are the official languages. In Canada, about 60 percent speak English and 24 percent speak French, with 16 percent speaking Italian, Chinese, German, Portuguese, Polish, or Ukrainian.

Since the majority of Canadian immigrants are bilingual, most have no linguistic problems when settling in the United States, which is also true for French Canadians, Acadians, Tilingit, and other groups that originate in Canada but have separate classifications. These groups often identify with their individual ethnic community in the United

States, rather than with a general Canadian community. As a result, language maintenance programs are organized according to the needs of the respective ethnic groups.

Cultural Characteristics

The economic patterns of Canadians entering the United States depends on the time. In the early twentieth century, Canadians worked in American industries, with about 60 percent in highly skilled jobs—a number that has been growing since the 1950s. In the middle twentieth century, Canadian-born immigrants tended to settle in the Northeast, Florida, and California. In New England, many French Canadians were brought in as bricklayers or to work in cotton mills. Others were temporary workers who returned to Canada in winter. Their presence was debated, for they were perceived as strike breakers accepting low wages and poor working conditions; thus business leaders and staff defended them, while unions and laborers argued against them.

Beginning in the 1960s, the majority of Canadians settling in the United States were professionals, skilled artisans, technicians, managers, salespeople, or service workers. Newer positions being filled by Canadians are classified as clerical, professional, executive administrative, and managerial. In the latter two categories, the figures are higher than for the U.S. average.

Housing and residence patterns for Canadians are not distinctive. Generally, they maintain a nuclear residence pattern, with parents and children in the same dwelling. In the United States, being Canadian is subservient to identity based on ethnicity. For example, immigrants from Canada who claim Ukrainian origins will tend to associate, and some may live in Ukrainian neighborhoods. But generally Canadians in the United States do not tend to maintain ethnic or social boundaries based on Canadian identity.

Religion has traditionally been a major building block of Canadian society. The Roman Catholic and Anglican churches dominate, while there is substantial representations by the United Church of Canada as well as by the Jewish, Muslim, Evangelical Lutheran, and Pentecostal faiths. The names may change, such as Anglican being Episcopalian, but the beliefs and rituals are similar.

The worldview of Canadians has distinct differences from those prevalent in the United States. Being Canadian does not imply a monolithic identity but encompasses many different groups. There is a greater acceptance of hierarchy in the society, whereas the people of the United States espouse equality, whether it is actually practiced or not. Also, Canadians are less distrustful of central authority than people in the United States. However, there are negative feelings concerning the strong economic and cultural influence the United States has on Canada. However, Canadians perceive of Canada as an international player, but this has been done by being active in the United Nations. They have focused on gaining influence by means other than using military and economic power.

Concerning marriage, 58.9 percent of the Canadian females in the United States more than fifteen years of age are married, which is close to the average in Canada. However, twice as many Canadian Americans are divorced (6.8%) as compared to those in Canada (3.1%). Also, twice as many Canadian-American women are widowed (20.5%) than in Canada, which indicates the elderly position of the Canadian-American population.

There are no documented health problems unique to Canadian immigrants to the United States. However, for those Canadians who are used to the public health system, the cost of medical services in the United States is shocking. Because the American system is more lucrative for physicians, however, some medical personnel have left Canada for the higher salaries south of the border.

Canadian Americans have had little involvement in U.S. politics. The major exception was Jerry Simpson, who served three terms in Congress as a Populist Party representative. Canadians have been more active in labor movements. Some of the international unions with the largest Canadian participation are the United Steel Workers of

America, the United Food and Commercial Workers International Union, the International Association of Machinists and Aerospace Workers, and the Brotherhood of Electrical Workers. Of course, these unions have locals in Canada, but immigrants from Canada continue participation when they arrive in the United States.

Statistics on Canadian immigrants are lacking because Canadians tend to identify with their genealogical origins. For example, French Canadians unite as a unit, and Italians immigrating from Canada identify with Italian associations in the United States over organizations concerned purely with Canadian issues.

As is clear from the above, cultural behavior of immigrants from Canada to the United States is not monolithic. Their identification with an ethnic community is of the highest priority, followed by region of residence in Canada. An overall Canadian identity is present, but it is generally described according to the cultural framework of British Canadians.

Assimilation and Cultural Persistence

Although there is variation according to ethnic origins and place of residence in Canada, assimilation to the United States is very easy. There is generally no language barrier, the two countries are close neighbors, and many people cross back and forth across the border. In addition, many U.S. citizens live in Canada. And the Canadian immigrating to the United States is not only close to home, but also has easy access to his home in Canada. Therefore, the assimilation of Canadians to life in the United States is probably the easiest of almost any community.

See also: ACADIANS AND CAJUNS; FRENCH CANADIANS

Bibliography

Doran, C. E., and Babby, E. R., eds. (1995). *Annals of the American Academy of Political and Social Science,* Vol. 538: *Being and Becoming Canada.* Thousand Oaks, CA: Sage Publications.

Ducharme, J. (1943). *The Shadow of the Trees: Story of French Canadians in New England.* New York: Harper & Brothers.

Fleras, A., and Elliott, J. L. (1992). *Multiculturalism in Canada: The Challenge of Diversity.* Scarborough, ON: Nelson Canada.

Gould, D. M. (1991). *Immigrant Links to the Home Country: Empirical Implications for U.S. and Canadian Trade Flows.* Dallas: Federal Reserve Bank of Dallas.

Hansen, M. L., and Brebner, J. B. ([1940], 1970). *The Mingling of the Canadian and American People.* New York: Arno Press.

International Seminar on North American History (1989). *From "Melting Pot" to Multiculturalism: The Evolution of Ethnic Relations in the United States and Canada.* Rome: Bulzoni Editora.

Keats, R. (1993). *The Border Guide: The Canadian Guide to Investment, Immigration, Tax, and Retirement in the United States.* Windsor, ON: Ontario Motorist Publications.

Lines, K. (1977). *Canadian and British Immigration to the United States Since 1920.* Ph.D. diss., University of Hawaii.

Lipset, S. M. (1990). *Continental Divide: The Values and Institutions of the United States and Canada.* New York: Routledge.

Marchand, S. A. (1943). *Arcadian Exiles in the Golden Coast of Louisiana.* New Haven, CT: Yale University Library.

Parker, J. H. (1983). *Ethnic Identity: The Case of the French Americans.* Washington, DC: University Press of America.

Samuel, T. J. (1969). *The Migration of Canadian-Born Between Canada and the United States of America.* Ottawa: Research Branch, Program Development Service, Department of Manpower and Immigration.

Schwab, J. G. (1979). "Migration Between Canada and the United States with Particular Reference to Professional and Intellectual Classes." M.A. thesis, McGill University.

Truesdell, E. (1943). *The Canadian-Born in the United States.* New Haven, CT: Yale University Press.

Wright, C. D. (1882). *The Canadian French in New England.* Boston: Rand, Avery.

ARTHUR W. HELWEG

CAPE VERDEANS

The inhabitants of the Cape Verde Islands (a crescent-shaped Atlantic archipelago approximately 350 miles off the west coast of Senegal) who have immigrated to the United States constitute a little-known racial-ethnic group known as Cape Verdean Americans. Though relatively small in number, these Afro-Portuguese settlers are of particular significance as the only major group of Americans to have made the transatlantic voyage from Africa to the United States on their own initiative.

Most historians agree that the Cape Verde Islands were uninhabited until the mid-fifteenth century, when Portuguese explorers landed there. Almost from the very beginning of settlement, West African slaves were brought to the Cape Verdes, initially to labor on sugar and cotton plantations, but the arid climate of these Sahelian islands prevented truly successful commercial cultivation of the land. What soon became more important to the Portuguese than agricultural production was the strategic location of the archipelago as a crossroads in the expanding slave trade. Situated near the Guinea coast and on the trade winds route to Brazil, the islands served as an entrepôt for the distribution of goods, for supplying foreign vessels with needed supplies and salt, and for transporting slaves to the New World.

As these exchanges were taking place, the sparse Portuguese population intermingled with the greater numbers of West Africans to produce a rich and distinctive society and culture.

In this mesh of African ancestry, Catholicism, and Western presence, it has not always been possible to discern whether the European or the African influence predominates. Rather, the interweaving has been so complete that it is most appropriate to speak of the evolution of a separate culture with its own distinctive customs, folklore, cuisine, music, literature, and finally, language. Though based on Portuguese and several West African languages, the mother tongue of the Cape Verdean people is a full-fledged, creolized language of its own, called Crioulo. Although varying in dialect from one island to another, Crioulo has become a defining feature of the Cape Verdean cultural identity that has been transplanted to the United States and other parts of the world.

The Cape Verde Islands have always been plagued by scanty and erratic rainfall, and the effects of the dry climate there were exacerbated by colonial mismanagement of the land, so that by the end of the eighteenth century the people of the islands experienced severe and recurrent drought, with its resulting famine and high mortality. Unable to escape overland to more favorable conditions, the young Cape Verdeans seized the chance to leave home in search of a better life as crew aboard U.S. whaling ships that were beginning to arrive at the archipelago's protected harbors, particularly on the island of Brava.

Especially as American seamen began to lose interest in whaling due to decreasing profits in the industry, the ship captains looked to the Cape Verde Islands to recruit hands who could be paid less money than their American counterparts. At the same time, because of the impoverished conditions, the men of the archipelago were eager to obtain a berth on a whaler, no matter what the pay, to escape the constant suffering. The Cape Verdean seamen earned a reputation as disciplined and able crews. Despite their skill as whalers, however, they were routinely allotted the lowest rates in the division of profits and were frequently subject to harsh treatment in the mariners' hierarchy because of discrimination based on race and ethnicity. Their exploitation at sea foreshadowed a similar prejudice they would face once the immigrants began to settle more permanently in the United States.

By the late nineteenth century, with the advent of steamship travel and the decline of the whaling and sealing industries, the old sailing vessels had become obsolete and were available at very low cost. Some of the early Cape Verdean immigrants took advantage of this opportunity to buy these old Essex-built "Gloucester Fishermen." They pooled their resources and converted them into cargo and passenger ships, used as packet boats that regularly plied between the Cape Verdes and the ports of New Bedford, Massachusetts, and Providence, Rhode Island. With the purchase of a sixty-four-ton fishing schooner, the Nellie May, Antonio Coelho became the first Cape Verdean–American packet owner. He hired a former whaleman as captain and set sail for Brava in 1892. Before long, Cape Verdean–American settlers came to own a fleet of these vessels. Thus, in a situation unlike that of most immigrant groups, the Cape Verdeans had control over their own means of passage to the United States.

During this same period, cheap sources of labor were being sought for the expanding textile mills, in the cranberry bogs, and in the maritime-related occupations of southern coastal New England. Increasing numbers, including women and children, arrived to fill the demand, fleeing their land of continual hunger. The movement continued steadily until the enforcement of the restrictive immigration laws of the early 1920s, which curtailed the influx.

Demography and Patterns of Immigration

As a by-product of a society organized on the basis of a rigid binary racial structure, official government records such as those compiled by the U.S. Census or the Bureau of Immigration have been hopelessly deficient regarding multiracial populations such as the Cape Verdeans. Entrenched standards of "black" and "white" formed the basis of classification when Cape Verdeans began arriving in larger numbers during the latter part of the nineteenth century. Routinely grouped under other broader categories, those looking phenotypically most European or "white" were listed as "Portuguese," while the remainder were grouped under the labels of "black Portuguese," "African Portuguese," or "Atlantic Islanders." Many of the Cape Verdean immigrants did not at first identify themselves as hailing from the Cape Verde Islands. Rather, they were more likely to see themselves as natives of their particular island of origin, (e.g., Bravas or Fogos).

Like other immigrants who do not fall readily within the dualistic confines of the U.S. system of racial classification, official population records have been completely inadequate in providing accurate demographic data on the Cape Verdeans. However, analysis of information recorded on the packet ship passenger lists has made it possible to calculate solid estimates of the numbers of Cape Verdean entrants and to construct a population profile of this group. Between 1820 and 1975, some 35,000 to 45,000 Cape Verdeans immigrated to the United States, with the islands of Brava and Fogo providing more than 60 percent of the newcomers. In the years of the heaviest inflow, between 1880 and 1920, the overwhelming majority were male migrants (83.4%). After the islands became an independent nation in 1975, an average of 900 arrivals entered annually, thanks to the continued liberal immigration policy of the United States. In 1995, the estimated number of Cape Verdeans and their descendants living in the United States stood at 350,000, slightly more than the total population of the home country itself.

Because of the packet trade, transatlantic passage was readily available for both new immigrants and return visitors, facilitating a significant flow of remittances, communication, and cultural exchanges between New England and the islands. At its height, three varying patterns of immigration had emerged. One common pattern was to make at least one return trip, perhaps to marry a girl from home or to arrange to bring other family members back to New England. The immigrant then returned to the United States, having made a more conscious decision to permanently relocate. Another scenario was that of temporary residence in the United States, when the original intention to return to Cape Verde after several years' working abroad was realized. Finally, there was a certain amount of shuttling back and forth, particularly among cranberry and maritime workers. The packet trade enabled seasonal cranberry pickers who would finish the harvest in late fall to return on the last boats out of New Bedford in November so they could spend the winter in Cape Verde. Between 1900 and 1920, one out of three arrivals had

Immigrants on the Savoia (which included 155 passengers and 28 crew) arrive in New Bedford, Massachusetts, on October 5, 1914, from Fogo Island. (Old Dartmouth Historical Society, New Bedford Whaling Museum)

traveled to the United States more than once. The connection between the Cape Verdean–American community and the Cape Verdes was so strong and transportation back and forth so accessible that the typical immigrant, upon leaving for the United States, was not required to make a final commitment to resettlement. This eased the anguish of separation, but it also slowed the process of setting down new roots.

Cape Verdeans are still primarily concentrated in southeastern New England, with the city of New Bedford remaining the hub of the Cape Verdean–American community. Significant proportions of the residents in the cranberry district on upper Cape Cod are also of Cape Verdean descent. However, Pawtucket, Rhode Island, and the areas around the cities of Brockton and Scituate, Massachusetts, have drawn larger numbers of the post-1975 influx

of new immigrants. When Cape Verdeans do migrate out of New England, they tend to follow the patterns of other Portuguese settlers and thus are also clustered in California, especially in the Sacramento area.

Employment

Contrary to the popular images of local Yankee families embarking on a Sunday's outing of cranberry picking, the cranberry industry early began to require a large and intensive agricultural work force, particularly during the autumn cranberry harvest. Italians, Poles, and Finns all provided the necessary labor in turn, but by 1910, Cape Verdean immigrants completely dominated the harvest. Approximately one-quarter of the total arriving immigrants listed Plymouth County, the heart of the cranberry district, as their intended destination. Most originated from the island of Fogo. Although the economic success of the cranberry industry became completely dependent on their labors, very few became owners of these productive bogs. For the most part, the bogworkers remained seasonal laborers, residing off-season in nearby urban areas. All of the hardships characteristic of migrant labor were experienced by the Cape Verdean pickers. Yet, in comparison to adaptation to factory work, to congested city life, and to unemployment and discrimination in employment, the weeks of the cranberry harvest were a welcome change for many. Not only were these former peasants able to work the land again, but also the wages that one could accumulate during a good season would be sufficient to take them through the cold winter months, with extra to send back to the old country or, in some cases, to make the return trip themselves.

Women also worked the bogs and were the primary labor force to harvest Cape Cod strawberries during the spring picking. Because of discrimination based on race and gender, Cape Verdean immigrant women were rarely employed in the local cotton mills, and thus, contributed to the family economy through berry picking in the rural areas and through domestic service in the homes of wealthier families in the cities. Their male counterparts were also confined to unskilled labor, particularly in maritime-related occupations such as seamen on merchant vessels, longshoremen, riggers, and dockside construction workers. When the factories did employ Cape Verdean immigrants, they usually held the most menial positions.

There were exceptions to this pattern of manual and seasonal labor, however. A few of the Cape Verde Islanders were able to purchase wetlands and convert them into cranberry bogs. These are the primary success stories of this immigrant group. Brought up as peasants on the islands, their connection to the land has endured. At the same time, with the cranberry industry still booming well into the end of the twentieth century, they have been able to achieve economic security. Their children may not choose to stay in the cranberry

business, but they typically go on to college and achieve middle-class occupations. This is no small feat, particularly in a society where people of color who have worked the land have traditionally been able to do so only as slaves, tenants, or sharecroppers, not as proprietors, and have otherwise been ghettoized in the larger cities.

Ethnic Identity

The Cape Verdean settlers brought with them a distinctive cultural identity, immigrating freely to New England as Portuguese colonials, thereby initially defining themselves in terms of ethnicity. However, because of their mixed African and European ancestry, they were looked upon and treated as an inferior racial group. Although the Cape Verdeans sought recognition as Portuguese Americans, white society, including the other Portuguese immigrants, excluded them from their social and religious associations. They suffered similar discrimination in housing and employment. At the same time, the Cape Verdeans chose not to identify with American blacks. Their Catholicism tended to keep them apart from the primarily Protestant African-American population, but, more powerfully, they quickly perceived the adverse effects of racism on the upward mobility of anyone considered nonwhite in the United States.

One noteworthy exception to this pattern is illustrated by the life of the flamboyant and charismatic evangelist leader "Sweet Daddy" Grace, perhaps the most famous Cape Verdean American immigrant. Founder of the United House of Prayer for All People, by the late 1930s, he had established hundreds of these Protestant congregations throughout the United States, with an estimated 500,000 followers, primarily African Americans. In the process he amassed hundreds of thousands of dollars, and by 1952 *Ebony* magazine called him "America's richest Negro minister." On the subject of race, Sweet Daddy declared, "I am a colorless man. I am a colorless bishop. Sometimes I am black, sometimes white. I preach to all races." Born Marceline Manoël da Graça in 1881 he sailed at age nineteen from his native island of Brava to

New Bedford. Among the bishop's many teachings was the singular claim that along with his own immigration, God, too, first arrived in America in 1900.

For the Cape Verdeans, the method of distinguishing them from the moment of their arrival in the United States on the basis of racial characteristics rather than their place of birth or last residence was the beginning of a pattern to which the newcomers would have to adjust repeatedly in the course of their settlement in the United States. As early as 1924, the leaders of the Cape Verdean community in New Bedford began to prefer the designation of Cape Verdean rather than being classed as Portuguese and certainly as an alternative to being known as black Portuguese. This marked the beginning of the long-standing pursuit by various members of the Cape Verdean–American community over the years to be recognized by the wider society as a distinct ethnic group with a specific cultural heritage. Not until many years later, on the 1980 U.S. Census forms, was it possible for Cape Verdean Americans to officially identify themselves as such.

As is characteristic of other nonwhite immigrants to the United States, issues of identity among the Cape Verdeans are ever-evolving and complex matters. Confusion about identification crops up often in literature about and by Cape Verdeans. Neither black nor white, but sometimes white, at other times black, African, Portuguese, brown, even labeled green by one reporter who took literally the translation of Cape Verde, this is a population continually in the process of redefining its identity. And it is not simply a matter of changing self-definitions. In terms of successful adaptation, how they are defined by others often has had greater social and economic significance than how they see themselves.

During World War II, service in the military was often a critical juncture for many Cape Verdean–American men of enlistment age. Joining the armed forces meant a first step out of the protective shelter of their local communities in southern New England and brought them face to face with the existence of segregated troops and a wider society that did not know or care about the ethnic identity of a Cape Verdean. Most were sent to black regiments, where they were forced to deal directly with the issue of race, both in terms of the racist treatment they received in the military and in having to confront the question of their own racial identification. Some were assigned to white units, where they were not accepted either. For those stationed with white troops in the southern states, it was especially painful to try to come to terms with the ambiguity of their own ethnic and racial background and the rigid racial barriers of their surroundings.

The 1960s were also watershed years for Cape Verdean Americans as the rise of black nationalism and its attendant emphasis on pride in one's African heritage had a transformative effect on many. The domestic social changes coincided with the struggles for liberation from Portuguese colonialism on the continent of Africa as well. At the time, the Cape Verde Islands, under the great revolutionary leader Amilcar Cabral, in collaboration with the Portuguese colony of Guinea-Bissau, were engaged in a protracted armed conflict to procure their independence. They did find some support for their cause among Cape Verdean Americans but there was also much resistance to the idea of Cape Verde breaking its long-standing ties with Portugal and switching to an African-identified political and cultural ideology. The process of rethinking racial identifications touched most Cape Verdean–American families in this period, often creating intergenerational rifts between parents and grandparents, who were staunchly Portuguese, and their children, who were beginning to ally themselves with the African-American struggle not only in political thought but also in cultural expression.

Shortly after gaining its independence in 1975, the Republic of Cape Verde presented the United States with the gift of the schooner Ernestina, the last Cape Verdean packet boat in existence. In 1986, at the tall ships celebration of the Statue of Liberty centennial, the vessel took its place at the front of the flotilla, in recognition of its unique history as the only surviving ship in the parade that had carried immigrants to the United States.

See also: AFRICAN AMERICANS; PORTUGUESE

Bibliography

Beck, S. (1992). *Manny Almeida's Ringside Lounge: The Cape Verdeans' Struggle for Their Neighborhood.* Providence, RI: Gavea-Brown.

Busch, B. C. (1985). "Cape Verdeans in the American Whaling and Sealing Industry, 1850–1900." *American Neptune* 45(2): 104–16.

Carreira, A. (1982). *The People of the Cape Verde Islands: Exploitation and Emigration,* trans. by Christopher Fyfe. Hamden, CT: Archon Books.

Cohn, M., and Platzer, M. K. (1978). *Black Men of the Sea.* New York: Dodd, Mead.

Ellen, M. M., ed. (1988). *Across the Atlantic: An Anthology of Cape Verdean Literature.* North Dartmouth, MA: Center for the Portuguese-Speaking World, University of Massachusetts.

Halter, M. (1993). *Between Race and Ethnicity: Cape Verdean American Immigrants, 1860–1965.* Urbana: University of Illinois Press.

Hayden, R. C. (1993). *African-Americans and Cape Verdean-Americans in New Bedford: A History of Community and Achievement.* Boston: Select Publications.

Lobban, R. A. (1995). *Cape Verde: Crioulo Colony to Independent Nation.* Boulder, CO: Westview Press.

Lobban, R.; Coli, W.; Connor, C.; Guglielmo, C.; Steffanci, C.; and Tidwell, R. J. (1985). "Patterns of Cape Verdean Migration and Social Association Through Obituary Analysis." *New England Journal of Black Studies* (5): 31–45.

Machado, D. M. (1981). "Cape Verdean Americans." In *Hidden Minorities: The Persistence of Ethnicity in American Life,* edited by J. H. Rollins. Washington, DC: University Press of America.

Nunes, M. L. (1982). *A Portuguese Colonial in America, Belmira Nunes Lopes: The Autobiography of a Cape Verdean American.* Pittsburgh: Latin American Literary Review Press.

Pap, L. (1981). *The Portuguese-Americans.* Boston: Twayne.

Ramos, L. (1981). "Black, White, or Portuguese? A Cape Verdean Dilemma." In *Spinner,* Vol. 1: *People and Culture in Southeastern Massachusetts.* New Bedford, MA: Spinner Publications.

Reid, I. D. (1939). *The Negro Immigrant: His Background, Characteristics, and Social Adjustments, 1899–1937.* New York: AMS Press.

MARILYN HALTER

CARPATHO-RUSYNS

The name "Carpatho-Rusyn" derives from the term *rusyny,* the name the people call themselves in their own language. The prefix "Carpatho-" defines the geographic location of their European homeland along the southern and northern slopes of the Carpathian Mountains. The name "Carpatho-Rusyn" was given prominence by writers and other cultural activists during the nineteenth-century national revival, and it is the term used by most secular and religious organizations associated with the group in the United States today.

The territory where Carpatho-Rusyn villages are located is often referred to as Carpathian Rus (Karpathska Rus). Because many countries have ruled the area, the Carpatho-Rusyn homeland also has had many names given to it by ruling powers: Ruthenia, Carpatho-Russia, Subcarpathian Rus, Carpatho-Ukraine, and Transcarpathia among others. The following ethnonyms result from the various names applied to this region: Byzantines, Carpathians, Carpatho-Russians, Carpatho-Rusyns, Carpatho-Ukrainians, Lemkos, Rusnaks, Rusyns, Ruthenians, Slavish, Subcarpathian Rusyns, Uhro-Rusyns.

The wide variety of names used to describe Carpatho-Rusyns and their homeland is in part related to the fact that the group has never had an independent state. Since the early Middle Ages they have lived as a minority in various countries, each of which used a different name to describe them.

Location and Cultural Characteristics

During the last decades of the nineteenth century, when Carpatho-Rusyns first began immigrating to the United States, Carpathian Rus was part of the Hapsburg-ruled Austro-Hungarian monarchy. About three-quarters of the group lived on the southern slopes of mountains that were part of the Hungarian kingdom, the remaining one-quarter on the northern slopes, within the Austrian province of Galicia. After World War I, Carpatho-Rusyns south of the mountains found themselves in the new state of Czechoslovakia, those on the northern slopes in Poland.

World War II brought new changes of international boundaries to Carpathian Rus. Beginning in 1945, and for nearly four decades until the political changes of 1989–1991, Carpatho-Rusyns were ruled by Communist regimes. Those living south of the mountains were divided between the Soviet Union (specifically the Transcarpathian oblast of Soviet Ukraine) and Czechoslovakia (specifically the Prešov Region of northeastern Slovakia). Those living north of the mountains in the so-called Lemko region of Poland were between 1945 and 1947 deported to other parts of that country but most especially to the Soviet Ukraine. Today, Carpatho-Rusyns may number about 850,000 and live primarily in three countries: Ukraine (650,000), Slovakia (130,000), and Poland (60,000). There are also smaller numbers in neighboring Romania and Hungary as well as immigrant communities in the Czech Republic, Croatia, and Yugoslavia (in Serbia's Vojvodina region). Because of the complex political history and changes of borders in their European homeland, many Carpatho-Rusyns, especially those who emigrated abroad, describe themselves according to the country in which they or their forbears were born. Therefore it is quite common in the United States to find Carpatho-Rusyns who call themselves Austrians, Hungarians, Czechoslovaks, Russians, Slovaks, Poles, or Ukrainians.

Carpatho-Rusyns are distinguished by their language, religion, culture, and political traditions. They speak a series of East Slavic dialects that at various times in the twentieth century have been codified into a distinct Carpatho-Rusyn literary language. The language uses the Cyrillic alphabet, which is in sharp contrast to the Roman alphabet officially used by the government and administration in all countries where Carpatho-Rusyns have lived (except for Ukraine after 1945). Carpatho-Rusyns have traditionally been adherents of Eastern Christian churches, either Greek (Byzantine rite) Catholic or Orthodox, and this has set them apart from the neighboring Roman Catholic or Protestant Slovaks and Hungarians, the Roman Catholic Poles, and the Jews (primarily Orthodox Hasidic) who have lived in their midst.

At first glance, Carpatho-Rusyns may seem similar to Ukrainians, who speak East Slavic dialects related to Rusyn and also attend Eastern Christian churches. Nevertheless, the Carpatho-Rusyn spoken and written language forms differ from literary Ukrainian, and Carpatho-Rusyn churches are jurisdictionally separate, with practices (in particular, Carpathian plainchant) that are quite distinguishable from those in Ukrainian churches. Finally, Carpatho-Rusyns have a distinct political culture. Whereas they never had an independent state, they have experienced a tradition of autonomy that reached its height during the interwar years of 1919 to 1939, when the eastern region of Czechoslovakia, called Subcarpathian Rus, functioned as an internationally recognized Rusyn autonomous province. A sense of political distinctiveness related to a specific autonomous land has remained alive among Carpatho-Rusyns in their homeland and in the United States. For instance, in the course of the December 1991 referendum on Ukrainian independence, 78 percent of the inhabitants of Transcarpathia voted for autonomy for their region.

Immigration and Settlement

The first large-scale immigration of Carpatho-Rusyns to the United began in the 1880s. Since that time there have been four distinct periods of immigration: 1880s to 1914, 1919 to 1939, 1945 to 1950, and 1980 to the present. By far the largest number of immigrants, an estimated 225,000, arrived during the first period. In virtually all cases the reasons were economic. The Carpatho-Rusyn homeland was an underdeveloped rural area of Austria-Hungary where the population eked out a livelihood from subsistence-level farming, livestock grazing (especially of sheep), and forest-related work. There were no industries or factories nearby, and the local economy could not absorb a rapidly increasing population. Young men in particular sought to improve their economic situation by going to work in the United States.

During the nearly half century before World War I, Carpatho-Rusyns settled primarily in the industrial Northeast. They found work in the coal mines of eastern Pennsylvania and Ohio, the steel and related industries around Pittsburgh, and as unskilled laborers in the factories of New York, New Jersey, Connecticut, Ohio, Illinois, and Minnesota. Many of the newcomers during this first period were interested in working only for a couple of years and then returning home. Therefore it was not uncommon to find in the decades before 1914 Carpatho-Rusyns sojourning between the United States and Europe two or three times. The annual return migration rate between 1899 and 1914 was as high as 17 percent.

After World War I the number of Carpatho-Rusyn immigrants to the United States declined substantially, and since then it has remained relatively small. During the interwar years, only about twenty thousand more arrived, about half from eastern Czechoslovakia (mostly women and children joining their husbands who immigrated before the war) and half from the Lemko region of southeastern Poland. World War II interrupted further immigration; then after hostilities ceased, about four thousand displaced persons arrived between 1945 and 1950, mainly from camps in Germany and Austria where they had found themselves as a result of the war. The postwar onset of

A traditional Easter morning blessing of baskets is given by the American Orthodox Saint Alexis (Toth) in front of St. Mary's Church in Minneapolis around 1890. (Paul Robert Magocsi)

Communist rule in all countries where Carpatho-Rusyns lived effectively blocked any further emigration. The only exceptions were the brief periods of political liberalization in Czechoslovakia (1968) and Poland (1980–1981), which allowed for about three thousand new emigrants to flee political oppression. Since the fall of communism and the political changes of 1989–1991, perhaps another two thousand Carpatho-Rusyns have immigrated to the United States.

Demography and Settlement Patterns

The vast majority of Carpatho-Rusyns in the United States today are third-, fourth-, or fifth-generation descendants of immigrants who arrived before World War I. Estimates based on immigration records and membership data from community organizations suggest that today there are 600,000 to 625,000 Americans who have at least one ancestor born in a Carpatho-Rusyn village. Most, however, identify with the country of their ancestor's birth (Czechoslovakia or Austria-Hungary in particular), so that in the 1990 U.S. Census just under thirteen thousand persons reported their identity as specifically Carpatho-Rusyn.

The settlement pattern established by the first wave of immigrants remains for the most part the same today. Between 1910 and 1920, as many as 79 percent of Carpatho-Rusyns lived in urban areas of the middle Atlantic states, in particular Pennsylvania (54%), New York (13%), and New Jersey (12%), followed by Ohio, Connecticut, and Illinois. Since the 1970s, there has been a trend toward resettlement in the Sunbelt states of Florida, California, and Arizona, which provide warmer climates for retired persons and economic opportunities for younger people.

Language

When Carpatho-Rusyns arrived in the United States, they spoke their local East Slavic dialects within the family household and at community gatherings. Of particular importance for Old World language maintenance were the printed media (newspapers and magazines) and the churches, which organized classes that taught Carpatho-Rusyn as part of the parochial school system or in special after-hours classes. Several Rusyn-American grammars and readers were published especially for what were popularly known as "Rusyn schools." Newspapers began to appear as early as the 1880s, and among the most important were the weekly *Amerikanskii ruskii viestnik* (American Rusyn Messenger, 1892 to 1952), the daily *Den'* (The Day, 1922 to 1927), and the weekly *Karpatska Rus'* (Carpatho-Rusyn', 1939 to the present). In the early decades, all of these Rusyn-language publications used the Cyrillic alphabet, but by the 1930s, many began to switch to the Roman alphabet. After World War II, English gradually became the dominant language of the press, so that today only one newspaper, *Karpatska Rus'*, is published partially in Carpatho-Rusyn. Analogously, by the 1950s, Rusyn-language school classes ceased to function and Eastern Christian church services, which had for decades been conducted in Rusyn and in a liturgical language known as Church Slavonic, were systematically being replaced by English. The process was completed by the 1980s.

Cultural Characteristics

In the European homeland, religion was traditionally an integral part of Carpatho-Rusyn life. Until the onset of Communist rule in the late 1940s, the whole village life-cycle was governed by the church, and the local priest — or his wife — reinforced the importance of religion through their role as elementary school teachers. It is not surprising, therefore, that Carpatho-Rusyn immigrants, the vast majority of whom had entered the United States before World War I, tried to recreate religious institutions that were similar to those they left behind.

Almost all Carpatho-Rusyn immigrants who arrived before World War I were Greek, or Byzantine Catholics. This meant that they were jurisdictionally within the framework of the Catholic Church and that they recognized the authority of the pope. They were different from the vast majority of Catholics who were of the Roman rite, however, in that they were permitted to maintain certain Eastern Christian rites and customs their ancestors had practiced before the seventeenth century, when Carpatho-Rusyns were part of Orthodox Christendom. Among the Eastern practices were Church Slavonic instead of Latin as the language of religious services; the liturgy according to St. John Chrysostom; the old Julian calendar, in which fixed feasts such as Christmas came two weeks later than by the western calendar; and a married priesthood.

Practices such as these, most especially the possibility that priests could be married, were vehemently opposed by the American Catholic hierarchy. Rusyn immigrants responded by demanding that their historic rights be recognized in the New World. In cases when this did not happen, they decided to return to the Orthodox faith of their ancestors, where such practices were the norm. Consequently, from the 1890s through at least the 1950s, Carpatho-Rusyn life in America was dominated by religious controversies related to the difficulty of adapting European practices to the new American Catholic environment. In effect, the religious practices being questioned also became symbolic of one's nationality, so that the concern with the church was transformed into a defense of Carpatho-Rusyn identity.

In the end, Carpatho-Rusyn Americans became more or less evenly divided between adherents of Greek/Byzantine Catholicism and Orthodoxy. Today the Byzantine Catholics (195,000) are jurisdictionally part of a metropolitan province based in Pittsburgh, with other eparchies (dioceses) in Passaic, New Jersey; Parma, Ohio; and Van Nuys, California. Orthodox adherents (250,000) have had a more complex history. Until the 1930s, Greek Orthodox who left the church joined the Russian Orthodox Church, which three decades later was renamed the Orthodox Church in America. When, in the 1930s, a new, specifically Carpatho-Russian Orthodox Church was established (with headquarters eventually in Johnstown, Pennsylvania), thereafter disaffected Byzantine Cath-

olics had the option of joining different Orthodox jurisdictions.

Aside from spiritual and cultural needs, the early Carpatho-Rusyn immigrants were faced with practical concerns, such as unemployment because of layoffs, strikes, or physical incapacity due to accidents. To protect themselves against such eventualities, fraternal insurance organizations were founded, the oldest of which was the Greek Catholic Union, established in Wilkes-Barre, Pennsylvania, in 1892. This and other similar organizations — the Russian Orthodox Catholic Mutual Aid Society (est. 1895), the United Societies of Greek Catholic Religion (est. 1903),the United Russian Orthodox Brotherhood of America (est. 1915), and the Liberty Greek Catholic Carpatho-Russian Benevolent Association (est. 1918) — by their names alone revealed the degree to which they were closely related to the various Carpatho-Rusyn churches. In fact, as part of their cultural activity, each of the fraternals published newspapers that together with funding and other activity played a significant role in the Greek Catholic-Orthodox controversies that had so dominated Carpatho-Rusyn community life.

Some of the larger fraternals had, at least until the 1950s, active women's and youth divisions and sports clubs, and they were engaged in social work such as the orphanage supported by the Greek Catholic Union in Elmhurst, Pennsylvania. The fraternals also served as catalysts for political activity, especially that connected with the homeland. For instance, in 1918, the Greek Catholic Union and United Societies formed the American Council of Uhro-Rusyns, which was instrumental in conducting negotiations among the U.S. government, the Paris Peace Conference, and leaders in the homeland that led to the incorporation of "Rusyns living south of the Carpathians" into the new state of Czechoslovakia. The Paris Peace Conference guaranteed Rusyns their own autonomous province, called Subcarpathian Rus (in Czech, Podkarpatská Rus), whose first governor, appointed by the Czechoslovak government, was the head of the Pittsburgh-based National Council and an American citizen, Gregory I. Zhatkovich. The fraternals

The Epiphany Byzantine Ruthenian Catholic Church was built in 1982 in Roswell, Georgia, in the traditional Carpathian wooden style. (Paul Robert Magocsi)

continued to play a role in the European homeland by sending money and criticizing Czechoslovak and Polish policies during the interwar years and by supporting the war effort against Nazi Germany and its supporters during World War II.

Since the 1950s, the fraternals have become essentially insurance companies whose various lodges may also sponsor social events such as bowling and golf. Because of its size (forty thousand members in 1992) and financial solvency ($210 million in assets), the Greek Catholic Union is today able to maintain a resort and retirement community at its headquarters in Beaver, Pennsylvania, northwest of Pittsburgh.

Assimilation and Cultural Persistence

Because of their relatively small numbers, Carpatho-Rusyns were generally never singled out in the United States for discrimination based on their specific national origin. They were, however, often lumped together and labeled along with other eastern Europeans as "Hunkies" or "Polaks." These opprobrious terms implied a low level of culture, poor English speech, and the assumption that they were able to perform only manual labor. In fact, Carpatho-Rusyns have been able to break out of this generalized stereotype, so that by the second generation they found employment as skilled factory and clerical workers and by the third generation were in managerial and professional occupations (in nursing, as medical technicians, and in electronics).

A few offspring of Carpatho-Rusyn immigrants have had particularly successful careers, such as the geographer of the United States during 1980s, George J. Demko; the State Department's Russian translator for the office of the President, Dimitry Zarechnak; the head of the Worldwide Church of God in Pasadena, California, and editor in chief of *The Plain Truth,* Joseph W. Tkach; and film stars Lizabeth Scott (Emma Matzo), and Sandra Dee (Alexandra Zuk). Undoubtedly the most well-known American-born descendant of Carpatho-Rusyn immigrants was the pop artist and experimental filmmaker Andy Warhol, whose repetitive portraits of the twentieth century's rich and famous have been compared to the icons that graced the Carpatho-Rusyn churches he attended as a youth in Pittsburgh.

Carpatho-Rusyns have generally been successful in adapting to American society. They have done this, however, at the expense of giving up or actively rejecting their ancestral heritage. In particular, this has been the case among the American-born second generation, who tended to be embarrassed by their parents' broken English and Old World lifestyle; by the church controversies that frequently divided communities and even families; by the fact that their parents or grandparents came from a place that could not easily be found — if at all — on world maps; and by the reality that they were reluctant carriers of a "strange" Slavic culture unknown to fellow Americans. That some Carpatho-Rusyn leaders said they were Russians or Ukrainians, or that many identified with the country of their or their parents' birth (Austria, Hungary, Slovakia) and not their ethnic culture only confused the identity issue further. Quite simply, by the 1950s and 1960s most Carpatho-Rusyn Americans did not know or care about their ancestral heritage. At the height of this assimilationist, be-an-American-like-everyone-else-phase, the Byzantine Catholic churches began removing the culturally distinct iconscreens (iconostases) before the altar to make their interiors look like the "more normal" Roman Catholic churches.

By the 1970s, however, the assimilationist phase began to be reversed. This was a time when third-generation descendants of the original immigrants seemed to follow the proverbial principle of wanting to know what their grandparents knew so well but what their parents hoped so desperately to forget. Beginning in 1975, several new Carpatho-Rusyn dance ensembles were established (the most important remains Slavjane, based in Pittsburgh); the churches began to return to or put more emphasis on their Eastern Churches heritage; lectures and scholarly conferences on Carpatho-Rusyn culture and history were held at several universities (Harvard, Pennsylvania, John Carroll, Duquesne); scholarly and popular books about the group in America and the homeland were published; and a scholarly institution (the Carpatho-Rusyn Research Center) and quarterly (*Carpatho-Rusyn American,* 1978 to the present) devoted exclusively to the group were established.

The subsequent political changes of 1989–1991 and the fall of communism in the homeland also have had an important impact on fostering the Carpatho-Rusyn identity in the United States. For nearly half a century, Rusyn Americans had been cut off from their European roots by the disruptions of World War II followed by four decades of Communist rule that hampered or restricted entirely travel and even communication with family members. Since 1989, however, contacts have been steadily renewed at the family and organizational levels.

The recently founded Rusyn-American organizations have also played an active role in the post-1989 Rusyn cultural revival in Europe. The "Americans" are among the founding members of the European-based World Congress of Rusyns (est. 1991), and they have provided financial support for new Rusyn-language newspapers, books, and scholarly events in the homeland. The Andy Warhol Foundation has funded the Warhol Family Museum of Modern Art in a Rusyn town in eastern Slovakia, while both the Byzantine/Greek Catholic and Orthodox churches in America have helped financially the reconstruction of churches and seminaries in Slovakia and in the Transcarpathian region of Ukraine that were destroyed during the Communist era. Thus the cultural revival of the 1970s that was in large part linked to the general "roots fever" in the United States, and the fall of communism in 1989–1991 followed by a Rusyn revival in the European homeland have provided a new lease on life to Rusyn-American communities. More and more Americans of Carpatho-Rusyn descent have a clearer picture of the cultural heritage of their ancestors and of Carpathian Rus, the ancestral European homeland that is the source of that culture.

See also: AUSTRIANS; CZECHS; HUNGARIANS; POLES; RUSSIANS; SLOVAKS; UKRANIANS

Bibliography

Barriger, L. (1985). *Good Victory: Metropolitan Orestes Chornock and the American Orthodox Greek Catholic Diocese.* Brookline, MA: Holy Cross Orthodox Press.

Dyrud, K. (1992). *The Quest for the Rusyn Soul: The Politics of Religion and Culture in Eastern Europe and America, 1890–World War I.* Philadelphia: Balch Institute Press.

Greek Catholic Union of the U.S.A. (1994). *Opportunity Realized: The Greek Catholic Union's First One Hundred Years.* Beaver, PA: Author.

Gulovich, S. C. (1946). "The Russian Exarchate in the United States." *Eastern Churches Quarterly* 6:459–485.

Magocsi, P. R. (1978). *The Shaping of a National Identity: Subcarpathian Rus', 1848–1948.* Cambridge, MA: Harvard University Press.

Magocsi, P. R. (1989). *The Carpatho-Rusyn Americans.* New York: Chelsea House.

Magocsi, P. R. (1994). *Our People: Carpatho-Rusyns and Their Descendants in North America,* 3rd revised edition. Toronto: University of Toronto Press/ Multicultural History Society of Ontario.

Pekar, A. B. (1992). *The History of the Church in Carpathian Rus'.* New York: East European Monographs, Columbia University Press.

Simirenko, A. (1964). *Pilgrims, Colonists, and Frontiersmen: An Ethnic Community in Transition.* New York: Free Press.

Tarasar, C. J., and Erickson, J. H., eds. (1975). *Orthodox America, 1794–1976.* Syosset, NY:Orthodox Church in America.

Warzeski, W. C. (1971). *Byzantine-Rite Rusyns in Carpatho-Ruthenia and America.* Pittsburgh: Byzantine Seminary Press.

PAUL ROBERT MAGOCSI

CHAM

The Cham are a rather exceptional lowland minority people from Vietnam and Cambodia. Cham villages are clustered in southeastern Vietnam on the border at Chau Doc and in central Cambodia in the vicinity of Phnom Penh (the capital). Cham also reside in Kampong Cham and other major urban centers.

Historical Context

The Cham were once one of the most powerful of Hinduized Southeast Asian peoples. Their maritime trade dominated much of the South China Sea. Their ritual center at My Son rivaled Angkor Wat in sacred symbolism. Cham towers of mortar and brick were arrayed along the south and cental Vietnamese coast, symbols of the power and influence of a great trading empire. Cham kingdoms were organized according to Hindu concepts of state and kingship and expressed linguistic and cultural affinity with the peoples of the Malay world in the Philippines and Indonesia. In Champa, the first of the great civilizations to be influenced by Hinduism, descent was matrilineal (goods and names were reckoned through the female line). The areca nut clan in the north and the coconut clan in the south continually vied for control of the Cham state while fighting off the empire of Vietnam to the north and the kingdom of Cambodia to the west.

In the thirteenth century, when Marco Polo is said to have visited the Cham capital on his way back to Italy from China, new currents of religious thought coursed through Southeast Asia. By the dawn of the fifteenth century, Muslim and Hindu rulers in Champa contested for the throne and the allegiance of the common people. In 1471 Champa was finally and irrevocably conquered by Vietnam. As their independent nation came to an end, many members of the Cham nobility fled to safe haven across the Annamite Cordillera mountain range to neighboring Cambodia, where they secured their allegiance to Islam, often serving as special armed guards for members of the Cambodian royal family. Cham farmers remaining in Vietnam were often forbidden from speaking the Cham language, forced to adopt Vietnamese names, and ordered to substitute Vietnamese traditional costumes for those of their ancestors. In southeastern Vietnam, between the towns of Phan Rang and Phan Thiet, approximately 180,000 vestigial Cham reside today. The population there is thought to be approximately 65 percent Hindu and 35 percent Muslim.

In the nineteenth century, France moved to exercise colonial control over Cambodia, Laos, and Vietnam (collectively referred to as French Indochina). The French, as was the case for the British and Dutch in their colonies in Southeast Asia, sought to "divide and rule." The colonial armies were disproportionately manned by members of ethnic minority groups. Minorities were often used to gather information and intelligence relevant to the suppression of anticolonial nationalist movements. During this colonial era, the Cham fared relatively well. In Vietnam, the Cham were granted a measure of cultural freedom; restrictive Vietnamese codes asserting policies of forced assimilation were abrogated by the French. In Cambodia, the Cham were accorded rights to organize their own Muslim schools.

Aftermath of the Vietnam War

The special attention and largesse that the Cham minority had received during the French and later American eras in Vietnam came to an end with the Communist victory in the Vietnam War.

On April 20, 1975, several thousand Cham fled their Vietnamese homeland as boat people to find refuge in Malaysian refugee camps. In Cambodia, the postwar fate of the Cham was more tragic. The Khmer Rouge regime of Democratic Kampuchea (April 1975–January 1979) was determined to wipe all foreign influence from the land. Cham communities became special targets for Khmer Rouge reprisal because they were viewed as a double threat. First, because of their unique language, dress styles, and village culture, they were immediately suspect as aliens within an increasingly xenophobic Cambodian state. Second, the strong, largely Orthodox Islamic beliefs and ritual practices were viewed as a challenge to the Maoist Marxist orthodoxy promoted by the new government of Pol Pot, the leader of the Khmer Rouge. Cambodian Muslims, like their Buddhist neighbors, were forbidden to practice their religion. The Khmer Rouge destroyed mosques, unprooted and relocated villagers, forbade daily prayers, and enjoyed the practice of Muslim dietary restrictions. Some estimates place the losses of the Cambodian Cham during this period at 50 percent of the total prewar population.

Due to the harsh conditions experienced in both Cambodia and Vietnam, Cham peoples joined the rush of more than 1.5 million refugees who fled Indochina between 1975 and 1995. From Vietnam, a handful of Cham officials joined the first-wave exodus in the spring of 1975. As Cham enclaves in Vietnam are generally situated near the coast, it was relatively easy to gain access to boats and escape routes to Malaysia, where contacts between Malaysian Islamic schools (especially in the state of Kelantan) and Cham communities in Vietnam and Cambodia had always been strong. Malaysia, motivated by this strong compassion for Muslim refugees, admitted approximately sixty thousand Cham as permanent refugees. In fact, the Cham became the only instance of a people being accepted as permanent refugees by first asylum states (Thailand, Malaysia, Indonesia, and Hong Kong) in Southeast Asia.

As the Vietnam War inexorably drew to a close in 1975, it was expected that a relatively small group of local Cambodian, Laotian, and Vietnamese elites would flee their homelands to find safe haven in America. In the course of twenty years of refugee admissions, a veritable cross section of the local populace has fled to countries of first asylum and subsequently been resettled in the United States. This means that not only former generals and mayors, but also rice farmers, urban Chinese business people, and rural minorities (such as the Cham and a host of highland tribal peoples) have been resettled in the United States. As Vietnamese armed forces swept into Cambodia in January 1979, hundreds of thousands of starving farmers from western Cambodia fled to safe haven in Thailand. Among this number were several thousand Cham. As clandestine boat departures from Vietnam accelerated after the Chinese invasion of Vietnam in February 1979, Cham coastal people were also among those fleeing their homeland for safe haven in Malaysia.

Life in the United States

Because Cham refugees were admitted to the United States as either Vietnamese or Cambodian nationals, no precise figures are available concerning the size of the Cham community in America. A fair estimate of the Cham population, however, is approximately seventy-five hundred people, most of whom live in California, Texas, and Washington State.

As the Cham immigrated to the United States from both Cambodia and Vietnam, there remain significant differences between these two groups

Cham dancers perform in Berkeley, California, in 1991. (Eric Crystal)

and within the Vietnamese Cham community as well. Although Cham in Vietnam are evenly split between Hindu and Muslim religious affiliations, the Cham from Vietnam in the United States are largely (although not uniformly) Muslim. Muslim Cham from Vietnam received significant assistance from international Muslim organizations to promote conversion of Hindu Cham to Islam in the United States. Increasingly, then, Cham identity in the United States is tied to Muslim identity. Cham from Cambodia and Vietnamese Cham from the western Cambodian border area around the city of Chau Doc practice Orthodox Islam. Cham from coastal southeastern Vietnam, the site of the last Cham kingdom at Panduranga, are more syncretistic in religious belief and cultural practice. Cham from this area are committed to preserving core identity through the promotion of Cham language study, the promotion of Cham dance and music, and the organization of conferences and cultural events. More Orthodox Muslim Cham eschew the dance, music, and costume traditions that inevitably evoke reflections of Hindu culture.

The Cham community in the United States has faced several unique problems and confronted many problems common to refugees from Cambodia, Laos, and Vietnam. The most significant problem has been identity and recognition. Unlike the highland Hmong refugees from Laos, who were recognized as a distinct group from the time of their first arrivals in the United States in 1976, the Cham have encountered much difficulty in establishing an identity as a unique refugee group. Because most Muslim Cham in America have adopted Arabic language names, the Cham are oftentimes confused with immigrants from other parts of the world. Few Americans were aware of this minority group prior to the establishment of Cham communities in cities such as Seattle, San Francisco, San Jose, Santa Ana, and Fullerton, California. As Muslims, Cham refugees encountered a double set of prejudices. First, they, along with other refugees from Indochina, inevitably encountered competition and resentment in the struggle for housing and entry-level jobs. Second, Muslims in America have often been forced to contend with ignorance and discrimination concerning their religious beliefs, problems that have been exacerbated by tensions between the United States and certain nations and groups in the Middle East.

Cultural Preservation

In the fall of 1993, the Cham community in the United States, with the support of a grant from the National Endowment for the Arts, organized a large public "Katey" festival, celebrating traditional Cham New Year. Staged in an auditorium at San Jose State University, the event drew Cham participants from across the United States and Canada. Organized by the International Office for Champa (an indigenous community group led by Cham from the Phan Rang coastal area of Vietnam), the event displayed a full panoply of modern and traditional song and dance. Videos of contemporary conditions in the Cham homeland in Vietnam were screened. Costumes and musical instruments used in the celebration had been recently commissioned and purchased from Cham villagers in Vietnam.

The Cham New Year festival was a statement of commitment to the preservation of the tradition and culture of a unique American immigrant community. Once isolated from their homeland and unrecognized within the United States, this small, unique community of refugees has begun to make its mark in business and higher education. Whether this community remains intact will depend on the rate of intermarriage and non-Cham Muslims. No further immigration of Cham from Vietnam and Cambodia can be anticipated in the future. For the present, the Cham may be justly regarded as a unique group of refugees resulting from the conflict in Indochina. The Cham are highly conscious of their role as inheritors of a great tradition, as a living vestige of a vanquished empire, and as determined bearers of an ancient culture.

See also: CAMBODIANS; VIETNAMESE

Bibliography

Becker, E. (1986). *When the War Was Over: The Voices of Cambodia's Revolution and Its People.* New York: Simon & Schuster.

Chanda, N. (1986). *Brother Enemy: The War After the War.* San Diego, CA: Harcourt Brace Jovanovich.

Coedes, G. (1968). *The Indianized States of Southeast Asia,* translated by S. B. Cowing. Honolulu: East-West Center Press.

Collins, W. (1996). *The Chams of Cambodia.* Phnom Penh, Cambodia: Center for Advanced Study.

Hickey, G. C. (1982a). *Free in the Forest: Ethnohistory of the Vietnamese Central Highlands, 1954–1976.* New Haven, CT: Yale University Press.

Hickey, G. C. (1982b). *Sons of the Mountains: Ethnohistory of the Vietnamese Central Highlands to 1954.* New Haven, CT: Yale University Press.

International Center for Ethnic Studies. (1995). *Minorities in Cambodia.* London: Minority Rights Group.

Kiernan, B. (1985). *How Pol Pot Came to Power: A History of Communism in Kampuchea, 1930–1975.* London: Verso.

LeBar, F.; Hickey, G. C.; and Musgrave, J. K. (1964). *Ethnic Groups of Mainland Southeast Asia.* New Haven, CT: Human Relations Area Files.

Maspero, G. (1949). *The Kingdom of Champa.* New Haven, CT: Yale University Press.

Stanton, G. (1993). "The Khmer Rouge Genocide and International Law." In *Genocide and Democracy in Cambodia: The Khmer Rouge, the United Nations, and the International Community,* edited by B. Kiernan. New Haven, CT: Yale University Press.

ERIC CRYSTAL

CHILEANS

Chile is a long, narrow strip of land located on the southwest coast of South America. The country is bordered by the Atacama desert in the north, the Andes Mountains to the east, and the Pacific Ocean to the west and south. As a result, Chile is practically an island, and its original inhabitants, the Araucanian Indians, were well protected from attacks by the neighboring Incas from Peru and the Spanish conquistadores. Today, the Chileans are a very homogenous people, a mixture of Indian and European ancestry, with a predominance of Castillian. The country is united by common use of the Spanish language and by the dominant influence of the Catholic Church.

Although Chile is the most distant Latin American country from the United States, its inhabitants have been immigrating to the United States since the beginning of the nineteenth century. The country's movement to obtain independence from Spain started in 1810, but even before that date, evidence exists of Chileans taking up residency in the United States. American whalers sailing the South Pacific put into Chilean ports to obtain supplies and often enlisted young Chilean men to replace losses or to serve as additional crew. Some of these Chilean sailors landed in Massachusetts or Maryland and settled there. Similarly, Spanish colonial ships that plied the South American route to California brought Chilean immigrants to the West Coast. In addition, ships involved in the tallow and hide trade between East Coast ports and California brought Chilean sailors and traders to California. It was natural then that, when gold was discovered in California in 1848, Chile was immediately affected by the Gold Rush. In the first six months of 1849, the Chilean Foreign Office issued six thousand passports to travel to California. However, half of the passengers to California did not bother to get travel documents, which lead the Chilean Congress to pass a law authorizing citizens to travel to California without passports. More than seven thousand Chileans have been documented as having arrived in California in 1848 and 1849. During that period, a significant number of American residents of Chile also traveled to California accompanied by their Chilean wives, children, and servants. The first wave of Chileans arrived in California ahead of all other nationalities except the Mexicans from Sonora who arrived by land.

Chileans in California

There were three distinct groups of Chileans, known also as Chilenos, who arrived in California.

The first group consisted of the experienced miners, men who knew how to dig shafts and tunnels. They collected, borrowed or stole money to buy a boat ticket to be part of the Gold Rush. When they could not get enough funds, they hired themselves out to rich entrepreneurs who were willing to pay passage. There were also those who became sailors, stewards, cooks, and even musicians so they could get on board a ship. The Chileno miners were recognized as experts. They knew how to mine gold, crush the ore, wash it in the streams, or use a "dry wash" method. Chilean stone cutters created the Chilemill, a rock crushing system, that became very popular in the West. The second group consisted of the merchants and entrepreneurs, people who had dealt with shipping and exporting and brought most of the stock of their Valparaiso stores with them. The third group consisted of the adventurers, people from all walks of life who wanted to make a fast buck. Among the third group was a contingent of prostitutes from the brothels of Valparaiso and Talcahuano. Some of these ladies, such as Mina and Clementina, are remembered in the names of streets in San Francisco. Others abandoned their profession, married, and became respectable matriarchs of California families.

In San Francisco, the Chileans established themselves at the bottom of Telegraph Hill, and the district became known as Chilecito, or Little Chile. Bound by Montgomery, Pacific, Jackson, and Kearney streets, the place was a hollow filled with little wooden huts. According to eyewitnesses, the women appeared to be always washing, but the vocation of the men was a puzzle to passersby. It has been impossible to determine the number of Chileans that actually arrived in San Francisco, since the 1850 and 1852 U.S. Censuses do not include San Francisco or Santa Clara counties, where the bulk of the Chilean population resided. Calaveras and Tuolomne counties, however, show heavy Chilean populations. In June 1849, Chilecito was sacked by a group of ruffians who called themselves the Hounds. The tents were destroyed, and fires were set to everything that would burn. Many of the residents ran up to the surrounding hills, and some even took refuge aboard the ships anchored in the bay. On the next morning the outraged citizens of San Francisco took action, forming the first group of Popular Justice Militia and arresting the leaders of the Hounds.

The Chilean miners fared well until 1850, when Americans claimed the mines and expelled the Chilean miners. A few Chilean, French, and Mexican miners remained in remote areas or at diggings that proved low yield. Later, a foreign miner's tax made even these efforts unprofitable, and they were forced to leave the mines permanently. Contemporary accounts describe "thousands" of Chileans returning to San Francisco. Some returned to Chile, but approximately half of them became employees of mining enterprises, lending their expertise to gold mining, farming, cattle ranching, retail business, and even serving as members of the clergy. Other Chileans expelled from the mines took to banditry. Some of these bandits, like the famous Narrato Ponce, left a trail of crimes through the mines and ranches of California's central valley. Others joined gangs of horse thieves captained by Mexican outlaws. The notorious bandit Joaquin Murrieta, however, contrary to popular belief, was not a Chilean. Other Chileans succeeded in business, founded towns, farmed large tracks of lands, and engaged in other activities. As late as 1890, there were active Chilean Patriotic Clubs in California. The influence of these early Chilean immigrants can be seen in place names such as Chilicamp, Chile Gulch, and Chileno Valley and in street names such as Valparaiso, Santiago, and Almendral.

Expanding Immigration

With the advent of steam navigation and the establishment of the Chilean Steamship Line, Chileans began immigrating to the United States in small numbers. By 1910, small Chilean colonies could be found in Boston, New York, Baltimore, New Orleans, and Los Angeles. A small group of

Chilean graduate students entered the United States during World War I when the universities in Europe were not accessible to them. Many of these immigrants became teacher assistants and eventually faculty members at some of the most prestigious universities in the country. Professors such as Arturo Torres Ríoseco, Eduardo Neal Silva, Francisco Aguilera, and Carlos Hamilton, were pioneers in the study of Latin American literature in the universities of the United States. Gabriela Mistral, Chile's Nobel Prize–winning poet, took up residence in New York during World War II.

In 1938, when Chileans voted into power a leftist government (the Popular Front), a number of wealthy Chileans, fearing political turmoil, immigrated to the United States. During World War II the size of the Chilean community in New York and Los Angeles grew steadily. There are some records of clubs and associations and even publications going back to the 1920s. The largest and most active group was the Club Obrero Chileno, which existed in New York until World War II. No immigrant quota was in effect for people from Latin America, and it was fairly easy for Chileans to obtain a permanent U.S. resident visa.

The election of Salvador Allende to the presidency of Chile in 1970 was the cause for numerous Chileans to emigrate. Some of them, who were employees of American companies, managed to obtain positions in the United States. They found employment in Utah, Nevada, Montana, New York, and parts of California, such as Los Angeles and San Diego. After the military coup of 1973 in Chile, many of these people returned, but a new wave of immigrants managed to find their way to the United States.

Chilean immigrants numbered 17,600 between 1971 and 1980. Thousands of them, claiming refugee status, settled permanently in the United States. Their arrival with new political ideas and understandable bitterness toward the new Chilean government caused friction with the established community to the point where some of the long-established Chilean clubs and associations disbanded. In some areas, the Chilean community was divided into two camps; they staged different cultural activities and issued publications. Although threats have often been exchanged, no violence has been recorded.

The number of Chileans in the United States increased by 23,400 between 1981 and 1990. Due to improved economic conditions in Chile and the return of democracy, immigration to the United States has slowed down considerably, registering 4,800 in 1991–1992 and 1,800 in 1993.

The Chilean-American Community

Today, there are about 73,000 persons of Chilean origin in the United States (50,322 according to the 1990 U.S. Census); about 10 percent are illegal aliens. The largest concentration of Chileans is found in California; 18,034 have been reported in that state. The Consulate General in New York, which covers a large area of the Northeast, claims 26,025 Chileans under its jurisdiction. The Los Angeles area accounts for 11,000 Chileans, and Miami accounts for 10,000. Smaller groups can be found in San Francisco, Las Vegas, New Orleans, and Seattle.

Chilean clubs and associations have been formed in most of these cities. Some of these clubs are sports oriented, mostly soccer teams with such patriotic names as Club Chile, Los Cóndores, and Colo-Colo. The most prominent club in Los Angeles is a rifle club. The oldest of these groups in continuous existence is the Lautaro Club in San Francisco, dating to 1957, which publishes the monthly *La Gaceta*. Other monthly Chilean publications include *Andes* in Miami and *La Aurora del Sur* in Los Angeles.

Chileans love to dance their national dance (*la Cueca*), and dancing groups regularly perform in San Francisco, Los Angeles, and other cities. Chilean food is mildly spicy and can be found in restaurants in Los Angeles, New York, and Houston. Very few Chileans have reported cases of racial discrimination. This may be due to the influence of European ancestry among Chileans. The main obstacle for recent Chilean immigrants is coping with a lack of English-language skills.

Bibliography

Beilharz, E., and López, C. U. (1976). *We Were Forty-Niners! Chilean Accounts of The California Gold Rush.* Pasadena, CA: Ward Ritchie.

López, C. U. (1974). *Chilenos in California, A Study of the 1850, 1852, and 1860 Censuses.* Palo Alto, CA: R & E Publishers.

Loveman, B. (1988). *Chile: The Legacy of Hispanic Capitalism,* 2nd edition. New York: Oxford University Press.

Pereira Salas, E. (1974). *Los Primeros Contactos entre Chile y los Estados Unidos, 1778–1809.* Santiago, Chile: Andrés Bello.

Sater, W. F. (1990). *Chile and the United States: Empires in Conflict.* Athens: University of Georgia Press.

U.S. Bureau of the Census. (1993). *Statistical Abstract of the United States,* 113th edition. Washington, DC: U.S. Government Printing Office.

U.S. Bureau of the Census. (1993). *1990 Census of Population, Persons of Hispanic Origin in the United States.* Washington, DC: U.S. Government Printing Office.

CARLOS U. LÓPEZ

CHINESE

Most of the Chinese in the United States were traditionally Cantonese from the Guangdong Province of southern China. After the implementation of the U.S. Immigration Act of 1965, however, there were significant changes in the Chinese immigration population. Cantonese continue to dominate the Chinese immigrant population in the United States today, but there are also Fujianese (Fukienese), Taiwanese, Shanghainese, and Chinese from the northern regions of China.

Stories of the immigrants, their failures and successes, were circulated in their home communities in China. Since the new immigration laws of 1965 emphasized family reunification, the home communities of these early immigrants were favored sources of new immigrants, who often had kinship connections and were linked to the established ethnic community in the United States.

The History of Chinese Immigration

Some sources claim that the Chinese were present in America as early as the fourth century C.E., long before Christopher Columbus. Other sources claim that the Chinese arrived in the tenth century C.E. However, according to reliable historical records, the first large influx of Chinese immigrants to America dates from the 1850s. The number of immigrants steadily increased over the years, peaking in 1890 with a population of 107,488. Discriminatory legislation such as the Chinese Exclusion Act of 1882, the anti-Chinese Scott Act of 1888, and the Geary Act of 1892 were designed to prohibit the entry or reentry of Chinese immigrants who were laborers, thus ending the influx of Chinese immigration. By 1920 there were only 61,639 Chinese in the United States. Racism and fear of economic competition from the Chinese were the principal factors contributing to discriminatory legislation. It was not until after World War II that Chinese immigration recommenced, although significant influxes did not become apparent until the passage of 1965 immigration laws. By 1990 the Chinese population had grown to 1,645,472.

Initially, in the 1850s, the Chinese settled on the West Coast, where they found jobs as railroad workers, miners, farmers, and domestics. They have been a presence in the state of California ever since. Upon completion of the Central Pacific Railway in 1869 and the closing of many mining companies, Chinese and white laborers alike had to look for other forms of employment in California. Economic competition with whites led to various anti-Chinese campaigns in California and the passage of discriminatory legislation. One example of anti-Chinese legislation was the Sidewalk Ordinance of 1870, which outlawed the Chinese pole method of peddling vegetables and carrying laundry. Traditionally, the Chinese carried heavy loads balanced on a pole that rested on their shoulders. The pole functioned as a fulcrum.

The Sidewalk Ordinance was directed specifically against the Chinese since non-Chinese people used wagons or carts to peddle their goods. There were ordinances against the use of firecrackers and Chinese ceremonial gongs, which were important symbols of luck and necessary implements for Chinese festivities. In 1871 the Cubic Air Ordinance was enacted, requiring each adult to have at least five hundred cubic feet of living space. The law was specifically directed against the Chinese who were living in cramped quarters in extended family living situations. The Queue Ordinance, passed in 1873 in San Francisco, was another example of legislation specifically targeting Chinese. Under Manchu law, Chinese men were required to comb their hair into long braids called queues. Cutting off their queues was a serious violation of Chinese Law. After the passage of the anti-Queue law, gangs began to attack Chinese people with long hair, cutting off their braids and wearing them as trophies on their belts and caps.

There were numerous laws prohibiting the Chinese from working in federal, state, county, or city governments. The Chinese were barred from the fishing industry. There were laws prohibiting the education of Chinese children in the public schools, as well as laws prohibiting the use of Chinese people as witnesses against white defendants in court. Chinese were barred from purchasing property outside of San Francisco's Chinatown. In addition to these laws, in 1882 Congress passed the Chinese Exclusion Act, which prohibited Chinese laborers from entering the country.

The Chinese responded to these sentiments and legislative acts by entering into businesses, such as Chinese restaurants and laundries, that were not directly competitive with white enterprises. They organized self-help, community, and protective societies. Many moved to the major metropolitan areas of the United States, such as San Francisco, Los Angeles, and New York City, where they could attract a large clientele for their

Chinese workers put the finishing touches on a trestle in the Sierra Nevada Mountains for the Southern Pacific Railroad in 1877. (Library of Congress/Corbis)

ethnic businesses. As a result of this movement, Chinese enclaves known as Chinatowns developed. From the 1880s to 1965, the Chinese depended entirely on ethnic businesses for their survival. In Chinatown they developed an ethnic economy that catered to both Chinese and non-Chinese customers. Their protective societies and associations were based on kinship, friendship, place of origin, trade, and dialect. Through these associations the Chinese mediated their own disputes, promoted their own economic interests, and socialized among themselves. Although the establishment of Chinatowns proved to be an adaptive strategy, their creation was necessary as a result of racism. Discrimination, nonacceptance, and exclusion of the Chinese by the larger society compelled them to engage in limited economic activities within the confines of Chinatown. By 1940, there were twenty-eight Chinatowns in the United States. As discrimination against the Chinese diminished and they became more accepted by the larger society, Chinese were able to move out of the Chinatowns and to pursue other economic activities. By 1955 there were only sixteen Chinatowns remaining in the United States. With the influx of new immigrants after 1965, some Chinatowns expanded. The already existing Chinatowns of San Francisco, Los Angeles, and New York all got a boost to their populations as new arrivals tended to move into preexisting Chinatowns. In San Francisco, 20 percent of the Chinese live in Chinatown; the rest of the Chinese population is dispersed throughout the city. Similar phenomenon occurred in the Chinatowns of New York, Chicago, and Los Angeles. Additionally, a new Chinatown in Monterey Park, near Los Angeles, has been created by the new Chinese immigrants.

Among the new Chinese immigrants, many are highly educated and trained in various professional careers. Professionals tend to live outside of Chinatowns in the metropolitan areas of cities such as New York, San Francisco, Los Angeles, Houston, San Diego, Dallas, Boston, and Chicago. According to the 1990 U.S. Census, in terms of spatial distribution, among the 1,645,472 Chinese in America, 704,850 live in California, and 284,144 live in New York. Hawaii, Illinois, New Jersey, and Texas also have more than fifty thousand Chinese each.

Language

Before 1965 the Chinese in the United States were a rather homogenous group in terms of place of origin and linguistic background. Most of the Chinese immigrants came from the rural area of the Guangdong Province in southern China, particularly the Sze Yap and the Sam Yap districts. The various dialects from Sze Yap and San Yap were used. However, the lingua franca used in the Chinese community in the United States was the Taishan dialect. Since 1965, with the arrival of the new immigrants from different parts of China, the most commonly used dialect in the Chinese immigrant community is the standard Cantonese used in the areas of Hong Kong, Macao, and Guanzhou. However, there are also Mandrian, Shanghainese, or Fukienese speakers in the community. Many of the new immigrants are bilingual or even multilingual; they speak English and one or more Chinese dialects. Since the writing system is uniform throughout China, it is understandable to all Chinese immigrants regardless of where they came from. In general, first-generation Chinese immigrants can speak and write in Chinese. As times goes on, the second generation tends to lose the ability to read and write Chinese. Although some can still speak a Chinese dialect, many have become monolingual English speakers. With the recent emphasis on multiculturalism and the emergence of China as a world power, some second-generation Chinese Americans are learning the official language of China, namely, the Mandarin (or Pu Tung Hua dialect.)

Since 1965 most of the immigrants have come from either the Cantonese- or Mandarin-speaking area of China, causing these two dialects to become the dominant ones. The Chinese television stations in New York and San Francisco have programs in both Cantonese and Mandarin. There are many Chinese newspapers circulated among the immigrant Chinese. The two most important ones are *Sing Tao Daily* and the *World Journal.* The

A 1990 Cantonese opera performance takes place at the Luck Ngi Musical Club in Seattle's International District. (Kevin Morris/Corbis)

former caters principally to the Chinese from Hong Kong and China, while the latter one caters to the Chinese from Taiwan. There are different political persuasions among the immigrants. Some identify with the Kuomingtang of Taiwan, some are sympathetic with the People's Republic of China, and some are for establishing roots in the United States. These different political persuasions are reflected also in the ethnic press of the Chinese. There are more than five dailies in New York's Chinatown and four dailies in San Francisco's Chinatown. Additionally, Chinese newspapers from mainland China, Taiwan, and Hong Kong are available in the major Chinatowns in the United States. Chinese immigrants are sensitive to domestic and international events and are eager to learn about the different perspectives.

All the Chinese language newspapers have impressive news coverage. *Sing Tao Daily* has an English supplement with news specifically targeted to young Hong Kong Chinese who have difficulty reading Chinese characters. Apart from local and American news, the contents of *Sing Tao Daily* are transmitted from Hong Kong via satellite. The *World Journal* is a pro-Taiwan newspaper that receives daily communications via satellite as well. The new immigrants in general are quite well educated and have an international mind-set. The Chinese newspapers inform immigrants about their homelands and provide reliable coverage about the social and political events around the world and in the United States.

The Old Immigrants and the New

The coastal regions of southeastern China, principally the provinces of Fujian and Guangdong, have been the main suppliers of Chinese immigrants. Traditionally, the South Seas had been a favorite destination for the Fujianese. Most of the Chinese of Guangdong Province, however, immigrated to the United States. Today the new Chinese immigrants come from different parts of China. Immigrants from Taiwan and mainland China face separate quotas imposed by the United States. The People's Republic of China has a quota of twenty thousand immigrants per year, while Taiwan has a separate quota of twenty thousand. Hong Kong, as a colony of Great Britain, had a colonial quota of six hundred slots per year. This quota for the Hong Kong natives was increased by the United States in August 1985 to five thousand per year. However, residents of Hong Kong who were born in China are included in the quota for mainland China.

Legal immigrants are admitted into the United States on three types of visas. One is the family reunion quota, the second is the special talents quota, and the third is the quota for political refugees. Illegal entrants from China do exist, but the number is relatively small as many of them have relatives in the United States. As it turns out, the illegal Chinese immigrants tend to be those from the economically deprived rural area of Fujian Province. In 1985, 95 percent of all visa applications cited family reunification as their classification preference. Since 1965, there has been a drastic increase of Chinese immigrants in the United States. There are several reasons that account for the increase. First, the Immigration Act of 1965 started to treat the Chinese more equitably. An equal quota was extended to nations from different parts of the world. Second, educational, political, and economic factors played important roles.

There are vast motivational differences between immigrants from Taiwan and Hong Kong and those from mainland China. Immigrants from mainland China seek economic opportunity and political freedom, whereas many immigrants from Hong Kong and Taiwan leave a strong economic situation to find political stability and educational opportunities in the United States. University education is highly competitive in the homeland of the Chinese. There are only two major universities in Hong Kong, and they can admit only eight hundred students per year, from a population of five million. For years Taiwan has sent many students to the United States to receive higher education, as Taiwan also has a limited number of universities; many do not even give doctoral degrees. These educational and political considerations of the new Chinese immigrants differ significantly from the overriding economic concerns of the nineteenth-century Chinese immigrants.

The kinds of structural principles used to organize the immigrant Chinese community in the United States were those common to rural China: kinship, place of origin, regionalism, and dialect similarities. During the pre-1965 era, many immigrants were sojourners who had no intention of staying in America permanently. They reasoned that after they had made enough money in America they would return to China to become entrepreneurs or they would lead blissful lives of retirement.

Initially, the Chinese worked mostly as laborers. After 1884, Chinese financial survival was entirely dependent on ethnic niche businesses such as Chinese restaurants, laundries, grocery stores, and gift shops. In general, the early immigrants were less educated than post-1965 immigrants and mostly came from rural areas of southern China. They were predominantly men who had left their families in China, as various pre-1945 immigration laws prevented the entry of Chinese women into the United States. After 1945 however, the War Bride Act and the G.I. Fiancees Act enabled Chinese women to enter the United States. Still, only Chinese G.I.'s benefitted from these new legal provisions. As a result, in the pre-1965 era, the sex ratio between males and females was highly uneven, with males dramatically outnumbering females. The Chinese community was labeled a "bachelor" community. The lack of family life and children was a principal reason that juvenile delinquency was not a problem.

Since 1965 the Chinese community in the United States has changed dramatically. Of major importance was the enactment of the Immigration Act of 1965, which abolished "national origins" quotas and established a system of preference whereby immediate relatives, skilled and unskilled workers, refugees, scientists, and technical personnel were listed under different categories of preference. For the first time Chinese immigrants were treated equally with other nationalities by United States immigration law, thus ending some eighty-five years of bias against the Chinese. How has the 1965 law affected Chinese immigrants? First, any Chinese citizen who has family connections in America can be sponsored for migration by their relatives in the United States. Family reunions are a major way in which these immigrants can immigrate to the United States. New immigrants can also bring their spouses and children under the age of twenty one. This practice helped to even out the sex ratio between males and females.

Another effect of the new immigration law has been the influx of skilled immigrants. This law specifically favored the entrance of skilled persons trained in science, technology, the arts, and other professions. New immigrants are relatively well-educated, and many are from urban areas of China: Taiwan, Hong Kong, or Macao. The new immigrants are also interested in making America their permanent home; they are not sojourners. The new immigrants' attitudes toward the United States is reflected in the phrase *Lo Di Sheng Gen* (after reachng the land, grow roots). Whenever they can, these new immigrants apply for United States citizenship. In fact, 48 percent of the Chinese in the San Francisco Bay Area are United States citizens. These immigrants wish to establish roots and commit themselves entirely to their new country, and they come relatively prepared to do so. The majority of the Chinese from Hong Kong belong to the middle class, and some arrive with a significant amount of savings or capital.

Given their resources, many of the new immigrants avoid traditional paths to employment through ethnic businesses such as restaurants, groceries, or gift shops. Some own or are employed in garment factories. Some are employed in Caucasian establishments. Others have branched out to areas of manufacturing, transportation, construction, wholesaling, finance, insurance, and agricultural services. Thus, there is more diversity in the economic pursuits of these new immigrants. The traditional images of Chinese coolies and penniless immigrants do not apply to the majority of the new Chinese immigrants. However, economically disadvantaged immigrants do exist, especially among those from mainland China.

Chinatowns in the United States

Today, there are about a dozen Chinatowns in the major metropolitan areas in the United States. While immigrants in the past tended to confine themselves in Chinatowns, the new immigrants who speak English and are professionals neither live nor work in the traditional Chinatowns. However, the Chinese immigrants who do not speak English still tend to move to Chinatowns or Chinese neighborhoods in the major metropolitan areas. These immigrants also depend on the traditional ethnic niche of the Chinese composed of Chinese restaurant, garment factories, gift shops, grocery stores, and laundromats. The ethnic economy of the Chinese and Chinatowns in the United States are an adaptation of the Chinese in the United States and, at the same time, the vestiges of racism and discrimination.

According to the 1990 U.S. Census, the San Francisco Bay Area's Chinese population was 315,345, while the Chinese population in the New York Metropolitan Area was 261,722. The Chinatowns in these two cities are the symbols of Chinese culture in the United States, housing many of the traditional Chinese organizations that coordinate many cultural activities relevant to the immigrant culture. Most of the traditional Chinese associations in various Chinatowns have their headquarters in New York or San Francisco.

Chinatown U.S.A. is a neighborhood, a work place, a social center, and a place that helps immigrants to adjust to a new land. It is an entry port for newcomers to the New World and, as such, is continually replenished with the traditional culture of the homeland. The newly arrived immigrants to the community get their first experiences with the United States and learn how to obtain employment, a social security card, open a bank account, sign up to learn English, understand their rights and obligations as members of U.S. society. America's Chinatown is an acculturation agent for the new immigrants. The community has bilingual social service agencies, translation services, Chinese stores, familiar food supplies, Chinese mass media, and information networks. All these social agencies and institutions fill the needs of the new immigrants. Newcomers can visit traditional herbal medicine stores, temples, and churches, which provides tremendous security to new Chinese immigrants, especially those who do not speak English.

Chinese restaurants are a visual part of San Francisco's Chinatown. (Bernard P. Wong)

Chinese Associations

Chinatown's traditional social structure was organized according to principles that are familiar to the immigrants. Everyone in the community has an opportunity to join one or more of these associations. There are also modern associations such as alumni associations, labor unions, social agencies, political parties.

Traditional Associations. In all the major Chinatowns in the United States, there are the traditional associations organized according to the traditional principles of kinship, clanship, place of origin, dialect, trade, and regionalism. These associations formed themselves into an associational structure. At the top of this structure is the Consolidated Chinese Benevolent Association (CCBA), known in San Francisco as the Chinese Six Companies. At one time, the CCBA, an overall community organization established in 1869, functioned as a consulate for the Chinese. The Chinese Six Companies in San Francisco were composed of Chinese from the six major district associations: the Ning Yung, Kong Chow, Young Wo, Shiu Hing, Hop Wo, and Yan Wo. The Six Companies served as spokesmen for the Chinese in San Francisco. Before the establishment of the Chinese Chamber of Commerce in 1910, the Six Companies also regulated the business activities of the Chinese, mediating business disputes and arbitrating conflicts between various family and district associations. The Six Companies arranged the shipment of bones of deceased immigrants back to China for reburial. They also issued clearance for immigrants to return to China, making sure that all returnees first paid their debts in America. The Chinese Six Companies still run a hospital and Chinese schools. They also are responsible for organizing the celebration of the Chinese New Year and various fundraising activities for the community. Although many of their functions are no longer needed, the Chinese Six Companies remain the highest authority, at least symbolically, of the San Francisco Chinese community. This is also the case of the CCBA in other Chinatowns in the United States.

The CCBA adopted an anti-Communist stance and are strong supporters of Nationalist China. This is perhaps because the CCBAs are controlled by the older Chinese who either suffered under Communism or embraced an anti-Communist ideology. Historically, the CCBA assisted the Kuomintang in their overthrow of the Manchu government in China. The CCBA in various Chinatowns have been under attack from radical students and community workers for being too slow to adapt and meet the needs of the new immigrants. Most of the traditional associations were established before 1965 to serve the needs of the adult, male Chinese, and they are not prepared to tackle contemporary social problems such as housing, Medicare, and juvenile delinquency.

The various family or clan associations in Chinatowns recruit members on the basis of common surname. The largest family associations are the Lee, Chan, and Wong. Within the family name associations are the *Fongs*, which group people according to both common surname and common village or place of origin. The family name or surname group in China was a clan group whose members were assumed to have descended from a common ancestor, and members addressed each other as "clan brothers." In China, the Fongs were a localized clan group and membership was based on patrilineal clansmen and descent from a common ancestor associated with a village. Many family name associations in San Francisco also maintain temporary lodging quarters for their members. These common lodging rooms are called common Fong. Thus the word "Fong" has two meanings: (1) common kinship origin in China and (2) the living quarters in the family name associations. What is significant here is that kinship has been used as a principal of social organization to address the needs and problems of the Chinese community. Within the family name associations, there were once informal credit-rotating clubs (*hui*). In the past, some members of a family name association could voluntarily participate in a hui. Members of the hui would agree on the amount of the deposit. Thus, for instance, ten

The Chinese Consolidated Benevolent Association building in San Francisco. (Bernard P. Wong)

members of the hui might agree to deposit $1,000 each and form a total pool of $10,000. The member entering the bid of the highest interest rate would get the money for his use. In return, he promised the $1,000 in return to each member plus interest. After repayment to all of the members, say, in ten months, the hui will be dissolved. This kind of informal credit arrangement is no longer practiced by the family name associations for it is rather risky and is not enforceable by law. Credit unions and banks are now the institutions for loans for the new immigrants. One association, the Lee Family Association, has its own credit union for members.

Multifamily name associations exist among the Chinese in the United States. One of the most important multifamily name associations is the

Four Brothers Association, which was organized by the Liu, Kwan, Chang, and Chao families because their forebears swore brotherhood by the Peace Garden Oath two thousand years ago for the purpose of saving the Han Dynasty. Another multifamily name association is the G. Ho. Oak Tin Association, which is composed of the Chan, Hu, Yuan, and Wang families, all of whom claim descent from the Shun Emperor. Chee Tuck Same Tuck Association is composed of the Wu, Tsai, and Chow families who were once neighbors in China. Similarly, the historical friendships among neighbors in China led to other associations; Loui, Fong, and Kwon families united to form Soo Yuen Association, and the Gon, Lai, and Ho families became the San Yick Association. Perhaps the most interesting of all is the Chew Lun Association, which united the Tam, Tan, Hsu, and Hsieh families based on a similarity (a common radical) in the Chinese characters used to spell their names.

In all the family name associations, both single family and multifamily, kinship ideology has been deliberately embraced, and kinship terms are used to address one another. The family name associations still exist today, attracting mostly older immigrants, to provide recreational facilities such as reading rooms and mahjong tables, to perform limited relief services, and to organize scholarship funds and ancestor worships.

Another level of organization is that of regional associations, which are composed of members from a certain county or region in China. The functions of the regional associations are similar to those of the family associations. They are basically mutual aid societies rendering welfare and employment assistance; the larger associations generally offer temporary lodging facilities, and some provide aid for burial service. The Vietnam Chinese Association has an informal insurance company that collects fees from members to form a fund to help families afford funeral services.

Business and trade associations form another cluster of associations in the social structure of Chinatown. The Chinese Art Goods Association, Chinese Chamber of Commerce, Chinese Apparel Contractors Association, Chinese Laundry Association, and Golden Gate Neighborhood Grocers' Association are some examples. These associations often negotiate with the larger society on matters of concern to Chinese businesses. As information centers, they channel information and regulations on taxes, sanitation, wages, licenses, and legislation. For example, the Chinese Chamber of Commerce voiced community-wide concern about the removal of Highway 480 in San Francisco, asking for the city government's assistance with the traffic flow through Chinatown and for parking facilities for customers of Chinatown businesses.

Another group of associations are called Tongs. The Tongs had much notoriety in the Tong Wars days. The Tongs have their roots in China as secret societies that fought against the Manchu government. In the past, the Tongs in Chinatown were involved in many illegal activities such as prostitution, gambling, and opium smoking. The Tongs have dissociated from their criminal past and today many call themselves fraternal organizations or merchant associations. On Leong Association, Suey Sing Merchant Association, Hip Sing Association, Yee Ying Merchant Association, and Ying On Association are some examples of Tongs.

Many of these traditional associations were important in the past, but they are gradually being replaced by modern associations such as alumni associations, political parties, social agencies, and the like. Organizations such as the Chinese American Citizens Alliance, Chinese for Affirmative Action, Chinese Newcomers Service Center, Chinatown Youth Center, Chinatown Neighborhood Improvement Resource Center, and On Lok Health Services for the elderly now play an important role in the life of the new immigrants.

The traditional Chinese associations exist mostly for social and recreational purposes. Some of these associations offer scholarships to students and maintain a place for ancestral tablets; some even have cemeteries. In fact, these associations tend to be particularly significant for the Chinese who have leadership capabilities or aspirations but have no opportunity to join any civic or social organizations in the larger society due to a lack of

English fluency. Many well-to-do Chinese are particularly interested in joining the associations and aspiring to leadership positions that will bring recognition or prestige. In general, the new immigrants from Hong Kong and Taiwan who speak English and live outside the confines of Chinatown have little or no interest in becoming members of these Chinese associations.

New Associations.   The second, larger block of formal organizations are called the new associations, for they differ from the traditional associations in many respects. First, the new associations have been organized recently and are not included within the umbrella of CCBA. Second, the new organizations recruit members from different social, economic, and educational backgrounds. Due to the influx of immigrants since 1965, the new associations have multiplied in size and number. New regional associations, alumni, political, commercial, and religious associations have been established, such as the Taiwan Association, the Hong Kong Student Association, the Lingnam University Alumni Association, and the Taiwan University Alumni Association. These associations have many highly educated members with cosmopolitan outlooks. Thus they differ markedly from the old sojourners who filled the rank and file of the traditional associations. The principal functions of most of these associations are generally social and recreational. Although all of them proclaim to protect the interests of Chinese Americans, these associations are generally apolitical. A small number of these associations, however, are actively concerned with Chinese civil rights. The notable ones are the Organization of the Chinese Americans, the Association for Progress, the Association for Equal Employment, and Chinese for Affirmative Action.

Social Agencies and Labor Unions.   Social agencies and labor unions are oriented to the larger society and have their roots in the U.S. society. In fact, many of these organizations have direct connections with the government, churches, labor unions, and nonprofit and charitable organizations of the larger society. They serve as bridges between Chinatown and U.S. society. The emergence and proliferation of their social services were related to the new resources available to the Chinese since 1965, including manpower and new funding available through the Economic Opportunity Act; consciousness of ethnicity; and the multiplication of social problems as a result of the influx of the new immigrants since 1965.

Cultural Continuity and Culture Change

The Chinese in the United States are not homogeneous. In terms of cultural identity, some adhere to the Old World culture, some are in favor of assimilation, and others are for the development of a hybrid identity (i.e., the Chinese-American identity). Politically, some are pro-Kuomintang, some are for the People's Republic of China, and some are committed to establishing roots in the United States. Increasingly, the trend is toward greater participation in the social, political, and economic life in America. In recent years, there has been an emphasis on diversity and multiculturalism in America, which encourages the celebration of one's ethnic roots and traditions. Among the Chinese, some want to be accepted wholeheartedly by the larger society and still retain their cultural heritage as Chinese. This tendency of emphasizing ethnic pride and at the same time wanting to be accepted by the larger society has met some practical difficulties. First, there is the problem of lack of education about the Chinese culture. Many second-generation Chinese Americans are so much concerned with economic mobility in the United States that they have not paid attention to learning the Chinese language and culture. In recent years, some of the American-born Chinese are taking ethnic studies courses. However, their knowledge of Chinese language and culture tend to be limited. Second, the residents of Chinatown who are new immigrants are more comfortable in speaking Chinese and are more at ease in following the Chinese patterns of interaction than the American ones. These new immigrants are so busy trying to make ends meet that they are not interested in the multiculturalism movement. The old immigrants are die-hard followers of old Chinese traditions.

Some of these old immigrants suffered severe discrimination in the past, and they see nothing worthwhile in assimilating to American life.

However, two important political changes in the larger society have affected the lives of the new immigrants. One is the enactment of the Immigration Act of 1965. The second is the civil rights movement in the United States and the subsequent passage of the Equal Opportunity Act and the Affirmative Action Program. The new Immigration Act of 1965 abolished the inequitable national quota system. Chinese and non-Chinese were to be treated equally under the new law. Chinese immigrants were no longer barred from bringing along their families. Since the new immigrants arrived with their spouses, they were also responsible for

A merchant sorts through a basket of ginseng root for an apothecary in San Francisco. (Phil Schermeister/ Corbis)

a new generation of native-born Chinese Americans. By 1996, there were more native-born Chinese Americans than any time before. The estimates of many experts about this population are around half a million. These native-born Chinese Americans will be the facilitators for future integration of the Chinese in America. As indicated by many social scientists, the local-born members of an ethnic community have always played an important role in the assimilation of minority populations.

Today, as a whole, there is more willingness among the Chinese immigrants to participate in American society than previously. Several reasons explain this kind of willingness to be part of America. First, they now immigrate to the United States with the intention of staying permanently. Second, many of them come from urban backgrounds. They are thus Westernized and more in tune with Western lifestyles. Many, in fact, want to assimilate into American culture and are looking forward to participating in American democracy. Third, many are well educated and knowledgeable about the American political process. They are eager to use American methods such as voting, petitioning, and demonstrating to pursue the "good life" in America. Thus there is a predisposition among the new immigrants to participate fully in American society, politically and socially. This kind of attitude will indeed help them enter into the larger society.

Politically, there have been relatively more new immigrants participating in U.S. politics than old immigrants. This is partly because new immigrants are better educated and more familiar with the political process in modern states. The new immigrants realize that they are rooted in Chinese culture but not in Chinese politics. They want to establish themselves in America, to protect their new life, and to obtain equal treatment in U.S. society. These new immigrants are eager to exercise their political rights. New organizations have been formed to sponsor political rights, to sponsor political candidates for elected offices, and to lobby for the interests of Chinese Americans. These organizations are not merely indications of the

Chinese interest in establishing themselves politically; their participation in the democratic process is an important index of integration.

The normalization of the relations between China and the United States affected the assimilation of the Chinese in the post-1965 era. First, the People's Republic of China advocated explicitly that overseas Chinese should acquire the nationality of the host country. Second, as a result of normalization of relations, Chinese Americans became keenly aware of their peculiar situation. They live in America and are committed to its lifestyle. Culturally, however, their roots are Chinese. Socially and economically, they embrace the American system. They became convinced that America was their true home when confronted with the question of "belonging." Thus, contrary to popular perception, Chinese Americans, especially the new immigrants, have not become more "sinicized" or developed more allegiance to the People's Republic of China as a result of normalization of relations. Instead, as a whole they have become more Americanized, increasing participation in U.S. society. This kind of change has had a great deal to do with the awakening of their ethnic identity in the midst of the triangular relations among the People's Republic of China, Taiwan, and the United States.

The economic conditions of the Chinese Americans have improved. However, there are three major aspects that need to be clarified. First, there is a relatively large group of professional Chinese people. This group of people are high wage earners. Second, there is a group of people among the immigrants from China who have to toil in the labor intensive ethnic enterprises such as restaurants and garment factories. The in-

A young child gives an offering to the costumed lion at a Chinese New Year celebration in Seattle. (Dean Wong/ Corbis)

come for these immigrants is relatively meager. Third, there are elderly immigrants who depend on the U.S. welfare system, although the size of this group is relatively small. These divisions still allow the average income of the Chinese immigrants to look better than many other ethnic groups. It is misleading, however, to use the term "model minority" to describe the Chinese immigrant group as a whole, for it obscures the social and economic differences among the Chinese.

Many second-, third-, or fourth-generation Chinese Americans have attended college or professional schools, and after graduation they usually prefer to work for American establishments according to their professional capacity. In fact, the professional Chinese tend not to be related to Chinatown economies and thus not to be connected to Chinatowns in general, living instead in middle-class neighborhoods.

Working and living among middle-class Americans allows the Chinese to have more contacts with U.S. society through education, institutions, careers, neighborhood connections, professional associations, churches, and other secondary institutions. They even have the same middle-class aspirations: better jobs, better housing, better cars, better education for their children, better household appliances, and better economic mobility. Even the family system resembles that of the majority of middle-class Americans: a neolocal residence and the nuclear family. Siblings are no longer required to address each other by traditional kinship terminology. Relationships within the nuclear family focus on the husband and wife bond rather than the father and son bond that exists in the traditional Chinese family. The lifestyle of these professionals who are not connected to Chinatown is principally a product of their careers, which are intimately connected with the American economy and society. There is also a significant increase of interracial marriages between the Chinese and members of the larger society; the increase of out-marriage among Chinese males went from 7.4 percent (1940–1949) to 13.5 percent (1950–1959) to a high of 17.7 percent (1960–1969). Correspondingly, the out-marriages among the Chinese females for the same periods rose from 5.6 percent to 10.2 percent and finally to 18 percent. Increased interracial marriage among the Chinese is also an indication of their increased assimilation. Furthermore, Chinese professionals with a higher education are more likely to marry interracially, another example showing that Chinese professionals are more assimilatable than other Chinese in the Chinese ethnic enclave.

Forces for maintaining the culture in the ethnic enclave emanate from a variety of sources, one of which is the Chinese press. Others include the Chinese school, the traditional associations, and their leaders. The influx of the new immigrant also serves to reinforce Chinese culture in America. Last, but not least, is the celebration of traditional festivals in various Chinese communities. Some of these festivals are celebrated in public, and others are celebrated privately, either at home or in association halls. Cultural festivities in various Chinatowns tend to unite the inhabitants and are symbols of Chinese culture in America. The major festivals are the Chinese New Year, Chingming (Festival of the Tombs), Chungyang (Festival of the Kites), the Dragon Boat Festival, and the Mid-Autumn Festival. By far, the most popular of them all is the Chinese New Year, which attracts many tourists to the Chinatowns of New York and San Francisco.

Barriers to Further Assimilation

Increased participation in U.S. society by the Chinese since World War II should not imply that discrimination against the Chinese has ceased. While there has been great improvement, the Chinese still experience legal, social, and economic discrimination. Even the Chinese who are U.S. citizens find obtaining federal employment extremely difficult; the fact that their mother country is a communist country is a barrier for many government jobs. It is still assumed in some quarters that the Chinese are clannish and cannot be made good citizens of the United States, in spite of the fact that they have fought and died for the United States in World War I, World War II, the Korean War, and the Vietnam War. Some Chinese families have been in America for five or six generations, yet they are often considered foreigners because of their Chinese ethnicity. Socially, there are educational institutions that still turn away qualified students of Chinese descent. In the job market, Chinese often encounter subtle discrimination. Once employed, Chinese workers often find it difficult to be promoted to higher rank, especially to managerial positions. This phenomenon has been referred to as "topping out," meaning that they have reached the point where further promotion is extremely unlikely. This explains why some Chinese leave their jobs after working many years for a company. Realizing that it is a "dead-end" job, they leave and open their own firms. This strategy of becoming self-employed echoes the old strategy of the Chinese during the exclusion era; in adversary climates, their forebears withdrew from competition with the white labor market by opening their own ethnic restaurants or laundries. Economically, the lifeline for many Chinese immigrants is still tied to the ethnic niche. The 1990s also saw an increase in the number of "hate" crimes committed against the Chinese. Poverty still exists in various Chinatowns, but the model minority image created by the media often obscures the social reality of the Chinatowns' pressing problems: a decaying housing situation, crowding, aging, juvenile delinquency, deficient health care, underemployment, and restrictive economic opportunities.

As a whole, in examining the social and economic conditions of the Chinese, improvement can be seen. The gradual elimination of social, legal, and economic injustices throughout the years by legislative means has helped foster Chinese participation in American society. The continued elimination of these external barriers will likely entice further participation and contribution by Chinese Americans.

See also: CHINESE-VIETNAMESE; TAIWANESE

Bibliography

De Guignes, J. (1761). *Researches Sur Les Navigations des Chinois du Cote de L'Amerique.* Paris: Academie des Inscriptions.

Fang, Zhongpu. (1980). "Did Chinese Buddhists Reach America 1,000 Years Before Columbus?" *China Reconstruct* 29(8):65.

Hsu, F. L. K. (1981). *American and Chinese: Passage of Difference.* Honolulu: University Press of Hawaii.

Lee, R. H. (1947). "The Chinese Communities in the Rocky Mountain Region." Ph.D. diss., University of Chicago.

Lee, R. H. (1960). *The Chinese in the United States of America.* Hong Kong: Hong Kong University Press.

Sandmeyer, E. E. (1973). *The Anti-Chinese Movement in California.* Urbana: The University of Illinois Press.

Steiner, S. (1979). *Fusang: The Chinese Who Built America.* New York: Harper & Row.

Wong, B. P. (1979). *A Chinese-American Community: Ethnicity and Survival Strategies.* Singapore: Chopmen Enterprises.

Wong, B. P. (1982). *Chinatown: Economic Adaptation and Ethnic Identity of the Chinese.* New York: Holt, Rinehart and Winston.

Wong, B. P. (1988). *Patronage, Brokerage, Entrepreneurship, and the Chinese Community of New York.* New York: AMS Press.

Wong, B. P. (1994). "Hong Kong Immigrants in San Francisco." In *Reluctant Exiles?,* edited by R. Skeldon. Armonk, NY: M. E. Sharpe.

Wong, B. P. (1996). *Ethnicity and Entrepreneurship: Immigrant Chinese in the San Francisco Bay Area.* Boston: Allyn & Bacon.

Wu, C.-T. (1958). "Chinese People and Chinatown in New York City." Ph.D. diss. University of Michigan, Ann Arbor.

BERNARD P. WONG

CHINESE-VIETNAMESE

Chinese-Vietnamese, also known as Sino-Vietnamese, ethnic Chinese from Vietnam, or Viet Hoa, are persons who immigrated to the United States from Vietnam but trace their ancestry to

China. Nearly all entered the United States between 1978 and 1985 as refugees from the Vietnam conflict. In the two thousand years of relationship between China and its southern neighbor, thousands of Chinese have immigrated to Vietnam, making their community, which numbered about 1.5 million in the 1960s, South Vietnam's largest ethnic minority group. Most had relatives who left China's Guandong Province, directly north of Vietnam, in the late nineteenth and early twentieth centuries in search of economic opportunity.

Prior to exit, Chinese-Vietnamese communities were highly organized, most often on the basis of their dialect and region of origin. A major settlement was Cholon (Big Market), Saigon's massive Chinatown where schools and even a hospital served the ethnic concentration. Within such communities, regional/dialect groups included Cantonese, Chao-Zhou, Hainanese, Fujianese, and Ha'kanese. Members of the population could generally speak several Chinese dialects as well as Vietnamese. Their degree of assimilation to Vietnamese culture varied considerably, ranging from near total, to those who lived in Chinese enclaves, sent their children to Chinese schools, and spoke Chinese dialects rather than Vietnamese. Many Chinese-Vietnamese were self-employed, and occupational specialization often took place among various dialect groups. Like overseas Chinese in other Asian nations, Chinese in Vietnam occupied a classic middleman role due to their own entrepreneurial orientation, as well as a result of the "divide and rule" policy of French colonists. As a group, the Chinese-Vietnamese were much less likely than the Vietnamese to have served in the South Vietnamese military during the war years.

While China and Vietnam share numerous cultural, religious and technological similarities, the two nations are also parties to a history of antagonism that goes back two thousand years. In fact, a major element of Vietnamese national identity can be traced to its conflict with its powerful northern neighbor. As a result, people of Chinese ancestry living within Vietnam experienced discrimination both because of their links to a hostile nation and their role as middleman traders. Under the Diem regime (1958–1963), various laws were enacted to encourage assimilation, including the requirements that Chinese serve in the military and take on Vietnamese citizenship. The transformation of Vietnam from capitalism to communism did not mean the end of persecution for Chinese-Vietnamese. As Communist nations, North Vietnam and China were allies during the Vietnam War. However, soon after, hostilities heated up again when Vietnam invaded Cambodia, China's ally.

As a result of the Vietnam-China conflict, the Hanoi government decided to rid Vietnam of its Chinese minority. Three reasons are cited for Vietnam's ejection of the Chinese. First, the loyalty of the Chinese was doubted. Second, the Communist government was in the process of rebuilding Vietnamese society in a socialist vein and wished to remove this staunchly capitalistic minority group. Finally, by charging the ethnic Chinese hundreds or thousands of dollars in gold as an exit fee, the new government was able to obtain badly needed financial resources. During this period the ethnic Chinese were informally allowed to leave Vietnam, and numbers of ethnic Vietnamese even assumed a Chinese identity to facilitate their own flight. Most escaped as boat people, but some 250,000 Chinese-Vietnamese living in North Vietnam entered China. Similar factors resulted in the exit of smaller flows of ethnic Chinese refugees from Cambodia and Laos, with whom the Chinese-Vietnamese often associate upon resettlement in the United States.

The size of the Chinese-Vietnamese population in the United States, itself divided by political and linguistic differences and varying degrees of assimilation to Vietnamese culture, is difficult to determine, partly because U.S. government agencies responsible for refugee resettlement collect data only by nationality and not ethnicity, making Chinese-Vietnamese indistinguishable from Vietnamese. An estimate by Rubén Rumbaut that is based on 1990 U.S. Census data suggests that their total numbers are 135,000 or more. However, even census data are flawed because Chinese-Vietnamese often report their ethnicity simply as "Chinese" on census forms.

Chinese-Vietnamese business mall in Los Angeles's Chinatown. (Steven J. Gold)

Arrival as Boat People

While the elite of South Vietnamese society began to enter the United States immediately after the fall of South Vietnam in the spring of 1975, only a handful of Chinese-Vietnamese persons—business leaders, soldiers, government officials, and those working for the United States—arrived among the first wave. Most Chinese-Vietnamese broached the United States following the outbreak of the Vietnam-China conflict of 1978. Of those in the United States in 1990, 29 percent entered between 1975 and 1979; 31 percent between 1980 and 1981; and about 33 percent between 1982 and 1990. Finally, approximately 2 percent were in the United States prior to 1975, and 5 percent were born in the United States.

Called boat people, these refugees often lived for three or more years under communism—sometimes laboring in "reeducation" camps or remote "new economic zones" before leaving Vietnam. Their exit, involving open sea voyages in leaky, overcrowded boats or long journeys on foot across revolution-torn Cambodia to Thailand was subject to attacks by pirates and military forces. Reportedly up to half perished in flight. Those lucky enough to survive spent several months in overcrowded refugee camps in Thailand, Malaysia, Indonesia, the Philippines, or Hong Kong before entering the United States. In refugee camps, various ethnic and nationality groups were housed together, often exacerbating long-standing antipathies and provoking strife among the various ethnic and nationality groups who were forced to flee the region.

Refugees selected for eventual resettlement in the United States received three months of training in English and American culture at one of two refugee processing centers (RPCs) in Galang, Indonesia, or Bataan, Philippines, to foster adaptation. Following their term in the RPC, refugees boarded charter flights for the United States, where they were met by representatives of resettlement agencies or sponsors and set up with apartments in refugee neighborhoods.

Due to the dangers of escape, more young men left Vietnam as boat people than did women, children, or the elderly. However, the Chinese-Vietnamese community has a higher rate of intact families than is the case among other groups of Southeast Asian refugees. U.S. Census data for 1990 indicate that the population is 50.4 percent male and 49.6 percent female. Because the vast majority of Chinese-Vietnamese entered the United States as refugees, they received government assistance and were exempt from nationality quotas and waiting periods that restrict voluntary immigrants. However, also as refugees, they experienced a traumatic exit, which is associated with physical and mental health problems, that prevented most from bringing financial assets, personal belongings, and even vital documents, such as diplomas, with them.

To distribute their impact, Southeast Asian refugees were initially resettled throughout the

United States. However, refugees soon relocated to California and a few other states where the climate, economy, and ethnic mix were to their liking. Unlike the ethnic Vietnamese, who had almost no presence in the United States prior to 1975, the Chinese-Vietnamese were able to join coethnic communities and sometimes even relatives in the United States. Consequently Chinese-Vietnamese refugees often gravitated toward American Chinatowns, where they found a remotely familiar environment and subsistence-level employment, often in restaurants, garment factories, or as laborers. Others, however, remained more closely affiliated with Vietnamese communities. As of 1990, 68 percent lived in California, 5 percent in New York, 4 percent in Texas, and 3 percent in Washington State, with the remainder distributed throughout the United States. The great majority of Chinese-Vietnamese are concentrated in just three metropolitan areas: 36 percent live in Los Angeles, Orange, and Riverside counties in Southern California; 26 percent in the San Francisco Bay Area (including Oakland and San Jose); and 4 percent in New York City.

Culture

The cultural orientation of the Chinese-Vietnamese is shaped by several factors, including their Chinese origins, the Vietnamese folkways in which they were immersed prior to immigration, and their experience as an ethnic minority group. Their religious outlook is most influenced by two belief systems, Buddhism and Confucianism. Mahayana Buddhism emphasizes the ethical principle of "good works" toward all living things. It argues for detachment from the material world, viewing wealth, power, and status as corrupting forces that cause suffering. For the Buddhist, true peace or Nirvana is achieved by the renunciation of worldliness. A process of reincarnation, whereby a person achieves his or her station in life as a result of good or bad deeds in previous lives, is also a major postulate. Buddhist priests (bonzes) were figures of influence in Vietnam and retain some authority in the United States. By the early 1980s the financial-

ly strapped refugee community had funded the creation of several Buddhist temples in the United States. In addition, Chinese-Vietnamese refugees participate in Buddhist churches organized by other Chinese communities in the United States. Their monks are sources of guidance, healing, and emotional support to the refugee population.

Confucianism—really a philosophy of life rather than a religion—is a second major influence on the Chinese-Vietnamese. Confucianism is generally regarded to be a conservative social tradition that posits the patriarchal family as the ideal human institution. It requires each man's and woman's obedience to higher authorities—rulers, parents, husbands, and older siblings. Modeling politics after its view of the family, the Confucian image of a good society is one of loyal citizens following the dictates of the father-emperor. Confucianism places great value on education and encourages parents to make sacrifices so their children might achieve. Accordingly, Chinese-Vietnamese families generally appreciate the opportunities for higher education that are available in the United States and, when resources permit, do their best to encourage children's academic pursuits.

The Chinese-Vietnamese Family

Chinese-Vietnamese religious cosmology, influential in itself, also shapes another institution of central importance: the traditional Chinese family. It is perhaps the most basic, enduring, and self-consciously acknowledged form of national culture among refugees. The Chinese-Vietnamese family is customarily a large, patriarchal, and extended unit, including minor children, married sons, daughters-in-law, unmarried grown daughters, and grandchildren under the same roof. Individualism is discouraged, while collective obligations and decision making are warranted. Rights and duties—such as inheritance or care for the elderly—are prescribed according to age, gender, and birth order. A vocabulary far more extensive than that available in the English language describes a complexity of relationships among siblings, cousins, and other relatives on both sides of the family. Deceased family members are also venerated; hence death constitutes no real departure from family life.

The eldest male has primary responsibility for the well-being and moral guidance of the entire family unit and supervises ancestor worship rituals. He is likely to make decisions for family members, choosing their occupations or marriage partners. Further, family finances are generally collectivized, with the father determining how individual earnings should be spent for the aggregate good.

Chinese-Vietnamese in the United States often consider themselves to be more traditional and "old-fashioned" than either Vietnamese or other Chinese groups, describing their reliance on traditions as a means of helping families survive the refugee experience, adapt to the United States, and keep children in line. However, like other immigrant and refugee groups, they also experience significant problems of family adjustment, often associated with economic difficulty, generational conflicts, and role reversals between men and women and between parents and children.

According to the 1990 U.S. Census, the average Chinese-Vietnamese household consists of approximately six persons. For persons age sixteen or over, 51 percent are married (48 percent of men, 55 percent of women), 1.9 percent are divorced, and 42.5 percent have never been married. Due to the effects of war, almost 5 percent of women are widowed, five times the figure for men. Reflecting the relative shortage of Chinese-Vietnamese (and Vietnamese) women in the United States, men reveal a much higher rate of having never been married (48 percent) than women (36 percent). The Chinese-Vietnamese are a relatively young population. As of 1990, 28 percent were nineteen or younger, 55 percent were twenty to forty-four, 13 percent were forty-five to sixty-four, and 3.7 percent were sixty-five or older.

Patterns of Economic Adaptation

Ethnic Chinese refugees from Vietnam occupy a paradoxical economic position within the South-east Asian refugee community in the United States. Relying on past experience and sources of capital and goods from overseas Chinese communities, a fraction of the Chinese-Vietnamese have been able to reestablish their role as entrepreneurs in America. Many of the most successful entrepreneurs among Southeast Asian refugee communities are of Chinese ethnicity. A mere seven or eight years after their arrival on U.S. soil, informed observers estimated that a large fraction—up to 40 percent—of businesses in refugee enclaves such as Orange County's Little Saigon (the largest Vietnamese community outside of Southeast Asia) and San Francisco's Tenderloin were Chinese-Vietnamese. Some Chinese-Vietnamese immigrants have become quite prosperous in garment manufacturing, food, and import/export. More often they run small "mom and pop" retail businesses such as restaurants, liquor stores, and beauty parlors. According to the 1990 U.S. Census, 9.2 percent of Chinese-Vietnamese in the United States, age twenty-five to sixty-four, were self-employed or worked in family businesses. While this figure is lower than the 10.2 percent average for all ethnic groups, it exceeds that of Vietnamese (8%), demonstrating the entrepreneurial orientation of the Chinese-Vietnamese.

However, lacking a Western-style education and English skill, and sometimes subject to discrimination from ethnic Vietnamese in the United States, as a group, the Sino-Vietnamese resettled in the United States are still doing less well in terms of social and economic adaptation when compared with Vietnamese refugees, including those who arrived at the same time with similar backgrounds. According to the 1990 U.S. Census, almost 13 percent of Chinese-Vietnamese age twenty-five to sixty-four have no education, 16 percent have completed elementary school, 21 percent have some high school, 16 percent are high school graduates, 25 percent have some college, and 9 percent have a bachelor's degree or higher. Men and women have generally similar levels of education, except a slightly larger fraction of women have no education, and a somewhat greater number of men are college graduates. In terms of language, 51 percent of those age twenty-five to sixty-four speak English "well," "very well," or exclusively, while 49 percent speak English "not well," or not at all. At home, among Chinese-Vietnamese of all age groups, 3.5 percent speak English, 76 percent speak a Chinese dialect, and 19 percent speak Vietnamese.

Statistics that report the economic status of refugees by ethnicity are relatively rare, but those that do exist indicate that the ethnic Chinese confront considerable difficulties and are marked by distinct patterns of education, residence, and occupational distribution. A 1982 University of Michigan study of 1,384 Vietnamese, Chinese-Vietnamese, and Lao refugee families who entered the United States after 1978 found that of the three groups, the Chinese-Vietnamese had the lowest rate of employment and were the least likely to be self-supporting. Moreover, Chinese-Vietnamese who were working earned less per hour than

employed Vietnamese and had relatively high rates of dependence on public assistance. Field studies document this trend as they describe refugees' difficulties in finding well-paid, stable work in either coethnic business or the larger economy. Hence the Chinese-Vietnamese are relatively unique among Asian immigrants, as they constitute an ethnic population that includes both affluent business owners as well as poverty-stricken, welfare-dependent refugees.

According to the 1990 U.S. Census, more than 28 percent of Chinese-Vietnamese were below the poverty line and 8 percent age twenty-five to sixty-four were unemployed, while another 23 percent were not in the labor force. Of those twenty-five to sixty-four who had jobs, the most common were low-level clerical work (11%), service jobs (20%), and factory jobs (26%). About 8 percent of Chinese-Vietnamese had managerial or professional employment. The average wage and salary

Members of a Chinese-Vietnamese family in their herb and tea shop in Westminster, California. (Steven J. Gold)

income for Chinese-Vietnamese individuals in 1989 was $9,139. Their total household income, at $42,563, was amassed by an average household size of just under six persons. Although the Chinese-Vietnamese have low incomes and are heavily concentrated in cities with the highest housing prices in the country, a full 46 percent owned their own homes as of 1990.

Community Formation

Two factors are central for understanding the community formation activities of Chinese-Vietnamese in the United States. The first is their experience as a "twice immigrant" group—one that was accustomed to being ethnic outsiders and minorities even before arrival in the United States. The second is their traditional emphasis on self-employment as a livelihood. Drawing on this heritage, Chinese-Vietnamese are familiar with ethnic and family-based organizations intended to facilitate their own cultural and economic survival. Within their communities, successful entrepreneurs play important roles in providing jobs and benefits to family members and coethnics. Because most Chinese-Vietnamese in the United States lack capital and other resources, their organizations often receive support from more established Chinese based in the United States and in several overseas communities such as Taiwan, Thailand, Singapore, and Hong Kong.

One major goal of the Chinese-Vietnamese associations is to aid coethnics in their resettlement in the United States. While a network of resettlement agencies and mutual assistance agencies (MAAs), generally run by elite Vietnamese, offered services during the years when thousands of Chinese-Vietnamese arrived in the United States, most Chinese-Vietnamese found Vietnamese organizations unsatisfactory. Both Vietnamese and Chinese-Vietnamese informants claimed that Chinese-Vietnamese were not treated fairly by Vietnamese-run resettlement agencies. To the Chinese-Vietnamese, agency managers (who were often former officers of the South Vietnamese Army) reminded them of the military men who had harassed them and demanded bribes during

the Vietnam War. Further, elite Vietnamese often scapegoated the Chinese-Vietnamese by claiming that criminals and other deviant members of the refugee population were of Chinese origin. Thus the needs of Chinese-Vietnamese were not met by existing MAAs and resettlement agencies. However, few ethnic Chinese had college degrees or spoke English fluently. As a group they lacked the credentials and connections required to take leadership of government-funded, refugee-run resettlement agencies.

Instead, relying on their long history of minority self-help in Vietnam, Chinese-Vietnamese created various associations, often based on dialect and regional origins. A Chinese-Vietnamese resettlement worker staffing such an agency in San Francisco described its mandate:

> We feel a lot of discrimination from the Vietnamese. They did it in Vietnam and they do it here, too. We describe our background as Chinese, not Vietnamese. We know from experience that the refugee agency—which the Vietnamese people run—won't do too much to help us. We are people in a common position, so that's why we joined together and started this association for Indochina Chinese refugees.

In addition to creating ethnic associations for resettlement, Chinese-Vietnamese also cooperate for economic purposes. Business owners describe how family-based networks are used to raise money, obtain inventories, access business advice, and secure trustworthy employees. Members of extended families and other networks sometimes develop cooperative arrangements to limit the cutthroat competition common to ethnic business districts. Chinese-Vietnamese use their linguistic and cultural skills and overseas connections to import consumer items of the type desired by Asian shoppers in the United States. Since labor costs are much lower in Asian countries, imported agricultural and manufactured goods are often inexpensive when compared to those available in the United States. Because certain Asian products preferred by Vietnamese consumers are not generally exported to the West, personal contacts are vital for organizing their acquisition and shipment. Importers claim that organizing international trade in perishable commodities is extremely difficult and would be virtually impossible without their competence in Chinese, coethnic connections, and travel to Asia. Further, since the ethnic Vietnamese generally lacked international business experience and had ties only to Vietnam—a Communist nation that prior to the mid-1990s could not trade with the United States—the Chinese-Vietnamese were almost without competition in their role as purveyors of goods to almost a million Southeast Asians living in the United States.

While their heavy emphasis on self-employment would appear to be economically beneficial to the entire Chinese-Vietnamese population, available data suggest that the large majority of this group continues to have financial problems. Studies by several scholars that compare employment and ethnicity within Southeast Asian refugee populations conclude that Chinese-Vietnamese are disproportionately involved in an ethnic economy— working for coethnics and relying on ethnic connections for job referrals much more frequently than the ethnic Vietnamese. In addition, these studies find that Chinese-Vietnamese have lower incomes, more part-time work, more limited opportunities for advancement, and fewer benefits than ethnic Vietnamese. For the Sino-Vietnamese community, the heavy orientation toward the ethnic economy appears to be a mixed blessing. Those able to run successful businesses do relatively well. For a larger group, however, reliance on coethnic employment seems to offer inadequate opportunities for upward mobility, at least in the short term. Nevertheless, as the Chinese-Vietnamese spend more time in the United States, their rates of self-employment have increased, so there is reason to believe that benefits from the ethnic economy will "trickle down" to assist a broader group.

Conclusions

Entering the United States as refugees from the Vietnam War, Chinese-Vietnamese refugees are characterized by a unique series of resources and liabilities. Maintaining a strong sense of family and community rooted in their experience as an ethnic minority in Vietnam, they possess certain skills for adapting to life in the United States. Moreover, their background in self-employment and their links to coethnic Chinese both in the United States and overseas provide some of the refugees with resources for establishing economic self-sufficiency in the United States. At the same time, however, the Chinese-Vietnamese are marginal to the larger Vietnamese-American community, and many reveal poverty and high levels of dependence on public assistance. Finally, it is probable that in the future, members of the Chinese-Vietnamese population will develop broader forms of ethnic identification and merge into the larger Vietnamese-American or Chinese-American communities.

See also: CHINESE; VIETNAMESE

Bibliography

Chen, K. C. (1987). *China's War with Vietnam, 1979: Issues, Decisions, and Implications.* Stanford, CA: Hoover Institution Press.

Desbarats, J. (1986). "Ethnic Differences in Adaptation: Sino-Vietnamese Refugees in the United States." *International Migration Review* 20(2): 405–427.

Gold, S. J. (1992). *Refugee Communities: A Comparative Field Study.* Newbury Park, CA: Sage Publications.

Gold, S. J. (1994). "Chinese-Vietnamese Entrepreneurs in California." In *The New Asian Immigration in Los Angeles and Global Restructuring,* edited by P. Ong, E. Bonacich, and L. Cheng. Philadelphia: Temple University Press.

Purcell, V. (1965). *The Chinese in Southeast Asia.* London: Oxford University Press.

Reimers, D. M. (1985). *Still the Golden Door: The Third World Comes to America.* New York: Columbia University Press.

Rumbaut, R. G. (1989). "The Structure of Refuge: Southeast Asian Refugees in the United States, 1975–1985." *International Review of Comparative Public Policy* 1:97–129.

Whitmore, J. K. (1985). "Chinese from Southeast Asia." In *Refugees in the United States: A Reference Handbook,* edited by D. Haines. Westport, CT: Greenwood Press.

STEVEN J. GOLD

CIRCASSIANS

The Circassians are also known by Turkish designation Cherkess. They call themselves Adyghé, with various tribal designations, such as Kabardians, Besleneys, Shapseghs (often erroneously Shapsughs), Bzhedukhs, Abadzakhs, and Chemgwis being most common within the ethnic designation. Living among them can also be found Abkhaz (also known by the Russian designation of Abazins and by the Turkish one of Abazas), who call themselves Apswa, as well as a few descendants of the Ubykhs, a small but distinct people who also called themselves Adyghé.

The Circassians and their kin are indigenous to the northwestern region of the Caucasus Mountains of what is today southern Russia and modern Georgia. They were distinguished from the other numerous ethnic groups of the Caucasus by several features. They were famous for their beauty and strength. Many among the Circassians and Ubykhs were distinguished by fair complexions, light eyes, and blond or red hair. Their languages formed a unique family, characterized by extremely complex grammar and enormous consonantal inventories accompanied by only two or three vowels. They had complex and varied societies, with a range of economic activities, from hunting in the mountains, to farming, pastoralism, handicrafts, and trading in the lowlands. The social order was extremely stratified with what seems to have been a caste system of princes, nobles, freemen, and peasants. The princes practiced a mystic discipline that involved spiritual visions and physical feats of a martial character. The peasants were often captives of war or the descendants of such captives.

Coupled to this caste hierarchy was an elaborate kinship system that was organized into regionally based tribes, each with its own divergent dialect. These in turn were overlain by a network of clans within which were found collateral assemblages ("blood frames") and lineal descent groups ("man's trace"). Many of these clans crossed ethnic divisions to embrace Ubykh and Abkhaz families as well. These peoples were capable of mounting a fierce defense of their homelands in times of war, and some have even characterized their societies as natural military organizations. Many of the men were known for their consummate skill at stalking game or their enemies. One peculiar form that this stalking took was a socially sanctioned practice of theft in which men would take items from each other in an effort to be as stealthy as possible. Being caught was a great disgrace.

Along with other peoples of the Caucasus, the Circassians and their kin showed a love of dancing, reverence for their elderly, respect toward women, religious and racial tolerance, loyalty to clan, hospitality to guests, a love of elaborate feasting, great equestrian skill, a fine sense of style and design reflected in elegant clothing and artifacts, a strict sense of social decorum, and a well-developed herbal medicine tradition, which seems to have reached its peak among the Ubykhs.

Immigration and Settlement History

The original homeland of the Circassians extended from the center of the North Caucasus, near the modern city of Vladikavkaz, westward to the Black Sea coast, with the Kuban River as a northern boundary, then south over the mountains and along the coast to the Ingur River in western Georgia. The Circassians shared the northern regions with the Tuallar, mountain Turks who are today's Karachays and Balkars. The Abkhaz formed a small population in the center of Circassian territory but resided primarily south of the mountains, along the coast, with the Ubykhs, confined to the coast, occupying a transitional zone between their two larger groups of kinsmen.

Starting in the late eighteenth century the Caucasus came under attack from the expanding Russian Empire. When Moscow tried to annex the Circassians and their kin in 1810, a war erupted that was to last until 1864. Because of the tenacity of their resistance, the czar ordered much of the population expelled in 1865. May 21 is still commemorated by the Circassians and their kin as the anniversary of this exodus. The Ottoman Empire

Circassian Americans dress in traditional costumes to perform a national dance. (M. Hilmi)

accepted them and based them in the Balkans, where they were used against Serbian insurrections. During the Russo-Turkish War of 1877–1878, the Circassians played a heavy role in an attempt to reclaim the Caucasus. At the Congress of Berlin in 1878 the Ottomans agreed to withdraw the Circassians into the Asian portion of the empire and to accept more refugees from the Caucasus. Further mass expulsions began in Russian and continued until 1905. At this time Circassians could be found in large numbers in the heartland of Turkey itself, with smaller communities in what are today Jordan and Israel, with only a fraction left behind in the homeland. Subsequent immigration to the United States reflects the geographic proportions of this large diaspora.

The first Circassians arrived in America in 1922 as refugees from the Russian Revolution. These refugees belonged to the large Natirba (Russian Natirbov) family, which is still one of the most prominent in the community. After this the first large wave of Circassians, roughly 100 men, arrived in the years after World War II. These had been prisoners of war taken by Nazi forces in battles with the Russians. Many of these men took German wives before immigrating. This small nucleus underwent a major expansion twenty years later, when roughly eighteen hundred families emigrated from Syria in a second wave. The people of this wave of the early 1970s had been driven to Damascus from their homes in the Golan Heights of Syria during the 1967 Arab-Israeli War. Their immigration to the United States was assisted by the Tolstoy Foundation. In addition to these two main waves, others have immigrated since the early 1950s from diaspora communities in Turkey, Jordan, and Israel.

The Circassians in the United States habitually live and associate with other peoples from the North Caucasus: with their kin the Abaza or Abkhaz, with the Turkic Karachay, Balkar, and Noghay, with the Iranian-speaking Ossetians, with the Chechen-Ingush, and with the various Daghestanis. Thus, in New Jersey there are roughly 3,500

Circassians, 200 Abaza or Abkhaz, 150 Ossetians, 250 Ingush or Chechens, and 300 Daghestanis of various ethnic background, but fully 3,500 Karachays and Balkars, with a sprinkling of Noghays. A small community of 300 Circassians and Abaza exists outside Los Angeles, in the Anaheim area, and another of roughly 100 people resides in Dallas and Houston. A unique community of Circassian-speaking Jews lives in Brooklyn but maintains some contact with their Muslim compatriots.

Languages

The Circassians of both waves spoke one of several forms of Circassian, predominantly Kabardian (an eastern dialect), or Bzhedukh, Shapsegh, or Abadzakh (western dialects). A few, because of mixed parentage or childhoods spent in mixed communities, spoke several dialects in addition to other Caucasian languages. All spoke second languages as well. Those of the first wave spoke Russian fluently, as well as some German. Those of the second wave spoke Arabic, and frequently Turkish. Those of the first wave could also read and write in a literary form of Circassian (Kabardian or Adyghean). All have acquired a command of English.

Speech interaction among the dialects shows an interesting skewing. Kabardian is quite different from the western dialects, with a distance greater than that between Dutch and German, for example. Members of the community often acquire a multilingualism at the dialect level. In mixed conversations each uses his or her own dialect, and the level of comprehension is generally high, although speakers of a western dialect generally understand Kabardian better than the Kabardians understand them. This is due to the fact that Kabardian has lost many of the contrasts preserved in the west, with the result that the Kabardians have trouble understanding what a speaker of a western dialect is saying.

Knowledge of Circassian has died out among children of the first wave due, in part, to the fact that they had mixed parentage. Usually they speak

German and English, abiding by the universal trend to learn the mother's language. Those of the second wave understand the language but rarely use it. Magazines and newsletters have appeared in a mixture of English and Circassian, such as *Adyghe Zhwaghwe* (The Circassian Star) from California and *Adyghe Maq* (The Circassian Voice) and its successor the *Circassian Times*, both from New Jersey. Since 1992, with the wars in the Caucasus, many young people have taken a renewed interest in their language and original homeland. Kabardian classes are now offered on weekends at the Community Center in Wayne, New Jersey, and they are well attended by both adults and children. Literacy problems hampered by disputes over orthography have clouded the issue of language maintenance so that prospects for survival of the language are not promising. It has yet to find a social setting where its use is habitual, and this bodes poorly for its future.

Cultural Trends

First-wave immigrants generally have greater access to their heritage because of their literacy and their education in Circassian primary schools in the Soviet Union. Unfortunately, their knowledge has generally not been passed on to their own children, because of language problems, or to the members of the second wave because of schisms within the community.

Immigrants of the second wave come from a diaspora that is more than one hundred years old and has endured cultural and linguistic suppression. Only in Israel has Circassian been written or taught in the schools. Limited cultural and linguistic rights in Turkey and Jordan came long after most immigrants had resettled in America. Thus, this group, along with other Caucasians, is literally engaged in an effort to rediscover its identity against the backdrop of turmoil and war in the Caucasus.

In both waves the individuals have come to occupy a range of economic niches. Some have become doctors; others, teachers or successful businesspeople. Most are workers. Many have shown extraordinary manual dexterity and have found careers as skilled machinists. Others have drawn upon time-honored martial customs and have entered the military, law enforcement, or the FBI. Younger people are pursuing high levels of education and will occupy generally higher economic positions than their parents did. In economic pursuits the community has been aided by a tradition of hard work, a respect for learning, and a high sense of personal integrity. The group has been hampered, however, by the general destruction of its old social structure of rank or caste. This has led to competition and rivalry within the community for prestige and influence, which in turn have led to schisms and hostilities. While individuals who have achieved wealth are usually ranked highly, wealth alone is not sufficient to assure social position. Devotion to heritage (however defined), integrity, hospitality, and generosity are also essential for a social leader, man or woman.

A number of customs have survived. Love of the dance thrives and is reflected in dance troupes for adults and children. Traditional male and female costumes are used in the dance and for other important ceremonies. Hospitality is still a vital aspect of domestic culture. Feasting remains important, but its scale has shrunk, as has the scale of the family or clan that hosts the feast. A *t'hamada* (toastmaster) still is chosen to head such gatherings. Such small feasts have traditional food, walnut paste, chicken with walnuts, corn mush, beef or lamb, and, in secular contexts, wine. Often the whole Caucasian community, including non-Circassian Caucasians, gathers for such feasts in restaurants, where the food is American and speeches are made throughout the meal. Gatherings of a more secular penchant will also offer toasts, but for all, drunkenness and boasting are scorned.

Women enjoy high regard and substantial freedom throughout the community. It falls to the women to maintain traditional cuisine and household dynamics. In their penchant for elegance the Circassian women carry on, by modern fashions, the traditional strengths of styling and beauty that

characterized the older material culture. Young women enjoy substantial freedom and choice, and ties between brother and sister remain very close. Kinship patterns have not altered except that the bond between husband and wife, traditionally formal and highly structured, seems to have grown more flexible and spontaneous. Marriage by mock abduction still occasionally takes place, but it is followed by the more usual Islamic or civil ceremony. Partners are predominantly drawn from within the community of recent immigrants. Funerals are now conducted by Islamic norms. Elders are still honored, everyone in a room standing upon their entry. Assimilatory trends are shown by a tendency to be flexible in the observance of social etiquette, expanding an older cultural pattern of conviviality. The old pattern of socially sanctioned theft has been reduced to a child's game in which baked goods are to be snatched without the housewife catching the culprit. If caught, the culprit is disgraced and soundly spanked. The youngest members of the community often show adolescent rebellion and insolence, even toward elders. This causes great dismay and confusion and is seen not merely as a passing trait but as a challenge to the survival of the group itself, since methods of social control, chiefly shaming, do not work for such young people, and their behavior is seen as utterly uncontrollable and beyond the pale.

Assimilation

Other basics of culture have been lost or are moribund. The Nart sagas, the old myths of the North Caucasus, appear to be known to only a few of the elderly. Epics centering around historical figures have also fallen from the repertoire. Children's rhymes and stories, however, are being reintroduced from sources in the Caucasus. The rich tradition of herbal medicine that drew upon the varied flora of the Caucasian forests and alpine meadows is moribund, but steps are being taken to codify what remains so that it might serve future generations. The terms for the stars, the seasons, the points of the compass, and for many of the fine details of handicrafts or animal husbandry have become the restricted knowledged of a few or have simply vanished. Such loss of folkloric and lexical richness reflects a shift away from traditional culture.

The most serious cultural stress within the community, however, involves the role of Islam in ethnic identity. First-wave immigrants were generally secular in their outlook, having been affected both by Soviet attitudes and by the general tolerance of the Caucasus. While a wide range of religious attitudes is exhibited, immigrants of the second wave generally see Islam as central to their community. Even among the most religious, however, Circassian identity is not to be compromised. Rather, preservation of ethnic identity takes precedence over all other goals, even when the content of that identity is nebulous. Religious tolerance still prevails.

Another aspect of assimilation that is emerging is that of mixed marriages. Circassians marry among themselves without regard to clan and will even marry other Caucasians. Young people, however, are occasionally marrying Americans of other ethnic backgrounds. Such marriages cause substantial stress for the family because they represent a challenge to the survival of the ethnic group, which is seen as endangered. Efforts are made to bring the non-Circassian spouse into Islam and to

ensure that the children of the union will retain a Circassian ethnic aspect, at least as a component of their identity. With the content of ethnic identity already compromised by dispersal and suppression both in the Caucasus and the Middle East, and with surviving elements of culture being lost or changed, it is unclear how such children will carry on the ethnic identity. Clearly a unique form of Circassian-American presence and self-conception is forming. Its success and viability are matters that only the future will determine.

Institutions and Links

A number of cultural organizations exist for social activity and the expression and preservation of culture. There is a cultural center in California and two in New Jersey: the Circassian Benevolent Association and the North Caucasus Center. The Circassian Benevolent Association has a large community center in Wayne, containing a mosque, a school, and a social center. This association also owns a summer camp in upstate New York, where families enjoy rural activities and reinforce the pastoral values that were once central to their culture.

The wars in the Caucasus, most particularly the Georgian-Abkhazian War of 1992–1993 and

The members of a Circassian-American soccer team. (M. Hilmi)

most recently the Russo-Chechen War, have galvanized the entire Caucasian community. The Circassians and the other Caucasians now have an umbrella organization, the North Caucasian Heritage Foundation. This group has staged peaceful demonstrations in Washington, D.C., and has lobbied members of Congress. Social rivalries are momentarily set aside for common goals. Circassians, like all Caucasians, feel the threat of extinction and are bewildered by what they see as Western indifference to and ignorance of their historic plight. This sense of neglect is at odds with their general love of America and its freedom, which resonates with their own deep love of freedom. Caucasian Americans are just beginning to enter into the active democratic processes offered by their new homeland and to use its democratic institutions to sustain and further the interests of their own community.

One of the most interesting and complex ties is between Circassians and their original homeland in the northwestern Caucasus. In 1989, the Soviets began a repatriation program that permitted anyone of Circassian descent to obtain a passport and go to one of the three Circassian republics: Adygheya, Karachai-Cherkessia, or Kabardino-Balkaria. This program attracted many visitors and even a few who set up vacation homes there. The program itself was administered by the International Circassian Congress, which is now called the International Cherkess Congress, a change of name that permits it to include any North Caucasian. Meetings have been held every other year, starting with 1987 in Amsterdam, 1989 in Ankara, 1991 in Nalchik (Kabardino-Balkaria), and 1993 in Maikop (Adygheya). The 1995 meeting was canceled because of the Russo-Chechen War. The last meeting was attended by Caucasians of all ethnic types, including many Kuban and Terek Cossacks, and ethnic groups from the Urals, such as the Tatars.

With the collapse of the Soviet Union, repatriation patterns took on a commercial form. Even before 1989, the Caucasus was seen not only as offering business opportunities but also as a natural repository for cultural treasures. Thus when the most famous diaspora Circassian writer, Kube Shaban, died in 1973 in New Jersey, his substantial literary estate was sent back to Maikop, the capital of Adygheya, where it was deposited in the Adyghé Institute for Languages and Literatures. It has since been published as a multivolume collection by this same institute, but it is in storage there, without significant distribution outside the republic.

The homeland is still seen as a geographical focal point of identity, as a repository for all things Circassian. Trade links, cultural ties, kinship relations, visits, vacations, and even sojourns of academic study or work are made to one of the three republics or neighboring regions, but little resettlement has taken place. Since the unrest caused by the start of the war in Chechnia in December 1994, the repatriation program has been suspended. The International Cherkess Congress persists, and visiting has continued. Since relocation was minimal, this suspension has had little tangible effect on Circassian relations with the homeland.

In their relationship to their ancestral land Circassian Americans are entering into a pattern set before them by numerous others who have fled persecution and war and found their way to America. They are yielding up some of their past to embrace a future, keeping much that is dear, creating some that is new, and paying homage to a homeland that will always be as dear as it is far away.

Bibliography

Colarusso, J. (1979). "Northwest Caucasian Languages." *The Modern Encyclopedia of Russian and Soviet Literature*, Vol. 3, edited by H. Weber. Gulf Breeze, FL: Academic International Press.

Colarusso, J. (1989a). "Myths from the Forest of Circassia." *The World & I*, December, pp. 644–651.

Colarusso, J. (1989b). "Prometheus Among the Circassians." *The World & I*, March, pp. 644–651.

Colarusso, J. (1989c). "The Woman of the Myths: The Satanaya Cycle." *The Annual of the Society for the Study of Caucasia* 2:3–11.

Colarusso, J. (1991a). "Circassian Repatriation." *The World & I*, November, pp. 656–669.

Colarusso, J. (1991b). "Two Circassian Tales of Huns and Khazars." *The Annual of the Society for the Study of Caucasia* 3:63–75.

Colarusso, J. (1992). *A Grammar of the Kabardian Language*. Calgary, AL: University of Calgary Press.

Henze, P. B. (1990). *The North Caucasus: Russia's Long Struggle to Subdue the Circassians*. Santa Monica, CA: RAND.

Luzbetak, L. J. (1951). *Marriage and the Family in Caucasia*. Vienna: St. Gabriel's Mission Press.

Wixman, R. (1984). "Circassians." In *The Muslim Peoples*, 2nd edition, edited by R. V. Weekes. Westport, CT: Greenwood Press.

JOHN COLARUSSO

COLOMBIANS

Colombians (or Colombian Americans) are individuals whose national origins can be traced to Colombia, a republic in northwestern South America. Colombian Americans are part of the broader ethnic group of Hispanics (or Latinos), which refers to Americans with Spanish surnames and/or those who trace their national origins to Spanish-speaking cultures. Colombians rank sixth (after Mexicans, Puerto Ricans, Cubans, Dominicans, and Salvadorans) in terms of size among the individual Hispanic groups in the United States but represent more than one-third of all immigrants from South America living in the United States. In spite of their growing importance among Hispanics, Colombians are often lumped together with other South American groups in statistical data, with the entire group being referred to as South Americans.

In the past, the rough mountain terrain of Colombia made transportation and communication between regions of the country difficult, thus creating distinct regional characteristics among its people. Because of these distinctions, Colombians sometimes prefer to identify themselves according to their specific region of origin. The principal subgroups found among Colombians in the United States include (1) Costeno, referring to those individuals from northwestern Colombia, where the cities of Cartagena and Barranquilla are located, (2) Valluno, identifying individuals from the western department (state) of Valle de Cauca, with its capital in Cali, (3) Paisa, referring to individuals from Antioquia in the northwest, where the city of Medellin is located, and (4) Cachaco, identifying those who trace their origins to the central Andean region, where Bogota, the capital of Colombia, is located.

Immigration Patterns

Prior to 1900, the United States experienced only an insignificant influx of South American immigrants. After 1900, however, South American immigration, including Colombian immigrants, increased; the immigrants became more and more attracted to the expanding economic opportunities available in the United States. During the first three decades of the twentieth century, more than 101,000 South American immigrants were admitted to the United States, with about one-fourth of them being Colombian.

Although immigration declined sharply during the Great Depression of the 1930s, it started picking up again in the post–World War II years, which once again saw improved employment opportunities. Colombian immigration to the United States continued to increase gradually each year after that, reaching an annual total of 5,733 in 1963. From 1964 to 1971, fueled by U.S. economic expansion brought about by the Vietnam War, more than eight thousand Colombian immigrants entered the United States each year. Although the annual number of Colombian immigrants declined somewhat between 1971 and 1977, the number has remained stable since 1977 with an average of ten thousand Colombian immigrants being admitted to the United States each year.

The vast majority of Colombian immigrants in the United States are legal immigrants, but it cannot be overlooked that a significant number are illegal immigrants. Most of the latter individuals entered the United States legally with nonimmigrant visas; they became illegal immigrants only when the visas expired and they chose to stay in the United States. As part of the Immigration Reform and Control Act of 1986, 24,596 Colombian immigrants obtained legalized status; this number represents only 1.5 percent of all "illegals" who adjusted their status under the act. Throughout the late 1980s, however, the number of illegal Colombian immigrants continued to rise, and by 1992, the Colombian illegal alien population in the United States was estimated at seventy-five thousand. This figure makes Colombians the ninth-largest illegal alien population (based on country of birth) in the United States.

Colombian immigrants come from urban areas, primarily Bogota, Medellin, Cali, and Barranquilla, Colombia's four largest cities. The immigrants are relatively well educated, and during the 1950s, more than 13 percent of all Colombian immigrants reported professional or technical occupations. Although the percentage had fallen to about 4 percent by the mid-1990s, the group's occupational skills remain high, with most reporting white-collar, skilled, or semi-skilled occupations.

Because of their urban background, Colombians tend to settle in large urban areas upon arriving in the United States. From the beginning, the preferred place of settlement for Colombian immigrants was the state of New York. In fact, up until the late 1970s, about 40 percent of all Colombians in the United States resided in New York. By 1990, only 28 percent of all Colombians (103,377 individuals) lived in New York. Florida, with 22 percent of the Colombian population (83,634 individuals), had become the state with the second-largest Colombian community. Other states with large portions of the Colombian population include California (11%), New Jersey (13%), and Texas (4%).

Demographics

The 1990 U.S. Census reported that 378,726 Colombians were living in the United States, and a large percentage of this Colombian population, more than 74 percent, was foreign born. In contrast, only 8 percent of the entire 1990 U.S. population was foreign born. The percentage of foreign-born Colombians is even high when compared only to the percentage of foreign-born Hispanics in the United States, which is 36 percent. Part of the reason for the large foreign-born Colombian population is the fact that the bulk of Colombian immigration to the United States has occurred since 1980. In fact, almost 52 percent of all foreign-born Colombians in the United States in 1990 had arrived during the 1980s.

This relatively recent arrival of the Colombian immigrants also accounts in part for the fact that the Colombian population in the United States tends to be younger (with a median age of 30.4 years) than the national population (which has a median age of 33.0 years). On the other hand, the Colombian population tends to be slightly older than the Hispanic population as a whole (which has a median age of 25.6 years). Still, almost 60 percent of all Colombian immigrants fall into the 25–60 age range, which is a significantly higher percentage than for either the national or Hispanic populations. In fact, less than 4 percent of all Colombians in the United States are older than 65, compared to 12.5 percent for the national population and 4.8 percent for the Hispanic community. Females make up more than 52 percent of the Colombian population in the United States, a percentage that is not significantly different from the percentage for the national population as a whole (51.3%) but is greater than that for the Hispanic population (49%). Although fertility among Colombian women in the United States is slightly lower than that of U.S. women as a whole and substantially lower than that of Hispanic women as a whole, a larger portion (56%) of Colombian females are in the childbearing age bracket, compared to the national and Hispanic populations.

In the past, new immigrants have overwhelmingly been the source of population growth among Colombians in the United States; while 145,567 Colombians entered the United States during the 1980s, only around forty-four thousand Colombian-American children were born during that decade. As the Colombian immigrant community consolidates, however, it should begin to experience more endogenous population growth.

Group Characteristics

Colombians in the United States are predominantly Catholic, and they respect strong family ties. In fact, almost 60 percent of the Colombian-American females over the age of fifteen are married, although only around 55 percent of the males are married.

The 1990 U.S. Census showed that there were 112,227 Colombian households in the United States. The average household size was 3.3 persons, accounting for the overwhelming majority (97.4%) of Colombian Americans. Almost 80 percent of these households were "family" households, with both husband and wife being present in 54.2 percent of the cases. The percentage of Colombian households headed by a female (17%) was higher than the national average for such households (13%) but lower than that for Hispanic households as a whole (20.4%).

Colombians in the United States are relatively well educated, especially when compared to Hispanics as a whole. More than 67 percent of all Colombians who are twenty-five years of age or older have at least a high school diploma or its equivalent, whereas only 50 percent of all Hispanics hold high school diplomas. More important, while around 31 percent of Hispanics over twenty-five years of age have less than a ninth-grade education, only 17 percent of Colombians in the same age range fall into this category. Nevertheless, the percentage of Colombians with a high school diploma or its equivalent is far lower than the analogous percentage for the entire U.S. population over twenty-five years of age (75%). When higher education is considered, however, the percentages are not quite as different. In fact, 40 percent of the Colombians in the United States have a postsecondary degree, compared to 45 percent of the overall U.S. population.

The labor force participation rate in 1990 for Colombian-American males over sixteen years of age was 83.2 percent, almost 10 percentage points higher than the nationwide average for all males and slightly higher than the 78.8 percent of participation for Hispanic men as a whole. Colombian-American women had a 1990 labor force participation rate of 64.3 percent, compared to 56.8 percent for all American women and 55.9 percent for Hispanic women as a whole. Most Colombians in the United States, around 67 percent, are employed in white-collar or service occupations. An additional 12 percent are employed as skilled laborers, while 21 percent hold unskilled labor positions. The industry that employs the most Colombians is the manufacturing industry, which employs 22 percent of all Colombians over sixteen years of age. The retail trade industry provides positions for more than 17 percent of all Colombians, and an additional 16.8 percent are employed in the professional and related services industry. Colombians rely almost entirely on the private sector for employment, with 86 percent employed in the private sector as wage and salary earners. An additional 6.3 percent of Colombians are self-employed, while slightly more than 7 percent are employed in government occupations (the majority of which are local government positions).

As a group, the Colombian community is economically better off than the more general Hispanic community. The median household income for Colombians in the United States in 1989 was $29,171 (only about $885 less than the national median household income for that year). For Hispanics as a whole, however, the median household income in 1989 was only $24,156. Although the Colombian households enjoy an income level similar to that of the rest of the United States, the fact that Colombian families on average tend to have more children places them at a comparative economic disadvantage. In fact, the per capita income for Colombians in the United States in 1989 was more than $3,000 less than the average U.S. per capita income. Other measures of economic well-being confirm that although they are economically better off than Hispanics as a group, the Colombians in the United States lag behind the rest of the nation. For example, 13.1 percent of Colombian Americans fall below the poverty line, which is lower than the 22.3 percent of Hispanics but greater than the 10 percent national average. On the other hand, only 7.3 percent of all Colombian-American households received public assistance income in 1989, compared to the 7.5 percent of all U.S. households receiving public assistance income that year.

Colombian-American Communities

The three largest Colombian immigrant communities in the United States are located in the New York City, Miami, and Los Angeles areas. The ethnic enclaves established in these areas have allowed for the replication of the Colombian lifestyle and cultural habits. Numerous businesses catering to Colombian immigrants have been founded. Colombian grocery stores, pastry shops, and nightclubs are abundant. A wide choice of restaurants featuring the distinct Colombian cuisine is available.

Although newspapers from Colombia are available in the larger ethnic enclaves of the United States and are read regularly by many immigrants, the Colombian-American ethnic press has flourished. The numerous weekly newspapers being published by and for Colombians in the United States include *El Colombiano* in Los Angeles, *Noticiero Colombiano* and *El Popular* in New York, *Al Dia* in Philadelphia, and *Acontecer Colombiano* in Miami. In addition, radio and television programs directed specifically at the Colombian immigrant community are broadcast by local stations in these areas. In Miami, affiliates of Colombia's two media networks (Radio Cadena Nacional and Caracol) own and operate two radio stations: Radio Klarida (WRMQ) and Radio Caracol (WSUA).

Most Colombians maintain close ties to their home country. A large percentage of Colombians in the United States send money periodically to family members still living in Colombia. Many immigrants also make periodic trips back to their homeland. As a result, the businesses that are involved in the process of maintaining these close personal ties with Colombia (e.g., travel agencies, international courier services, air cargo companies,

money transfer agencies) have prospered. The growing Colombian community in the United States has also been one of the factors contributing to the increase of trade between Colombia and the United States. Many Colombian Americans have jobs directly tied to the bilateral trade, and binational chambers of commerce have been established in California, Florida, Texas, and Illinois to promote further trade between the two countries.

Organizations

In general, Colombian immigrants have not involved themselves to any great degree in U.S. political, social, or community affairs. Much of this lack of involvement can be attributed to the fact that Colombian immigration to the United States has been a relatively recent phenomenon. It can also be attributed to the nature of this immigration; Colombians consider themselves economic immigrants and are primarily concerned with achieving a better standard of living. A third contributing factor to the low levels of participation is the fact that fewer than 36 percent of the Colombians over twenty-one years of age residing in the United States are American citizens. Even among Colombians who have resided in the United States for more than ten years, only 46.7 percent have been naturalized. The reluctance to adopt American citizenship prior to 1991 was partly due to the fact that Colombian law required those individuals who became American citizens to forgo their Colombian citizenship. In 1991, however, a new Colombian constitution was adopted that allowed Colombians to hold more than one citizenship.

Although few Colombian immigrants belong to or participate in American community organizations, the number of Colombian organizations in the United States has grown. Some of these organizations have been spurred by the desire to promote a more positive U.S. image of Colombia and Colombians. This is reflective of the fact that opinion surveys have reported that more than 80 percent of all Colombian immigrants in the United States believe that other Americans hold a negative image of Colombians. Other Colombian organizations promote contact and interchange among members on a professional basis. Such organizations include the Colombian American Bar Association and the Asociacion Medica Colombia/USA. In U.S. cities with large Colombian populations, service clubs such as the Lions Club and Kiwanis have even created Colombian chapters.

As Colombian communities in the United States grow and consolidate, there is increasing evidence that Colombians are becoming more and more involved in the political and social affairs outside their enclaves. Republican and Democratic Colombian-American clubs are being organized, and more Colombians are participating in pan-Hispanic organizations.

Conclusion

Colombian assimilation into mainstream American life has been very slow. Their close ties to the home country and their relatively short history in the United States make them a fairly isolated group holding to its traditions. One public opinion survey among Colombian immigrants found that 99 percent felt it was very important for their children to speak and write Spanish well, speak Spanish at home, and hold on to their Colombian heritage and culture. As has been the case for other immigrant groups, however, assimilation might be inevitable. The 1990 U.S. Census reports that while 90.5 percent of Colombian immigrants who were five years of age or older spoke Spanish, only 71 percent of Colombians who fell under the same age restrictions *and were born in the United States* spoke Spanish.

Bibliography

Cornelius, W. A., ed. (1976). *The Dynamics of Migration: International Migration*. Washington, DC: Interdisciplinary Communications Program, Smithsonian Institution.

Gutierrez, R. C., and Velasquez, S. R. de. (1980). *El Exodo de Colombianos: Un Estudio de la Corriente Migratoria a los Estados Unidos y un Intento para Propiciar el Retorno*. Bogota, Colombia: Colciencias.

Redden, C. A. (1980). *A Comparative Study of Colombian and Costa Rican Emigrants to the United States*. New York: Arno Press.

Strategy Research Corporation. (1994). *The U.S. Colombian Market Study*. Miami: Colombian Accuracy Project, Colombian American Chamber of Commerce.

U.S. Bureau of the Census. (1993). *Persons of Hispanic Origin in the United States*. Washington, DC: U.S. Government Printing Office.

U.S. Immigration and Naturalization Service. (1958–1977). *Annual Report of the Immigration and Naturalization Service*. Washington, DC: U.S. Government Printing Office.

U.S. Immigration and Naturalization Service. (1978–1995). *Statistical Yearbook of the Immigration and Naturalization Service*. Washington, DC: U.S. Government Printing Office.

U.S. Immigration and Naturalization Service. (1991). *Immigration Reform and Control Act: Report on the Legalized Alien Population*. Washington, DC: U.S. Government Printing Office.

U.S. Immigration and Naturalization Service. (1994). *Immigration Fact Sheet*. Washington, DC: U.S. Government Printing Office.

MARIA DOLORES ESPINO

COPTS

See EGYPTIAN COPTS

CORNISH

Cornwall, the Cornish homeland, is the long, narrow toe of England that pushes out into the Atlantic Ocean. From earliest times these Celtic peoples had mined tin and, at least as early as 500 B.C.E., exported tin and copper. By 1838 there were two hundred mines in Cornwall employing thirty thousand people, producing both quantities of tin and two-thirds of the world's supply of copper, and making huge profits for the owners. Mining families shared little of this wealth and, to survive economically, miners' wives, daughters, and younger sons worked aboveground processing the ore; at ten years of age, boys joined their fathers underground.

Mining families lived precariously, depending on the potatoes and other vegetables they could grow, fish from the nearby ocean, and the pig or cow they could keep on the patch of land surrounding their leased cottages. Nevertheless, the population increased. In the 1840s the potato blight forced reliance on grain products such as break, but speculators kept grain prices high throughout the decade. Families were faced with more children to feed and higher food costs. At the same time, life in the mines was hazardous, and the death rate was high. Furthermore, depressions in the price of copper were not unusual; the closing of less economic mines might mean starvation for whole families. Seeking a better life, a few miners sold their belongings; borrowed from friends and relatives; and left for North or South America, South Africa, or Australia.

After 1863, due to the increased efficiency of mining methods as well as the mineowners' greed for greater production and greater profits, copper lodes were becoming exhausted. At the same time, the discovery of great new deposits near Lake Superior in the United States and increased production in South American mines brought a fall in the price of copper. By 1867 most copper mines in the west of Cornwall had closed; others had laid off men and cut wages; and though tin mining continued, it could not provide employment to the laid-off copper miners. With savings accumulated during the boom years, the men in the family left, many to join uncles or cousins who had emigrated during the previous three decades. As they in turn found work, they sent for other relatives. According to the Royal Statistical Society's 1888 report, one-third of the mining population of Cornwall left the county between 1871 and 1881. Emigration continued into the twentieth century, dwindling away by the 1950s.

The New World

Although there were Cornish in Colonial America, mass immigration did not occur until the nineteenth century. In 1827 the lead mines of Mineral Point, Wisconsin, first attracted Cornish to the Midwest. By then there were also Cornish farmers breaking land in the new prairie settlements. In the 1840s, Cornish miners were working the copper and iron deposits of Upper Michigan. After 1849 hundreds left for the gold fields of California. Some mined mercury, essential for processing gold. After 1865, the gold and silver deposits of the western and southwestern states attracted great numbers of Cornish.

Cornish miners were known for their technical skills; their independence and initiative; and their strong kinship ties, often characterized as "clannishness." It was said that every time a Cornishman got a job, he would ask the mine superintendent, "'ave 'e got a job for my cousin Jack?" So, in the U.S. mining communities, all Cornish were called "Cousin Jacks." The origin of the female equivalent "Cousin Jennie" (or "Cousin Jinnie") is obscure.

Language, Demographics, and Kinship

While the rest of England was invaded by Romans, Danes, Angles, Saxons, and Normans, Cornwall remained isolated, preserving its native language and culture. Cornish, a Celtic tongue allied to Breton, was generally spoken until the end of the eighteenth century. Today Cornish survives in place and family names and in terms used in the mining industry, such as "kibble" (a bucket used for hauling up ore) and "winze" (a small internal mine shaft). Revival of the language is encouraged by the annual *Gorsedd*, which features Cornish choirs, poetry, dance, and drama under the auspices of more than two hundred bards from Cornish communities in the United Kingdom and abroad.

It is impossible to estimate the number of people of Cornish heritage in the United States. The Cornish-American Connection, a project to research the history of Cornish immigration to North America, now has more than fifteen thousand names of immigrants to either the United States or Canada. In the United States, the Cornish-American Heritage Society has nearly five hundred active members.

Cornish-American men and women are to be found in every walk of life. The second and continuing generations of immigrant stock were encouraged to seek higher education, and many hold professional positions.

Many fourth-generation Cornish-American families have kept in touch with their relatives "back home" as well as elsewhere in the world. *Tam Kernnewick*, the quarterly newsletter of the Cornish-American Heritage Society, regularly reports on exchanges of visits between Cornish cousins and their American relatives.

Social and Political Organizations

Today the Cornish are firmly ensconced in the middle class. Earlier immigrant men joined ethnically based societies such as the Sons of St. George, or benevolent associations such as the Odd Fellows and the Ancient Order of Foresters, while their wives' and daughters' social activities involved family and church affairs. Their descendants are likely to belong to any organization that attracts middle-class Americans, from the PTA to the Rotary Club. A good many still maintain ties to their Cornish origins by joining the English-Speaking Union, or, for women, the Daughters of the British Empire. In recent years interest in their roots has led many Cornish Americans to join the Cornish-American Heritage Society (founded in 1982) or to send family information to the Cornish-American Connection.

Cornish political activity was inhibited by three factors. First, the system of employment led to competition rather than cooperation. Until the end of the nineteenth century, Cornish miners functioned as independent contractors. Either they were paid a set amount per unit of work, or they competed against others for the pitch they would work and were paid a proportion of the value of the ore extracted. This set teams of men against each other rather than against the mineowners, and even when conditions in the mines were at their most dangerous, the Cornish rarely united in political action.

The structure of Cornish society also inhibited political action. Within the same family, some might be miners and some "captains" or superintendents, or even mineowners. This, and a long-term tradition of respect for the large, landowning families, made it difficult to take an adversarial position against the mineowners.

Not the least important, the teachings of John Wesley had received the wholehearted endorsement of the Cornish. Wesley had emphasized that life was brief and hard, merely a preparation for the world to come. The exhortation "Look not to the things of this world" may have restrained any attempts to change the status quo.

In the United States, the Cornish were initially compensated through their familiar system of contracts achieved through individual rather than collective bargaining. As the wage system replaced the contract system, the Cornish did join unions, which became both the representative units for bargaining with the owners and important benevolent and social organizations. On the whole, however, the Cornish, because of their superior skills, were better paid than most miners and tended to distrust union organizers as much as they did mineowners. By the 1870s, many superintendents and some mineowners were Cornish; thus, they were part of management.

Strikes that occurred were to protest the introduction of new mining methods, to demand an eight-hour day, or to obtain better pay. But the owners' threats to bring in cheaper immigrant labor invariably forced the miners either to return to work for less pay and more hours, or to move elsewhere. Many Cornish abandoned mining and sought livelihoods in other fields.

Few Cornish today seem very interested in political office. However, as in the past, most follow local, national, and international affairs and conscientiously vote. Their Methodism encourages social liberalism, but they tend to be fiscally conservative; most vote Republican.

Social Control and Conflict

The people of Cornwall, due to widespread poverty were often tempted to engage in smuggling, or even the deliberate luring of ships onto the rocks, where cargoes could be "salvaged." However, by the mid-nineteenth century the pervasive influence of the Methodist Church had engendered a mostly law-abiding, sober, and deeply religious population. Wherever they settled in America, Cornish miners built churches and, with rare exceptions, these were of the Methodist denomination.

Some Cornish Americans were able to accumulate "pensions" for their old age by "high-grading" or smuggling gold out of the mines. However, fantastic stories of huge fortunes amassed by high-graders may owe more to literary embroidery than to actual fact. Most miners retired in relative poverty, with many succumbing to early deaths from silicosis acquired from years of inhaling pulverized rock.

There were conflicts between Cornish Americans and members of other ethnic groups. The Cornish would work only with other Cornish, and they used their considerable influence to drive out Irish and Chinese miners. Brawls between Cornish and Irish made headlines in most mining towns. The Irish believed, with good cause, that mine captains favored hiring Cornish miners and that the Cornish were overly straitlaced and far too frequently willing to preach to others how to behave and how to worship. Today men and women of Cornish descent are quite likely to have married those from other ethnic groups.

Religious Belief

In Cornwall, early belief in the Celtic nature gods was subsumed into, but never quite replaced by, Christianity introduced by Irish missionaries. St. Ives, St. Kea, St. Keverne, and many other of these "saints" are still commemorated in the names of Cornish towns and villages. In 1549 the Latin Mass was replaced by a new prayer book in English, a language many Cornish still did not speak.

In protest, ten thousand Cornish marched on Exeter. The brief revolt was put down and its leader executed. Thereafter, many Cornish, deprived of the emotional consolation of the Catholic rituals, once again sought solace in the magical powers to be found in sacred wells, oak groves, and hilltops.

By the eighteenth century, the Church of England had almost abandoned its Cornish parishes. The Methodist Society was founded in 1739, and in 1743 both Charles and John Wesley arrived in Cornwall, where their revivalist preaching attracted large numbers. Methodist teaching centered on repentance, the hellfire that awaited those who did not repent, and the glory of heaven for those who suffered on this earth. The emotionalism of revivalist preaching appealed to the Cornish, and in spite of some initial opposition, Methodist chapels could be found in the smallest villages by the 1870s.

The Church of England continued to have adherents, especially among the gentry. Parishes with charismatic individual pastors, some of them classed as "High Anglican," remained viable, as did parishes that were generous with help in times of need.

Another form of religious expression was introduced when William Booth, a Methodist minister, founded the Salvation Army in 1865. Seen as a movement that supplemented, rather than replaced, the Methodist Church, the Salvation Army immediately attracted Cornish followers. Families might attend the Methodist Church on Sunday morning and the Salvation Army service in the evening. In addition, the Salvation Army's sponsorship of brass bands appealed to the Cornish love of music.

The Cornish brought their Methodism to the United States, and early immigrants remained faithful to the tenets of the Methodist Church, including strict observance of the Sabbath, teetotalism, and the prohibition of card playing and dancing.

The Salvation Army, introduced to the United States in 1880, also attracted many miners' families. However, there were some problems because in the United States the Salvation Army was considered to be a church, and its American officers did not understand that the Cornish did not want to make the Army Hall their exclusive place of worship.

Today links between the Cornish and the Methodist Church are still strong; however, some families of Cornish descent have inevitably joined other denominations.

One other religious denomination early on attracted Cornish adherents. Mormon missionaries arrived in Cornwall in 1835 and converted many Cornish. Helped by the Mormon Emigration Fund, some four hundred English, including Cornish, arrived in Salt Lake City, Utah. Many of their descendants became pillars of the Mormon Church.

The Arts, Celebration, and Folklore

Music was the most important artistic expression for the Cornish. There was a tradition of choral music, encouraged by the Methodist Church, and of "silver" and brass bands, which were the pride of the towns and villages. This musical tradition was continued in the United States, where many mining towns boasted both bands and fine choirs.

Cornish towns celebrate May Day with maypole dancing and the crowning of a queen. Padstow features dancers and a hobby horse. Later in May, Helston holds its "Furry Dance" ("Furry" from the Latin *feriae* or feast). Midsummer Night is celebrated with bonfires.

Perhaps because the nineteenth-century Methodist Church forbade theatrical performances and dancing, these traditions were never imported into the New World. However, the Cornish did have an outlet for their love of parades on July 4, when the streets of mining towns were decorated, as were the wheeled vehicles, which later included cars, that took part in the grand parade.

In Grass Valley, California, the Miners' Union (later the Mineworkers' Protective League) organized a Labor Day Miners' Picnic. All stores closed, and the whole town went out to the park to take part in sports and watch Cornish wrestling, where local wrestlers competed with teams from as far away as Nevada.

Food played a part in all these events, and the tradition of certain Cornish food specialties has been maintained in U.S. mining towns, where the Cornish still bake Cornish pasties, a triangular pastry filled with meat and potatoes, and flavour cakes and buns with saffron, a very costly spice supposedly introduced to Cornwall by Phoenician tin traders.

A rich tradition of folklore is nearly forgotten, but most Cornish Americans believed in "Tommy Knockers," small people who lived in the mines and warned of impending disaster.

Death and Afterlife

Death was no stranger to the Cornish. Whether in Cornwall or in the United States, men died from accidents or from silicosis, and women from the hazards of childbirth. In addition, epidemics were perennial, and "summer cholera," whopping cough, measles, and other illnesses killed many infants and small children.

Methodist beliefs offer solace to those beset by the ills of this world. Sermons and tracts, and especially hymns, give a firm promise of a heavenly afterlife to those who gain grace by their willing acceptance of earthly suffering. This promise encourages the belief that death is merely the gateway to a glorious life to come.

Bibliography

Berry, C. (1949). *Cornwall*. London: Robert Hale.

Burke, G. (1986). "The Decline of the Independent Bal Maiden: The Impact of Change in the Cornish Mining Industry." In *Unequal Opportunities: Women's Employment in England 1800–1918*, edited by A. V. John. Oxford, Eng.: Basil Blackwood.

Cook, J. (1984). *Close to the Earth: Living Social History of the British Isles*. London: Routledge & Kegan Paul.

Dexter, T. F. G. (1926). *Cornish Names*. London: Longmans Green.

Ewart, S. (1989). *Cornish Mining Families in Grass Valley, California*. New York: AMS Press.

Jenkin, A. K. H. (1927). *The Cornish Miner*. London: Allen and Unwin.

Jenkin, A. K. H. (1945). *Cornwall and Its People*. London: J. M. Dent & Sons.

Lingenfelter, R. (1974). *The Hardrock Miners: A History of the Mining Labor Movement in the American West 1863–1893*. Berkeley: University of California Press.

Rowe, J. (1953). *Cornwall in the Age of the Industrial Revolution*. Liverpool: Liverpool University Press.

Rowe, J. (1974). *The Hardrock Men: Cornish Immigrants and the North American Mining Frontier*. London: Barnes & Noble.

Rowse, A. L. (1969). *The Cousin Jacks: The Cornish in America*. New York: Charles Scribner's Sons.

Todd, A. C. (1995). *The Cornish Miner in America*. Seattle: Arthur H. Clark.

SHIRLEY EWART

CROATIANS

Croatians are a South Slavic people who inhabit Croatia, one of the republics of the former Yugoslavia that declared its independence in 1991. Croatians also live in Bosnia-Herzegovina, where they were 31 percent of the population before the 1992 war, and in Serbia, where they are 2 percent of the population. Croatia is bordered by Slovenia and Hungary to the north, the Adriatic Sea to the west, and Bosnia-Herzegovina and Serbia to the south and east. In English they are called Croatians or Croats; in the Croatian language they refer to themselves as Hrvati, which is an Iranian or Celtic word.

There are about 1.5 to 2.5 million Americans of Croatian descent in the United States, the third largest Slavic group after Poles and Czechs. According to the highly inaccurate U.S. immigration figures from 1880 to 1914, about 400,000 Croatians arrived in the United States, excluding Dalmatians (from Croatia's Adriatic coast) and the unregistered, which might amount to half of all Croatian immigrants. Croatians flocked to Pittsburgh; Chicago; New York City; Cleveland; Kansas City, Missouri, Gary, Indiana; and California. The new arrivals were peasants from the interior, 95 percent of whom were unskilled and 36 percent of whom were illiterate. This was the period of the largest influx of Croatians who would ever arrive in America; but between 1900 and 1914, from 33 to 40 percent of Croatian immigrants returned to Europe because they were either disabled, sick, or lonely.

After World War II a well-educated group of Croats escaped Yugoslavia when Josip Broz Tito's Communist government took power after defeating the fascist forces. Since 1945 a total of forty-two thousand Croats have immigrated to the United States, with two to three thousand arriving each year from the 1970s on. Pennsylvania, with 180,000, has the largest concentration of Croatians, followed by Illinois (Chicago has fifty thousand), California, New York, Minnesota, and Missouri.

Settlement

Dalmatians first began to settle along the Gulf Coast of the United States in small numbers as early as the eighteenth and nineteenth centuries. By the time of the Civil War there were three thousand in the South. A number of them flocked to California during the Gold Rush of 1849 and played an important role in developing the West. Then, in the 1870s, inland Croats from Severin, on the Kupa River, immigrated to work at unskilled jobs in the dangerous copper mines of what would become Calumet, Michigan. Via chain migrations and transatlantic voyages, Croats then began settling in Pennsylvania, New York, New Jersey, and Illinois in great numbers from the 1880s onward. Croatian working-class neighborhoods formed in the large industrial cities of the Midwest and East. Large, anonymous cities such as Pittsburgh, Chicago, Cleveland, and New York compelled Croatian immigrants to join together, forge ethnic parishes, and out of self-protection preserve their traditions and language.

Before and after the turn of the twentieth century, Dalmatians were farming California's Santa Clara, Pajaro, and San Joaquin valleys. They moved into southern California, and Croatians even established themselves in the mining areas of the Southwest, but World War I stopped the flow of immigrants. From 1921, when Congress passed acts restricting the number of immigrants from southern and eastern Europe, until 1930, only thirty thousand Croatians were allowed to enter the United States.

The Croats who had immigrated to the United States before the 1930s had built strong communities that were an important but unrecognized part of the American scene. In contrast to the early pioneers, most of whom had only a fourth-grade education, greater numbers of Croatian children finished high school and a substantial minority went on to higher education and became professionals. Their ranks were increased with the influx of World War II displaced persons, who settled and worked in large cities of the Midwest and East. Young and educated, they added a dynamic element to the ethnic consciousness of Croatians. Since the Yugoslav government allowed free immigration in 1965, Croatians have immigrated to the United States mainly for economic opportunities.

Economy

In the first half of the nineteenth century, Dalmatians began developing the oyster industry in Louisiana. In 1849, many Dalmatians went to California during the Gold Rush to pan for gold, while other bought stores, restaurants, or saloons. In that same year John Tadich took over the restaurant his uncle had opened in San Francisco; the restaurant is still in operation, on California Street. From the 1890s until after the turn of the century, Dalmatians cultivated grape vines and planted apple orchards in the San Joaquin and Pajaro valleys. They also became important in the fishing industry, establishing a large fishing fleet in Los Angeles' port of San Pedro as well as in Washington State. They moved on to Nevada to

mine silver and New Mexico to take up coal mining; and in Michigan they labored in the copper mines of the Upper Peninsula while the ore of Butte, Montana, attracted Croats who later became ranchers or restauranteurs.

In the 1880s landless peasants from Croatia's interior started immigrating to Pennsylvania to perform backbreaking work for the railroads and in construction, the steel mills, and anthracite coal mines. New York and New Jersey drew large numbers as men found jobs on the vast harbors and waterfronts. Protestants viewed the Roman

Annie Clemenc, who lead the Michigan copper miners in daily marches in the 1913 strike of the Western Federation of Miners. She was injured by the militia and risked her life to retrieve the American flag that was knocked from her hands. The strike was finally settled, but the union was disbanded. (Superior View)

Catholic Croats as a challenge to their domination, and great resentment against the immigrants soon developed among nativists in the population, who considered the immigrants to be inferior and a threat to the American way of life.

Many Croatians labored eighty hours a week for about $1.50 a day with no benefits except one day off every sixth day. They began to join labor unions well after the turn of the twentieth century, playing a pivotal role in the important strike by thirteen thousand copper miners in Calumet, Michigan, in 1913.

Along with the key positions they hold in America's various industries, succeeding generations of Croatians have moved into the fields of education, health services, engineering, and other professions.

Organizations, Newspapers, and Politics

The first Croatian organization in the United States was the Croatian Illyrian Mutual Benevolent Society, founded in San Francisco in 1857 and still in existence. It was followed in 1874 by the United Slavonian Benevolent Association in New Orleans. These mutual assistance organizations gave immigrant workers and their families financial help during sickness or after accidents or death. Other associations, mainly dealing with insurance but branching off into sports and music, spread among the Croatian settlements. Sokol (Falcon), which first began in Chicago in 1908, is an example of an athletic society.

The Croatian Union began in what is now Pittsburgh in 1894, offering health and life insurance to six hundred members. Three years later, after changing its name to the National Croatian Society, it joined with other fraternal organizations and became the Croatian Fraternal Union in 1925. It is the largest Croatian organization in the country (with 100,000 members and lodges in principal cities in twenty-eight states), provides scholarships to its members' children, offers Croatian-language classes, and sponsors many youth orchestras to promote Croatian folk music. Among other organizations is the Croatian Catholic Union, which

was founded by a number of priests in Gary, Indiana, in 1921 to combat the perceived left politics of the National Croatian Society. In 1994, the Croatian Fraternal Union and the Croatian Catholic Union joined with twenty-two other Croatian groups to form the National Federation of Croatian Americans, an umbrella organization to support Croatians in the United States and abroad and defend an independent Croatia and Bosnia-Herzegovina.

The Croatian Fraternal Union publishes the *Zajednicar* (Fraternalist), which goes to forty thousand households throughout the United States. It began publication in 1896 under the masthead *Napredak* (Progress). Until its demise in the early 1920s, *Narodni List* (People's Journal) was also a very successful daily, published by Frank Zotti. It was nationalistic in tone and attacked the newly formed Kingdom of the Serbs, Croats, and Slovenes, which was created in the aftermath of World War I and which became Yugoslavia in 1929. Other Croatian-language newspapers that continue to be published are the Croatian Catholic Union's *Nasa Nada* (Our Hope), *Hrvatski Kalendar* (Croatian Almanac), and *Danica* (The Morning Star), the latter two produced by the Croatian Franciscan Press of Chicago.

Croatian-American relations with the former Yugoslavia caused much divisiveness after the creation of the South Slav state in 1918. The older immigrants tended to approve of the state, although they were mistrustful of Serb dominance prior to World War II. They clashed over endorsing the Communist regime, and this became exacerbated with the arrival of many political refugees who had fled to the United States after the Communist victory. Many of the old immigrants had not accepted the World War II fascist Ustasha regime (led by Ante Pavelic), which the displaced persons had supported. Throughout the postwar period these new immigrants had voiced their opposition to the Tito government, even resorting to terrorism. With the creation of an independent Croatia in 1991, support has now coalesced around rebuilding a war-ravaged economy.

Although members of the Democratic party for the most part, the early immigrants did not get involved in the American political process unless it was to strike for better working conditions or salaries. But as they became more assimilated, they went into the political arena, creating governors, mayors, city councilmen, and congressional representatives of Croatian descent.

Family and Religion

The early nineteenth-century Dalmatian seafarers in America were single young men who assimilated quickly and married Irish, Spanish, or Mexican women. The peasant immigrants who arrived in the mass migrations after the turn of the century increasingly began to bring their wives and families. Because they came from small villages, they relied on the Croatian language and formed ethnic enclaves to help them and their families deal with the strangeness and complexity of urban life. These communities also protected them from discrimination and violence at the hands of Americans who had themselves recently immigrated and who were afraid of losing their jobs to the newcomers. They labeled these neighborhoods "Hunky-towns" and called the Croatians "slabs," "strams," "modgies," or "crows."

Contrary to American individualism, Croatians from the same villages tended to join cooperative households such as boardinghouses. These were patterned after the *zadruga*, a commune of eighty to ninety members. The emphasis on cooperation and the family helped them to survive very difficult living conditions and eventually allowed their children to obtain the education that would enable them to get higher-paying jobs.

Until the 1940s, Croatian society preserved traditional peasant beliefs from the eighteenth century. The Catholic religion and the basic family structure were very important, and religious values, social control, and discipline were part of this traditional life. Around the beginning of the century, family units became smaller and consisted of the nuclear family, with the father as the ulti-

mate authority. Women were not as important and were considered the possession of males; women's roles were to bear sons and obey their husbands. The community dictated that mothers take responsibility for their daughters, which they did because they desired a better life for their daughters, whereas the fathers were less involved with the children and took much more interest in the sons' education than in the daughters'.

Croatians in the United States have assimilated into the American mainstream as the younger generations have become more removed from their cultural heritage. They tend now to get married at an older age. The large wedding celebrations of the past, which took place in ethnic halls and which were hosted by the groom's family, have given way to more American-style receptions that are catered and less identifiable as Croatian.

The Roman Catholic faith has played a central role in the Croatians' religious and cultural expression. There is a strong adherence to Catholic dogma, and the ceremonies surrounding baptism, marriage, and death. Devotion to the Virgin Mary is strong, exemplified by the chapel dedicated to Our Lady of Bistrica at the National Catholic Shrine in Washington, D.C.

The Croatians did not have a tradition of anticlericalism, as did the Italians, who were very reluctant to send their children to parochial schools in the early decades of the twentieth century. Like the Poles, Croatians tended to foster parochial schools and ethnic parishes, although they were much slower in adopting them than were the Poles. As with other eastern Europeans, they regarded the priest as the arbiter in political as well as in religious matters. Here they came into conflict with the Irish Catholic hierarchy, who accepted the Protestant ideal of the separation between religion and politics.

The first Croatian parish was established in what is now Pittsburgh in 1901, and there are now thirty-three in the United States. Due to the post–World War II immigration, a number of Croatian parishes have welcomed young people who have emigrated from the former Yugoslavia.

Culture and Science

Music and folk dances are essential parts of Croatian cultural expression. Croatian traditional music features the tamburitza, a pear-shaped wooden instrument in the lute family that has a fretted neck and four to six pairs of strings. Accompanied by tamburitzas, vocalists from Croatia or the diaspora sing their ballads at picnics and other celebrations across the country. The Croatian Fraternal Union, which celebrated its one hundredth anniversary in 1994, sponsors many youth orchestras to foster Croatian culture. The kolo (circle dance) is performed during folk festivals where richly embroidered regional costumes are worn. During Christmas, choral groups sing the *koleda*, secular songs that hearken back to Slavic pagan winter solstice festivities during which youths visited houses and sang songs in return for food and drink. Croatian music and folk art are being preserved in the immigrant archives at the University of Minnesota through the valuable bequests of Zlatko Kerhin.

In the fine arts, Ivan Mestrovic, the preeminent Croatian sculptor of the twentieth century, produced fine works in wood, plaster, stone, and bronze, as well as in architecture. Some of his art includes the statue of Native Americans in Chicago's Grant Park and his Pietà at Notre Dame University.

Nikola Tesla, although not as well known, is the equal in the scientific community of Thomas Edison and Guglielmo Marconi. Born of Serb parents in the Lika region of Croatia, Tesla developed alternating current, the radio (his contributions are perhaps more important than those of Marconi), the polyphase electric motor, the vacuum tube, a system of transmitting electric power without wires, and the bladeless steam turbine.

There has been an increased interest in ethnic identity among Croatians in the United States since the 1960s. The second and third generations have tried to maintain the Croatian language. They have also sought to keep in contact with relatives in Croatia and have even visited their parents' or grandparents' towns or villages to maintain a cultural link with the homeland of their ancestors.

See also: SERBS; SLOVENES

Bibliography

Adamic, L. (1940). *From Many Lands*. New York: Harper & Brothers.

Allen, J., and Turner, E. (1988). *We the People: An Atlas of America's Ethnic Diversity*. New York: Macmillan.

Balch, E. (1969). *Our Slavic Fellow-Citizens*. New York: Ayer.

Eterovich, F., and Spalatin, C., eds. (1964). *Croatia: Land, People and Culture*. 2 vols. Toronto: University of Toronto Press.

Govorchin, G. (1961). *Americans from Yugoslavia*. Gainesville: University of Florida Press.

Lovrich, F. (1971). *The Social System of a Rural Yugoslav-American Community: Oysterville*. San Francisco: Ragusan Press.

Meler, V. (1972). *The Slavonic Pioneers of California*. San Francisco: Ragusan Press.

Nyrop, R., ed. (1982). *Yugoslavia: A Country Study*. Washington, DC: U.S. Army.

Preveden, F. (1962). *A History of the Croatian People*. New York: Philosophical Library.

Prpich, G. (1971). *The Croatian Immigrants in America*. New York: Philosophical Library.

Prpich, G. (1978). *South Slavic Immigration to America*. Boston: Twayne.

Shapiro, E. (1989). *The Croatian Americans*. New York: Chelsea House.

Singleton, F. (1993). *A Short History of the Yugoslav Peoples*. Cambridge, Eng.: Cambridge University Press.

DANIEL CETINICH

CUBANS

The rise of Cuban Americans as the third-largest Hispanic community in the United States effectively started in 1959, with the massive exodus from the island after the rebel movement headed by Fidel Castro overthrew the government of Fulgencio Batista. Before this time sizable Cuban communities thrived in the nineteenth century in New

York, Key West, New Orleans, and in Ybor City, on the outskirts of Tampa. New York, which contained one of the earliest Cuban-American communities, was still the premier destination for immigrants from the island in the period between World War II and the rise of the Castro government. Miami, largely because of its youth and weak economic structure, was never the principal destination of Cuban immigrants to the United States.

While Miami did not have the employment opportunities required by the Cuban immigrants during the first half of the twentieth century, it did receive those seeking refuge from the shifting fortunes of the island's turbulent political history. Two deposed Cuban presidents—Gerardo Machado and Carlos Prío Socarrás—made their home in Miami. A prominent Cuban politician of the 1940s, Bobby Maduro, built and gave his name to Miami's baseball stadium. Even Castro spent time in Miami in the 1950s, and as leader of the 1959 revolution he initiated a process of revolutionary change that, in its rapidity and pervasiveness, alienated large sectors of the Cuban population and contributed to the creation of the Cuban-American community in the United States.

This pattern of immigration changed with the creation of rail and highway links between Miami and Key West and their extensions to Havana by way of regular ferry service. Air service between Miami, Key West, and Havana dates back to the 1920s and represents a pioneering effort in the history of passenger aviation. Those transportation links served to make Miami the principal staging area for the increasingly close relationship developing between Cuba and the Florida peninsula. In 1948, for example, Cuba led all countries in the world in the volume of passengers exchanged with the United States.

Patterns of Influx

The pattern of Cuban emigration since 1959 reflects primarily the availability of the means to leave Cuba. From 1959 to 1962, when the Cuban Missile Crisis of October eliminated regular commercial air traffic between the United States and

A single, worn boat honors the Cuban refugees who risked their lives in 1962 to obtain a better life in Key West, Florida. (Nik Wheeler/Corbis)

Cuba, some 200,000 persons left Cuba. The U.S. government facilitated their entry by granting them refugee status, allowing them to enter without the restrictions imposed on most other nationality groups. This favored treatment continued until shortly after the termination of the 1980 boatlift.

The Cuban Missile Crisis ended all contact between the two countries, slowing down considerably the pace of Cuban immigration in 1964 and 1965. Persons leaving Cuba during those years were doing so clandestinely, often in small boats, or through third countries, usually Spain or Mexico.

In the fall of 1965, in a move that responded to internal pressures for emigration and that was to be repeated fifteen years later, the Cuban government opened a port and allowed persons from the United States to go to Cuba to pick up relatives who wanted to leave the country. Some five thousand Cubans left from the port of Camarioca before the United States and Cuba halted the boatlift and agreed to an orderly airlift. The airlift, popularly known as the "freedom flights," started in December 1965 and lasted until 1973. The twice-daily flights brought 260,500 persons during those years.

The termination of the airlift brought another period, during the mid- to late 1970s, of relatively low emigration from Cuba. By 1980, however, the pressures for emigration once again caused the Cuban government to open a port for unrestricted emigration. The port was Mariel, giving the name to the boatlift that lasted for six months and brought, in a manner uncontrolled by the United States, more than 125,000 Cubans.

The end of the boatlift and the onset of restrictions on Cuban immigration brought about a lull in the exodus during the 1980s. The activation of an immigration agreement between the United States and Cuba in November 1987 provided for the admission into the United States of about twenty thousand persons from Cuba each year. Priority was given to those who would qualify for political asylum. Most of the persons who arrived after that date—a number well below the projected figure of twenty thousand—were former political prisoners and their families.

In 1994 another crisis ensued, and a massive wave of *balseros* (rafters) landed on Florida's shores. In August of that year the Cuban government ceased to patrol its coastal waters, giving a green light to anyone courageous enough to build a raft and set off across the Straits of Florida. From August 12 to August 23 the U.S. Coast Guard intercepted nine thousand Cubans attempting the dangerous crossing in homemade rafts. The U.S. government, fearing another Mariel, implemented unprecedented measures. The Clinton administration announced that the United States would no longer automatically accept rafters or other illegal immigrants from Cuba. Rafters intercepted in the

Straits of Florida would be sent to makeshift refugee camps established at Guantánamo naval base, on the southeastern tip of the island of Cuba, or to Panama. This decision did not discourage those intent on leaving the island. From August 13 to September 13, when the Cuban government resumed patrolling its borders, approximately thirty six thousand Cubans fled the island. More than twenty-eight thousand of them ended up in Guatánamo or Panama temporarily; most were eventually accepted into the United States.

The two governments reopened discussions on the issue of immigration on August 23, resulting in a new immigration agreement, signed on September 9. The agreement established as a minimum quota what used to be the maximum, twenty thousand, not including cases where Cubans on the island wanted to be reunited with immediate relatives living in the United States. Both governments agreed to expedite requests to assure a regular and regulated flow. The Cuban government agreed to reestablish strong border controls, while the U.S. government agreed to suspend its automatic admission of illegal immigrants. In this fashion, the Clinton administration became the first Democratic administration to restrict entry of Cuban immigrants into the United States.

Settlement Pattern

It is now axiomatic to view the final destination of Cubans, either coming from Cuba or resettling from other points of the diaspora, as Miami. But this process of concentration was preceded by an intentional dispersion throughout the United States engineered by the Cuban Refugee Program.

The Cuban Refugee Program was established in February 1961 as a federal effort to provide assistance in handling the large influx from Cuba. With the explicit goal of easing the impact of the Cuban exodus on Miami, the progam resettled some 300,000 Cubans throughout the United States from 1961 to 1978. The bulk of the resettlements took place during the early years of the airlift in the 1960s and were directed to New York, New Jersey, California, and Illinois.

Almost as soon as the resettlements began, however, a "trickle back" to Miami was already under way. Data from the U.S. Census show that the communities that received larger numbers of resettled Cubans during the 1960s are precisely the communities that have been losing a greater number of Cubans to Florida since the mid-1970s. By 1980, the U.S. Census found slightly more than 52 percent of U.S. Cubans living in Greater Miami; the 1990 figure approached 60 percent. The concentration of Cubans in southern Florida increased during the 1980s as the majority of Mariel entrants settled in Miami, where they could find employment within a familiar cultural environment and use their native language.

It is likely that the process of concentration in Miami will continue throughout the 1990s. The principal factor in sustaining that trend will be entry into retirement age of the large middle-aged cohort in the Cuban-origin population, many of whom were young heads of households who were resettled away from Miami in the 1960s. It is likely that many of those who have not yet returned to Miami will do so when they retire in the years ahead.

Despite the fact that southern Florida now accounts for a majority of the U.S. Cuban population, it is important to remember that not all Cubans live in Miami and that there are sizable Cuban-American communities throughout the United States. The largest concentration outside Miami is in New Jersey across the Hudson River from New York City, especially in Union City and West New York. Overall, Cubans living in those industrial communities tend to be concentrated in blue-collar occupations, tend to register as Democrats, and seem to hold somewhat more liberal views on the issue of relations with the homeland.

U.S. Cubans are urbanites. They surpass the total U.S. population, as well as every other major Hispanic group, in the proportion who reside in urban areas. Within metropolitan areas Cubans are more likely, in comparison with other populations, to reside in the suburbs.

Other significant Cuban-American communities exist in the largest U.S. cities, such as Los Angeles and Chicago. In comparison with Cubans living in the two major communities of Miami and New York–New Jersey, Cubans residing in other cities are more likely to be professionals and to have higher incomes. One explanation for this phenomenon is that those who upon resettlement elsewhere were able to obtain good employment were not as likely to abandon those opportunities to join the flow back to Miami. Those Cubans living in communities with few of their compatriots also exhibit a higher degree of cultural assimilation to U.S. society; this is especially true for their children. Devoid of the insularity that the enclave in Miami provides, that second generation of Cuban Americans is less likely to speak Spanish well and more likely to marry non-Cubans.

The Cuban Enclave in Miami

As of the mid-1990s, persons born in Cuba or of Cuban descent represent Miami's largest ethnic group. Cubans account for 56 percent of Greater Miami's foreign-born population, and persons of Cuban origin constitute the bulk—nearly 70 percent—of all Hispanics in the area. About 50 percent of the population of Dade County (including Miami) is of Hispanic birth or descent.

Cubans can be found throughout most of Greater Miami, including predominantly white non-Hispanic neighborhoods. Hispanic-Anglo segregation is not as high as one would expect. That is not the case for Hispanic-black segregation; the two populations exhibit considerable spatial distance. Blacks in Miami tend to live in fairly confined areas, segregated from both Hispanics and Anglos.

Miami's Cuban community is regarded as the foremost example, in the United States, of a true ethnic enclave—a distinctive economic formation characterized by the spatial concentration of immigrants who organize a variety of enterprises to serve their own ethnic market and the general population. The basis of the enclave is highly differentiated entrepreneurial activity. Miami is the metropolitan area in the United States with the highest per capita number of Hispanic-owned busi-

Cuban waiting staff at the Versailles Restaurant in Miami's Little Havana. (Tony Arruza/Corbis)

nesses, most of them Cuban. The community's entrepreneurial base was established largely by Cuban immigrants, especially those who arrived in the first wave in the early 1960s and possessed the complex of skills and attitudes that eventually made possible their entry into a wide range of self-employment.

Strong and diversified entrepreneurial activity is responsible for the enclave's most important overall feature: institutional completeness. Cubans in Miami can, if they wish, literally live out their lives within the ethnic community. The wide range of sales and services, including professional services, available within the community makes possible its completeness.

Consequences of the Enclave

To understand Cubans in Miami it is important to trace the implications of the structural organization of the enclave. Foremost among them is the well-studied influence on the process of economic adjustment, but the enclave also affects such important areas as acculturation, interethnic relations, and political participation.

Economic Adjustment. Most of the research on the Miami enclave deals precisely with its relationship to the relatively successful economic position of Cuban immigrants. The enclave somewhat insulates the immigrant against the usual processes of the segmented labor market. In contrast to Mexican immigrants, who must join the open labor market in peripheral sectors of the economy throughout the country, many recent Cuban immigrants enter the U.S. labor market mainly through the large number of businesses in Miami that are owned or operated by members of their own group who arrived earlier. While compensation may not be higher in the enclave, ethnic bonds provide for informal networks of support that facilitate the learning of new skills and the overall process of economic adjustment, thereby blurring the usual differences between the primary and secondary labor markets. The enclave's positive implications for economic adjustment are seen as a factor that has maintained the Cubans' socioeconomic position as relatively high in comparison with that of many other immigrant groups.

Acculturation. The existence of the enclave also has evident implications for the process of acculturation. The completeness of the enclave has the effect of slowing down that process, for it tends to insulate the immigrant from the "dominant" society and culture, allowing for the retention of the culture of origin. Using language as one indicator of the degree of acculturation, one study found that most Cubans use only Spanish at home and in many of their daily activities.

The institutional completeness of the enclave has made Spanish a public language in Miami, one that is not confined to the intimacy of the family or the peer group. It is the lingua franca for conducting a wide range of business and personal matters beyond one's primary group. This pervasiveness has made language use as such a critical—and often explosive—issue in Miami, one that is the frequent battleground for interethnic conflicts. It is not a coincidence that the "English only" movement was born in Miami.

The retention of the language and cultural patterns of the country of origin are also attributable to the fairly recent arrival of most Cubans in the United States. The overwhelming majority of Cubans in Miami, as in the rest of the United States, are immigrants, with an overrepresentation of the middle-aged and the elderly. The bulk of the population has arrived in the United States only since the mid-1960s.

Another factor that retards the process of acculturation among Cubans in Miami, especially important in the early stages of the exodus, is the perception many U.S. Cubans have of themselves as reluctant immigrants, compelled to leave their country but with the expectaton of returning, and consequently with little desire or motivation to assimilate into the mainstream society.

It is also important to remember that there have been periodic waves of massive arrivals from Cuba. The new arrivals are fresh from the culture of origin, and they renew and reinforce that culture within the immigrant community.

Interethnic Relations. A third major consequence of the enclave is in the arena of interethnic relations. In a metropolitan area in which the various ethnic groups—especially blacks—are spatially segregated, the existence of an institutionally complete community among Cubans makes it even less likely that Hispanics and blacks will create the basis for a better understanding and a common agenda. There are, of course, many causes for this social distance, but the ability of the Cubans to live largely within their own community is undoubtedly one of them. Compared to American blacks, Cubans in Miami have a far greater likelihood of being able to work with coethnics, shop in stores owned and operated by coethnics, and obtain professional services from coethnics.

Political Participation. Although participation in the political system of the United States, at all levels, has traditionally taken a back seat to the politics of the homeland, the 1980s saw the rapid and massive entry of Miami's Cubans into the realm of electoral politics in the United States.

One factor that encouraged Cubans in Miami to become citizens and register to vote was the candidacy of Ronald Reagan. The ideology of the Republican candidate on foreign policy was appealing to many Cubans, and it served to join exile politics with registering and voting in the United States. Participation in the U.S. political system, therefore, is not necessarily an abandonment of the concern with the political status of the homeland, but may actually be an extension of those exile concerns.

More than 50 percent of Cubans born in Cuba but living in the United States are U.S. citizens. Of *all* Cuban Americans, more than 64 percent are U.S. citizens.

The size of the Cuban community in Greater Miami and its fairly high turnout rates during elections have produced a boom in the number of Cubans in elected positions at all levels of government. Cubans are mayors of the incorporated areas of Miami, Hialeah, Sweetwater, West Miami, and Hialeah Gardens, all within Greater Miami. Cubans comprise a majority in the commissions or councils of those cities. Cubans also are the managers of the largest municipalities in Dade County, and in 1995, a Cuban was selected to be the overall county manager, probably the most powerful position in the region.

When the 1990s started there were already ten Cubans in the Florida legislature—seven in the House and three in the Senate. In 1989, a Cuban reached an elective office at the federal level when Ileana Ros-Lehtinen was elected to the U.S. Congress, succeeding longtime congressman Claude Pepper. Another Cuban, Lincoln Diaz-Balart, was elected to Congress in 1992.

The Cuban voting block has to be considered by any candidate seeking countywide office. The 1990 countywide elections for Metropolitan Dade County's Commission emphasized the strength of a unified Cuban voting bloc. During these elections two of the non-Cuban victors, one of whom was a black Republican, owed their success to the support garnered among the Cuban electorate. Nowhere else in America, nor even in American history, have first-generation immigrants so quickly and so thoroughly appropriated local political power.

Explaining the Cuban Phenomenon

Three factors can be identified as promoting Miami's Cuban economic and political activity: structural factors arising from the human capital Cubans brought with them and their geographical concentration in Miami, the role of the U.S. government in providing aid to the arriving Cuban refugees, and the creation of a collective Cuban-American identity arising from the interplay of the U.S. state and Cuban exile counterrevolutionary organizations.

The first wave of Cubans has been labeled the "Golden Exiles," the top of Cuban society who were most immediately threatened by a socialist revolution. Many had already established a footing in the United States, and when the revolution came they simply abandoned one of their residences for another across the Straits of Florida. Before the revolution, for example, one Cuban shoe manufacturer produced footwear for a major U.S. retail chain. He obtained his working capital from New York financial houses. After the revolution the only change was that the manufacturing was done in Miami rather than Havana. In most cases, even if they could not transfer their investments, their human capital—their knowledge and experience—came with them.

Second, the U.S. government created for the arriving Cubans unprecedented direct and indirect assistance programs. The Cuban Refugee Program spent nearly $1 billion between 1965 and 1976. The federal government provided transportation costs from Cuba, financial assistance to needy refugees and to state and local public agencies that provided services for refugees, and employment and professional training courses for refugees. Even in programs not especially designed for them, Cubans seemed to benefit. From 1968 to 1980, Latinos (almost all Cubans) received 46.9 percent of all Small Business Administration loans in Dade County.

Even more important was indirect assistance. Through the 1960s, the University of Miami had the largest CIA station in the world, outside of the organization's headquarters in Virginia. With perhaps as many as twelve thousand Cubans in Miami on the CIA payroll at one point in the early 1960s, it was one of the largest employers in Florida. It supported what was described as the third-largest navy in the world and more than fifty front businesses: CIA boat shops, CIA gun shops, CIA travel agencies, CIA detective agencies, and CIA real-estate agencies. This investment served far more to boost the Cubans economically in Miami than it did to destabilize the Castro regime.

This favorable reception by the U.S. government translated itself not only into millions of dollars of resettlement assistance but also into a "direct line" of Cuban exile leaders to the centers of political power in Washington, D.C. Unlike other immigrant and ethnic minorities who struggled painfully for years or even generations to gain access to the corridors of power, this was available to Cuban leaders almost from the start.

This window of opportunity greatly boosted the Cubans and the Miami economy in general in the 1960s. Waves of Cuban immigrants stimulated demand and received substantial subsidies from the federal government. With a high rate of labor force participation, especially among women, the Cubans also contributed significantly to productivity growth.

There is equally no doubt that not all Miami Cubans are rich and powerful businessmen. Even the fact of business ownership is somewhat misleading. Of the nearly twenty-five thousand businesses owned and operated by Latinos in 1982, only 12 percent had paid employees, and together they generated only about eighteen thousand paid

jobs, about the same number of Cubans in Dade County who belonged to unions at that time. Moreover, most of the Cuban and other Latino employment growth during the 1970s was directly attributable to population growth. Latinos (as well as blacks) were underrepresented in Miami's fastest-growing industries, especially the financial services.

Trends in the Cuban-American Community

Although, as noted previously, the enclave tends to favor the retention of the culture of the homeland, delaying the process of acculturation, it is unlikely that the Cuban community in the United States will be an exception to the usual intergenerational shift toward greater acculturation and assimilation. English is the principal language among Cubans who have lived all or most of their

Workers make cigars at El Credito, a Cuban cigar factory in Miami's Little Havana. (Dave G. Houser/Corbis)

lives in the United States. The 40 percent of the community that lives outside of Miami uses English almost exclusively.

Similarly, there are sharp intergenerational differences among Cubans in the level of acculturation, with early adolescents demonstrating the highest scores of all age groups in measures of behavioral acculturation. Furthermore, males evidence greater acculturation than females. An exaggerated acculturational gap is a major source of intergenerational conflict. Alienation between parents and children is usually found in Cuban families with interactional problems.

An important focus of intergenerational tensions is conflicting value orientations with respect to dependence and independence. Cuban culture promotes the continued dependence of children on their parents, even in the teenage years and beyond. However, children are more likely to have internalized the norms of independence commonly found in U.S. society.

One adaptation that reduces intergenerational tension is "biculturality," by which each generation adjusts to the other generation's cultural preferences. Parents learn how to remain loyal to their ethnic background while becoming skilled in interacting with their youngsters' Americanized values and behaviors, and vice versa.

Coming up rapidly behind that large cohort of first-generation entrepreneurs who created the enclave are those Cuban Americans born in the United States or who arrived as children from the island. Largely educated in the United States, the influentials in that group are less likely than the older generation to be entrepreneurs and more likely to be professionals.

The advent of that dramatic intergenerational shift is already evident in the participation of Cubans within the traditional Anglo institutions that hold true economic power in Miami (banks, law firms, insurance companies, real estate, advertising, professional services, and the public bureaucracies). At the upper levels there are few Cuban faces in those institutions, especially in the private sector. At the lower and middle-management levels there is a critical mass of young Cuban

professionals. Their training, as well as their bilingual and bicultural skills, have made them very attractive to those institutions, particularly as more and more firms strive to serve the growing Hispanic population of the area. Furthermore, "Anglo flight" from Dade County has removed the Cubans' Anglo contemporaries from competition for those jobs.

Those younger professionals have the credentials to break out from the ethnic enclave and obtain employment in the larger firms and institutions outside the ethnic community. If this is the case, then it is obvious that a rapid change will take place in the years ahead in the economic basis of the Cuban community, from a community dominated by first-generation entrepreneurs to one of second-generation professionals. Such a shift will alter the Cuban community's relationship with the rest of the city and the country.

Removed somewhat from their Cuban origins, the new generation of Miami Cubans will think like immigrants rather than exiles, will have a new agenda, and will easily find common ground and solidarity with other ethnic groups in the community, especially the growing number of non-Cuban Latins.

Cubans have transformed Miami in many ways. This transformation is forcing a reevaluation of ideas about how urban centers develop and how immigration affects this development. The Cuban-American experience in Miami shows that newcomers to an American city can achieve unparalleled power and prestige in one generation if six conditions are met. (1) The receiving city must be relatively small, with a weak established leadership structure. This condition can be most beneficial to the newcomers if leadership as well as the population have a tradition of being transient. (2) A substantial portion of immigrants are particularly rich, either in material or human resources. (3) The immigrants have had previous contact with the city, preferably as tourists, political exiles, or businesspeople, not as economic immigrants. (4) The ethnic category of the immigrants is not overly represented in the poor segments of the established resident population. (5) A large number of immigrants from the same country of origin flood into the area and, perhaps more important than sheer numbers, they are able to create a differentiated class structure within the receiving city. This allows for the potential to create an economic enclave as the middle and upper classes generate and use their capital by paying for the labor provided by coethics in the lower classes. (6) The development of this enclave, in turn, is aided by the allotment of development aid (direct or indirect) from the receiving government, the restructuring of the economy in a way that increases the value of certain characteristics of the immigrant group (e.g., billingualism and international contacts), and the relative absence of a strong economy before the arrival of the immigrants.

Although these dynamics are able to work in the Cuban-American success story, they are unlikely to be repeated in any other region in the United States with any other immigrant group in the foreseeable future.

Bibliography

Boswell, T. D., and Curtis, J. R. (1983). *The Cuban-American Experience: Culture, Images, and Perspectives*. Totowa, NJ: Rowman & Allanheld.

Diaz-Briquets, S. (1984). "Cuban-Owned Businesses in the United States." *Cuban Studies* 14(2):57–68.

Didion, J. (1987). *Miami*. New York: Simon & Schuster.

Fagen, R. R.; Brody, R. A.; and O'Leary T. J. (1968). *Cubans in Exile: Disaffection and the Revolution*. Stanford, CA: Stanford University Press.

Ferree, M. M. (1979). "Employment Without Liberation: Cuban Women in the United States." *Social Science Quarterly* 60(June):35–50.

Grenier, G., and Stepick, A., eds. (1992). *Miami Now! Immigration, Ethnicity, and Social Change*. Gainesville: University Press of Florida.

Maier, F. X., and McColm, R. B. (1981). "Nation in Our Midst: The Cuban Diaspora." *National Review* (February 20):148–152, 184.

Mohl, R. A. (1983). "Miami: The Ethnic Cauldron." In *Sunbelt Cities: Politics and Growth Since World War II*, edited by R. M. Bernard and B. R. Rice. Austin: University of Texas Press.

Mohl, R. A. (1985). "An Ethnic 'Boiling Pot': Cubans and Haitians in Miami." *The Journal of Ethnic Studies* 13(2): 51–74.

Muir, H. (1953). *Miami, U.S.A.* Coconut Grove, FL: Hurricane House Publishers.

Pedraza, S. (1995). "Cuba's Refugees: Manifold Migrations." In *Origins and Destinies: Immigration, Race, and Ethnicity in America*, edited by S. Pedraza and R. Rumbaut. Belmont, CA: Wadsworth.

Pedraza-Bailey, S. (1985). *Political and Economic Migrants in America: Cubans and Mexicans*. Austin: University of Texas Press.

Pérez, L. (1985). "The Cuban Population of the United States: The Results of the 1980 U.S. Census of Population." *Cuban Studies/Estudios Cubanos* 15:1–18.

Pérez, L. (1986). "Immigrant Economic Adjustment and Family Organization: The Cuban Success Story Reexamined." *International Migration Review* 20:4–20.

Portes, A. (1981). "Modes of Structural Incorporation and Present Theories of Labor Immigration." In *Global Trends in Migration: Theory and Research of International Population Movements*, edited by M. M. Kritz, C. B. Keely, and S. M. Tomasi. New York: Center for Migration Studies.

Portes, A., and Bach, R. L. (1985). *Latin Journey: Cuban and Mexican Immigrants in the United States*. Berkeley: University of California Press.

Prieto, Y. (1987). "Cuban Women in the U.S. Labor Force: Perspectives on the Nature of Change." *Cuban Studies/Estudios Cubanos* 17:73–91.

Rieff, D. (1987a). *Going to Miami: Exiles, Tourists, and Refugees in the New America*. Boston: Little, Brown.

Rieff, D. (1987b). "A Reporter at Large: The Second Havana." *The New Yorker* (May 18):65–83.

Wilson, K. L., and Martin, W. A. (1982). "Ethnic Enclaves: A Comparison of the Cuban and Black Economies of Miami." *American Journal of Sociology* 88:135–160.

Wilson, K. L., and Portes, A. (1980). "Immigrant Enclaves: An Analysis of the Labor Market Experiences of Cubans in Miami." *American Journal of Sociology* 86:295–319.

GUILLERMO J. GRENIER
LISANDRO PEREZ

CYPRIOTS

Cypriots form one of the smallest ethnic groups in the United States. The term "Cypriots" is used to refer to immigrants from the island of Cyprus, the third-largest island of the Mediterranean Sea in area (after Sicily and Sardinia). Because Cyprus is inhabited by Greeks, Turks, Armenians, and Maronites, the term "Cypriot" can be used to describe any one of those people. The United States ranks as the third most popular destination of Cypriot emigrants, after the United Kingdom and Australia. Place of birth rather than ethnicity is the main criterion for the identification of Cypriots as a distinct ancestral group.

Immigration Patterns

While archaeological excavations have established that population movement to and from Cyprus dates to the eighth millennium B.C.E, modern emigration from Cyprus is mainly a twentieth-century phenomenon. Although the record of Cypriot emigration is incomplete, especially for the first half of the twentieth century, the emigration flow from Cyprus can be subdivided into five phases, based on the major events associated with each period: early beginnings (1900–1954), emergency years (1955–1959), mass exodus (1960–1963), intercommunal strife (1964–1974), and the invasion and its aftermath (mid-1974–1986).

During the first phase (1900–1954), the flow of Cypriot emigrants was maintained at low levels and was driven by the drought of 1902, the severe drought (astohia) of 1932–1933, and the uprising of October 1931 against British rule. Clearly these upheavals in Cyprus affected the rural regions of the island, which traditionally supplied the bulk of emigrants. During the period 1924–1927, a total of five thousand Turkish Cypriots immigrated to Turkey, taking advantage of a provision in the Treaty of Lausanne. However, many of those who opted for Turkish nationality under terms of the treaty later returned to Cyprus. The British rulers of the island discouraged immigration of Turkish Cypriots to Turkey, because potential interethnic tensions between Greek Cypriots and Turkish Cypriots could be used to maintain British control of the island. The major destinations of Cypriot immigrants during the 1920s were Egypt, Greece, Australia, the Belgian Congo, Argentina, Britain, and the United States. In 1930, more than one thousand Cypriots entered the United States.

The second phase of Cypriot emigration (1955–1959) coincided with the years of emergency when the Greek Cypriots launched an armed campaign against British colonial rule and in favor of union (enosis) with Greece. A total of 29,135 Cypriots left the island because of the political upheaval. Paradoxically, while the Greek Cypriots were fighting to rid the island of British rule, 85 percent of the emigrants settled in the United Kingdom. By 1959 the anticolonial campaign ended without achieving union with Greece. Cyprus was granted independence and was proclaimed a republic on August 16, 1960. The first three years of independence were marked by a massive exodus of the population of Cyprus. The propelling forces behind this migratory flow were the political uncertainty that surrounded the new republic, high unemployment, and the Commonwealth Immigration Act of 1962, which restricted immigration to the United Kingdom and went into effect in July 1962. Many Cypriots immigrated to the United Kingdom to beat the closing of the gates. Friends and relatives who were already in the United Kingdom played a major role in facilitating Cypriots' immigration there.

The fourth phase of emigration (1964 to mid-1974) was characterized by interethnic violence between the island's Greek and Turkish communities, and emigration fluctuated significantly, reflecting the rise and fall in the level of interethnic fighting.

The fifth phase followed the military invasion of the island by Turkey on July 20, 1974. As a result of the invasion, the island was divided into a Turkish-occupied North and a Greek-dominated South. The economy of the government-controlled

South was dealt a severe blow, and unemployment reached an unprecedented high level because of the influx of refugees from the North. Because of these catastrophic events, emigration peaked once more in 1976. That was the record year for Cypriot immigrants (971) arriving in the United States; following dramatic improvements in the Cypriot economy, the immigratory flow was reduced to levels of about two hundred or less per year in the 1980s. Anecdotal information suggests that return migration, particularly from Britain and South Africa, has been occurring for some time.

As the record suggests, Cypriots mainly emigrated in waves that closely reflected the political upheavals on the island, and, to a lesser extent, the poor economic conditions that prevail periodically because of droughts there. The passage of restrictive legislation by the British Parliament played a major role in curtailing the number of Cypriot emigrants to the United Kingdom.

The patterns of Cypriot immigration can be conceptualized in terms of chain migration. A member of the family, usually male, migrated first. He was followed by other immediate family members, relatives, and friends from the same or neighboring villages, mainly because of positive information feedback regarding the destination and support that the established emigrant would provide for the newcomers. Although the places of origin of Cypriot emigrants cannot be ascertained with any degree of accuracy for the first half of the twentieth century, the majority emigrated from rural areas. The United Kingdom is the most popular destination of Cypriot emigrants (58.2%), followed by Australia (15%), and the United States (3.5%). Other destinations include Greece, Canada, South Africa, Zaire, Nigeria, and Zimbabwe.

Demography

The long demographic record of Cyprus dates to Neolithic times. Eteocypriots, as the first inhabitants of the island were called, probably arrived from the Syrian coast. During the second millennium B.C.E. Mycenean Greek traders and Achaean colonists introduced Hellenic culture and influ-

ence to the island. Subsequently Cyprus was conquered by Assyrians, Egyptians, Persians, Alexander the Great, Romans, Byzantines, English, Lusignans, Venetians, and Turks.

Among the many events that influenced the demographic history of the island, two are most important: (1) the introduction of Hellenic culture during the second millennium B.C.E. and (2) the occupation of the island by the Ottoman Turks from 1571 to 1878, which introduced the Turkish component in the population matrix of the island. By the time of independence in 1960, following eighty-two years of British rule, the 1960 Cypriot Census reported that the Greeks outnumbered the Turks by four to one. The existing record of Cypriot emigration shows that Cypriots emigrated according to their relative size in the population. The United Kingdom and especially London was a popular destination for both Greek and Turkish Cypriots. During the period 1953–1994, a total of 11,921 Cypriots immigrated to the United States. The 1990 U.S. Census reported 10,060 foreign-born Cypriots in the country.

Early waves of Greek Cypriot immigrants to the United States were predominantly young males. This predominantly male migratory flow was echoed among early waves of Greek immigrants throughout the United States. Given the extremely low levels of female immigration, it is not surprising that as many as half of the Cypriot immigrants married outside the Cypriot as well as Greek communities. This pattern has continued to rise, and the rate of intermarriage for Greek Americans reached 62.4 percent, based on church records, for the period from 1991 to 1994.

Despite their rural origins, Cypriot immigrants showed a strong spatial bias for the large urban centers in the northeastern part of the United States. According to the 1990 U.S. Census, there were 10,060 foreign-born Cypriots in the country; they were distributed by region as follows: Northeast, 5,758 (57%); South, 2,209 (22%); West, 1,082 (11%); and Midwest, 1,011 (10%). Given that Greek Cypriots create their identities around the Greek Orthodox Church, they are spatially distributed in ways that resemble those of the

Cypriot dancers in traditional folk costumes perform at an event in New York. (Stavros T. Constantinou)

rest of Greek Americans. Although there is no documented evidence about residential shifts from the northeastern to the southwestern United States, anecdotal evidence suggests that such a movement is under way.

A further examination of the spatial distribution of foreign-born Cypriots in the United States by state corroborates this observation. As in the case of Greek concentrations, the largest cluster of foreign-born Cypriots is in the state of New York, most specifically in New York City. Other states with large concentrations are New Jersey (1,482), California (898), Florida (518), and Virginia (486). While New York City has the largest number of Cypriots, Los Angeles, Norfolk, and Detroit are some of the other urban centers with large concentrations of Cypriots.

Linguistic Affiliation

The Greek Orthodox inhabitants of Cyprus speak Greek, the Muslims speak Turkish, the Armenians speak Armenian, and the Maronites speak a mixture of Arabic and Greek. According to the 1960 Cypriot Census, the last official undisputed census of the population of Cyprus, the proportion of the population by religion was as follows: Greek Orthodox, 77 percent; Muslim, 18.3 percent; Armenian-Gregorian, 0.6 percent; Roman Catholic, 0.8 percent; Maronite, 0.5 percent; and other, 2.8 percent. Although some Muslims spoke Greek, and some Greeks spoke Turkish, the census did not tabulate the results by language. As one would expect, more members of the minority communities spoke Greek than vice versa.

Given that Cyprus was under British control from 1878 to 1960, a significant proportion of Cypriot emigrants (irrespective of ethnic group affiliation) was bilingual, because English was taught for six years as a subject in the secondary school curriculum. Moreover, English was used widely in official government business and as the common medium of communication among the island's educated classes.

The Greek language and orientation to place of birth are the prime definers of Cypriot identity among Cypriots in the United States. The members of the second generation define their identity mostly in terms of religion and their participation in the life of the church, much like the rest of Greek America, especially since there are no separate Cypriot parishes or communities. Maintenance of the Cypriot dialect is not possible, especially given the widespread geographic distribution of the Cypriots in all but six states (Montana, Nebraska, North Dakota, South Dakota, West Virginia, and Wyoming).

While there is no separate Greek Cypriot newspaper published in the United States, Cypriots own one (*Proini*) fo the two major national Greek newspapers in the country. The Greek-language press as well as the English-language press have been covering developments surrounding the Cyprus problem extensively because of its importance to Greek foreign policy. The Cyprus question has unified and mobilized the Greek Cypriot and Greek communities in the United States, especially following the Turkish military invasion of the island in 1974.

History and Cultural Relations

Like Greek immigrants, Cypriots have sought employment predominantly in the restaurant and confectionary businesses, a handful of immigrants branched out into other areas, such as farming, insurance, architecture, and even furniture restoration. Over the years, anecdotal evidence suggests that employment patterns have shifted to the professions. A significant number of the recent immigrants were students who, after finishing their studies, chose to stay in the United States and seek employment in their chosen fields of study.

Cypriot family life, like the Greek, revolves around the Greek Orthodox Church calendar. Celebrations of major church holidays such as Christmas, Easter, and holidays of the saints, form an integral part of family life. The family unit is of the nuclear traditional type, with the father, mother, and children having well-defined roles. Many times the family provides support for other members and is instrumental in bringing more members into their community.

Assimilation and Cultural Persistence

As a group, Cypriots have integrated themselves socially within the Greek communities of the states where they settled. In areas where Cypriots clustered in large numbers, they organized their own voluntary associations based on place of origin. The organization of such local societies (*topika somateia*) parallels developments among Greek immigrants from other parts of the country. The *Yearbook*, published annually by the Greek Orthodox Archdiocese of North and South America, listed twenty-six Cypriot organizations in the United States in the 1996 edition. Some represented people from certain villages, others had a regional appeal, while still others appealed to all Cypriots. The tendency to form societies of local, regional, and national scope in the United States is also characteristic of Cypriots in the United

Kingdom and Greeks in other parts of the world, including Greece proper. These societies helped early immigrants adjust to their new surroundings. Often members engaged in philanthropic activities and sent aid to people in their place of origin.

Cypriots, much like Greek immigrants and other ethnic groups, have experienced the forces of assimilation. While the first generation defines ethnicity around language and orientation toward the place of birth, the second generation defines ethnicity around the Greek Orthodox religion. The degree of ethnic identification varies from individual to individual, from generation to generation, and from community to community. Some communities are more ethnic than others; some are more American than others. However, there is a certain core of values revolving around the institution of the church that is common to all Greek communities. It is this core that provides the common reference and sense of belonging.

See also: ARMENIANS; GREEKS; TURKS

Bibliography

Anthias, F. (1992). *Ethnicity, Class, Gender and Migration: Greek-Cypriots in Britain.* Aldershot, Eng.: Avebury.

Constantinou, S. T. (1990). "Economic Factors and Political Upheavals as Determinants of International Migration: The Case of Cyprus." In *Proceedings of an International Conference on Cypriot Migration: Historical and Sociological Perspectives* (in Greek), edited by Ministry of Education. Nicosia, Cyprus: Imprinta.

Diamantides, N., and Constantinou, S. (1989). "Modeling the Macrodynamics of International Migration: Determinants of Emigration from Cyprus, 1956–85." *Environment and Planning A* 21:927–950.

Georgiades, G. (1946). "The Cypriot Community of Norfolk, U.S.A." (in Greek). *Elefthera Foni* (Free Voice) 25(December):4.

Georgiades, G. (1947). "The Cypriot Community of Norfolk, U.S.A." (in Greek). *Elefthera Foni* (Free Voice) 1(January):4.

Great Britain Colonial Office. (1931). *Cyprus 1930,* London: Her Majesty's Office.

Great Britain Colonial Office. (1932). *Cyprus 1931.* London: Her Majesty's Office.

Percival, D. (1949). *1946 Census of Population and Agriculture.* London: Crown Agents for the Colonies.

Republic of Cyprus, Ministry of Finance, Department of Statistics and Research. (1989). *Statistical Abstract 1987 & 1988.* Nicosia, Cyprus: Printing Office of the Republic of Cyprus.

U.S. Department of Commerce, Bureau of the Census. (1983). *1980 Census of Population, Ancestry of the Population by State: 1980.* Washington, DC: U.S. Government Printing Office.

STAVROS T. CONSTANTINOU

CZECHS

The term "Czechs"—they call themselves Češi or Čechové (the singular forms are Čech for a male and Češka for a female)—refers to people whose mother tongue is Czech. The Czech-speaking people are natives or inhabitants of Bohemia (Čechy) and Moravia (Morava). The use of the geographic term "Bohemian" to refer to Czech ethnicity is misleading. The term does not include the Moravians, who also speak Czech, but takes in members of several small minorities who also live in Bohemia but whose native languages are other than Czech (primarily Slovak, Romany, Polish, and German).

The Czech-speaking inhabitants of Bohemia and Moravia together form the major ethnically distinct population of the Czech Republic, the state that came into being in 1993 when the Slovaks of the Czech and Slovak Federative Republic established their own independent republic, Slovakia. The most pronounced badge of Czech ethnic identity is the Czech language, a member of the West Slavic subbranch of the Indo-European language family. Czech is most closely related to Slovak, with which it is mutually intelligible. The population of the Czech Republic in 1995 was 10.4 million, about 94 percent of whom were Czech-speakers.

The crowning of the first Bohemian king took place in 1085, with the title becoming hereditary in 1198. The peak of medieval civilization in the kingdom was attained during the fourteenth century with the establishment in Prague (Praha) in 1348 of the first university in central Europe. In 1620—the same year in which the Mayflower landed at Plymouth—the Bohemian Kingdom lost its independence in the Battle of White Mountain (Bílá hora), and its provinces were declared to be the hereditary property of the Hapsburg family. Forcible re-Catholicization of the population, who followed the teachings of the fifteenth-century Bohemian religious reformer Jan Hus (John Huss), gave rise to emigration, which, together with the effects of the Thirty Years' War and the epidemics of plague and other diseases, may have reduced the population of Bohemia by as much as one-half and that of Moravia by one-fourth. Independence was not regained until 1918, with the breakup of the Austro-Hungarian Empire. The newly established Czechoslovak Republic, or Czechoslovakia, included not only the territory of the historic Bohemian Kingdom (Bohemia, Moravia, and part of Silesia) but also Slovakia and, in the extreme east, Carpathian Ruthenia.

Immigration History

The first Czech immigrant to North America whose name is known was Augustin Heřman, also spelled Augustine Herrman). He left Bohemia during the Thirty Years' War, settled in the Netherlands, and made several business journeys to America. Eventually he settled in the New World and began in 1661 to take part in the administration of New Amsterdam (renamed New York in 1664). Among his various activities was the making of the first map of Virginia and Maryland, which appeared in 1670. As a reward Heřman received from Lord Baltimore several large grants of land, one of which he named Bohemia Manor.

There must have been others either visiting or settling in North America during the remainder of the seventeenth century, but their numbers would have been quite modest. After 1620, thousands of members of the religious reform movement in Bohemia and Moravia (the Czech lands) who traced their origin to the fifteenth-century Hussites had fled to the Netherlands, England, Sweden, and other countries. Some of the Swedish expeditions to North America to what was then called New Sweden (around Delaware Bay) very likely included some exiles from the Czech lands. Many members of the Unity of Brethren, a Reformation church in the Czech lands severely persecuted after 1620, went into exile in Saxony, Poland, and several other European countries. Some of those who settled in Saxony later immigrated to America, but they must have been thoroughly Germanized by the mid-1700s when they founded colonies in Georgia, Pennsylvania, and North Carolina.

Although about three hundred Czech Jesuit missionaries were sent to the New World to convert Native Americans to the Catholic faith, emigration from the Czech lands to North America was quite limited in scope until the second half of the nineteenth century. From that time on, emigration increased substantially, in part as the consequence of the revolutionary nationalist movements in western and central Europe in 1848.

The Austrian Empire, which included a dozen different nationalities and was already one of the most densely peopled areas of Europe, was about to experience a marked increase in population growth. In the Czech lands alone the population rose from 6.5 million to well over 10 million between the mid-1840s and 1910. Moreover, the Revolution of 1848 marked the beginning of many social and economic changes. For example, serfdom was abolished in the empire, giving the peasantry freedom to move, and industry began rapid development.

Industrialization in the Czech lands soon reached large-scale proportions, but despite new job opportunities, population pressure was such that many people had little choice but to look for employment and a new life abroad. Most of the emigrants, whose flight from their homeland had become a mass phenomenon by the beginning of the 1860s, went either to Lower Austria—especially Vienna, the imperial capital—or to the United

States. The first waves of emigrants were from the poor, largely mountainous border regions—for example, northern Bohemia, where the cottage weaving industry was being replaced by factory production. But there were other reasons as well. In peasant families the heir was customarily the oldest son, and because the holdings of small peasants were too modest to be divided, some of the younger sons also had reason to seek a new life abroad. Consequently, the flight from rural southern Bohemia became a general phenomenon during the 1880s.

By this time, considerable information was already available about life in the United States, not only from letters of the earlier emigrants but also from newspaper articles and from stories and songs in the popular press. Some songs indulged in gross exaggeration, but the texts were simply ex-

A young girl in 1942 works with her teacher on a Czech-language lesson to aid in the retention of her native language. (Library of Congress/Corbis)

pressions of astonishment at the unlimited possibilities in a country where in 1871, for example, an acre of Nebraska prairie land could be purchased for $1.30. One of the early popular songs, "The New Song About America," published in Olomouc (Moravia) in 1856, in its twelve stanzas described America as a land where "dumplings grow on trees, with ponds of butter under these trees . . . pigs grow already roasted . . . and fences are made of sausages." Then, perhaps to tone down such enthusiastic testimonials, the song reminded the singer and the listener that "an American must not be lazy" because there, too, "one must work to stay alive." Advertising by shipping companies and land agents contributed to the growing interest in immigrating to the New World.

Until about 1880, many of the Czech-speaking immigrants to the United States were farmers. They settled in some of the prairie states of the Mississippi Valley and in Nebraska, Kansas, and Texas. Of those who arrived later, some found jobs in coal mines, iron and steel mills, and glass factories. Others worked for the railroads that began to connect the many distant locations on the North American continent; still others continued in the trades they had practiced in the old country. During the pre–World War I period, the tendency of Czech immigrants to settle in or near the communities where they already had relatives or friends explains the many pockets of significant Czech population.

As of 1920, most of the immigrants who claimed Czech as their mother tongue lived in Illinois; fewer than half as many lived in Ohio, Nebraska, New York, Texas, and Wisconsin, and still fewer in Minnesota and Iowa. In the larger cities Czech was listed as mother tongue by 106,428 people in Chicago; 43,997 in Cleveland; 43,839 in New York; 11,416 in Omaha; 9,723 in St. Louis; 8,694 in Baltimore; 6,745 in Milwaukee; 4,576 in St. Paul; 4,519 in Detroit; and 3,563 in Pittsburgh—the ten cities with the largest Czech-speaking populations.

Emigration from the German-governed Protectorate of Bohemia and Moravia from March 1939 until May 1945 was nearly impossible. Some

Czechs did manage to escape, and a few Czech Jews obtained permission to emigrate during the early months of the German occupation before Adolf Hitler attacked Poland on September 1, 1939. However, the majority of Czech Jews, who either did not have the opportunity to leave the country or who simply could not conceive of what the future held for them, did not survive the Nazi concentration camps.

Immigrants from Bohemia and Moravia who entered the United States during the post–World War II period of Communist dictatorship (1948–1989) were for the most part professionals who settled wherever they happened to find a suitable position. They tended to be young adults or in early middle age. Very few people at or near retirement age chose to leave their home country, most preferring not to attempt the adjustment to life in a new country.

Of those who spent most of the period of the Communist regime in the United States, very few decided to relocate permanently to the Czech Republic after 1989, although many return periodically to visit their native country. By contrast, some of the immigrants to the United States during the nineteenth century arrived without their families and then returned after having earned a sufficient amount of money to make a good start in their home country.

Demography

Precise demographic information concerning the last century and a half of Czech immigration to the United States is not easy to come by. There are several reasons for this lack of data: (1) The earliest figures apply to the Austrian Empire as a whole; (2) later data for the Czech lands do not distinguish between Czech- and German-speaking immigrants; (3) post-1918 statistical tables do not always separate the population of the Czech lands from the Slovaks and Carpatho-Rusyns, treating the population of Czechoslovakia as a whole; and (4) no figures were ever published concerning the many thousands of refugees from postwar Communist-dominated Czechoslovakia because such

statistics would have been embarrassing to the Communist regime. The following information has been compiled from a variety of sources.

Immigrants from the Austrian Empire, including the Czech lands, who were residing in the United States in 1860, numbered 24,880. The majority were probably from Bohemia and Moravia (although perhaps some of these spoke German as their first language). Immigrants from the Czech lands residing in the United States totaled 40,287 in 1870; 85,361 in 1880; 118,197 in 1890; 156,809 in 1900; 228,738 in 1910; 234,564 in 1920; 201,138 in 1930; and 159,640 in 1940. The steadily rising figures through 1920 indicate that the number of newcomers outweighed by far the deathrate among the aging early immigrants. The very modest increase in immigration during the decade ending in 1920 was, of course, a consequence of World War I. During the subsequent decade, 1921–1930, Congress passed laws (in 1921 and 1924) sharply restricting immigration by setting national origin quotas. And immigration during the decade ending in 1940 was affected by the worldwide economic depression of the 1930s.

Beginning with 1900, year-by-year statistics concerning immigration from the Czech lands to the United States yield the following figures: 3,060 in 1900; 3,766 in 1901; 5,590 in 1902; 9,591 in 1903; 11,911 in 1904; 11,757 in 1905; 12,958 in 1906; 12,554 in 1907; 10,164 in 1908; and 6,850 in 1909. This totals 88,201 people, or an average of 8,820 annually.

Corresponding figures for the decade of 1910–1919 continue for several years at annual totals of eight to eleven thousand, but then drop back during the years of World War I to 1,651 for 1915 and to as low a number as 74 during 1918, the final year of the war. The total for the decade was 49,942.

The figures available for the three decades from 1921 through 1950 are 27,296 from 1921 to 1930; 1,682 from 1931 to 1940; and 14,969 from 1941 to 1950. The last figure reflects the fact that a great many Czechs left Czechoslovakia, mostly illegally, in 1948 and 1949 after the Communists seized the government in February 1948. Many of the refugees were people whose factories, businesses, or properties were nationalized or confiscated by the new regime. They were joined by diplomats, journalists, artists, scientists, and others who had family members or relatives already abroad. During the 1950s Czechoslovak borders with non-Communist states were so carefully guarded that illegal crossing to the West was very difficult, with dangerous consequences for those caught. Finally, during the first half of the 1960s, some loosening occurred. Permission to travel was issued to relatives of people residing abroad, and some others were permitted to emigrate. The occupation of Czechoslovakia in August 1968 by the armies of the Warsaw Pact countries again resulted in large numbers of people leaving the country, both legally and illegally. Reliable figures are not available, but it is estimated that from that year until the end of Communist rule in 1989, about 350,000 persons left Czechoslovakia to settle in Europe, Australia, Canada, and the United States. The number of immigrants to the United States from Czechoslovakia as a whole between 1961 and 1986 was about 37,800, and 13,797 were admitted as permanent residents under refugee acts; these, of course, included Slovaks, although the majority would have been Czechs.

The tendency of Czechs has been to immigrate primarily to America, and as a consequence the largest Czech émigré population is in the United States. As of the early 1990s a total of 1.3 million people in the United States claimed Czech background, with an additional 300,000 claiming Czechoslovak background. Some of the latter would surely have to be counted as Czechs—that is, as having their roots in Bohemia or Moravia.

Cultural and Social Characteristics

Prior to World War I, the great majority of immigrants settled where relatives or close friends were already established. During that period intermarriage with non-Czechs was rare. Wherever there was an appreciable concentration of Czech immigrants, and especially if they were engaged in farming, the older generation retained Czech as their primary language of communication. Their children learned it at home as their first language and spoke it with their peers of the same background, but learned English in school. Moreover, during the latter part of the nineteenth century, in quite a few communities with a substantial Czech component, classes in Czech were held after school or on Sundays. Members of the second generation were typically bilingual, but for those of the third generation the first language was almost invariably English and their knowledge of Czech superficial, with vocabularies in many instances limited to topics concerning domestic matters. Most children born in this country to post–World War II immigrants have only passive knowledge of conversational Czech, if that much, and those who study Czech in the few universities where it is offered find it difficult.

Ethnic revival programs that have characterized the activities of many ethnic groups in the United States since the 1970s also have been organized in many of the towns where the Czech component is strong enough to warrant such efforts (e.g., in Iowa, Nebraska, and Texas). These programs have been more successful in reviving Czech traditional observances related to the church calendar than in inducing people to learn Czech or to improve their Czech language skills.

Most of the early Czech immigrants—those who arrived in the 1850s through the 1870s—were farmers. From about the 1880s, the number of those eager to engage in trades, crafts, and the professions began to increase. The 1905 record of occupations lists the following as the most frequently reported by arriving Czech immigrants: domestics, day laborers, farm laborers, farmers, carpenters, tailors, miners, shoemakers, butchers, locksmiths, masons, blacksmiths, bakers, seamstresses, clerical workers, storekeepers, ironworkers, weavers, glassworkers, house painters, millers, and musicians and music teachers. In contrast, the overwhelming majority of immigrants who arrived after World War II were professionals—scientists, professors, engineers, and businesspeople.

Czech-American miners in Hazelton, Pennsylvania, wait to begin the day's work. (Library of Congress/Corbis)

The early immigrant families devoted their energies to acquiring their own farm and house, and a great many of them succeeded after years of real hardship. Those who settled in large cities initially rented, some for many years, but later were able to afford their own housing. Postwar professionals, once they acquired a relatively permanent position, were able to buy a house in the suburbs like other Americans.

Except for Czech Jews, the majority of immigrants were Christians, many of them registered as Roman Catholics. However, a fair number were freethinkers—people forming their opinions on the basis of reason rather than political or religious dogma. In general, Czech immigrants were practical and hardworking people who, despite their modest beginnings, became successful members of the American middle class. While in their home country the effective kin group was limited to only close relatives, a more extended family network operated in the early decades of immigration, when those already in America were expected to assist even distantly related newcomers to adjust to a new social, cultural, and physical environment.

Compatriotic associations have been of two general types: those that were organized and maintained by the immigrants who arrived before World War I; and, since 1938, those whose members were political refugees. The most recent immigrants, especially after 1968, settled throughout the United States rather than in Czech-American enclaves. Trying to assimilate as rapidly as possible, they tended not to search out associations of compatriots.

One of the oldest and at one time the most significant organization of Czechs in the United States was the patriotic gymnastic organization Sokol (Falcon), patterned after an old pre-Communist organization of the same name. But there were many other organizations, mostly local, that sprang up in the Czech ethnic enclaves. The Czechoslovak National Council of America has served as the umbrella organization for several hundred associations and clubs with a total membership approaching 250,000. Many of the professional people who immigrated to the United States after World War II became members of the Czechoslovak Society of Arts and Sciences in America, founded in 1956.

Over the years a large number of periodicals and newspapers serving Czech immigrants sprang up around the United States. Close to seven hundred published in Czech are listed in Esther Jerabek's *Czechs and Slovaks in North America: A Bibliography* (1976), with more than two hundred of them originating in Chicago, and some going back as far as the 1870s. A few of these publications lasted for several decades, but most had a relatively short existence.

The Czechs have assimilated well into American society—only elderly persons with extensive social networks in their home country found it difficult to adjust. Some of the early immigrants, many of whom were laborers or domestics, may have been looked down upon, as reflected in the disparaging term "bohunk," used in the United States especially for unskilled laborers of central European origin. (The term is a blend of *bo*, from "Bohemian," and *hunk*, altered from "Hungarian.") Post–World War II immigrants, highly educated professionals, have achieved positions comparable to those of well-educated Americans, and their social and professional ties are much like those of other middle-class citizens of the United States.

See also: AUSTRIANS; SLOVAKS

Bibliography

Barton, J. J. (1977). "Religion and Cultural Change in Czech Immigrant Communities, 1850–1920." In *Immigrants and Religion in Urban America*, edited by R. M. Miller and T. D. Marzik. Philadelphia: Temple University Press.

Bicha, K. D. (1980). *The Czechs in Oklahoma*. Norman: University of Oklahoma Press.

Capek, T. ([1920] 1969). *The Čechs (Bohemians) in America: A Study of Their National, Cultural, Political, Social, Economic, and Religious Life*. New York: Arno Press.

Dvornik, F. (1962). *Czech Contributions to the Growth of the United States*. Chicago: Benedictine Abbey Press.

Jerabek, E. (1976). *Czechs and Slovaks in North America: A Bibliography*. New York: Czechoslovak Society of Arts and Sciences in America.

Karytová-Magstadt, Š. (1993). *To Reap a Bountiful Harvest: Czech Immigration Beyond the Mississippi, 1850–1900*. Iowa City, IA: Rudi Publishing.

Kutak, R. I. ([1933] 1970). *The Story of a Bohemian-American Village: A Study of Social Persistence and Change*. New York: Arno Press.

Laska, V., comp. and ed. (1978). *The Czechs in America, 1633–1977: A Chronology & Fact Book*. Dobbs Ferry, NY: Oceana Publications.

Machann, C., ed. (1979). *The Czechs in Texas: A Symposium*. College Station: Texas A&M University Press.

Machann, C., and Mendl, J. W. (1983). *Krásná Amerika: A Study of the Texas Czechs, 1851–1939*. Austin, TX: Eakin Press.

Rosicky, R. (1929). *A History of the Czechs (Bohemians) in Nebraska*. Omaha: Czech Historical Society of Nebraska.

ZDENEK SALZMANN

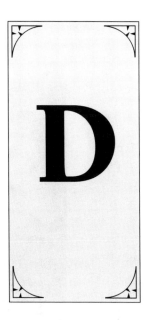

DANES

Danes, Norwegians, and Swedes were all drawn to the rich farmlands and homesteading opportunities of the American Midwest in the late nineteenth century. There they made their mark on the development of states such as Wisconsin, Minnesota, Michigan, Nebraska, and Iowa. Because of the common Nordic heritage and geography, they are often grouped as Scandinavians, but each of the three nationalities has distinct histories and immigration experiences.

Danes come from the kingdom of Denmark, which consists of the Jutland Peninsula and several islands, including Bornholm, in the Baltic Sea. In the past, the Kingdom of Denmark also included Iceland (which became a republic in 1944) and Schleswig-Holstein (lost to Prussia by war in the 1860s). The Danish language is the official language of the kingdom, which also included Norway until 1814. Denmark was the most urbanized and industrialized of these Nordic regions, smallest in size and most densely populated. It sits at the northern crossroads of Europe and is an important political, cultural, and trading center in northern Europe.

Immigration and Settlement

A few Danes immigrated to America in 1619 with Jens Munk's Hudson's Bay expedition seeking the Northwest Passage. There were Danes in New Netherlands, along with the Dutch, as early as 1624. Danes like to point to Jonas Bronck, the Dane who purchased a large tract of land from the Indians, land later referred to as the Bronx. Danish Moravians settled in Bethlehem, Pennsylvania, in 1736. Danes explored and settled the Danish West Indies (Virgin Islands), which were later sold to the United States in 1917. An early Danish pathfinder is Peter Lassen, who led a party of pioneers over the Rocky Mountains to California for gold. Lassen Peak in California is named for him. Latter-Day Saints missionaries brought parties of Danes to Utah starting in 1850, where they introduced agricultural methods and became the second-largest ethnic group in the state.

The earliest Danish settlements appeared on the East Coast in New York City, Brooklyn, Philadelphia, Baltimore, and Perth Amboy, New Jersey. Danes engaged in trade and manufacturing, established factories, and employed their newly arrived countrymen. Some stayed, of course, but others worked a year or two in the Danish terra-cotta industry or ironworks before heading west.

People in all three of the Scandinavian countries were attracted to the opportunities for work, land, and living conditions in America. Unemployment, scarcity of available farmland, and overpopulation in the homeland drove them to look elsewhere. A few of these immigrants were seeking religious freedom, but this was less so for Danes than the others. Danes joined the emigration stream from western Europe, sailing from ports in Denmark, Norway, and Great Britain. Between 1820 and 1975, about a tenth of the native population, or 366,000 Danes, left for America. More Swedes (1,270,000) and Norwegians (855,000) immigrated to America during the same time, representing a quarter to a third of their populations. The peak migration year for all Scandinavians was 1882, when 88,132 Danes came to the United States. The U.S. quota after 1920 allowed just under 6,000 annually for Danes, an amount they did not always fill.

Several characteristics differentiated the Danes from other Scandinavian immigrants. There were fewer of them. They arrived later and spread out even more widely. Fewer came as families. During the peak migration era not more than 11 percent of the Danish immigrants settled in any one state, while 19.6 percent of the Swedes and 28.6 percent of the Norwegians, for example, settled in Minnesota alone. Danes settled more in urban areas, intermarried more with American nationals, had one of the highest rates of naturalization for citizenship, and were one of the first groups to drop their native tongue. Although they are the most rapid of Scandinavians to assimilate, the 1990 U.S. Census found 34,999 Danish-born and 1,634,600 Americans who claim primary Danish ancestry.

Danes scattered widely across the United States, in cities and in the country. Although more than half of the Danes came from rural areas, the highest *rate* of migration when compared to the total population was from the Danish cities. A typical pattern was to leave the farm in search of work in the nearby city, and from there to emigrate. About a fifth of the Danish emigrants left the

A street in Solvang, a city in California that was settled almost exclusively by Danish, Dutch, and Bavarian immigrants. (The Purcell Team/Corbis)

capital city of Copenhagen; the rest were about evenly divided between Jutland and all the other islands. As health conditions improved in the nineteenth century, more children survived to adulthood, putting great pressure on the economy. The earliest emigration from rural Denmark was in just those areas in the southeast with the richest farmland, where ownership by large estates made the dream of owning land impossible for poor farmworkers.

The Danish emigrants traveling before 1890 tended to be in family groups and came mostly from southeastern Denmark (Lolland, Falster, and Bornholm). During the 1880–1900 mass emigration, young male adults between ages fifteen and twenty-nine made up 55 percent of the emigration.

The largest group of those (43%) were rural farm laborers, while 25 percent were domestic and industrial workers and 18 percent were craftsmen (smiths, joiners, carpenters, bricklayers, bakers). Emigration from the Jutland Peninsula increased after 1885 when the reclaimed heathlands became fully occupied. Few young single women emigrated until late in the century, when there was a demand for house help in America. Typically a young man left first to find work and/or land and was later joined by wife, bride, or family, or he found a marriage partner in America. The marriage age in Denmark around 1900 tended to be twenty-nine, and most of the single female immigrants were between ages thirty and forty.

Conditions in Denmark certainly shaped the emigrants. They came from a nation that was moving from absolute monarchy to liberal democracy in which farmers and city people participated actively in the growing political parties. Denmark had switched from grain export to butter, eggs, and bacon after the 1870s, when world grain surpluses drove the market down. The 1848 Constitution guaranteed universal suffrage for men. Illiteracy was nearly eradicated as a result of compulsory public school attendance for children aged six to fourteen since 1814. Industrialization starting in the 1850s created jobs that attracted rural people to cities. Economic, political, and social conditions were better in Denmark than in the rest of Scandinavia in the late 1800s, but the increasing population created new social problems. Unemployment, hunger, and breadlines became familiar urban experiences. Labor and socialist movements joined the liberals to press for more reforms to help the common people. But the class structure was entrenched, and there was little chance of ordinary citizens crossing those boundaries. Danes in America liked the fact that no worker had to take off his cap to the boss or landowner. And they believed the American dream that hard work and industry would lead to success.

As the number of emigrants with experience in America grew, people back in Denmark learned more about life in the New World. Personal letters described the kinds of jobs that were easy to find,

the good soil, the precise cost, and the availability of land. The letters were encouraging but realistic. The message was that the immigrant could improve his or her living standard but must expect to work hard. These letter writers said they now had farms, homes, and jobs they could never have hoped to attain back in Denmark. These letters from America, some of which were published in the newspapers, confirmed the propaganda of the agents for railroads, steamship lines, and midwestern states that promoted immigration.

Clusters of Danish immigrants appeared in neighborhoods in New York City, Perth Amboy, Chicago, Omaha, and Racine, Wisconsin, where jobs were plentiful. Danes at first often had to join with Norwegians and Swedes to form social clubs, and established newspapers and social insurance organizations, but soon they were able to form Danish organizations, which were strongest at the start of the twentieth century, when immigrants and their first-generation children were most numerous. By 1920, there were 189,154 Danish-born immigrants in the United States, and in 1930, Danish immigrants and their children reached a peak total of 529,142.

One study of Danish emigration divides the movement into five phases: 1820–1850, pathfinders, individuals who sought adventure; 1850–1870, family and Mormon group migration; 1870–1895, mass migration to the American Midwest; 1895–1910, town migration to the urban Midwest and West; post-1910, "know-how" professionals who came under reduced American quotas.

The Danish settlements in Wisconsin increased significantly from 1870 on, making Racine the American city with the largest Danish population at the turn of the century. Rural settlements of Danes in Wisconsin at New Denmark and West Denmark were just clusters of log cabins at first, but gradually the Danes cleared patches of land for farming and dairy cattle. Small groups of Danes formed farm settlements in Montcalm County, Michigan, in the 1840s and 1850s. Rural areas in Minnesota, Iowa, Nebraska, Kansas, and the Dakotas attracted Danes who were part of the late nineteenth-century migration. There was even a mall settlement in Texas, but generally the Danish immigrants avoided the southern states.

Wisconsin led the states in numbers of Danish up to 1890. After that the lead moved to Iowa, with a large concentration in the religious centers of Elk Horn and Kimballton, and finally to California in 1920, where it remained. More than a third of all the Danish in the United States, according to the 1990 U.S. Census, live in California, which also has the last Danish settlement, Solvang, founded in 1911 in Santa Barbara County by Danes who moved from the Midwest. Solvang is nationally known for its Danish-style architecture, authentic windmill, and Danish food and festivals.

By the early twentieth century, Danes could be found in every state in the Union. In cities their early neighborhoods were visible but multiethnic. They built churches and social halls, such as those in Racine, Chicago, Omaha, and Minneapolis. Danish bakeries, florists, and gift shops still mark many of these old neighborhoods. In the countryside, Danes made an impact with successful dairy and butter cooperatives. They worked on the farms, in the trades, industry, the arts, and the professions. Only a few became leaders in politics.

Organizational Life

Danish religious and social organizational life is filled with dissention and breaking off of new groups. The church is frequently the strongest force for holding an ethnic group together, but Danes in America were divided among Lutheran, Mormon, Adventist, Baptist, and Methodist sects. At most only 35 percent of the Danish immigrants were members of these churches, but the church did foster a sense of Danishness, especially in rural areas, where it was the main social center. Clubs and fraternal organizations brought Danish Americans together in the city. There are no studies that document the numerous Danish immigrants who married outside the group, dropped the language, and settled into the new culture without making strong ethnic social ties. The ethnic activities associated with first- and second-generation Danes in America do not wholly reflect the experience of a people noted for its rapid assimilation.

In Denmark, the Lutheran Church accommodated differing views on church matters, but in America those differences caused a split in 1894 into the Grundtvigian and the Inner Mission (pietistic) branches, each with its own college, religious publications, and societies. The Lutheran settlement at Elk Horn, founded in 1875, had a folk school and church-supported orphanage. People in the town spoke Danish, owned the businesses, and developed cooperatives. Elk Horn and Kimballton, five miles apart, illustrate the sharpness of the church split. Elk Horn became Inner Mission, and Kimballton became Grundtvigian; they were bitter rivals, fought, and broke off old contacts. Their two colleges also competed. Dana College in Blair, Nebraska, grew from an Inner Mission seminary into a four-year liberal arts college. Not far away, Grand View College (founded in 1896) in Grand View, Iowa, begun for the Grundtvigians, was accredited by the state as a junior college in 1938 and became a four-year college in 1976. Both have extensive archives and libraries reflecting their Danish-American origin. The Grundtvigians, smaller in number, stressed the value of Danish language and cultural studies, while the Inner Mission encouraged English and assimilation. By the 1920s, English was being used in both Sunday schools, and by the 1940s, even the Grundtvigians adopted English for the church services. But the debate over Danishness and Americanization fueled many a newspaper column during those years.

The Grundtvigian folk high school movement in Denmark, named for pastor N. F. S. Grundtvig, provided residential schools for boys and girls from farms to learn basic subjects such as history, math, geography, language, and literature, along with gymnastics and folk dancing, in a religious atmosphere. Immigrants carried on this tradition, founding six such schools, the first at Elk Horn in 1878 and the last in Solvang in 1911. Although they had served a total attendance of only 10,000 to 12,000 young people before they closed in the 1930s, they were significant in maintaining Danish language and culture in a rapidly assimilating group. Experts in adult education have studied the Danish model and incorporated some of its features.

Despite their small numbers, Danes in America founded clubs; published weekly newspapers as well as magazines and books in Danish and English; held Constitution Day (June 5), midsummer, and Christmas festivities; and formed social insurance and singing groups. The Danish Brotherhood began in 1872 as a veterans group of those who fought against the Germans in 1848 and grew to provide life insurance, burial aid, and help for the sick and the aged among its 11,000 members. The Danish Sisterhood, its auxiliary, was founded in 1893. The Dania Society, started in California in 1874 as a social group, also offers aid and supports an old-age home.

The Danish colony in Chicago more than doubled between 1870 and 1880, from 1,243 to 2,556. More than half the Danes in Chicago between 1880 and 1890 worked in manufacturing and trades; about a quarter in personal and domestic services; and others in transport, communication, and clerical jobs. Chicago attracted a number of prominent Danes from social and business circles, and one group of these men met regularly at a local pub downtown. The "invited" regulars were business men, a brewer, artists, and writers. The Chicago Danish-American colony was an active urban group whose enthusiasm for the old homeland led to the formation of the Danish-American Society in 1906 to promote cultural ties. In 1909, they purchased a tract of heathland in Jutland, and in 1912, they began the annual American Fourth of July celebration in the Rebild Hills; this celebration has been held continuously since then except during World War II, when Denmark was occupied. This group also established the permanent Danes Worldwide Archives in Aalborg in 1932. This archive carries on an active research and publication schedule.

Danes in America produced fifty different weekly newspapers reflecting religious, political, and local interests. *The Danish Pioneer*, founded in 1872, reached a circulation of 30,000 in 1914, serving the Midwest from its Omaha base. It is still

A Danish Brotherhood group in Idaho gathers around a campfire in 1941 at the Cherry Springs Campground in the Caribou National Forest. (USDA-Forest Service/Corbis)

being published from Chicago. The *Pioneer*'s editor, Sophus Neble, was a liberal democrat whose paper covered events in Denmark and America and encouraged cultural exchange. He favored Americanization but also wished to pass on some Danishness to the younger generation. Two world wars brought pressure on American immigrant groups to demonstrate their loyalty and give up speaking foreign languages. Neble and others argued that Danes could be patriotic and loyal to America without abandoning affection for their native land and Danish. But decreased immigration and increasing Americanization in postwar America led to a sharp drop in Danish-language readers. Circulation of the top seven Danish-American newspapers dropped from 72,000 weekly in 1910 to 7,700 in 1960. Only two papers were still publishing in the 1990s (*Pioneer* and *Bien*). The use of the English language and tabloid formats converted *Pioneer* and *Bien* in California into ethnic-interest publications for a far-flung group of readers with interests in things Danish, most of whom communicate in English.

Ethnic Revival

Along with other early immigrant groups in America, Danish Americans revived interest in their ethnic heritage in the 1970s. After World War II there was an increasing flow of trade, travel, and study abroad. Danish heroism in smuggling its Jewish citizens out of occupied Denmark to neutral Sweden was internationally recognized. Denmark was part of the North Atlantic Treaty Organization and the United Nations. Danish design and modern Danish culture were admired. Many second- and third-generation Danish Americans found new interest in getting in touch with their roots, even if they could not speak Danish. The Danish language and, in some cases, Danish heritage were no longer conditions for membership in Danish ethnic associations. Ethnicity became of academic interest and stimulated new research and publications that expanded on the first crop of books of history and personal recollections by the pioneers.

The Danish-American Heritage Society, which was founded in 1977 to explore and record the history of Danish immigrants, publishes *The Bridge*, the first journal of ethnic history for this group. Danes first talked about an ethnic museum in 1916, but only in the 1980s were they able to incorporate the diverse interests and affiliations among them in the planning process. The Danish Immigrant Museum was founded at Elk Horn in 1994. The museum contains relics from famous Danes such as Victor Borge and Jakob Riis, but the focus is on typical immigrants who came, struggled, survived, or flourished in their new homeland, bridged old and new cultures, and felt the highs and lows of that experience. The museum's mission is to pass along that cultural heritage.

See also: NORWEGIANS; SWEDES

Bibliography

Hvidt, K. (1975). *Flight to America*. New York: Academic Press.

Hvidt, K. (1976). *Danes Go West*. Copenhagen: Rebild National Park Society.

Larsen, B. F., and Bender, H., eds. (1992). *Danish Emigration to the U.S.A.* Aalborg, Denmark: Danish Worldwide Archives.

Lovoll, O. S. (1993). *Nordics in America*. Northfield, MN: Norwegian-American Historical Association.

Marzolf, M. T. (1979). *The Danish-Language Press in America*. New York: Arno Press.

Nielsen, G. R. (1981). *The Danish Americans*. Boston: Twayne.

Stilling, N. P., and Olsen, A. L. (1994). *A New Life*. Aalborg, Denmark: Danish Worldwide Archives.

MARION T. MARZOLF

DOMINICANS

Dominicans are immigrants and the descendants of immigrants from the Dominican Republic, a Caribbean nation of some 7.5 million people. During the 1960s, the first decade of massive Dominican immigration to the United States, Dominicans were seldom recognized as a distinct cultural group. As immigration surged in the 1970s and 1980s, Dominicans gained increasing visibility as an ethnic group. By the 1990s, they represented the fourth-largest Latino population in the United States (after Mexican Americans, Puerto Ricans, and Cubans).

Settlement and Immigration History

Dominicans are an overwhelmingly urban population, with New York the principal destination for most immigrants. About three-quarters of all Dominicans in the United States live in the Greater New York area, where they form the largest immigrant group by nationality to have settled in New York since the mid-1960s. Among Latino groups in New York, Dominicans are second in number only to Puerto Ricans. Within New York, Dominicans are among the residentially most concentrated of the city's new immigrant groups. More than half of New York's Dominicans live in Manhattan, forming distinctive neighborhoods in upper Manhattan and, to a lesser extent, on the Lower East Side. Significant numbers also live in Queens, the South Bronx, and Brooklyn. In far lesser numbers, Dominicans also have settled in such New Jersey cities as Newark, Union City, and Hoboken, as well as in Miami; Boston; Lawrence, Massachusetts; and Providence, Rhode Island.

Puerto Rico, a U.S. territory governed by U.S. immigration laws and regulations, is another important destination for Dominicans. An estimated 10 percent of Dominican immigrants reside in Puerto Rico, with most concentrated in the capital, San Juan. Separated from the Dominican Republic by the narrow Mona Passage, Puerto Rico is similar in culture and language. For many Dominicans, Puerto Rico represents a stepping-stone to the mainland United States, but for others it is an alternative destination.

The great majority of Dominican immigrants are legal resident aliens, having entered the United States primarily through family reunification provisions of the immigration law. In 1992, the U.S.

Immigration and Naturalization Service estimated that only about forty thousand Dominicans resided in the United States without appropriate documentation (i.e., less than 10 percent of the foreign-born Dominican population). Until recently, Dominicans also had a fairly low rate of naturalization. This began to change in the early 1990s, and the number of Dominicans seeking U.S. citizenship doubled from 6,545 to 12,274 between 1990 and 1993.

Dominican immigration is characterized by an intense circulation of people between the United States and the Dominican Republic. On holidays such as Christmas, Holy Week, and Dominican Mother's Day, the island is flooded with immigrants who fly back for brief visits. On such occasions these "Dominican Yorkers," as they are often called, not only renew their social and cultural ties to the island but also make a significant contribution to the tourist industry, the republic's economic mainstay.

Most Dominican immigration is motivated by the desire to improve social and economic standing in the Dominican Republic. However, there always has been an important fraction of immigrants who were politically motivated. Before 1961, the number of Dominicans immigrating to the United States was relatively small. During the long and repressive regime of Rafael Trujillo (1930–1961) there were severe restrictions on population movement. Opponents of the dictator sometimes managed to flee to New York, where they lived as political exiles. Others, who had social connections to Trujillo, were able to evade his restrictions and leave. Between 1950 and 1960, some ten thousand Dominicans immigrated to the United States. After Trujillo was assassinated in 1961 and the restrictions were removed, Dominican immigration increased sharply. The defeat of the popular revolt of 1965 and the subsequent U.S. occupation of the Dominican Republic resulted in another large increase in the number of immigrants. Since the mid-1960s, the economic and political uncertainties surrounding election years in the Dominican Republic often have been accompanied by increases in the number of Dominicans leaving for the United States. The rapid deterioration of Dominican economy since the 1980s has given additional impetus to immigration. This deterioration, which has been accompanied by increasingly difficult living conditions, has been exacerbated by the country's large international debt repayments, the enactment of austerity measures, and the drastic reduction in U.S. foreign aid in the late 1980s. In the 1980s, an average of more than twenty-two thousand Dominicans a year entered the United States, up from about fourteen thousand a year in the 1970s. The 1990s have witnessed an even larger increase in Dominican immigration, with the number nearly doubling from 1989 to 1990. Between 1990 and 1993, an average of 42,750 Dominicans immigrated to the United States each year. There are indications that during this period, undocumented immigration increased as well.

Although immigrants come from all strata of Dominican society, members of the country's urban middle classes tend to predominate. The fact that the republic does not share a land border with the United States makes immigration a process that requires substantial resources, both in terms of money and appropriate family connections with which to obtain a resident visa. It also makes undocumented entry more difficult; thus, most Dominicans enter the United States via a process of "chain migration" in which they are sponsored by relatives who are legal immigrants or citizens.

Demography

Despite its small size, the Dominican Republic had become the fourth most important source of new immigrants to the United States by the mid-1990s. On a per capita basis the Dominican Republic is the world's largest contributor to U.S. immigration.

According to the 1990 U.S. Census, 520,151 Dominicans resided in the United States, of whom 70 percent were foreign-born. Since the onset of immigration, the number of women has been consistently, if only slightly, greater than the number of men. With a median age of twenty-seven, the great majority (70%) of Dominicans are in the peak productive years between fifteen and sixty-four. Fewer than 4 percent are sixty-five or older. Among these older immigrants, women outnumber men by more than two to one, reflecting not only the greater longevity of women, but also the strong cultural preference for sponsoring the immigration of older women to take care of grandchildren while mothers work. The U.S.-born population is composed largely of first-generation Dominicans, three-quarters of whom are less than fifteen years of age. Fertility rates for Dominicans are comparable to those of other Latinos in the United States and are only slightly higher than the overall national rates.

Health

For economic reasons, Dominicans may often bring health problems to local hospital emergency rooms for treatment. Affordable prenatal care is an especially important health concern for many women. In addition to biomedicine, some Dominicans may seek alternative health care, such as spiritualist healers (*espiritistas*).

Language

Spanish, with distinctive regional and rural/urban variants, is the language spoken in the Dominican Republic. The existence of a densely populated ethnic enclave in New York and the presence of a large Latino population make possible the continued use of Spanish after immigration. According to the 1990 U.S. Census, the great majority of foreign-born Dominicans living in the United States reported speaking English "not very well." Most Dominicans do acquire some knowledge of English, however.

Economic Features

Dominicans in the United States mostly work at low-paying, semiskilled or unskilled jobs in industry and services. Dominican women work in numbers comparable to U.S. women generally and are more likely to be employed outside the home than they were in the Dominican Republic prior to immigrating. Dominican women most often work in manufacturing, especially in the New York garment industry, which is the single largest employer of Dominican women in that city. Dominican men tend to cluster in manufacturing and in services such as restaurants, hotels, and hospitals. Dominican immigration to Puerto Rico differs from that directed to the mainland in its much higher component of skilled and professional workers.

Average earnings for Dominicans are among the lowest for immigrant groups in the United States. According to the 1990 U.S. Census, one-third of Dominican families earned incomes below the official poverty level. To make ends meet, and to save for the eventual return to the Dominican Republic to which many aspire, some may work at more than one job.

Distinctive businesses often associated with Dominican immigrants are *bodegas*, small neighborhood grocery stores that stock the food specialties of the Hispanic Caribbean; garment shops that employ other Dominicans on the sewing machines; and nonmedallion or "gypsy" cabs that service immigrant neighborhoods in New York. Since the mid-1980s, a vicious stereotype has emerged that identifies Dominicans with the crack-cocaine drug trade in New York. While sections of upper Manhattan are important arenas for this trade, only a tiny fraction of Dominicans are engaged in drug traffic. The great majority of Dominicans work hard at largely low-paying jobs.

Marriage

On the whole, Dominican immigrants are a young group, and many marry for the first time in New York. Marriage occurs most often with other Dominicans, but a sizable minority intermarry with non-Dominicans, particularly with Puerto Ricans. Marriage is ideally stable and monogamous,

with authority ideally vested in the oldest male. In practice, however, there are notable social class differences in marriage practices. Monogamous unions sanctified by a church wedding are most characteristic of middle-class Dominicans. An alternative, multiple-mate pattern also exists in which women tend to exert authority throughout a series of consensual unions. In the United States a third, more cooperative and egalitarian pattern of marriage relations appears to be emerging as both women and men work outside the home and pool their incomes into a joint household fund.

Family and Kinship

Dominican kinship is bilateral, with equal importance attached to both the mother's and the father's kin. There is a strong cultural expectation of mutual aid within the family and a privileging of family interests over those of the individual. "Fictive" forms of kinship, such as the bonds of coparenthood created through the ritual of baptism of a child or through other means (*compadrazgo*), and informal adoption (*hijos de crianza*), are also considered important. Both fictive and biological ties represent important resources that may be mobilized to meet the substantial costs of immigrating to the United States.

After immigrating, many Dominicans continue to conform to the cultural expectation to help out family members left behind by sending them money regularly. By the mid-1990s, immigrants' remittances were estimated at $1 billion a year. Remittances have become vitally important to the island's economy, far surpassing the amount earned by the country's principal export crop, sugar.

Religion

Most Dominicans are Roman Catholic. There are few Dominican priests, however. Catholic churches in Dominican neighborhoods in New York frequently offer masses in Spanish. A number of Dominicans have converted to evangelical Protestant sects.

Cultural Characteristics

In the earliest years of immigration, Dominicans were seldom recognized as a distinct cultural group. In New York, they were often lumped together with Puerto Ricans. This low profile was reinforced by the fact that initially most Dominicans' political activity in the United States was oriented toward the Dominican Republic. Orientation toward home country politics was reinforced by a strong ideology of return and the intense circulation of people between the United States and the Dominican Republic. During this period some community leaders emerged in New York, but they tended to be members of the economic and social elite and had only a limited following. Numerous ethnic associations with a broader appeal began springing up in the 1970s. The vast majority of these were hometown associations, essentially social clubs whose members shared a common geographical origin in the Dominican Republic. In addition to organizing recreational events, these organizations often engaged in fundraising for public works projects in their home communities.

Beginning in the 1980s, Dominicans intensified their participation in U.S. political life, particularly in New York politics. Initially the hometown associations provided a platform of support that could be mobilized for political participation at the local level. Some associations also provided such human services as assistance with finding employment, job training, and language instruction.

A new ethnic leadership has emerged out of community-based efforts to deal with the major problems facing Dominicans, such as housing, education, and the discrimination they have encountered as both Latinos and people of color. Since the mid-1980s, Dominicans living in New York have run for a variety of elected offices, most notably in upper Manhattan, where their numbers are greatest. The emergence of Dominicans as a distinct ethnic group is thus a recent phenomenon, and has come about largely as the result of pressure from Dominican leaders and organizations intent on securing government recognition and resources to improve the quality of life in the immigrant community.

The Arts

Only a few distinctively Dominican publications have been established in the United States. In New York the easy availability of a variety of daily newspapers from the Dominican Republic and the presence of well-established Spanish-language dailies may have discouraged the development of immigrant Dominican newspapers. Beginning in the mid-1980s, the Dominican dailies, aware of their large immigrant readership, devoted increasing attention to reporting the news of the Dominican community in the United States. *Diario de la Prensa*, a Spanish-language daily published in New York, also has a substantial Dominican readership. Magazines devoted to Dominican literature have fared better. The magazines *Alcance* and *Punto 7* both publish poetry, fiction, and essays by Dominican authors.

In the 1980s, Dominican culture began to exert a growing presence in the United States after years of near invisibility. One of the most notable contributions to cultural life outside the Dominican immigrant community has been the music and dance of the merengue. Despite the many stylistic changes it has undergone since the onset of massive immigration, merengue remains a key symbol and banner of Dominican identity and nationalism. The merengue bands that sprang up in New York following the onset of immigration have provided one of the most important cultural links between the U.S. ethnic community and the Dominican Republic. Some merengues offer commentary on immigrant life in the United States that reaches a wide audience in the Dominican Republic. Since the mid-1980s, merengue also has become widely popular among non-Dominicans in the United States, as well as among Latin American and European audiences. This national and international success has reinforced merengue's place as a central symbol of Dominican identity. Outside New York, where boundaries among Latino populations are less sharply drawn, merengue has come to be regarded by some non-Dominican Latinos as a symbol of pan–Latin American identity.

New York–based folkloric groups frequently perform a variety of Dominican dances in both New York and the Dominican Republic. Until lack of funds forced its closing in 1990, Casa Dominicana was perhaps the most important institution for the diffusion of Dominican culture and art in New York. Established with initial support from the Dominican government in 1985, Casa Dominicana organized numerous literary conferences, exhibitions, and poetry and theater workshops. Also in the 1980s, New York–based Dominican writers achieved wider recognition with the publication of works by such authors as Daisy Cocco de Filippis, Franklin Gutiérrez, José Carvajal, and Alexis Gómez. The novelist Julia Alvarez, who writes in English on Dominican themes, has achieved national acclaim.

The most visible special event associated with Dominicans is the annual Dominican Day Parade, held each August on or around Dominican Restoration Day (August 16). Modeled on the Puerto Rican precedent, the parade is not only a cultural event of considerable importance to the community but also represents an attempt to augment group visibility to city and state governments. Tens of thousands of people attend the parade, in which the mayor and other New York political figures, as well as politicians from the Dominican Republic, march. Besides the floats and festive banners, placards often call attention to the immigrants' social and economic problems in such critical areas as housing, education, and immigrants' rights. Because the parade constitutes an important arena for the projection of Dominican identity and presence in New York, control over the Dominican Day Parade Committee is hotly contested among political factions in the Dominican community.

Education

Education is a concern of considerable importance to Dominicans in the United States. With the intense overcrowding of its schools, upper Manhattan in particular has been the site of parents' repeated efforts to improve the quality of education. Dominicans have been elected to, and on occasion directed, the local community school board. The City University of New York also has been a significant educational institution for Dominicans, providing a route for the acquisition of skills and credentials necessary for social, economic, and political advancement. Dominican student organizations have long been active in the city university system, and a program in Dominican Studies has been established.

Assimilation and Cultural Persistence

Among Dominican immigrants, the presence of a large ethnic community and an even larger Spanish-speaking population in the northeastern United States has facilitated the retention of language and culture. Nevertheless, English words have entered the daily vocabulary, and only a minority of second-generation Dominicans do not speak English. Rates of naturalization have steadily increased since the early 1980s. Members of the growing second generation often identify more closely with African-American culture than with the dominant white culture. A common experience of racial discrimination, residence in the same or contiguous neighborhoods, and attendance at the same public schools as African Americans have fostered a common identification, common linguistic features, and a shared style of youth culture. The sense of a common Latino identity across national-origin lines is also steadily growing. It is likely that only a small proportion of the second generation of Dominicans in the United States will decide in the future to settle in the Dominican Republic.

See also: PUERTO RICANS

Bibliography

Austerlitz, P. (1993). "Local and International Trends in Dominican Merengue." *World of Music* 36(2):70–89.

Bray, D. (1984). "Economic Development: The Middle Class and International Migration in the Dominican

Republic." *International Migration Review* 18:217–236.

Duany, J. (1992). "Caribbean Migration to Puerto Rico: A Comparison of Cubans and Dominicans." *International Migration Review* 26:46–66.

Georges, E. (1987). "A Comment on Dominican Ethnic Associations." In *Caribbean Life in New York City: Socio-Cultural Dimensions*, edited by C. Sutton and E. Chaney. New York: Center for Migration Studies.

Georges, E. (1990). *The Making of a Transnational Community: Migration, Development, and Cultural Change in the Dominican Republic.* New York: Columbia University Press.

Georges, E. (1992). "Gender, Migration, and Class in the Dominican Republic: Women's Experiences in a Transnational Community." *Annals of the New York Academy of Sciences* 645:81–99.

Gilbertson, G. (1995). "Women's Labor and Enclave Employment: The Case of Dominican and Colombian Women in New York City." *International Migration Review* 29:46–66.

Gilbertson, G., and Gurak, D. (1993). "Broadening the Enclave Debate: The Labor Market Experiences of Dominican and Colombian Men in New York City." *Sociological Forum* 8:205–222.

Grasmuck, S., and Pessar, P. (1991). *Between Two Islands: Dominican International Migration.* Berkeley: University of California Press.

Gurak, D. (1987). "Family Formation and Marital Selectivity Among Dominican and Colombian Immigrants in New York City." *International Migration Review* 21:275–298.

Hendricks, G. (1974). *The Dominican Diaspora: From the Dominican Republic to New York, Villagers in Transition.* New York: Teachers College Press.

Pessar, P. (1987). "The Dominicans: Women in the Household and in the Garment Industry." In *New Immigrants in New York*, edited by N. Foner. New York: Columbia University Press.

EUGENIA GEORGES

DRUZE

"Druze" is a term denoting a religious identity of a sect that branched out from Shi'a Islam. The high-ranking spiritual leaders of this faith prefer to be called "Unitarianists," and consider the name "Druze" a misnomer because it is a sobriquet for a rebellious proselyte who tried to lead them astray during the nascent period of their religious movement in the twelfth century. In spite of that, the label "Druze" has remained the most persistent and characteristic of this group. A Druze in the United States is anyone who adheres to the Druze religious faith, has an Arab surname, comes from an Arabic-speaking background, and has ties to Lebanon, Syria, Jordan, or Israel.

The Druze population in the United States is predominantly Lebanese and ethnically Arab. As such it comprises a small section of Arab Americans and shares historical, cultural, and linguistic ties with both Arab and Muslim communities. A few Lebanese Druze started to immigrate to the United States in the late nineteenth century in pursuit of better economic and educational opportunities for their families. The largest wave of Druze immigration, however, occurred between 1975 and 1990, with the exacerbation of regional conflicts and the outbreak of violence and civil strife in Lebanon. Hundreds of Lebanese Druze suffered human and financial losses and were forced to flee their homeland for a safer and stable future.

Smaller communities of Druze in America originated in southern Syria in a region known as Jabal al-Duruz (Druze Mountain), Jordan, and Israel. The varied socioeconomic structures of these societies and their historical experiments have shaped each Druze community differently and molded its conception of its identity and tradition.

Arabic is the unifying language of all the Druze of Middle Eastern countries, and it is within the rubric of Arab-Islamic history that the Druze situate their heritage and interpret their cultural development. Despite the constant exhortation by their spiritual leader in Lebanon to preserve the Arabic language and pass it to their children, the American Druze did not develop language maintenance programs for the purpose. Generational differences and forces of assimilation have confounded the issue of linguistic ties even further.

Immigration and Settlement

The earliest record of Druze immigration to the United States dates to 1881, a decade after the advent of the first emigration wave of Syrian and Lebanese Christians. The early Druze communities increased steadily and spread out in various American cities and towns. Early pockets of Druze settlements in the United States appeared in the eastern states, the Pacific Northwest, and the Midwest. Many Druze faced strenuous economic conditions and social circumstances, especially those who took up manual labor or worked in the Midwest as peddlers. Eventually the Druze succeeded in founding homes and creating lasting roots in North Carolina, Kentucky, Tennessee, West Virginia, Connecticut, Pennsylvania, Michigan, Iowa, and Missouri.

In the early 1980s, civil strife and the erosion of the Lebanese economic infrastructure drove hundreds of Druze to North and South America, Australia, and West Africa. Druze communities can also be found in the Philippines and the West Indies. Compared to the Druze in Latin America and West Africa, who exhibit a pattern of circular migration, there has been a much smaller rate of return migration to Lebanon by the Druze of the United States and Australia.

As of the mid-1990s, Los Angeles, Houston, and Dearborn, Michigan, have the largest Druze settlements in the United States.

The first formal organization for American Druze, the American Druze Society (ADS), was founded in 1907 in Seattle, Washington. As of 1996 the ADS counted 27,000 Druze members. The number of non-ADS Druze range from 5,000 to 6,500. Since the mid-1960s the number of American Druze emigrants has increased dramatically, but its composition has remained predominantly middle-class Lebanese.

Economy

Small groups of Druze Americans have fared well in business enterprises and professions. Possessing little skill or training, many nonetheless refrained from industrial, mine, farm, railroad, or construction labor, preferring to work as peddlers or to set up small shops. Like many Arab immigrants, the Druze entrepreneurs own family-operated shops and stores. Among the educated middle-class male population the professions of engineering and medicine predominate. On the other hand, the educated female population has exhibited varied interests, taking up academic, medical, and administrative careers and investing more in artistic endeavors.

The economic constraints of American life and its impact on Druze immigrants has caused a significant increase in the percentage of women wage earners and heads of households. Economic improvements and social mobility alongside the expansion of educational and professional resources among the Druze have molded gender roles, allowing Druze women a more assertive role and a sense of empowerment, which remains a source of tension in the traditional patriarchal system.

Kinship, Marriage, and the Family

As for all Arabs, pedigree and genealogical descent is not a matter of indifference to the Druze, among whom 10 percent are families claiming aristocratic descent. To be sure, the American Druze have been able to a greater extent to overcome the hegemony of the aristocratic families over their political organizations than have the Druze in Lebanon.

The average age of marriage for the Druze is lower than the overall average in the United States. Adherents of the Druze faith uphold marriage within the group as an ideal rule of conduct; those who violate it expect to become socially ostracized. This ideal, however, is a function of class and status, because one tends to find among the more Westernized, upper-class members along with working-class families a higher tendency for marriage outside the group. It is usually the middle-class traditional Druze who have more rigorously forced the principle of marriage within the group on their offspring. On the one hand, women seem to carry the brunt of the severe restrictions against interfaith marriages, as many of them prefer to remain single rather than risk social and economic alienation from their communities by marrying a non-Druze. On the other hand, it is more common and acceptable for Druze males of the first and second generation to marry Christians than it is for females. The annual conventions that the Druze hold in the United States have facilitated intra-Druze marriages but nonetheless have revealed generational conflicts in opinion and social values.

Few Druze households have been able to maintain a closely knit, cohesive, and extended family in the United States. Americanization has reinforced the nuclear family and weakened ties of kinship, rendering them secondary to the values of individualism, competitiveness, and material success. There persists, however, a strong sense of family responsibility and respect for parents and relatives. Neolocal residence is largely manifest and is usually dictated by spatial mobility and economic opportunities for husband and wife. Although the patriarchal system forces male-female relations to be responsive to male dominance, several Druze women have increasingly questioned the subordinate position allotted to them and have made independent choices about their lives and careers.

Variations in class, social background, and educational level reveal dramatic differences in child-rearing methods and approaches to American culture. Nevertheless, pride in Arab heritage, socializing with other Druze and Arabs in general, and respect and affection for parents are highly stressed. The Druze awareness of the need to transmit the Arabic language to their children is nonetheless overshadowed by the tendency to emphasize the children's successful integration into American society. Typical of most traditional immigrant communities is the parents' complaint of their weakened control over their children's conduct and their inability to make them comply with their decsions or advice.

In concordance with Islamic law, though with slight variations, Druze law specifies that in the absence of a will, every two female offsprings receive half the share of their male sibling. It is,

however, common for a Druze parent to write a will specifying to whom the inheritance will go. In this case a female may even inherit all of her parents' possessions to the exclusion of her brothers if the will states that.

Sociopolitical Organization

Recent immigrants have expressed little state or national allegiance, turning inward to the activities and tasks of their community associations. It is usually with the second-generation American Druze that one witnesses active participation in the American political process, voting, and nationwide discussions and debates of domestic issues. First-generation immigrants are naturally more concerned with sociopolitical developments in their homeland and the foreign policy of the United States toward the Middle East and the Arab world. The most central and primary issue to most immigrants is the U.S. government's stand on the Arab-Israeli conflict and the Palestinian question. The Druze feel especially alienated by what they feel is the United States' alliance to Israel and the propagation of its politicoeconomic ambitions and interests.

The Druze are hardly effective at the state, federal, or local levels, and they are still caught in internal Druze politics, which reinforces factional and regional divisions, replicating those in Lebanon. The Druze political structure in Lebanon is dominated by the two opposed factions: the Yazbakis and the Junblatis. This schism is reflected in the political outlook and affiliations of the ADS participants. Independent, secularist, and more progressive political trends usually find representation outside the confines of the ADS and sectarian establishments.

Religion

The Druze religious faith is an offshoot of Shi'a Islam. It can be traced to Fatimid Ismailism in Egypt during the reign of the enigmatic and highly controversial eleventh-century caliph al-Hakim bi-Amr Allah. Within Ismaili theology and its inherent messianic expectations emerged the belief in the divinity of al-Hakim and in his being the expected savior. In 1017, al-Hakim publicly proclaimed that he was the manifestation of the deity and summoned his followers to embrace this belief in their religious worship. Although Druze apologists tend to cite him as an outstanding sociopolitical reformer of his times, al-Hakim's excessive restrictions against orthodox Muslim practices and Christian and Jewish presence marked him as a capricious ruler who strove to unite the Islamic world under his leadership. By the time of his death in 1021, he had neither advanced nor formulated a coherent Druze creed, a task that fell to his courtier and Persian theologian, Hamza ibn Ali. Druzism found permanent roots in the northern frontier of the Fatimid Empire and the mountainous region of present-day southern Lebanon. By the end of the Fatimid caliphate in 1174, no traces of Druzism in Cairo could be detected.

It is believed that some of al-Hakim's courtiers, with the design and approval of his sister Sitt al-Mulk—whom he had accused of immoral conduct—murdered him. Druze spiritual leaders, however, maintain that he did not die but was in occultation at the mount of al-Muqattam in Cairo.

The Druze interpretation of the Islamic *shari'a* and revelation has taken such an esoteric and exclusive course that the Druze today, especially those living in the United States, are divided on whether they consider themselves to be Muslim or not. The assumed secrecy of Druze theology and cosmology along with the impermissibility of conversion to Druzism have demarcated Druze sectarian boundaries and reinforced Druze separateness. A number of spokespersons for the American Druze proclaim that while the tenets of the Druze faith are part and parcel of Islam, the Druze are not considered orthodox Muslims in that they do not adhere to the Koran, enact the rituals of praying in the direction of Mecca, or undertake pilgrimage or fast during the holy month of Ramadan. Notwithstanding, increased efforts have been invested to reconcile Druzism with the wider Islamic milieu, mostly out of expediency and under contingent political pressures.

The Druze believe in reincarnation. The Day of Judgment for the Druze is a definite period in time during which the soul experiences repeated reincarnations, striving toward its actualization and perfection. Unlike in the teachings of Islam, the afterlife rewards are not encapsulated in a paradise of Earthly delights but rather in the experience of the beatific vision of the divine. Hell is no more and no less than the failure to hold this vision. The Druze are ardent supporters of the principle of free will and refute the concept of predestination.

Assimilation

The Druze endorse a rigorous work ethic, which has helped them cope with their new economic, religious, and cultural situation in the United States. Since the 1970s, a number of Druze intellectuals have called for change in the secretive nature of the Druze religion, in accordance with the open religious atmosphere in the United States. Instead of facilitating total absorption in American culture, the dynamics of socioreligious exchange and forces of Americanization have instead reinforced the formation of a distinct Druze awareness perpetuated by a vague and diffuse understanding of creed and Scripture. For many of the early immigrants, a professed integration in the dominant culture meant proclaiming to be Christian (mainly Presbyterian or Methodist) and dissociating one's identity from "Islamicness." As part of the Arab-American population, the Druze continue, however, to face forms of cultural and racial discrimination and stereotyping in their everyday contacts, through the media, or within the framework of the government's policy on the Middle East.

See also: JORDANIANS; LEBANESE CHRISTIANS; LEBANESE MUSLIMS; SYRIANS

Bibliography

Abu-Izzeddin, N. M. (1984). *The Druzes: A New Study of Their History, Faith, and Society.* Leiden, Netherlands: E. J. Brill.

Alamuddin, N. S., and Starr, P. D. (1980). *Crucial Bonds: Marriage Among the Lebanese Druze.* New York: Caravan Books.

Al-Najjar, A. (1982). "The Druzes' Role and Dilemma in America." *Our Heritage* 2(4):23.

Betts, R. B. (1988). *The Druze.* New Haven, CT: Yale University Press.

Beynon, E. D. (1944). "The Near East in Flint, Michigan: Assyrians and Druses and their Antecedents." *Geographical Review* 24(2):239–274.

Bryer, D. (1975, 1976). "The Origins of the Druze Religion." *Der Islam* 52:47–84; 53:4–27.

Dana, N. (1980). *The Druze: A Religious Community in Transition.* Jerusalem: Turtledove.

Haddad, Y., and Smith, J. (1993). *Mission to America: Five Islamic Sectarian Communities in North America.* Gainesville: University Press of Florida.

Hirschberg, J. W. (1969). "The Druzes." In *Religion in the Middle East: Three Religions in Concord and Conflict*, 2 vols, edited by A. J. Arberry. Cambridge, Eng.: Cambridge University Press.

Layish, A. (1982). *Marriage, Divorce, and Succession in the Druze Family.* Leiden, Netherlands: E. J. Brill.

Naff, A. (1985). *Becoming American: The Early Arab Immigrant Experience.* Carbondale: Southern Illinois University Press.

Oppenheimer, J. W. S. (1980). "'We Are Both in Each Others' Houses': Communal and Patrilineal Ideologies in Druze Village Religion and Social Structure." *American Ethnologist* 7:621–636.

Perillier, L. (1986). *Les Druze.* Paris: Éditions Publisud.

RULA ABISAAB

DUTCH

Compared to other European countries, the Netherlands did not see many of its inhabitants go to the United States as immigrants. The nation had a reputation for social and economic stability, as well as a long history of tolerance; relatively few of its citizens responded to the lures of life in the New World. By 1996, fewer than 300,000 Dutch immigrants to the United States had been recorded, compared to more than a million each from the smaller nations of Sweden and Denmark and far greater numbers from Germany, England, and Ireland.

Early Immigration

From the American Revolution until 1845, the number of Dutch immigrants to America averaged fewer than one hundred a year. These early immigrants, arriving in small groups of individuals or in families, sometimes found homes in the well-established Dutch colonial community of upstate New York, which had begun in the days when New York City was still called New Amsterdam. More often, however, Dutch immigrants settled in small towns or isolated agricultural enclaves; North Carolina, Ohio, Wisconsin, Texas, and Oregon were among their destinations. Such immigrants typically merged into the existing population and, except for their surnames, retained little of their Netherlandic culture.

Between 1847 and 1857, in contrast, more than a thousand people a year arrived, establishing towns and farming communities, and setting up cultural institutions that continued to welcome new immigrants, in even greater numbers, for more than a century. These midcentury arrivals were mostly Calvinists, members of a group (the Seceders) that had broken away from the state church of the Dutch government. To understand their situation, it is necessary to outline a bit of their history in the Netherlands. The Dutch government, reacting to rationalist influences and a new monarchy in the years after Waterloo, had changed the way the church was run.

William I had appointed key people to the Synod, a centralized ruling body, thus diminishing the autonomy of local congregations. The Synod had changed the songbooks used during worship by adding hymns, which struck many people as being less holy than their traditional Psalms taken from the Genevan Psalter. It had also tinkered with the doctrines of historic Calvinism, especially the Canons of Dort and the Belgic Confessions, whose strong hostility toward Catholics and Baptists had become something of an embarrassment to the Crown. For a time in the 1830s, in fact, the government had imposed a regimen of fines, harassment, and imprisonment on those Seceders who protested too loudly. By 1840, however, under a new set of religious laws and a new king, the harsh treatment had largely disappeared.

Although it is not accurate to say that the Seceders were the only American immigrants to flee a spirit of tolerance in their native land, it has often looked that way. The image of the Netherlands as a prosperous, open-minded, humane, and stodgily progressive nation has persisted to the present. This brief spate of official intolerance was very much out of character in a land where since the age of Erasmus (a Catholic humanist), Spinoza (a secular Portuguese Jew), and Rembrandt (an Anabaptist), people of widely divergent ideas had lived together peacefully. Much of the Seceders' resentment was aimed at the treatment the government guaranteed to Catholics, Baptists, and Jews, who enjoyed social and legal rights often lacking in other European nations.

The outlines of these ideological disputes should not obscure the issues of bread and butter. To Albertus Van Raalte and Hendrik Scholte, pastors who became the most influential leaders of Dutch settlers in America, the need for freedom of religion (as they saw it) was of utmost importance. But many of their followers were poor, and in their view the trip across the Atlantic offered a new economic beginning as well. Especially in the aftermath of the potato blight, which had hit the Netherlands with demoralizing thoroughness in the summer of 1845, poverty was a compelling reason for considering emigration. Many rural Hollanders had seen their entire potato crop destroyed and, with the blight still raging in the summer of 1846, there was little hope for a quick recovery. Complicating the farmers' plight were a profound change in European economies; a high rate of taxation; and an outmoded, fragmented national infrastructure.

The port cities of Amsterdam and Rotterdam dominated the nation's economy. The outlying provinces did not keep pace with market requirements and found themselves increasingly isolated from the centers of activity. For many farmers life was becoming difficult, sometimes desperate. Even those who could avoid poverty were worried about the future. Prospects for their children were bleak.

Van Raalte and Scholte, each working separately with other prominent leaders of the Seceders, formed cooperative associations, sought financial support, and began looking into possible places to live in America. Van Raalte was the first to leave the Netherlands. Late in the summer of 1846, he led several hundred settlers to the United States, intending to purchase land in Wisconsin, where a few Hollanders had already achieved a foothold. Travel delays, an early winter, and a chance meeting with Dutch Catholics on their way to Wisconsin helped persuade him to remain in Michigan. He soon explored the land around what is now the city of Holland, Michigan, and there he established a *kolonie*, which, over the ensuing decades, attracted thousands of Dutch immigrants. In 1847, Scholte followed Van Raalte; however, Scholte was unwilling to bring his band of people into Michigan, despite several invitations. The land in western Michigan was swampy and heavily wooded, making it difficult for agriculture. Scholte preferred the rolling plains of northwestern Iowa, and chose to settle there, in what became the city of Pella. Western Michigan and northwestern Iowa thus became the centers of a new sort of Dutch colony, based on agriculture, with churches and schools controlled by Calvinist Seceders.

Fewer than one in five of the immigrants came from cities, the rest having lived in rural provinces. In the century of great European emigration, when entire regions of countries such as Ireland were depopulated, the proportion of Hollanders to join the tide never amounted to as much as 1 percent of the population, although the land was small and crowded.

Those settlers who immigrated to America were not desperately poor. More than 65 percent of them were from the middle classes, although as many as one-fifth had sought public assistance from the Dutch government. In some ways, however, they followed traditional patterns. Like most immigrants, they normally arrived in groups rather than as individuals. They moved as part of an extended chain forged by family and church. They followed the folkways they had known back home and, despite the strangeness of the new land, found

A Dutch shoemaker and a hotel maid dance together wearing wooden clogs as part of the celebration of Dutch National Day in San Diego, California. (Earl Kowall/Corbis)

much that was familiar to them. Many letters tell of meeting old neighbors or long-lost relatives from the Netherlands:

> "I took a trip to the colony," says Marcus Nienhuis in 1854, in a letter back home, "and met a friend of yours. I saw the woman standing in her doorway and asked some directions. As soon as she opened her mouth, I could tell that she was from Drenthe and I asked if she was the wife of Harm Smidt. In surprise she answered, 'Yes'" [Brinks, 1986, p. 36].

People continued to speak in their regional dialects, and formed villages that were virtual trans-

plants from the rural provinces of the Netherlands. Within a few years of the first arrivals, the towns around Holland had sprouted Dutch names: Overisel, Drenthe, Vriesland, Staphorst, Harlem, and Groningen, among others. Sometimes as many as two hundred people would arrive at once, putting a strain on the welcome that was extended to them. However, they kept coming.

Settlement Patterns

Van Raalte had chosen the land around Holland partly because of its isolation—in that way he thought he would keep "foreign" influences on his flock at a minimum. The very difficulty of the place appealed to him. Although the Treaty of Chicago (1833) had displaced most Native Americans from this part of Michigan, there were a few Indians still living in the region. Aside from occasional clearings and oak openings, the land was heavily wooded and swampy. Existing farms were scarce, but since farming was the only way of life most of the settlers knew, and since it was the desire even of those who could not afford land in the Netherlands, they worked clearing acreage and planting crops. By 1900, these settlers and their offspring had acquired more than two thousand square miles of land in Michigan, an immense tract by Dutch standards. In their homeland, thirteen thousand square miles had been parceled out among eleven million inhabitants.

Being primarily agricultural people, or at least aspiring to that condition, the settlers utterly failed to comprehend the ways of the Indians they met, a loosely mixed group of Ottawas and Catholic Potawatamies. Now and then a Hollander would find a deer hanging in a tree and take it home. More often the newcomers would gather up items the Indians had apparently abandoned in the woods, such as axes or troughs for making maple syrup, not knowing that the owners intended to return and use them the next year. Van Raalte, among his other duties as church father, oversaw the return of several thousand maple troughs, with negotiated settlements being reached for those items that had been lost or destroyed.

It was from individual Indian landowners that many of the original tracts of land were purchased, and the settlers worked at maintaining good relations with them, despite misunderstandings. But the late 1840s was a time when the Indian presence in Michigan was diminishing. Most of the Potawatamies had been resettled outside of the state, and the Ottawas were being pushed toward enclaves farther north. An outbreak of fevers, some of them malarial, in the summers of 1847 and 1848 speeded the process of Indian displacement. Some settlers saw God's will behind the high rate of Indian mortality during these bouts of sickness; more likely, however, the cause was a combination of low resistance and a folk remedy for fever that included sudden immersion in cold water.

New settlers kept arriving in a steady stream. Holland, the heart of the kolonie, with about fifteen hundred people in 1850, was spreading its influence through the surrounding villages and had sent many young workers and families to urban satellite communities. The Dutch in Michigan, despite their hardships, were living out an American success story.

Religious Conflicts

Scholte, in Iowa, seemed to favor a less isolationist approach to the experience of America than his counterpart in Michigan, but Scholte, too, wanted his followers to remain true to the vision that had brought them to America. He recognized that if people moved in sufficient numbers and stayed together, they would be able to control the institutions of religion, education, and local government, allowing them to retain the religious and social stability they desired. His followers in Iowa, settling on land that did not require clearing and draining, created productive farms almost immediately, and established trading relations with towns and cities as far away as St. Louis, Missouri. Both these leaders, and many others in smaller towns, insisted on the religious nature of their community. Title deeds routinely required that the owners be Christians, with the added proviso (in practice if not in writing) that they could not be Catholic.

Despite, or perhaps because of, such doctrinal strictness, religious conflicts soon arose in the new communities. The Dutch had long been known for a proclivity to theological squabbling. "Is there a mongrel sect in Christendom," asked one seventeenth-century onlooker, "which does not croak and spawn and flourish in their Sooterkin bogs?" "They are so generally bred up to the Bible," said another, "that almost every cobbler is a Dutch doctor of divinity . . . yet fall those inward illuminations so different that sometimes seven religions are found in one family" (Schama, 1987, p. 266). Religion did lend a special cast to the earliest settlements. Although fewer than 2 percent of the Dutch population belonged to this fringe religious group, Seceders accounted for almost 50 percent of the immigrants before 1850. Even among these conservative folk, however, more than 90 percent listed economic reasons, not religion, as foremost among the causes for their move.

Assimilation and Cultural Persistence

Concerning secular issues, there was virtually no disagreement. A certain amount of assimilation was inevitable and was welcomed. A commitment to a new country cannot be founded simply on disaffection with the old. The farmers worked to adopt current American agricultural practices, which sometimes differed from the Dutch ways, and their letters home show genuine pride in their accomplishments. The villages hired English-speaking teachers for both adults and children to ensure the removal of language barriers.

They established relationships with "Yankee" merchants in nearby cities. They showed a uniquely northern American sentiment on the issue of slavery, going so far in 1855 as to request "humbly and kindly" that a group of southern churches founded by Dutch-American slaveholders be kept out of their religious fellowship. And when the Civil War began, just thirteen years after the founding of Holland, Michigan, hundreds of their young men fought for the Union. These people were dedicated to the idea of becoming Americans—not merely Hollanders on foreign soil—and of making contributions to the life of their new nation. R. T. Kuiper expressed his feelings in a letter to the Netherlands:

"Life is more roomy here," [he wrote], "freer, easier, more common; there is more open-heartedness.... There are far fewer formalities and rules of conduct. Everyone associates on a more equal level. True, everyone is called 'mister,' but no one 'sir,' with the exception of the preacher, who is still addressed as 'Dominie.' But no one removes his hat for him" [Brinks, 1986, p. 231].

In one respect, then, they assimilated quite successfully.

However, another attempt at assimilation met with shattering opposition. The earliest Dutch churches affiliated themselves with the Reformed Church of America (RCA), a denomination whose history went back to the days of Peter Stuyvesant. In the eyes of many settlers, the RCA had become too Americanized (i.e., impure in doctrine); this group, almost half the existing community, formed the Christian Reformed Church (CRC) in 1857. Debates about minor details of religious doctrine and practice raged within the community, leaving outsiders mystified. It seems apparent to most historians that these family quarrels were less about religion than about ethnic identity. One group (the RCA) wished to effect a rather significant level of assimilation, while the other (the CRC) emphasized the need to retain moral purity by remaining separate. The real question was how to be American yet Dutch, or vice versa.

By 1900, more than 100,000 new immigrants had been added to the midwestern Dutch communities. The scarcity of available farmland in the original settlements caused two clear changes: First, many new farm villages sprang up in northern areas of Michigan and Wisconsin, on the lowlands to the east of Chicago, in southern Minnesota and South Dakota, and in settlements around Lynden, Washington, and Bellflower, California; second, many families found themselves settling in cities instead of on farms. During this era the communities gained an increasing economic and cultural self-sufficiency, creating or consolidating many of their institutions—hospitals, nursing homes, churches, and schools. Because of divided loyalties between the RCA and the CRC, these institutions tended to develop in pairs. Even the smallest villages supported two churches; the community also developed parallel systems of higher education. The RCA founded Hope College (1866) in Holland, Michigan; the CRC countered with Calvin College (1876) in Grand Rapids, Michigan. Both colleges added seminaries for the training of clergymen.

The divergent strategies of these two conservative cultures appear, in a superficial way, in the makeup of the student bodies at their respective schools. Today, Hope College in Holland enrolls about 40 percent of its students from the Dutch community, while Calvin in Grand Rapids attracts

The Crystal Cathedral in Garden Grove, California, is the home of the Reformed Church in America. (Lynn Goldsmith/Corbis)

twice the percentage of undergraduates with Dutch surnames. Both communities remain somewhat precariously related to their Dutch heritage and to each other. The expending of so much energy on parochial issues continues to reinforce their insularity.

When historians describe the Dutch communities of Michigan, they are either scrupulously dispassionate or modestly glowing in their assessments. Neat and amply reasoned documents, well-ordered and comprehensible patterns of development, have an innate appeal to historians. Novelists of Dutch descent, writing about the same community, arrive at radically different conclusions, many of them unflattering. In dozens of short stories and novels, Peter De Vries has spent a sizable portion of his narrative time lampooning the midwestern Dutch. Especially in *The Blood of the Lamb*, he shows a society with infinite talent for fragmentation along doctrinal lines. The protagonist's father, in fact, sees this tendency as a sign of health: "Rotten wood you can't split," he boasts.

Novelists such as Feike Feikema and David Cornel De Jong emphasize the painful crushing of independent spirits by a narrow, often boorish culture, doom-ridden and bleakly ministerial. The filmmaker Paul Schrader, screenwriter and director of such films as *The Last Temptation of Christ*, *American Gigolo*, *Raging Bull*, and *Cat People*, often has fun with the community in sly visual asides.

Historians and artists perceive the community in vastly different ways. The nature and purpose of a well-organized society is to promote group survival, not to nurture individual talent. This quality is what historians—students and employees of cultural institutions—seek and admire. Artists, on the other hand, approach society from the bottom up, often finding their identity in the delicious freedom to revolt and rebel.

Artists, despite the fact that they constitute only the tiniest segment of a community, suggest the possibility of a third immigrant strategy for coping with American society: to maintain a certain distance from the ethnic community without exactly losing touch. Population figures show that Dutch descendants in the United States in 1996 numbered about four million, mostly clustered in the areas of the historical settlement, where they prospered in a wide variety of economic pursuits. Ethnic membership in the RCA and the CRC combined amounted to approximately 500,000.

Continued Contributions

Traditional immigration from the Netherlands slowed to a trickle in the years after World War II, but in the early 1980s there was one notable exception. A group of dairy farmers from the northern provinces of the Netherlands began moving to West Texas, where they established family farms that were well funded and technologically sophisticated.

These farm families, more than four hundred of them by 1996, with religious and cultural connections to midwestern Hollanders, helped move Texas from thirty-fifth place to sixth place in the volume of its milk production, adding yet another small piece to America's cultural mosaic.

See also: FRISIANS

Bibliography

Bratt, J. D. (1984). *Dutch Calvinism in Modern America: A History of a Conservative Subculture.* Grand Rapids, MI: W. B. Eerdmans.

Brinks, H. J. (1986). *Write Back Soon: Letters from Dutch Immigrants in America.* Grand Rapids, MI: CRC Publications.

De Jong, G. F. (1975). *The Dutch in America, 1609–1974.* Boston: Twayne.

Hinte, J. v. ([1928] 1985). *Netherlanders in America: A Study of Emigration and Settlement in the Nineteenth and Twentieth Centuries in the United States of America*, translated by A. De Wit. Grand Rapids, MI: Baker Book House.

Lucas, H. S. (1955). *Netherlanders in America.* Ann Arbor, MI: University of Michigan Press.

Mulder, A. (1947). *Americans from Holland.* Philadelphia: Lippincott.

Schama, S. (1987). *The Embarrassment of Riches: An Interpretation of Dutch Culture in the Golden Age.* New York: Knopf.

LARRY TEN HARMSEL

EAST AND SOUTHEAST ASIANS

See BUDDHISTS; CAMBODIANS; CHAM; CHINESE; CHINESE-VIETNAMESE; FILIPINOS; HMONG; INDONESIANS; INDOS; JAPANESE; KHMU; KOREANS; LAO; MIEN; OKINAWANS; TAIWANESE; THAI; TIBETANS

ECUADORIANS

The number of Ecuadorians living in the United States reached 191,000 in 1990 and constituted 2.0 percent of all foreign-born Spanish-speaking residents. Although their population is relatively small, these immigrants represent the exodus of a significant sector of the South American nation of Ecuador, whose population was estimated at ten to eleven million in 1989.

The majority of Ecuadorians are relative newcomers and are few in number relative to other minority groups. As a consequence, they are essentially absent from the literature on U.S. minorities until the 1970s. By 1980, when 6,133 Ecuadorians were legally admitted to the United States, their population had reached 64,000 and they accounted for one out of five U.S. residents of South American origin.

Legal entrants more than doubled in 1990, when 12,476 were admitted. Most were young adults: The average age of new arrivals changed from 25.5 years in 1960 to 28.8 years in 1980. At that time 72.3 percent of Ecuadorian U.S. residents were between ages 16 and 64, 56 percent were high school graduates, and 9.3 percent were college graduates.

Ecuadorian immigrants tend to concentrate in the northeastern United States and to settle predominantly in urban areas. As of 1990, the largest populations were found in the states of New York (89,838), California (29,953), Florida (14,679), New Jersey (27,572), and Illinois (8,659). Virginia, Massachusetts, Connecticut, and Texas all registered more than 2,000 Ecuadorian residents.

Almost one-half of Ecuadorians entering the United States between 1965 and 1989 (the largest immigration occurred in the 1970s) settled in New York City, primarily in the boroughs of Brooklyn and Queens. In fact, New York has been called Ecuador's third city because, as of 1990, New York's population of Ecuadorians was exceeded only by the inhabitants of Quito and Guayaquil, Ecuador's two largest cities.

The Native Land

Ecuador derives its name from the equator, which crosses it. Although the country is relatively small, it is geographically, climatically, and ethnically diverse. The nation is divided into three major ecological zones: the Costa (the Pacific coastal plain), the Sierra, (the highland valleys lying between the double chain of the Andes Mountains), and the Oriente (the Andean piedmont and the lowlands of the eastern Upper Amazon region). The Pan-American Highway is the major transportation artery, and prior to the 1970s, access to rural communities not located near that road could be difficult, especially during the rainy season. Regional loyalties are strong, and often, so is group-identity. Native Americans living in the highlands and the Oriente have resisted strong pressures to assimilate in the wider society (i.e., to "mestizoize"); they struggle to conserve their unique cultures.

Since the 1960s, the national and provincial governments have affected dramatic improvements in rural communities' access to potable water, electricity, health care, and education. Literacy in the mid-1980s was estimated at 85 percent. Although the combined sectors of agriculture (35%) and services (50%) employ 85 percent of the Ecuadorian workforce, virtually no immigrants entering the United States between 1982 and 1989 declared an occupation in agriculture, and roughly a quarter of all immigrants declared occupations in the service sector.

Ecuadorians have emigrated primarily for economic rather than for political reasons. Waves of emigration coincide with economic crises in their native land, and consequent unemployment or underemployment. The majority of emigrants have come from the populous city of Guayaquil.

Reasons for leaving vary with region of origin. Lack of market demand for the exceptionally fine Ecuadorian-made straw hats (the so-called Panama hats) led many artisans to emigrate from the provinces of Azuay and Cañar in the 1970s. Immigrants from Pacific coastal provinces also left in the 1970s

and 1980s due to declines in the fishing industry. The rise in immigration to the United States during the 1980s and 1990s is linked to drastic declines in Ecuador's manufacturing and construction industries and (from 1986 to 1990) an almost 30 percent decline in real wages.

Ethnonyms

In Ecuador, apart from a small black minority (5%), there are three global ethnic categories with which people self-identify: the *blancos* (Spanish-speaking "whites," an estimated 10 to 15 percent of the population), the *runas* (Quichua-speakers, often bilingual, estimated at 40 percent of the population), and the mestizos (Spanish-speakers of mixed Hispanic and runa heritage, an estimated 40 percent of the population). In polite usage, runas are termed "indigenes"; pejoratively, they are called "Indians." Quichua (*runa simi*) is an expressive and beautiful native language that predates the sixteenth century Spanish invasion. At least thirteen dialects are spoken in Ecuador. Mestizos who are peasant farmers are pejoratively called *cholos* by some urbanites.

These terms and the ethnocultural categories they designate are associated closely with social class and with corresponding economic opportunities. Although the term *blanco* connotes the "Spanish" social elite, the term is appropriated by mestizos throughout the Sierra to assert a non-indigenous identity. Blancos (used here in the term's widest sense) occupy the upper, middle, and lower-middle classes. Runas generally are in the lower classes and are socially stigmatized by the wider society. Certain Otavalo weavers and Saraguro cattle-farmers, however, may be wealthier than their mestizo neighbors, and Ecuador's most famous, and wealthiest artist, Guayasamin, proudly proclaims his "Indian" origins and portrays the suffering and poverty of the runas in his internationally acclaimed work. Runas primarily are found in the highlands and the Oriente. Mestizos work in all three ecological zones but reside predominantly on the coast or in the highlands.

Ecuadorians in the United States

The regional, ethnic, and class factors discussed above are important in determining the composition of the immigrant population. Apart from bilingual Otavalo runas, the majority of immigrants to the United States have been Spanish-speaking middle- or lower-middle-class mestizos from the coastal and highland zones. Small numbers of Otavalos from the highland province of Imbabura have immigrated to U.S. cities that are centers for tourism (e.g., New York, Miami, New Orleans). Otavalo men, famous for their skilled production of tapestries and other textiles, also sell woven items made by other indigenous groups such as the Salasaca of Tungurahua Province. Expatriate Otavalo men often retain their elegant ethnic costume and are readily recognized by their white, mid-calf-length trousers; blue or gray wool ponchos; and hair arranged in a long, single braid.

In New York City in 1990, Ecuadorians had the lowest rate of naturalization (18%) among immigrant groups. Fewer than 2,000 Ecuadorians living in the United States were naturalized each year from 1980 to 1989. Analysis of a sample drawn from the 1990 U.S. Census found that among 2,020 Ecuadorian immigrants (over age eighteen and residents of the United States for at least five years) 27.1 percent were naturalized.

These people had experienced an average of 13.3 years of schooling, and 61.8 percent of them spoke good English. Their average annual income was $8,441; 36.7 percent were homeowners, 2.8 percent were self-employed, 67.8 percent had children, and 70.6 percent lived in urban areas.

In the 1970s and 1980s, many undocumented aliens gained illegal entry. Prior to the passage in 1986 of the Simpson Rodino Immigration Reform and Control Act, no law prohibited the employment of illegal immigrants in the United States. People entering on a tourist visa could "disappear" for a few months and earn money that helped establish them in some enterprise upon their return home. A survey of illegal immigrants found that Ecuadorians paid a higher average fee ($2,880) to achieve illegal entry compared to average costs to Peruvians ($2,620) or Colombians ($1,796). The undocumented Ecuadorians in this survey had experienced an average of 9.7 years of education.

Ecuadorian Workers in the United States

Many recent immigrants in the New York urban area who have yet to become citizens have been employed in lower-paying service-sector jobs. If one compares data from the 1990 sample of immigrants reported above, it appears that Ecua-

TABLE 1 Selected Sectors of Employment in New York City (1982–1989)[a]

	Executive Administration (Managerial)	Professional Technical	Administrative Support[b]	Precision Production (Crafts/Repairs)	Operators Fabricators Laborers[c]	Service
Men (%)	5.6	7.2	16.0	16.5	21.3	25.8
Women (%)	4.4	6.2	35.0	9.1	21.3	18.0

Source: Salvo and Ortiz, 1992, pp. 151–152.

[a]For natualized men and women between eighteen and sixty-four years of age.

[b]"Administrative Support" includes jobs such as clerks, typists, and secretaries.

[c]"Operators, Fabricators, Laborers" includes many women who were sewing machine operators.

dorians' average earnings have dropped since 1980, even though in the United States at that time their median annual earnings ($12,000) were lower than the $14,000 median reported for all other Central and South American immigrants. As a group, female Ecuadorians (age sixteen to sixty-four) fared worse, earning a median income of $8,005. Although proficiency in English differentiates earning potentials for male workers, it has less effect on the potential of female workers. This may be due to women's recourse to low-paying domestic employment or other service jobs.

During the period from 1982 to 1989, many Ecuadorians entered the United States as students (20.9% of men and 18.2% of women), but most came as workers. The majority of male immigrants to New York City (68.6%) and almost half of female immigrants (43.8%) reported having an occuption. Table 1 shows how naturalized Ecuadorian New Yorkers in the 1980s were distributed among selected occupational categories.

Although hard data are lacking, some of the employment outside the service and administrative sectors that have attracted Ecuadorians in the metropolitan areas of Washington, D.C. and Chicago include travel, real-estate, insurance, car repair, shoe repair, jewelry-making, and musical and artistic productions.

Cultural and Social Life

Though few in number, Ecuadorian immigrants have created the means to maintain vital cultural communities and a dual identification with both Ecuadorian and U.S. societies. Community news is disseminated in newsletters published by immigrants in Atlanta, New York, Chicago, Los Angeles, and other cities, and many of the 140 U.S. radio stations that broadcast exclusively in Spanish include Ecuadorian national news as well as reports of immigrants' club events and social calendars.

Ecuadorian restaurants in the cities mentioned above serve traditional foods, including such specialties as fried pork (*fritada*) with hominy (*mote*); roast guinea pig (*cuy*); and the delectable

Ecuadorian soups of corn, potatoes, or *caldos* (meat broths) accompanied by hot sauce (*aji*). Tamales stuffed with chicken and/or vegetables; sweet, steamed, corn-cakes (*quimbolitos*), and cheese-filled potato pancakes (*llapingachos*) are but a few typical foods.

Clubs play a significant role in immigrant social life. Wherever immigrant Ecuadorians settle, they form organizations that celebrate their culture and offer social and instructional programs for members. Ecuadorian generosity is well known, and many clubs raise money to support charitable institutions in Ecuador; women's auxiliaries are especially noted for support of day-care centers and aid to impoverished or orphaned children.

Festivals offer opportunities to affirm and articulate self-identity and common group values. Mother's Day is an important occasion for immigrant Los Angeles families (as it is in Ecuador) and features the election of a local woman as the "Symbol of Ecuadorian Motherhood." Ecuador's national holidays and the fiestas peculiar to specific native locales are celebrated with programs of music, poetry readings, and dances in native costumes, to which the wider community may be invited. An example is the August celebration of Ecuadorian independence in Arlington, Virginia, organized by the Ecuadorian Cultural Brotherhood, whose members, garbed as indigenes, serve typical foods to the crowd.

Clubs sponsoring festivals may import traditional musicians, singers, or dancers from Ecuador; however, immigrant performers also are in demand. Audiences nostalgic for the richness of traditional Ecuadorian culture enjoy *pasillos*, songs of love and loss, and runa music and dances. Musicians play native instruments such as the *bombo* (drum), *zampoña* (a large pan-pipe), *quenas* (flutes), and *charango* (a stringed, mandolin-like instrument).

Athletic clubs and games are important social venues for men. *Ecuavoley*, the strenuous Ecuadorian version of volleyball, competes with soccer as the most popular men's sport. Ecuavoley is played with nine-foot-high nets and three-man teams. In the parks where the games take place, spectators also gather to play *cuarenta* (a popular Ecuadorian card game) or to grill meat for picnic lunches.

Regional loyalties that differentiate populations in Ecuador often provide bases for club membership in the United States. Social clubs named for Ecuadorian cities or provinces attract immigrants from those locales. Examples include Club Ambato, found in cities in Virginia, California, New York, and New Jersey; Fundación Cuenca, Club Damas Manabitas, and Club Atlético Guayaquil in Los Angeles; and Sociedad Tungurahuences in Brooklyn, New York. Where the immigrant populations are smaller, the membership is pan-Ecuadorian (such as Club Social Ecuatoriana in Baltimore, Maryland).

In Ecuador, the February celebration of Carnival is a time for play—mostly for dancing, drinking, and feasting, and dousing friends, family, and unsuspecting strangers with cold water. The water play is eschewed in Ambato and replaced by the more decorous Festival of Fruit and Flowers notable for its parties, public performances, and grand parade with beauty queens (*reinas*) elected by each neighborhood (*barrio*). All the queens are candidates for the hotly contested title of Reina of Ambato.

In the United States, this festival is an annual Club Ambato event. The Los Angeles club elects a reina (whose parents must have been born in Ecuador), and club members travel with her to Ecuador to participate in the Ambato festival. Members who stay home celebrate with dancing, music, and traditional foods.

The Day of the Dead is celebrated in Ecuador in November. Graves of deceased relatives are cleaned and decorated with flowers and crepe paper. In the past, families shared a meal at the gravesite, drinking corn beer (*chicha*) or other alcoholic beverages and consuming the deceased's favorite foods. Food and children's toys are central to this holiday. Food, sold in the streets or prepared in homes, includes breads shaped as swaddled babies and *colada morada*, a beverage made from ground purple corn and berries (said to simulate blood). Toys are sold in tented booths that fill the streets. Plastic toys largely have replaced the traditional ones made of low-fired clay. Some immigrant Ecuadorians do not publicly observe Finados, though many families make *colado morada*, give their children toys, and attend the Catholic Mass.

Ties to Ecuador: Dual Citizenship

Many local clubs and other special-purpose organizations are linked to overarching organizations. The Ecuadorian United Front (Frente Unido Ecuatoriano, FUE), in Los Angeles, affiliates eleven groups. The Chicago-based Federation of Ecuadorian Organizations in the Exterior (Federación de Entidades Ecuatorianas en el Exterior, FEDEE) has an international membership that unites 600 groups in the United States, Canada, Mexico, Venezuela, and Puerto Rico. FEDEE holds annual congresses; the first of its newsletter, *Equatorianidad*, was published in July 1994.

Maintenance of strong ties to Ecuador and the attainment of dual citizenship for immigrants have been major FEDEE goals. Together with other expatriate organizations such as the Ecuadorian Civic Committee, FEDEE successfully lobbied the Ecuadorian government to hold a plebiscite on the question of dual-nationality. Ecuadorians voted to amend their constitution, and Ecuadorian citizenship became "unrenounceable" on January 24, 1995, when the amendment was published in the Official Register.

Family and Gender Roles

Family ties are strong, especially between parents and children. Of the 12,476 Ecuadorians who immigrated in 1990, 1,639 were parents, spouses, or children of U.S. citizens.

Barring individual and ethnic variations, Ecuadorian family structure generally follows a patriarchal pattern. More than a quarter of female immigrants to New York City (28.4%) categorized themselves as homemakers. In cultural ideology, the husband is master of the household, and his activities are his own business. The wife is his helpmate, subject to his orders.

The idealization of female roles is part of the immigrants' cultural tradition. Young women are idolized and given temporary "center stage" through the election of reinas and in quinceañeras—the often-elaborate parties given on a girl's fifteenth birthday. Celebrations of Mother's Day honor the women's self-sacrifice for their families.

Gender roles are conserved in the home but are changing slowly in the workplace. Many educated Ecuadorian women have entered the professions. Among immigrants to New York City from 1982 to 1989, 5.3 percent of the women worked in a professional or technical specialty, and 2.6 percent worked as executives, administrators, or managers. Women take prominent positions in some urban social clubs and organize separate auxilliaries. As U.S. society moves toward gender equality, we might expect corresponding alterations in gender roles among Ecuadorian immigrant groups.

Bibliography

Astudillo, J., and Cordero, C. (1990). *Los Huayrapamushca*. Quito: Imprenta El Conejo.

Bean, F., and Tienda, M. (1987). *The Hispanic Population of the United States*. New York: Russell Sage Foundation.

Carasquillo, A. (1991). *Hispanic Children and Youth in the United States: A Resource Guide*. New York: Garland.

Cortés, C. (1993). "Power, Passivity and Pluralism: Mass Media in the Development of Latino Culture and Identity." *Latino Studies Journal* 7:3–22.

Hanratty, D., ed. (1991). *Ecuador: A Country Study*. Washington, DC: Federal Research Division, Library of Congress.

Mahler, S. (1995). *American Dreaming*. Princeton, NJ: Princeton University Press.

Pooley, E. (1985). "Little Ecuador." *New York* 18(Sept. 16):32.

Reddy, M., ed. (1993). *Statistical Record of Hispanic Americans*. Detroit: Gale Research.

Salvo, J., and Ortiz, R. (1992). *The Newest New Yorkers*. New York: City of New York Department of City Planning (DCP 92-16).

U.S. Bureau of the Census. (1990). *Persons of Hispanic Origin in the United States*, CP-3-3. Washington, DC: U.S. Government Printing Office.

U.S. Bureau of the Census. (1990). *Persons of Hispanic Origin in the United States*. Census of Population and Housing, Subject Summary Tape File (SSTF)3. Washington, DC: U.S. Government Printing Office.

U.S. Bureau of the Census. (1993). *Hispanic Americans Today*. Washington, DC: U.S. Government Printing Office.

Valenzuela, A. (1991). "Hispanic Poverty: Is It an Immigrant Problem?" *Journal of Hispanic Policy* 5:59–84.

Winkelman, M. (1993). *Ethnic Relations in the U.S. A Sociohistorical Cultural Systems Approach*. Minneapolis/St. Paul: West Publishing.

Yang, P. (1994). "Ethnicity and Naturalization." *Ethnic and Racial Studies* 17:593–618.

LAURIS MCKEE

EGYPTIAN COPTS

The name "Copt" is traditionally used to refer to the Christian inhabitants of Egypt, descendants of the ancient Egyptians. It is derived from the Egyptian Het-ka-Ptah, or the divine house of the *ka* (spirit) of Ptah, a name of the principal sanctuary in northern Egypt in ancient times. The name was adopted by the Greeks, who transformed it into Aigytos. With the coming of Arabs in the seventh century C.E., the term was Arabized to Gipt/Qipt. Toward the end of the sixteenth century C.E. European travelers, in their quest for manuscripts from Coptic monasteries in Egypt, revised the term to Copt.

Aside from some ethnic mixing with Syrians, Lebanese, and Armenians who lived in Egypt and shared the Christian faith of the Copts, the Copts have kept ethnically separate. Otherwise they would have lost their religion to the majority Egyptian Muslims who surround them.

Egyptian Copts (also known as Egyptian Christians and Coptic Orthodox) are identified by being Christian and for the most part Orthodox. Since 451 C.E., they have existed apart from Greek

Orthodox, Roman Catholics, and other Christians for political and religious reasons. Socially they are characterized by being diligent and upwardly mobile, with higher than average education and success in private enterprise. This has been how the Copts have dealt with the oppressive attitude to which they have been repeatedly subjected by the Muslim majority since the seventh century C.E.

Immigration History

The Copts have always been loyal to Egypt for religious and ethnic reasons. They have considered Egypt to be Umm Al-Duniah (Mother of the World). Traditionally this made their travel outside its borders rare and short, but things changed after the 1952 Nasser revolution, which abolished the monarchy and instituted a socialist republic. This political change brought land reform, and the gentry lost their social power. Wealthy Christians stood to lose more by their financial downfall than their Muslim counterparts. The financial security that buffered them from the oppressive practices of the Muslims was gone. This prompted some of these families to send their children abroad, seeking a better life. In the mid-1950s, many went to Europe, but some made their way to the United States. These early immigrants settled for the most part in the New York–New Jersey area in the East, and southern California in the West.

This first wave was joined, though slowly, by other members of the Coptic gentry class and others who enrolled in American universities and pursued academic and other professional careers. Such opportunities were rarely available to them in Egypt because of their minority status. The newcomers settled wherever the academic opportunity was available. So in addition to the previously mentioned areas, they settled in the Midwest as well as the South.

Following the 1967 Arab-Israeli War, educated Copts of all classes and ages found limited opportunities in Egypt, so they turned toward new lands of opportunity—the United States, Canada, and Australia. This immigration wave was orderly and legal. As the cream of the crop applied to become a productive part of a society other than that of their ancestors, the U.S. government admitted the cream of that cream. This occurred from 1967 to 1971. This more substantial group tended to settle mostly where the early settlers of their community went—New York–New Jersey and southern California. However, other individuals settled in Illinois, Michigan, Florida, Texas, Ohio, and other places.

Around 1972, another major wave of Coptic immigration occurred. This time it was organized under the auspices of the World Council of Churches, Catholic Missionary Services, and others. This wave came by way of Lebanon, the only Middle Eastern country with a ruling Christian government. Copts were granted visas as refugees fleeing from religious (Islamic) persecution in Egypt. The composition of this wave was more varied. It included blue-collar craftsmen as well as university graduates. It also included Muslim families who had converted to Christianity but who never would have been allowed to leave for America directly from Egypt. They settled in the same geographical districts as the previous waves.

By 1973 and thereafter, those immigrants became U.S. citizens. They then applied for permanent residence for other members of their families: parents, siblings, uncles, aunts, cousins, nephews, and nieces. Constantly worsening conditions for the Copts in Egypt guaranteed a steady flow of immigrants. The majority of the immigrants came from the major cities of Cairo and Alexandria.

Demography and Settlement History

The number of Copts is not accurately known, because most statistics do not distinguish them from Muslim Egyptians. In the 1970 U.S. Census, however, Copts were estimated to be about 25,000 of the 31,358 Egyptian immigrants recorded. Estimates in the mid-1990s range as high as 265,000. Those twenty to forty-five years of age constitute the majority of this population. Copts less than fifteen years of age are the second largest group. Those forty-five to sixty and fifteen to twenty years of age are about equal in number, while those more than sixty years old are about 5 percent of the total. The male-majority population of the early immigrants has dwindled to probably a simple majority. The birth- and deathrates are not currently known, but judging by the numbers of baptisms versus funerals in Coptic churches in the United States, the birthrate is much higher.

The distribution of Copts in the United States is substantially the same as it was in the early 1970s. The major areas of concentration, according to the number and size of Coptic churches are New York–New Jersey and southern California, with 40 to 50 percent of the total between them. Other areas of concentration are Illinois, Michigan, Ohio, Pennsylvania, Texas, and Florida. Smaller numbers are found in Massachusetts, Rhode Island, Virginia, Wisconsin, Minnesota, Maryland, Washington, Arizona, and Connecticut. Small pockets of Copts, accounting for less then 5 percent of the total, are scattered in many other states.

Language

The Coptic language, relegated to secondary status among the group, is used mainly in liturgical services of the Coptic churches in the United States. However, a few families speak Coptic in the home.

Arabic is the language spoken by the group in Egypt and is generally used in their homes in the United States. American-born children of immigrants speak English predominantly in and out of the home. Children who immigrated with their parents are more bilingual. Those fifteen to forty-five years of age are the most bilingual of the group. The majority of older members in that age category tend to retain a distinctive accent, especially if they arrived after 1967. Older members of those forty-five to sixty use more Arabic than English in the home, and their accent is heavier. Those over sixty years speak Arabic with little or no English for the most part. The presence of Coptic churches with liturgical services in Arabic keeps the Arabic language alive.

Cultural Characteristics

The Coptic community in the United States has a high percentage of professionals and university graduates. This results from their traditional belief that they can succeed only if they achieve the highest level of education. Families are closely knit, monogamous, and keep close to their roots in Egypt. Their social activities are for the most part associated with the Coptic churches, which function as the major focus for the community, with the priest leading.

The high professional level of the group affords its members adequate health coverage. If insurance or government cannot help, the church can aid through the many established physicians among its members. Respiratory and coronary diseases are common among those over forty-five due to the fat-rich Middle Eastern diet coupled with heavy smoking among many in that age category. Community work is restricted to social welfare and religious activities. Cultural or arts activities do not mix well with the overwhelmingly religious atmosphere that binds the group. This makes political activities very difficult to start. Virtually no elected official at any level of government belongs to the Coptic community. However, increasing numbers of Copts are getting involved in the voting process and attempt to elect members from among them to political offices. Several Arabic-English newspapers are published by members of the group. There are also a few lay religious organizations to preserve the mainly religious heritage of the community.

Assimilation and Cultural Persistence

Assimilation of Egyptian Copts into American society has been slow and partial. Mastery of spoken English has not been easy for those over twenty-four years old. This, along with their mostly dark complexion has made them stand out as foreigners, though not of any particular group. First-generation immigrants did not usually marry outside their group but were at ease with others from the Middle East, Latinos, and Filipinos because of shared traditional values (e.g., the dominant role of males, close family ties, respect for elders, and strong religious affiliation). Second and subsequent generations have been more receptive to marriage with other ethnic groups, though many have chosen to marry within their own group.

Copts in general have kept away from Muslims, especially Egyptian Muslims, because of the ill treatment they were subjected to in their homeland on religious grounds. They have tended to keep socially within their own group if their number was large enough in one region to make this possible. They do not have a history of open complaint about discrimination against them in the United States, especially since the signing of the 1979 Camp David peace accords between Egypt and Israel.

See also: EGYPTIAN MUSLIMS

Bibliography

Assad, M. (1991). "Mission in the Coptic Orthodox Church—Perspective, Doctrine, and Practice." *International Review of Mission* 80:251–261.

Brown, L. G. ([1933] 1969). *Immigration: Cultural Conflicts and Social Adjustments.* New York: Arno.

Partrick, T. H. (1996). *Traditional Egyptian Christianity: A History of the Coptic Orthodox Church.* St. Cloud MN: North Star Press.

U.S. Bureau of the Census. (1994). *Statistical Abstract of the United States,* 114th edition. Washington, DC: U.S. Government Printing Office.

U.S. Department of Justice, Immigration and Naturalization Service. (1933–1977). *Annual Report of the Immigration and Naturalization Service.* Washington, DC: U.S. Government Printing Office.

U.S. Department of Justice, Immigration and Naturalization Service (1978). *Statistical Yearbook of the Immigration and Naturalization Service.* Washington, DC: U.S. Government Printing Office.

U.S. Department of Justice, Immigration and Naturalization Service. (1993). *Immigration and Naturalization Service Fact Book.* Washington, DC: U.S. Government Printing Office.

Watterson, B. (1988). *Coptic Egypt.* Edinburgh: Scottish Academic Press.

HANY N. TAKLA
MAGED S. MIKHAIL
MARK R. MOUSSA

EGYPTIAN MUSLIMS

Muslim Egyptian Americans come from the Arab Republic of Egypt, a nation located at the northeastern corner of Africa. Egypt is 386,000 square miles in area—larger than Texas but smaller than Alaska, and almost entirely arid except for the Nile River valley, which runs through the country from south to north. The Nile Valley comprises only about 15,000 square miles—4 percent of Egypt's surface area—and is about twice the size of New Jersey. Ninety-nine percent of Egypt's population of fifty-eight million live in this area. By comparison, New Jersey, one of the most densely populated states in the United States, has a population of nearly eight million. But even this comparison understates the crowdedness of Egyptian cities, particularly the capital, Cairo. Close to half of Egypt's population is urban, and approximately eleven million—one-fifth of the total population (unofficial estimates claim even more)—live in Greater Cairo. This concentration of population makes Egypt as a whole one of the most densely populated countries in the world, and Cairo (the point of origin for most Egyptian immigrants to the United States) one of the most densely populated urban areas.

As a group Muslim Egyptians refer to themselves, in their own language, as Egyptians (Misriyeen), as Muslims (Muslimeen), or in some situations as Arabs (Arab). None of these self-appellations is mutually exclusive. Egypt's national identity is complex. Geographically Egypt is African, but modern Egyptians do not see themselves as having strong cultural links to sub-Saharan Africa. In cultural terms modern Egypt is oriented toward the Arabic-speaking world, including the Levant, the Arabian Peninsula, the Persian Gulf, and Arab North Africa. Cultural links to these places are primarily religious and linguistic; the majority populations in all these countries are Muslim, usually Sunni (as is Egypt) rather than Shi'a (various groups that adhere to a different variant of Islamic doctrine than Sunnis), and all are Arabic-speaking. Egypt is 90 to 94 percent Muslim, the rest being primarily Coptic Christian.

Although Egypt's Muslim and Arabic-speaking character aligns it with the Arab world, there are also unique elements of Egyptian identity. The Nile River valley is a more geographically distinct area than in most other Arab countries. Egyptians are well aware of the environmental bond created by their common orientation to the river. Historical continuity back to pharaonic times is both a source of pride and a pillar of official nationalist ideology. Orthodox religious practices of Egyptian Muslims are very similar to those of other orthodox Muslims, including, minimally, profession of faith in one God, daily prayer, almsgiving, fasting during the Islamic month of Ramadan, and pilgrimage to Mecca for those who are able. However, the popular religious practices of Egyptians are highly distinctive, particularly in their carnival-esque celebrations of Muslim saints' birthdays known as *mulids*. Literate Egyptians learn a modernized version of classical (seventh to tenth century C.E.) Arabic, which is shared by all literate Arabs. However, spoken Egyptian Arabic is distinct from other Arabic vernaculars and forms a potent element of national identity. Cairo has historically been the most important center for radio, film, and television production in the Arab world, and Egyptians have often proved more willing to use their distinctive spoken vernacular in the new media than have other Arab states. In summary, while Egyptians can and sometimes do define their identity in terms of connections to coreligionists or other Arabic-speakers, such identification is highly contextual. Egyptian iden-

tity can be subsumed by Islamic or Arab culture, or distinguished from either or both.

Emigration

Historically, emigration from Egypt has been quite low. This has sometimes been attributed to a fierce attachment to the land. Egypt has, until recently, been primarily an agricultural society and strongly dependent on the Nile. Also, for much of the twentieth century there have been relatively few economic pressures favoring emigration. At the turn of the century Egypt had a population of about ten million living on substantially the same arable territory in the Nile River valley that the current population of fifty-eight million occupies. Until the 1980s, when population increase dramatically outstripped agricultural production, Egypt was self-sufficient in most of its basic food

An Egyptian man and his child participate in singing patriotic songs as part of a U.S. citizenship ceremony. (UPI/Corbis-Bettmann)

crops. Also, within the Arab world Egypt was a pioneer in developing modern institutions. Like most of the non-Western world, Egypt's modern history included European occupation (by England, from 1882 to 1952). Despite the inevitable underdevelopment that accompanied forced dependence on Europe, Egypt was unusually successful in establishing modern educational and economic institutions on its own soil. By the time of independence from England, Egypt's role in the regional economy was to supply technical and professional expertise to less-developed Arab countries. Under such conditions pressure for Egyptians to emigrate was relatively light.

The volume of Egyptian emigration began to change in the 1960s. Political repression and large-scale economic nationalization carried out by the regime of President Gamal Abdel Nasser resulted in some increase in emigration—primarily wealthy Egyptians who were threatened by Nasser's nationalizations, or who had been closely identified with the previous English-backed regime. The Nasser government balanced its unfavorable policies toward members of the old regime by guaranteeing jobs to all college graduates. Between expansion of the public sector and a generally restrictive policy on emigration, few Egyptians aside from those who were out of favor with the Nasser government were able to leave or, indeed, wanted to leave.

The turning point in Egyptian emigration was 1967, when Egypt suffered a catastrophic military defeat at the hands of Israel. That year was a psychological watershed for Egypt. The military debacle and an ensuing war of attrition, culminating in another massive war in 1973, caused enormous economic and social dislocation, which undoubtedly contributed to the desire of some Egyptians to emigrate. After the 1973 war, conditions became far more favorable for emigration. The early 1970s saw a shift in regional power away from Egypt and toward the petroleum-rich Persian Gulf states. Gulf capital acted as a magnet to all classes of Egyptians. By 1974, the Egyptian government was no longer able to provide work for college graduates and was unable, or unwilling, to expand the private sector to absorb excess labor. Bowing to the inevitable, the government lifted restrictions on labor emigration dating from the Nasser era. The trickle of emigration quickly turned into a flood.

Egyptian immigrants to the oil-rich states of the Middle East dwarfs that to the United States and Europe. Estimating the total size of any immigrant/ethnic group in the United States is problematic because of the difficulty in counting the offspring of immigrants. The United States has no census category for Arabs; therefore, children born in America of Arab parents simply disappear from official statistics. The problem in counting Arab Americans is exacerbated by wide differences in the degree to which groups identify with the country of origin after the first generation. The *Statistical Abstract of the United States, 1993,* estimates that between 1961 and 1991 a total of seventy-nine thousand Egyptians immigrated legally to the United States (by comparison, the total number of Egyptians estimated to have been working abroad in a single year peaked in 1983 at more than three million). Estimates for the total Arab-American population of the United States vary from eight hundred thousand to two million. The numbers are derived by extrapolating from immigration data to account for natural increase in the community. Since other Arab groups in the United States have much deeper historical roots than the Egyptian community—back to the mid-nineteenth century in some cases—one may assume that the natural increase in the size of the Egyptian community has been comparatively small. Furthermore, Egyptians, unlike other Arab immigrants to the United States, show little propensity for "chain migration" (migration to places where kin have already been living for some time), which makes the Egyptian community more diffuse and harder to count than other Arab communities.

Egyptian immigration to the United States is much more likely to be described as a "brain drain" than as a labor immigration. Most Egyptians who immigrated to the United States are well educated, work in professional occupations (such as engineering, medicine, or computer science), and are urban (mostly from Cairo). Those who go to Persian Gulf states must be satisfied with temporary work, since Persian Gulf states' attitude toward permanent immigration is extremely negative. By contrast, Egyptians who immigrate legally to the United States can and generally do stay. U.S. immigration law, which favors professionals, helps to reinforce the number of educated Egyptians among the relatively small number of Egyptian immigrants.

The majority of the Egyptian immigrants to the United States are Christian rather than Muslim, even though the proportion of Christians in Egypt's population is quite small. Part of the reason for this is that Christians, while on average somewhat more prosperous than the Muslim population as a whole, are nonetheless informally blocked from access to the highest levels of institutional power. An increase in religiously motivated politics since the 1970s (a phenomenon that affects both the Muslim and the Christian communities) has also made the position of Christians in Egypt appear less tenable. Furthermore, it is both easier and in some ways more feasible socially for Muslims to work in the Persian Gulf than for Christians. Consequently many Muslims in the first generation of Egyptian labor emigration who might have had the means and the required level of education to immigrate to the United States have chosen the Gulf instead. Demographers, however, suggest that the character of Egyptian emigration is changing rapidly and that the future will bring an increase in Egyptian immigration to the United States. Cairene elites of both religions—the group most likely to be able to immigrate to the United States—now express a preference for immigrating to North America or Europe rather than to the Persian Gulf. The generation of Egyptians who began emigrating in the 1970s and 1980s has essentially "broken the ice," and the younger generation fully intends to follow in their footsteps, although not necessarily to the Persian Gulf, whose countries have proven less hospitable to coreligionists in practice than in theory and have begun replacing Egyptian and Arab labor

with nationals or with more compliant labor from the Indian subcontinent. The trend, therefore, is toward greater Egyptian immigration to the United States and a higher proportion of Muslim immigration than has historically been the case.

Community Life in America

Most Egyptian immigrants live in large metropolitan areas such as Washington, D.C., Chicago, New York, or Los Angeles. Community life for many Egyptian Muslims centers around mosques, which occasionally cater to a single national community but need not do so. Egyptian Muslims also participate in nonsectarian Egyptian organizations, particularly in New Jersey, New York (especially Brooklyn), and Maryland. However, some of these organizations are primarily Christian. There are no Egyptian neighborhoods on the order of, for example, the Arab community of Dearborn, Michigan, where as many as two hundred thousand Arab Americans (few of them of Egyptian origin) live in a relatively compact area. Dearborn is sufficiently Arab that many of the signs on local businesses are written in Arabic. Parts of New Jersey and New York are the most likely candidates for eventually attracting enough Egyptian immigrants to constitute a Dearborn-like Arab community, but as a rule the Egyptian community is spatially diffuse and maintains whatever coherence it has through a communications and transportation infrastructure. Computer technology is becoming an increasingly important means of knitting together far-flung members of the community.

The social organization of Muslim Egyptian immigrants bears many similarities to that of Christian Egyptians. Family structure is essentially nuclear, closely knit, and patriarchal. Families in Egypt give greater emphasis to connectivity with cousins and other extended kinship networks than do Egyptian families living in America. This is at least partly due to the educational requirements for immigration to the United States, which emphasize the professional qualifications of individuals over family networks. In both Egypt and America, neighbors can provide physical and moral

Two Egyptian Muslim cousins stand in front of their family-owned-and-operated deli in Long Island City, New York. (Kathleen Butler/William Kavanah)

support that is formally expected of kin. Like many other Middle Easterners, Egyptians sometimes express a theoretical preference for marriage to children of the father's brother. However, real marriages do not often conform to the stated preference. Cousin marriage — both real and theoretical — is less emphasized among educated Egyptians than among the less educated and rare among children born to immigrants. The incidence of marriage to non-Egyptian or non-Muslim Americans is high and is another factor that makes estimating the total size of the community difficult. The rate of intermarriage is far higher for men than for women because Muslim men can marry non-Muslim women, with the understanding that the children are to be raised Muslim, whereas Muslim women are prohibited from marrying outside the faith.

Egyptian immigrants are not a physically marked group within American society. Although a long robelike garment called a *galabiyya* might be characterized as the national dress, very few educated Egyptians wear one in public in Egypt or America. Skin color and facial features of Egyptians vary, in America ethnic terms, from black (African American) to Caucasian. In consequence, Egyptians' physical appearance is ambiguous in terms of American racial stereotypes. The typically high educational attainment of Egyptian immigrants (including, in many cases, facility in English) also militates against the most overt manifestations of American racial stereotyping.

Egyptians encounter few overt barriers to assimilation. There are, however, significant caveats to the ease with which Egyptian Muslims assimilate into American society.

Assimilation and Cultural Persistence

It is increasingly common for Egyptian Muslim immigrants to prefer to maintain an identity distinct from what they see as mainstream American society. Many Egyptians regard certain aspects of American society with suspicion. Egyptian mass media portray American society as highly commercialized, alienating, amoral, and secular to the point of sacrilegiousness. Although many Egyptians, both immigrants and in Egypt, express admiration for the personal freedom afforded by American society, they also insist on drawing a line between freedom and what they view as mere licentiousness. Immigrants fully intend to resist those aspects of American life that they see as crossing into licentiousness, and while the reality of American society may not conform to media imagery, many immigrants arrive with preconceptions that are not entirely favorable. Parents, in particular, are likely to display a concern for raising children who are not overly "Americanized." The results of such efforts to resist what are perceived to be threatening aspects of "Americanization," however, are highly unpredictable. Older and younger generations of immigrants inevitably have differences of opinion on what "Americanization" means.

An even greater problem is that assimilation for Egyptian Muslim immigrants requires that they suppress both Arab and Muslim identity. Among other Middle Easterners suppression of Arab identity by Egyptians is possible, and Muslim identity, in the absence of large numbers of non-Muslims, is not an issue. But in an American context suppression of Arab and especially Muslim identity is unacceptable to many immigrants. Americans in general are much more likely to associate Egypt with pharaonic civilization than with Arab society, and while Egyptians do not necessarily deny their cultural continuity with ancient Egypt, they are nonetheless well aware of the links between their

society and Arab culture. Prejudice against Arabs is extreme in American society. Furthermore, American prejudice against Arabs often emphasizes religion, which is the most unproblematic and undisputed element of shared Muslim Egyptian and Arab identity. The American media, in particular, commonly make ludicrously simplistic equations of terrorism, militant religious extremism, and Islam. Consequently, when an incident such as the bombing of the World Trade Center in New York City in 1993 happens — an incident that did involve Egyptians and Muslims — the media treat it as typical of the entire Muslim community, even though most Muslims condemned the action. The American media do not extrapolate group character from atrocities committed in the name of religion for any other faith. Such terms as "Christian terrorist" or "Jewish terrorist" are nonexistent in American media language, even though terrorism has been committed in the name of Christianity and Judaism, just as it has been committed in the name of Islam. "Muslim terrorist" or "Islamic terrorism," however, are exceedingly common terms in the American media. A particularly noteworthy example of media distortion came in the aftermath of the Oklahoma City bombing in 1995. The Muslim and Arab community was tried and convicted by the media within hours. The World Trade Center incident and its Egyptian and Muslim perpetrators were often invoked in this swift media trial. But when later investigations revealed no Middle Eastern connection, there were few, if any, public apologies to justifiably offended Muslims. One result of systematic and egregious distortion of Islam in the American media is that American Muslim immigrants, including Egyptians, feel duty bound to defend their religion.

Aside from the extreme bias of American media against Islam, it is also true that the intensification of religious identification among Muslims parallels a similar phenomenon in other faiths throughout the world since the mid-1970s. It is inevitable that Egyptian-American Muslims would be affected by this tendency regardless of any media distortions or social pressures exerted by their adopted country. In Egypt many participants in Islamic cultural, political, and social groups (which are no more predisposed to violence than, for example, American high-school Bible-study clubs or the Chabad-Lubavitch movement) work in the technical professions. The technical professions are also heavily represented among Egyptian immigrants to the United States, which suggests that an emphasis on Islamic identity among Egyptian immigrants is both sociologically rooted and unsurprising.

See also: AFRICAN MUSLIMS; EGYPTIAN COPTS

Bibliography

Abu-Laban, S. (1989). "The Coexistence of Cohorts: Identity and Adaptation Among Arab-American Muslims." *Arab Studies Quarterly* 11(2–3):45–63.

Araby, Kadri, M. G. el-, and Arafat, I. S. (1977). "Egyptian Muslims." In *The New Jersey Ethnic Experience,* edited by B. Cunningham. Union City, NJ: Wm. H. Wise.

Haddad, Y. (1991). *The Muslims of America.* New York: Oxford University Press.

Kayal, P. (1987). "Counting the 'Arabs' Among Us." *Arab Studies Quarterly* 9(1):98–104.

Keck, L. (1989). "Egyptian Americans in the Washington, DC, Area." *Arab Studies Quarterly* 11(2–3):103–126.

McCarus, E., ed. (1994). *The Development of Arab-American Identity.* Ann Arbor: University of Michigan Press.

Metz, H. C. (1991). *Egypt: A Country Study.* Washington, DC: Federal Research Division, Library of Congress.

Nasr, S. H. (1993). *A Young Muslim's Guide to the Modern World.* Chicago: Kazi.

Sayyid-Marsot, A. L. (1985). *A Short History of Modern Egypt.* New York: Cambridge University Press.

Sell, R. (1990). "International Migration Among Egyptian Elites: Where They've Been; Where They're Going." *Journal of Arab Affairs* 9(2):147–176.

Shaheen, J. (1984). *The TV Arab.* Bowling Green, Ohio: Bowling Green State University Popular Press.

Terry, J. (1985). *Mistaken Identity: Arab Stereotypes in Popular Writing.* Washington, DC: American-Arab Affairs Council.

U.S. Department of Commerce. (1993). "Immigrants by Country of Birth." In *Statistical Abstract of the United States, 1993.* Washington, DC: U.S. Bureau of the Census.

WALTER ARMBRUST

ENGLISH

England, the homeland of the English, is unlike Scotland, Wales, or Northern Ireland because it does not constitutionally exist; it has no separate rights, administration, or official statistics. The Church of England is its main distinctive institution. The English in England maintain their separate identity in sports (soccer, cricket, and rugby) and heritage, which are manifest in the monarchy, aristocracy and associated pageantry, Parliament, pride in their country, and love for their local community (with the local pub being an integrating institution). Also, English poetry, prose literature, and art are distinctive.

Although there are a lot of similarities, English culture differs from that of the United States in that the English place greater emphasis on maintaining traditions, self-restraint, control of aggression, discipline, insularity from Continental Europe and other cultures, and pride in their ability to deal rationally with diverse situations.

In the United States, an English person is one who has emigrated from or traces ancestral roots to England, even if the ancestry is not exclusively English. Unlike American ethnicity, which is based on the concept of soil (because of the inherent definition of the United States as an immigrant nation), English ethnicity is based on the concept of blood. In other words one had to trace one's blood or ancestry to those who claimed to be and were accepted as being racially English.

Immigrants from England have a unique place among the ethnic communities in America because their initial and ongoing cultural influence has been pervasive. Because English culture has survived as the base of U.S. culture, a unity has been maintained in spite of the cultural diversity resulting from immigration. Specifically, English culture forms the basis for U.S. society and culture in terms of language, literature, social customs, law, and political thought.

In addition to the English cultural concepts that contributed to the early success of the United States, people of English descent such as George Washington, John Adams, and Benjamin Franklin contributed directly by signing the Declaration of Independence and providing leadership for the drafting of the U.S. Constitution and Bill of Rights.

English culture continues to exert its influence, if somewhat less obviously, on American society. For example, WASP (white Anglo-Saxon Protestant) continues to connote traditional wealth and power, and assimilation to U.S. culture is still referred to as "Anglo-conformity." Some, like the "Boston Brahmins," take special pride in their English ancestry and the contribution their English ancestors have made to the growth and development of the United States, but the English-based foundation is being challenged by the ideology of multiculturalism.

Immigration and Settlement History

England constitutes the largest land area and has the highest population density of any of the four units of the United Kingdom. It is also the most intensely industrialized region. Located off the western coast of Continental Europe, it is bounded on the north by Scotland and on the west by Wales. Geographically, England constitutes 50,332 square miles, or 53 percent of the land area of the United Kingdom.

Other than the Native Americans, the English were the first to settle what is now the United States. They established the first permanent colony at Jamestown in 1607; other early settlements were at Plymouth and Massachusetts Bay in 1620–1622. Many immigrated to obtain cheap land and avail themselves of better economic opportunities, although others were looking for religious freedom. Most colonies came under royal control, established the Church of England, and had the English system of law, governmental administration, education, commerce, financial management, agriculture, arts, and entertainment.

Three settlements emerged as social models: Pennsylvania, where all white Europeans would be welcomed on equal terms; Massachusetts, where the "religiously pure" would be accepted; and the Virginia structure, where a plantation economy based on cheap workers, especially slaves, developed. The Pennsylvania model eventually became the basis for the U.S. Constitution and American society.

The settlements in southern New England, with their emphasis on Puritan ethics and conformity, possessed a zeal for democracy, a passion for education, and an intention for their values to be the values of the entire nation. Divergence was more characteristic of the indentured workers and relatives of indentured workers who lived in the settlements of the Tidewater region of Virginia and Maryland. However, tobacco dominated the economy of these middle Atlantic settlements, making the settlers dependent on the English market and perpetuating their ties to the homeland. The settlements of Pennsylvania emphasized "acceptance," creating a greater heterogeneity among their population. The distinctive traits of these three original settlement regions followed their residents who moved west. New Englanders migrated across New York and through northern Ohio to form settlements in Michigan, Wisconsin, northern Indiana, and northern Illinois. The Tidewater people moved across Pennsylvania to southern Illinois and down into the hill country of Kentucky and Tennessee. Pennsylvanians followed a similar pattern, moving into southern Indiana and Illinois.

Initially, single men were sent to America by the Virginia Company to find gold (which did not materialize) and create a profitable trade. By the late 1620s, agriculture and tobacco-raising stabilized and became profitable, while England began to suffer economically, all of which resulted in several thousand individuals immigrating annually, a stream that included women and children. In the Chesapeake to Charleston region, indentured servants trained as farmers, tradesmen, laborers, and craftsmen were the primary immigrants. Indentured servants who brought their families to or joined their families in America were likely to remain. But the indenture system was

Delegates to the Second Continental Congress in Philadelphia in 1776 sign the Declaration of Independence, stating the separation of the thirteen American colonies from England. (Library of Congress/Corbis)

gradually replaced by slavery, which provided cheaper labor.

In 1690, 90 percent of the seaboard colonies were English by birth, and in the 1790 U.S. Census, 60 percent of the population of that region had English names.

Between the American Revolution and 1825, England's involvement in India, Latin America, and the War of 1812 ("America's Second War of Independence") contributed to a reduction in English immigration. Also, it was a period when London restricted the number of English craftsmen and settlers each ship could transport to America. Except for the period during the U.S. Civil War, however, English immigration increased steadily after 1825 and peaked in the 1880s. Family units became more prominent in the immigration stream after 1835. English immigration increased to 60,000 a year by the 1860s and rose to 75,000

annually in 1872, after which it began to decline. This wave that began in the 1820s was largely due to unrest in England caused by tenant farmers and urban laborers fleeing depressed areas affected by industrial changes. Although some people had dreams of a utopian society, most were attracted by new land, textile factories, railroads, and the expanding mining industry. By the end of the nineteenth century, the middle Atlantic states had the largest number of English Americans, followed by the north-central states and New England. However, a growing number were moving to the West, the Pacific Coast, and the South.

Despite the fact that England was the largest investor in American land development, railroads, mining, cattle ranching, and heavy industry throughout the nineteenth century, the English comprised only 15 percent of the great nineteenth-century European immigration to America. In fact, of those who left England between 1820 and 1920, only 10 percent went to America. During the first four decades of the twentieth century, English immigration declined to 6 percent of the total influx because there were better economic opportunities and favorable immigration policies in Australia and Canada. The percentage of skilled workers and professionals entering the United States, however, increased dramatically. It was a time when English culture, literature, and family connections were desired—the marriage of wealthy Americans to English aristocrats was well publicized, and colleges and universities emphasized America's English heritage in history and literature courses.

During the Great Depression of the 1930s, more English returned than entered the United States, although it was a time when more English women entered than men. The decline reversed in the decade after World War II, when more than 100,000 people, many of them war brides, entered the United States. This was less than 12 percent of the European influx. In the 1960s, the term "brain drain" was coined to refer to the outflow of English engineers, technicians, medical professionals, and other specialists being lured to America by large corporations. Thus, since 1970, partly due to the implementation of the Immigration Act of 1965, English immigrants have been about 12 percent of the total flow arriving from Europe. These individuals, usually unmarried and professionally trained, have, like their predecessors, continued to merge almost imperceptibly into American society. This is true not only because of their cultural compatibility but also because the immigration stream is dominated by professionals, managers, and technically skilled people who have found good jobs in metropolitan areas.

Demography

A total of 25,836,397 Americans claim English as their first ancestry, and 10,819,382 claim it as their second ancestry; in 1980, a total of 23,748,772 claimed it as their single ancestry. The type of immigrant has changed over the years.

Initially settlers were primarily single males, with a large number being indentured laborers. In the nineteenth century, families and technically skilled individuals became more prominent. It was a time when there was a push factor of poor economic conditions and social unrest in England and the pull of opportunities in the United States. As of the mid-1990s, the highest percentage of English settlers is found in the counties of the Appalachian Mountains, especially in Tennessee, Kentucky, and southwestern Virginia. The English are the third-largest ethnic group in the United States (after the Germans and the Irish). The southeastern region of the United States has the largest number of people claiming English descent, while California, Texas, Florida, New York, and Ohio host the largest number of English Americans among individual states.

Language

When English immigrants arrive in the United States, they enter a country where the national language is the same as their own: English. The English language is of the Indo-European family. Its parent tongue is the West Germanic group of Proto-Indo-European. The nearest related languages are German, Netherlandic, and Frisian. There is considerable dialectal variation, the most distinctive in England being in Lancashire, Cornwall, and parts of East London.

English spoken by recent immigrants from England is identifiable by the accent. The accent, however, is largely lost after several decades in the United States. The greater distinction between English spoken in England and that spoken in the United States has to do with several hundred vocabulary words. Some of the differences include petrol for gas, crisps for potato chips, and ring off for hanging up the telephone.

Cultural Characteristics

The English are indistinguishable from the mainstream of American white society. Besides, American culture is based on English values and institutions; thus American institutions and behavioral patterns are similar to those of the comparable class in England. As a result, adjustment to life in the United States for English immigrants is minimal. They do not form residential enclaves, nor are their houses or lifestyle noticeably different from other Americans of a comparable class. The English in America do not have visible symbols that distinguish them from mainstream American society.

During the nineteenth and early twentieth centuries, English immigrants tended to be technically trained or agriculturalists. Most worked in industry. Small groups of English skilled workers in industrial and mining communities in the East and Midwest did attempt to form labor unions, but the unions were generally short-lived. During the post–World War II period, especially after the Immigration Act of 1965 was implemented, English immigrants were not numerous—in fact, the quota from England was seldom filled—but they were generally highly skilled and technically trained. Their contribution to the quality of life and the high technological position of the United States was and is very high.

English family life focuses on the nuclear family of husband, wife, and children, with an occasional relative living with them. This structure was set during the Colonial era. Even separatist groups, such as the Puritans, were comprised of nuclear families. In New England, laws such as Sunday "blue laws" were designed to sanctify the Sabbath by prohibiting drinking, dancing, and work-related activities on the Sabbath while at the same time encouraging prayer, charity, and missionary activities. Outside of New England, entertainment in the forms of dancing, sports, and singing were not only more prevalent but often were sponsored by the church. During the large waves of nineteenth-century immigration, English immigrants joined communities of other English in small towns and re-created the traditional pub as well as choral societies, sports clubs, self-help societies, and fraternal organizations.

Generally, women dominate the domestic and social life of the family as well as relations with friends and extended family. It is their role to maintain connections with relatives in England. Men control the business and public aspects of family life. This sexual division of duties in the English-American family has been decreasing since World War II, especially in the 1970s and 1980s, when the women's liberation movement gained a following in the United States. English-American women, like the rest of the American female population, joined in the cause of obtaining equal rights for females, which had the side effect of decreasing the sexual division of duties within the English-American family.

For most English immigrants, the church is central to their identity. Virtually all Christian religious denominations present in England are also present in the United States, and the liturgy and Scriptures are similar in both countries. Therefore, most English immigrants can practice the same form of religious expression in America that they practiced in England.

Another institution emphasized by the English immigrant is education. Many groups, including the Quakers and Puritans from England, advocate free public education for all. Professionals favor private schools and colleges; they also value sending their sons for a junior year abroad at a British university. Thus there are many endowments to subsidize education in England, the most famous being the Rhodes scholarship program.

Higher education has been a concern of English immigrants since the Colonial era. Thus a large percentage of early colleges in America were founded by British immigrants or their descendants, especially in New England and the Southeast. In many of these colleges, they emphasized traditional English sports such as sculling (team rowing) and rugby. However, three English aristocratic pastimes that enjoy the greatest popularity in America and have "become American" are tennis, horse racing, and sailing. Also, scattered throughout the United States are rugby, cricket, and English football (soccer) teams, where the uniquely English sports heritage is kept alive.

English immigrants and their descendants have included many leading philanthropists who have supported museums, colleges, medical soci-

A cricket match in Van Cortlandt Park in New York City illustrates the continued presence in America of an "English" sport. (Michael S. Yamashita/Corbis)

eties, cultural organizations, and academic exchange programs.

Assimilation

The English in the United States have become a "hidden community" in that they have not developed or maintained an identity that is distinctive from the mainstream of American society. In fact, since the beginning of the civil rights movement, the English have become more "hidden" because identifying with or being WASP (a derogatory term also used to imply being English) resulted in connotations of being a racist or an exploiter. Because they have blended so easily into the American mainstream, there is very little written about the English as an ethnic community.

See also: CORNISH; IRISH; SCOTCH-IRISH; SCOTS; WELSH

Bibliography

Berthoff, R. T. ([1953] 1968). *British Immigrants in Industrial America, 1790–1950*. New York: Russell & Russell.

Blumenthal, S. (1980). *Coming to America: Immigrants from the British Isles*. New York: Delacorte Press.

Boston, R. (1971). *British Chartist in America, 1830–1900*. Manchester, Eng.: University of Manchester Press.

Campbell, M. (1955). "English Emigration on the Eve of the American Revolution." *American Historical Review* 61:1–20.

Cohen, R. (1994). *Frontiers of Identity: The British and Others*. London: Longman.

Erickson, C. ([1972] 1990). *Invisible Immigrants: The Adaptation of English and Scottish Immigrants in 19th-Century America*. Ithaca, NY: Cornell University Press.

Johnson, S. C. ([1914] 1966). *A History of Emigration from the United Kingdom to North America, 1763–1912*. New York: E. P. Dutton.

Kirk, R. (1994). *America's British Culture.* New Brunswick, NJ: Transaction.

Noble, A. G., ed. (1992). *To Build a New Land: Ethnic Landscapes in North America.* Baltimore, MD: Johns Hopkins University Press.

Robertiello, R. C. (1988). *The WASP Mystique.* New York: Donald I. Fine.

Shepperson, W. S. (1957). *British Emigration to North America.* Minneapolis: University of Minnesota Press.

Shepperson, W. S. (1965). *Emigration and Disenchantment: Portraits of Englishmen Repatriated from the United States.* Norman: University of Oklahoma Press.

Snowman, D. (1977). *Britain and America: An Interpretation of Their Culture, 1945–1975.* New York: New York University Press.

Taylor, A. M. (1965). *Expectations Westward: The Mormons and the Emigration of Their British Converts in the 19th Century.* Ithaca, NY: Cornell University Press.

Yearly, C. K. (1957). *Britons in American Labor: A History of the Influence of United Kingdom Immigrants on American Labor, 1820–1914.* Baltimore, MD: John Hopkins University Press.

ARTHUR W. HELWEG

ERITREANS

See ETHIOPIANS AND ERITREANS

ESTONIANS

Estonians come from a country that is one of the Baltic group encompassing Latvia, Lithuania, and Estonia, on the eastern coast of the Baltic Sea and on the southern side of the Gulf of Finland. Estonia is the most northerly of the three Baltic countries, which are all bordered by the former USSR. The Estonian language belongs to the Balto-Finnic section of the Finno-Ugric language group, so called because of the two largest tribes that first inhabited Estonia, the Finns and the Hungarians.

The Estonians are an ethnic group by virtue of their language, religion, and national origin.

History

The thirteenth century marks the beginning of Estonia's struggles against conquerors. Under the pretext of Christianization, Swedes, Danes, the Teutonic Order of Knights, and Russians fought over the land. In 1227, Estonia was conquered and divided by the order, bishops, and Danes until it was dissolved in the sixteenth century. The Treaty of Altmark in 1629 gave Estonia to Sweden but left the resident German nobility with privileges in local government. During this time the University of Tartu was founded, the first books and grammars appeared, and every parish had a few schools.

In 1700, the Great Northern War broke out, causing Sweden to relinquish all its provinces on the eastern Baltic shore to Russia, and Estonia was divided in half. This war left ruin and devastation as well as isolation from the Western world. The peasantry fell into bondage that lasted until the middle of the nineteenth century.

The University of Tartu, which had been closed, reopened in 1802 as a Baltic-German cultural center. At this time nationalism was a phenomenon all over Europe, and Estonians asserted their rights. Those with higher education joined together in a cause that would lead to a national movement, part of which was the founding of the Estonian Learned Society in 1838. The activities of this group helped to influence a national awakening. Newspapers began to appear in addition to music festivals, which are a part of Estonian tradition to this day, despite government obstacles such as censureship under czarist rule and Soviet domination.

During this time, Russian authorities initiated a policy in the Baltic provinces aimed at Russification of their inhabitants. However, in spite of the many impositions experienced during the Russification period, the time between the Russian Revolution of 1905 and World War I in 1914 saw much economic and cultural growth. Industry, shipping, and commerce flourished and the number of those receiving a higher education rose considerably. Life for Estonians did not improve after the Bolshevik Revolution, but they worked hard to declare their independence. Unfortunately, this came at a time of impending occupation of Estonia by German forces.

The independence of the Republic of Estonia was proclaimed in Tallinn, the capital, in February 1918. German troops entered Tallinn the day after the proclamation, recognizing neither the independence of Estonia nor its government. However, the proclamation of independence proved to be a great moral force and helped shape Estonian attitudes during this period of German occupation. After Germany's defeat in November 1918, its occupation of Estonia collapsed, and power was turned over to Estonians, not Soviets.

Independence was short-lived. The Nonaggression Pact of 1939 between Germany and the then Soviet Union preceded the start of World War II. The Estonian government was forced to sign the Mutual Assistance Pact, resulting in complete Soviet occupation of Estonia. This pact also had been signed by Latvia and Lithuania. Life was not easy during this time, and mass deportations were evident. More than ten thousand people, including women, children, and the elderly, were herded into boxcars and sent to northern Russian and Siberian slave camps. Estonia was occupied by Germany in 1941 and then reoccupied by the Red Army in 1944.

However, rather than live under Stalinist repression, more than 100,000 Estonian citizens fled westward crossing the Baltic Sea in small fishing boats and motorboats. Thousands of these "Viking boat" refugees lost their lives during this flight through enemy action and crossing the stormy Baltic Sea.

Immigration

The first country to invite Estonians and other refugees after World War II was the United Kingdom; between 1947 and 1948 nearly six thousand Estonians were working in hospitals and undermanned industries there. Those who had to flee to chaotic Germany began to leave for Australia. The United States also opened its doors to displaced persons, and nearly eleven thousand Estonians found asylum there and in Canada.

The period from 1945 to 1952 saw the arrival of Estonian political exiles in the United States. Those arriving during this period had suffered through a year of Soviet rule in 1940–1941, followed by three years of German occupation and then Soviet reoccupation.

According to the 1990 U.S. Census statistics, more than twenty-five thousand people identified themselves as members of the "Estonian ancestry group," with at least one parent of Estonian origin, and more than sixteen thousand listed both parents as Estonians. Estonians can be found in almost every state, with heavy concentrations in New York, California, New Jersey, Illinois, Florida, Connecticut, and Ohio. A 1984 study of New Jersey Estonians revealed a settlement of nearly six hundred living in the Jackson area.

An Estonian family peels apples in their home near Jewett City, Connecticut, in 1942. (Library of Congress/ Corbis)

Employment

Estonians in exile were, with rare exception, forced to accept employment in manual work. The most tragic was the position of the intellectuals. University professors, artists, writers, musicians, journalists, teachers, clergymen, medically trained personnel, engineers, qualified technicians, and those who had occupied leading positions in economic life and politics had to find work in trades not previously considered. The Estonian communities in the United States and Canada found good opportunities for employment, however, mainly in manual labor. It was not uncommon for Estonians to be employed as maids, butlers, construction workers, bakers, dairy farmers, cooks, chauffeurs, or hotel workers.

Organizations

In all countries where they live, Estonians have founded central organizations that lead their social, educational, and national-cultural activities. The oldest and best known among these is the Estonian Committee, founded in 1944 in Sweden. In the United States the Estonian National Committee, the Estonian World Council, and the Committee for a Free Estonia have flourished. Similar organizations are found in Germany, Great Britain, Canada, and Australia. Close cooperation among these central organizations of Estonians in exile existed because the aim of all of them was the fight for the liberation of Estonia from foreign domination; this was finally achieved with the dissolution of the Soviet Union in 1991.

Education

Because of centuries of oppression and a desire to preserve their free national and cultural traditions, Estonians value education. Wherever Estonians sought refuge, Estonian schools were established within a few months after settlement. In the United States, supplementary schools have also been established to teach Estonian language, history, geography, and literature. Besides supplementary schools, virtually every Estonian congregation has its own Sunday school, which provides the Estonian children with instruction in both religion and Christian morality in their mother tongue.

Estonians have maintained a lifestyle closely aligned with the middle class in the United States. Because World War II had interrupted the educational aspirations held by Estonians who had to leave their studies behind, there is a determination by this group to obtain higher education and training to compete in the global workplace. Unlike other immigrant groups who arrived in the United States with little or no education, Estonian immigrants were members of a professional class. It is hard to find children in the second generation who have not upgraded themselves with some form of advanced education.

Language

Language for Estonians is a strong mechanism for identification and maintenance of identity. Estonian is often still spoken at home, and printed material in the language is supported. The language is necessary to participate in activities such as scouting, where the language is required. Because Estonians interact with each other in a more global way, the language is necessary for communication. Being able to read newspapers in the language keeps Estonians abreast of the latest political, social, and economic movements in the home country.

In many instances, religious services are still held in Estonian; in confirmation rites, both English and Estonian are used. Estonians espouse the teachings of the Evangelical Lutheran Church and the Apostolic-Orthodox Church.

Because the language for Estonians is still useful socially, for religious reasons, in interaction with friends and relatives, and for educational purposes, maintaining it for functional purposes is necessary. The language has provided a bond of unity among its speakers.

The Albany-Schenectady Estonian Society folk dance group performs in traditional costumes. (A. Merend/Estonian Archives)

Group Characteristics

Estonians exhibit a strong sense of self and belonging. A past history is shared and maintained through social, religious, and organizational structures. There is a strong tie to an ancestry, religion, and common language. Having an ethnic identity that is strong fortifies family foundations and causes individuals to consider themselves as more unique and less as one of the host crowd. Lives are conducted around their ethnic group. Parents who had to leave their homeland have made a conscious effort to transmit the culture to their children from their early childhood through adolescence and into adulthood, ensuring that the children would have a clear understanding of who they are in terms of Estonian ethnicity. Estonians have always had a pride in their heritage and did not go through periods of submerging their identity and then reidentifying with the culture. There is consistency in the degree and focus of maintaining their ethnic identity. Kinship and friendship networking patterns, common occupational positions, residential stability or ethnic neighborhoods or areas, and concentration and dependence on common institutions and services have reinforced the maintenance of this group.

Although it may appear to be a closed value system, it is not constraining on its members. There is room for individuals to make choices concerning movement away from the group for economic reasons or because of marriage outside the group.

Activities sponsored through Estonian clubs and groups reinforce the history through dance, music, and special holiday observances. Thus solidarity takes place on a continuing basis. These activities are important to the socialization experiences of the group and involve interaction with other Estonians from other states and countries, since annual festivals are held in the United States, Canada, and abroad.

Family factors appear to exert the most important influences on ethnic identity. Parents play a primary role in inculcating ethnic identity among children. Parents speak the language in the home and relay the customs and traditions associated with the group. Extended family situations foster language acquisition, and folk stories and songs are part of ethnic transmission.

Marital patterns of parents exert an influence in the direction of ethnic identity among their children. Marriage outside the group is not an issue now but may pose a problem in the future. Intermarriage rates for the Estonian group may be critical to the maintenance of ethnic identity and also may be critical for maintenance of the Lutheran faith within the group.

Assimilation

When Estonians first arrived in America, their first task was to begin building new lives for themselves and their families. Regardless of their background, education, and experience, the newcomers had to accept whatever employment was available. Through hard work and persistence, the newcomers soon established themselves in communities across the nation and began making significant contributions to local economies. Physically and culturally, Estonians are not dissimilar to others in the American middle class. While there is evidence to show that discrimination and prejudice in the host society against the foreign-born retard assimilation by forcing the group to retain ethnic social ties, this is minimal in the case of Estonians.

After the Estonians had secured themselves in their fields of employment and established their own homes, they involved themselves in local charitable, professional, political, and social fields.

Cultural Persistence

Estonians have maintained their ethnic identity through a past-oriented ethnicity based on ancestry and origin. No matter where Estonians are located, they share commonly held traditions. Language is a major component in the maintenance of a separate ethnic identity. It appears that the second generation has a strong sense of Estonian pride and identification. The transmission of ethnic values through religious, social, educational, and community orientation has been successful by first-generation Estonians. Those who left their dreams and aspirations in one country have effectively transmitted a full and rich ethnic identity to their offspring in their new country.

Bibliography

Parming, T. (1969). "The Second-Generation Hypothesis: An Appraisal." Ph.D. diss., Princeton University.

Pennar, J. (1975). *The Estonians in America, 1627–1975.* Dobbs Ferry, NY: Oceana.

Rank, G. (1976). *Old Estonia: The People and Culture.* Bloomington: Indiana University Press.

Raum, T. U. (1991). "The Reestablishment of Estonian Independence." *Journal of Byelorussian Studies* 22:251–257.

Raun, T. U. (1994). "Post-Soviet Estonia, 1991–1993." *Journal of Byelorussian Studies* 25:73–79.

Roos, A. (1993). *Introducing Estonia.* Tallinn, Estonia: Kommunaalprojekt.

M. ANN WALKO

ETHIOPIANS AND ERITREANS

Ethiopians and Eritreans are Afrcan immigrants from predominantly agrarian and pastoral societies whose semifeudal social structure remained intact until the 1974 revolution in Ethiopia. Eritrea was an Italian colony from 1889 to 1941. The British defeated the Italians during World War II and occupied Eritrea from 1941 to 1952. In 1952 the United Nations federated Eritrea with Ethiopia. Eritrea remained an autonomous but integral part of Ethiopia until 1991. Most Eritrean and Ethiopian immigrants arrived in the United States as refugees escaping from the terror, violence, torture, and persecution they experienced or feared they might experience in their homeland.

This fear was a product of the revolutionary military government run by the Armed Forces Coordinating Committee, commonly known as the Dergue (meaning "committee" in Amharic), which ruled Ethiopia from 1974 to 1991. In May 1991, a coalition of two antigovernment movements, the Ethiopian People's Revolutionary Democratic Front (EPRDF) and the Eritrean People's Liberation Front (EPLF), ended the Dergue's reign of terror. The thirty-year war for the independence of Eritrea from Ethiopian rule ended with the Eritrean nationalists defeating the Ethiopian army. On May 24, 1993, Eritrea officially declared its independence from Ethiopia. Soon after, it was admitted to the United Nations. In spite of this division in Africa, most Ethiopian and Eritrean immigrants in the United States share a common historical legacy: They claim descent from distinct people known as Abyssinians (Habesha). The Abyssinians are the core of the population in Ethiopia and a politically dominant group in Eritrea. They have considerable power in both Eritrea and Ethiopia. The Abyssinians in the United States are deeply aware of their long, unique cultural and ethnic history. They consider themselves both related to and separate from other Africans, as well as from African Americans.

Immigration and Settlement History

The first Ethiopian and Eritrean refugees to resettle in the United States legally were 169 refugees admitted in 1979 as seventh-preference immigrants. Until the passage of the Refugee Act of 1980, the U.S. government had no official policy of allowing Africans to enter the United States as refugees. After the enactment of the Refugee Act of 1980, the number of refugees increased dramatically. From 1976 to 1994, about 33,195 Ethiopian and Eritrean refugees resettled in the United States. In addition, there were around 4,643 Ethiopians and Eritreans granted asylum from 1980 to 1994. Of the 43,727 Africans allowed to enter the United States between 1982 and 1994 as refugees, the majority (around 68%) were Ethiopians and Eritreans. Although Ethiopians and Eri-

treans constituted the overwhelming majority of African refugees between 1980 and 1991 (the data from 1982 to 1991 show that about 93 percent of the African refugees were Ethiopians and Eritreans), other Africans, especially Somalis and Sudanese, began to enter the United States as refugees in large numbers in 1992. By 1994, the Somalis replaced Ethiopians and Eritreans as the largest of African refugees to resettle in the United States. Out of the 5,856 Africans admited to the United States in 1994, about 61 percent were Somali, around 21 percent were Sudanese, and only about 5.6 percent were Ethiopian and Eritrean.

Once they arrived in the United States, most of the refugees were resettled and assisted by nongovernmental agencies. A survey conducted in Washington, D.C., in 1984 reported nongovernmental resettlement agencies helped 85 percent of the Ethiopian and 95 percent of the Eritrean refugees. The U.S. Catholic Conference helped the largest number, 45 percent of both nationalities. The Church World Service aided 18 percent of the Ethiopians and 10 percent of the Eritreans. The U.S. government and its authorized resettlement agencies followed the dispersal model in the resettlement of refugees from Ethiopia and Eritrea. The major concentrations of resettled Ethiopian and Eritrean refugees were located in California, Washington, D.C., Maryland, Virginia, and Texas. Between 1983 and 1990, there were 16,157 Ethiopian and Eritrean refugees resettled in the United States. The initial resettlement of these refugees was as follows: 22.3 percent in California, 12.5 percent in Texas, 6.6 percent in Maryland, 5.8 percent in New York, and 4.7 percent in Washington, D.C. After their initial resettlement, many Eritrean and Ethiopian refugees moved to major metropolitan centers where they could meet their compatriots. This secondary migration has led to concentration of the exiles in a few major urban centers: Los Angeles, Dallas, New York City, and Washington, D.C. (which has the largest population of Ethiopians and Eritreans in the United States).

Since the 1960s, Washington, D.C., has been a hub for the Ethiopian elite and their children, who attend local schools. Around this core have gathered other ex-students who arrived looking for jobs. The reputation of Washington, D.C., as the center of the Ethiopian and Eritrean presence increased as it became the center of Ethiopian and Eritrean political activism. More and more students and ex-students joined their friends and families in the area, and most of the students combined attendances at local colleges with their work and political activism. The large service sector in the Washington, D.C., area provided ideal opportunities for employment.

Demographics

Since Eritrea broke away from Ethiopia and became an independent state only in 1991, most Eritreans officially entered the United States as Ethiopians. Therefore, the data on Eritreans is often included with Ethiopians, making it difficult to make demographic distinctions between the two populations. In 1991, the number of Ethiopians and Eritreans living in the United States was estimated to be between 50,000 and 75,000. The total was estimated to have reached 100,000 in 1995. Ethiopian and Eritrean immigrants have some unique demographic characteristics. Men make up the overwhelming majority of the immigrants; of those who arrived as political refugees in 1992, 62 percent were male and 38 percent were female. Ethiopian and Eritrean societies are patriarchal and favor males over females in almost all spheres of public life, including education, employment, government, and business. Males predominate among those who are educated and employed in the modern sector. Therefore, men in greater numbers then women met the complex criteria set by the U.S. officials in the refugee processing sites in the Sudan and Europe.

In addition, even though the majority of the refugees in the Sudan were Eritrean Muslims, most of the refugees who resettled in the United States were Amharic-speaking Ethiopians and Tigrinya-speaking Eritreans, with some Tigrinya-speaking Ethiopians and some Oromos. Most of these resettled refugees were Christian, although a few of the Eritrean refugees were Muslim. The explanation for the discrepancy between the two populations is complex. The Ethiopian and Eritrean refugees allowed into the United States were those whom the U.S. government defined as able to integrate into the society quickly and successfully. This included those who were Christian, those who were not involved in supporting armed political movements, those who were better educated or young, and those who were deemed to contribute most to the host society or had work experience in the modern sector of the economy. The greatest influence in granting refugee status was the refugee's educational background. For instance, while less than 4 percent of the refugees from Ethiopia living in the Sudan had attended a university, nearly 20 percent of the household heads resettled in the United States had attended a university. The Amharic-speaking Ethiopians were the most preferred for immigration to the United States because they had greater access to educational and occupational resources in Ethiopia, they were less likely to be associated with armed political organizations, and they were mostly Christians. Therefore, these refugees were perceived to be the most likely to integrate successfully into U.S. society.

Language

All Ethiopians and Eritrean immigrants in the United States speak languages derived from a large language superfamily known as Afro-Asiatic. The Afro-Asiatic languages include Chadic, Berber, Ancient Egyptian, Semitic, Cushitic, and Omotic. Most Ethiopian immigrants speak Amharic as their national language. Amharic, derived mostly from Semitic mixed with some Cushitic, is a language originally spoken by Amharas, an ethnic group found in the central and northwestern parts of Ethiopia. Amharas are the major creators of the modern Ethiopian state, and throughout the twentieth century they played a major role in running the bureaucracies of the state. In spite of the transfer of power from Amharas to Tigrinya-speaking Ethiopians in 1991, the government offices are still controlled by Amharas. The original home of the Tigrinya-speaking Ethiopians is Tigray, the northernmost region of Ethiopia; thus, they are known as Tigreans. Their territory borders a Tigrinya-speaking region of Eritrea. Geez, an ancient Semitic language belonging to the Afro-Asiatic language family, is the origin of Tigrinya and Amharic. Oromos speak a language called Oromo, a Cushitic language belonging to the Afro-Asiatic language group as well. The Oromo people are the largest ethnic group in Ethiopia, but they are not a politically powerful group.

In contrast to Ethiopians, most Eritrean immigrants speak Tigrinya; Tigrinya-speakers are also the dominant ethnic group in Eritrea. There are a small number of Tigre- and Belein-speaking Eritrean immigrants in the United States. Tigre is a Semitic language, and like Amharic and Tigrinya, it is derived from Geez. Belein belongs to a Cushitic language family. Almost all Tigrinya-speakers, even those from Eritrea, can communicate in Amharic.

Most Ethiopian and Eritrean immigrants know how to speak and read English before their arrival in the United States. They generally speak their native languages with one another in their homes, at work, and during leisure time, but they are usually able to communicate with the mainstream American society in English. With some exceptions, their children mostly speak English as their first language. The first generation's attempt to train the second generation to speak Amharic or Tigrinya has failed. Members of the second generation speak to one another in English and barely understand the native languages spoken by the first generation.

Cultural Characteristics

Most Eritreans and Ethiopians now in the United States are descended from Abyssinians. The Abyssinians are the product of the blending of indigenous Nilotic and Omotic peoples, Cushitic and Semitic immigrants who arrived in the region presumably more than three thousand years ago. The Abyssinians developed a unique culture that adapted ancient Christianity to local conditions. They created their own written language, called Geez. From Geez emerged many languages spoken in Ethiopia and Eritrea, including Tigrinya, Tigre, Amharic, and Gurage. The Oromos, believed to be more numerous than the Abyssinians, constitute the largest ethnic group in Ethiopia, accounting for almost 50 percent of the population. Oromos were first colonized by Abyssinian rulers. Historically, Oromos have been pastoralists specializing in cattle raising. A widely dispersed population, Oromos are found in every province of Ethiopia. In many regions of Ethiopia, Oromos have intermarried with Amharas and assimilated into Amhara culture.

Once in the United States, Ethiopians and Eritreans undergo a shift in their social position from being members of the dominant majority groups in their own societies to being among the nondominant immigrant minority groups. The reversal of their social status causes identity conflict among the immigrant generation. The identity conflict manifests itself in gender and family relations, race relations, and generational frictions. This means that Ethiopians and Eritreans feel pressure to find a new sense of identity that blends their sense of worth and honor from their homeland with their immigrant status in the United States.

Often these refugees find communal support in the areas of high concentration such as Los Angeles, Washington, D.C., and Dallas. The earlier immigrants provide an opportunity for the newer immigrants to socialize, eat ethnic food, listen to ethnic music, use their own language, and share their experiences. In spite of these opportunities, most refugees still experienced loneliness and isolation because the number of Ethiopians and Eritreans in the United States is small, and they are dispersed in different cities. These refugees are also divided along ethnic, political, and, in the case of Eritreans, religious lines. Most suffer from the absence of family support and the lack of elders with authority to direct and advise them. The alienation is most severe for single males in their twenties.

In the Eritrean and Ethiopian cultures, the older generation is respected because of its age and rank. Conversations follow a pattern in which the higher status is assigned to older men, followed by older women, followed by younger married men and married women, followed by the eldest sons, followed by the eldest daughters, and so on. In such gender- and age-based hierarchies, the needs of younger children are hardly addressed; they are expected to keep quiet and obey the orders of the adults. Individuals do not have an identity separate from kinship, friendship, or family. An individual's concerns are regarded as secondary to communal concerns. Individuals are expected to conform to the general values and norms of the community. Often communal tensions arise when individuals, usually those born in the United States, assert their individuality.

In most cities of the United States, the refugees cope with the reversal of status by participating in all-Eritrean and all-Ethiopian political and cultural organizations and support groups. Males participate in soccer teams that have been active in the United States since the mid-1980s. Other organizations, such as friendship circles and peer groups, meet and play and socialize on weekends. Many participate in Ekub, a traditional Abyssinian rotating credit association. Ekub allows individuals to accumulate capital while socializing with their compatriots. Very often, spouses participate together in networks of friendship, family circles, and political organizations. Many locally based small ethnic organizations have emerged in many cities in the United States. These ethnic organizations also provide religious services for the adults and classes for teaching Tigrinya and Amharic to the second generation.

Assimilation and Cultural Persistence

Most Ethiopian and Eritrean immigrants face many difficulties in assimilating into American society. The primary barrier to their assimilation is finding jobs that matched their educational and occupational qualifications. They generally enter the U.S. economy as low-wage workers in the service sector, a pattern that started with Ethiopians and Eritreans who were students in the late 1960s and early 1970s and working part time in various jobs: parking lot and gas station attendants, waitresses and waiters, dish carriers, taxi drivers, night guards, hotel and hospital maintenance personnel, nurse's aides, and providers of other services. Most refugees originally hoped to return to their homeland and work in occupations based on their new qualifications. They treated their stay and their work in the United States as temporary until they finished their education or training. As the political crisis in Ethiopia worsened, and as new refugees arrived in the United States as permanent residents, their dream of returning to their homeland faded. Many continued in their previous jobs, and the earlier residents helped the newcomers find jobs that required only minimum skills in the service sector. As a result, there occurred a cultural division of labor in which most Ethiopians and Eritreans specialized in low-paying service jobs that required only minimum interaction with the host society. A few who have saved enough capital have broken from this trend and opened their own businesses, including liquor and convenience stores, restaurants, gas stations, taxi cabs, real estate agencies, and computer and printing services. Many Ethiopians and Eritreans have succeeded in creating a niche for Ethiopian and Eritrean restaurants in most major American cities. These restaurants generally specialize in Abyssinian cuisine because of its nature as a cultural practice shared by both Eritrean and Ethiopian immigrants.

Male and female immigrants experience the new society of the United States differently. Eritrean and Ethiopian women gain greater financial and personal independence and security than they had in their homeland. Women experience greater freedom and rights in the home and at work in the United States. Men, on the other hand, find their dominant position challenged both at home and at work. They often resist changing their attitudes and behavior. They avoid helping their wives in the kitchen when visitors come to their home, even if they do help when there are no visitors.

Most single men do their own cooking and other necessary domestic duties, but once they marry the gender roles tend to be sharply defined. They are mainly concerned about their culturally defined male image as the patriarch of the family.

The ideal of gender equality in the United States generates tensions within the refugee families, and between males and females in general. The number of cases of wife battery has risen along with divorce rate. The dilemma for a battered woman is that her husband or male partner is often the only person she knows in the United States; the fighting husband and wife often have no mediating community or family to which they can turn to reduce tension and lessen isolation. In addition, marriage in Ethiopia and Eritrea represents the bringing together of two extended families, so it is hard for a woman to imagine that she has the right to break the relationship on her own. Still, there is relative gender equality in the United States compared to the glaring inequality in their homeland. This gives the women some hope of improving themselves and attaining the American dream of a secure middle-class lifestyle — with or without their male partners — in the long run. In the short run, most of the refugee women work in low-paying service jobs.

In the eyes of the first generation of immigrants, the issue of race relations is not a major concern. They are aware of the racial divide in American society and face racial prejudices in everyday life, but they do not acknowledge that racial issues affect their lives. Instead, they relegate the racial issue to a private and often secondary level of concern. This pattern continues even when the significance of race increases as they set up families and their children grow up in American society. The first-generation immigrants continue to center their energies on "making it," acquiring basic survival skills such as language, vocational, and professional skills, as well as higher education. They emphasize national and regional ethnic identity as a way of mitigating the black identity assigned to them by American society. They do not protest any race- or class-based discrimination they experience in the United States. They do not feel they are entitled to speak on these issues because they came to the United States as voluntary immigrants. Therefore, Eritreans and Ethiopians focus mostly on the well-being of their families, relatives, and friends in the United States and other parts of the world.

Ethiopian and Eritrean immigrants feel a sense of panethnicity with Somali and Sudanese immigrants, constituting a panethnic group known as peoples from the Horn of Africa. The Horn of Africa is a unique cultural area occupying the northeastern parts of Africa including Ethiopia, Eritrea, Somalia, Somaliland, Djibouti Republic, and Sudan. The region is a junction that links Asia and the Middle East to Africa. Historically, it served as a crossroads for people going from Africa to Asia and vice versa. From their early beginnings, three major world religions (Islam, Christianity, and, to some extent, Judaism) have shaped the evolution of the unique culture of the Horn of Africa. The region has witnessed widespread ethnic and racial mixing, religious conversions, migrations, conquests, wars, and redefinition of boundaries. Therefore, the culture of the Horn of Africa is an exceptional blending of these diverse cultural influences. Eritreans, Ethiopians, Somalis, and Sudanese are aware of their cultural links and feel a sense of affinity with one another.

However, there is no unique culture among the second-generation Ethiopians and Eritreans. The parental generation has in general been unable to pass its culture, its language, and, to a large extent, its religious orientations to the second generation. This failure to educate the children about their culture, faith, and language has been a source of great anguish to the parents. Instead, the second generation has constructed and negotiated its own identity, blending its American and African cultural influences. The refugees' children are more individualistic and less bound to ethnic culture than are their parents. Most members of the second generation confront American society as black persons with Ethiopian or Eritrean parents. What these youths become varies depending on their neighborhood, class background, and personal choice of friends and lifestyles. Some identify themselves as Eritrean/Ethiopian, Abyssinian (Habesha), or African, and some identify themselves as blacks. Many individuals assume different cultural identities depending on the social context, using ethnic and racial identities as resources to manage socially challenging and often uncomfortable situations.

Members of the first generation have a strong pride in their national and ethnic heritage. Such a sense of honor and worth may help to give members of the second generation a strong basis for negotiating a meaningful ethnic identity in the United States.

Bibliography

Buxton, D. (1970). *The Abyssinians.* New York: Praeger.

Cichon, D. J.; Gozdziak, E. M.; and Grover, J. G., eds. (1986). *The Economic and Social Adjustment of Non-Southeast Asian Refugees.* Dover, NH: Research Management Corporation.

Human Rights Watch. (1991). *Evil Days: Thirty Years of War and Famine in Ethiopia.* New York: Author.

Kibreab, G. (1985). *African Refugees.* Trenton, NJ: African World Press.

Koehn, P. H. (1991). *Refugees from Revolution: U.S. Policy and Third World Migration.* Boulder, CO: Westview Press.

Markakis, J. (1987). *National and Class Conflict in the Horn of Africa.* Cambridge, Eng.: Cambrige University Press.

McSpadden, L. A., and Moussa, H. (1993). "I Have a Name: The Gender Dynamics in Asylum and in Resettlement of Ethiopian and Eritrean Refugees in North America." *Journal of Refugee Studies* 6(3):203–225.

Moussa, H. (1993). *Storm and Sanctuary: The Journey of Ethiopian and Eritrean Women Refugees.* Dundas, Ontario: Artimis Enterprises.

Office of Refugee Resettlement. (1993). *Report to the Congress: Refugee Resettlement Program.* Washington, DC: U.S. Department of Health and Human Services.

Selassie, B. H. (1980). *Conflict and Intervention in the Horn of Africa.* New York: Monthly Review Press.

U.S. Committee for Refugees. (1983, 1991, 1993, 1994). *Refugee Reports.* Washington, DC: Author.

Woldemikael, T. M. (1993). "The Cultural Construction of the Eritrean Nationalist Movements." In *The Rising Tide of Cultural Pluralism: The Nation-State at Bay?*, edited by C. M. Young. Madison: University of Wisconsin Press.

Woldemikael, T. M. (1996). "Ethiopians and Eritreans." In *Refugees in America in the 1990s: A Reference Handbook,* edited by D. W. Haines. Westport, CT: Greenwood Press.

TEKLE MARIAM WOLDEMIKAEL

EUROPEAN JEWS

See JEWS, EUROPEAN

FILIPINOS

Filipinos in the United States are descendants of immigrants and political refugees from the Philippine Islands. They are also known as Tagalogs, Visayans, Cebuanos, Negrenses, Hiligaynons, Ilongos, Ilocanos, Pampanguenos, Samarenos, Masbatenos, Cavitenos, Bulaquenos, and Batanguenos, among others, according to language or province of origin. Filipinos' homeland comprises more than 7,100 islands with a total land area of 115,707 square miles. The largest islands are Luzon, Mindanao, and the Visayas. Small coral islands extend south into the Sulu Sea toward Indonesia. The Philippine archipelago first became a single country under Spanish colonial rule, fell under American rule after 1898, and became an independent nation-state in 1946. With rocky outcrops, flowing coconut trees, and white beaches, the islands are inhabited by more than one hundred different populations who speak mutually non-understandable Malayo-Polynesian languages and have distinct cultures and traditions. These include indigenous mountain people and descendants of settlers from China or the west. Extensive sea trade established language and cultural commonalities between inhabitants of adjacent islands' shores, while interior areas were isolated by their deep forests and mountain terrain (*bundok*). Thus the origin of the term "boondocks," which crept into American usage after World War II.

Before 1900, Philippine populations of Malayo-Polynesian background were categorized as "Indios" by the Spaniards, in contrast to "Chinese," "Chinese mestizos," and "Spaniards" (a category that included Spanish mestizos). The term "mestizo" referred to the offspring of intermarriage between Indios and Chinese. After 1900, with the formation of a Philippine state under American rule, a new term "Filipino," became the formal appellation for the bulk of the Philippine population composed primarily of local Indios and of former Chinese mestizos, who had by then become members of the Philippine elite. "Mestizo" then came to refer only to mixed Spanish-native ancestry. A distinct category of "Chinese" was used to refer to more recent immigrants from China and Taiwan, even though they too were intermarrying with native populations.

This usage continued after the Philippines gained independence in 1946. The term "Filipinos" continued to identify racially and ethnically the bulk of the Philippine citizenry (i.e., people speaking Malayo-Polynesian languages and living on agricultural lowlands). Lowlanders speak seventy distinct Malayo-Polynesian languages, nine of which are used by about 90 percent of the Philippine people. The "Chinese" continued to be kept distinct despite intermarriage and the increased use of local languages and cultural practices. Twentieth-century China-born immigrants, but also their Philippine-born children and grandchildren, were until 1975 not legally entitled to Philippine nationality because of the strict enforcement of citizenship regulations based on *jus sanguinis* (the blood of the father rather than the place of birth). Despite the 1975 policy shift, Chinese still encounter difficulties in processing citizenship applications.

The culturally diverse upland populations and the racially distinct aboriginal Negritos ("Aetas") have acquired right to citizenship only recently and often still imperfectly. The southern Muslim populations repeatedly resisted government intervention and claim the right to be a separate nation.

Political unification and extensive internal migration during the twentieth century have constructed elements of a unified "national culture" in which issues of regional difference and linguistic hegemony are, however, still actively debated. The ethnonym "Filipino" is thus primarily the artifact of a long history of Western-imposed cultural categories and of the construction of a twentieth-century nation-state searching for its roots in precolonial times.

Filipinos in the United States

Location. Filipino immigrants to the United States first moved to Hawaii and California. In both the 1980 and 1990 U.S. Censuses, about two-thirds of the overall Filipino population, both foreign- and native-born, resided on the West Coast and in Hawaii—mostly in Los Angeles, San Francisco, and Honolulu—52 percent in California and 12 percent in Hawaii in 1990. There are growing percentages, however, in the large urban areas of the East Coast states (13.7% in 1990), with

the largest concentrations in New York, New Jersey, Maryland, and Virginia; in Illinois (4.6% in 1990); and in Texas (2.4% in 1990).

Predominantly urban, Filipinos were the fastest growing population during the 1980s among Asian-Pacific Americans, themselves the nation's fastest growing minority group, measured in percentage growth. By 1990, Filipinos represented 20.4 percent of all Asian Americans (who numbered 6,908,638 in 1990, a 99% increase since 1980), and were second only to the Chinese (23.8%).

Demography. Filipino immigrants, whose numbers, as in the case of other Asian-American immigrant populations, had grown relatively slowly in the pre-World War II period, have been increasing at a rapid pace since 1965. In only five years, between April 1, 1980, and September 30, 1985, the proportion of Asian-Americans in the total U.S. population increased from a little over 1.5 percent to 2.1 percent. It had reached 2.9 percent by 1990. While no Asian group in the United States numbered more than a million in 1980, by September 1985, the Filipinos, with an estimated 1,051,000, has almost overcome the Chinese, estimated at 1,079,000. By 1990, the Filipinos continued to be the second largest Asian-American population in the United States, with an estimated 1,409,362 as compared to 1,644,255 Chinese. Given their proportionally large numbers, they have been relatively understudied.

Since 1965, Filipinas have steadily exceeded Filipinos. By 1990, there were 86 males for each 100 females.

Linguistic Affiliation. All Filipino languages are Malayo-Polynesian, close to Malay or Indonesian and part of the large Austronesian family of languages. Filipinos had a Sanskrit-based writing system before European contact. They continued to develop their separate literary styles even though Spanish became the formal language of the colonial administrators and of religious training. The American occupation in the early twentieth century brought a great emphasis on education. By the 1970s, Filipino men and women had the

A Filipino boy works with a labor gang in a cauliflower field near Santa Maria, California, in 1937. (Library of Congress/Corbis)

highest levels of education and best English proficiency in Asia.

In 1990, 63.7 percent of foreign-born Filipinos in the United States spoke English very well and easily at home as opposed to less than half that number in the case of most other foreign-born Asian or Latin-American immigrants. Filipinos continued, however, to speak one or more of their native languages in family interactions. In addition, Filipinos have the highest level of education of all foreign-born immigrants, including Europeans.

History and Cultural Relations

For the first two hundred years of Spanish colonial rule (1565–1780s), the Philippines remained very much at the periphery of the world system, with Manila functioning as an entrepôt for the then profitable Spanish galleon trade between Mexico and the Far East. There were few Spaniards on Philippine soil and practically no emigration of Philippine inhabitants. Tobacco, indigo, sugar, and abaca industries were developed at the turn of the nineteenth century and rapidly capitalized by British and American interests, then in expansion. It was mostly children of this nineteenth-century Filipino and Chinese-mestizo colonial class, who later went to Spain for their education, learned how to best undermine the Spanish colonial hegemonic control, and ultimately contributed to the termination of Spain's rule.

After the Philippines formally became an American colonial territory in 1902, there was surprisingly limited immigration to the United States even though Philippine citizens, as members of the colony, were not submitted to quotas. They obtained American passports when leaving their country and roamed freely across the United States. (But they still were not easily granted American citizenship.) Starting with the first 160 Filipino male workers recruited as agricultural labor for Hawaii in 1906, some eighty thousand Filipinos, mostly single working males, but also some students and merchant marine crewmen, were residing in the United States by 1929. This first wave consisted mainly of males who were predominantly unschooled, unskilled, and of low socioeconomic status. They were hired by Filipino contractors in rural areas to offset agricultural labor shortages in Hawaii, California, and Alaska, shortages that other Asian immigrants, less favorably treated by immigration laws at the time, could not fill. Even though these Philippine immigrants were often very poorly rewarded for their hard work, were racially discriminated against, and led difficult and lonely lives, most remained in the United States.

The number of overall Philippine immigrants to the United States had risen only to 125,000 by 1940 and 176,000 by 1960. Slowed down by the Depression of the 1930s, their immigration further decreased with the passage of the Philippine Independence Act in 1934, which made the Philippines a country under U.S. Commonwealth protection and thus defined Filipinos as aliens. From 1935 to 1946, Filipinos had an immigration quota of fifty persons a year. From 1946 to 1964, after the Philippines had become an independent nation-state, the quota rose to one hundred persons a year, and immigrants were granted naturalization rights. During World War II, immigration had formally stopped, but many Filipinos who served in the U.S. military or were the wives of U.S. servicemen were later granted immigrant status.

Given the slow immigration of Filipinos to the United States, despite their close ties, their sudden influx after 1965 is particularly striking. The 1965 changes to the U.S. immigration policy facilitated a wave of well-educated professionals and technical workers who could then bring their families to the United States under the family reunification regulations. By 1969, in four years time, India and the Philippines had replaced all European countries as the leading source of scientists, engineers, and physicians in the United States, with the Philippines as the major source of physicians. Since the greatest demand was for medical and other health-related professions (physicians, nurses, medical technicians, food professionals), women also steadily outnumbered men.

By the late 1970s and 1980s, with the increased deterioration of the Philippine economy leading to a negative gross national product (GNP) in the mid-1980s and the growth of overseas opportunities, emigration from the Philippines sharply increased and expanded beyond the United States while assuming a somewhat different character. Aside from professionals and technically trained people, an increasing number of well-educated Filipino immigrants to the United States were service workers, office staff, domestic helpers, nightclub entertainers, and even mail-order brides. Professionals and technicians also left for other labor-absorbing countries (e.g., Canada and Australia). At the same time Filipinos quickly responded to the industrial boom of the Middle East (requiring construction, manufacturing, and industrial workers) and subsequently to the need in

that region for educated service workers as office support staff, nurses, pharmacists, and domestic helpers. Domestic helpers, construction workers, seamen, nightclub entertainers, prostitutes, and mail-order brides also started to leave for Europe and Japan, with increasing numbers immigrating to Hong Kong, Malaysia, and Singapore.

This emigration from the Philippines was officially sponsored by the government early on. By 1974, a new Philippine Labor Code was established by President Ferdinand Marcos through presidential decree, and the martial law government started to issue licenses to state-recognized labor recruiting agencies. It also established a workers' assistance and adjudication office to "look after the welfare" of overseas workers and their families and facilitate procedures for remittances. Subsequent presidential decrees in 1980 and 1982 further consolidated the role of different government agencies sponsoring emigration.

By 1983, there were 1,023 recruiting agencies in the international labor export business paying the government an annual license fee. By 1988, branches of the Ministry of Labor in provincial cities and in Manila advertised on their bulletin boards lists of potential jobs overseas that they administered directly. This was the practice for contract jobs to the Middle East as well as to the United States, Canada, Australia, Europe, and the rest of Southeast Asia. Combined with the U.S. individual and family reunification policies, this state-sponsored emigration helps account for the soaring numbers of educated Philippine immigrants in the United States.

Between 1974 and 1985, about two million Filipinos had left for the United States or the Middle East as temporary or permanent workers. More than half a million were working in Europe, Japan, Hong Kong, Singapore, Canada, and Australia, and almost another half a million contract workers were employed in some 130 other countries around the world. The Philippines had become a leader in the international export of manpower. By 1995, from a population of nearly seventy million Filipinos, some 3.5 million worked overseas, mostly in the United States and Saudi

Arabia, according to conservative Philippine government figures. This labor trade proved to be quite helpful to the overpopulated, underemployed Philippines. Overseas Filipinos became an unexpected source of valuable foreign exchange as dollar remittances reached the billion dollar level for the first time in 1983 and had tripled, according to official banking figures, if not sixtupled (if one includes money flows through private finance companies and other channels), by the end of 1994.

Economy

Filipinos in the 1990 U.S. Census were mostly employed in technical, sales, and administrative support occupations (36.7%), managerial and professional specialties (26.6%), and services (16.8%); the rest were operators and laborers (11.0%), crafts and repairs (7.4%), and farming, forestry, fishing (1.5%). They had a diverse employment profile. However, while 36.3 percent of entering immigrants in 1969 had been employed at professional or managerial level, the figure had declined to 7.6 percent by 1985. In 1980, the proportion of Filipinos employed as professionals, managers, and executives was about the same as that of white Americans, but the percentage of service workers (16.5%) was already higher than that in the white population (11.6%).

The median family income of Filipino-Americans is higher than that of the general population, particularly among the foreign-born, but there are more workers per family. In fact, the median income for an individual white American worker was almost 14 percent higher than for a Filipino American. Filipino women are more often employed than other Asian women and more often in the professions. As an average, Filipinos had, in 1990, the lowest poverty rate of other Asians and

A Filipino brick cleaner in Seattle stands before the remains of the Puget Sound Hotel in 1993. (Dean Wong/Corbis)

of white Americans because of their professional presence. There are, however, considerable differences in income among Filipino Americans, although possibly less than among Chinese Americans. In addition, a Filipino's income is lower if he is a recent immigrant.

As undocumented immigrants, Filipinos are the most frequently apprehended and deported Asian Americans, a shift that occurred during the 1980s. Before 1965, the undocumented Asian Americans were predominantly Chinese.

Filipino immigrants, despite their particularly rapid naturalization rates, preserve strong transnational ties with their country of origin. They make frequent trips to the Philippines, reinvest in houses, land, or businesses, and send remittances, with strong government encouragement. Under the special category of "balikbayan" (i.e., returnees) created by Marcos in 1974, trips back to the Philippines by Filipino Americans are facilitated even when they are already American citizens. They can send balikbayan boxes full of household appliances, electronic equipment, and even cars back to the Philippines almost tax-free. Numerous Filipino businesses with branches in both countries have been created to facilitate these exchanges.

Kinship, Marriage, and Family

Kinship. Lowland Philippine kinship groups and descent, though somewhat variable across different language groups, are bilateral, with a strong presence historically given to the female line. Women held important positions, owned land and power, and imposed their sexual preferences in precolonial lowland Philippine society as noted with astonishment by Spanish writers. When the Americans came to the Philippines, women had retained some economic and political independence despite centuries of Spanish Catholicism that attempted to mold them and refused to educate them. Even in the fiercely Muslim southern Philippines, women (until recently) did not veil their faces at marriage, still roamed freely and had considerable economic independence. Relatedness

is considered through a wide circle of relatives through both the mother and the father, as well as through widely used forms of "fictive" kinship such as *compadrazgo* and sponsorship.

Marriage. Filipino marriages are monogamous and in general quite stable after the couple has begun having children. They are based on a free choice of spouse and on romantic love. There is considerable intermarriage between language groups, facilitated by extensive migration within the country since the 1960s. It is thus not uncommon for Filipinos to speak three or four different Philippine languages in addition to English. Which one they self-identify as their primary language varies according to their personal situation.

Domestic Unit. The family structure of Filipinos in the United States remains close knit and intergenerational, even though households may be scattered in different locations. The average number of persons per household (4.0) is significantly higher than the U.S. average and may include some grandparents, siblings, and cousins. It is common, especially among foreign-born families, to have some close family members, such as siblings or older married children or parents, still living in the Philippines. Immigrants thus stretch their families and households over long distances, often at great emotional cost.

Inheritance. Among Filipino Americans, inheritance is bilateral, as it usually is in the Philippines. In fact, women feel quite independent from their husbands with regard to decisions about their own property. This often creates misunderstandings in mixed marriages with Westerners who generally feel they should be consulted about such matters before major decisions are made.

Socialization. There are considerable social class differences in child rearing in the Philippines. However, personal honor, respect for the aged, proper courtship behavior, and appropriate demeanor remain very important among most Filipino Americans. There is evidence of weakened parental control when the children and grandchildren of foreign-born immigrants are studying away from home. Most young Filipino Americans, especially daughters, are raised quite strictly and feel somewhat alienated from their foreign-born parents. They are strongly pressured to perform well in school (school performance, advertised in the Filipino-American newspapers, enhances the parents' social status). However, they are not equally encouraged to achieve when they select a college and a career away from home. There was evidence of high suicide rates among Filipino-American public high school students, especially girls, in San Diego in 1995.

Sociopolitical Organization

Social and Political Organization. Filipinos live quite scattered in the large U.S. metropolitan areas where they are located. They interact on the job (especially where they are highly concentrated in a single profession, such as nursing) or in school (if they are students), but they mostly meet at Sunday Masses and at parties and social affairs. Religious festivities and other celebrations are advertised in the Filipino-American newspapers.

Filipinos have formed myriads of organizations in the United States, including hometown associations, social clubs, cultural clubs, religious groups (Charismatics), professional and vocational Filipino-American organizations, civic organizations (Lyons, Rotary, Jaycees), advocacy groups, former alumni networks, and philanthropic groups. These organizations, which have their own meetings and activities, have often become transnational, with branches in both the United States and the Philippines.

Filipinos, having become an important voting bloc in the United States, are now courted by both American politicians and Philippine political candidates. In fact is is not uncommon for candidates to the Philippine Senate or House of Representatives to electioneer in New York or on the West Coast.

Social Control and Conflict. Filipinos come from a highly segmented pyramidal society where class differences are considerable. Spain and the United States ruled the Philippines through local leaders who profited in the process. After independence, a few families monopolized economic and political resources, leaving a large bloc of the population in dire poverty. Some of these families have become political refugees in the United States, where their presence is then felt, as during the Marcos-Aquino conflict. The majority of the Filipino Americans, however, came from the educated urban provincial middle classes who were not satisfied with the opportunities they could find in the Philippines or are the upwardly mobile children of farmers and leaseholders. In the United States, the leadership of Filipino-American organizations is often in the hands of well-to-do immigrants. Although a wide range of political ideologies is represented, there is factionalism within organizations and infighting among the leaders.

As "little brown brothers," Filipinos were subject to U.S. paternalism in their own country and to the strict miscegenation laws of the pre–World War II period in the United States, which prohibited intermarriage with whites. In response, Filipinos became close allies of Hispanic labor leaders during the unionization efforts by agricultural workers in California. Post-1965 immigrants experience racial discrimination on the job and as Asians may enter into conflicts with blacks or Hispanics. Filipino youth bands are part of the California urban scene.

Religion and Expressive Culture

Religious Beliefs. The Philippine Islands were conquered by Spain during the late sixteenth century after Miguel Lopez de Legazpe established the first permanent Spanish settlement in Cebu in 1565. Spanish soldiers, heavily armored, conquered scattered local settlements and Arab coastal statelets. For more than three hundred years (1565–1898), colonization by Spain occurred through the missionizing presence of Catholic orders (Jesuits, Dominicans, and Augustinians) whose priests were the main Spanish presence throughout the countryside and in Manila, aside from a few Spanish administrators and soldiers. Many Filipinos were resettled around a plaza with a church. Lowland Filipinos, christianized for cen-

Lowland Filipinos practice their religion while maintaining syncretic elements of their animistic beliefs and continuing to practice local medicine and magic. Town people participate in healing ceremonies where local practitioners dance on live coals throughout the night behind the church without interference from the priest. Elements of syncretism remain in the Filipino-American belief system, reinforced by frequent exchanges with the homeland.

Religious Practitioners. Religious leaders called *baylan* (Tagalog) or *babaylan* (Ilongo), usually women, practice healing ceremonies for various forms of illness (including mental illness). Through possession by familial or local spirits, they provide diagnosis and cure. These "dancing" healers became powerful leaders of anticolonial uprisings during the nineteenth century, threatening the weakened Spanish colonial government. Their dances contain Catholic elements (references to God, Jesus, etc.) as well as memories of armed conflicts (shields and spears). Black magic and love potions are also common.

Ceremonies. In the Philippines the church functions as a focus of sociability and cohesion, where some mediation between rich and poor can take place. Filipinos in the United States remain active churchgoers. Weekly services, weddings, anniversaries, christenings, funerals, and other religious celebrations are important opportunities for social interaction and ethnic reinforcement. Santacruzan and Flor de Mayo combine pageants where young people parade in fancy, often traditional, clothes with elaborate preparations of national foods, singing, and dancing. Political meetings or beauty pageants are also very popular. These events facilitate networking, mark Filipino-American class differences, and allow youngsters of both sexes to meet and interact. Intermarriage with other Filipinos is still strongly preferred by many foreign-born parents.

Arts. There is a multiplicity of Philippine traditional and newly created folk arts. Upland and lowland populations wove their own clothes in a

Members of a female Filipino dance company wear traditional attire during a public performance in Seattle. (Morton Beebe-S.F./Corbis)

turies, are thus predominantly Catholic. In 1902, a splinter group initiated an independent nationalistic Church, named after Bishop Gregario Aglipay, and not formally recognized by the Vatican, which remains attractive to the poorer populations. When annexed by the United States after a successful Filipino-led anticolonial struggle, some Protestant churches (Baptist, Presbyterian) established branches, and after World War II, numerous Christian sects (Mormons, Seventh Day Adventists, Jehovah's Witnesses) successfully proselytized in the Philippines. Numerous cults developed during the twentieth century, including the cult of José Rizal, who was a national hero and martyr at the end of the Spanish era.

variety of threads, designs, and colors, often combined with tie-dye or embroidery. Expert gold and silver smiths, lowlanders also learned embroidery and silver work from Spain. There is writing on bamboo; elaborate Spanish and Chinese influenced furniture; wood sculptures including "santos"; Christmas Chinese-style lanterns of bamboo and multi-colored paper; songs, literature, and theater in English and Philippine languages. Special ceremonies, such as the yearly Ati-Atihang in honor of the Aetas (the interior people) on the island of Panay, have been reconstructed or invented for tourists.

Medicine. Folk medical practitioners who sell curative herbs, roots, sea shells, minerals, and bones in the weekly markets in the Philippines readily refer their clients to local medical doctors or pharmacists, depending on the type of illness. Local midwives practice in poor neighborhoods. Although modern medicine is well developed in the Philippines, it is still combined at times with these folk practices, even in the United States.

Death and Afterlife. Filipinos combine beliefs in a Christian afterlife with animistic beliefs that allow dead family members to come back to haunt or help their descendants. They live in a world in which an ant hill or a rock could conceal an easily angered spirit and where *tamawo* (Ilongo for people-like spirits), light-skinned and high-nosed, live in high-rise cities on top of tall trees and court attractive young Filipinos whom they ultimately take to their other world.

Funerals are week-long celebrations, including food and gambling, where visitors contribute money to the family. Much of this has been simplified in the United States, especially when funerals are held in funeral homes.

Bibliography

Basch, L.; Glick-Schiller, N.; Szanton Blanc, C. (1994). *Nations Unbound: Transnational Projects, Post-Colonial Predicaments and Deterritorialized Nation-States.* New York: Gordon and Breach.

Fast, J., and Richardson, J. (1979). *Roots of Dependency: Political and Economic Revolution in 19th Century Philippines.* Quezon City, Philippines: Foundation for Nationalist Studies.

Gardner, R. W.; Robey, B.; and Smith, P. C. (1985). "Asian Americans: Growth, Change and Diversity." *Population Bulletin* 40(4):5–7.

Hing, B. O. (1993). *Making and Remaking Asian America Through Immigration Policy, 1950–1990.* Stanford, CA: Stanford University Press.

Karp, J. (1995). "Migrant Workers: A New Kind of Hero." *Far Eastern Economic Review* 158(13):42–45.

Ong, P.; Bonacich, E.; and Cheng, L., eds. (1994). *The New Asian Immigration in Los Angeles and Global Restructuring.* Philadelphia: Temple University Press.

Phelan, J. L. (1959). *The Hispanization of the Philippines: Spanish Aims and Filipino Responses, 1565–1700.* Madison: University of Wisconsin Press.

Pido, A. J. A. (1986). *The Filipinos in America: Macro/Micro Dimensions of Immigration and Integration.* New York: Center for Migration Studies.

Szanton Blanc, C. (1990). "Collision of Cultures: Historical Reformulations of Gender in the Lowland Visayas, Philippines." In *Power and Difference: Gender in Island Southeast Asia*, edited by J. M. Atkinson and S. Errington. Stanford, CA: Stanford University Press.

Szanton Blanc, C. (1996). "The Thoroughly Modern 'Asian': Culture, Transnationalism, and Nation in Thailand and the Philippines." In *Ungrounded Empires: Cultural Politics in Modern Chinese Transnationalism*, edited by A. Ong and D. Nonnini. New York: Routledge.

Takaki, R. (1989). *Strangers from a Different Shore: A History of Asian Americans.* New York: Penguin.

U.S. Department of the Census. (1993). *Asians and Pacific Islanders in the United States.* Washington, DC: U.S. Government Printing Office.

U.S. Department of the Census. (1993). *The Foreign-Born Population in the United States.* Washington, DC: U.S. Government Printing Office.

U.S. Department of the Census. (1993). *We the American Asians.* Washington, DC: U.S. Government Printing Office.

CRISTINA SZANTON BLANC

FINNS

Until the late nineteenth century, Finns were little known in the United States as only a few had settled in Delaware in the New Sweden colony of 1638. In the mid-1800s, Henry Wadsworth Longfellow, Thomas Conrad Porter, and others discovered the Finns through Finland's epic poem *Kalevala,* and American and English travelers subsequently wrote about their stopovers in Finland en route to St. Petersburg. Popular resistance to Russification at the end of the nineteenth century also brought Finland to the sympathetic attention of American editors. In the long run, however, the onset of modern immigration to the United States from Finland in the 1860s did the most to introduce Finns to Americans

Finnish History

The Finnish people descended from tribes originating in the Ural Mountains and Volga Valley of Russia. The tribes belonged to the Finno-Ugrian language group and came from the south and east to Suomi (Finland), which is the northernmost European nation and has an area comparable to that of Great Britain or Italy. Finland's name derives from the tribe known as the Suomalaiset (people of Finland), who settled in the southwestern part of the country. Another tribe was the Karjalaiset (people of Karelia) in eastern Finland and the adjacent Russian territory. The third tribe, the Hämäläiset (people of Häme), settled in the central region. Later the descendants of these tribes developed cultural differences, particularly dialects that deviated from the standard Finnish language.

After Finland was acquired by Sweden in the twelfth century, Swedish migrants moved to the country's southwestern settlements and created a landed aristocracy. The newcomers introduced Swedish governmental administrative practices; for instance, they later followed their homeland's model in establishing what became the Evangelical Lutheran State Church of Finland. Swedish became the official language of government and education, though the masses only spoke Finnish. This process of Swedization even changed Finnish surnames. The Finnish-born Swedish-speaking descendants became known as Swede-Finns.

The Swedish reign of Finland, which lasted almost six hundred years, came to an end in 1809 when Russia gained the country through war and established it as a Grand Duchy with autonomy over internal affairs. No attempt was made to replace Swedish with Russian as the official language, so Swedish-speaking Finns dominated the governmental bureaucracy. By the 1830s and 1840s, however, young educated Swede-Finn romantic nationalists became apprehensive about their own national identity. They now identified themselves with the Finnish-speaking masses to unite the nation. Among these nationalists was Elias Lönnröt, a young doctor, who in 1835 published the first volume of his *Kalevala,* based on runes that he had collected in Karelia to show the historic roots of the vernacular language. Another nationalist was Johan Snellman, who became a member of the government bureaucracy and championed recognition of the Finnish language. Fearing that Russians might eventually impose more control on Finland, Snellman wanted to enlist the Finnish masses in shaping the nation's destiny. In 1863, the Russian government agreed to make Finnish coequal with Swedish as an official language during a twenty-year period. By 1890, the Swedish-speaking people made up only about 15 percent of the population.

While the nationalist movement gained strength between the 1860s and World War I, Finland underwent other dramatic changes. Its population increased between 1850 and 1900 by more than 60 percent to 2,655,900, with the urban sector growing faster than the rural one. By 1901, fewer than a fourth of the heads of rural households owned their land. Thousands of the growing landless people had to migrate to work in sawmills and other industries in southern cities such as Helsinki. Concurrently, pietistic and evangelical as well as secular movements challenged the state church. The temperance movement also gained strength, and by the 1890s, the labor movement was making headway.

This popular ferment further intensified the nationalist movement that, though divided, grappled with Russification between 1899 and 1906. The Russian czar attempted to pacify the nation by authorizing a popularly elected one-house parliament to replace the diet of four estates that had represented only 10 percent of the population. After replacing the socialist parliamentary majority, the bourgeois nationalist parties proclaimed Finnish independence from Russia in December 1917. In the four-month Civil War of 1918 the socialists failed to gain control of the new nation.

Immigration to the United States

Another consequence of changes in Finland was emigration. In the mid-1880s, the first influx of modern Finnish immigrants reached the United States. The Calumet and Hecla Company recruited them along with Norwegians from the copper mines of Norway to work in its mines around Calumet and Hancock, Michigan. Other Finns followed from Finland itself to work in the mines as well as to find employment in states stretching from New England to the Northwest. Usually the immigrants traveled via the port of Hanko in Finland to England, where they boarded ships for the translantic trip to New York. Upwards of 300,000 Finns had immigrated to the United States by 1920, with the greatest number arriving between 1899 and 1914. Until 1900, the U.S. Bureau of the Census enumerated these immigrants as Russians, while Americans often called them Finlanders.

The majority were unmarried, young, and from rural backgrounds; of the 273,366 passport recipients between 1893 and 1920, 86.5 percent were from rural communes. Nearly half of these immigrants were either cottagers and landless farm workers or the children of landowners and tenants; fewer than 10 percent were landowners and tenants. The rest came from other occupations or did not report any. Of those who received passports

from 1901 to 1920, 69 percent were between the ages of sixteen and thirty. One-fourth of the Finnish immigrants were married, and initially men outnumbered women by almost two to one. In short, they were mainly young landless workers unable to find land or work in Finland. The more remote Oulu and Vaasa provinces sent more immigrants than any others.

Most immigrants settled in a northern tier of thirteen states ranging from New England through the Midwest to the Pacific Coast. In 1900, 62 percent of the 62,641 Finns lived in Michigan, Minnesota, Massachusetts, and New York; the first two states alone accounted for almost half of the population. Another 27 percent lived in nine states: Ohio, California, Washington, Wisconsin, Oregon, Montana, Pennsylvania, Illinois, and New Jersey. In 1920, the Finnish immigrants reached

A Finnish farmer lives in the sub-marginal farm area of Ramsey Hill, New York, in 1940. (Library of Congress/Corbis)

their peak of 149,824. Of this population, 40 percent lived in Michigan and Minnesota, while New York and Massachusetts increased their share and thereby kept these four states still at the top with 58 percent. The rank order of the other nine states changed somewhat, but together with the top four they accounted for 91 percent of all Finns. More than 53 percent of these immigrants were classified as urban, and almost 47 percent were classified as rural residents, though no more than half of the latter probably lived on farms. Michigan, Minnesota, and Wisconsin had the highest ratios or rural to urban Finns, while the reverse was true in Massachusetts, New York, Ohio, and California.

Obtaining employment was the first need of most immigrants. No other topic received more attention in their letters from America to friends and relatives back in Finland. While newcomers followed the early copper miners to Michigan's Upper Peninsula, others found their way to newly opened iron mines in Minnesota and coal, copper, and silver mines in the Rocky Mountain states. Still others worked in such industries as the steel mills of Pennsylvania and Ohio and the quarries and chair factories of Massachusetts, as well as the lumber camps from the Midwest to the Pacific Coast. While men also found work as carpenters in urban centers such as New York City, thousands of women worked in the same places, often as domestic servants. Although shopkeeping and other businesses lured Finns from industry, farming became the main alternative for miners and factory workers. Initially, the new farmers got homesteads in Minnesota and elsewhere, but later they more commonly established farms on cutover lands where the trees had been cleared. In 1920, Finnish farmers numbered 14,000, two-thirds of them located in Minnesota, Michigan, and Wisconsin.

Finnish Organizations

Because only a fourth were married at the time of arrival, most Finns did not have families to support. At first the men, who outnumbered the women, often lived in cooperative or private rooming and boarding houses, "boys' houses" (*poika-talot*). Courtship soon became a major feature in immigrant culture as men and women socialized in newly established churches and halls and even through advertisements seeking correspondents with marital interests. By 1920, the sex imbalance was becoming less pronounced, and family life was established. The 152,161 American-born children of immigrants soon outnumbered their parents. All the parents of 90 percent of the children were from Finland, and the rest of the children had one Finland-born parent each. Although family life provided more community stability, parents often still moved, as indicated by the different birthplaces of their children.

In addition, the Lutheran churches reinforced community life. Newcomers competed to establish congregations on a voluntary basis in the absence of state support. In the 1870s, Michigan's copper miners formed the first Apostolic Lutheran congregation. They were pietistic followers of Lars Laestadius, who preferred lay preachers over the trained clergy of Finland's state church. Subsequently, in 1890, Finland state church supporters organized the Finnish Evangelical Lutheran Church, or Suomi Synod, and six years later they established Suomi College to train clergymen. In 1898, other Evangelical Lutherans who regarded the Synod as authoritarian formed the Finnish National Evangelical Lutheran Church (with the word "national" meaning "people's"). In 1916, these three groups had 245 congregations with 33,000 first- and second-generation members, with the Suomi Synod in the lead. Finns also formed Congregational and other non-Lutheran churches.

Sooner or later each community also set up temperance, labor, and other competing organizations. For about thirty years, from the 1880s to the 1900s, the Finnish National Temperance Brotherhood held sway despite the inroads of rivals such as the Friends of Temperance. In the 1890s workers formed mutual benefit societies such as the Imatra Aid Society of Brooklyn, while the Knights of Kaleva promoted nationalistic cultural purposes. In 1899, the socialists emerged and, seven years later, formed the Finnish Socialist Federation. In 1913, the federation had 260 local chapters, though it lost some to the Industrial Workers of the World on the eve of World War I. After the socialists prominently supported the Minnesota iron mine strike of 1907, nationalistic-minded church people and others denounced labor activism as undermining Finnish reputations. This division widened further after the Michigan copper strike of 1913–1914. Whatever the nature of the organizations, however, each sponsored as many cultural activities as possible consistent with its values. Finnish cultural life flourished, therefore, with drama, music, poetry, gymnastics, publications, and polkas.

These organizations relied particularly on newspapers to keep contact with their supporters. Only 2 percent of the immigrants were classified as illiterate, because Finland's state church had required communicants to know how to read the Bible and the catechism. After the first short-lived newspaper, the *Amerikan Suomalainen Lehti* (American Finnish Journal), appeared in 1876, it was followed by others such as the *Uusi Kotimaa* (New Homeland) that were published by proprietors. In 1899 the Suomi Synod supporters started their own paper and began the shift to organization-sponsored ones. Four years later the socialists began the *Työmies* (Workingman), the first of three labor papers. Another early paper was the *New Yorkin Uutiset* (New York News), which started in 1906. All relied on local correspondents, reported organizational activities, and translated material from the American press.

Although maintaining a Finnish-language cultural life, the immigrant community was not isolated from the dominant American culture. The workplace, if nothing else, introduced it to new ways of doing work. Domestic servants learned new ways of cooking for employers. Public schools taught English to immigrant children for whom immigrant organizations published readers to help them retain parental language. Also both parents and children created a hybrid of the two languages known as Finglish. By adapting themselves to the dominant culture, immigrants became less likely to

return home after their first five years in the United States. By 1920, 39 percent of the eligible men were naturalized. But it was still possible to name children after *Kalevala* characters such as Aino and Väinö, bake *pulla* or *nissua* (buns), build log barns in Old Country ways, and bathe weekly in the steam bath or *sauna*. Indeed, Finns and their children were becoming Finnish Americans by World War I.

After Finnish immigrant numbers peaked in 1920, the communities remained somewhat static until World War II. In the 1920s, the influx of 16,691 newcomers kept the decrease in immigrant numbers to about five percent. In contrast, only 2,146 Finns immigrated during the 1930s, when the first generation declined by 18 percent; the decrease resulted partly from the exodus of Finns to Soviet Karelia. No major settlement changes occurred generally, however, in the thirteen states that had initially attracted most immigrants. Almost 60 percent still resided in Michigan, Minnesota, Massachusetts, and New York. Internal migration lured men from Michigan's declining copper mines to Detroit's automobile factories, and others purchased farms in cutover areas. Only 27.5 percent were rural farm residents.

The second-generation Finnish Americans, however, helped to keep up the Finnish presence. In the 1920s, their numbers increased 17 percent to a high of 178,058 in 1930 and then decreased 6 percent to 167,080 in 1940. Thus the combined total number of the first- and second-generation Finnish Americans declined ony 5.8 percent between 1920 and 1940. Almost 80 percent of the second-generation group had two Finland-born parents each, and the rest had one each.

The immigrants managed to maintain somewhat the pre–World War I level of their community activism, more so in the 1920s than the 1930s. The decline of the temperance movement after World War I was offset by the cooperative movement, especially in midwestern rural areas where the Central Cooperative Wholesale had seventy-one local stores and branches by 1928. Although the socialists were split over communism after the war, the left and right wings regrouped while the industrial unionists also maintained their activism. The left created the Finnish Workers Federation. Likewise the three Lutheran groups worked hard to recruit the second generation. In addition, Finnish newspapers had a peak circulation of 104,000, or two issues for every three immigrants. The Great Depression of the 1930s, however, curtailed organizational life. Four newspapers disappeared, though the rest still had more than eighty thousand subscribers. Even mortgage foreclosures led to the loss of meeting halls. In 1938, most major organizations, regardless of the ideological spectrum, united to celebrate the three-hundredth anniversary of the settling of New Sweden. During the Russo-Finland War of 1939–1940 the same groups, except for left elements, united to support their former homeland.

Community Decline

From the close of World War II to 1970, the immigrant communities went into decline. Thousands retired to collect social security benefits, and many settled in the Lake Worth area of Florida. Others suffered the infirmities of old age, and newspapers frequently published obituary notices. During the 1940s, immigrant numbers decreased 18 percent to 95,686, and in the next two decades they declined 52 percent to 45,499 in 1970. Overall, between 1940 and 1970, when the average of 441 new immigrants arrived annually, the decrease was 61 percent.

Consequently, organizational activism declined. In 1948, the suspension of one of the oldest proprietary papers, *Päivälehti (Daily Journal)* foretold the fate of most other newspapers. While the National Lutherans were merging with the non-Finnish Missouri Lutheran Synod, the Synod Lutherans joined what became the multiethnic Evangelical Lutheran Church in America, though they formed a Finnish conference group within it. In 1963, the Central Cooperative Wholesale likewise merged with a non-Finnish organization. Labor activitsts, too, lost many of their meeting halls and suffered from the postwar Red Scare. While reducing the scale of their

organizational activities, Finns attempted to preserve the record of their past. In the 1950s, the Minnesota Finnish American Historical Society and similar groups initiated projects to collect immigrant records and publish histories of their communities.

In contrast, the second-generation Finnish Americans increased modestly in number between 1940 and 1960 before decreasing to 158,327 in 1970, about 5 percent below the level reported thirty years previously. The group aged fourteen to twenty-four numbered only 9,346 in 1960, while 157,490 were twenty-five years of age or older. Most had finished their schooling; 21 percent had completed only the eight grade of elementary education and 30 percent had four years of high school education. Those with four or more years of college education totaled 10,975 (6.5%). It was this schooling that enabled second-generation Finnish Americans to pursue middle-class professions more easily than their parents.

Except for the immigrants still living after 1980, Finnish descendants are now identified by ethnic ancestry regardless of generation. In 1990, the immigrant generation numbered only 23,313, while all Finnish descendants, whether foreign born or not, totaled 658,870, an increase of 7 percent during the 1980s. In 1980, more than half of the descendants had at least one other ancestry group than Finnish, which indicated ethnic intermarriages, particularly beyond the second generation.

By 1990, Finnish Americans were more geographically dispersed than ever before. As late as 1960, 86 percent of all immigrants and their children were still in the thirteen states that had first attracted Finnish immigrants. In 1990, only 75.6 percent of all Finnish Americans lived in these states. Five of the thirteen states, including Michigan and New York, had net losses, while relatively high increases occurred in states that had never before drawn many Finns, such as Arizona, Virginia, Texas, and Florida. Both retirement living and professional opportunities drew Finns away from old immigrant areas.

Since the 1970s, it has become more difficult to bring together the descendants of Finnish immigrants. Finnish Americans are more dispersed from the historic centers of community activism. Here and there in such places as Fitchburg, Massachusetts, some immigrant societies survive thanks to second-generation Finnish Americans. No new national organizations, however, have replaced the old Finnish ones that had kept immigrants in close contact with each other. The merged religious and cooperative organizations became increasingly multiethnic, and the newspaper networks virtually disappeared. However, the English-language *Finnish American Reporter* has twenty-five hundred subscribers, and since 1983, FinnFest has provided an annual event somewhat similar to the summer festivals that immigrant organizations sponsored in the past. This event brings together several thousand Finnish Americans to remember their Finnishness on college campuses with three or more days of drama, concerts, lectures, exhibits, arts and crafts, films, and other activities. Because FinnFest has attracted mainly middle-age, second-generation Finnish Americans, the absence of many later generation descendants has aroused comment.

The fact that most Finnish-American descendants do not come together as did their immigrant ancestors does not mean, however, that they have all forgotten the ancestral culture. Many second- and third-generation Finnish Americans visit Finland, trace their genealogy, and collect Finnish mementos. Their visits also enable them to do historical research at the Finnish American Historical Archives at Suomi College and the Immigration History Research Center at the University of Minnesota. Some have even made pilgrimages to the monument marking the arrival of Finns in New Sweden. Other activities include visits to pioneer farmsteads that have been preserved in Oregon and Minnesota. All of these activities have served to foster a nostalgic sense of a bygone Finnish legacy of community activism. It is still to be seen, however, whether later generations of Finnish Americans will remember and foster that legacy.

See also: SWEDE-FINNS

Bibliography

Hannula, R. N. (1979). *Blueberry God: The Education of a Finnish-American.* San Luis Obispo, CA.: Quality Hill.

Hoglund, A. W. (1960). *Finnish Immigrants in America, 1880–1920.* Madison: University of Wisconsin Press.

Hummasti, P. G. (1979). *Finnish Radicals in Astoria, Oregon, 1904–1940: A Study in Immigrant Socialism.* New York: Arno.

Jalkanen, R. J., ed. (1969). *The Finns in North America: A Social Symposium.* East Lansing: Michigan State University Press for Suomi College.

Jalkanen, R. J., ed. (1972). *The Faith of the Finns.* East Lansing: Michigan State University Press.

Karni, M. G., ed. (1981). *Finnish Disapora,* Vol. II. Toronto: Multicultural History Society of Ontario.

Karni, M. G., and Asala, J., eds. (1994). *Americana, 1978–1994.* Iowa City: Penfield Press.

Karni, M. G., and Jarvenpaa, A., eds. (1989). *Sampo the Magic Mill: A Collection of Finnish-American Writings.* Minneapolis: New River.

Karni, M. G., and Ollila, D. J., Jr., eds. (1967). *For the Common Good: Finnish Immigrants and the Radical Response to Industrial America.* Superior, WI: Tyomies Society.

Kaups, M. (1976). "From Savusaunas to Contemporary Saunas: A Century of Sauna Traditions in Minnesota, Michigan, and Wisconsin." In *Sauna Studies: Papers Read at the VI International Sauna Congress in Helsinki on August 15–17, 1974,* edited by T. Harald, Y. Collan, and P. Valtakari. Helsinki: Finnish Sauna Society.

Kero, R. (1974). *Migration from Finland to North America in the Years Between the United States Civil War and the First World War.* Turku, Finland: Turun Yliopisto.

Kivisto, P. (1984). *Immigrant Socialists in the United States: The Case of Finns and the Left.* Rutherford, NJ: Fairleigh Dickinson University Press.

Kolehmainen, J. I. (1977). *From Lake Erie's Shores to the Mahoning and Monogahela Valleys: A History of the Finns in Ohio, Western Pennsylvania, and West Virginia.* Painsville: Ohio Finnish-American Historical Society.

Kolehmainen, J. I., and Hill, G. W. (1951). *Haven in the Woods: The Story of the Finns in Wisconsin.* Madison: State Historical Society of Wisconsin.

Puotinen, A. E. (1979). *Finnish Radicals and Religion in Midwestern Mining Towns, 1865–1914.* New York: Arno.

Ross, C. (1977). *The Finn Factor in American Labor, Culture, and Society.* New York Mills, MN: Parta Printers.

Ross, C., and Wargelin Brown, K. M., eds. (1986). *Women Who Dared: The History of Finnish American Women.* St. Paul: Immigration History Research Center, University of Minnesota.

Wasastjerna, H. R., ed. (1957). *History of the Finns in Minnesota,* translated by T. Rosvoll. Duluth, MN: Finnish-American Historical Society.

A. WILLIAM HOGLUND

FRENCH

French-born immigrants in America are sometimes called "Franco Americans." This term, however, characterizes essentially French Canadians. The term "French American" stresses that these immigrants came directly from France and cannot be mixed with other French-speaking groups in the United States (i.e., Louisiana Cajuns, Creoles, and French Canadians). The history, language, and culture of the French Canadians and Louisiana Cajuns often differ from those of the French Americans. Other French-born immigrants came as members of groups seldom associated with France (e.g., Amish and Mennonites) and share their history with these groups. The history of French-speaking immigrants from other countries (e.g., Switzerland and Vietnam) is also comparable to that of other immigrants from these areas. It is sometimes difficult to differentiate the contributions of the members of each of these groups.

Discovery and Settlement

"America," the name of the entire continent containing the United States, appeared in print for the first time in 1507, in Saint-Dié-des-Vosges (France), when the authors of the *Introduction to Cosmography* named the lands mapped earlier by Amerigo Vespucci. French merchants soon came to the realization that this discovery offered a potential source of income. In 1523, the French king Francois I sent Verrazano on a discovery mission. The first French explorers who ventured into the newly discovered lands followed the rivers (the Saint Lawrence River in particular). Members of the Jesuit order, the only religious group allowed in the French colonies at that time, came along with traders and explorers. The Jesuits' goal was to convert the Indians to Roman Catholicism; the goal of other Frenchmen in North America was to develop trade with the Indians. These two approaches were contradictory; the Jesuits often disrupted trading activities because they saw them as detrimental to the spiritual well-being of the Indians. The Jesuits enjoyed their monopoly until 1698. Their efforts brought limited results and often led to violence and warfare between Indian tribes or between the French and the Indians.

The regions of North America where French explorers, soldiers, and missionaries were active became known as New France. It included eastern Canada, the Great Lakes, and the valleys of the Ohio and Mississippi rivers. The seventeenth century marked a key period in the development of New France. The French king Louis XIV oversaw a transformation of the administrative structures of these regions that led to an increase in French efforts at discovery and trade. In addition to a reinforcement of the French presence in what is today the Canadian province of Quebec, the French colonies of Illinois and Louisiana emerged during this period.

The *coureurs des bois* (literally, "messenger of the woods"; here it means traders, in contrast to explorers and Jesuits) were the first Frenchmen to reach many of the Indian tribes during the westward development of New France They were often associated with explorers and Jesuits. The coureurs des bois accused the Jesuits of hampering their trade efforts; the Jesuits accused the coureurs des bois of corrupting the Indians with their alcohol

A French trapper skins muskrats in his camp in the marshes of Delacroix Island in Louisiana in 1941. (Library of Congress/Corbis)

and their bawdy lifestyle; the explorers saw the other two groups as necessary but unreliable allies. The best-known French figures of this period were explorers. In 1673, Jacques Marquette and Louis Jolliet were the first to enter the Mississippi River and travel southward until reaching the Arkansan tribes; Daniel Greysolon, sieur du Luth, explored Lake Superior in 1678; Cavelier de la Salle descended the Mississippi to the Gulf of Mexico in 1682; and Étienne Venyard, sieur de Bourgmont, explored Kansas in 1724. These early explorations did not bring immigrants but led to the creation of a few military and trading outposts. In addition to Quebec and its surrounding regions, the only noticeable areas of French settlement in the late seventeenth and early eighteenth centuries were the Illinois and Louisiana areas.

The evolution of the Illinois region during the second half of the seventeenth century was atypical. After several decades marked by hunting, fishing, and trading, the area (including the valleys of the Ohio and northern Mississippi rivers) became an agricultural region, thus entering the second stage in the development of the frontier. The creation of these French settlements complicated the military protection of French interests. The Fox Indians had been opposed to the French and renewed their attacks on the Illinois settlements. From 1712 to 1737, the French army waged an unsuccessful war against the Fox.

In Louisiana, the late seventeenth and the early eighteenth centuries were marked by military actions against the Indians (the Natchez Wars) and by efforts to attract settlers to ensure the survival and the growth of the colony. The French authorities deported poor men and women, robbers, and other French prisoners to Louisiana. They also provided the poorest women with a "dowry" so they could find a husband once they arrived in America. In addition, the French brought black slaves from Haiti to add to their work force. In 1727, the Ursuline Sisters established a convent in New Orleans (founded in 1718), introduced strict education among Creole and French young ladies, and contributed to an in-depth transformation of French society of Louisiana. The emergence of a moneyed class of traders and planters accelerated the establishment of slavery following enactment of the Black Codes in 1724.

The Seven Years' War began in 1754 in America with the defeat of George Washington at Fort Duquesne, near present-day Pittsburgh. After encouraging actions in 1756 and 1757 against the British, the French forces were progressively put on the defensive. Quebec fell on September 18, 1759, and the rest of New France crumbled progressively. In 1763, the Treaty of Paris took away all the French possessions in America and gave Louisiana to Spain.

Other Early French Settlers

During the early sixteenth century, Protestantism attracted a significant number of French followers. The opposition of the Catholic Church and edicts of the French king encouraged the French

Huguenots to look for other places of settlement. Between 1555 and 1559, groups of explorers sailed without success to Brazil, Florida, and Canada. Jean Ribaut's first expedition to Florida failed; a second, more successful one was launched in 1564.

French Huguenot immigration to America began in earnest during the seventeenth century. The first French Huguenots left from Holland (the Dutch had founded New Amsterdam between 1610 and 1620) and, progressively, from French ports (La Rochelle in particular). By the late seventeenth century, several thousand French Huguenots had sailed for America. They settled in British colonies around New York City (New Rochelle in particular), in New England (Oxford, Salem), in Virginia, and in the Carolinas. The impact of these French-born Huguenots was hardly noticeable in America because they were readily assimilated by the society in which they had found refuge. The Colonists usually welcomed these French newcomers. The "Americanization" of the majority of French Huguenots was thorough because of their religious beliefs and because of their social standing (many French Huguenots were nobles or skilled craftsmen). Today, however, there is still an identifiable trace of the French Huguenot heritage in South Carolina (in and around Charleston).

Revolutionary Years

The revolutionary years include the 1770s, 1780s, and 1790s, when revolutionary wars spread in America and France. The French involvement was significant during the American War of Independence. Military support from the French army and navy as well as financial support from the French Crown sustained the American efforts until the British surrendered at Yorktown (in 1781). The results of these actions were felt differently by the French who were in America. The Marquis de Lafayette's popularity throughout the newly founded United States was a direct result of his own involvement in the War of Independence. For the French settlers in Illinois and the northern Missis-

sippi River valley, these decades meant the end of their independence and prosperity. Their lands in Illinois and Missouri were progressively taken away from them by American settlers, and by the end of the eighteenth century, there were no significant French settlements left in the northern Mississippi River valley.

During the late 1780s and 1790s, the French Revolution forced French nobles out of France, and many found refuge in America. They settled primarily in urban areas (New York, Boston, Philadelphia, Charleston, New Orleans), with a few venturing westward. Several outlandish schemes were concocted by these nobles. One such example was Asylum, a settlement built in northeastern Pennsylvania with the hope of bringing Queen Marie Antoinette to America and re-creating a version of the French court of Versailles. By the early 1800s, as soon as the revolutionary violence diminished in France, most of these émigrés had abandoned their American homes and projects and had returned to France.

Nineteenth and Early Twentieth Centuries

The number of French settlers in the United States at the beginning of the nineteenth century was small and increased slowly during the nineteenth and early twentieth centuries (54,000 in 1850; 116,402 in 1870; 104,197 in 1900; 153,000 in 1920). This minimal increase was due to several reasons. First, since the Treaty of Paris, the French had no lands left in North America. Second, France had never had a strong pattern of immigration. Third, the French colonies easily absorbed those who wanted to try their luck outside France.

Several factors contributed to the arrival of noticeable small French groups to the United States. The development of maritime transportation during the nineteenth century helped French immigrants cross the Atlantic to eastern harbors (New York City, Boston, Philadelphia) and southern ports (New Orleans, Mobile). The defeat at Waterloo led to the arrival of former Napoleonic soldiers who tried to create self-sufficient settlements in Alabama (Démopolis and Aigleville) and in Texas (Champ d'Asile). Those experiments, however, failed rapidly. The second group was composed of French whose goal was the creation of settlements in new lands where a new lifestyle would lead to happiness and well-being. Whether disciples of Étienne Cabet (the Icarians) who settled in Illinois, Iowa, and Missouri, or followers of Charles Fourier (the Phalanxists) who settled in Texas, these small groups encountered limited success. Some remained where they had settled and were absorbed into the neighboring American society; others returned to France after their failure. The third group included the French "forty-niners" who arrived in California during the Gold Rush. These immigrants were attracted by the promise of riches. Their impact, however, was felt only indirectly. After the rush, those who stayed behind planted vineyards and helped establish California's wine country.

A fourth group came later in the nineteenth century and attempted to organize workers in factories, mines, and workshops. These were socialists and anarchists who settled primarily in and around New York City and spread into the neighboring regions in the 1870s and 1880s. Their small numbers and pressures from their bosses as well as workers from other ethnic groups limited their success. The utopians came from urban locales where they were artisans and industrial workers; they attempted to create rural utopias in America and failed. The socialists and anarchists were also industrial workers or miners, and their efforts in America resembled those of their European counterparts. Their success was limited among a varied work force in a climate of uncertainty and tension.

Only a few areas of France provided significant numbers of immigrants. Four provinces sent identifiable contingents to the United States during the nineteenth century. Central France provided a stream of immigrants during the last decades of the nineteenth century; several areas in Brittany also sent regular groups to America. The largest groups came from northeastern France (Alsace, Lorraine, Franche-Comté). Alsace had been confiscated by the Germans after the French defeat of 1870–1871. Migrants from Alsace settled in rural zones between the East Coast and the frontier or in urban areas (Denver, Chicago, Detroit, etc.), where they often associated with German-speaking people, whose language they shared. The Basque migration that began in the 1880s was smaller,

Young French women who married American soldiers during World War I arrive in Boston after the war to reunite with their husbands. (Library of Congress/Corbis)

more focused, and confined primarily to Nevada and California, where the newcomers played an important role in raising and herding sheep and cattle.

French-born immigrants made a noticeable contribution to the history of Roman Catholicism in the United States. Between 1800 and 1900, many newly created dioceses were headed by French-born bishops. This trend is noticeable, as the creation of these dioceses paralleled the westward expansion of the United States. These early French-born bishops were often succeeded by bishops reflecting more closely the ethnic makeup of the Roman Catholic congregations within the diocese. During the nineteenth and early twentieth centuries, other French-born immigrants came alone, sometimes for specific reasons (Civil War volunteers, scientists, artists), and were often assimilated into the surrounding American society, whether they encountered fame or not.

From the 1920s to the 1990s

The impact of World War I caused a total break in the French migration patterns. There was a great need for workers, scientists, farmers, and teachers in France, and emigration slowed. In addition, the American Immigration Act of 1924 limited the number of French immigrants to 3,000 per year. The 1920s and 1930s were somber decades for French Americans. Their overall influence was waning, the cohesion of their communities was diminishing, and French-language publications began to disappear. With the growth of American public education, the active use of the French language became confined to familial or fraternal surroundings and diminished progressively. The end result was the assimilation of the French Americans.

World War II brought a new wave of French immigration to America. Artists, writers, actors, intellectuals, and politicians from diverse political allegiances (from Gaullists to socialists and collaborationists) fleeing Nazism settled in eastern cities. Many continued their original activities and brought an aura of distinction to the French-

American group. After the war, French-born brides of American soldiers constituted a noticeable group of new immigrants.

The general migration patterns of French Americans changed during the postwar decades. Many French who immigrated to America after 1950 were active in teaching and abstract research (in secondary schools and universities), business and commerce (restaurant owners, chefs, designers), and industrial or applied research (computer specialists, software designers). In 1980, among the 120,200 French Americans, there were 160 women for every 100 men, settled primarily in the states of California (23,764) and New York (20,852); there were, however, French Americans in every state of the United States. The French Americans were part of the 2.6 million French-speaking Americans making up the fifth-largest linguistic group in the country.

Conclusion

The overall impact of French Americans was limited in past centuries. Today their impact on the social, scientific, artistic, and intellectual life of the United States is hardly noticeable. There is no French-language press of national scope in the United States, and French Americans have few relational or organizational networks (the Alliance Française seems to be an exception). They wield little power within the American political, religious, and economic systems. In 1980, 67 percent of French Americans had become American citizens; the "melting pot" had really led to their absorption into American society.

See also: ACADIANS AND CAJUNS; FRENCH CANADIANS

Bibliography

Allain, M., and Conrad, G., eds. (1973). *France and North America: Over 300 Years of Dialogue.* Lafayette, LA: University of Southwestern Lousiana Press.

Allain, M., and Conrad, G., eds. (1974). *France and North America: The Revolutionary Experience.* Lafayette, LA: University of Southwestern Louisiana Press.

Allain, M., and Conrad, G., eds. (1978). *France and North America: Utopia and Utopians*. Lafayette, LA: University of Southwestern Louisiana Press.

Creagh, R. (1988). *Nos cousins d'Amérique: Histoire des Francais aux Etats-Unis*. Paris: Payot.

Golden, Richard M. (1988). *The Huguenot Connection*. Doordrecht, The Neth.: Martinus Nijhoff.

Louder, D., and Waddell, E., eds. (1993). *French America: Mobility, Identity, and Minority Experience Across the Continent*. Baton Rouge, LA: Louisiana State University Press.

McDermott, J. F., ed. (1969). *Frenchmen and French Ways in the Mississippi Valley*. Urbana: University of Illinois Press.

Mathy, J.-P. (1993). *Extrême-Occident: French Intellectuals and America*. Chicago: University of Chicago Press.

Nasatir, A. P. (1945). *French Activities in California: An Archival Calendar Guide*. Stanford, CA: Stanford University Press.

Parkman, F. (1851–1892). *France and England in North America: Being a Comprehensive History*. Boston: Little, Brown.

Zoltvany, Y. F. (1969). *The French Tradition in America*. New York: Harper & Row.

ANDRÉ J. M. PRÉVOS

FRENCH CANADIANS

French Canadians define themselves as French-speaking individuals born in Canada. They are the descendants of the French who settled in the northern part of the North American continent in the early seventeenth century. They are mainly concentrated in Quebec, one of Canada's ten provinces. However, other concentrations exist outside Quebec, particularly in the provinces of Manitoba, Ontario, and New Brunswick. The exact number of French Canadians living in the United States before 1890 are not known, since the U.S. Census did not differentiate between Canadians of French or of British origin. French Canadians were first labeled "French." Then, in the late nineteenth century the ethnonym "Franco-American" appeared: it is still used to describe people of French-Canadian birth or ancestry living in the United States. In general, Franco-Americans remain one of the country's least visible and least known minorities.

French Canadians immigrated to several regions of the United States. In the nineteenth century most of them lived in the six New England states of Connecticut, Maine, Massachusetts, New Hampshire, Rhode Island, and Vermont. A smaller number went to California, the Midwest (particularly Michigan, Illinois, Wisconsin, and Minnesota), and New York. Since World War II, French Canadians have dispersed throughout the country as a consequence of greater linguistic integration. Since the 1970s, Florida has become a place of residence for some 700,000 Quebecois.

By the 1990s, more than thirteen million Franco-Americans lived in the United States, 3 million of them in the Northeast. More than 1.5 million spoke French at home, including around 400,000 in New England and New York.

Economic Background

The first French Canadians immigrated to the United States for political reasons. Those who had supported the American rebels in the invasion of Canada in 1775–1776 had to go into exile when the invasion failed. Numbering one hundred, they received land from the American government in the northern part of New York State. Later, the failure of nationalist rebellions in Canada in 1837–1838 forced several French-speaking *patriote* leaders to find refuge in Vermont and New York.

However, these movements are small in comparison to the wave that began in the 1840s because of Quebec's deteriorating socioeconomic conditions. Since the early nineteenth century, the socioeconomic reality of the continent's Northeast had been changing. In Quebec, a high birthrate and the rarity of good agricultural land had exerted pressure on landholdings. French Canadians were faced with the following options: subdivision of farms; moving to cities; or seasonal work in the lumber industry, which had been developing since the early part of the century. But the process of modernization of agriculture, in which few French Canadians could participate, worsened the situation. Agriculture was hurt by a series of natural disasters in the 1830s and 1840s. The financial depression of 1837 strongly affected England and the United States, the two main markets for Canadian agricultural and forestry products. In the 1840s, Great Britain ended its protectionist policy that had provided a ready market for Canadian wood and grain. This decision plunged Quebec into a depression from 1846 to 1850, while the lumber industry—the only profitable sector of the economy—had to adapt to the new marketplace. Many farmers who combined agriculture with lumber found themselves in a difficult position. Some borrowed to buy the machinery necessary to remain competitive in a continental market. Others sold their farms and moved to new territories on the fringes of the settled area or to the eastern parts of Quebec, where land was plentiful and cheap. But many considered immigration to the United States to improve their condition.

Quebec's economic situation remained difficult after 1860. In agriculture, the penetration of the market economy forced farmers to make more adjustments. Although some tried to modernize production by using credit and converting, with more or less success, to dairy farming, those who could not had to sell their land. Some of these displaced farmers became agricultural laborers, while others moved to cities. In industry, the development of manufacturing was slower in Quebec than in New England, and wages generally were lower. Under these conditions, the decision to immigrate to the United States often became self-evident. The booming American manufacturing industry and its need for labor allowed French Canadians to find temporary jobs and save the money necessary to pay their debts or remain on the land. But progressively, given Quebec's sluggish growth, this temporary immigration became permanent as more and more French Canadians, both rural and urban, decide to stay in the United States.

Immigration

From 1840 to 1860, the destination of French Canadians bound for the United States was divided almost equally between the Midwest and New England. Farmers who still had savings went to the Midwest to settle on fertile land, while those without money went to New England to find temporary work as farm laborers or lumber workers. The development of cotton manufacturing in Massachusetts, Rhode Island, New Hampshire, and Connecticut and its huge demand for unskilled labor attracted a growing number of French Canadians. Estimated numbers of immigrants in New England showed a constant increase: 8,700 in 1840, 19,380 in 1850, and 37,420 on the eve of the Civil War. As for the Midwest, there were approximately 3,500 in Michigan in 1850 and 9,000 in 1860. In California, the Gold Rush of 1848 attracted thousands of French Canadians. But from 1860 on, the Northeast emerged as the privileged destination.

After the Civil War, New England became highly industrialized, and the number of French Canadians increased notably, growing from 103,000 in 1870 to more than 200,000 in 1880, 365,000 in 1890, and 573,000 in 1900. In Michigan, the French-Canadian population increased from 23,000 in 1870 to 37,000 in 1880, 57,000 in 1890, and 82,000 in 1900. French-Canadian immigration remained cyclical. Although it accelerated after the Civil War, it decreased in the depression years of 1873–1879, 1882–1885, and 1894–1896. Emigration slowed at the beginning of the twentieth century until the end of World War I. A total of 100,000 French Canadians are estimated to have immigrated to the United States between 1900 and 1910 and 80,000 in the following decade, bringing their numbers in New England to 624,154. This decrease was caused by improved living and working conditions in Canada, where economic growth kept potential emigrants at home. In addition, from the end of the nineteenth century, New England textile mills were faced with stronger competition from the South. Northeastern manufacturers modified their working conditions to decrease production costs, which caused many strikes that did not help French-Canadian immigrants in search of a stable labor market. Immigration resumed in the early 1920s, when 130,000 French Canadians joined their compatriots. European immigration was strongly restricted after the passage of U.S. immigration laws in 1921 and 1924. However, these laws did not apply to immigrants from North America. In the mid-1920s, the economic situation in Canada improved, and emigration tapered off. By 1930, 743,219 French Canadians had immigrated to the United States. Finally, the Great Depression closed the chapter on a process that had drained almost one million French Canadians from Canada since 1840.

The Quebec government tried to take advantage of the depression of 1873 and the immigrants' trend toward voluntary return to enact a policy to repatriate French Canadians living in the United States. In 1875, the government gave free land in the Eastern Townships to returning immigrants. However, this policy had little success. Quebec's economic situation did not improve, and returning immigrants were faced with the same difficulties that had prompted them to leave years earlier. Few settled in the Eastern Townships, and once the depression was over, a good number of them returned to the United States.

Community

French-Canadian communities in the United States were started by the first temporary immigrants. As early as 1850, the parish of St. Joseph in Burlington, Vermont, was founded by French Canadians who broke away from the local Irish Catholic parish. The petitioners explained to church authorities that they were unable to worship properly in a language they did not understand well. This will to re-create structured communities calls into question the reaction of Quebec's clerical and political elites, who always viewed emigration as a straight path to assimilation. Some even vilified emigrants by calling them "traitors" to the nation. The clergy later tempered

their criticism and decided to go into the Anglo-Protestant stronghold of New England to minister to their French-Canadian parishioners. Quebec's ideology of survivance (preservation of the French-Canadian culture) was transposed to New England as elites sought to isolate French Canadians from the "evil" influence of American society. Structured communities were set up in New England's largest manufacturing centers: Woonsocket, Rhode Island; Fall River, Lowell, Lawrence, Holyoke, and Worcester, Massachusetts; Manchester and Nashua, New Hampshire; and Biddeford-Saco and Lewiston, Maine.

Only three French-Canadian parishes existed prior to 1860, but between 1860 and 1900 more than eighty parishes were set up, mainly in Massachusetts, Rhode Island, and New Hampshire. In 1900, immigrants worshiped in 147 national (only French Canadians) or mixed (French Canadians and other Catholics) parishes, participated in more than two hundred national societies, and attend some one hundred parochial schools. The number of parishes grew more slowly in the first two decades of the twentieth century but rose significantly in the 1920s, when twenty-eight new parishes were founded, fourteen of them national.

Working Conditions

The majority of French Canadians found employment in New England's cotton mills. At first they occupied the least-skilled and worst-paid jobs. Work was demanding and conditions were harsh. The work was repetitive and dangerous, the days long and tiring. Shops were poorly lit; the noise from the machines was deafening; and cotton particles floating in the air caused respiratory problems, headaches, and eye irritation. Women and children made up the majority of the labor force in this industry. Men, who could command higher wages, were employed in foundries, machine shops, or shoe factories. Families with several children of working age had an advantage in this type of labor market. Many parents lied about their children's age so they could work at the mill.

The children and wife of a French Canadian potato farmer in 1940 in Soldiers Pond, Maine, stand among barrels that are to be filled with the harvest. (Library of Congress/Corbis)

This behavior has long been criticized. However, the immigrants' objective was to save as much money as possible to return home; they considered all means to reach that goal as good. In addition, family employment at a factory was a continuum from the farm, where boys ten to twelve years old were expected to participate in chores. So it is not surprising that parents wanted their children to work in New England.

Despite difficult working conditions, French Canadians were generally satisfied with their situation in the United States. They earned more money than in Quebec and considered that emigration had improved their standard of living. French-Canadian workers were not attracted by trade unions in the nineteenth century. The clergy criticized unions, and unionism in the immigrants'

minds meant strikes and lost wages, which ran counter to their economic interests. This attitude changed as temporary immigrants decided to settle permanently in the United States and improve their living conditions. However, working conditions in the textile industry deteriorated after World War I, with wage cuts, longer hours, and several strikes, the most famous for French Canadians being the one at the Amoskeag Company of Manchester, New Hampshire, in 1922, in which they played an active role. French Canadians who immigrated in the 1920s did not hesitate to cross picket lines, and tensions erupted between new arrivals and earlier French-Canadian immigrants, who were more aware of the deterioration of working conditions and the need to mobilize to maintain working conditions at a respectable level.

Kinship and Family

If migration before 1860 was often individual and temporary, afterward it was more on a family and permanent basis. Early immigrants convinced relatives and friends to join them, arranged employment for them, initiated them into factory work, and housed them or found them a place to stay. This type of immigration, called chain migration, explains the growth of the movement after 1860 and the immigrants' concentration in specific neighborhoods within industrial towns. The family occupied center stage in the immigration process; it was the basic unit that eased immigration and adaptation to a new society and industrial work. Company policy that encouraged hiring relatives allowed family solidarity to persist for some time despite immigration.

Religion and Social Institutions

Religion motivated the creation of French-Canadian communities. Defining themselves as French-speaking Catholics first, immigrants tried early on to re-create a structure similar to the one they had left behind in Quebec. The Catholic parish was the community's foundation. The parish priest represented authority, and it was essential for immigrants that he be of the same ethnic origin as themselves. This caused persistent conflict with the Irish Catholic hierarchy.

The parish priest oversaw construction of the French-speaking church and parochial school. He also helped create national societies—mutual-aid groups that, on payment of dues, assisted members in case of illness, accident, or death in the family. These societies were also standard-bearers of the faith and promoters of French in the United States. They numbered twenty-one in 1870, seventy-three in 1880, and more than two hundred in 1890. The main ones were the Société Saint-Jean-Baptiste and the Union Saint-Jean-Baptiste d'Amérique.

The press also played an important role in the life of these "Little Canadas." Its mission was to assist the clergy faithfully in the maintenance of the immigrants' way of life and propagation of the ideology of survivance. Prior to 1900, almost 150 French-language newspapers were established in New England, but most of them were short-lived. French Canadians were poor, mobile, and often illiterate, and the few who could read newspapers were more attracted to the American press.

Sociopolitical Organizations

French Canadians in New England became politically active at several levels, especially toward the end of the nineteenth century, when their numbers and concentration in some towns or states allowed them to send compatriots to political office. Fall River, Massachusetts, was the third-largest French city in North America in the early twentieth century, and Woonsocket, Rhode Island, was nicknamed "the Quebec of New England." Aram-J. Pothier from Woonsocket was governor of Rhode Island from 1908 to 1915 and again from 1925 to 1928. Other Franco-Americans were elected to public office, such as judges, state senators, and representatives in many regions of New England.

External and Internal Conflicts

On arrival in the United States, French Canadians often had to join existing English-speaking parishes. The will to set up separate and autonomous French-speaking parishes caused constant friction with the Irish Roman Catholic establishment, who had the last word in approving new parishes. It preferred to keep control over a single mixed parish, while French Canadians wanted a national parish where they could speak their own language and keep their culture. Internally, sporadic conflicts within some Franco-American parishes erupted in the nineteenth century between those advocating wider involvement in American society and those wishing to remain isolated to keep their French-Catholic identity. But starting in the early twentieth century, the high walls that elites built around the immigrants started to crumble. The rise of the second and above all the third generation polarized conflicts and questioned more acutely the ideology of survivance. The new generation was increasingly attracted to the "American way of life" and wished to integrate more fully into mainstream society culturally and linguistically. In addition, with the resumption of mass immigration after World War I, American society questioned its ability to integrate, or even assimilate, large numbers of immigrants. In this view, any foreigner was viewed as a potential troublemaker who must be quickly assimilated to maintain social order. Immigrants were pressed to become "100 percent American" and adopt the English language. French Canadians, like other immigrant groups, were met with open hostility from the population. French parochial schools were constantly pressured to increase teaching in English. In 1922, the Peck Act was adopted, providing that private schools would be directly supervised by the state instead of by local school boards. Only private schools that taught in English the same subjects as public schools and in a manner satisfactory to the authorities would be allowed to operate. Despite their unhappiness, Franco-Americans abided by the law.

But another crisis was to divide French-Canadian communities even more dramatically. The *Sentinelle* crisis, as it was called, lasted from 1922 to 1929. At first it was a fight between Franco-American militants and the Irish Roman Catholic bishop of Providence, Msgr. William Hickey, over management of parochial schools. However, this crisis rapidly became a struggle between the partisans of survivance and those who were more open to American influences. In 1922, the bishop decided to oversee Catholic high schools in Providence to make them more attractive and more competitive with the public school system. These schools were placed under the diocese's direct authority and were supported financially by all the diocese's parishes. This decision elicited a strong reaction from Franco-Americans. The opposition's leader, Elphège-J. Daignault, stated that the diocese's policy negated the parents' right to educate their children as they saw fit and the parishioners' right to manage the schools that they themselves

funded. But above all, he asserted that the policy threatened French-Canadian survival, since the parish has always been the institution that allowed the immigrants to retain their ethnic identity. What the Irish Catholic clerical authorities wanted, according to Franco-Americans, was to take away their power in this basic institution to weaken and then destroy it.

The fight against the authorities' decision was lead by the newspaper *La Sentinelle*. From 1923 to 1929, Franco-Americans petitioned Rome several times to obtain the pope's opinion on the question. They even used the courts, a dangerous gesture that could lead to excommunication. In 1927, the *Sentinellistes* were defeated in the courts, and the bishop obtained permission from the Council of Rome's Sacred Congregation to excommunicate those who sued him. The decision was announced in April 1928 and destroyed the movement, which disappeared in 1929.

The crisis had a major impact not only on relations between the Irish episcopate and French Canadians but also within Franco-American communities. Moderates on the issue of survivance learned from this episode that submission to the laws of the church comes first, while radicals saw it as the ultimate attempt by the English-speaking Catholic clergy to silence the French-speaking element. In addition, immigrants who arrived in the 1920s fanned tensions between the old guard and the rising generation by sharing the views of the first generation on the primacy of survivance. This confrontation weakened the Franco-American community. In 1930, the Great Depression put a virtual end to immigration. Only people who had guaranteed jobs or sponsors able to support them could immigrate. The practical end of immigration marginalized radicals even further and allowed for the ascendancy of moderates who believed in continuity within wider participation in American society.

The virtual end of immigration had a negative effect on the Franco-American community. From 1930 to 1960, communities and institutions were weakened by the lack of newcomers. English gained more ground among the population, parishes were less and less French, and newspapers and institutions declined and gradually abandoned the goals of survivance.

However, the 1960s were marked by an ethnic renewal in the United States. Franco-Americans took advantage of this climate to revitalize their institutions to defend their culture and their language. New elites emerged. New organizations were set up, such as the Franco-American Resource and Opportunity Group (FAROG), founded by students at the University of Maine at Orono in 1971 with the goal to make English-speakers aware of the French-speaking reality, and the Council for the Development of French in New England (CODOFINE), created in Manchester, New Hampshire, in 1973. Traditional organizations such as the Association Canado-Américaine, the Union Saint-Jean-Baptiste, and the Fédération Féminine Franco-Américaine still hold annual conventions. Since 1980, the French Institute of Assumption College in Worcester, Massachusetts, has organized an annual conference where academics present papers on various aspects of Franco-American life. A few French-language newspapers are still being published, including *Le Journal* in Lowell, Massachusetts. The Franco-American community has given birth to individuals who have marked American history. Many do not know that the Beat Generation's most eloquent voice, Jack Kerouac, was born in Lowell of French-Canadian parents. Even if some cultural traits are maintained and reinforced, linguistic assimilation seems irreversible. Franco-Americanness becomes more a matter of local identification. Some New England towns, such as Woonsocket in Rhode Island, Manchester in New Hampshire, and Van Buren, Madawaska, and Fort Kent in Maine, continue to highlight their Franco-American roots by holding traditional cultural and French-language activities. If the trend toward localization continues, one can expect that Franco-Americans will become even less visible in American society.

See also: ACADIANS AND CAJUNS; CANADIANS; FRENCH

Bibliography

Anctil, P. (1979). *A Franco-American Bibliography: New England.* Bedford, NH: National Materials Development Center.

Brault, G. J. (1986). *The French-Canadian Heritage in New England.* Hanover, NH: University Press of New England.

Cumbler, J. T. (1979). *Working-Class Community in Industrial America: Work, Leisure, and Struggle in Two Industrial Cities, 1880–1930.* Westport, CT: Greenwood Press.

Freeman, S. L., and Pelletier, R. (1981). *Initiating Franco-American Studies: A Handbook for Teachers.* Orono: Canadian/Franco-American Studies Project, University of Maine.

Hareven, T. K., and Langenback, R. (1978). *Amoskeag: Life and Work in an American Factory-City.* New York: Pantheon.

Louder, D. K., and Waddell, E. (1983). *French America: Mobility, Identity, and Minority Experience Across the Continent.* Baton Rouge: Louisiana State University Press.

Quintal, C. (1983). *The Little Canadas of New England.* Worcester, MA: French Institute, Assumption College.

Ramirez, B. (1983). "French-Canadian Immigrants in the New England Cotton Industry: A Socio-economic Profile." *Labour/Le Travail* 11:125–142.

Ramirez, B. (1991). *On the Move: French-Canadian and Italian Migrants in the North Atlantic Economy, 1860–1914.* Montreal: McClelland & Stewart.

Roby, Y. (1990). *Les Franco-Américains de la Nouvelle-Angleterre, 1776–1930.* Sillery, Quebec: Septentrion.

Vicero, R. D. (1968). "Immigration of French Canadians to New England, 1840–1900: A Geographical Analysis." Ph.D. diss., University of Wisconsin.

JEAN LAMARRE

FRISIANS

During the early medieval period, the North Sea was often called Mare Frisicum, and even today most Frisians in Europe (also known as Friesians,

Friesian Islanders, and Friesens) live on the off-shore islands, or near the coast, of that body of water. By the late medieval period, however, linguistic and cultural distinctions that persist to the present became evident among West, East, and North Frisians. The West Frisians live primarily in the Dutch province of Friesland, in the north-western part of the kingdom of the Netherlands; East Frisians in the German territory of Ostfriesland, along the North Sea between the Dutch border and the Weser River; and North Frisians just south of the German-Danish border, along the western Jutland Peninsula, and on the adjacent offshore islands.

Though documented as a distinct people for some two millennia, Frisians claim no single national homeland in Europe and hence are frequently identified as Dutch, German, or even occasionally as Danish. Most educational efforts, official transactions, and religious celebrations are carried out in the language of the dominant culture rather than in Frisian. These circumstances have led to a polarization, in both Europe and North America, between those reticent Frisians who identify themselves simply as Dutch or German and more vocal proponents of a distinct Frisian linguistic and cultural identity. In contrast to some European minorities, however, the Frisians tend to disavow political separatism.

Although Frisian enclaves exist in the United States, it is virtually impossible to cite accurate population figures. For the 1990 U.S. Census, "Frisian" and "Friesian Islands" were offered as possible ancestry codes for respondents. No "Frisians," however, appear in the U.S. Bureau of the Census's *Detailed Ancestry Groups for States*. Rather, they constitute part of the undifferentiated fifty-eight million German Americans and six million Dutch Americans reported in the documentation of the census.

Frisians have been present in North America at least since the seventeenth century. Two governors of New Amsterdam, including Peter Stuyvesant, were West Frisians. In the 1680s, Frisians were among the earliest settlers of Germantown, Pennsylvania. In that same period the utopian Labadist community, with a strong West Frisian contingent, settled in Maryland. Serious influxes of Frisian population did not begin, however, until the mid-nineteenth century.

West Frisians

Frisian seceders from the state church, organized by Maarten Anne Ypma, arrived in southwestern Michigan in 1847 and soon founded the settlement of Vriesland. In the same year, Sjoerd Aukes Sipma attempted to gain as many followers as possible to join the colony at Pella, Iowa, founded by the religious separatist Hendrik Pieter Scholte. Eventually, Pella claimed a *Vriesche buurt* (Frisian neighborhood) on the northern edge of town, where many Frisian Americans settled primarily as agriculturalists.

Many West Frisians were adherents of the Reformed faith, and settled in the 1850s and 1860s in enclaves such as Friesland (Columbia County) or New Amsterdam (formerly Frisia, north of La Crosse), Wisconsin. Other denominations are, however, represented among this ethnic group. Since the founder of the Mennonite faith was from Friesland, it is appropriate that in the mid-1850s strictly observant Frisian Mennonites immigrated to the United States, settling in New Paris, near Goshen, Indiana.

Frisians are typically strong proponents of their belief systems, even if as agnostics. It is therefore noteworthy that the one West Frisian settlement founded (primarily for economic reasons) on ideals of social progress never prospered. The group, headed by Worp van Peyma at Lancaster, just east of Buffalo, New York, in the late 1840s and early 1850s, failed to attract new members and eventually disbanded.

In addition to Vriesland, Michigan, there are, or once were, communities named Friesland in Minnesota, South Dakota (now Platte), and Wisconsin, as well as a number of towns named for Frisian cities, such as Harlingen, New Jersey. With the exception of enclaves such as those in or near Whitinsville, Massachusetts; Paterson, New Jersey; Rochester, New York; and Lynden, Washington, most West Frisians live in the areas of greatest general Dutch-American concentration: southwestern Michigan, northern Indiana, Greater Chicago, southern Wisconsin, south-central and northwestern Iowa, Pennsylvania, New Jersey, and New York, the states of the Pacific Northwest, and south-central Los Angeles County, California. Since World War II Canada's more lenient immigration policies have led to a dramatic increase in the West Frisian population of that country.

Many, but certainly not all, of these Frisian Americans can be identified by surnames ending in -ma (e.g., Jaarsma, Talsma) or -stra (e.g., Dykstra, Hofstra). They typically affiliate, as do many Dutch Americans with roots in the various provinces of the Netherlands, with the Reformed Church in America or the Christian Reformed Church. A number of once-popular Frisian organizations have experienced a decrease in membership, and West Frisians who choose to belong to a heritage organization often choose the more general Dutch International Society in Grand Rapids, Michigan.

East Frisians

East Frisians immigrated to America for purely economic reasons. Failed grain and potato crops as well as waning opportunities for off-season migrant laborers in the nearby Netherlands led to initial settlement in the 1840s in Illinois' German Valley: Stephenson, Ogle, Winnebago, and Carroll counties. Further enclaves followed in Adams, Chippewa, and Iroquois counties. Virtually wherever swampy land could be found at reasonable prices, the East Frisians seized the opportunity, employed their skills in irrigation and drainage, and established profitable agricultural enterprises.

In 1854, members of the Illinois settlements migrated to Grundy County, Iowa. It is estimated by some (not altogether implausibly) that there are more persons in Iowa actively claiming East Frisian ancestry than in Germany. The main concentrations are in Butler, Grundy, and Hardin counties and in the north-central and northwestern part of the state. From 1882 to 1972, the *Ostfriesische Nachrichten* (later the *Ostfriesen-Zeitung*) was published at Breda, Iowa. The East Frisian Genealogical Society continues to be active in George, Iowa, and the Ackley Heritage Society in Ackley, Iowa, provides resources for the study of East Frisians in the United States, primarily in Iowa. Cultural programs and heritage festivals are sponsored by the Ostfriesian Heritage Society in Grundy Center, Iowa.

Further westward migration by East Frisians took two distinct paths. The Reformed (the majority among American East Frisians, albeit the minority in the European homeland) moved primarily northward to Minnesota (Chippewa County) and South Dakota (Turner, Cook, and Lincoln counties). The Lutheran East Frisians (the majority in Europe, but the minority in the United States) moved west and south to Nebraska, particularly to Gage County. It was especially the Nebraska East Frisians who perpetuated the tradition of reclaiming swampland for profitable agriculture.

East Frisian land stewardship patterns have been studied in the United States because of the strong group preference for farming and because strenuous efforts to keep land within families, or at least within the East Frisian community, provide scholars with an unusual opportunity to investigate attempts at continuity in cultivation and conservation policies.

Language maintenance is unusually vigorous among East Frisians, and it is not uncommon for a person removed three or four generations from the immigration experience to have a functional command of the language (typically a Frisian-based form of Low German). In 1995, for example, Buffalo Center, Iowa, and the cooperating communities of Ackley, Grundy Center, and Wellsburg, Iowa, raised funds to host an East Frisian theater group from East Friesland, Germany. The cast presented five performances in the ethnic language to packed auditoriums.

Group cohesiveness is enforced by a reported tendency toward endogamy (marriage within the group) and a loyalty to religious roots. A frequently cited example of the latter comes from Flatville, a town in Champaign County, Illinois, that does not appear on many maps. The traditionally East Frisian congregation of Immanuel Lutheran Church claims more than one thousand members, most of whom do not actually reside in Flatville but who desire to maintain affiliation at the church of their forebears.

Along with various Reformed and Lutheran sects, the United Church of Christ claims a number of East Frisian members. An exception to the dominant rural Protestantism of the East Frisians is offered by the Catholics, originally from the Saterland area, whose most prominant concentration is in and around Cincinnati, Ohio.

North Frisians

Some of the North Frisians on the U.S. East Coast trace their ancestry to colonial-era seafarers, merchants, or immigrant tradesmen. The peak of North Frisian immigration to the United States, however, came during the last third of the nineteenth century. Most settled in the northern Midwest, especially in or near east-central Iowa, though a number settled on the East and West coasts.

Quite commonly, North Frisians think of themselves as North Germans, Low Germans, or Schleswig-Holsteiners in America rather than as North Frisians per se. If they affiliate with a heritage association it may be with the American Schleswig-Holstein Heritage Society of Davenport, Iowa, whose membership draws heavily upon the concentrations of Low Germans in east-central, north-central, and northwestern Iowa.

One reason for the assimilation of the North Frisians into the larger German-American population lies in the historical background for their relatively heavy nineteenth-century immigration to the United States. In response to Prussia's annexation of Schleswig-Holstein in 1865 under Otto von Bismarck and the ensuing Austro-Prussian (1866) and Franco-Prussian (1870–1871) wars, young men often attempted to leave Germany between their confirmation registry at age fourteen and eligibility for military conscription at sixteen. Others came in their early twenties, after fulfilling

military obligations. The relatively young age of immigrants, their resultant dependence on sponsors or support networks in the United States, and their aversion toward the political regime in the European homeland all contributed to accelerated acculturation by North Frisians to life in late nineteenth-century rural America and fostered strong patriotic ties to the United States. These circumstances led to a prevalent view that identification with other German Americans, with a traditionally German congregation for worship, and often with agricultural related professions was more important than maintenance of North Frisian or sectarian particularism.

In 1995, the American Schleswig-Holstein Heritage Society hosted a conference in De Witt, Iowa, on Low Germans in the United States. The conference drew participants from throughout the United States (albeit primarily from the Midwest) and from Germany. Participants with North Frisian connections appeared to be attending out of broader interests in Low German-American culture rather than because of specific North Frisian concerns.

Conclusion

Scholars have pointed out that a song popular among Frisians in the nineteenth century and comprehensible in most varieties of the Frisian language summarizes much of the sentiment of the Frisian immigrants to the United States. Those who sang "*Amerika, du lan fan dream en winsken*" (America, you land of dreams and wishes) immigrated with aspirations of success and self-actualization in the new country. Though proud of their heritage and eager to maintain group ties, these were not refugees driven from the European fatherland primarily by persecution or ideological intolerance. Hence Frisian Americans may maintain communication with relatives in Germany or the Netherlands but do not consider themselves to be part of a Frisian diaspora on American soil. Rather, they see themselves as Americans who place a high value on, and vest major confidence in, such values as hard work (often in a rural setting), fiscal conservatism, communal interdependence, active religious affiliation, and the practice of personal piety. While seldom attracting attention by social or political activism, they tend to be visible in various areas of the country because of their preference for living near other group members. Although immigration quotas and changing demographic factors on both continents led to a marked decline in the rate of immigration to the United States during the twentieth century, Frisian Americans as a group represent the realization of the dream espoused by so many European immigrants who arrived in the United States in the last half of the nineteenth century.

See also: DUTCH; GERMANS

Bibliography

Droege, G. B. (1979). "Frisians, Ethnicity and America in Twelve Questions and Answers." *Europa Ethnica* 36:28–42.

Frizzell, R. W. (1982). "Reticent Germans: The East Frisians of Illinois." *Illinois Historical Journal* 85:161–174.

Galema, A. (1991). "Transplanted Network: A Case Study of Frisian Migration to Whitinsville, Mass., 1880–1914." In *The Dutch in North America*, edited by R. Kroes and H.-O. Neuschäfer. Amsterdam: Free University Press.

Galema, A. (1996). *Frisians to America, 1880–1914: With the Baggage of the Fatherland*. Groningen, Netherlands: REGIO Project Uitgevers.

Hiller, E. T.; Corner, F. E.; and East, W. L. (1928). "Rural Community Types." *University of Illinois Studies in the Social Sciences* 16(4):490–624.

Hoogstraat, J. (1990). *Von Ostfriesland nach Amerika: Aus dem Leben ostfriesischer Auswandrer des 19. Jahrhunderts*. Norden, Germany: Bibliothek Ostfriesland 3, Soltau-Kurier-Norden.

Lucas, H. S. (1955). *Netherlanders in America: Dutch Immigration to the United States and Canada, 1789–1950*. Ann Arbor: University of Michigan Press.

Lüpkes, W. (1925). *Ostfriesische Volkskunde*. Emden, Germany: Schwalbe.

Pauseback, P.-H. (1990). "Zur Auswanderung as dem norfriesischen Raum nach Nordamerika in königlich-preßischer Zeit." *Zeitschrift der Gesellschaft für Kanada-Studien* 10(2):97–100.

Poortinga, Y. (1958). "Emigaesje út Westerlauwersk Fryslân nei en festiging yn'e Foriene Steaten (oant likernôch 1900 ta)." *Friesisches Jahrbuch* 32:89–109.

Saathoff, J. A. (1930). "The Eastfrisians in the United States: A Study in the Process of Assimilation." Ph.D. diss., University of Iowa.

Schnucker, G. (1986). *The East Friesens in America: An Illustrated History of Their Colonies to the Present Time*, translated by K. De Wall. Topeka, KS: Jostens Printing and Publishing.

U.S. Bureau of the Census. (1992). *1990 Census of Population. Supplementary Reports. Detailed Ancestry Groups for States*. Washington, DC: U.S. Government Printing Office.

PHILIP E. WEBBER

GARIFUNA

The Garifuna are an authentically American immigrant group that spring from the Caribbean soil of Middle American geography. They originate in the so-called New World, just as do immigrants from Panama, Jamaica, Canada, or Argentina. Unlike these others, however, Garifuna draw their identity primarily from their own particular ethnic and racial history, sensibilities, and cultural heritage, rather than from the political and territorial entity of a nation-state such as Haiti or Mexico. Garifuna have constructed an identity that straddles categories normally considered to be discrete. They can legitimately claim to be indigenous American, black, Latin American, or West Indian. Apparently unique and exotic, Garifuna actually embody commonly found processes of cultural movement, combination, and invention that are typical of the histories and peoples of the Western Hemisphere.

These immigrants hail from many nations. They emerge from a diaspora that began at the end of the eighteenth century, when the people were dispersed from the eastern Caribbean island of St. Vincent. A tiny remnant population lingers in St. Vincent, but almost all Garifuna arriving in the United States call one of several Central American nations home, including Nicaragua, Honduras, Guatemala, and Belize. Moreover, Garifuna claim both a Native American identity as well as an African-American one. Their physical appearance, culture, language, religion, and history all attest to their combined heritage as black and indigenous.

When they settle in the United States, Garifuna may choose to affiliate (1) with men and women from their nations of origin, whether or not these compatriots are Garifuna; (2) with already resident Latin American or Caribbean immigrant communities; (3) with other Garifuna, even though they may originally come from different Central American countries. Alternately, Garifuna may exercise the option of connecting with resident African-American communities as well as resident and immigrant Native Americans. Not all of these potentially desirable neighbors are equally hospitable toward their Garifuna sisters and brothers. Among the factors determining reception are socio-economic status, regional differences within the United States, linguistic preferences, and levels of racial prejudice. This is an extremely complex and variable situation that changes over time and must be examined on a case by case basis.

Caribbean History

In the 1630s, European travelers in the eastern Caribbean island of St. Vincent reported seeing mixed groups of similarly dressed people, some of whom seemed to be African and others Caribbean Indian. It appears that shipwrecked Africans joined the resident Carib Indians, and these amalgamated communities became favored destinations for escaped Africans fleeing nearby European slave-holders. It should be noted that some contemporary Garifuna believe they are, in fact, the descendants of a pre-Columbian African presence that antedates the onset of African slave trading in the Caribbean. In either case, the Garifuna people represent one of the first free black populations established in the African-American diaspora.

Equally significant, the contemporary Garifuna also represent the indigenous pre-Columbian presence in the Caribbean. Their ancestors were the South American Carib and Arawak Indians who migrated to the Caribbean archipelago from the mainland, beginning with the eastern Caribbean islands immediately off the South American Atlantic coast, moving through these smaller islands and on to the larger islands sometimes known as the Greater Antilles. The sizable Arawak settlements in the largest islands welcomed Christopher Columbus and the first Europeans arriving in the region. Unlike the Arawak, the foreparents of modern Garifuna remained behind and settled on the smaller islands. Known as the Island Carib Indians, these new people emerged from the extensive contact between the two original South American groups during their sojourn in the Caribbean. After the Europeans documented the existence of the free African-American population that chronicles came to call the Black Caribs, these same reports began referring to the Island Caribs as the Red Caribs, or occasionally the Yellow Caribs. No one knows exactly how the so-called Black Caribs and Red Caribs may have formed combined or segregated communities over time. It is known, however, that they eventually divided the island of St. Vincent into two separate enclaves. Yet they probably had some continued association, and they may even have assisted each other in occasional mutual defense against their European common enemies.

Eventually the existence of an armed free black population proved too debilitating for the slave-holding communities on St. Vincent, so the British authorities decided to take action to bring about the end of years of chronic Garifuna raids and intermittent military skirmishes. In 1796, the English troops finally and decisively defeated the Garifuna forces. The surviving Garifuna were detained, exiled, and abandoned off the east of Spanish-occupied Honduras in 1797. Over the next two hundred years, Garifuna settled along the Caribbean coast of Central America from Nicaragua to Belize, the northernmost of the Middle American homelands. This centuries-long diaspora spawned a transnational consciousness that enables modern Garifuna of different nationalities to acknowledge and reinforce their shared ethnic heritage. These Central American Garifuna now number 300,000 to 400,000, and they are recognized by other Centro-Americanos as a distinct ethnic group.

Ethnic and Racial Markers and Emblems

The salient characteristics emblematic of Garifuna identity are socially constructed, and consequently they are contested, vary in different social situations, and have changed over time. Nevertheless, certain features are most often emphasized by both outsiders and the Garifuna themselves. The Garifuna language is one of the most frequently recognized characteristics. The language, unique to this group, is a subtly modified version of the Island Carib language spoken by those Indians in the seventeenth century. Although the vocabulary clearly originates in pre-Columbian Native South American lexicons, phonetically—even to an untrained ear—the language sounds "West African." Centuries of contact with other groups have also produced many cognates imported from French, Spanish, standard West Indian English, and West Indian Creole English. In Honduras, the heart of Garifuna Central America, where the majority of Central American Garifuna live, most children learn Garifuna as their first language. In St. Vincent and Nicaragua, language loss is almost complete. Between these extremes, the Guatemalan Garifuna are usually fluent in both Garifuna and Spanish, while, in addition to standard and Creole English, most Belizean children learn a variety of Garifuna heavily laced with the Creole *lingua franca* of the nation. Many Belizean Garifuna children are also encouraged to acquire some fluency in Spanish. Indeed, throughout the region Garifuna are known for their unusual ability to speak many languages. They celebrate this as a part of their identity, which demonstrates intelligence as well as adaptability.

Like most Central Americans, Garifuna are almost all at least nominal Catholics, but many are also active in the more esoteric religion unique to Garifuna. Like other syncretic belief systems, such as Shango or Santeria, Garifuna religion incorporates elements of Catholicism with African components. Garifuna syncretic religion is also explicitly oriented toward ancestors and includes many elements directly traceable to South American Indian shamanic belief systems. Few outsiders know many details of Garifuna syncretic beliefs and practices, just as very few outsiders have more than a slight familiarity with the Garifuna language. However, both these markers are recognized as important by Garifuna themselves, and non-Garifuna as well. Moreover, just as some Garifuna are not fluent in the Garifuna language, some do not actively participate in the Garifuna syncretic religion. Whether language and religion are actual lived experience, potent symbolic markers, or both, they remain two of the most often noted signals of Garifuna identity.

Garifuna people are also associated with the sea. Their Central American settlements are almost exclusively coastal, and they are respected sailors, navigators, and fishers. The technology of boat building and crafting nets and traps for turtles, crabs, and other marine animals, as well as seafood cuisine, are associated with the Garifuna. Their staple food, cassava, has gradually been displaced by wheat, rice, and corn. Nevertheless, the increasingly rare but distinctive Garifuna cassava bread and the equipment required to process the manioc tuber and produce the bread serve as emblems of Garifuna heritage and identity. Additional identity markers reflect the experiences of a dispersed people. Throughout their Middle American diaspora, Garifuna are known for their independence, group solidarity, and status as outsiders—members of a distinct, numerically small minority. Non-Garifuna have sometimes labeled them as wild, clannish pariahs. Within the group, Garifuna celebrate their persistence despite the dispersal and hostility of others—their ability to survive, adapt, and thrive whatever the circumstances.

The racial and ethnic dimensions of Garifuna identity unfold differently in the different Central American homelands. In Belize—historically a predominantly black country—within the African-American racial category, ethnic distinctions such as language, religion, lifestyle, and worldview have distinguished the Garifuna from the majority black Creole population. Belizean Garifuna have also emphasized their indigenous American Indian identity to underscore the contrast between themselves and Belizean Creoles. In the past, Belizean Garifuna have been the targets of discrimination by Creole and other Belizeans. As the mestizo population of Belize grows, talk of a pan-ethnic Afro-Belizean identity has also accelerated. The incipient Afro-Belizean category must overcome lingering doubts and tensions spawned during the years of strife between the two black ethnic groups. Undoubtedly, new alliances will develop, including possible affiliations between Garifuna Belizeans and other indigenous Central American Indian Belizeans.

Outside Belize, an African-American racial identity becomes salient in predominantly Latin and mestizo countries. In addition to the discrimination directed toward the Garifuna as black people, Indians in these mestizo countries have also suffered from unfair treatment. Garifuna enjoy the distinction of dual claims to infamy based on their concurrent membership in two stigmatized racial-ethnic groups. Often Garifuna people's perceived status as *Moreno* or *Negro* overshadows their coincident Indio identity. Nevertheless,

Garifuna are activist members in organizations of Native Middle American Indians, regional black organizations, regional multiethnic multiracial coalitions, and national and international Garifuna organizations.

Experiences in the United States

Upon arriving in the United States, things change radically for Garifuna. The majority of Americans have never even heard of the Garifuna and know little or nothing about the details of their history, culture, and racial/ethnic markers. Assumptions made based on the African-American appearance of most Garifuna actually obscure many of the ethnic realities of their identity and virtually obliterate their Native American racial descent. General ignorance about the facts of Garifuna life also become entangled with the actual category-bursting characteristics of this amalgamated diasporan identity. This snarl constructs a high hurdle of confusion for immigrants to surmount.

Nevertheless, Garifuna are very resourceful in the face of this challenge. As the following examples demonstrate, they craft their U.S. identities to take advantage of the many options available to them. For instance, in 1992, the five hundredth anniversary of the arrival of Columbus in the Caribbean, Garifuna invoked their Carib Indian roots to join with other indigenous people to fight for native peoples' rights. This connection also spurred their involvement in a Smithsonian project on the music and culture of Native South American rainforest groups. Southern California politicians frequently used Garifuna as translators when mediating disputes in Los Angeles Latin American communities. As black Centro-Americanos they were linguistically and culturally sensitive but essentially impartial, since they were not themselves members of the Mexican, Salvadoran, or other enclaves. The Garifuna are especially well-positioned to act as ethnic brokers in a variety of situations. Their mixed race and transnational heritage strain the confines of notions about identity and confer an extraordinarily situational litheness to the enactment of Garifuna identity in the United States.

For example, Garifuna could legitimately check three of the five standard census categories: African American, Native American, and Hispanic, not to mention an incipient "Other" category. This also makes it very difficult to get an accurate count of the size of the community. Concerns about legal status and perceptions of a hostile climate toward immigrants also lead to the kind of undercounting common among many immigrant communities. Nevertheless, reliable estimates place the size of the U.S. Garifuna population at around 120,000. While this number represents one of the smaller groups among U.S. immigrants, it holds vital significance for the Garifuna themselves. This tiny segment of the total U.S. population comprises at least 25 percent of the total Garifuna population worldwide. Significantly, more Garifuna from different parts of the diaspora come together in the United States than in any other place where Garifuna live.

While Garifuna live in cities all over the United States, the largest communities are located in New York, Los Angeles, Chicago, and Houston. The New York community is the oldest and the largest, established just after World War II. Chain migration slowly augmented this community throughout the 1950s, with a surge in the 1960s, and there has been steady growth since then. The next largest community, the Los Angeles community, grew slowly until the 1970s when far larger numbers began arriving and continued at higher levels throughout the 1980s. The New York community totals between 75,000 and 100,000, with 75 percent to 80 percent of the immigrants arriving from Honduras. In Los Angeles, the community is at least 80 percent Belizean and numbers between 15,000 and 25,000. Unlike the two largest Garifuna enclaves numbering in the tens of thousands, only an estimated 5,000 to 10,000 Garifuna live in Chicago, and no more than 3,500 Garifuna live in Houston.

Regional differences are also important, with the New York community being more heavily Honduran and oriented toward a black Latino identification, while Los Angeles, being more Belizean, leans toward a Caribbean, Afro-Indian, or African-American emphasis. These are only tendencies, and the hallmark of Garifuna identity is the broad and flexible repertoire of affiliation available in different situations. It should be noted that Garifuna can as easily activate identity to create distance as to create alliances. For example, Los Angeles Garifuna may highlight their indigenous or Latino identity to distinguish themselves from West Indians or black U.S. residents. Finally, the seemingly limitless options available to Garifuna individuals require the collaboration of other individuals and groups to be really useful, and the adoption of certain identifications may limit the extent to which others will accept any future assertions Garifuna may take.

Within U.S. immigrant communities, many other Central American immigrants know something about the Garifuna, such as the religion, language, or lifestyle details mentioned above. This knowledge will structure relations with the Garifuna for good or ill and contrast with the general ignorance characteristic of most resident Americans. While this ignorance enhances the flexibility of Garifuna identification, the knowledge of other Centro-Americanos may curtail Garifuna options. Fellow immigrants sometimes bring imported racial and ethnic tensions from their former home. For example, black Belizean immigrants may retain or reinvent the old animosities between Creole and Garifuna Belizeans that characterized black Belizean interethnic relations at the time many immigrated to the United States. In other instances racial dimensions will likely obscure ethnic distinctions. This scenario is most likely when immigrants meet who are from mestizo Central American nations such as Guatemala or Honduras. Similarly, the salience of race often structures interactions with resident Americans. They, like mestizo immigrants, associate black (as well as Indian) identity with markedly minority status. In these immigrant communities divisions are most often revealed among Garifuna and non-Garifuna from the same Central American homeland. Conversely, the Garifuna community itself

may fragment along national lines, although other divisions emerge as well. Notable among these are village or region of origin, generational distinctions, gender, and socioeconomic position.

Among these distinctions, socioeconomic differences are significant for several reasons. Most important, hopes of economic advancement provide the primary goal for the vast majority of Garifuna immigrants. Those Garifuna with technical or professional skills often experience downward mobility, at least initially. They may also encounter difficulties as immigrants, Latinos, or people of color due to biases built into the American economy. Many are never able to move beyond entry-level positions, but a sizable segment—at least 10 percent to 25 percent—achieve real economic security for themselves and the ability to support dependents back in Central America. Sometimes their status as foreign-born African Americans gives them certain advantages over their U.S.-born counterparts.

Socioeconomic divisions intersect with gender and generational distinctions in interesting ways. As immigrants arrive in the United States, women often have an easier time finding entry-level points—most often as domestic workers—than their male counterparts. Eventually, these differences level off or begin to favor male immigrants following the strata of general gender biases built into the American economy. Many Garifuna women are just beginning to extricate themselves from an oppressively patriarchal set of restraints. This idealized patriarchal power has always been confronted by the reality of a number of outspokenly autonomous professional women as well as numerous female household heads earning modest but independent wages. This household configuration has persisted in the United States as one of a range of arrangements, including nuclear families that usually have two wage earners. Both nuclear and extended family forms are threatened by the sequential immigration to the United States that characterizes most immigrants' histories. Ultimately, even extended families may be fully reconstituted in the United States, but more often, the youngest and the oldest family members may remain in or return to Central America. They receive financial contributions from adult male and female providers working in the United States.

Garifuna have long practiced migratory wage labor. Historically, Central American Garifuna men were most likely to supplement their families economically through migration, but since the 1950s, women have been increasingly likely to travel in search of work. Like many other Caribbean and Middle American immigrants, the practice of seeking work away from home and possibly fragmenting families to do so, predates the North American experience. U.S. immigrants are simply extending their search for work further than in the past.

Socioeconomic and generational distinctions have coincided in a focus on upward mobility. A general emphasis on educational opportunity and technical training has been bolstered by annual Career Day events that recognize the achievements of ambitious youths, highlight the accomplishments of successful Garifuna adults, and establish mentoring programs to assist and inspire young people. The committee that organizes Career Day event includes members who work for these goals throughout the year. In fact, this focus on youths is most prominent in efforts to resist assimilation, prevent language loss, and encourage strong identification with Garifuna heritage and contemporary issues.

Assimilation, Transnationalism, and Garifuna Self-Determination

Garifuna efforts to define their own identity and influence their fortunes as a group appear frequently and spontaneously. Once again, regional differences determine relevant issues. In New York City, for example, Garifuna have successfully won bilingual assistance for students learning English as a second language in the public school system. In Los Angeles, where so few children can claim Garifuna as a mother tongue, activity focuses more on providing opportunities for Garifuna-language use and acquisition to forestall the very real possibility of total language loss.

The linguistic needs of Garifuna young people contrast from one community to another. However, concerns about appropriate conduct and the dangers of city life characterize Garifuna across regions. Parents and guardians hope to use Garifuna identity to insulate young people from these urban evils. Explicit strategies range from activities like Career Day events, mentioned above, to encouraging membership in cultural organizations, dance groups, drumming classes, and language classes. The simplest techniques involve reminding youngsters that they are "different" and come from a proud tradition of mobile, persistent people who succeeded in maintaining their particular legacy over the centuries, in numerous nations, despite hostile physical and social environments.

For so many Garifuna, their young people are the precious embodiment of the future and consequently the focus of efforts to preserve and perpetuate group identity. The Garifuna go beyond this, however. Their worldview emphasizes the connectedness of the generations. The living have specific obligations to their descendants as well as to their ancestors. Within Garifuna religious cosmology, indiscretions are believed to have consequences not only for the perpetrator but also for other family members, again including the deceased and the unborn. Garifuna history includes couvade activities that prescribe and proscribe the behavior of expectant fathers who even undergo onerous parallel labor experiences. Deceased relatives prove almost as troublesome as the newborns, demanding ritual baths, food drinks, and increasingly elaborate ceremonies with insistent regularity over the course of years or decades.

Just as it is difficult to maintain linguistic fluency in the United States, it is virtually impossible to perform the full range of religious practices. Nevertheless, U.S. residents remain connected to their homelands through religious ceremonies held in Central America that require either the financial support of family members living in the United States, their physical attendance, or both. Supernatural obligations and sanctions reinforce family and community ties back to these Central

American homelands as well as forging links with Central American Garifuna from other countries within the diaspora. Their common identity as Garifuna religious practitioners provides a point of contact for residents of different regions in the United States—such as Chicago and Houston—or for immigrants from Guatemala, Belize, and Honduras who may come together in New York or Los Angeles.

One of the most spectacular examples of the public display and celebration of Garifuna identity is the holiday called variously Garifuna Settlement Day, November Nineteenth, or simply Nineteenth. This event was formally observed in the United States in the early 1970s in Los Angeles. Since then the holiday has spread to other U.S. communities. Settlement Day originated in Belize in the early 1940s as a commemoration of the nineteenth-century arrival of the first Garifuna immigrants to what was then the colony of British Honduras. In the United States, Settlement Day is an occasion to portray Garifuna identity to a wider audience and to rally Belizean and non-Belizean Garifuna and strengthen their connection with the group. There is a pageant and a queen associated with Settlement Day, in addition to dances, dinners, Catholic services, cultural fairs, house parties, and more. A Settlement Day committee works all year to produce this fall event. In addition to Settlement Day, Garifuna are active in local organizations such as folk dance groups, cultural preservation societies, and the national Garifuna USA organization founded in 1992. These groups have produced occasional newsletters, weekly radio programs, and inclusion in cultural and ethnic celebrations at the neighborhood, city, and state levels.

Garifuna efforts to negotiate and maintain a distinct identity are similar to strategies used by many other immigrant groups. Garifuna are different from other immigrants in that Garifuna identification can only be understood in the context of their centuries-old diaspora. As other immigrants grapple with the imminent transnational realities of their North American experience, Garifuna identity is already immanently portable. Many recent U.S. immigrants struggle to craft an identity that can be tailored to the new contexts yet remain recognizable as distinctive and connected to their particular heritage. For Garifuna, neither immigration itself nor the flexible accommodation to changing conditions threatens their sense of peoplehood. Rather this successful adaptable immigrant status is an integral part of their history and a cornerstone of their identity. The specter of assimilation has stalked the Garifuna community for many years, in many lands, yet they continue as an identifiable distinct people.

Conclusion

The Garifuna diaspora, begun in the late eighteenth century, has produced a transnational group whose identity is not anchored by any one political entity or geographic territory. Moreover, that same diaspora is manifested most spectacularly in the United States, where Garifuna from many countries come together. These immigrants arrive with a history of mobile persistence. When Garifuna say, as so many immigrants do, they will go "home" to Central America to retire, or when they and their families circle back and forth between Central America and North America, they are activating long-standing migratory patterns. So many other immigrants must struggle to create a new identity as they go along, that is as life in the United States challenges, rewards, and confounds them. In contrast, even as Garifuna craft new U.S. identities, this novel permutation joins a medley of already established versions of being Garifuna. Forged in the crucible of a historic diaspora, while melding black and indigenous heritages, Garifuna immigrants arrive in the United States primed to deal with both the threat as well as the promise of their new lives in North America.

See also: HONDURANS

Bibliography

Coelho, R. (1955). "The Black Carib of Honduras: A Study in Acculturation." Ph.D. diss. Northwestern University.

Gonzalez, N. (1969). *Black Carib Household Structure*. Seattle: University of Washington Press.

Gonzales, N. (1979). "Garifuna Settlement in New York: A New Frontier." *International Migration Review* XIII:255–263.

Gonzales, N. (1988). *Sojourners of the Caribbean: Ethnogenesis and Ethnohistory of the Garifuna*. Urbana: University of Illinois Press.

Kerns, V. (1983). *Women and the Ancestors: Black Carib Kinship Ritual*. Urbana: University of Illinois Press.

Macklin, C. (1972). "Aspects of Black Carib Religion." Honors thesis, Harvard University.

Macklin, C. (1986). "Crucibles of Identity: Ritual and Symbolic Dimensions of Garifuna Ethnicity." Ph.D. diss., University of California, Berkeley.

McClaurin, I. (1996). *Women of Belize: Gender and Change in Central America*. New Brunswick, NJ: Rutgers University Press.

Palacio, J. O. (1988). "Caribbean Indigenous Peoples Journey Towards Self-Discovery." *Cultural Survival* 13(3):49–51.

Sanford, M. (1971). Disruption of the Mother-Child Relationship in Conjunction with Matrifocality: A Study of Child-Keeping Among the Carib and Creole of British Honduras." Ph.D. diss., Catholic University of America.

Taylor, D. M. (1951). *The Black Carib of British Honduras*. New York: Wenner-Gren Foundation.

Young, V. H. (1993). *Becoming West Indian: Culture, Self, and Nation in St. Vincent*. Washington, DC: Smithsonian Institution Press.

CATHERINE L. MACKLIN

GEORGIANS

The people generally known as Georgians call themselves Kartvelebi and their country is Sakartvel-o, "the land of the Kartvelebi." The word "Georgia" probably comes from the Turkish word "Gurji," which is what Turks call Georgians. Other theories suggest the name comes from the Greek *georges*, meaning farmer, or from the name of the Georgians' patron saint, St. George. The dominant Kartveli tribe gave its name to the new state, but

Georgian regional groups, such as the Mingrelians and Svans, who speak their own distinct languages at home, still retain their own identities. However, they identify themselves as Georgian and speak Georgian in public communications.

The country of Georgia occupies 27,657 squares miles (approximately twice the size of Belgium). On its northern border lies the Russian Federation. To the south are Turkey and the Republic of Armenia, and to the west and east are the Black Sea and the Republic of Azerbaijan, respectively. The northern part of the country is dominated by the Greater Caucasian Mountains (Elbruz is the highest mountain at 18,480 feet) and in the south by the Southern Georgian Highlands. Despite its geographical location in "Asia," Georgians have been historically and culturally influenced by Meditarranean powers as well as by those of Asia and the Middle East. Throughout the centuries, because of its strategic location as a crossroads between Europe and Asia, Georgia was invaded and settled by Greeks, Romans, Persians, Turkish tribes, Arabs, Mongols, and Russians. Georgia was also on one of the branches of the Silk Road, which carried trade from China and India to Europe. The Georgian people have been occupied over the centuries by a multiplicity of foreign armies, but Georgian culture, with its polyphonic music, folklore, spectacular dance, poetry, and literature, retained its uniqueness. The first literary works in Georgian are from the fifth century C.E., and Georgia played an important role in Byzantium and the spread of Christianity in the east. Georgians can trace their statehood to the sixth century B.C.E., when the kingdoms of Colchis (the land of the golden fleece) and Iberia were known to both the Persians and the Greeks. Physically, Georgians resemble the Greeks and the Italians, and they think of themselves as part of Mediterranean culture.

Georgians share their country with various ethnic minorities who have settled in the region over the centuries. While Georgians made up 70.1 percent of the population in 1989, this percentage is increasing as ethnic minorities begin to emigrate from the region. The largest ethnic minorities in

1989 were the Armenians (8.1%), Russians (6.3%), Azeris (5.7%), Osetians (3.0%), Greeks (1.9%), and Abkhazians (1.8%). In the past, most ethnic groups in Georgia lived peaceably together, and the country was cosmopolitan in culture. But since the collapse of the Soviet Union, Georgia has been torn apart by secessionist wars. Both the Abkhazians, an indigenous Caucasian group related to the Adyghe and Cherkess nations of North Caucasia, and the Osetians, who speak an Iranian-based language, wish to secede from Georgia.

Georgians in the United States

It is hard to estimate how many Georgians are living in the United States today. In the pre-Soviet period Georgians would have been classified as Russian, as they were subjects of the Russian Empire. In the Soviet period, they would have been categorized by U.S. immigration authorities as stateless or as former Soviet citizens. There was no separate category for foreign-born Georgians in the U.S. Census before 1991. It is only since the collapse of the Soviet Union in 1991 and the re-establishment of an independent Georgian state that they have been recognized by the U.S. government as a separate group, but even then there have still been problems in counting them. Georgians only make up 70 percent of their country's population, and legalized aliens in the United States since 1991 are still categorized by country of birth. Thus, some individuals classified as Georgian may not consider themselves as such. But from informal surveys of the Georgian community and additional statistics released by the U.S. Immigration and Naturalization Service (INS) and the U.S. Bureau of the Census, it can be estimated that there are between 3,000 and 4,000 Georgians in the United States (up to 12,000 if the Georgian Jews are included). Since the 1992–1995 period, 2,217 citizens from the Georgian Republic have arrived in the United States, probably the largest wave of legal immigrants from Georgia in U.S. history.

The number of legal immigrants is small for a number of reasons. Georgians have traditionally been reluctant to leave their republic in Caucasia due to strong family and kinship ties, the favorable climate and productive land, relative prosperity, and a strong sense of pride in their culture. Soviet statistics in 1989 revealed that 95.2 percent of all Georgians living in the Soviet Union lived in Georgia, while only 66.7 percent of all Armenians and 85.4 percent of all Azerbaijanis were living in their respective homelands. Second, Georgians have had few opportunities to emigrate. As subjects of the Russian Empire, emigration was extremely difficult, although some Georgian revolutionaries made their way to the United States before 1917 to escape czarist persecution. One such revolutionary was Alexis Gogokhia, who arrived in the United States in 1900 and became a prominent socialist activist and a founding member of the American Communist party in 1919. Emigration was almost impossible during the Soviet period. The rare opportunities for Georgians to leave their country during the twentieth century were between 1918 and 1921, a period of brief Georgian independence; after World War II, when some Georgian prisoners of war managed to avoid repatriation to the Soviet Union; during the 1970s, when Jews, many of them Georgian, were permitted to emigrate as part of the Helsinki Agreements; and finally after 1991, when Georgia regained its independence. A third factor that discouraged Georgian immigration to the United States was the attraction and physical closeness of Europe. Most Georgian emigrants in the past settled either in Russia, Poland, France, Turkey, Iran, or Germany. Both Munich and Paris were popular havens for Georgia political émigrés. Before the 1930s, many Georgian political émigrés belonged to the Georgian social democratic movement (although a sizable minority preferred the more nationalistic National Democratic Party), which had established strong links with European socialist parties in Germany, Belgium, and France. After the invasion of Georgia by the Red Army in February 1921, President Jozef Pilsudski of Poland, a former member of the Polish Socialist Party, invited many Georgians to settle in Poland. The largest and longest established Georgian community remains in Paris.

Settlement History

The first Georgians who immigrated to the United States were a group of horse riders invited in the 1890s to join Buffalo Bill Cody and his Wild West Congress of Rough Riders of the World. For more than twenty years, they toured the United States and Europe with this group and others like it, such as Pawnee Bill's Historic Wild West and the Cole Younger and Frank James Wild West. The Ringling Brothers Circus, one of the largest at the time, was sufficiently impressed to sign up approximately thirty Georgians after 1900. Georgians in these touring shows were often referred to as Cossacks. A very small number of Georgians who wished to escape military service during the 1904–1905 Russo-Japanese War or who were attracted by railway construction jobs in California trickled into the United States in the decade before World War I.

During the period of Georgian independence, informal diplomatic links were established with the United States, and Georgia was recognized *de jure* by the Supreme Allied Council (although not by the United States) in February 1921. After the Red Army invasion of Georgia in 1921, many Georgians fled to Europe, Turkey, Poland, and China. Approximately 150 of these exiles, mostly former officers, government officials, or aristocrats, immigrated to the United States. They were often members of Georgian princely families such as the Bagrationis, Mdivanis, Eristavis, Dadianis, and Chavchavadzes (Prince Paul Chavchavadze, for example, was married to a niece of Czar Nicolas II). Many of the new arrivals assimilated into the American upper class. Prince Archil Gurieli married Helena Rubenstein, a famous perfumer, and the Eristavis became linked through marriage to the family of J. P. Morgan, a well-known financier. George Matchabeli, the founder of the Matchabeli perfume group, arrived at this time, as did Alexander Kartvelishvili (Kartveli), an aeronautical engineer and founder of Republic Aviation, one of the largest aircraft manufacturing companies during and after World War II. He designed the Thunderbolt fighter plane (P47) and the Thunderjet (S84).

The latter was known as the workhorse of the Korean War. The small Georgian community of the 1920s was concentrated in New York City. At that time, Prince Simon Sidamon-Eristoff (Eristavi in Georgian) played a leading role in the community.

The next significant wave of Georgians arrived after World War II and consisted mostly of former émigrés from Europe, especially from France and Poland, but there were also individuals from South America. These émigrés were joined very soon afterward by Georgian prisoners of war (POWs). More than 600,000 Georgians were in the Red Army during World War II, and many ended up in American POW camps. Settled under the terms of the Displaced Persons Act of 1948 or the Refugee Relief Act of 1953, most of them were former Soviet soldiers, although a number of them had

A Georgian potter sells his wares. (Stephen Jones)

been members of the émigré National Committee for the Liberation of Georgia or had fought in the Georgian Legion and other military units under German command in an endeavor to liberate their homeland from Soviet occupation. A few even came from Soviet-occupied Poland and from the French Foreign Legion. Unpublished Georgian memoir materials indicate many of these immigrants had a hard time in the early postwar years, although others, especially former émigrés from Europe and South America, assimilated relatively quickly. The Tolstoy Foundation and the Church World Service are remembered by many Georgians as charitable organizations that helped them find employment. The Tolstoy Foundation was led for many years by Prince Teimuraz Bagration and later by Constantine Sidamon-Eristoff, both of Georgian descent.

In the 1970s, there was a third wave of Georgian immigration. This wave consisted of Georgian Jews, with the first families arriving in 1973–1974. Two more larger groups of Georgians Jews, many from Israel, followed in 1978–1980 and in the mid-1980s. They were helped to settle by the Hebrew Immigrant Aid Society and the New York Association for New Americans. The majority (perhaps 80%) of the 7,000 to 8,000 Georgian Jews in the United States live in Queens in New York City, and to a lesser extent in Brooklyn. They have built their own synagogue and publish a community newsletter in Georgian, Hebrew, and English. They also produce a magazine, *New Life,* in both Georgian and Russian. Some Georgian Jews have established themselves in the jewelry trade, and more are involved in the food retail business. The children of first-generation immigrants are more likely to pursue professional rather than business careers. There are also significant Georgian Jewish communities in Philadelphia, Baltimore, and Washington, D.C. Emigration from Israel and Georgia has increased in the 1990s due to the serious unemployment in both countries.

Since 1991, the Georgian community has received a new infusion, the fourth wave, through the arrival of students and scholars on exchange programs and through the presence of Georgian diplomats and their families in both Washington, D.C., and New York City. Both the Georgian embassy in Washington, D.C., and the Permanent Mission of the Republic of Georgia at the United Nations in New York City were established in 1993. There is a particularly high concentration of Georgian students at Emory University (particularly in the schools of business, medicine, law, and public health) as a result of Atlanta's city program with Tbilisi, Georgia's capital. The sister city program began in 1989 and focuses on cultural exchanges and developmental aid, especially in the medical field. There is a community of 150 to 200 Georgian residents in Atlanta.

Georgians have become more geographically scattered throughout the United States, but according to INS figures for 1992–1995, the vast majority still prefer to settle either in California or New York. In 1995, for example, 27 percent of legal immigrants from Georgia settled in California, and 33 percent settled in New York.

Language, Religion, and Cultural Life

The Georgian language is part of the southwest Caucasian group of languages that includes Zan (Mengrelo-Chan), Svan, and Georgian proper (Kartuli). It does not belong to any of the world's major language categories (e.g., Indo-European, Semitic) and is incomprehensible to all neighboring peoples. Georgian has its own alphabet from at least the fifth century C.E., influenced by Phoenician-Aramaic and Greek scripts, although there have been two major modifications since that time. The latest alphabet, called *mkhedruli,* has thirty-three characters and is written from left to right. Language is central to Georgian national identity. In 1978, when Georgia was still part of the Soviet Union, students organized a large demonstration to defend their language from the threat of Russification (substituting Russian language use for Georgian). In the 1990s, 98.2 percent of Georgians considered Georgian their native tongue, and all business, politics, and most cultural activities within Georgia were conducted in Georgian.

Georgia's multiethnic content is reflected by a multiplicity of religions. Most Georgians belong to the Georgian Orthodox Church, a branch of Eastern Orthodoxy. East Georgia was converted to Christianity by St. Nino of Cappadocia in 330 C.E. St. Nino and St. George share a special popularity among Georgians. According to the Georgian Church, it became autocephalous (led by its own Patriarch) in the fifth century. The church has always been a symbol of national unity to Georgians. It held the country together when it was territorially divided for centuries in the late middle ages. There are also Georgian Catholics (a small number) and Georgian Muslims (a larger number) in Achara in southwest Georgia and along the state's southern periphery. The Osetians and Abkhazians are mostly Eastern Orthodox (although some Abkhazians are Muslim); the Azeris, Assyrians, and Kurds are mostly Muslim; and the Armenians, Greeks, and Russians are Gregorian, Greek Orthodox, and Russian Orthodox, respectively. Georgia has always been a place of religious tolerance and Tbilisi has many synagogues and churches and at least one mosque.

The Georgian-American community, unlike other Soviet national groups, such as the Armenians, Latvians, or Ukrainians, has never had the numbers or resources to organize a political lobby. It has been unable to finance Georgian-language schools or even its own church. Georgian immigrants display a fierce loyalty to their language, but their children find it hard to retain a knowledge of Georgian without community support. There are Georgian-language programs at a number of universities (e.g., Indiana University at Bloomington, Columbia University, and Emory University) taught by Georgian immigrants, but these courses serve the academic rather than the native community. The absence of financial resources is a serious problem for the Georgian community. Most Georgian immigrants are Georgian Orthodox, but they have no separate church building in which to pray. The Georgian community is served by the Georgian Orthodox Mission of St. Nino, founded in 1992 and led by a Georgian priest under the jurisdiction of the Georgian Patriarchate in Tbilisi. Services are held twice a month in the Cathedral of the Orthodox Church in America on Second Street in New York City. The congregation in New York City is small (twenty to twenty-five members); but despite its size the mission serves as an important meeting place for Georgians on important festival days like St. Nino's, and it has also organized food donations to the Republic of Georgia.

Georgians have been more successful in establishing newspapers and associations, although this activity has also been plagued by insufficient finances. The first Georgian organization in the United States was the Kartuli Sazogadoeba (Georgian Society), founded in San Francisco in 1924. In 1930, the Allaverdy (Caucasian Society) was formed to unite different Caucasian groups. In the 1950s, it ran a vacation home, and it still runs a summer camp. Its offshoot, the Allaverdy Foundation, provides scholarships for Caucasian students who wish to study in the United States. In 1931, the Kartuli Sazogadoeba Amerikis Sheeretbul Shtatebshi (Georgian Association in the United States of America, Inc.), which was more exclusively Georgian, was founded by, among others, Prince George Matchabeli, Prince Simon Sidamon-Eristoff, Paul Kvaratskhelia, and Prince Irakli Orbeliani. In the 1950s, many of the new immigrants became enthusiastic supporters of U.S. anti-Communist policies. More politicized than their predecessors, they formed leagues and parties: the Kartuli-Amerikuli Liga (Georgian-American League), the Kartuli Erovnuli Kavshiri (Georgian National Union) and Sakartvelos Damoukideblobis Amerikuli Sabcho (American Council for Independent Georgia). The Georgian-American League published the newspaper *Voice of Free Georgia* from 1953 to 1958 and, following its closure, *Iveria* from 1970 to 1980. The American Council for Independent Georgia published *Chveni Gza* (Our Path) in 1953. Between 1955 and 1975, the community was also served by the newspaper *Kartuli Azri* (Georgian Opinion). In 1951, after pressure from Georgian émigrés such as Guivy Zaldastani, Georgians were given their own radio section on *Voice of America*, which still functions today with a staff of five Georgians.

The Georgian Association in the United States of America, Inc., which in the 1960s had a loose membership of more then five hundred, is the longest serving Georgian organization in the United States. Until the 1970s, it ran a shelter for needy Georgians known as the Georgia House, and its presidents included Paul Kvaratskhelia, Sandro Baratheli (active in settling Georgian Jews in the 1970s), Guivy Zaldanstani, and Othar Zaldastani. Since 1991, it has renewed its charitable and cultural activities in the United States with a new vigor. It organizes annual celebrations on St. Nino's Day (January 26) and Independence Day (May 26, marking the Declaration of Independence of the first Georgian Republic of 1918–1921). Two other charitable Georgian associations have been founded since 1991 to help Georgian society through a period of economic deprivation and chaos: American Friends of Georgia (1994), based in New York and Massachusetts, and Georgian Foundation, Inc., in California. Both are run by Georgian immigrants or their descendants and have concentrated on humanitarian aid to fight tuberculosis, support orphanages, distribute food packages for the poor and books for libraries.

Given the small size of the Georgian community in the United States, it is being linguistically assimilated. Exogamous marriage is common, and most young Georgian Americans achieve good professional careers. There have been some great Georgian successes in American cultural and political history despite their small numbers. In the 1940s, George and Helen Papashvily wrote one of the most popular books of the time, *Anything Can Happen* (1945), which was an account of a new immigrant's experience in the United States in the 1930s. The book was subsequently made into a film, and George Papashvily went on to become a well-known sculptor.

There is no discrimination or "ghettoization" of Georgians. The strong sense of Georgian kinship and solidarity still brings the scattered community together during Georgian national holidays. Most Georgians are strong supporters of tradition and the family that has helped them, despite their small numbers and geographic spread, retain a sense of Georgianness. The community has been rejuvenated by their country's independence, the arrival of Georgian diplomats and students, and the activity of new associations. Georgians will never reach the numbers or strength of, for example, the Armenian diaspora in the United States, but since independence they have successfully raised the profile of the Georgian community within the United States and are now being replenished with younger members.

See also: RUSSIANS

Bibliography

Allen, W. E. D. ([1932] 1971). *A History of the Georgian People: From the Beginning Down to the Russian Conquest in the Nineteenth Century.* London: Routledge & Kegan Paul.

Anderson, B. A., and Silver, B. D. (1996). "Population Redistribution and the Ethnic Balance in Transcaucasia." In *Transcaucasia, Nationalism, and Social Change: Essays in the History of Armenia, Azerbaijan, and Georgia,* revised edition, edited by R. G. Suny. Ann Arbor: University of Michigan Press.

Gachechaladze, R. G. (1995). *The New Georgia: Space, Society, Politics.* London: University College Press.

Jones, S. (1992). "Revolutions in Revolutions within Revolution: Minorities in the Georgian Republic." In *The Politics of Nationality and the Erosion of the USSR,* edited by Z. Gitelman. New York: St. Martin's Press.

Papashvily, G., and Papashvily, H. W. (1945). *Anything Can Happen.* New York: Harper & Brothers.

Suny, R. G. (1989). *The Making of the Georgian Nation.* London: Tauris.

STEPHEN JONES

GERMANS

Traditions remain firmly rooted among many transplanted German Americans. More than a century and a half after settlement, Lutheran parishioners from Frankenmuth, Michigan, maintain routine contact with their parent congregation in the old country. As they have through the decades, church members still start each written letter with the same Old-German greeting, "I send you greetings in the name of the Father and Son and Holy Ghost." However, outside of a few enclaves such as Frankenmuth and in the "German triangle"—the areas between Cincinnati, Milwaukee, and St. Louis—and in Pennsylvania, German languages and customs have disappeared. For most contemporary Germans, social isolation and the ethnic tie to a small clan have been largely extinguished. Ethnic diversity among fellow Germans, religious and political differences, and two world wars fought against Germany encouraged German Americans to assimilate rapidly. The same forces also caused others to withdraw into isolated rural and urban ethnic enclaves. Diversity and fragmentation within German-American societies challenge those who intend to construct a common history of German settlement in America. Generalizations must be made carefully, stereotypes questioned, and historical observations often must be made with caution and qualification.

Today, ethnic traditions among Germans, when they do exist, are selective. The best German characteristics are often celebrated as part of tradition and economics—to attract visitors to Old World celebrations. German immigrants, better than most, successfully struggled and sacrificed to provide their children with a sense of belonging. Once later generations mastered the English language, secured employment, and transcended local parochialism, they looked back at their heritage. Most German Americans did not prolong ethnic sentimentality, and they should be viewed as descendants of those who struggled to become real Americans.

The contradictory image between cultural preservation and assimilation among German-speaking peoples is best explained by the sheer number of German immigrants and their places of origin. In 1990, fifty-three million Americans claimed some degree of German descent. Between 1820 and 1900, nearly five million immigrants from Germany settled in the United States. Between World War I and 1963, German arrivals outnumbered those from any other single country. In the last quarter of the twentieth century only Britain could claim more ethnic offspring (14% of all Americans) than those identifying themselves as descendants of Germans (12%). Nearly seven million Germans, settled in America, or 15 percent of the total immigration. Their numerical strength made it inevitable that sizable numbers would readily Americanize.

Besides numbers, religious, cultural, and geographic heterogeneity also encouraged assimilation. Nineteenth- and twentieth-century wars continuously shifted the boundaries of Germany and made it difficult to identify all Germans geographically. For the purpose of this entry, German immigrants are defined as those arriving from the territory of imperial Germany as formed in 1871, and the state that succeeded it after the Treaty of Versailles in 1919. Unless they arrived in masses as religious congregations or villages from one province and settled together in America, cultural differences among Germans coupled with widespread geographical settlement patterns in America dispersed common culture identity and facilitated acculturalization.

Germans are also exceptional among immigrant groups because of their religious differences. The most obvious religious identity divided northern Germans, dominantly Protestant Lutheran, from southern Germans and Rhinelanders, mostly Catholic. Even within these broad geographical zones, smaller sects were central to German identity. Moravians, Mennonites, Pietists, and Jews often were motivated by religious intolerance or missionary zeal to emigrate. Religion reinforced group identity in the New World and buttressed German churches, schools, and languages, especially in the mid-Atlantic and midwestern settlements.

German immigrants were politically and economically diverse. They were not all conservatives from an authoritarian empire, but freethinkers, political reformers, and some revolutionaries. And unlike poverty-driven Irish or Poles, many Germans arrived in America with some major or

German Americans wear traditional costumes for the German Village Fair in New York in 1904. (Museum of the City of New York/Corbis)

substantial savings and agricultural or mechanical skills. Also, many German immigrants had acquired some education.

Eighteenth-Century Immigration

Initially German settlers arrived in Virginia, recruited by the London Company; however, it was not until seventy years later, in 1681, that William Penn brought thirteen German and Dutch Mennonite families to settle Germantown, Pennsylvania. Although this was the earliest specifically German settlement, large-scale immigration did not begin until the early eighteenth century, in 1709, when heavy taxation and harsh winters led several thousand Palatinate Germans to immigrate, via England, to the Hudson River region of New York and to Pennsylvania. Word-of-mouth promotion, letters, and "newland" agents persuaded thousands of southwestern Germans to travel to

America. Perhaps as many as half to two-thirds arrived in America as "redemptionists"—individuals bound to New World masters as servants, usually for four years, for payment of their passage across the Atlantic.

German immigration continued, reaching a peak in midcentury, until the Seven Years' War (1756–1763), imperial prohibition in 1768, and the American Revolution (1775–1783) brought it to a fifty-year standstill. The immigrants entered mostly through Philadelphia, and, like the experiences encountered in later centuries, these eighteenth-century pioneers immigrated to America for a variety of reasons.

The early Germantown settlers were Dutch and Swiss German-speakers, and mostly Lutheran and Reformed Church members. And while religious motives played a role in emigration—some Mennonites, Baptists, Dunkers, Schwenkfelders, and Moravian Brethren arrived before 1740—

economic factors overwhelmingly motivated most German newcomers. Old Country inheritance customs that continuously divided small land parcels forced many farmers into marginal existence by the 1730s. Skilled and semiskilled artisans, day laborers, and former landholders were attracted to the opportunities in America promoted by ship captains, advertisements by proprietors in America, and "letters from Pennsylvania."

Those seeking a better life crowded the port city of Rotterdam, Holland. Often with little savings left after their four-week trip down the Rhine from southwestern Germany, these refugees remained willing to hazard the last of their resources on the transatlantic voyage; 7 to 10 percent of them died in crossing or shortly after their arrival. It is estimated that as many as 50 percent of the young children whose families attempted to settle along the tidewater coast between Baltimore and South Carolina also died.

Most German-speakers, though, fanned out in and around Philadelphia. The early arrivals took the best farmland or settled into the skilled or market trades in Germantown. In time others moved westward into Lancaster County and down the Shenandoah Valley into Virginia and South Carolina. New York, Maryland, and New Jersey also attracted significant numbers. Benjamin Franklin, just before the Revolutionary War, estimated that German-speaking settlers made up one-third of Pennsylvania's population. Still, while they were one of the largest sources of immigration, only about 100,000 Germans arrived in the colonies. In the 1790 U.S. Census, about 8.6 percent of the population in the United States was of German decent.

Franklin expressed the anxiety evident among many Pennsylvanians, where an alarming number of Germans threatened traditional English-speakers: "Why should *Pennsylvania* founded by the *English*, become a colony of *Aliens*, who will shortly be so numerous as to Germanize us instead of our Anglifying them?" (Dinnerstein and Reimers, 1988, p. 2). To assimilate the newcomers the state set up a number of English-language-only schools.

German-speakers assimilated into the cultural mainstream at a moderate pace in the eighteenth century. Rural areas originally settled by church groups or village migrations maintained their ethnic identity. The German language was used in the home and at religious services. A German press that supported thirty-eight German newspapers prior to 1800 flourished in urban areas. Many German-language schools and societies also were established to resist secularization and loss of the language. Marriage partners remained largely German-speakers at the end of the century, although patterns of religious commonality in marriage were beginning to break down.

As rural German settlements grew and settlers moved away from the cities, integration diminished German culture. The English language was necessary for trade and commerce, law, and politics. Germantown residents began to Anglicize their names, and church and business records were soon kept in English. German immigration, almost nonexistent for half a century at about the time of the American Revolution, encouraged assimilation as ties with Germany were loosened or severed.

Nineteenth-Century Immigration

Large-scale emigration from the German provinces began again after the Napoleonic wars in 1815. Until 1834, southwestern Germany continued to provide the bulk of the emigrants. They still departed from Dutch port cities; however, by the 1830s, Antwerp, Rotterdam, and Amsterdam acquired poor reputations because residents frequently exploited emigrants by charging high fees for provisions and lodging during the long wait for passage. On January 1, 1834, provincial toll barriers between German states were lowered nationwide. The Zollverein, or tariff union, facilitated movement to the German harbors of Bremen and Hamburg. Now others, both paupers and the more prosperous, joined the southwesterners on the journey to America.

By midcentury, passengers arrived in German port cities from the Rhineland, Westphalia, Oldenberg, and Saxony. The eastern regions of Prussia and Mecklenburg, heretofore recipients of German émigrés, likewise began to export people to America. Steamship and cheap, subsidized railway travel further diverted emigrants from the Rhine River corridor to Bremen and Hanover. American insistence on clean and safer ships, coupled with the efforts German emigration societies made for shorter waiting periods—only three or four days before departure—quickly dispelled many hazards once associated with the legendary journey.

Geographical diversification also reflected a change in the socioeconomic status of the travelers. Impoverished, surplus populations of the Southwest continued to emigrate, but now an increasingly more prosperous emigrant emerged from the North. Here farms and small shops could be passed on in total to heirs. Those who did not benefit through inheritance, as well as craftsmen, small merchants, and manufacturers who could not compete within a changing industrial economy, saw their future in the New World. Emigration for these people was a way to preserve and sustain Old World family and economic habits. Between 1830 and 1850, a higher proportion of comfortable, skilled, and educated emigrants left Germany than in any other period.

War and military service also influenced emigration. Decades-long conscription terms in the provincial armies coupled with frequent wars fought for German unification after midcentury spurred thousands of young men to travel abroad. "Forty-eighters," men who fled as fugitives from the aborted democratic revolutions in 1848 and 1849, likewise numbered several thousand. Bavarian Jews—some 10,000—fled from the Southwest to escape social and religious discrimination. Pietists continued to leave; they settled in communal societies such as Harmony and Economy, Pennsylvania; Amana, Iowa; Ora Labora, Michigan; and Zoar, Ohio. Chancellor Otto von Bismarck's *Kulturkampf* against Catholics encouraged many clergy and religious individuals to leave.

Albert Wolff, a "forty-eighter" who was the commissioner of emigration from Minnesota, reported from Bremen in 1870 that the city remained "alive with emigrants." Shipping firms, he noted, were able to dispatch emigrants quickly to America. Two passenger liners left for New York each week, and while many travelers seemed to know their destinations, an equal number were perfectly set "to go wherever they pleased." Wolff reported that these were often the better classes, well educated, and well dressed. The coming war between Prussia and France in 1870 "frightened thousands of well-to-do and peaceable people" (Johnson 1981, p. 160).

While there was a diversity of motives compelling emigration, annual numbers fluctuated sharply throughout the century. From 1820 to 1860, the numbers moved steadily upward—nearly a million German-speakers arrived in the peak decade prior to the U.S. Civil War. Immigration dropped off slightly in the 1860s and 1870s but resumed to more than a million in the 1880s. A sharp downturn occurred in the last decade of the century, but movement increased until World War I. Thereafter in the twentieth century it continued at reduced levels.

The most effective nineteenth-century factor in spurring German immigration is now believed to have been chain migration. One immigrant cluster, family, or church would write, encouraging letters to friends and relatives in Germany. These "letters from America" would bring others to an established midwestern settlement, and gradually more would follow in this chain to create a community of like-minded immigrants.

German settlement patterns in the New World depended not only on chain letters, but also on time of arrival, transportation routes to the interior, economic opportunities, and nineteenth-century advertising and state-recruitment efforts. Some German settlers continued to stop in the mid-Atlantic states and the Northeast. Only a few were attracted to the South, except for Texas and New Orleans. Most were drawn to the Midwest: Ohio, Michigan, Illinois, Wisconsin, Minnesota, and Missouri became the new centers of German settlement.

The earliest arrivals, those before the Civil War, followed migration chains to the open and free farmlands and frontier cities of the Midwest.

Flowing from western Pennsylvania down the Ohio, Germans settled in Cincinnati and Louisville. They continued down the Mississippi to Missouri and northward into Illinois. The Erie Canal and the Great Lakes pointed them to Michigan, Wisconsin, and Minnesota. Later, railroad companies such as the Northern Pacific advertised the upper Midwest through thousands of brochures distributed by land agents hired by Michigan, Wisconsin, or Minnesota. Soon a chain of urban German communities stretched from Buffalo to Detroit to Milwaukee and into Minnesota. In between, they created hundreds of mostly rural, small agricultural communities often bound together by common religion, family, or place of origin.

The chain migration westward often was tied to immigrant churches. Though the churches seldom directed recruitment efforts, new arrivals frequently were of the same religion, geographic region in Germany, and social-political disposition. These strong religious affiliations explain the persistence to this day of certain settlement patterns. But deeply divided religious differences among German-speakers served to isolate antebel-

lum German immigrants from one another as well as from Americans. Even among concentrations of Germans, Catholics, Pietists, or Lutherans—with their various synods—had little to do with one another. A good many of these small settlements represented religious theocracies, where the minister often remained a benevolent overlord. Also, because many of these midwestern settlements were peopled by immigrants with some means, skills, or entrepreneurial experience, they were easily able to establish and maintain self-supporting agricultural villages. These villages clung to their form of the German language and established parochial schools to protect their culture. Well into the twentieth century rural settlements such as Frankenmuth, Michigan; Saint Nanzcanz, Wisconsin; and Stearns County and New Ulm, Minnesota, remained largely isolated German enclaves.

After the Civil War, German-speakers settled more often in urban areas. Fewer farming opportunities (except for the Volga Germans of Colorado, the Dakotas, and Michigan's reclaimed Saginaw Valley), more skilled immigrants, and individualistic immigration trends channeled settlers toward pockets of German-speakers in the cities. Mid-

Two German-American brothers in Kansas prepare shocks of wheat during a harvest in the 1920s. (Albert and Blanche Neuenschwander)

western urban centers often became characteristically German. In Milwaukee and St. Louis, more than 30 percent of the residents were German-born by the Civil War. Cincinnati, Louisville, and to a lesser extent Chicago, Detroit, Cleveland, and Toledo also maintained important German communities.

Obviously, the reception given German-speakers varied according to religious affiliation, origin, and place of settlement in the new land. Those who arrived as family units and settled as groups often talked of building a new Germany in the United States. Although these efforts at state-building failed, many unassimilated pockets of Germans remained in the rural Midwest. In the cities, by the late nineteenth century, German dominance created sections known as *Kleindeutschlands* (little Germanys). These ethnic pockets boasted Lutheran or Catholic German-speaking churches, German newspapers, beer gardens, and a number of German mystical, fraternal, and mutual-benefit societies. Educational clubs, political societies, and patriotic organizations, modeled on similar groups in Germany, also dotted the Kleindeutschland neighborhoods.

Americans often defined rural Germans by their church, while urban Germans were more commonly identified by the clubs, social, or political organizations they joined. Regardless of the identity, these concentrations of Germans—both rural and urban—increased nativist fears that the Germans were unwilling to assimilate into traditional American culture. Nativists warned that the German colonies were put together without any mixing with Americans and were controlled by their ministers or politicians. Traditionalists also worried that monolithic German voting blocs would upset traditional party alignments.

Many nativists in the middle Atlantic and lower New England states, fearing alien influences, especially by German Catholics, joined the Know-Nothing party at midcentury. The Know-Nothings, who received their name from their familiar denial, "I know nothing," when asked about attacks on German Catholics, were opposed to any immigrant holding public office and to continued immigra-

tion, and they supported a naturalization period of up to twenty-one years. By 1856, following the formation of the Republican party in 1854, the Know-Nothings were absorbed by the new political organization.

Although German-speakers had a reputation for political apathy, when they did get involved, they generally supported Democratic candidates. Prior to the Civil War some Germans abandoned the Democrats for antislavery fusion parties and later the young Republican party. However, in the 1860 Presidential election, only in states such as Missouri, Illinois, and Minnesota, where the Republicans were not identified with the nativists, did the Germans support Abraham Lincoln in significant numbers. Elsewhere, and through the rest of the nineteenth century, the Republicans' support for prohibition, their affiliation with anti-clerical German liberals, and the party's defense of the freedmen kept conservative Lutherans and German Catholics in the Democratic party. Only in 1896 did sizable numbers of Germans shift to the Republican party, out of concern for William Jennings Bryan's moralism and free silver advocacy.

Nativism carried over into surges of moralistic legislation against customs and institutions associated with German-speaking immigrants. Anti-liquor legislation and temperance movements flourished in Wisconsin, Ohio, and Nebraska in the 1870s. The spread of German-language parochial schools encouraged state legislators to require English-only public schools; however, so loud was the public outcry that most of those laws were quickly repealed. Not until World War I was the German language largely removed from public and parochial schools.

By the turn of the twentieth century, second-generation Germans, especially in the cities, were rapidly melding into the American mainstream. The pace of assimilation, though, varied by region. In the eastern port cities skilled workers found more employment opportunities, but competition from unskilled, immigrant labor often forced common German laborers to move to midwestern cities. Here, where the pace of assimilation was slower, the sons of German immigrants now found white-collar employment in increasing numbers. In businesses such as breweries, food-related industries, export-import businesses, and chemical and machinery manufacturers, Germans found entrepreneurial success. German women and their daughters did not enter the work force as often as other immigrants, but when they did, they began as laborers, servants, peddlers, shopkeepers, or tailors. Most German women avoided factory jobs; by century's end a good many found employment as nurses, clerical workers, salesladies, and teachers—opportunities that required education and the ability to speak English. For both men and women, economic opportunities spurred patterns of assimilation that continued into the twentieth century.

Even as German Americans experienced upward mobility, the family unit remained strong. The father, always a dominant figure, maintained that role despite a working wife and public-school-trained offspring. Nonetheless, children left school early—at twelve to fourteen years old—to take jobs to support the family. Germans, more often than many other immigrant groups, relied on child labor. Kinship and ethnicity enabled German city dwellers to survive hard times and eventually to build and buy homes. By the turn of the twentieth century, Germans owned their own homes at rates higher than similar-status immigrants or native-born urban residents. The nuclear family persisted despite children beginning to marry outside the ethnic clan. Lutheranism or Catholicism nurtured the family circle and provided some continuing identity among German Americans in the larger cities.

Distinctive patterns of German culture persisted in insular and isolated rural communities into the twentieth century. Centered around the local Lutheran or Catholic church, the German language, education, and family orientation marked the tightly contained German rural social unit. Since Germans owned nearly 11 percent of all American farms in 1900, there were sufficient numbers to perpetuate for four and five generations these agricultural communities. By 1950, German descendants were still the single largest immigrant group engaged in agriculture. Even at the end of the twentieth century there are several remnants in the Midwest of these rural, self-contained, German religious and social enclaves.

The Twentieth Century

As World War I approached, there was a popular revival among both urban and rural German Americans of interest, preservation, and pride in things German. The paradox within the German community was evident: Gradual but persistent assimilation encouraged many people now to glorify and defend the fatherland. The German press—dependent on a readership that was rapidly diminishing—almost unanimously supported the German Empire and demanded strict American neutrality. The German-language press, which peaked at almost 800 newspapers in 1894, had shrunk to 554 in 1910. World War I was about to accelerate that decline, but in the meantime the press became even more stridently pro-German as it attempted to keep America out of the war and defeat the Anglophile Woodrow Wilson in 1916.

The German-American Alliance, a loose federation of more than three million members in forty states, led the heightened ethnic consciousness. Originally founded as a league to fight prohibition, it was financed by German brewers and led by businessmen, clergymen, journalists, and educators. The alliance and other organizations lobbied for an arms embargo, sponsored rallies, collected for German war relief, and organized speakers and writers to oppose American involvement. To many Americans, the activities of the alliance and the ethnic press implied German disloyalty.

When the United States joined the Allied powers against Germany in 1917, American patriots received a mandate to eradicate any semblance, especially among Germans, of any dual allegiance. Rumors about sabotage and disloyalty began to circulate throughout the states with significant German populations. Local defense committees, the National Americanization Committee, and the American Protective League created a climate of harassment and distrust. Communities

HIS IRON CROSS

Given in Return for Hospitality.

A 1915 cartoon of a German American holding an iron cross after having put a bomb at the base of the Statue of Liberty is illustrative of the anti-German sentiments in American during World War I. (Library of Congress/Corbis)

by the hundreds dropped the German language from their schools; renamed streets, foods, and towns; banned German music; and burned German books. A German in Collinsville, Illinois, was even lynched in April 1918.

In response to the anti-German hysteria many Germans withdrew into their ethnic communities and at the same time tried to reassure themselves and their neighbors of their loyalty. Religious pastors were divided. Some remained openly against the war while others often encouraged young men to show their patriotism by enlisting. German voters switched to the Republican party to vote against President Wilson, and German cultural and social organizations quickly disappeared. German-language newspapers shrunk by half by 1919. The war finally forced assimilation on many urban and rural German churches that dropped the use of the native language and closed parochial schools.

Following the war, and until 1932, some 500,000 German-speakers entered the United States. The war, industrial expansion, and rapid cultural dissipation eliminated German communities in many cities. German identity was rapidly set aside when status as an American was challenged. Some resentment, economic mobility, and industrial leaders who preached acculturation encouraged many Germans to move out of cities to residential areas in and around large industrial communities. The automobile and improved roads abetted assimilation in urban as well as rural areas.

During the Great Depression years of the 1930s, some postwar German immigrants and "unchastened" second-generation residents were attracted to the racial views and anti-Semitism of the Nazi party. Father Charles Coughlin, Detroit's "radio priest," attracted thousands of German listeners in the Midwest with his neo-isolationist views and attacks on international bankers and Jews. The German-American Bund also attracted support among postwar immigrants. Fritz Kuhn, a decorated German war veteran, who immigrated to Detroit in 1927, organized the bund in 1936. Kuhn reportedly worked for the Ford Motor Company, where Henry Ford's anti-Semitism and strong anti-unionism encouraged hate groups, especially during the union-organizing years among the autoworkers in the 1930s. Membership in the bund reached twenty-five thousand and was concentrated in Detroit and the Northeast, especially New York, where many unmarried and unemployed postwar immigrants settled. Kuhn moved to New York in 1936 but was convicted and imprisoned in 1939 for embezzling bund funds. Only a small percentage of German Americans ever joined the bund. Unlike during World War I, German ethnicity was not rekindled by Nazi success or failure. Little repression was evident as the remnants of German America were quickly disappearing.

The discovery of a "new ethnicity" in the 1960s enabled some third- and fourth-generation Germans to revive their Old World heritage. "Little Bavarias" sprouted as tourist attractions, German Day was still celebrated in Chicago, harvest processions, Oktoberfests, and singing festivals were

A German-American man dressed in traditional clothing plays a clarinet. (Buddy Mays/Corbis)

common wherever Germans gathered. Folk customs and crafts experienced a revival, and whole towns redesigned themselves as German village replicas. Churches continued to preserve traditional customs and imagery.

The collapse of East Germany and the reunification of the homeland in 1990 likewise sparked a renewed interest in Germany's past. The establishment of a reunited and economically strong Germany as a leader among nations has finally enabled many German Americans to set aside the ethnic cloud of two world wars. Confronting and apologizing for the Holocaust likewise lessened the burden of German history. A resultant surge in genealogical research also occurred that revived interest and pride in things German.

Still, there is only a passing revival of interest in German-American culture. At the end of the twentieth century German Americans still essentially choose their ethnicity. Although little of the paradox between assimilation and cultural preservation remains, some Germans painstakingly—especially in rural areas—struggle to maintain their identity. In celebrating their ethnicity the lost culture is remembered, but what also should not be forgotten is that Germans, unlike any other immigrant group, in sheer numbers successfully transcended ethnicity and helped to define Americanism. Millions of German-speakers thoroughly assimilated and became Americans, but in doing so they contributed to that constantly changing identity of what it is to be an American.

See also: FRISIANS; GERMANS FROM RUSSIA; HUTTERITES; MENNONITES; SWISS

Bibliography

Bennett, D. H. (1988). *The Party of Fear. From Nativist Movements to the New Right in American History.* Chapel Hill: University of North Carolina Press.

Conzen, K. N. (1976). *Immigrant Milwaukee, 1836–1860. Accommodation and Community in a Frontier City.* Cambridge, MA: Harvard University Press.

Dinnerstein, L., and Reimers, D. (1988). *Ethnic Americans: A History of Immigration and Assimilation,* revised edition. New York: HarperCollins.

Faust, A. B. ([1909] 1969). *The German Element in the United States,* 2 vols. New York: Arno Press.

Gatzke, H. W. (1980). *Germany and the United States. A "Special Relationship"?* Cambridge, MA: Harvard University Press.

Hawgood, J. A. ([1940] 1970). *The Tragedy of German-America.* New York: Arno Press.

Johnson, H. B. (1981). "The Germans." In *They Chose Minnesota,* edited by J. D. Holmquist. St. Paul: Minnesota Historical Society Press.

Keil, H., and Jentz, J. B., eds. (1983). *German Workers in Industrial Chicago, 1850–1910: A Comparative Perspective.* De Kalb: Northern Illinois University Press.

Levine, B. (1992). *The Spirit of 1848: German Immigrants, Labor Conflict, and the Coming of the Civil War.* Champaign: University of Illinois Press.

Luebke, F. C. (1990). *Germans in the New World. Essays in the History of Immigration.* Champaign: University of Illinois Press.

O'Connor, Richard. (1968). *The German Americans.* Boston: Little, Brown.

Trefousse, H. L., ed. (1980). *Germany and America. Essays on Problems of International Relations and Immigration.* Brooklyn, NY: Brooklyn College Press.

Trommler, F., and McVeigh, J., eds. (1985). *America and the Germans. An Assessment of a Three-Hundred-Year History*, 2 vols. Philadelphia: University of Pennsylvania Press.

JEREMY W. KILAR

GERMANS FROM RUSSIA

The many thousands of Germans from Russia who live in the United States comprise a diverse and far-flung ethnic group. Yet, despite important regional and religious differences, all of the Germans from Russia share a common characteristic: They are descendants of German-speaking settlers who once dwelled in the Russian Empire.

Today, even third- and fourth-generation members of this ethnic group prefer to be known as "Germans from Russia," regardless of the fact that they may never have set foot on Russian soil. Although the group is frequently referred to as German-Russians or Russian-Germans, there still is resistance to use of the term "Russian" as an identifying label. In the German scholarly literature, Germans from Russia are described as "Russlanddeutsche" (literally, Russia Germans). In Anglo-American circles other terms sometimes are used: Catherine Germans, Czar's Germans, Russo-Germans. Curiously, the German emigrants from Russia seldom used any of these monikers. Many simply referred to themselves in dialect German as Unser Leit (Our People).

In reality, the Germans from Russia are more easily identified by their specific areas of origin in Russia (e.g., Black Sea Germans, Caucasus Germans, Volga Germans, Volhynian Germans) or by their religious affiliations (e.g., Hutterite Brethren, Russian Mennonites, Swiss Volhynian Mennonites). Since the late 1960s, however, the term "Germans from Russia" has gained steady acceptance by both insiders and outsiders.

Historical Background

German-speaking settlers in Russia have a history that spans more than four centuries. In the late 1500s, German artisans and workers established a German suburb in Moscow that remained culturally distinct until World War I. Czar Peter the Great, in his efforts to Westernize the Russian Empire, invited many Germans to settle in St. Petersburg and other Russian cities.

In the 1760s, Czarina Catherine the Great ascended the Russian throne. Although the German-born czarina embraced many Russian ways, she sought to strengthen her new empire by recruiting foreign settlers from the West. In 1762 and 1763, Catherine issued official invitations, urging families from the German states and other parts of Western Europe to settle in the Russian Empire. The 1763 manifesto proved most successful, for it guaranteed special privileges to all colonists who answered Catherine's call. The privileges included thirty-year tax exemptions, generous tracts of land, exemption from civil and military service, and full religious freedom. To thousands of war-weary peasants, the 1763 manifesto seemed like a godsend.

Within five years, approximately thirty thousand colonists settled on the steppes of the Lower Volga. In many respects this region was a wilderness due to frequent attacks by bands of thieves and wandering Asian tribes. Despite early hardships, more than one hundred mother colonies sprang up on both sides of the Volga River. Most of the Volga German colonists came from Hessen, Bavaria, and the Rhineland-Palatinate. In nearly every case, each colony was founded along strict denominational lines. Thus Protestants and Roman Catholics established separate colonies that eventually became known by distinctly German-sounding names: Balzer, Frank, Herzog, Mariental,

Seewald. In some cases, Volga German colonies included a curious upper and lower village arrangement (*oberdorf/unterdorf*) that reflected dialect differences and fierce rivalries.

Early in their history, the Volga Germans adapted the *mir* system of Russian land tenure, whereby each male villager received an equal allocation of land. The land, however, was considered communal property and thus switched hands every few years. The mir system made it practically impossible for non-Germans to move into the colonies and take up residence. Consequently the in-group consciousness of the Volga Germans became increasingly stronger. As the colonist population grew, however, the land allotments available to the villagers became correspondingly smaller.

In the eyes of Russian officials, the Volga German colonization of the 1760s was a success. For decades afterward, more Germans entered Russia and established agrarian colonies. In 1770, a small group of Hutterites was permitted to settle near Chernigov. By the late 1780s, German-speaking Mennonites from West Prussia founded villages in the Chortitza area near Zaporozhye. Eventually more Mennonites came to Russia and established numerous villages in the Molotschna region of South Russia.

In 1804, Czar Alexander I signed a document that was similar to the 1763 manifesto of Catherine the Great. This time, however, Alexander sought to lure German settlers into "New Russia"—the Ukraine. Most of those who accepted the invitation were Protestant and Catholic families from what is now southwestern Germany and northeastern France. These colonists, who settled near the port city of Odessa, became known as the Black Sea Germans. Settlements also mushroomed in the Crimea, Bessarabia, and the South Caucasus. Unlike the Volga Germans to the north, the Black Sea Germans were not nearly so isolated and often mixed freely with neighboring Jewish, Tatar, and Ukrainian peoples. Instead of adopting the mir system, the Black Sea Germans sought to acquire private lands in addition to the allocations made available to each colonist family by the government. This "land hunger" eventually resulted in the acquisition of millions of acres by the Black Sea Germans.

More Germans moved into Russia between 1816 and 1875. Most of these settlers did not enjoy the special privileges of earlier colonists and established small settlements in Volhynia. These Volhynian Germans were especially numerous in eastern Volhynia, near the cities of Novograd-Volynsky and Zhitomir.

Altogether, more than three thousand ethnic German settlements once dotted the lands of the Russian Empire. By 1912, some villages numbered only a few families, while other colonies included nearly fifteen thousand inhabitants. The vast majority of all the Germans in Russia were Lutheran (76%), followed by smaller numbers of Roman Catholics, Mennonites, and Baptists.

With the onset of World War I in 1914, the Germans in Russia became targets of fierce anti-German campaigns. Problems for the ethnic German minority continued during the Communist era under Vladimir Lenin and Joseph Stalin. By the end of World War II, nearly all of the three thousand German settlements in Russia had been emptied of their German-speaking inhabitants. The embittered survivors were exiled primarily to Kazakhstan and Siberia, where many German-Russian descendants still live today.

Immigration to the United States

In 1871, Czar Alexander II abrogated a number of the German colonists' special privileges. Most distressing to the colonists was the realization that they would have to march in the czar's army like other Russian subjects. Military service was frowned upon by the Germans in Russia, especially the Hutterites and Mennonites, who objected to war on moral and religious grounds. Most German colonists, however, simply felt that compulsory military service was a violation of Catherine the Great's 1763 manifesto.

Along with the widespread dissatisfaction under Alexander II, there were also economic factors that prompted emigration. In both the Black Sea

Traditional clothing for a German-Russian wedding. The bride wore a dark dress and an elaborate, hand-made bridal wreath. The groom often wore a long ribbon pinned to his right lapel. (Emil Retzlaff and Timothy J. Kloberdanz)

Similarly, a Volga German minister from Norka, Russia, worked as a missionary in Kansas and Missouri in the 1860s. Upon his return, Reverend Wilhelm Stärkel shared information with any villager who was hungry for information about America. Soon large groups of Protestant and Catholic Volga German immigrants followed.

Most of the Germans who left Russia and immigrated to the United States settled in the Plains states. This great immigration was that of a farming people who literally went "from the steppes to the prairies." In Russia, they had adjusted to life on the treeless grasslands so thoroughly that they preferred the level, unobscured horizons on the New World.

One of the great ironies of German-Russian immigration history, however, it that upon reaching the United States, most Volga Germans went south into Nebraska, Kansas, and Colorado. The Black Sea Germans, who were accustomed to a somewhat milder climate in South Russia, headed north into the Dakotas and the Canadian prairie provinces. Dakota Territory was crisscrossed by the great Missouri River, and this frontier region resembled in many ways the Volga River region in Russia. But Dakota Territory became a major settlement of the Black Sea Germans rather than the Volga Germans.

In the late 1800s, Black Sea Germans were attracted to the Dakotas by the availability of free homestead land. The Volga Germans, on the other hand, pursued work opportunities in various parts of the central Great Plains states. Many Volga Germans worked for American farmers as day laborers or sugar beet workers until they acquired tenant farms or permanent places of their own.

Most Germans from Russia settled in the western United States, especially the Great Plains region. As in Russia, large groups of settlers who shared the same regional and religious characteristics tended to cluster together in America. A recurring pattern of immigration among the Germans from Russia involved a scout, emissary, or male family member who first surveyed the New World situation before sending for others. The Germans from Russia chose to immigrate and settle to-

and Volga regions there were severe shortages of land to accommodate the ever-increasing German colonist population. Because the Germans in Russia emphasized wheat growing and the cultivation of other grains, the demand for large tracts of level farmland was great.

As early as the 1840s, a few Germans from Russia immigrated to the United States. Under the leadership of colonist Johann Ludwig Bette, a small group of Black Sea Germans settled on Kelleys Island, near Sandusky, Ohio. After becoming successful in the United States, Bette returned to the Odessa area in the 1870s and told his fellow villagers all about America. By 1872, Black Sea German immigration to the New World was under way.

gether as large family units, thus maintaining their important Old Country social ties, dialects, and religious identities.

Group Composition

It is difficult to estimate how many Germans from Russia immigrated to the United States. The immigrants did not always identify themselves as subjects of Russia, and in later years some families tried hard to conceal the facts of their ethnic background. Richard S. Sallet, in his study *Russian-German Settlements in the United States* (1974), estimated that by 1920 approximately 303,000 Germans from Russia (of the first and second generations) lived in the United States. Sallet studied the population data for counties in states that were known to have large numbers of Germans from Russia. Most of the Volga German immigrant communities were concentrated in Nebraska, Kansas, and Colorado. The Black Sea Germans could be found primarily in North Dakota, South Dakota, and Washington State. In the early 1950s, many German refugees from Russia fled communism and made their way to the United States.

Today, possibly as many as 2.5 million Americans trace their ancestry to Germans from Russia. In some states, the German-Russian presence is very strong. In 1920, for example, seventy thousand German Russians lived in the sparsely populated and largely rural state of North Dakota. Today it is estimated that one out of every five North Dakotans is a descendant of Germans from Russia.

Language

For generations the German colonists in Russia emphasized maintenance of the German language in church, school, and home. Relatively few colonists learned the Russian or Ukrainian languages unless they had served in the Russian Army or interacted regularly with their Slavic neighbors. Russification efforts in the 1870s required that Russian be taught in all colonist schools, but the campaign met with mixed success. Even as late as 1914, many of the Germans from Russia who entered the United States spoke only German.

The Germans from Russia conversed in one of many German dialects, depending on their area of origin in Germany and their place of settlement in Russia. The Volga Germans spoke a largely Hessian dialect, while many Black Sea Germans spoke either Schwäbisch (Swabian) or Low German. Thus, when Volga and Black Sea Germans exchanged words, distinct dialectal peculiarities were much in evidence. Volga Germans, for example, referred to a horse as *gaul*, but many Black Sea Germans preferred the term *ross*. Both of these dialect words were completely different from the Hochdeutsch (Standard German) term *pferd*.

Although the Germans from Russia clung to their native dialects, Standard German was used in church and school. The language of the Bible, religious hymns, and even German-Russian newspapers was *Hochdeutsch*. Outside the church and schoolhouse, dialect German prevailed. For the Germans from Russia, their distinctive dialects did much more than serve as colloquial forms of expression. The dialects helped set the people apart from German-speaking immigrants who came directly from Germany.

In the United States, a number of German-language newspapers focused on the interests and needs of the Germans from Russia. One of the most important was the *Dakota Freie Presse*, founded in Yankton, Dakota Territory, in 1874. The masthead of this newspaper proudly billed itself as the most widely circulated German-Russian newspaper "in the entire world." By 1920, the *Dakota Freie Presse* had a circulation of nearly fourteen thousand readers. The newspaper was nondenominational and reached large numbers of Black Sea Germans, Volga Germans, and other German Russians. Thus it helped create a sense of peoplehood among all Germans from Russia, whose settlements stretched across the United States—from the Black Sea German settlement of Lodi, California, to the Volga German hamlet of Pine Island, New York.

In 1954, the eighty-year-old *Dakota Freie Presse* ceased publication. The date of the ethnic newspaper's demise roughly corresponds to the time that many German-Russian families began shifting to English. In the aftermath of the two world wars, the sons and daughters of the German immigrants from Russia put aside their ethnic newspapers and tried hard to master the language of their adopted country.

Today, the great majority of German-Russian descendants in the New World no longer speak or understand the dialects of their ancestors. There are, of course, notable exceptions in certain parts of the United States. All of the colony-dwelling Hutterites of the Great Plains continue to use German to such an extent that English remains a second language. In Ellis County, Kansas, many Volga German Catholic families still use the distinctive dialects of their immigrant forebears—most of whom left Russia as long ago as the mid-1870s.

Cultural Life

The main cultural institution of the German immigrants from Russia was the church. In the first years of settlement, churches served both the religious and social needs of the Germans from Russia. This was equally the case among Black Sea German homesteaders on the Dakota prairies and Volga German factory workers in the heart of Chicago.

In German-Russian churches, males traditionally sat on the right half of the church and females on the left. This separation of the sexes persisted in some congregations until well after World War II. In the Catholic churches of the immigrants, even statues of the Blessed Virgin Mary were placed on the "women's side."

Along with many official religious practices, the Germans from Russia kept alive a large number of folk religious practices as well. Within the home, families observed seasonal customs that related to the church calendar. On New Year's Day, groups of German Russians would go from house to house reciting lengthy verses in German. Almost always these rhymed wishes concluded with the

hope that the recipient would one day enjoy eternal happiness in "*dem Himmelsreich*" (the Kingdom of Heaven). At Easter, families used dried onion skins and other natural substances to dye eggs in a variety of hues. Some immigrant families baked special breads and carved paschal lambs out of homemade butter. Perhaps the most sacred time of the year was Christmas Eve, when many German Russians believed ordinary water left outside turned to wine. On Christmas Eve two masked visitors entered the family home and inquired about the children's behavior. These mummers were known as the Belznickel (Furry Nicholaus) and Christkindl (Little Christ Child). Curiously,

On Christmas Eve, German-Russian children pray before a veiled woman in white who represents the Christkindl (Little Christ Child). (Timothy J. Kloberdanz)

the role of the Christkindl was always played by a woman who wore a veil and a long white garment. Well-behaved children who could pray in German received candy and words of praise. Those children who could not recite their German prayers to the satisfaction of the mummers were whipped with willow branches. These and many other folk customs strengthened the ethnic identity of the Germans from Russia and emphasized the importance of language, proper behavior, and tradition.

The social organization of the Germans from Russia was characterized by close family ties that included godparents and members of the extended family. Older individuals were accorded respect, and any elderly man or woman was addressed accordingly—*Vetter* (uncle) or *Bas/Wes* (aunt). The Volga Germans even referred to their cousins as *Halbgeschwister* (literally, half brothers and half sisters). In the first years of settlement in the United States, the Old Country institutions of marriage within the group and marriage arrangements prevailed. Among the Lutherans and Catholics, wedding celebrations were lavish affairs and sometimes lasted three days.

Ethnic Persistence

The first Germans from Russia who settled in the United States experienced various forms of discrimination. In the early 1900s, they were derided as "dumb Russians" or "dirty Rooshuns." By the time that the Germans from Russia finally convinced their American neighbors that they were culturally "German," World War I began with Germany. In northern Colorado, many Germans from Russia who worked in the sugar beet fields as stoop laborers lived in segregated settlements. These ethnic communities were known by various names: the "Rooshun Corner," Little Russia, Saratov, St. Petersburg, the Jungles, and "the Pansy Bed"—due to the brightly painted houses of the immigrants. In the mid-1920s, Colorado's German-Russian minority became targets of anti-immigrant harassment by the Ku Klux Klan.

Due to their sequestration and distinctive speech patterns, the ethnic identity of the Germans from Russia was fairly obvious to their neighbors. Intermarriage with mainstream Americans was so uncommon in the early years that the mere possibility inspired novels such as Hope Williams Sykes's *Second Hoeing* (1935) and Mary Worthy Breneman's *The Land They Possessed* (1956).

Today, the descendants of the Germans from Russia no longer live in segregated settlements or tolerate exclusion. While most present-day German Russians seldom speak their ancestral dialects or observe three-day wedding celebrations, they have not forgotten the ways of their elders. Many now use higher education and computer technology to research and preserve aspects of their ethnic heritage. For example, college courses on German-Russian history and culture have been offered at Colorado State University, North Dakota State University, and other institutions. Following the collapse of the Soviet Union, partnerships were created between German-Russian scholars in the United States and the former USSR. In 1968, the American Historical Society of Germans from Russia (AHSGR) was founded in Colorado. Today this large organization has its headquarters in Lincoln, Nebraska. The society publishes books, journals, maps, genealogical guides, and hosts a yearly international convention. In 1971, the Germans from Russia Heritage Society (GRHS) was established in Bismarck, North Dakota. Like its sister organization AHSGR, the North Dakota group publishes a wide range of German-Russian materials and holds annual meetings for its membership.

The creation of two German-Russian ethnic societies will not halt the forces of assimilation, but AHSGR and GRHS have succeeded in emphasizing a sense of German-Russian peoplehood— much as the *Dakota Freie Presse* did in the early 1900s. These ethnic organizations help remind people that the German-Russian community includes well-known individuals who have contributed to American life and culture—for example, entertainer John Denver, movie actress Angie Dickinson, *USA Today* founder Al Neuharth, and bandleader Lawrence Welk. Many present-day

German Russians are determined to record their history, publicize their cultural contributions, and celebrate their persistence as a distinctive ethnic group. Whether German-Russian culture will be an integral and vibrant part of America's future remains to be seen.

See also: GERMANS; MENNONITES

Bibliography

Arends, S. F. (1989). *The Central Dakota Germans: Their History, Language, and Culture.* Washington, DC: Georgetown University Press.

Breneman, M. W. ([1956] 1989). *The Land They Possessed.* Brookings, SD: South Dakota Committee on the Humanities and the South Dakota Library Association.

Eisenach, G. J. (1948). *Pietism and the Russian-Germans in the United States.* Berne, IN: Berne Publishers.

Fleischhauer, I., and Pinkus, B. (1986). *The Soviet Germans: Past and Present.* New York: St. Martin's Press.

Giesinger, A. (1974). *From Catherine to Khrushchev: The Story of Russia's Germans.* Battleford, Saskatchewan: Marian Press.

Kloberdanz, T. J., and Kloberdanz, R. (1993). *Thunder on the Steppe: Volga German Folklife in a Changing Russia.* Lincoln, NE: American Historical Society of Germans from Russia.

Koch, F. C. (1977). *The Volga Germans: In Russia and the Americas, from 1763 to the Present.* University Park: Pennsylvania State University Press.

Long, J. W. (1988). *From Privileged to Dispossessed: The Volga Germans, 1860–1917.* Lincoln: University of Nebraska Press.

Marzolf, A. H. (1995). *That's the Way It Once Was: Black Sea German from Russia Experiences.* Bismarck, ND: Germans from Russia Heritage Society.

Sallet, R. S. (1974). *Russian-German Settlements in the United States*, translated by L. J. Rippley and A. Bauer. Fargo: North Dakota Institute for Regional Studies.

Stumpp, K. (1971). *The German-Russians: Two Centuries of Pioneering.* Lincoln, NE: American Historical Society of Germans from Russia.

Stumpp, K. (1980). *Das Schriftum über das Deutschtum in Russland.* Stuttgart: Verlag Landsmannschaft der Deutschen aus Russland.

Sykes, H. W. ([1935] 1982). *Second Hoeing.* Lincoln: Unversity of Nebraska Press.

Williams, H. P. (1975). *The Czar's Germans*, edited by E. S. Haynes, P. B. Legler, and G. S. Walker. Lincoln, NE: American Historical Society of Germans from Russia.

TIMOTHY J. KLOBERDANZ

GHANAIANS

The Republic of Ghana was the first African country to achieve independence. On March 6, 1957, the Gold Coast became formally independent from Britain and was renamed Ghana. Like all African countries, Ghana was constructed in the colonial period as an arbitrarily bounded entity; its borders were determined by Europeans at the 1884–1885 Berlin Conference. Following centuries of trans-Saharan trade that linked the Mediterranean and Islamic North Africa with the peoples of western Africa, European contact with what is now Ghana began in the fourteenth century when the Portuguese established the first of many forts that were built along the Atlantic coast. First used for trading gold and spices, these coastal forts and castles became ports for the slave trade and were used as military posts in the European competition for control of trade and access to the interior. Millions of enslaved persons—800,000 recorded from what was then the Gold Coast in the eighteenth century alone—were transported to the Americas through these forts by the Portuguese, Danish, Germans, Swedes, French, Dutch, and British, joining millions more from the entire Atlantic coast of Africa. The British finally wrested control over the coastal forts from their European rivals, and in the nineteenth century, after a series of wars with the Asante, in which the British deported the king and burned the capital of Kumasi, they took control of the interior forest region and proceeded north to gain a foothold in the savanna.

Ghana contains a number of ethnic and linguistic groups. The Asante, an Akan group whose home is the forest region in the central part of the country, are the largest, but they have shared political and economic power without major conflicts with others, including other Akan people from the Brong-Ahafo and Fante regions, the Ewe and Ga in southern Ghana, and the Dagomba, Gonja, and Mamprusi people in the north, to name just a few of the major groups. Some of these people, including the Asante, Dagomba, Gonja, and Mamprusi, were organized into states in precolonial times; others were clan and lineage based. Many traditional rulers were subordinated or removed from office by the British but remained strong in terms of local allegiances. Today, traditional rulers play an important part in local government and in religious and ceremonial affairs.

Ghana's economy is based on agriculture (50 percent of the gross national product), with cocoa and timber being the main export crops. Ghana also has important gold mines; the Ashanti Goldfields Company began trading on the New York Stock Exchange in 1996. Bauxite, diamonds, and manganese are also mined. The economy did poorly in the 1970s and 1980s, with inflation reaching almost 150 percent, but the nation has responded well to an economic recovery program launched in 1983, followed by a structural adjustment program carried out under the auspices of the World Bank.

History of Immigration

While the enslaved people and their descendants were severed from any contact with their homeland, elements of African culture nevertheless have been retained. These are evident in music, folklore, religion, family and community relationships, and aesthetics. These cultural retentions coexist with a new recognition of Ghanaian influence in African-American identity. Kente cloth, now seen as emblematic of African-American identity, is based in part on the narrow loom strip-weaving traditions from Ghana. In certain communities, paticulary in Jamaica and Surinam, many Ghanaian traditions have been kept alive. Today some African Americans have begun tracing their roots back to Ghana and, in some instances, have had success in finding connections to their ancestral homes. There is also a significant wave of tourist travel to Ghana on the part of African Americans.

Throughout the colonial period, a small number of Ghanaians were sent to Great Britain for higher education. Many returned to Ghana, but some immigrated permanently to Britain or to Canada. A small number of Ghanaians immigrated to the United States via Great Britain before independence. Ghana's first president, Kwame Nkrumah, received his bachelor of science degree in economics and sociology from Lincoln University in 1939 and his bachelor of theology and masters in education in 1942 from the University of Pennsylvania. As president, Nkrumah invited W. E. B. Du Bois to live and work in Ghana, further enhancing the ties with African Americans. (In 1963, Du Bois renounced his American citizenship and officially became a citizen of Ghana.)

A small number of nonstudent Ghanaians immigrated to the United States during the three decades before Ghana gained its independence. Urbanites who had been influenced by American movies, literature, and jazz, as well as by the civil rights movement and black consciousness movements in the United States, made the Atlantic crossing by working on or stowing away on boats and ships. Frustrated by what they saw as slow progress to independence, yet not equipped with higher education, these Ghanaians attempted to join artistic communities such as those established in New York and known collectively as the "Harlem Renaissance." Few of these people were accepted into the African-American civil rights movement, which had little room for "outsiders" at the time. In any case, this wave of immigration probably only amounted to a few hundred immigrants who settled mainly in New York and Chicago. Many worked in factories and took menial jobs; some ended up in the army and served in the Korean War.

A few thousand Ghanaians entered the United States in the 1960s in the aftermath of independence. The Convention People's Party awarded scholarships to students to attend American and Russian universities. While some of these people returned to Ghana, degrees in hand, to fill the many vacancies in government service that opened up in the years following independence, many remained in the United States.

Poor economic conditions in Ghana in the 1970s and political unrest between 1979 and 1983 led to further immigration; accurate statistics for the total number of documented and undocumented immigrants during this period are not available. Some of these immigrants followed a pattern of chain migration, receiving tickets and funds from relatives who were already in the United States. These people were young (often educated at least through elementary school), and they were prepared to compete in the American economy. In 1981–1982, there was widespread hunger and deprivation in Ghana, and this further enhanced emigration. Children were sent to relatives in Europe or the United States, and many people emigrated from Germany and Britain to the United States as immigration regulations tightened in those countries. Some of these people took jobs that did not require formal education and became taxi drivers, factory workers, hospital orderlies and attendants, and security guards. Others married African Americans and became entrepreneurs or went to school to get further training.

Later in the 1980s, a second generation of Ghanaian lawyers, doctors, academics, and other professionals immigrated to the United States, mainly because of the lack of employment in Ghana. In the 1990s, people from an even broader educational base began to immigrate because of the lottery system in the United States and family attachment and associations. Quite a few people in this group are entrepreneurs—restaurant owners, seamstresses, hair dressers, boutique owners, and teachers. There is a growing market for the cultural knowledge and skills of Ghanaians in the African-American community.

Language

English is the official language of Ghana, and all Ghanaian children learn English in school. While a very small minority of Ghanaians arrive in the United States without being able to speak English, most Ghanaian immigrants speak English, and many can read and write it as well. All Ghanaians speak one or more Ghanaian languages and continue to speak these languages with friends and relatives in the United States. In Ghana, it is estimated that the language distribution is as follows: Akan, including Twi, 45 percent; Gur, 16 percent; Ewe, 14 percent; Ga/Adangme, 10 percent; Guan, 20 percent. Ghanaian children born in the United States learn English, but almost all of them also learn at least one Ghanaian language. There is a large Ghanaian Muslim community whose members speak Hausa; many of these people are literate in Arabic, the language of religious worship and study.

Ties with Ghana

Remittances from Ghanaian immigrants in the United States are important to relatives in Ghana. One estimate puts bank transfers for 1995 at $300 million. It is not uncommon for a man to have a spouse in the United States as well as one or more wives and children in Ghana, all of whom will expect and may receive support. Telephone contacts are frequent, and Ghanaians in the United States often are involved in local events in Ghana, such as community leadership disputes, through phone and mail contact.

The Ghanaian community includes both Christians (Catholics or various Protestant denominations) and Muslims. A significant number of these people also follow traditional religious customs, particularly those ceremonies associated with naming, coming of age, marriage, funerals, and honoring the ancestors. Funerals are celebrated both in the United States and in Ghana; many families even transport the deceased to Ghana for funeral services and burial. In addition, many immigrants in the United States return to

Ghana for the funerals of relatives who remained in Ghana.

Demographics

The 1990 U.S. Census shows 20,889 foreign-born Ghanaians living in the United States, including 15,709 noncitizens and 5,180 naturalized citizens. Informal estimates are considerably higher, by a factor of at least ten. Of the enumerated Ghanaians, most (19,901) come from urban or peri-urban areas in Ghana, but in the United States, most have settled in urban areas. Almost half (40.3%) were enumerated in the mid-Atlantic states, 75 percent of these in New York State (6,337). Other states with high proportions of the total enumerated Ghanaian immigrant population are California with 7 percent, and Maryland, Virginia, and the District of Columbia with a total of 18.8 percent.

In 1994, there were 1,458 Ghanaians admitted to the United States; 809 of them were immediate relatives of U.S. citizens, 434 were admitted through family sponsorship, and 153 were admitted through employment-based preferences. There were only 37 refugee and asylee adjustments for Ghanaians in that year. There are many more people in Ghana who would like to immigrate to the United States in search of educational and economic opportunities, but their main problems are finding sponsorship and obtaining visas.

Associational Life

The strength of associational activities, including social service support and recreational activities, in the Ghanaian community is striking. In Washington, D.C., and in the New York–New Jersey–Connecticut area, there are Ghanaian newspapers. In July 1996, *Asenta*, a New York newspaper, listed forty-three Ghanaian associations grouped under the umbrella of the National Council of Ghanaian Associations. Some of the associations are ethnically based, while others are based on place of residence in the United States and common occupational activities. These associations include, for example, the Executive Women's Club, the Ghana Development Club of New Jersey, the Veteran's Club of the USA and the Akan Association of the USA. Many of these associations have regional groups in other parts of the country. In addition, there were two children's schools listed and twelve Christian churches that had Ghanaian ministers. Many Ghanaians belong to more than one association. Almost all of these groups organize social services for their members, arrange social events, and disseminate information and news about Ghana. There are a number of Ghanaian home pages on the World Wide Web that facilitate commerce and communication.

A number of the ethnic associations are connected to traditional ethnic communities in Ghana. The head of the Asanteman Association, for example, seeks recognition from the Asantehene in Kumasi, Ghana, and the same is true of many of the other associations. The officers in the United States are elected, and offices are often hotly contested. Some of the contestants travel to Ghana to obtain recognition from traditional rulers in Africa. In some cases, when these rulers visit the United States they adjudicate disputes over association offices and many other types of civil complaints.

See also: AFRICAN AMERICANS

Bibliography

Asante, M., and Mattson, M. (1992). *The Historical and Cultural Atlas of African Americans*. New York: Macmillan.

Anderson, S. E. (1995). *The Black Holocaust for Beginners*. New York: Writers and Readers.

Du Bois, W. E. B. (1968). *Autobiography of W. E. B. Du Bois: A Soliloquy on Viewing My Life from the Last Decade of Its First Century*. New York: International Publishers.

Kuada, J. E., and Chachah, Y. (1989). *Ghana: The Land, the People, and Their Culture*. Copenhagen: African Information Centre.

Nkrumah, K. (1979). *Autobiography of Kwame Nkrumah*. London: Panaf Books.

Smertin, Y. (1987). *Kwame Nkrumah*. New York: International Publishers.

Schildkrout, E. (1996). "Kingdom of Gold." *Natural History* 105(2):36–47.

U.S. Bureau of the Census. (1990). *1990 Social and Economic Characteristics.* Washington, DC: U.S. Government Printing Office.

ENID SCHILDKROUT
AMA B. BOAKYEWA

GREEKS

Greeks began arriving in America in significant numbers starting in the 1890s. At that time, more Greeks lived outside of Greece than in Greece proper. Greece had achieved independence from the Ottoman Empire in 1821, but it was only after World War I that the modern Greek state attained the borders that approximate it today. Many Greek immigrants thus came from the remaining parts of the Ottoman Empire, the surrounding Balkan countries and Egypt. Greek immigrants also came from Cyprus, which did not become independent from British rule until 1960.

All told, an estimated 800,000 Greeks have crossed over to the United States. About two-thirds of these arrivals made America their permanent home. Whether from Greece proper or outside, the Greek immigrants were culturally a relatively homogeneous group. Nearly all were adherents of the Greek Orthodox faith and spoke standard Greek, with only a few years of grammar school being common. The small number of Slavophones, Vlachs (Romanian-speaking), and Jews coming from Greece proper were by and large removed from the Greek-American community. Thus the Greek-American community from its inception was remarkably homogeneous in its ethnicity. Only when intermarriage occurred in significant numbers in recent decades was this homogeneity altered.

Immigration Periods

Greek immigration can be divided into five distinct periods. More than 500,000 Greeks migrated to the United States during the great wave (1890–1924), which ended when congressional legislation severely restricted immigration. Thus the early community was in large measure a bachelors' community inasmuch as fewer than one in five Greek immigrants was a woman. The ratio of males to females among Greek-born Americans was a remarkably high 2.8 to 1 even in 1930 and a still disproportionate 1.6 to 1 as late as 1960.

The closed-door period (1925–1945) lasted through the end of World War II. Only some 30,000 Greeks migrated to the United States during that time; many were brides of immigrants already settled in America. Many such marriages were arranged across the ocean, with a goodly number being "picture brides," who came from the same or a nearby village of their prospective grooms. The usual pattern was for Greek immigrant women not to work outside the home, though there were always exceptions to this rule. In the early immigrant families, husbands were often much older than their wives, which gave a distinctive cast to the family constellation.

The third period, postwar migration (1946–1965), began after the doors opened somewhat under provisions for displaced persons. Some 75,000 Greeks arrived in the United States during the two decades following World War II. In addition to unskilled workers, the new immigrants also included a number of Greek professionals as well as young Greek students attending colleges and universities in America.

The new wave (1966–1979) occurred when immigration laws were changed to allow easier entrance for the relatives of persons already in the United States. About 160,000 Greeks arrived under the new legislation. Unlike previous eras, the sex ratio was fairly evenly balanced, with some of the immigrant families including young children, a first in Greek immigrant history.

The current phase, which began in 1980, is a period of declining immigration. During the 1980s, approximately 2,500 Greeks annually migrated to America. In the 1990s, the figure dropped to 1,500. Factoring in the probable number of returnees, there is no longer any net Greek increase in this country from immigration. Also to be noted, since the 1960s, a low birthrate means the American-born generations have not been replacing themselves. With no renewal of immigration in sight and with little likelihood of a rise in the birthrate, the Greek-American population will shrink in the years to come.

The 1990 U.S. Census listed approximately one million persons who claimed to be of Greek ancestry, of whom about two-thirds were entirely of Greek ancestry. Greeks were overrepresented in the Northeast, underrepresented in the South, and proportionately represented in the rest of the country. Well over half of all Greek Americans live in or near one of nine American cities: New York (250,000); Chicago (120,000); Boston and nearby mill towns (100,000); Los Angeles (45,000); Detroit (40,000); Philadelphia (25,000); and 20,000 each in Baltimore, Cleveland, and Pittsburgh.

By using available census and immigration figures and by making some assumptions on birth- and deathrates, the generational distribution of Greek Americans in the mid-1990s can be estimated as follows: first generation (immigrants), 200,000; second generation, 350,000; third generation, 300,000; and fourth generation, 150,000. The proportion of those with some non-Greek ancestry increases with succeeding generations.

History

The flood of Greek immigrants who arrived in America between 1890 and 1924 can be traced along three major routes: (1) Greeks going to western states to work on railroad gangs and in mines; (2) Greeks going to New England mill towns to work in textile or shoe factories; and (3) Greeks who went to large northern cities, principally New York or Chicago, and worked in factories or found employment as busboys, dishwashers, bootblacks, or peddlers. Thus, like most other immigrants, Greeks initially made up a proletarian class.

A store owned and run by a Greek family in Peru, Indiana, in 1916. (Hellenic Museum and Cultural Center)

A very few years after the start of mass migration, however, there also began within the Greek immigrant colony the process of internal social stratification that is characteristic of American society as a whole. The beginnings of a Greek-American middle class can be detected by 1910. By the 1920s, a considerable number of Greeks owned small businesses. The entrepreneurial ability of many of the Greek immigrants was consistently noted by every American observer of Greek immigrants in the early decades of the twentieth century. The early Greek shopkeepers were concentrated in a narrow but familiar range of enterprises: candy stores, bootblack and shoe repair parlors, dry cleaners, florists, produce stores, bars and taverns, and, most notably, restaurants.

The intent of the vast majority of immigrants to America was to make money and then return to their home villages to live lives of comfort. The immigration experience was a culture shock (to which it took many Greek immigrants years to adjust) for women and men alike. Some never did adjust. To move into an urban setting, not to know the English language, and to be targets of hostility by groups already in America was a painful transition. Yet almost all of the immigrants were able to make more money in America than they could in the old country. Slowly but inevitably the majority of the Greek immigrants realized that their future was in America.

Since World War II, but particularly since the 1960s, American-born Greeks have generally been an upwardly mobile ethnic group with levels of education and income surpassing that of Americans of northern European stock. Greek Americans have become prominent in the arts and sciences, but perhaps their visibility has been greatest in politics. Michael Dukakis, the son of Greek immigrants, was the first person of southern European ancestry to be nominated as a presidential candidate by a major political party. Three Greek Americans have served in the U.S. Senate, all the children of Greek immigrants: Paul Sarbanes (D., Md.), Paul Tsongas (D., Mass.), and Olympia Snowe (R., Me.).

The Greek Orthodox Church

When a sufficient number of Greeks had settled in one place, the practice was to establish a local Greek Orthodox church. Among the earliest church communities were those in New Orleans, New York, Chicago, and Boston. By 1916, there were about sixty Greek churches in the United States, and about 200 in 1930. In the early years, the Greek churches in America came under the authority of the Church of Greece. But political conflict in Greece carried over into America with vying bishops belonging to the various factions. Order came in 1931 when the Greek Orthodox churches in America came under the administrative as well as spiritual authoriy of the Ecumenical Patriarch of Constantinople in Istanbul, Turkey.

In the United States, the church is officially known as the Greek Orthodox Archdiocese of America, with headquarters in New York. From 1931 to 1948, Archbishop Athenagoras served as head of the archdiocese. When he was elevated to the patriarchate in 1948, his successor was Archbishop Michael. Following Michael's death in 1959, the leader of archdiocese was Archbishop Iakovos, who became a major religious figure in American society and assumed the role of ethnic spokesman for the Greek community in America. Iakovos retired in 1996 and was succeeded by Archbishop Spyridon, the first American-born archbishop.

By 1996, the Greek Orthodox archdiocese consisted of some 130,000 dues-paying families and close to 600 churches in the United States. (About thirty or so Greek Orthodox churches existed outside the archdiocesan framework.) A surprising development in the 1990s was the growing number—a dozen or so—of Greek Orthodox monasteries in the United States.

As American-born generations replaced immigrants as the numerically dominant group, a process of Americanization in the church became evident. English began to be introduced into the liturgy in the 1960s, and by the 1990s, a policy of "flexible bilingualism," with varying mixtures of

Greek and English dependent on the parish's linguistic makeup, seemed to be working fairly well.

Another development was a reassessment of women's role in the church, although it was not nearly as pronounced as the feminism appearing in mainstream denominations. The issue of ordination for women has not seriously emerged in the Greek Orthodox Church, but there is a growing sentiment to revive the ancient ecclesiastical order of female deacons, as has been done already with male deacons. Traditionally the major outlet for women in the church was the Philoptochos (Friends of the Poor), a female association. Since the 1970s, the overall trend has clearly been toward greater representation of laywomen in leadership positions.

Perhaps the strongest measure of the trend toward the Americanization of the church is in the increasing incorporation of non-Greeks. Some of

A priest stands in front of a Greek Orthodox church in Alaska. (USDA-Forest Service/Corbis)

these are converts from other Christian denominations, but most are non-Greeks converted to Orthodoxy for reasons of marriage. According to archdiocesan statistics, mixed couples accounted for three out of ten church marriages in the 1960s; by the 1990s, the figure was close to seven in ten. It must be kept in mind, however, that these numbers refer only to weddings conducted within the Greek Orthodox Church; virtually all Greek Americans who marry outside the Church marry non-Greeks. Now that intermarriage has become the rule rather than the exception, its meaning has been transformed. Intermarriage no longer carries a stigma in the community; thus it is much easier for exogamous Greek Americans and their spouses who marry into the church to continue active membership in the Greek community.

The Greek-American community has had to change its position on intermarriage in the face of its frequency. The initial edict of immigrant parents was to tell their children that all Greek potential marriage partners were better than all non-Greek. The next line of defense, typical of the second generation, was to acknowledge that there are equal measures of good and bad in all nationalities, but the sharing of a common Greek background makes for a better marriage. (Interestingly, the available archdiocesan data, though not conclusive, show a somewhat *lower* divorce rate among couples in which one of the partners was not ethnically Greek.) The final argument, a common recourse of the third generation, is that if one does marry a non-Greek, one must be sure that the spouse is able to adapt to the family kinship system and be willing to become Greek Orthodox.

In the mid-twentieth century, to be Greek American almost always meant to know the Greek language—for immigrants as a native tongue, for the children of immigrants with various degrees of fluency. But learning and using Greek require conscious effort, and this effort was by and large not being made by second-generation parents for their children, much less for the children of mixed marriages. Increasingly, Greek Orthodox affiliation rather than Greek language has become the defining trait of Greek ethnic identity in America.

As the church in America enters the twenty-first century, changes of some magnitude are evident. In addition to the demographic changes caused by intermarriage and the virtual end of immigration, there are signs of a move toward a more pan-Orthodox identity in this country—that is, through closer interaction with coreligionists coming from Russian, eastern European, and Arabic traditions. As the immigrant past fades, the move toward pan-Orthodoxy in America will undoubtedly continue to gain ground. This also corresponds with a move toward a more pious Orthodoxy as reflected in the appearance and proliferation of Eastern Orthodox monasteries in the United States in the 1980s and 1990s. The appearance of the Orthodox Christian laity in 1987 marked a major step toward greater democracy in the church and adaptation to American realities of language use.

Across the Generations

If the immigrant Greek family in America could not exactly replicate that of the old country, it was not for lack of trying. Husbands insisted on their moral authority over their spouses, though the formal submissions of the wife could mask her practical dominance in household affairs. Mothers and fathers tried to enforce a strict disciplinary code over their children, though this could be softened by frequent parental indulgences or subverted by clandestine activities with American friends outside the home. Spanking was common, but both parents were physically affectionate toward their offspring, with much kissing of young children. Children were included in adult activities, as age segregation was alien to the Greek immigrant mind. In their adolescent years, sons were given much more leeway, and they were much more likely to be supported in a university education than daughters. A generalized respect for elders is ingrained in both the Greek and Greek-American cultural norms. This is complemented by the notion that grandparents are expected to "spoil" their grandchildren.

A Greek sponge diver in Tarpon Springs, Florida. (Dave G. Houser/Corbis)

To be sure, assimilative processes are always at work. Even though most second-generation Greek Americans were familiar with the Greek language, and many could speak it quite well, English became the language of American-born Greeks in their own homes as well as on the outside. While vestiges of patriarchy persisted, egalitarin relations between the spouses became more the mode, along with much more equal treatment of sons and daughters. The major celebration accorded the nameday, the traditional day of the saint after which a person is named, gave way to the American custom of celebration of the birthday. Yet some patterns continued. A taste for Greek food and a liking of Greek music and dancing often carried over to members of the third and fourth generations.

The intersections among ethnicity, class, and family structure are complex ones. It is generally agreed, however, that those immigrant parents who displayed a more open attitude toward American influences were more successful in passing on Greek ethnicity than those parents who tried to resist all American encroachments totally. Efforts to rear children as though they were living in Greece were more common among blue-collar than middle-class immigrants. To pose the alternatives as all-or-nothing Greek, as many traditional parents were inclined, could lead some of their adult children to forsake their Greek background entirely. But the much more characteristic outcome has been one of continuing—though changing in form—Greek identity across the generations.

The family, which in the old country was a tightly knit unit that included uncles, aunts, and cousins, has become modeled after the nuclear family. Though an aged parent is much more likely to live with one of his or her grown children in a Greek-American setting than is typical of contemporary American society, the pattern of aged parents living on their own or in nursing homes has become more prevalent. Divorce, which was rare and brought shame to Greek-American families before World War II, approaches middle-class American proportions now.

No better illustration of the coexistence of Greek and American customs is found than in the Greek-American funeral. Attendance is high, including that of distant relatives and casual friends as well as close friends and relatives. If the deceased was an old person, there will not be excessive gravity. Before World War II, wakes were commonly held in the home of the deceased, and, following the funeral, a meal was prepared at home by some of the female relatives for the mourners. Today, the wake is held at a funeral home, always Greek-owned if such exists in the area. The next day there is a service at church, the internment at the cemetery, and a postfuneral meal at a restaurant. The entire funerary event remains—though now refracted through commercial establishments—a major manifestation of the collective consciousness of the Greek-American community.

Voluntary Associations

The first Greek associations to form in the United States were the *topika somateia*, groups of immigrants who came from the same village or region in the home country. The topika somateia gained a second wind in the late 1960s with the arrival of large numbers of new immigrants. Much of this momentum carried through into the 1990s along with the rise of second-generation leadership. Predictions of the demise of such parochial organizations have been premature.

Since its founding in 1922, the American Hellenic Educational Progressive Association (AHEPA) has been preeminent among Greek-American secular associations. Influenced by Masonic ritual, AHEPA represented the aspiration of a rising middle class and was committed to Americanizing its membership by adopting English as the official language. (The Greek-American Progressive Association [GAPA], a counterorganization that used Greek as its language, had become moribund by the 1960s.) AHEPA's annual conventions are the premier social events in Greek America. Since the 1970s, AHEPA has shifted its goals toward support of charitable activities and maintenance of Hellenic identity. In the 1990s, AHEPA began to have an image of an aging organization, an impression that will need to be corrected if AHEPA is to continue to be as effective in the future as it has been in the past.

Other organizational developments have reflected the rise of a new generation of business and professional persons. Usually covering a metropolitan area, these organizations hold fund-raisers and sponsor cultural programs. The United Hellenic-American Congress (UHAC), founded in 1975, is based in Chicago and has become a national organization. Other organizations formed in the 1970s to promote Greek-American causes and to serve as a forum for Greek-American issues are Krikos (Link) and Axios (Worthy) in Los Angeles. On a different scale is the Hellenic-American Neighborhood Action Committee (HANAC), which has evolved into one of the major social service agencies in the Greater New York area.

Also notable was the 1990 founding of the Greek-American Women's Network (GAWN), a departure from previous women's organizations, which were essentially auxiliaries of the male organizations.

The Press

The first Greek newspaper in the United States appeared in 1892 in Boston. Since that time more than a hundred Greek newspapers in America have appeared at one time or another. Two New York dailies, the conservative *Atlantis* (1894–1971) and the liberal *National Herald* (1915–present), dominated the national scene from their inception. Another Greek-language newspaper, *Proini*, began publication on a daily basis in New York City in 1977.

Over time, older Greek-American periodicals began to shift from Greek to English, and new ones emerged with English from the start. Among the more successful were *The Greek American* in New York, *Greek Press* and *Greek Star* in Chicago,

Greek-American children march in the 1990 Greek Orthodox Epiphany Parade in Tarpon Springs, Florida. (Nik Wheeler/Corbis)

Hellenic Chronicle in Boston, *Hellenic Journal* in San Francisco, and the *Greek American Monthly* in Pittsburgh. Professionally edited magazines with impressive artwork made their appearance in the 1980s: *Greek Accent* (which ceased publication in 1988) and *Greek-American Review*. Another high-quality magazine, *Odyssey*, first appeared in 1993 and is notable because while mainly geared to a Greek-American audience, it is published in Greece.

Greek Americans and Greece

During the Balkan wars of 1912–1913, some forty-five thousand immigrants returned to Greece to volunteer to fight in the Greek army. In the immediate post–World War I period, the political schism in Greece between the supporters of King Constantine I and the liberal prime minister Eleftherios Venizelos cleaved the Greek community in America as well. Following World War II the Greek-American community strongly supported the pro-Western government in the Greek civil war, though elements of leftist support for the Communist side were not absent. The Turkish invasion of Cyprus in 1974 affected the Greek-American community profoundly. One important consequence was the formation of what came to be known as the "Greek lobby." The major entities were the American-Hellenic Institute Political Action Committee (AHIPAC), which worked closely with AHEPA and UHAC with its close ties to the archdiocese. Though the two groups sometimes differed on strategy and though personality conflicts were not absent, they generally complemented rather than competed with one another. In addition to lobbying against the Turkish occupation of northern Cyprus, Greek-American leadership also took active roles in supporting the civil rights of the Greek minority in Albania and in opposing Turkey's expansionist moves in the Aegean Sea and the irrendentist claims of the Former Yugoslavia Republic of Macedonia to northern Greece.

Cooperation between the Greek-American establishment and the government in Greece was affected by the electoral victory of Andreas Papandreou and his Socialist party in 1981. Although cynics claimed that Papandreou's bark was worse than his bite, the prime minister's anti-American rhetoric disturbed Greek Americans as much as American officials. While important members of the Greek-American community have acted as a pro-Greek lobby in Washington, they have been less effective as a pro-American pressure group in Athens. After suffering an electoral defeat, Papandreou returned as prime minister in 1993, at which time he adopted a much more conciliatory attitude toward the United States. In 1996, upon Papandreou's retirement, Costas Simitis became prime minister. The Simitis government promised even more cordial relations with the United States.

The continuing support that Americans of Greek ancestry give to the causes of the old country, despite political differences between Athens and Washington, shows that they ultimately take their bearings not from developments in Greece, or even from Greece's foreign relations with the United States, but rather from a deep and abiding belief that what is good for America is good for Greece and vice versa.

For most Greek Americans, however, the ties with Greece are personal rather than political. A cardinal feature of Greek-American ethnicity is the trip back to the old country. The advent of relatively inexpensive air services has brought travel to Greece easily within reach of the Greek-American community. Among American-born Greeks, a large number, probably a majority, have visited the ancestral homeland at least once. New developments in the way of language and cultural courses offered in Greece for those of Greek ancestry born abroad are becoming new factors in reviving a flagging ethnic identification.

As Greek America approaches the end of the twentieth century, the end of the immigrants' story is in sight. Nearly all of them entered this country as unskilled workers, but a significant portion became proprietors of their own small businesses.

The children and grandchildren of the immigrants have moved, in the main, into middle-class vocations and into the professions. Although processes of assimilation are undeniable, there has been a persistent attachment to Greek Orthodoxy and a "Greek identity," however hard to define that might be, well into the second and third generations. How well this identity will fare in the fourth and later generations is yet to be known.

See also: VLACHS

Bibliography

Burgess, T. (1915). *Greeks in America.* Boston: Sherman, French.

Georgakas, D., and Moskos, C. (1991). *New Directions in Greek-American Studies.* New York: Pella.

Karanikas, A. (1981). *Hellenes and Hellions: Modern Greek Characters in American Literature.* Urbana: University of Illinois Press.

Kopan, A. T. (1989). *The Greeks in Chicago.* Urbana: University of Illinois Press.

Kourvetaris, G. A. (1971). *First- and Second-Generation Greeks in Chicago.* Athens: National Center for Social Research.

Moskos, C. (1988). *Greek Americans: Struggle and Success.* New Brunswick, NJ: Transaction.

Papaioannou, G. (1976). *From Mars Hill to Manhattan: The Greek Orthodox in America Under Patriarch Athenagoras I.* Minneapolis: Light and Life.

Papanikolas, H. Z. (1982). *Toil and Rage in a New Land: The Greek Immigrants in Utah.* Salt Lake City: Utah Historical Society.

Saloutos, T. (1964). *The Greeks in the United States.* Cambridge, MA: Harvard University Press.

Scourby, A. (1984). *The Greek Americans.* New York: Twayne.

Tavuchis, N. (1972). *Family and Mobility Among Greek Americans.* Athens: National Center for Social Research.

Vlachos, E. C. (1968). *The Assimilation of Greeks in the United States.* Athens: National Center for Social Research.

Zotos, S. (1976). *Hellenic Presence in America.* Wheaton, IL: Pilgrimage Press.

CHARLES MOSKOS

GRENADIANS

The island of Grenada (Isle of Spice; Spice Island) is really a three-island independent state in the southeastern Caribbean comprised of Grenada, the largest island, and two smaller islands to its immediate northeast: Carriacou, and Petite Martinique. Grenada lies between St. Vincent and the Grenadines to the north and Trinidad and Tobago to the south. Before gaining independence in 1974, Grenada belonged to a subgroup of British Caribbean islands known as the Windward Islands.

Grenada is located at the extreme southern end of the Caribbean archipelago that stretches for more than two thousand miles in an arc across the Caribbean Sea, from Cuba, near the tip of Florida, to Aruba, off the coast of South America. Many of the Caribbean islands, or the West Indies (the name that Christopher Columbus gave the region), were formed through intense volcanic eruptions that began at least one hundred million years ago. Grenada is very mountainous and contains three crater lakes and an active marine volcano, "Kick 'em Jinny," which often makes sea travel between Grenada and Carriacou very difficult.

Grenada's climate is maritime-tropical, and the annual average temperature is twenty-eight degrees Celsius (eighty-two degrees Fahrenheit). The heaviest rainfall months are June through December; annual rainfall ranges from 1,500 millimeters (60 inches) on the coast to 5,100 millimeters (150 to 200 inches) in the mountains. A central, thickly forested mountain ridge runs from the northeast down the middle of the island to the southwestern coast, so that the island's capital, St. George's, and all of its other towns are situated along the coasts. Carriacou and Petite Martinique are less mountainous and receive less rainfall than Grenada. The topography of the islands and their history of large-estate ownership and poverty have made acquisition of cultivable land impossible for the majority of the people. Since the 1850s many Grenadians have used regional and extraregional labor migration to access wage labor.

History and Demography

The indigenous Carib and Arawak native peoples were completely decimated by the French who arrived to settle the island early in the seventeenth century. The British finally captured Grenada from the French in 1796, but important vestiges of the French period are still evident, especially in people's surnames, in the many French place names, in a fast-fading French Creole, in Roman Catholicism (the predominant religion), and in several well-preserved seventeenth- and eighteenth-century French forts.

During the eighteenth and early nineteenth centuries, the British shipped West Africans into Grenada and enslaved them on estates to cultivate agricultural products for export to Britain. Britain emancipated the enslaved Africans in its colonies in 1834. However, on some islands, including Grenada, free slave labor was replaced with the wage labor of Asian, African, Maltese, and Portuguese indentured workers. The majority of Grenada's indentured workers were Asian Indians from Calcutta and Madras.

By far the largest racial group in Grenada consists of people of African descent. In 1921, Grenada's population was 66,302; Asian Indians numbered 2,082. The resident Asian Indian population was small and poor and in time became absorbed into the larger black racial group. According to the 1990 Grenadian Census, 82 percent of the island's population is of African descent, 13 percent classified themselves as being of mixed racial origin, and 5 percent classified themselves as white. The population of Carriacou is predominantly black. The island's relative isolation promoted the retention of strong aspects of West African culture introduced to the society during slavery. Grenada's population was 93,858 in 1971, but it declined to 89,088 in 1981, mainly due to heavy emigration. By 1991, the population had increased to 94,806.

Grenada's Economy. Sugar eventually became Grenada's cash crop, while cotton was grown on Carriacou, and both products were exported to

Britain. When sugar production became unprofitable in the middle of the nineteenth century, cocoa, nutmegs, cinnamon, and cloves were introduced as alternative postemancipation cash crops. Grenada is second only to Indonesia in the export of nutmegs and mace, the lacy orange membrane that covers the nutmegs. Spices and bananas are the island's chief export crops, but precarious and fluctuating prices for these products on the world market make economic planning for the island almost impossible, and the island's annual unemployment levels are often well over 20 percent. Since the 1980s, tourism has begun to rival agricultural production as the island's main source of revenue.

The island imports all of its manufactured goods and most of its food, but its export earnings are insufficient to meet its balance-of-payments debts. About 22 percent of its exports are to England, while about 33 percent of its imports are from the United States and 13 percent are from the neighboring island of Trinidad. Britain, the United States, and Trinidad are also major labor destinations for many emigrating Grenadians.

Island Politics. The island's government is modeled after the British parliamentary system, and general elections are held every five years. Since 1951, when adult suffrage gave every citizen over twenty-one years of age the vote, elections have been held regularly, except from 1979 to 1983, when a socialist-type experiment in government, modeled closely on that in Cuba, was tried. Bloody civil unrest erupted in St. George's in late October 1983, during which Prime Minister Maurice Bishop was assassinated. The United States used this period of instability to intervene and restore the traditional form of government. Since then, several elected governments have come and gone under the watchful eyes of the United States government, and the island seems to be experiencing relative political stability.

Labor Emigration

Grenadians and other Anglophone Caribbean people began using emigration as a survival strategy immediately after full emancipation in 1838. For decades, the most prosperous English-speaking island in the southern Caribbean, Trinidad, was the hub of much Grenadian emigration. Trinidadians coined the term "small islanders" to describe Grenadians, and they still use the term derogatively, even when they are immigrants together in the United States.

A second phase of Grenadian labor emigration took male workers to the "foreign" Spanish-speaking Caribbean and to Panama at the beginning of the twentieth century to build the Panama Canal. In the first decades of the twentieth century, Grenadians traveled to work in the sugarcane fields of Cuba and the Dominican Republic and later to Costa Rica and Nicaragua to work on the banana plantations. At that time, Grenadian men also traveled to Brazil and British Guiana (now the independent Guyana) to cut logs and look for gold. Many of these men turned up later in Venezuela and on the Dutch islands of Aruba and Curacao, sites of major oil refineries from the 1920s to the 1950s.

A century-long history of intraregional migration had stimulated the interests and ambitions of Grenadians, and they wanted access to consistent wage-earning opportunities. Only a few hundred Grenadian men had been able to find their way into the United States before World War I. They had done this by apprenticing on U.S. boats that transported bananas from Central America via Barbados and jumping ship once they docked in New York or Boston. The enlistment of U.S. servicemen in World War I opened up more employment opportunities to Caribbean men, but again only a small trickle of Grenadian men immigrated to the United States during these years.

It was the oil fields of the southern Caribbean and the U.S. naval base at Chaguaramas, Trinidad, that exposed Grenadian men and women to American entrepreneurship, work habits, and most of all high wages: the well-sung "Yankee dollar." Thousands of men (the majority from Carriacou), many of whom had been fishermen or captains of interisland schooners, worked on the tugboats and oil tankers that plied the oil fields in Lake

Maracaibo in Venezuela and incessantly crossed the twenty-mile-wide sea lane between the oil fields and the islands of Curaçao and Aruba, where giant oil repositories and refineries were located.

Grenadian women who had been employed as domestics in Venezuela, Curaçao, or Aruba and who had married male immigrant workers, or Grenadian nurses who had worked in the medical facilities in the oil enclave were among the first immigrants to the United States in the late 1950s. Grenadians were among thousands of Caribbean workers laid off and repatriated in the mid-1950s, when the oil refineries mechanized and downsized their operations. These restless men and women were determined to find their way into the United States, and they used various means. Some had made important job connections while working in the oil enclave or on the naval base and had been given references by American employers. Others had sent their children to U.S. schools, and once these children found jobs and sponsors to help them with the immigration requirements, they applied for permanent residence for their parents. Still others first found work on oil refineries in the U.S. Virgin Islands, or traveled first to England, and from there found their way, often via Canada, into the United States.

In the mid-1950s, Canada inaugurated a program under which eligible Caribbean women were sponsored by Canadian residents who employed them for two years as live-in maids, after which time the women were on their own. A few hundred Grenadian middle-class professional women used this program to get into North America. After the mandatory period, they found their way into the United States and became residents mainly of New York, Boston, and Washington, D.C. Early in the 1960s, U.S. immigration authorities developed a program under which domestic workers and nurses from the Caribbean were encouraged to seek entry into the United States by finding prospective employers. Hundreds of Grenadian women found sponsors. Poor Grenadian women who were lucky to have contacts in the United States found jobs as live-in nannies, especially in New York City. Grenada's two main hospitals were drained of their trained senior nurses as many of these women found positions in New York hospitals.

The largest wave of Grenadians immigrating to the United States began in the years immediately following enactment of the Hart-Celler Immigration Reform Act of 1965. This act changed the focus of U.S. immigration policy, which formerly had favored European nations, to include developing countries. By 1965, Britain had all but closed its doors to its former Caribbean colonists. However, U.S. foreign policy included a revived interest in the Caribbean, and U.S. presence and influence in the Caribbean increased all during the 1960s.

Caribbean immigration to the United States soared. The 1910 U.S. Census estimated that there were 11,757 foreign-born blacks in New York. The majority of these would have been Caribbean-born. The number rose to 67,655 by 1960. By 1980, however, there were 300,000 foreign-born non-Hispanic Caribbean blacks in New York.

Grenadian/Caribbean/Black Communities

It is very difficult to distinguish a Grenadian from a Caribbean person generally or simply from a black person in the United States. Racial politics and prejudice in the United States motivate black ethnic groups to live in contiguous neighborhoods. In addition, there is much intermarriage and cooperation within the English-speaking Caribbean immigrant community, and increasingly between Caribbean blacks and native African Americans. The most reliable figures are those that represent the numbers of arriving Grenadian immigrants over a time period, from which logical deductions may be made.

The statistics of the U.S. Immigration and Naturalization Service show that between 1960 and 1980 a total of 10,391 Grenadians had entered the United States legally. In a slightly overlapping period, 1971 to 1984, New York was the point of entry for 12,085 Grenadian immigrants. The pace of Grenadian emigration has been steady and is indicated in Grenada's population decline and subsequent low population increase during the 1980s and early 1990s. An average of 850 Grenadians have annually gained legal entry to and permanent residence in the United States since 1984.

The great majority of Grenadian immigrants to the United States have gained entry through family reunification, while others, whose applications for entry had been filed prior to the 1970s, were at last called to immigrate to the United States. However, many Grenadians who arrive ostensibly as tourists or students remain illegally to work. There is constant coming and going between Grenada and the United States for varying periods, especially among legal immigrants, so that any census misses hundreds who are visiting in Grenada.

A conservative estimate is that fifteen thousand Grenadians are permanent residents in the United States or are U.S. citizens. This number is a mere drop in the wider U.S. black population, but it is a significant percentage of Grenada's total population. The vast majority of Grenadians in the United States live in two cities: New York and Washington, D.C. In New York, Grenadians live within the major Caribbean communities around Nostrand Avenue in the Flatbush section of Brooklyn and in the Bronx.

The politics of race in the United States often forces blacks to downplay their ethnic differences and join in pan-Caribbean/pan-black coalitions. Although there is intense ethnic competition, evidenced in clannish black ethnic groupings, associations, and organizations, there is also ongoing cooperation among Grenadians, other Caribbean blacks, and African-Americans. They meet in churches, in the workplace, in parent-teacher organizations, in neighborhood watch committees, and at Caribbean Carnival festivities.

Transnationalism

Proximity to the United States, extensive U.S. tourism to the Caribbean, U.S. cable television in the Caribbean, and other modern methods of communication and transportation all tend to minimize borders between tiny Caribbean nations and their very powerful, politically active neighbor to the north. Grenadians fly out of Grenada and go to New York City, Washington, D.C., and Miami to visit and shop as if Grenada were a neighboring state.

"Transnationals" is a term coined by social scientists to describe immigrant people who live physically and emotionally between their sending societies and the host society where they make their living. There is ongoing debate about whether the transnational is a permanent immigration phenomenon or a feature of first-generation immigrant insecurity, felt among people who for racial or other reasons have not been readily welcomed by the host society. Others suggest that modern technology and aggressive international entrepreneurship have minimized the importance of state boundaries so that small, dependent states in the Caribbean, such as Grenada, effectively become extensions of a powerful neighbor such as the United States.

Grenadians remit millions of U.S. dollars through banks and the postal service and through the transfer of goods to relatives back in the sending country. Grenada's main post office in St. George's has constructed a large holding area to accommodate the barrels and boxes stacked with foodstuffs and clothing that arrive daily from New York and Washington, D.C.

Numbers of Grenada's small middle class, mainly professionals, also have been immigrating to the United States since early in the twentieth century. Others have experienced social mobility in the United States. However, social class demarcations are distorted by racial inequalities in the United States, and the vast majority of Grenadians in the United States are service workers whose average annual income is $20,000 to $30,000. Wages obtained by Grenadian residents in the United States are making significant contributions to Grenada's gross national product and maybe to its social and political stability as well.

Bibliography

Bogen, E. (1987). *Immigration in New York*. New York: Praeger.

Brizan, G. (1984). *Grenada: Island of Conflict*. London: Zed Books.

Kasinitz, P. (1992). *Caribbean New York*. Ithaca, NY: Cornell University Press.

Levine, B. B., ed. (1987). *The Caribbean Exodus*. New York: Praeger.

Portes, A., and Rumbaut, R. G. (1990). *Immigrant America: A Portrait*. Berkeley: University of California Press.

Richardson, B. C. (1992). *The Caribbean in the Wider World, 1492–1992*. New York: Cambridge University Press.

Schiller, N. G.; Basch, L.; and Blanc-Szanton, C. (1992). "Transnationalism: A New Analytic Framework for Understanding Migration." In *Towards a Transnational Perspective on Migration*, edited by N. G. Schiller, L. Basch, and C. Blanc-Szanton. New York: New York Academy of Sciences.

Sealy, N. (1992). *Caribbean World*. New York: Cambridge University Press.

Sunshine, C. A. (1994). *The Caribbean: Survival, Struggle, and Sovereignty*. Washington, DC: Ecumenical Program on Central America and the Caribbean.

Sutton, R. C., and Chaney, E. M. (1987). *Caribbean Life in New York City: Sociocultural Dimensions*. New York: Center for Migration Studies of New York.

U.S. Department of Justice. (1969, 1980, 1983, 1984). *Statistical Yearbook of the Immigration and Naturalization Service*. Washington, DC: U.S. Government Printing Office.

Wiltshire, R. (1992). "Implications of Transnational Migration for Nationalism: The Caribbean Example." In *Towards a Transnational Perspective on Migration*, edited by N.G. Schiller, L. Basch, and C. Blanc-Szanton. New York: New York Academy of Sciences.

PAULA AYMER

GUAMANIANS

"Guamanian" refers to the people residing on the western Pacific island of Guam, in the region of Micronesia. The term includes the descendants of the original inhabitants of the island as well as later arrivals who have become permanent residents. To distinguish themselves, descendants of the indigenous people of Guam call themselves Chamorro (also spelled Chamoru).

Spain claimed Guam as a colonial possession in 1565, and established a Catholic mission there in 1668. Spaniards initially referred to the natives as Indians, but later called them Chamorros. Both Chamorro and Guamanian are used to refer to the native inhabitants of Guam in the historical and social science literature. Laura Thompson, an anthropologist who carried out field work in Guam from 1938 to 1939, reported that the people prefer to be called "Guamanian" instead of the more correct term "Chamorro." Anthropologists refer to all of the original inhabitants of the Mariana Islands, of which Guam is a part, as Chamorro. Anthropologically, Chamorro refers to the indigenous culture of the Marianas, the people of that culture, and their language.

Guam's population became more diverse after World War II, with the immigration of large numbers of Americans and Filipinos. The influx of people to Guam from abroad continued in the decades that followed, so that by the 1990 U.S. Census, Chamorros comprised only 43.3 percent of the total population. The Chamorros' identification with the island's indigenous culture allows them to express their ethnic heritage and distinction from members of other ethnic groups (e.g., Filipinos, Koreans, Chuukese, and Palauan) now resident in Guam. Consequently, Chamorros are the largest ethnic group on the island. Since the 1970s, the term Chamorro-Guamanian has been used frequently to distinguish descendants of the native inhabitants from non-Chamorro immigrants to Guam.

Guam was captured by American forces during the war with Spain 1898. The native population, by then a hybrid population both in physical type and cultural heritage (a mixture of indigenous Chamorro, Spanish, Mexican, and Filipino traits), was recognized as American nationals and citizens of Guam. In 1950, the U.S. Congress designated Guam as an unincorporated territory of the United States, and Guamanians were granted U.S. citizenship. Therefore, movement of Guamanians to the U.S. mainland is properly termed migration rather than immigration. They are members of a culture that has been absorbed into the fabric of American society and thus represent an American subculture.

Migration and Settlement History

The earliest individuals to migrate from Guam to the mainland United States were those who enlisted in the armed services. Designated as American nationals after Guam was captured from Spain, Chamorros in 1937 were allowed to enlist in the U.S. Navy, but only as mess attendants. Enlistment into other branches of the military commenced after Chamorros were granted U.S. citizenship under the Organic Act of 1950 that established Guam as an unincorporated territory of the United States. Many enlisted personnel brought their families with them when based at mainland military installations and then settled in nearby cities, the principal ones being Long Beach, San Diego, and San Francisco in California, and Seattle, Washington. California has attracted the majority of Chamorros migrating to the mainland, with more than half of the nearly fifty thousand Guamanians (term used in the census) counted as mainland residents in the 1990 U.S. Census. Their distribution throughout the fifty states is not even, but Guamanians are resident in each state.

Military enlistment afforded individuals not only the opportunity to leave Guam, but it also was an avenue for gainful employment. Not all seeking to improve their economic opportunities did so through the military. Many Chamorros, facing limited economic opportunities and an increasing cost of living on the island, considered moving to the mainland their best chance for improving their life. This migration extended through the 1960s, 1970s, and 1980s. Still others migrated to pursue higher education or advanced professional training at mainland colleges and universities.

Guam experienced tremendous sociocultural change after World War II, specifically with regard to the expanded military presence. Three major events in the 1960s and 1970s brought on further change: Typhoon Karen in 1962; withdrawal of the military security closure of the island (this had limited economic growth and mobility) in 1962; and Typhoon Pamela in 1976. The federal government poured large amounts of money into the island's economy to repair damages inflicted by the storms. Tourism emerged as a major industry when travel restrictions were removed. Rapid economic development and increasing urbanization ushered in many negative consequences for the people of Guam, for whom life just a mere two or three generations before had been based wholly or in part on subsistence cultivation and strong family ties. The changes of the 1970s and 1980s produced increasing crime rates, drug trafficking, and disintegration of traditional family patterns. Regarding the rate of change as too rapid and unsatisfying, many Chamorros migrated to the mainland.

Whatever the reason for migrating, settlement patterns for Chamorros on the mainland were similar. First arrivals would subsequently serve as hosts for family or relatives arriving later. Typically the first arrival was military and had settled with immediate family in a community near the base. A sibling or surviving parent of the husband or wife would move from Guam to live with his or her mainland relatives. Once a sibling found employment and a residence, his or her family would then follow.

Chamorros in Guam would frequently decide after retirement to move to the mainland to be with adult children already residing there. Conversely, Chamorro military personnel based on the mainland would often return to Guam upon retirement from military service.

Some of those who leave Guam for the mainland in pursuit of higher education and professional training decide to stay because they believe life will be better than on Guam; others return.

Demographic Characteristics

The 1990 U.S. Census reports a total of 49,345 Chamorros resident in the United States. California hosts the largest number, with 25,059; cities in the state with the largest concentrations of

Chamorros are San Diego (2,643), Los Angeles (2,140), and Long Beach (1,051). Other states with significant numbers of Chamorros are Washington (3,779), Texas (2,209), Hawaii (2,120), New York (1,803), Florida (1,241), and Illinois (1,105). Chamorros are resident in all fifty states and the District of Columbia. In contrast to California, which has the largest population, Vermont hosts the smallest population of Chamorros, with 24. The number of Chamorros in the other states range from Wyoming's 35 to Virginia's 923.

There are nearly equal numbers of women and men among the Chamorro population in the United States. Of the 49,345 total in the 1990 U.S. Census, females account for 24,140 (49%) and males 25,205 (51%). These percentages are virtually uniform in the four regions reported in the census.

Census data for 1990 also report for Chamorros an average of 3.35 persons per household and an average of 3.79 persons per family. A majority of the population is 25 to 34 years old.

Language and Cultural Characteristics

Under American rule in Guam, English was the predominant language, and Chamorros were compelled to adopt it as their own. Despite American efforts to discourage Chamorros from speaking their native tongue, the Chamorro language continues to survive.

The first wave of Chamorros to arrive on the mainland prior to 1950 were familiar with English, but they faced difficulties communicating, as they were not yet fully bilingual. Subsequent arrivals, especially those during the later 1950s and the following decades, were more proficient in English. Research conducted in the early 1980s among Chamorros in northern California reports that many of those interviewed for the study spoke both English and Chamorro at home. Other studies indicate differences in the level of fluency in Chamorro between adults and children. Children born in the United States, or those who left Guam before age twelve, could understand but not speak Chamorro fluently.

Chamorros on the United States mainland make strong attempts to maintain their cultural heritage and identity. One means of doing this is through the formation of Guam clubs. Faye Untalan Munoz and Robert A. Underwood both point out that the principal aspect of traditional culture lost when Chamorros move to the mainland is support through extended family ties. To re-create a support network in mainland communities, Chamorros form clubs to establish relationships beyond kinship. For example, the Guam Territorial Society was established in 1952 among Chamorros who had moved to Washington, D.C., or the surrounding area. The group was comprised of persons serving in the military, their families, and Chamorro students attending colleges or universities in the area. By 1996, the Guam Territorial Society had become the Guam Society of America, Inc., recognized as the largest Guam club on the East Coast. Other Guam clubs existing in 1996 in other parts of the country include Sons and Daughters of Guam Club, Inc., San Diego; Guamanian Club of Bremerton and Vicinity, Port Orchard, Washington; Hafa Adai ("hello" in Chamorro) Club of Mississippi, Gulfport; and Texoma Chamorro Society, Lawton, Oklahoma. Social activities in these groups provide an avenue for maintaining traditional customs (such as fiestas), values, and communication through group newsletters. Some groups also maintain links to Guam by sponsoring a float in the annual Liberation Day parade, which celebrates Guam's liberation from the Japanese on July 21, 1944.

Among the traditional aspects of Chamorro culture Guam clubs help to maintain are obedience to and respect for elders (e.g., the kissing of the hand—and sometimes the cheek—of elders, called *mangnigni*); the importance of unity and support among family and friends; extending generosity and hospitality to guests; the Catholic religion and customs such as novenas, rosaries, and fiestas; and the Chamorro language.

Based on research carried out in the late 1970s, Munoz makes observations concerning family, marriage, and economic patterns among Chamorro migrants on the mainland. Migrants who arrived before World War II had few relatives on the mainland. However, they became focal points for family members who migrated in later years. When siblings and other relatives move to the mainland, they tend to live in close proximity to family members already resident. Among the first generation of migrants, marriage was usually with other Chamorros. Marriages among the second and third generation of migrants were increasingly with non-Chamorros.

According to Munoz, few Chamorros on the mainland hold professional positions. Instead, they engage in activities that range from unskilled or semiskilled work, custodial or clerical positions, to midlevel management. Men who had retired from the military but continue to work are employed as custodians, clerks, or cooks. Women who are employed tend to be engaged in service occupations, such as sales clerks, fish cannery workers, teacher's aides, or clerk/typists. Data from the 1990 U.S. Census indicate that Chamorros in the United States have a median household income of $30,503. Regionally, the median household incomes for Chamorros are: West, $33,843; South, $27,297; Northeast, $21,065; and Midwest, $20,919.

In addition to Guam clubs satisfying social needs, Underwood argues that some of them also afford mainland Chamorros a means of organizing politically. Initial political concerns were toward reaffirming their Chamorro identity on the mainland but now include a broader range of issues, such as participation in the ethnic politics of their home state or becoming active in groups promoting the interests of Pacific Islanders in the United States. This effort is aimed at fostering an identity distinct from that of Asian American or Asian Pacific American, categories frequently used by state and federal agencies.

Assimilation

Chamorro migrants to the mainland encounter interesting contrasts. They arrive with some degree of familiarity with American social life, being from a U.S. territorial possession that has become highly Americanized. There is familiarity with the language, economic system, school system, and other social institutions. Nevertheless, Chamorros are relatively unknown to other Americans, are usually mistaken for members of other ethnic minorities, and have suffered discrimination. Not all forms of discrimination, however, result from mistaken identity. When Chamorros were first allowed to enlist in the U.S. Navy, they could only be mess attendants. Thus Chamorros have been and, according to Munoz, are subjected to American institutionalized racism. Munoz notes that Chamorros are in the process of coping with a sense of insignificance and feel inferior to white people as a consequence of the long history of political and religious domination by Western nations. On the mainland this mentality is sometimes expressed in submissive behavior toward white people. An alternative explanation for such behavior is that Chamorros are expressing their traditional values of showing kindness and hospitality. Munoz concludes that even in these instances, Chamorros believe they are exploited and taken for granted by other Americans.

Guam clubs have long served as means for helping Chamorro migrants adapt to their new social environment. They facilitate the maintenance of traditional Chamorro culture, provide a formal mechanism for establishing political ties with other Pacific Islander groups in the United States, and are a vehicle through which Chamorros shed their anonymity and are able to proclaim their identity as part of a significant, vibrant American subculture.

See also: PACIFIC ISLANDERS IN HAWAII

Bibliography

Barrett, W., tr. (1975). *Mission in the Marianas.* Minneapolis: University of Minnesota Press.
Carano, P., and Sanchez, P. C. (1964). *A Complete History of Guam.* Tokyo: Charles E. Tuttle.
Mayo, L. W. (1987). "Urbanization in the Pacific and Guam." *City and Society* 1:99–121.

Mayo, L. W. (1992). "The Militarization of Guamanian Society." In *Social Change in the Pacific Islands*, edited by A. B. Robillard. London: Kegan Paul International.

Munoz, F. U. (1978). "Pacific Islanders: Life Patterns in a New Land." In *New Neighbors: Islanders in Adaptation*, edited by C. Macpherson, B. Shore, and R. Franco. Santa Cruz, CA: Center for South Pacific Studies, University of California, Santa Cruz.

Rogers, R. F. (1995). *Destiny's Landfall: A History of Guam*. Honolulu: University of Hawaii Press.

Souder, L. M. T. (1992). *Daughters of the Island: Contemporary Chamorro Women Organizers on Guam*. Lanham, MD: University Press of America.

Thompson, L. ([1947] 1969). *Guam and Its People*. New York: Greenwood Press.

Underwood, R. A. (1985). "Excursions into Inauthenticity: The Chamorros of Guam." In *Mobility and Identity in the Island Pacific*, edited by M. Chapman and P. S. Morrison. *Pacific Viewpoint* 26:160–184.

U.S. Bureau of the Census. (1992). *1990 Census of Population: General Population Characteristics, United States*. Washington, DC: U.S. Government Printing Office.

U.S. Bureau of the Census. (1993). *1990 Census of Housing: Detailed Housing Characteristics, United States*. Washington, DC: U.S. Government Printing Office.

LARRY W. MAYO

GUATEMALAN MAYA

The 150,000 Guatemalan Maya living in the United States are an unusual ethnic group in that they are Native American immigrants, even though they come from a Spanish-speaking country in Central America. As Mayan Indians they have a religious system that is a blend of Christianity and indigenous religion or *costumbre*; the corn they eat has sacred characteristics, and the languages they speak are related to other North American Indian languages. About half of the Guatemalan Maya are in the United States legally; the other half are in the process of obtaining legal status or temporarily working without papers. They are the living descendants of one of the most complex civilizations of the Americas. The Maya are people whose ancestors built the spectacular and extensive cities, pyramids, and empires throughout the countries of Mexico, Guatemala, Belize, El Salvador, and Honduras before the coming of the Spaniards to the New World. Chichén Itzá, Copán, Tulum, and Tikal are well-known archaeological sites of Mayan history that draw millions of tourists to places such as Cancún, Mexico. The Mayan area before the coming of the Spaniards in the sixteenth century was never a unified nation or country, but rather a series of confederations and empires connected by trade, marriage, and the political ambitions of Mayan rulers. Many people assume that the Mayan culture is a "lost civilization," a group of people who are no longer around. But Maya today are very much in touch with their own history and culture: They still speak the same languages as their ancestors; worship the forces of rain, the sun, and spirits of the forest alongside the Christian deity; and grow corn and other crops in the same way as they have been doing for three thousand years. Of course, those who have immigrated to the United States often cannot grow their own crops while they live in cities such as Chicago or Los Angeles, but when they can, such as in the large settlement of Maya in Indiantown, Florida, they are quick to plant gardens with their favorite Mayan spices and vegetables. The Maya in the United States are mostly from Guatemala, although there are representatives of the Mayan communities of the southern Mexican states of Chiapas and Yucatán as well.

One of the ironies of the Mayan civilization and the Maya today is that they seldom use the term "Maya" to refer to themselves. The term is really a name given by outsiders more than a century ago to the language the Maya speak. Maya themselves are much more likely to use the name of their hometown as the way of identifying themselves. If you ask a Guatemalan Maya, "Who are you?" he or she will answer, "I am from San Pedro," or "I am Jacaltec" (from the town of Jacaltenango). But in the United States, where ethnicity is more linked to someone's country of origin than to a town, younger immigrants are beginning to call themselves "Maya" or "Guatemalan." This is especially true of those people who were either brought to the United States when they were very young or were born in the United States.

Languages and Ethnic Identity

More than thirty-one Mayan languages are spoken in the Mayan homelands of Guatemala, Mexico, Belize, El Salvador, and Honduras. The country with the most Mayan languages is Guatemala, where there are twenty-one officially accepted Mayan languages or "dialects," as they are called. Guatamala has the greatest number of Maya, as about half of the nine million people there are of Mayan heritage. These different languages or dialects are for the most part not mutually intelligible, and so by this definition, they are true languages with differences among them like those among Spanish, French, and Italian. Like the languages derived from Latin, the Mayan languages also have common roots, but they have developed separately over the past three thousand years. The famous Mayan book of origin, the *Popol Vuh*, for example, was written in the Quiché Mayan language and so cannot be read by people who speak other Mayan languages, such as Jacaltec or Kanjobal. Many people who speak Spanish and are not Maya think of these more than thirty-one different languages as only dialects and mistakenly believe that all Maya can understand each other.

In Guatemala, the prestige of Spanish-speaking people is so high that even Maya often refer to their languages as "dialects" rather than the true languages they are. Also, the Maya, who have lived for close to five hundred years as subjects in Guatemala, have learned to identify themselves as Indios (Indians), a term that lumps them with all Native Americans. Another term Maya have adopted is *naturales* (natural people). This comes from the colonial era of the sixteenth and seventeenth centuries when Spaniards in the New World referred to people living outside the confines of European civilization as "natural people." In U.S. schools Maya are often categorized as "Hispanic," even though their first language is not necessarily Spanish, or even "Latino," a term that likewise better describes the people who have ruled over them rather than themselves. Since the term "Maya" is not accepted or even understood in many places, they often just call themselves "Guatemalan."

Immigration and Settlement History

Guatemalan Maya began immigrating to the United States in the late 1970s, although there were always a few people from Guatemala who traveled to the United States in earlier times. Large numbers began to arrive in the late 1970s and early

A Guatemalan woman practices her traditional weaving skills in southern Florida. (Nik Wheeler/Corbis)

1980s because of the civil violence that pervaded much of Guatemala at that time. A guerrilla insurgency that began in the 1950s became a strong force by the late 1970s; in the early 1980s, a particularly harsh military regime led by General Ríos Montt designed a strategy of ending the guerrilla movement by destroying their bases of support. This meant burning large tracts of isolated Mayan lands in the mountainous regions of northwestern Guatemala and killing many Maya. Montt had himself installed as president and offered a harsh choice to the Maya: Accept the food of the military (in this case beans) or accept their bullets. About 500,000 Maya (and other Guatemalans) left the country in the early 1980s. Mexico accepted 46,000 of them as official refugees; the rest quietly changed from their distinctive handwoven garments to Western clothes to blend into Mexican and later U.S. society. When these people enter the United States, they are identified only as Guatemalan, so there is no official number of Guatemalan Maya in the United States. There were 265,000 Guatemalans in the United States as reported in the 1990 U.S. Census; of these, 187,000 were born in Guatemala. But not all Guatemalans are Guatemalan Maya. Anthropologists and historians estimate that there are 150,000 Guatemalan Maya in the United States. The exact number is difficult to determine because many Guatemalan Maya are in the United States without legal immigration papers. Others are quick to respond that they are Guatemalan and do not necessarily claim to be Maya even if they speak a Mayan language.

The Guatemalan Maya in the United States are found in the major cities of Los Angeles, Denver, Phoenix, Houston, West Palm Beach, New York, and Chicago. They also have settled in many small towns; the best known is Indiantown.

The first pioneers of this refugee immigration went where some of their family members or friends had traveled before them: Los Angeles, Phoenix, and Houston received the first hundreds of families who fled the violence of Guatamala. These people were from small villages or *aldeas* in the mountainous regions of Guatemala, often from areas where the only transportation routes were footpaths. They were farmers, people who in the past had learned how to migrate to the coffee and cotton plantations to work in Guatemala. Now they immigrated to the United States, far from the Guatemalan coast. Once in the United States they entered the immigrant worker streams, traveling across the United States to places such as South Florida or up the West Coast as far as the Canadian border. Some places welcomed these immigrants. A good example of a welcoming community is Indiantown, which had a total population of three thousand in 1980, when the first group of Guatemalan Maya arrived. Indiantown (named after a Seminole Indian camp) and the area around it had become a leading citrus and vegetable producer in southern Florida. When a few Guatemalan Maya without legal papers arrived to work in the citrus groves in 1982, they were picked up and detained by the immigration authorities and then later released to a Catholic priest in Indiantown. These early arrivals were poor, spoke very little Spanish and no English, and yet had a strong desire to make their lives better within the safety of the United States. They applied for political asylum and were granted a year's time to prepare their cases. The local residents of Indiantown took pity on their plight and helped find them jobs, social services, and ways to recoup from the trauma of what they had been through in Guatemala. During that year the first Mayan immigrants contacted other family members who were still in Texas and Arizona about the hospitality of the local community. This led to a chain migration of other Guatemalan Maya to the area. Family members began to arrive daily, work in the rich agricultural lands around the town, and in turn call their family and friends to come there. Many of the Guatemalan Maya who had gone to large cities such as Los Angeles preferred the small-town atmosphere of Indiantown. The name itself seemed to be fitting, as the Maya knew that they were Indians. By the beginning of the 1990s, the Mayan population of the town had grown to more than three thousand, and the early pioneers began to buy houses and settle into being Mayan Americans.

In this way, Indiantown became something of an informal capital of the Guatemala Maya in the eastern United States. But as these immigrants gained legal status and became familiar with opportunities, Indiantown became less attractive. Guatemalan Maya began to move out to other small towns—first in Florida, then to other southeastern states to work in industries such as poultry and construction. Indiantown became somewhere to return to for the annual fiesta at the end of September. Similar processes have occurred in other major Guatemalan Mayan settlements in Houston, Phoenix, and Los Angeles. Those who were able, moved to small towns and cities where they could find work and fit into American culture without living in concentrated neighborhoods.

Community Changes

After ten years of immigration to the United States, the Guatemalan Maya had developed two kinds of immigrant communities. One was the community of farm labor: living in camps through the United States in family groups, following different agricultural labor needs for preparing lands, planting, and harvesting vegetables. The other kind of community was more stable and involved working in industries where dedication and close attention to detail made the Guatemalan Maya a favored kind of worker. Houston, Texas, for example, became a destination for many Guatemalan Maya who found work in grocery stores. West Palm Beach and communities around it attracted others through opportunities to work on booming golf course construction jobs in the area.

By the mid-1990s, the Guatemala Maya of the United States were divided not only by this division of labor but also by age, sex, and family affiliations. The early pioneer immigrants tended to be families who came to escape the persecution in Guatemala throughout the 1980s. Their more settled communities were characterized by ethnic clubs, celebrations, and social service organizations in which they played major roles. The second and much more mobile group consisted of young men who began coming in the late 1980s

and early 1990s to find work. This group tended to work more in agriculture and were highly mobile, moving between work throughout the United States as well as in Mexico. Sometimes there was friction between the two groups, as the older, family-orientated immigrants began buying homes, opening businesses, and making a life in the United States. The second group, the younger immigrants, did not plan on staying in the United States but were there to make enough money to buy land in Guatemala or sometimes just to survive because of the high inflation and rampant unemployment in Guatemala. Younger immigrants lived together in trailers, apartments, and rooming houses, often crowding many people into one room to save money. This has led the older families to resent the image that the younger Guatemalan Maya have portrayed in the United States. Like young people in many places who are away from their families, they quickly got a reputation for working hard but also for drinking and loitering. In contrast to these young people, the children of the first group of Guatemalan Mayan immigrants tended to adapt quickly to the advantages of education by working hard to finish high school and even go to college. Because the children of this pioneer group learned English and used it every day, they were at odds with the second wave of immigrants, the majority of whom spoke more Spanish than either English or their Mayan language.

The age distribution of Guatemalan Maya in the United States is heavily weighted toward younger people. For all Guatemalans in the United States in 1990, the median age was twenty-eight years. Close to 70 percent of the Guatemalan Maya in the United States are under age thirty-five, and of these, men outnumber women three to two.

Immigration, Work, and Kinship

The Guatemalan Maya in the United States have had to adapt their patterns of marriage and family to the needs of work in agriculture and other low-income jobs. Guatemalan Mayan men often save their money in order to return to

Guatemala, marry, and then return to the United States with their spouse. But extended families are not as common in the United States as they are in Guatemala, since few members of the parent or grandparent generation are in the United States. As a result, children born in the United States are sometimes sent back to Guatemala to be raised by their grandparents. Child care in the United States is an important issue, since both spouses usually work. Guatemalan Mayan women look to their friends and relatives to watch children, thus maintaining group identity and providing opportunities for women to earn income through the establishment of formal and informal day-care centers.

Guatemalan Maya in the United States are often trilingual, using Mayan among their family and acquaintances from their home villages, Spanish with other Guatemala Maya and other Latinos, and English whenever they are able to learn it through school or adult education programs. Some of the first wave of immigrant children speak only Mayan and English, especially as their families begin to move out of migrant labor occupations to more settled employment. This unique blend of trilingualism and Mayan-English bilingualism has contributed to settlement patterns among Guatemalan Maya in the United States that are different from those of other Latino groups. The attraction of foods and services of Latino neighborhoods is important, but because the Guatemalan Maya were known as indigenous people in Guatemala and have less facility with Spanish than their Mexican or other Latino neighbors, they often live in separate but close-by neighborhoods from the Spanish-speaking people around them.

Art and Culture

The Guatemalan Maya are known for their exquisite weaving skills. In some Guatemalan Mayan communities the women weave, while in others the men weave. Once in the United States, it has not been possible for the Maya to continue to weave, although in some of the new Mayan associations, such as Ixim in Los Angeles or Corn Maya in Florida, weaving, embroidery, and other

Two young Guatemalan Mayans participate in the Fiesta of San Miguel, held annually to promote cultural traditions. (Allan F. Burns)

artistic skills are being revived. Once the initial shock of immigrating to the United States was over, Guatemalan Mayan women began wearing traditional handwoven skirts or *cortes* as well as woven and embroidered blouses or *huipiles*. These important markers of identity have been brought by couriers who travel between U.S. Mayan communities and Guatemala. Marimba playing is another art of the Maya, and it continues to be an important source of group solidarity in the United States. Most Mayan communities in the United States have marimba groups that play for family weddings, baptisms, and funerals, as well as communitywide events such as fiestas. The marimba is a wooden xylophone that can be played by three or four people at once. While the marimba is tuned to the European scale, the way in which it is played reminds the community of their heritage. Playing is done very seriously, and performances can last up to twelve hours. The Mayan sacred book, the *Popol Vuh*, is represented in Guatemalan Mayan communities in the United States in the form of oral family stories. They are told by women, who tend to be the guardians of family culture.

Community Events

Guatemalan Mayan community events include extensive soccer matches that unite the different Mayan neighborhoods. Soccer teams are often organized along the lines of home communities in Guatemala and give young men a chance to engage in a very enjoyable sport. The matches, often held on Sundays, are also times when families come together and socialize, where young women feel at ease talking with their friends, and where Guatamalan Maya interact with other Latinos who have their own teams.

Guatemalan Maya festivals are a regular occurrence in the major settlements. These festivals include the Christian celebration of Christmas, celebrated by many Maya through the *posada,* a reenactment of the journey of Mary and Joseph looking for a place to stay before Jesus was born. Each village in Guatemala has a patron saint's day as well, and these have become important cultural events for the Guatemala Maya in the United States. Sometimes ethnic clubs sponsor the celebration of the fiesta of the village, while other times it is sponsored by a church. These fiestas have several elected queens who represent workers, the soccer teams, and the community. Often a soccer tournament occurs on the same weekend as a fiesta. Food is served, the marimba band plays, children perform folk dances, and people spend a day or two enjoying each other's presence. Outsiders are always welcome at these events, and often the performances include dancers from other Latino communities. The more settled Guatemalan Mayan communities are able to raise money to bring performers from Guatamala to be in their fiestas. When this occurs, masked dancers often perform dances recalling the Spanish conquest of the Maya world, or dances about deer and other animals.

Not all Maya are Catholic; about half of the Guatemalan Maya in the United States practice a Protestant religion. There are many Baptists and Seventh-Day Adventists among the Guatemalan Maya even though the community fiesta days appear to be closely linked to the Catholic Church.

Cultural Persistence and Assimilation

The indigenous identity of Guatemalan Maya in the United States has been a force for keeping their culture a vital and useful way of adapting to life as immigrants. Ethnic clubs and associations have provided services such as job referrals, emergency assistance, translation for filling out documents, and even housing. These clubs have also sponsored events such as fiestas, workshops, and meetings with other groups. The Guatemalan Maya often are discriminated against by other Latinos as well as by long-term residents in the communities where they live. Sometimes ethnic associations have held town meetings to look for solutions to discrimination in health care and schooling.

Guatemalan Mayan immigrants come from a country where banking is rare in indigenous communities, so many carry around their money, making them targets for robberies and muggings. Because many Maya live in poor areas of cities, they have been especially vulnerable to attacks by African Americans living in these same areas, making them fear meeting African Americans in other contexts. Ethnic clubs have helped solve this problem by bringing African Americans to meetings as well as by training people how to open a checking account at local banks.

As more young Mayan children attend schools, watch television, and spend more time in the United States, it is natural that they find it difficult to return to Guatemala, a country with a lower standard of living than the United States. While speaking a Mayan language in homes and at cultural events is continuing, it is always easier to speak either Spanish or English to the majority of people Maya meet who are not from their part of Guatemala. This trend is most pronounced among the Guatemalan Maya who live away from the larger settlements of Maya in the United States, where it is easier to spend time with people who

GUJARATIS

speak their language. Mayan clothing is also easier to maintain where there are many other Maya living. Young Guatemalan Maya do not want to be singled out in schools because of their clothing, especially if they are the only Maya in a school.

Assimilation is held in check among the Guatemalan Maya in the United States because migration continues to occur, bringing new people into communities from Guatemala. Assimilation is also slow because Guatemalan Maya regularly visit their families in Guatemala, as airfares are not expensive and driving through Mexico is easily possible. Finally, Guatemalan Mayan clubs in the United States regularly bring musicians, dancers, poets, and other cultural experts to fiestas in an effort to maintain identity. But the Mayan cultural persistence is not necessarily a barrier to their success in the United States. Both as communities and as individuals, the Maya are quick to take advantage of opportunities to learn and contribute to the United States as Mayan Americans.

Bibliography

Burns, A. (1993). *Maya in Exile: Guatemalans in Florida.* Philadelphia: Temple University Press.

Hagen, J. M. (1994). *Becoming Legal: A Maya Community in Houston.* Philadelphia: Temple University Press.

Loucky, J. (1988). "Central American Refugees: Learning New Skills in the U.S.A." In *Anthropology: Understanding Human Adaptation,* edited by M. C. Howard and J. Dunaif-Hattis. New York: HarperCollins.

Manz, B. (1988). *Refugees of a Hidden War: The Aftermath of Counterinsurgency in Guatemala.* Albany: State University of New York Press.

Menchu, R. (1984). *I. Rigoberta Menchu: An Indian Woman in Guatemala,* edited by E. Burgos-Debray, translated by A. Wright. London: Verso.

Montejo, V. (1991). *The Bird Who Cleans the World and Other Mayan Fables.* Willimantic, CT: Curbstone Press.

Rodriguez, N., and Hagan, J. M. (1989). "Undocumented Central American Migration to Houston in the 1980s." *Journal of La Raza Studies* 2(1):1–4.

Santoli, A. (1988). *New Americans: An Oral History.* New York: Viking Press.

Tedlock, D. (1985). *The Popol Vuh.* New York: Simon & Schuster.

ALLAN F. BURNS

GUJARATIS

Gujaratis are people who hail from Gujarat, one of the most highly industrialized and agriculturally fertile states of the Republic of India. Gujarat is located on the western coast of India, on the Arabian Sea. Gujaratis are the single largest ethnic group among Asian Indians in the United States, forming an estimated 50 percent of the total of 810,000 Asians Indians in the 1990 U.S. Census. In comparison, Gujarati-speaking people in India numbered 41 million, or fewer than 5 percent of the population, in the 1991 Indian Census.

Among the major subgroups of Gujaratis in the United States are Banias (Hindu and Jain), Patidars (or Kanbis), Parsis (or Zoroastrians), Kachchis, Bohras, and Ismailis.

Immigration History

The first Gujaratis in the United States were a few Parsis, who arrived in the nineteenth century with other scattered adventurers, seafarers, and merchants from India. In the first half of the twentieth century, there were a few Gujaratis among the Indian students who entered the United States for higher learning. It was not until the Immigration Act of 1965, which gave preference to highly skilled immigrants and their families, that the first significant wave of Gujarati immigrants arrived in the United States. Highly educated Gujaratis from engineering and medical colleges as well as other technical and research institutions took advantage of the new laws to immigrate. At first they were no more numerous than the other groups from different regions of India. But they took greater advantage of the family reunification clause of the 1965 legislation and sponsored the immigration of their less skilled relatives, establishing a pattern of chain migration that rapidly made them the most dominant of the Asian Indian ethnic groups. By 1995, Gujaratis had come not only from the major cities of Ahmedabad and Vadodara in Gujarat's central industrial belt but also from all regions of Gujarat.

Gujaratis also have immigrated to the United States from other parts of the world. They arrived from East Africa in the 1970s, following their expulsion by the Ugandan dictator Idi Amin and an uncertain political climate in Kenya and Tanzania. They also came from South Africa, England, and Fiji, especially after the 1987 Fijian coup threatened their economic and political security on that Pacific island. Thus the Gujaratis in the United States represent a wide spectrum of socioeconomic groups, with diverse places of origin.

Gujaratis have had a trading and business tradition since ancient times. Though most Gujaratis in India are engaged in agriculture, the business castes, who form a cohesive and prosperous trading community, are found all over the world. They plied their trade as early as the second century C.E. to the western coast of Africa, and later in the sixth and seventh centuries to the Far East. In the nineteenth century, British colonial administrators employed Gujaratis to work on the Ugandan railway. Gujaratis also went as free merchants to supply the colonies of indentured Indians in Africa, the Caribbean, Southeast Asia, and Fiji. After decolonization, descendants of these nineteenth-century immigrants themselves immigrated, to Europe (mainly England), Canada, Australia, and the United States.

Even after years of residing abroad, Gujaratis have a strong orientation to the homeland and visit Gujarat regularly for business, marriage, and religious pilgrimage. They also invest heavily in real estate and industrial ventures in Gujarat, and many return to the homeland for retirement.

Occupations

Though the ranks of Gujaratis include those trained in medicine, engineering, and other high-

technology fields, they prefer to go into business for themselves, since they regard self-employment as the most honorable form of occupation and one that enables them to contol their own destiny and gain wealth. They specialize in the hotel, real estate, retail, and wholesale trades, and are dispersed widely all over the United States, mainly in industrialized and urbanized areas, where economic opportunities are greatest.

There is a broad pattern in the spatial and occupational distribution of Gujaratis. In the northeastern part of the United States they are concentrated in the grocery, appliance, and newsstand businesses; in the Midwest they tend to own PC (printed circuit) board factories or fast-food franchises; while in the West and Southwest they dominate the hotel and motel industries. As the Asian Indian community in the United States be-

Gujaratis are a visible presence in the grocery business. The first Patel Brothers grocery store was opened in Chicago; it was later expanded into a national chain. (Mukul Roy)

came more numerous and prosperous and there was an increase in demand for ethnic goods and services, Gujaratis seized new opportunities for expansion by setting up national chains of grocery and jewelry stores. They are especially dominant in the diamond industry in Antwerp, from where they supply a worldwide market. With their extensive international network and global assets of capital and human resources they are able not only to survive the ups and downs of business but also to expand into new areas. They are well known for their thrifty ways and often are compared to Jews for their business acumen.

While many first-generation Gujarati immigrants ran small "mom and pop" operations such as grocery stores, newsstand concessions at train stations or street corners, or wayside budget motels, second-generation Gujaratis born in the United States have professionalized and upgraded the businesses, moving up to chain stores and luxury hotels. The Asian American Hotel Owners' Association has claimed that there were 8,000 Asian-American hoteliers in 1995, most of them Gujarati, with a business market value of $26 billion, 720,000 franchised rooms, and 175,000 independent rooms. The "hotel-motel-Patel" connection is well known, since the most common last name among Gujaratis in the hotel industry is Patel (the caste name of Patel is that of the traditional village headman). Another common last name is Shah. The Patels are considered extraordinarily enterprising and have a strong network of business support from their own community. The Shahs belong more to the professions and are likely to be doctors or engineers who go into business for themselves.

Languages and Ethnic Press

The Gujaratis are an extremely diverse group of many different faiths and affiliations held together by the common thread of the Gujarati language. Gujarati is an Indo-Aryan language with its own distinctive, cursive script, and it has several dialects based on region, caste, and community. There are small minorities of Kachchi- and Urdu-speaking Gujarati Muslims. English-language proficiency is generally lower among Gujaratis than among other Indian groups, even among professionals. There is greater native-language retention among immigrant Gujarati households in the United States than among other Indian groups. The 1990 U.S. Census reported that 102,000 persons spoke Gujarati at home. Gujarati-language classes are held regularly at temples and cultural associations but, as with other immigrant groups, language erosion is taking place among second-generation Gujaratis.

Gujaratis in the United States subscribe to Gujarati magazines and newspapers published in India. They also get *Gujarat Samachar,* a newspaper published in Ahmedabad and distributed nationally in the United States from New York by *India Abroad.* Early attempts in the 1970s to start a Gujarati-language press in Chicago failed when the latest Gujarati publications from the homeland became easily available in the United States. Gujarati-language television programs are broadcast regularly on TV-Asia on international cable channels. Because of rapid transportation and satellite communication and the up-to-date, continuous flow of current information from India, the Gujarati language continues to flourish in the United States, at least among first-generation Gujarati immigrants, even without the existence of a local ethnic press.

Religion

While the main religion of Gujartis is Hinduism (90%), there are also Muslims, Jains, and Zoroastrians among the Gujarati population.

Hindu Gujaratis are a devoutly religious people who build prominent worship centers or *puja* rooms in their own homes and donate generously to the building of temples in major cities across the United States. The Hindu religious sects can be broadly divided into those who worship one or more of the great traditional Vedic deities, and those who follow a more austere, modern religion, such as the Swadhyayas and the Swaminarayanis. Gujaratis also organize *yagnas* (public prayer gatherings) where thousands participate in ritual ceremonies.

Gujarati Jains, who number an estimated 70,000 in the United States, are extremely wealthy and occupy a prominent place in the society and economy of Asian Indians. The Parsis are a very small minority of Gujaratis (even in India, their number dwindled to 120,000 in the 1981 Indian Census, and in the United States they are no more than a few thousand). Muslim Gujaratis are a separate group who remain socially and culturally distinct from other Gujaratis, even in the United States.

Family and Kinship

The joint family, which consists of parents and their married as well as unmarried sons, is the norm among Gujaratis in India, though the situation is fast changing in India and even more so in the United States. However, the nuclear family consisting of only parents and their children is not necessarily the alternative. Many families include adult married siblings or cousins who live jointly, especially in the early phase of immigration, but who move on to establish separate households once they have achieved economic independence. In cases where large numbers of family members are involved in the same family business in the hotel, restaurant, or grocery industries, as often happens with Gujaratis, they may live jointly for convenience. Descent is patrilineal, and elderly parents of first-generation immigrants who join their children in the United States always make their home with their sons, who have a moral obligation to care for their parents in old age. The head of the family is usually the father, and generally speaking, males exercise more authority over the household than females. After marriage the man brings his bride home to be part of his family, while the woman leaves her home to join her husband's family. Gujarati women, whether highly educated or unskilled, are as likely to work outside the home as other Indian women. Gujarati women often work in the family business, attend to all the household chores, and are primarily responsible for bringing up the children.

Marriage Patterns

Even more than other ethnic Indian groups, Gujaratis observe narrow caste restrictions when it comes to marriage. In Africa, England, and Fiji they remained distinct from the host society for generations, marrying only within their own community and according to strict caste rules. In the United States they have maintained strong family and kinship ties by sponsoring their relatives from India or other parts of the world and have been able to maintain many of their old traditions of endogamy (in-marriage). Many Gujaratis arrange marriages for their children by locating spouses in India or from among the family of Gujaratis scattered worldwide.

There is much conflict between the first and second generations on the issue of arranged marriages. Second-generation Gujarati Americans would prefer to make their own marriage choices but are also reluctant to cross their elders. For this reason, innovative solutions have been worked out to suit the American context. The Charotar Patidars, a subsect of Gujarati Hindus who are numerous in the United States and are particularly fastidious about caste rules governing marriage, arrange annual conventions with an attendance of several thousand in major cities such as Chicago or Atlanta. Entire families belonging to the same caste or subcaste are brought together at these conventions so Gujarati Americans can get to know suitable eligible marriage partners. Each one of the following subsects is represented in the American Gujarati population: Six Gam, Vansol Vibhag Twenty-seven Gam, Bavis Gam, Chovia Gam, Five Gam, and Satyavis Gam.

Diet

Gujaritis are generally very strict vegetarians. Some sects, such as the Jains, even avoid root vegetables such as onions and potatoes. Gujaratis also believe in fasting. While some do it as regularly as once a week, others observe fasts only on religious occasions. Ritual purity and pollution rites associated with the cooking and eating of food are also observed by the more orthodox Gujaratis, especially the parents of immigrants.

Gujarati women dress in traditional clothing to participate in a garba contest. (Mukul Roy)

The Arts

Much of the folk culture of Gujaratis stems from the mythology surrounding Lord Krishna, and artistic traditions honoring him have flourished among the Gujarati community in the United States, especially those traditions that were easily transferable to a new country. Prominent among these traditions are the *ras* and *garba* folk dances, performed by both men and women. National competitions featuring scores of groups from different parts of the United States and Canada bring Gujaratis together annually. The women wear heavy skirts called *ghaghra*, with voluminous folds in startlingly brilliant colors, and a brief top or *choli*, which is emblazoned with embroidered mirrors. Dancers move in a circle, singing and clapping their hands and clashing together sticks called *dandia*. This vigorous dance has been synthesized with American-style rock-and-roll rhythms into a new dance form called *disco-dandia*, which is highly popular among Gujarati teenagers.

Another traditional art is *rangoli*, paintings in colored chalk done by women for festivals and other ceremonies. The intricate designs are floral or geometric, or depict characters from myths and legends.

The greatest burst of cultural and artistic activity for Gujaratis occurs during the festival of Navarathri or Dussehra, in the months of October and November. Diwali (Deepavali), which celebrates the return of the epic King Rama to his rightful kingdom of Ayodhya, is another religious festival celebrated with fervor by Gujaratis. This is also the time when the goddess Lakshmi, harbinger of wealth and prosperity, is worshiped by the merchant community. Houses are cleaned, new clothes are worn, there are spectacular fireworks displays, and there are song and dance performances in all the major temples across the United States. Shops are gaily decorated and display an abundance of sweets and other attractive wares. Diwali sales are as critical to ethnic Indian merchants as Christmas is to American retailers.

Account books are tallied to determine a store's profitability, and the new financial calendar begins. For the Asian-Indian immigrant community in the United States, and for Gujarati Hindus in particular, this is an auspicious time when their economy, art, culture, and religion come together in a seamless web and reach a glorious culmination.

Discrimination

When Gujaratis, along with other Indian immigrants, adopt a dispersed residential pattern in the city and suburbs, they do not attract much attention. But when they concentrate in a particular geographical area (e.g., in Edison, New Jersey) or establish a visibly successful business presence, they are in danger of incurring the hostility of the local population, especially in times of recession or unemployment. In the early 1990s, racist gangs called "dotbusters" (for the dot or *bindi* that Indian women wear on their forehead) attacked Indians in predominantly Gujarati neighborhoods in the New York–New Jersey area, murdering at least four individuals. Other Gujaratis who run newsstands, gas stations, or grocery stores in scattered locations are also very vulnerable to attacks and have been targets of what are believed to be hate crimes. However, discrimination based on ethnic origin is difficult to prove, and while there have been no indications of widespread or nationwide discrimination, the sporadic attacks have alarmed the entire Asian-Indian community and put them on alert.

Assimilation and Cultural Persistence

The Gujarati culture is perpetuated in the United States through many Gujarati associations, some of which are formed on the narrowest of sectarian interests based on the size and nature of the Gujarati population. In major cities such as New York, Chicago, Houston, or Los Angeles, there may be four or five Gujarati associations formed on the basis of religion, caste, professional or trade interests, or even country or origin, such as the association of Gujaratis from East Africa.

Graduates of engineering, medical, or scientific institutions have formed alumni associations that interact frequently with the homeland by setting up joint industrial ventures, transferring technological expertise, and donating charitable funds. While the connection to the homeland is strong for first-generation immigrants, the second generation is more rooted in the United States; however, their search for their own new identity is based on their Gujarati heritage.

See also: JAINS

Bibliography

Bhardwaj, S. M., and Rao, N. M. (1990). "Asian Indians in the United States." In *South Asians Overseas: Migration and Ethnicity,* edited by C. Clarke, C. Peach, and S. Vertovec. Cambidge, Eng.: Cambridge University Press.

Brown, R. H., and Coelho, G. V., eds. (1986). *Tradition and Transformation: Asian Indians in America.* Williamsburg, VA: College of William and Mary Press.

Fisher, M. P. (1980). *The Indians of New York City: A Study of Immigrants from India.* Columbia, MO: South Asia Books.

Helweg, A. W., and Helweg, U. M. (1991). *An Immigrant Success Story: East Indians in America.* Philadelphia: University of Pennsylvania Press.

Khandelwal, M. S. (1995). "Indian Immigrants in Queens, New York City: Patterns of Spatial Concentration and Distribution, 1965–1990." In *Nation and Migration: The Politics of Space in the South Asian Diaspora,* edited by P. van der Veer. Philadelphia: University of Pennsylvania Press.

Leonard, K. B., and Tibrewal, C. S. (1993). "Asian Indians in Southern California: Occupations and Ethnicity." In *Immigration and Entrepreneurship: Culture, Capital and Ethnic Networks,* edited by I. Light and P. Bhachu. New Brunswick, NJ: Transaction.

Pocock, D. F. (1972). *Kanbi and Patidar: A Study of the Patidar Community of Gujarat.* London: Oxford University Press.

Rangaswamy, P. (1995). "Asian Indians in Chicago: Growth and Change in a Model Minority." In *Ethnic Chicago: A Multicultural Portrait,* edited by M. J.

Holli and P. d'A. Jones. Grand Rapids, MI: William B. Eerdmans.

Saran, P. (1985). *The Asian Indian Experience in the United States*. Cambridge, MA: Schenkman.

Shah, A. M. (1974). *The Household Dimension of the Family in India: A Field Study in a Gujarat Village and a Review of Other Studies*. Berkeley: University of California Press.

Williams, R. B. (1988). *Religions of Immigrants from India and Pakistan: New Threads in the American Tapestry*. Cambridge, Eng.: Cambridge University Press.

Williams, R. B., ed. (1992). *A Sacred Thread: Modern Transmission of Hindu Traditions in India and Abroad*. Chambersburgh, PA: Anima.

PADMA RANGASWAMY

GUYANESE

Guyanese immigrants began arriving in the United States early in the twentieth century. With an accelerated flow after the 1960s, they became the fourth largest immigrant group in New York City by the 1990s. The Cooperative Republic of Guyana is located in northeastern South America, bordering on Venezuela, Brazil, and Suriname. With 90 percent of its population clustered along its 270-mile Atlantic coastline, Guyana faces toward the Caribbean, and the historical forces shaping its social order since the 1700s have linked Guyana to the West Indies despite its mainland location.

Guyana is known as the "land of six peoples." The ethnic diversity of its three quarters of a million inhabitants reflects the area's history of conquest, slavery, and indentured labor. Spanish, Dutch, and English explorers made early expeditions to the area, but it was Dutch settlers and traders who achieved control of the territories of Demerara, Essequibo, and Berbice — the three counties of contemporary Guyana — early in the eighteenth century. They developed a complex system of irrigation and drainage that permitted the establishment of sugar plantations in the low-lying coastal areas and brought West Africans as slaves to provide labor for the sugar estates. The British took control of the area in the late eighteenth century and united the three territories as the colony of British Guiana in 1831. Under British rule, the planters continued to rely on slave labor until emancipation in 1834, when labor shortages prompted the colonial government to bring indentured laborers from Portuguese Madeira, China, and the Indian subcontinent. Former slaves from the West Indies were also recruited as plantation workers. By 1966, when Guyana became independent, just over half its residents were Indo-Guyanese (known locally as East Indians), 43 percent were of African or mixed ancestry, and 5 percent were Amerindian descendants of the native populations of Caribs, Arawaks, and Warrau. The remaining 2 percent of the population included Portuguese (1.0%), other Europeans (0.3%), and Chinese (0.6%). The Republic of Guyana is thus a multiethnic society in which the language and societal-level institutions inherited from the colonial powers frame a diversity of cultural forms and historically-derived inequalities that continue to shape contemporary social and political struggles.

English is Guyana's official language. As in other English-speaking Caribbean countries, the standard British English that is the formal language of government and education coexists with Guyanese English or "Creolese," a continuum of linguistic forms that emerged from the linguistic encounter of Africans and English colonists. While Guyanese English is the first language of most Guyanese, the Hindi, Urdu, and Amerindian languages have not totally disappeared, and a renewed interest in learning Hindi emerged in the 1980s among East Indians. As English-speakers, Guyanese immigrants in the United States do not face the linguistic barriers to employment that other South American immigrants encounter.

Immigration and Settlement History

Throughout the nineteenth century, British Guiana was a major recipient of immigrants, as sugar planters imported laborers under indenture and contract programs. Immigration to the United States began around 1900, when Guianese joined the movement of Caribbean peoples seeking economic opportunities abroad. Most of the early Guianese immigrants were of African descent, and like other Afro-Caribbean newcomers, they settled within the racially segregated black neighborhoods of New York and other northeastern cities. In 1924, new U.S. policies restricted nonwhite immigration, and only 3,505 immigrants from British Guiana arrived in the United States between 1925 and 1960. Changes in U.S. policies in 1965 accelerated the flow of peoples from the Western Hemisphere. Between 1961 and 1990, the United States admitted close to 100,000 immigrants from Guyana. Like their predecessors, most settled in the Northeast, with the largest concentrations in the boroughs of Brooklyn and Queens in New York City. By the 1980s, Guyanese immigrants began moving to suburbs of the northeastern cities and to other parts of the country as well.

While Afro-Guyanese immigrants remain a significant proportion of Guyanese residents in the United States, Guyana's East Indian majority has been heavily represented in post-1965 immigration. The two groups occupy separate residential areas within New York City, although precise figures on their relative size and location are not available.

The 1990 U.S. Census enumerated 75,765 persons of Guyanese ancestry, including 64,602 (85.3%) born in Guyana. The median age was 30.6 years, and females comprised 53 percent of the population. Among those employed, 22.6 percent held managerial or professional positions; 35.4 percent worked in technical, sales, or administrative jobs; 19.8 percent were service workers; 8.7 percent worked in production or skilled crafts; and 12.4 percent were laborers or other unskilled workers. Guyanese immigrants have high levels of educational achievement; among those over age twenty-four, 90 percent were high school graduates, 20 percent were college graduates, and 5 percent had graduate degrees. In 1989, the Guyanese mean family income of $41,734 exceeded the national average.

Cultural Characteristics

Economic Activity. The large post-1965 influx of Guyanese immigrants began at a time when economic restructuring was transforming employment patterns in global cities such as New York. A decline in manufacturing and the growth of service employment—in both the high-paying corporate financial and management services and the low-wage domestic and personal service industries—shaped the economic opportunities available to Guyanese newcomers. Guyanese professionals have entered technical and educational fields. Within the service economy, Guyanese are represented in the municipal and state work force, as well as in health care and private household work. Smaller numbers are employed in retail and manufacturing. As the Guyanese population has grown, more Guyanese immigrants, particularly from the Indo-Guyanese community, have established businesses catering to the needs and tastes of their compatriots.

Housing. For Guyanese in the United States, as in Guyana, owning a home is a symbol of economic success. Guyanese immigrants have achieved notable rates of home ownership, with more than a quarter of all Guyanese households living in owner-occupied homes. In New York, neighborhood concentrations of Guyanese homeowners have emerged in several areas in the boroughs of Queens and Brooklyn.

Religion. Religious plurality characterizes the Guyanese immigrant community. Most Afro-Guyanese immigrants are Christians. Roman Catholics are the most numerous of the Christian groups, but many Guyanese Anglicans join Episcopalian congregations in the United States. Evangelical Protestant denominations and a variety of smaller independent Christian churches also have a following among Guyanese immigrants. The majority of Indo-Guyanese immigrants are Hindus, but Muslims and Christians are also represented. Guyanese Hindus have established more than forty temples in the New York area and have created a Pandits Parishad (council) to promote Hinduism, train new pandits, and encourage the study of

Hindi and Sanskrit. The temples are well attended on Sundays and holy days, and ceremonies conducted by Guyanese Hindus in their homes draw large groups of kin and neighbors. Guyanese immigrants celebrate Phagwah, known as Holi in India, with an annual parade in New York City that draws up to fifty thousand Indo-Guyanese participants.

Worldview. The ethnic composition of contemporary Guyana resulted from colonial efforts to satisfy the labor needs of the sugar industry. Colonial power was reinforced by the hegemony of British cultural concepts that invoked racial justifications for the Guyanese social hierarchy and privileged British definitions of proper language and social conduct. As in other plantation societies, an egalitarian counterideology emphasized the common status and predicament of subordinate groups, but egalitarianism coexisted with an acceptance of the differential value attributed to dominant and subordinate cultural forms. With independence, the Europeans ceased to be a numerically significant presence in Guyana, and an anticolonial socialist ideology was widely endorsed as an alternative to the colonial capitalist framework. But the departure of colonial elites did not fundamentally displace British-derived definitions of cultural value. In the struggle over the cultural definition of the emerging Guyanese nation, the major ethnic groups have variously drawn on the egalitarian tradition, ethnic cultural forms, and the heritage of colonial values as they pressed their competing claims for the power to define Guyanese national culture.

Ethnic conflict between East Indians, who predominated in rural agricultural areas, and the urban-based Afro-Guyanese characterized Guyanese politics in the years leading up to and following independence, and ethnicity continues to influence the worldview of Guyanese immigrants. While the experience of Indo-Guyanese immigrants in the United States has fostered new links to other peoples of Indian origin, it has also revealed the extent to which they share in Afro-Creole Guyanese culture. For Afro-Guyanese immigrants, the United States provides a context for an enlarged "Afro-Caribbean" identity and for discovering commonalities with the black American population. Whether emerging pan-Caribbean identities can incorporate the full range of Guyanese multiculturalism remains to be seen.

Family, Kinship, Interpersonal Relations. In Guyana, as in the island societies of the West Indies, the family forms that emerged from the plantation social order are based on bilateral networks of extended kin with highly elastic boundaries. Family networks build on a variety of lateral and intergenerational ties, including consanguinity, legal marriage, and other forms of conjugality. They are sustained by multiple transactions and a strong ideology of mutual support, and their links extend across households, communities, and national boundaries. Flexible Guyanese family networks support the efforts of members to pursue diverse livelihood strategies, including emigration, and to adapt to changing economic options in Guyana or abroad. Although East Indians who came to Guyana as indentured laborers brought family ideologies that emphasized patriarchal authority and more corporate economic endeavors, the imperatives of the plantation system transformed and creolized East Indian familial practices, limiting patriarchal authority and fostering an emphasis on bilateral kin links, thus reducing but not eliminating the contrasts between Afro- and Indo-Guyanese family forms.

Guyanese immigration to the United States is structured by the extended family networks that link immigrants to kin in Guyana. Earlier arrivals sponsor the immigration of other relatives, and transnational ties to kin in Guyana are maintained by the flow of remittances, gifts, and visits. Many immigrants invest their earnings from work in the United States in land and houses in Guyana, where they hope to eventually resettle.

For Guyanese immigrants in the United States, the workplace is a context for interaction with a variety of other groups—West Indian, African American, Latino, and U.S.-born whites of diverse backgrounds. But as the Guyanese population in the United States has grown, it has increasingly provided an encompassing context for immigrant social life, which centers heavily on ties to kin and coethnics in the Indo-Guyanese or Afro-Guyanese segment of the immigrant community.

Arts.   West Indian influences on U.S. cultural life are apparent in music, dance, literature, and theater, and Guyanese immigrants have contributed to the vibrant Caribbean artistic presence in the United States. Numerous West Indian writers have achieved critical recognition in the United States, among them Guyanese novelists such as Edgar Mittelholzer, Jan Carew, and Wilson Harris. And artists drawing on Guyana's unique melange of ethnic traditions are achieving visibility in sculpture and painting. Guyanese immigrants participate in New York's annual West Indian Day Festival, where Caribbean music, design, and theatrical arts are celebrated and displayed. The Phagwah parade of Guyanese Hindus is one of the newer additions to New York's public celebration of ethnic culture.

Social and Political Organization.   Throughout the twentieth century, voluntary associations have provided varied forms of mutual assistance for Caribbean immigrants. With the growth of the West Indian population in the second half of the twentieth century, associations of Guyanese immigrants have proliferated. In addition to groups based on occupation or school ties, a host of Guyanese social clubs and sports associations are active in New York and other urban centers where immigrants from Guyana reside.

These groups have played important roles in the often tumultuous post-independence politics of Guyana. Like other Caribbean countries, Guyana permits emigrants to retain Guyanese citizenship when they become citizens elsewhere. It has been distinctive, however, in allowing overseas nationals to vote in elections at home. Guyanese voluntary associations have been a vehicle for home-based parties and politicians to mobilize both financial and electoral support from constituents residing in the United States.

Two newer types of organizations emerged within the U.S. Caribbean community in the 1980s: Pan-Caribbean associations, which seek to mobilize West Indian constituencies around U.S. political issues of significance to the immigrant community, and groups such as the Indo-Caribbean Federation of North America, which promotes links among Indo-Caribbean peoples from Guyana, Trinidad, and Suriname, and the East Indian Diaspora Steering Committee, which seeks communality among immigrants from the Indo-Caribbean and the Indian subcontinent as people of Indian origin.

In New York, where local political activism has long involved the mobilization of ethnic constituencies, the new organizations give Caribbean immigrants greater visibility as a potential political force than do the individual country-based associations. Pan-Caribbean association emergence has both reflected and promoted growing West Indian involvement in the U.S. political arena, evident in 1996 when several Guyanese candidates from districts in Brooklyn and Queens sought election to the New York State Senate and Assembly. While this foray into electoral politics signals a new engagement with U.S. society, it also positions the Guyanese community to contest threats that new U.S. economic and political trends pose to Guyanese transnationalism.

Assimilation and Transnationalism

Afro-Guyanese immigrants who immigrated to the United States in the early years of the twentieth century, like other immigrants from the West Indies, maintained distinctive country-based organizations and favored socializing with compatriots. However, their experience of racial discrimination promoted involvement in struggles for racial justice, and while distinctive cultural identities had salience within the larger black community, this ethnic diversity was largely invisible to the white majority. Guyanese immigrants who became involved in broader social and political arenas in the United States were identified as blacks rather than as West Indians or Guyanese.

For post-1965 immigrants, events in both Guyana and the United States affect patterns of incorporation. In the 1970s and 1980s, Guyanese government efforts to take control of economic development processes were unable to offset the effects of declining world prices for the agricultural and mineral exports on which Guyana's economy depends. Deteriorating economic conditions and growing governmental authoritarianism propelled Guyanese immigration to the United States. Despite the election of a new government and signs of improvement in the economy, Guyana continues to grapple with issues of economic development, ethnic division, and national identity, and emigration remains high. At the same time, Guyanese immigrants in the United States face new pressures from corporate and public sector downsizing, heightened racial tensions, growing nativist sentiment, and anti-immigrant legislation. They have responded with increased engagement in the U.S. political arena, forming new alliances based on broadened Caribbean, Indian, and African diasporic identities. Yet strong family networks and the expansion of Guyana's "local" political field to encompass Guyanese citizens overseas have sustained the involvement of immigrants in the social and political life of Guyana and foster transnationalism as a strategy through which Guyanese immigrants pursue both livelihood and identity.

Bibliography

Basch, L., Glick Schiller, N., and Szanton Blanc, C. (1994). *Nations Unbound: Transnational Projects, Postcolonial Predicaments, and Deterritorialized Nation States.* Langhorne, PA: Gordon and Breach.

Colen, S. (1990). "'Housekeeping' for the Green Card: West Indian Household Workers, the State, and Stratified Reproduction in New York." In *At Work in Homes: Household Workers in World Perspective,* edited by R. Sanjek and S. Colen. Washington, DC: American Anthropological Association.

Conway, D., and Cook, T. J. (1996). "New York City: Caribbean Immigration and Residential Segregation in a Restructured Global City." In *Social Polarization in Post-Industrial Metropolises,* edited by J. O'Loughlin and J. Friedrichs. Berlin: Walter de Gruyter.

James, W. (1993). "Migration, Racism, and Identity Formation: The Caribbean Experience in Britain." In *Inside Babylon: The Caribbean Diaspora in Britain,* edited by W. James and C. Harris. London: Verso.

Jayawardena, C. (1963). *Conflict and Solidarity on a Guianese Plantation.* London: Athlone Press.

Kasinitz, P. (1992). *Caribbean New York: Black Immigrants and the Politics of Race.* Ithaca, NY: Cornell University Press.

Melwani, L. (1995). "What Are Over 200,000 Guyanese Hindus Doing in New York State?" *Hinduism Today* 18(8):3–7.

Palmer, R. W. (1995). *Pilgrims from the Sun: West Indian Migration to America.* New York: Twayne.

Smith, R. T. (1996). *The Matrifocal Family.* New York and London: Routledge.

Sutton, C. R., and Chaney, E. M., eds. (1987). *Caribbean Life in New York City: Sociocultural Dimensions.* New York: Center for Migration Studies.

Sutton, C. R., and Makiesky, S. (1975). "Migration and West Indian Racial and Political Consciousness." In *Migration and Development: Implications for Ethnic Identity and Political Conflict,* edited by H. I. Safa and B. DuToit. The Hague: Mouton.

Vertovec, S. (1993). "Indo-Caribbean Experience in Britain: Overlooked, Miscategorized, Misunderstood." In *Inside Babylon: The Caribbean Diaspora in Britain,* edited by W. James and C. Harris. London: Verso.

Watkins-Owens, I. (1996). *Blood Relations: Caribbean Immigrants and the Harlem Community, 1900–1930.* Bloomington: Indiana University Press.

Williams, B. F. (1991). *Stains on My Name, War in My Veins: Guyana and the Politics of Cultural Struggle.* Durham, NC: Duke University Press.

SUSAN MAKIESKY BARROW

GYPSIES

No common original name exists for all Gypsy groups, and each goes by its own designation. Since 1980, some writers have attempted to generalize the cumbersome label "Roma and Sinti," based on only two Gypsy groups, to all Gypsies. This usage ignores the individual identities of other Gypsy groups, each of which has its own history and culture. However, since in the English-speaking countries each group translates its own ethnic name as "Gypsy," and since this is also the label used by outsiders, we will continue to use it as the most general and convenient way to refer to this set of ethnic groups thought to be related by common origin.

At least five ethnically separate Gypsy groups exist in America, and isolated individuals or families of many other groups also may exist. The five major groups, here identified by their self-designations in order of size are (1) Rom, subdivided into the Kalderash, Machwaya, and Lowara groups, (2) Romnichels, or English Gypsies, (3) Ludar, or Romanian Gypsies, (4) Romungros, or Hungarian/Slovak Gypsies, and (5) Chikeners (German, *Zigeuner*), or German Gypsies. In addition, a few families of Spanish Cale Gypsies can be found in some of the larger U.S. cities. Various Romanian, Macedonian, and other eastern European Gypsies also have been arriving in the United States since the 1970s, but thus far, with the exception of the Lowara Rom (who began immigrating to the United States in the 1970s), they remain largely unstudied. Because of the lack of research or documentation on the other Gypsy groups, the description in this entry is limited to the above-mentioned three largest and best-known ones.

Definition

All American Gypsies make a distinction, first between themselves and non-Gypsies, who are lumped together under a single label (e.g., *gazhe, gorgios*), and then between their own and other

An 1851 illustration shows a small Gypsy camp near the Elysian Fields in New Jersey. (Gleason's Pictorial Drawing-Room Companion/Corbis)

Gypsy groups, who are not recognized as "our kind of Gypsies." The boundary between "us" and others is marked by a set of physical, cultural, and linguistic traits that vary by group. Most recognize a system of cleanliness rules as an important separator between themselves and non-Gypsies. Outsiders define Gypsies mainly by nomadism and are unaware of their division into separate ethnic units.

Immigration History

All groups considered Gypsies are descended from ancestors who left India around 900 C.E. and arrived in the Greek-speaking areas of southeastern Europe in the eleventh or twelfth century. As their population grew, they split into new groups that subsequently spread throughout the rest of Europe, lost contact with each other, and came to be influenced by different cultures, forming the ethnic divisions observable today.

Gypsies have been part of the American population since 1850. A few individuals may have come earlier, but no indisputable records of earlier arrivals have been found. So far two waves of Gypsy immigration to America are documented: the first from the British Isles beginning in 1850, and the second from eastern Europe starting about 1880. Unlike many other immigrants, the Rom, Romnichels, and Ludar immigrated as extended families; each moving as a single functioning social unit at once, instead of sending one member of the family first, to be followed by other members. Gypsies of all three groups continued to immigrate in small numbers at least until World War I. Although the extent of their return migration is hard to gauge, some families of all three groups did go back and forth, some several times. Why some groups left Europe and immigrated to America, while others did not, requires further investigation. The only generalization that can be made at this time is that Gypsies from various European countries seem to have immigrated at about the same time as other people from the same areas were leaving for America.

The Romnichels, from England, who were the first Gypsies to arrive in the United States and maintain a continued presence, began arriving in 1850. Many of the first arrivals returned to England to bring additional relatives. Several Romnichel families also moved to Canada for the duration of the Civil War. A few families continued to make trips to Canada after the war on horse trading business.

The Rom immigration began in 1881. Most came directly from German or English ports to New York City, after having traveled extensively throughout Europe. Many families also traveled through South and Central America or Canada before their arrival in the United States. One Rom entrepreneur, having successfully brought in his family and relatives from Brazil, returned three times to recruit other groups of Rom to immigrate. One of these groups embarked from Hamburg in 1897; another from Liverpool landed in Quebec in 1904, and later crossed the border to the United States. The last trip brought a group in 1917 from Veracruz, Mexico. The entrepreneur, who had gained experience in dealing with the bureaucracy, assisted the newcomers first in gaining admittance to United States and later in getting their citizenship papers. Several Rom families fled to Mexico at the onset of World War I and subsequently had considerable difficulty returning to the United States, as they could not prove they were American citizens.

The Ludar first came from southern European ports directly to New York, beginning in 1882. Some families traveled first through South America, Cuba, Mexico, or Canada. Some also returned to Europe or South America to bring additional relatives or to find wives.

Demography

The total Gypsy population in North America probably does not exceed sixty thousand. The Rom form the largest group, descended from nearly a dozen original clans whose adult members were born primarily in Serbia or Russia. The Rom clans are further divided into about fifty named lineages (*vitsas*), many of which have since formed off-shoots with their own names. Thus the Mineshti clan (descendants of Mina) now consists of nearly a dozen lineages, such as the Bimbuia, Gunareshti, or Michellesti. Other clans include the Rusuya, Fransuzuia, and Guneshti, each with its own named lineages. Initially the Machwaya was considered just another Rom clan, but over time it has developed into an independent group, albeit with numerous marriage connections to the Kalderash. The total population of the Rom is roughly between thirty and forty thousand. Their distribution is countrywide but constantly fluctuating as families move for various economic and social reasons. All major cities have concentrations of Rom roughly proportional to their population, and many smaller towns and even busy rural roads have at least one family.

The next largest group, the Romnichels, consists of about forty lineages. On the basis of current but admittedly still incomplete knowledge their numbers may be estimated at fifteen to twenty thousand. Most Romnichels traveled widely at first, but many families soon began to exploit specific territories or at least travel circuits with some stability. Other families continued to travel throughout the country. Overall they tend to be somewhat more rural than the Rom. Early Romnichel concentrations developed in Massachusetts, New Jersey, Ohio, Illinois, and California; southern states were initially visited during the winter months as part of a pattern of seasonal north–south migration. Today the southern states have a sizable percentage of the population.

The Ludar also number about forty lineages, but their population is considerably smaller. The documentation for this group is much poorer, but some older Ludar estimate their numbers to be in the four to five thousand range. Although the Ludar also traveled widely, they differ from other Gypsies in that they formed ethnic enclaves more readily, developing concentrations in the New York–Philadelphia–Baltimore area, and in the Midwest, where they traveled between major cities. After about three decades of camping in large groups, the Ludar established a sequence of shantytowns in Queens, New York; Chicago; and near Philadelphia. One enclave on the outskirts of New Orleans in the 1970s was still together in a group of about thirty families, this time in a trailer park. A portion of the Ludar population continues to travel, mainly as concessionaries with carnivals.

Language

The Rom speak an inflected Gypsy language belonging to an Indic branch of the Indo-European language family. This language, called "Romany" by linguists, is related to Sanskrit and modern Indian languages such as Hindi. It belongs to a group of Vlach, or Romanian-influenced, Gypsy dialects. All Rom are fluent in English, some in Spanish, and, in eastern Canada, French. The first immigrant generation also spoke the languages of the countries in which they spent some time before immigrating to the United States. These included Russian, Serbian, Portuguese, and Spanish; the last two were learned by families spending several years in South America.

All Romnichels speak English as their first language, but they have also preserved a creolized form of their original Gypsy language, now called Romnes, which consists of Gypsy words embedded in English syntax. The Ludar speak English and a dialect of Romanian as their first languages. They have also been reported to speak a form of Gypsy similar to the Rom dialect, but no samples have been collected to verify the claim. Both the Rom and the Romnichel forms of the Gypsy language, and the dialect of Romanian the Ludar use, serve the purpose of secret speech sufficiently so that there has been no need for them to develop argots, such as the Travelers (Scottish and Irish itinerants) use.

Culture

The primary economic organization of each of the three groups is currently referred to by scholars as peripatetic adaptation. It is based on the opportunistic exploitation of the surpluses of the host society by a wide variety of strategies. The specific strategies used fluctuate according to the popularity of certain pursuits, the skills possessed by the group, and the economic opportunities locally available.

The Romnichels, who had relied on a wide repertoire of peripatetic strategies in England, began concentrating on horse dealing as their primary activity soon after their arrival in the United States. Women's fortune-telling, peddling, and basketmaking continued to be used as supplemental strategies. When the horse trading began to decline after World War I, various secondary pursuits again assumed greater importance, until the 1950s, when the blacktopping and roofing trades became the dominant strategies.

The Rom were also engaged in horse trading, but their primary occupation on their arrival was coppersmithing, which lasted until the introduction of Monel metal and stainless steel replaced the formerly prevalent copper vats, steam jackets, and other industrial equipment. Women's fortune-telling, which had been a secondary activity at first, now became the chief source of income. The Rom remained nomadic during their first two decades in the United States, but by 1908, some families had begun to compete for and claim certain areas as spheres of influence. Over time, areas frequented by particular Rom became territories in the sense that they were restricted for exclusive exploitation by these families, for both sales and fortune-telling purposes. These territories are often contested, but they are also bought and sold as businesses. After the 1950s, some Rom took up blacktopping and related activities; others relied more on the sale of used cars and trailers. Fortune-telling remains one of the main economic strategies for most Rom.

The Ludar arrived with trained bears and monkeys and were ready to give public performances as soon as they got off the boat. Less is known about their other early pursuits, but at least some dealt in horses and did door-to-door peddling and fortune-telling. Some crafted rustic furniture for sale, and many families still continue this trade. Since the 1950s, many have become blacktoppers and roofers, while other families have remained in the entertainment industry, primarily in carnivals.

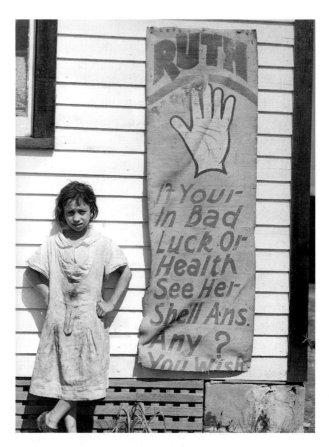

A Gypsy child stands next to a sign advertising palm reading near Salisbury, Maryland, in 1940. (Library of Congress/Corbis)

All three groups have used a sequence of wagons, tents, trailers, and campers as mobile dwellings; they also rented tenements, apartments, and private housing for winter layovers. Today many families also own or rent homes, but frequent visits to friends and relatives keep the populations highly mobile. From about 1914 until the 1990s, many urban Rom lived in storefronts that were also used as fortune-telling establishments. During travel families also frequently stay at campgrounds, motels, and hotels. Only a few families of each group are still primarily nomadic; most maintain a mixed travel/settlement mode of existence.

Before leaving England the Romnichels used the services of the Church of England; after immigrating they continued to use various Protestant churches in the United States until the 1970s, when many began to turn toward more charismatic

Pentecostal churches. The Rom and the Ludar were initially Serbian Orthodox. In America most Rom have used Roman Catholic churches; in about 1980, many Rom families also began turning toward the more evangelical Christian sects. Both the Rom and the Romnichels have founded their own Pentecostal churches, which they operate with their own pastors.

All three groups adhere, albeit to different degrees, to a system of purity regulations governing the handling of food, washing of clothes, and placement of household items according to clean and unclean zones within the household. Most Gypsies believe that the human body is unclean from the waist down, and anything associated with it would pollute the upper body. For the Rom these rules have meant the avoidance of certain types of work, such as plumbing, that would bring them in contact with polluting materials.

The social organization of the Rom and the Ludar is very similar, probably resulting from their long common exposure to Serbian and Romanian cultures. Both groups calculate descent through the male line, and possess patrilineal descent groups. Marriages are by arrangement, and bride-price is paid to the bride's parents. Postmarital residence is patrilocal, and the couple will usually remain with the man's parents, at least until their first child is born, or until other brothers marry and bring their brides into the household.

The traditional Romnichel pattern of marriage was by elopement followed by private marriage by a minister or civil authority. Postmarital residence is ambilocal (i.e., the couple can live with either the parents of the bride or the parents of the groom), or as the people expressed it, "That's the fifty-dollar question." Although descent is patrilineal, maternal kin also are an important part of a family's network.

The Rom system of leadership is based on a *Rom Baro* (Big Man), who speaks for his extended family and controls economic activities in a territory claimed by his family. The Kris, a Gypsy court of respected elders who are chosen ad hoc, adjudicates conflicts ranging from bride-price disputes to

division of earnings in work partnerships. The Romnichels have no equivalent institution or leadership. Disputes are settled either by the parties themselves, or, in the case of younger males, by their fathers. Little is known of Ludar political organization.

Cultural Persistence

Members of all three groups possess a strong sense of ethnic identity and a marked reluctance to associate with others not of their kind. Socialization instills a strong sense of ethnic pride in the children, and very few express any desire to be anything but Gypsies. Nevertheless, some attrition occurs, and intermarriages take place. Romnichels have the highest rate of intermarriage; the Rom have the lowest. Although all groups have always had some members leave and take up a more mainstream lifestyle, overall ethnic identity remains strong.

See also: TRAVELERS

Bibliography

Brown, I. (1929). "The Gypsies in America." *Journal of the Gypsy Lore Society*, 2nd series 8(4):145–176.

Fraser, A. (1992). *The Gypsies*. Oxford, Eng.: Basil Blackwell.

Gropper, R. C. (1975). *Gypsies in the City: Culture Patterns and Survival*. Princeton, NJ: Darwin Press.

Kaslov, S. (1995). "The Ways of My People." *Journal of the Gypsy Lore Society*. 5(1):15–37.

Lockwood, W. G., and Salo, S., eds. (1994). *Gypsies and Travelers in North America: An Annotated Bibliography*. Cheverly, MD: Gypsy Lore Society.

Miller, C. (1975). "American Rom and the Ideology of Defilement." In *Gypsies, Tinkers, and Other Travellers*, edited by F. Rehfisch. London: Academic Press.

Salo, M. T. (1979). "Gypsy Ethnicity: Implications of Native Categories and Interaction for Ethnic Classification." *Ethnicity* 6(1):73–96.

Salo, M. T. (1986). "Peripatetic Adaptation in Historical Perspective." *Nomadic Peoples* 21–22:7–36.

Salo, M. T., and Salo, S. (1977). *The Kalderaš in Eastern Canada*. Ottawa: National Museums of Canada.

Salo, M. T., and Salo, S. (1981). "Kalderaš Economic Organization." In *The American Kalderaš, Gypsies in the New World*, edited by M. T. Salo. Hackettstown, NJ: Gypsy Lore Society.

Salo, M. T., and Salo, S. (1982). "Romnichel Economic and Social Organization in Urban New England, 1850–1930." *Urban Anthropology* 11:273–313.

Salo, M. T., and Salo, S. (1986). "Gypsy Immigration to the United States." In *Papers From the Sixth and Seventh Annual Meetings, Gypsy Lore Society, North American Chapter*, edited by J. Grumet. New York: Gypsy Lore Society.

Salo, S. (1986). *Register of the Carlos de Wendler-Funaro Gypsy Reserch Collection c. 1920–1975*. Washington, DC: Archives Center, National Museum of American History, Smithsonian Institution.

Salo, S. (1992). "The Flight into Mexico." *Journal of the Gypsy Lore Society*, 5th series 2:61–81.

Sutherland, A. (1975). *Gypsies: The Hidden Americans*. New York: Free Press.

MATT T. SALO

HAITIANS

The Haitian population in the United States is composed of both persons born in Haiti and persons of Haitian descent. Some Haitians refer to themselves as members of "the Haitian community." Depending on the context, the term "community" may encompass the Haitians who have settled in a particular location such as New York or Miami, or all Haitian immigrants to the United States. The term "diaspora" has also become popular among immigrants. The word "diaspora" carries different meanings to Haitians, depending on where and by whom it is used. In the United States immigrants use it to convey their sense of belonging to a distinct group living in the United States because of the difficult political and economic situation in their homeland; but Haiti is still home. The term is also used by Haitian immigrants returning to Haiti as a way of differentiating themselves from those who remained.

Because the large-scale immigration of Haitians to the United States was precipitated by the civil disorder that accompanied the beginning of the Duvalier dictatorship in 1957, most of the newcomers saw themselves at first as transients and political exiles. This sense of impermanence, as well as long-standing divisions in Haitian society along class, color, and political lines, prevented Haitians from developing collective responses to problems they faced as immigrants in the United States. As immigration increased in the 1970s, U.S. political leaders and the media began to brand Haitians as undesirables, and the U.S. government refused to recognize Haitian immigrants as political refugees. In the 1980s, the U.S. Centers for Disease Control (CDC) classified Haitians as a risk group for the human immunodeficiency virus (HIV). Although the CDC later rescinded its inaccurate labeling, its action had important negative consequences on many Haitian immigrants, who lost their jobs or faced increased difficulties finding work or housing.

As a result of the discrimination they faced as Haitians and as black immigrants, many immigrants came to share a common and distinct Haitian identity. Haitians often also share a unique sense of blackness based on Haiti's history. Established in 1804 by the only successful slave uprising in history, Haiti was the first black nation in the Western Hemisphere.

Immigration and Settlement History

During the late eighteenth century many free black Haitians volunteered to the United States to fight in the American Revolution. These Haitian soldiers included a future leader of the 1804 Haitian revolution, Henry Christophe. With the abolition of slavery and the creation of the Haitian state, many slaveowners, accompanied by some of their slaves, took refuge in the United States. Haitians continued to arrive in the United States throughout the nineteenth century and settled in New Orleans, Philadelphia, and New York City, where they contributed to the cultural and economic development of these cities. Traces of this past immigration are found in traditions, lore, customs, and biographies of African-American families. In the 1920s and 1930s, some Haitian intellectuals, artists, and trade unionists were active participants in the Harlem Renaissance.

Until 1932, little is known about the volume of Haitian immigration because the U.S. government kept no records of Haitian immigration. From 1932 to 1950, only 5,544 Haitians entered the United States as immigrants. From 1959 to 1993, a total of 302,458 Haitians entered the United States with permanent resident visas and 1,381,240 Haitians arrived with nonimmigrant visas (most of these had tourist visas). Until the 1980s, a great number of the immigrants who arrived with tourist visas were able to regularize their status and become permanent residents.

Between 1971 and 1981, more than 60,000 Haitians arrived in South Florida by small wooden sailboats. A large number of men, women, and children drowned attempting to sail to the United States. Sometimes their bodies washed up on Florida's beaches, but this dramatic evidence of a people fleeing a repressive regime did not alter the U.S. policy of refusing Haitian refugees political asylum, placing them in prison camps, and deporting them. They were rejected because they were black and because the U.S. government supported the Duvalier regime. Haitians were portrayed as impoverished, illiterate, and diseased and labeled "boat people." The negative images ignored the diverse composition of the refugee population and of the Haitian communities in the United States and the presence of a significant middle class.

The brutal treatment of the Haitian refugees led to mass demonstrations of Haitians, class-action suits by U.S. civil rights advocates, and to increasing pressure by the Congressional Black Caucus. In 1980, U.S. public attention focused on Haitian immigration when approximately 12,500 Haitians and 125,000 Cubans arrived by small boats in South Florida within a few months. As a result, the Carter administration was forced to grant temporary admittance to both Haitian and Cuban refugees by creating a special Cuban-Haitian Entrant Status. The practice of deporting Haitians and denying them refugee status continued under the Reagan and Bush administrations. In addition, the U.S. Coast Guard began the practice of stopping Haitian boats at sea, sinking them, and returning Haitian refugees to Haiti.

The 1990 election of Jean-Bertrand Aristide to lead the first democratic government in Haitian history helped slow the immigration. However, when a military coup of generals with connections to the U.S. Central Intelligence Agency overthrew Aristide, Haitians again began to flee to the United States. Most of these persons were apprehended before they could reach the United States and were returned to Haiti to face the retribution of the military government. During 1994, the U.S. Immigration and Naturalization Service (INS) processed 10,400 applications of persons who filed for refugee status but approved only 18 percent of those received.

The Haitian immigration of the 1950s and 1960s contained members of the Haitian upper class as well as entrepreneurs, professionals, and skilled workers. Among those who arrived during this period were a relatively large contingent of affluent mulatto families as well as prominent members of the political class. The majority of these immigrants were urbanites, with most coming from Port-au-Prince, the capital. As political and economic conditions continued to deteriorate in Haiti from the 1960s to the 1990s, the social base of the immigration broadened: first

Two young Haitian women prepare to cook on a grill shortly after Hurricane Andrew knocked out power for much of Homestead, Florida, in 1992. (Raymond Gehman/Corbis)

Haitians who had been born in rural villages or in towns but had lived in Port-au-Prince, and then people directly from rural areas. Many of the latter immigrants had less skills, education, and money than the first arrivals.

The New York metropolitan area was the first region of dense Haitian settlement, and in 1993, more than one-third of the newly arrived Haitian immigrants continued to settle there. Beginning in the 1970s, Miami began to receive large numbers of Haitian immigrants. In 1993, another third of the newly arrived immigrants settled in either Miami or other cities and towns in South Florida. Boston, Massachusetts; Newark, New Jersey; Bridgeport, Connecticut; Orlando, Florida; and

Washington, D.C., also have sizable Haitian settlements. However, Haitian immigrants have been willing to settle wherever they can find employment, including cities in California and Illinois. Almost all Haitian settlements are in urban areas, although in the 1980s many Haitian immigrants were migrant farmworkers. They settled in areas such as Bellglade, Florida, but worked in agricultural areas along the East Coast.

There are no reliable figures on the number of Haitian immigrants and people of Haitian descent now in the United States. The 1990 U.S. Census reports 225,000 people born in Haiti who were living in the United States. This total does not include people of Haitian descent who were born in the United States and probably does not count the presence of undocumented immigrants in many households. In 1993, the INS estimated that there were 88,000 undocumented Haitians in the United States. Most researchers of Haitian immigration consider that the U.S. Census and INS figures considerably underrepresent the size of the Haitian population in the United States. It is likely tht one-fifth of Haiti's six million people live outside of Haiti, with the largest concentration settled in the United States.

Haitian immigrants are among the growing number of immigrants in the United States who live transnational lives. They have settled permanently in the United States yet maintain strong ties to Haiti, which they still call "home." People of all class backgrounds in Haiti live their lives across national borders, connected to family, friends, business associates, and political movements in Haiti. Most Haitians do not arrive in family groups but through a process known as chain migration. The immigration of one member of a family household is made possible through a pooling of the resources of those left behind. The immigrant then uses wages both to sustain family members still in Haiti and to provide money for the immigration of other members of the family. Until changes in the immigration law in the 1980s women often immigrated first because they could obtain permanent resident status by working as domestics. Remittances from Haitian immigrants sustain households throughout Haiti. As an unemployed man in Haiti put it, "When someone is in the United States, he is the wealth of people here."

The continuing familial, economic, religious, social, and political ties between Haitians in the United States and people in Haiti were formally recognized by the Aristide government in 1991. The territory of the Haitian state is divided into nine geographic divisions called departments; Haitians in the United States were designated part of the "tenth department" of Haiti. By implication the diaspora became part of the Haitian state. The designation of the "tenth department" gave public recognition to the fact that Haitian immigrants have participated in political processes that affect Haiti through lobbying, demonstrating, and organizing in the United States. Over the years increasing numbers of Haitians have decided to become U.S. citizens. In 1994, a total of 40 percent of Haitians with permanent resident visas and who had completed the requisite residency time became naturalized U.S. citizens.

Language

Immigrants educated in Haiti have different levels of knowledge of French, but all Haitians speak Kreyol. Until 1987, French was the only official language of the country and the one taught in schools. However, the majority of the people are unable to attend enough school to become literate and attain proficiency in French. Kreyol, as opposed to the more generic term "creole," is the Haitian language that developed when slaves integrated linguistic elements and structures from their different African languages, French, and several trading languages used in Africa and the Caribbean. It is a fully developed language for which linguists have developed a standardized system of orthography. However, it has not been taught in Haiti so that most Haitians, even if literate in other languages, do not know how to read or write in Kreyol.

In the 1970s, a group of exiled Haitian priests launched a campaign to legitimize the use of Kreyol and began to use it in the celebration of Mass and in other public events in the United States. This created a great deal of controversy among Haitian immigrants, in particular around the adoption of Kreyol as the language to be used in bilingual programs for Haitians students that began to be implemented in the New York public schools. By the 1990s, Kreyol had moved from being the language that Haitians used predominantly only among themselves to the language used at most Haitian meetings and public occasions in the United States. The transition from conducting public gatherings in French to Kreyol was hastened by the fact that young people born or raised in the United States do not know French and understand Kreyol more easily. Moreover, many of these young Haitians prefer to speak English and often refuse to respond to their parents when spoken to in Kreyol or French. About half of the first-generation Haitian immigrants can speak English well. Most Haitians learn some English.

In 1996, there were three major Haitian newspapers published in the United States, two based in New York (*Haïti Progres* and *Haiti Observateur*) and one based in Miami (*Haïti en Marche*). These papers also maintained offices and were distributed in Haiti. One of the New York papers has been published since the 1970s. Haitian periodicals are written predominantly in French, with a few articles in Kreyol and English in each issue.

Wherever Haitians have settled in significant numbers they have begun radio programs, most of which use Kreyol, although some programs broadcast in French. Haitian entrepreneurs have begun an innovative form of radio station that broadcasts on a frequency that can be heard only on special receivers bought from the company. Most of the radio programs have correspondents in Haiti who report directly on the most important events of the day or week.

Education

The Haitian immigrant population is more highly educated than the Haitian population as a whole. Because of Haiti's weak economy, further impoverished by years of political corruption and repression, many of Haiti's doctors, lawyers, engineers, and teachers are unable to find employment or obtain a decent standard of living in Haiti and are forced to emigrate. During their first years of settlement in the United States many of these professionals experience considerable downward mobility, impeded by linguistic and racial barriers. However, most Haitian immigrants with a professional education eventually are able to become part of the U.S. middle class. Beginning in the 1980s, when it became more difficult for foreign-trained doctors and nurses to obtain U.S. certification, Haitian doctors and nurses faced increased barriers to obtaining U.S. credentials.

Education continues to be a goal of Haitians after they immigrate, so that Haitian adults often attend school as well as work full-time. The 1990 U.S. Census reports that 41 percent of Haitian immigrants have less than a high school education, 48 percent have at least a high school education, and 11 percent have a college degree or higher. Women are about as likely as men to obtain a high school or college education. Of the Haitians with a professional degree, 63 percent are men.

Economic Integration

Like most other immigrant groups. Haitians enter the work force as low-paid wage workers who work long hours, often without benefits. Haitians as a group have a high level of employment. Women are employed almost as frequently as men. In 1990, a total of 34 percent of the population worked in service occupations, 21 percent as factory operatives, 21 percent as clerical or technical workers, 9 percent as professionals, 5 percent as managers, and 3 percent as farmworkers. In New York, for example, Haitians work in industries such as health care, hotels, office cleaning, and transport services. Women in particular work in the home health-care industry. Haitians participate very actively in trade union activities in the hospital and hotel industries.

Individual income is low, averaging $11,894 in 1989, with 21 percent of the families earning an income below the poverty line. However, the presence in households of several adult wage earners means that households are often able to pool resources, so that the mean household income in 1989 reached $32,161. Neighborhoods of dense Haitian settlement in Brooklyn and Miami provide a base for small Haitian businesses. These include record stores, travel agencies, restaurants, grocery stores, bakeries, and barber and beauty shops. Haitian doctors and dentists provide services for a Haitian clientele. The reduction in the number of manufacturing jobs, racial discrimination, and the difficulties they face in obtaining legal documentation force many immigrants to begin informal businesses. Vans operated by male drivers offer regular and inexpensive transportation services in areas with large concentrations of immigrants. Women use their kitchens to cater parties, weddings, and other social events. Their living rooms are transformed into day-care centers. People sell goods imported from Haiti from their homes and earn money by dressmaking, tailoring, repairing automobiles, and obtain commissions by transporting cash to Haiti.

Haitian businesses that focus on financial services and the flow of money, cargo, and travelers across international borders have been growing in size and significance. Services provided include insurance, accounting, and transfer of remittances and investments to Haiti. The largest Haitian businesses are cash transfer firms that send money and packages to Haiti as part of the ongoing pattern of maintaining transnational connections. By 1990, remittances sent through money transfer businesses totaled $125 million annually, which constituted about 30 percent of the Haitian state revenue.

Homeownership is important to Haitian immigrants and is made possible when several adults in a household work. Of people in Haitian households, 30 percent live in homes they own. Many people who buy homes in the United States also buy property and build homes in Haiti. However, many Haitian families live in overcrowded, poorly maintained apartments, where they pay high rents but are exposed to hazardous conditions that include lead-based paint, falling ceilings, and a lack of heat in winter.

Family

Two-thirds of Haitian adults marry, and marriage is an important and socially prestigious relationship for Haitians of all classes. Formal marriage is less common among poorer Haitians, who favor common-law marriages. Marriage is often seen as a project of mutual interest between a man and a woman rather than a source of friendship. Many changes occur with immigration to the United States, particularly among members of the middle class. Increasingly they tend to see husbands and wives as companions, yet there also is an increased rate of divorce. Most Haitian immigrants marry other Haitians, although there has been some intermarriage of Haitians with other Caribbeans, with African Americans, and with European Americans.

Households often include members of an extended family, including siblings, parents, aunts, uncles, or cousins of the husband and wife. Women rarely live alone with minor children. Extended kin beyond the household are also important in the daily life of immigrant families. Kinship networks are the primary support for Haitian immigrants when they resettle in the United States. Kin provide housing for new arrivals, assistance in finding housing and employment, and advice on U.S. culture. After the newcomer is settled, an extended network of kin continue to provide sources of companionship, assistance with child care, and support in times of illness, job loss, or the loss of a family member through death. Weekends are often spent at family gatherings. Husbands and wives often have their own kinship networks to which they look for support.

An equal number of Haitian women and men have immigrated to the United States. The degree to which Haitian women feel that immigration has improved their lives depends on a number of factors, including their class background in Haiti and whether they have been able to achieve edu-

cation or employment security in the United States. Most adult women work, and women find that they virtually have two full time jobs, since they are responsible for the housework and child care. Haitian men have been slow to contribute to the housework, although younger men do some cleaning and child rearing. Women often find their lives much more difficult in the United States because many immigrants had servants in Haiti. Some of the burden of work is relieved by having grandparents or other women in an extended family share the responsibilities of cooking or cleaning.

In poorer families children are sometimes sent back to Haiti to be raised by grandparents or kin so that their parents can work full time or hold more than one job. Such separations are often painful for both parents and children but are seen as necessary for the survival of all members of the family. Children are usually brought to the United States when they are teenagers so they can learn English, attend high school in the United States, and then obtain work. However, efforts are made to keep children within a Haitian family network because U.S. culture is seen as failing to teach children manners and a respect for kin, elders, and teachers.

Haitian children born or raised in the United States and living in inner-city neighborhoods interact most often with African-American children and tend to adopt the cultural patterns of their peers, especially clothing and hairstyles. Many Haitian parents, understanding the racist nature of U.S. society and its allocation of African Americans to the bottom of society, try to keep their children from assuming this identification. Parents say that they do not want their children to be "black twice." When they become young adults, second-generation Haitians often begin to use and enjoy their immigrant networks and family ties and often embrace some form of Haitian identity.

Religion

The majority of Haitian immigrants identify themselves as Catholics. Catholic parishes in areas of significant Haitian settlement such as New York, New Jersey, Miami, and Chicago have recruited Haitian priests. The celebration of Mass in Kreyol is often accompanied by Haitian drummers and Haitian music. Haitian immigrants have formed lay organizations to support the church and have looked to Catholic agencies such as Catholic Charities to provide assistance in settlement. In Haiti many more women attend Mass on a regular basis, but in the United States men also have begun to participate regularly in church services. Haitian Catholic priests emerged as important community leaders in the efforts to obtain democratic government in Haiti and contributed to the building of transnational political movements and in efforts to raise money for literacy campaigns in Haiti.

A growing minority of immigrants belong to Protestant congregations that include Baptists, Seventh-Day Adventists, Methodists, and the Church of God. At first Haitians joined multiethnic congregations, but in many instances they were assisted by Protestant church organizations to establish separate Haitian churches headed by Haitian ministers. Some of these congregations meet in established church buildings; others use storefronts. Haitian forms of healing using Protestant prayers and the assistance of *bon anj* (good souls) are practiced by some Haitian Protestants. Protestant churches have also assisted in immigrant settlement, providing health fairs, employment assistance, and English classes. Some congregations are linked to churches in Haiti and send money for community health projects and schools in Haiti. In general these congregations have kept their distance from Haitian politics.

The set of religious beliefs that Haitians call "serving the spirits," scholars refer to as Vodun, and the U.S. media label "voodoo" is also practiced

A Haitian woman reads from a prayer book at the Catholic Center in Little Haiti, Miami. (Tony Arruza/Corbis)

in the United States. Services are held in the home of the priest or priestess and often last throughout the night. In New York the basement of a private house is often converted to a place of worship. Singing is accompanied by the use of three drums. The spirits speak through the initiates, who go into a trance and provide guidance, comfort, and healing for immigrants who must deal with the difficulties of adjusting to their new life. Women and men of all generations as well as children participate. Because Haitian Vodun has been misunderstood and distorted by the media, most Haitians are reluctant to talk about their knowledge of Vodun. Children learn not to speak about their experiences in public. Haitian Vodun also fosters transnational connections. Some believers return to Haiti for initiation or to fulfill responsibilities to the spirits.

The Arts

Haitian painting has achieved an international reputation, and Haitian artists who have settled in the United States continue this tradition. Because Haiti is linked in the public mind with a particular "naive" art style of brightly colored paintings depicting the Haitian countryside and Vodun celebrations, Haitian artists who wish to pursue other art styles or to work in other media have had difficulties finding a place for their work. Ritual objects such as embroidered and sequin-covered flags depicting various spirits have been recognized as an art form and put on display in U.S. museums.

Since the beginning of large-scale immigration, bands from Haiti have toured in the United States, and recordings of their music are available in Haitian stores. The Haitian music industry has became transnational, so that recording for audiocassettes or videos may be done in Haiti, while production may take place in the United States. Older forms of dance music such as minijazz and *compas*, with lyrics focused on male-female relationships, are being replaced by a "roots-movement" in Haiti and among Haitian musicians in the United States. This music incorpor-

A pair of dancers perform a traditional Haitian dance in San Francisco. (Ted Streshinsky/Corbis)

ates Vodun rhythms and melodies into an exuberant music that combines an awareness of Haitian suffering with the joy of resistance. Some of the newer bands include Haitians born in the United States. This newer Haitian music has moved into public spaces as part of world beat radio programs and urban dance clubs. *Rara* music, traditionally a peasant Vodun music in which bands take to the streets during Lent, is now performed in parks in New York during the summer. Haitian immigrants from middle-class backgrounds who know little about peasant culture become acquainted with their cultural heritage through the performance of "roots movement" music, including the transformed rara.

Community Organizations

Haitian immigrants have formed a multiplicity of organizations. Participation in organized activities often helps immigrants reestablish a network beyond family ties and provides for social support. Haitian organizations also offer an arena in which social status can be obtained or validated, both in the United States and in Haiti. Organizations tend to be based in a single locality in which Haitians have settled rather than being regional or national in scope. However, many organizations in the United States carry out activities in Haiti. These organizations include soccer clubs and leagues; Masonic temples; associations of doctors, nurses, or other professionals; associations of artists, including dance troupes and theatrical groups; political organizations; community organizations; and hometown associations. Many of the community organizations were established with the assistance of U.S. philanthropic organizations or churches and have been dependent on financial assistance from these sources. The services they have provided to assist newcomers include literacy classes, English classes, and counseling on immigrants' rights. In contrast, hometown associations, which are often called "regional associations," unite people from the same village, town, or city in Haiti to organize activities to assist people "back home." Funds are raised for projects that include clinics, electrification, cemetery reconstruction, and literacy assistance.

See also: AFRICAN AMERICANS

Bibliography

Brown, K. (1991). *Mama Lola: A Voudou Priestess in Brooklyn*. Berkeley: University of California Press.

Buchannan Stafford, S. (1987). "The Haitians: The Cultural Meaning of Race and Ethnicity." In *New Immigrants in New York City*, edited by N. Foner. New York: Columbia University Press.

Buchannan Stafford, S. (1992). "Language and Identity: Haitians in New York City." In *Caribbean Immigrants in New York*, revised edition, edited by C. Sutton and E. Chaney. New York: Center for Migration Studies.

Charles, C. (1992). "Transnationalism in the Construct of Haitian Migrants' Racial Categories of Identity in New York City." In *Towards a Transnational Perspective on Migration: Race, Class, Ethnicity, and Nationalism Reconsidered,* edited by N. Glick Schiller, L. Basch, and C. Blanc-Szanton. New York: New York Academy of Science.

Chierci, R. (1991). *Demele, "Making It": Migration and Adaptation Among Haitian Boat People in the United States*. New York: AMS Press.

Glick Schiller, N., and Fouron, G. (1990). "'Everywhere We Go We Are in Danger': Ti Manno and the Emergence of a Haitian Transnational Identity." *American Ethnologist* 17(2):329–347.

Glick Schiller, N.; DeWind, J.; Brutus, M. L.; Charles, C.; Fouron, G.; and Thomas, L. (1992). "All in the Same Boat? Unity and Diversity Among Haitian Immigrants." In *Caribbean Immigrants in New York,* revised edition, edited by C. Sutton and E. Chaney. New York: Center for Migration Studies.

Laguerre, M. (1984). *American Odyssey: Haitians in New York*. Ithaca: Cornell University Press.

Stepick, A. (1991). "The Haitian Informal Sector in Miami." *City and Society* 5:10–12.

Woldemikael, T. (1989). *Becoming Black American: Haitians and American Institutions in Evanston, Illinois*. New York: AMS Press.

NINA GLICK SCHILLER
CAROLLE CHARLES

HASIDIC JEWS

See JEWS, HASIDIC

HINDUS

See BANGLADESHIS; BENGALIS; BIHARIS; GUJARATIS; MAHARASHTRIANS; MALAYALAM SPEAKERS; NEPALESE; PUNJABI MEXICANS; PUNJABIS; SINDHIS; SRI LANKANS; TAMILS; TELUGUS; TRINIDADIANS

HISPANICS

See ARGENTINEANS; CALIFORNIOS; CHILEANS; COLOMBIANS; CUBANS; DOMINICANS; ECUADORIANS; HONDURANS; MEXICANS; NICARAGUANS; PANAMANIANS; PERUVIANS; PUERTO RICANS; SALVADORANS

HMONG

The Hmong comprise one of several refugee groups from Southeast Asia that immigrated to the United States following the end of the second Indochinese War. The name "Hmong," which means "man" or "human being," contrasts with names given to the group by outsiders. The Han Chinese referred to the Hmong as Miao, which is sometimes translated as "barbarian." In Laos, the Hmong were called Meo by Laotian and French colonial administrators, a derogatory designation said to imitate the sound of their language (similar to the mewing of a cat). Miao is now widely used as a self-identifier by Hmong living in China.

More than five million Hmong live in mainland China, with the greatest concentration (more than half) in Guizhou Province in southern China. Another 80,000 Hmong live in mountain villages in northern Thailand. And while 75,000 Hmong refugees left Laos during the 1975–1979 period, the majority of Hmong chose to remain in the country, where an estimated 250,000 Hmong still live in the eastern highlands. Geographic isolation has resulted in cultural diversification of Hmong populations in China, Laos, and Thailand. Ethnic subgroups may be identified by differences in the dialect of Hmong spoken and by folklore and customs. There are two ethnic subgroups in Laos: the White Hmong (Hmoob Dawb) and Green Hmong (Hmoob Ntsuab). In the United States, the most common dialect (and ethnic subgroup) is the Green Hmong.

Definition of the Group

Using self-identification and linguistic criteria, researchers in the People's Republic of China counted more than five million Hmong in the 1982 census of ethnic minorities. In Laos and Thailand, the Hmong are identified by language and dress. It is often said that the Hmong have always been minorities, even in their own country, and this process of self-definition of difference from the dominant group has carried over to the United States. The Hmong recognize that they are but one of many Asian populations and identify themselves as different from other groups not just because of language and culture but by virtue of their role in the Vietnam War. For adults who fought in the war, regular meetings with prominent military leaders from that earlier era are an important part of local community life. Because of their relatively recent arrival in the United States, the maintenance of their home language, and the symbolic importance of their lost homeland, it is likely that the Hmong will retain a strong sense of ethnic identity. In the U.S. Census—where ethnic background is determined by self-identification—the Hmong are grouped as one of many ethnic populations under the more general designation of "Asian and Pacific Islander," while for other administrative purposes they are identified as one of several "Southeast Asian Refugee" populations.

Immigration and Settlement History

The earliest mention of the Hmong people is found in Chinese records when the Hmong (Miao) were living in the Yellow and Yangtze river plains in the central regions of China. Between 2700 and 2300 B.C.E. the Hmong were forced into mountains to the south by other groups who migrated into the central plains. In these mountains the Hmong formed autonomous kingdoms whose leaders were recognized by the Chinese emperor with titles of nobility. Each kingdom was dominated by a different clan and ruled by a hereditary *kaitong* (little king).

Hmong kingdoms in southern China came into conflict with the expanding Chinese imperial state during the transition from the Ming Dynasty (established 1368) to the Manchu Dynasty (established 1644). They waged unsuccessful rebellions against the Chinese state in the 1735–1740 and 1795–1806 periods. Repression following yet another failed rebellion (1855–1872) forced thousands of Hmong to flee south into northeastern Laos and the Vietnamese highlands.

Following Hmong rebellions in Laos and Tonkin during the War of Pa Tchai (1919–1922), the French colonial government divided the Long Het district of Xieng Khouang Province in northern Laos into two administrative areas, and powerful lineages representing the Lo and Ly clans competed for alliances with the French. Family groups associated with the Ly clan, which achieved political power in Xieng Khouang under the French, supported the constitutional monarchy established in 1949, while family groups associated with the Lo clan supported the nationalist Pathet Lao forces seeking formation of an independent state.

General Vang Pao earned the support of American military planners when he led his Hmong troops into the capital city of Vientiane in 1960 and overthrew a coalition government representing groups from both the right and the left. The Hmong were recruited by the Central Intelligence Agency (CIA) to serve as a "secret army" in Laos, where they fought a guerrilla war against Vietnamese and Laotian forces and rescued American pilots shot down over North Vietnam and Laos. The Hmong were uprooted from their home villages and relocated to military centers, where they became dependent on supplies flown in by the CIA. As many as 30,000 Hmong (fully 10 percent of the population) were killed during the war, and another 75,000 became refugees in their own land. Following the collapse of the American military effort in the spring of 1975, General Vang Pao, his support staff, and family members were flown from Laos to Thailand. Other Hmong who had been involved in the war fled across the Mekong River into northern Thailand, where they were held in refugee camps run by the United Nations. By the end of 1975, more than 40,000 "Lao hill people," most of whom were Hmong, were living in refugee camps awaiting resettlement in France, Australia, and the United States. The first group of 9,000 Hmong refugees arrived in the United States in the years immediately following the American withdrawal from South Vietnam (1975–1978). The collapse of the Pol Pot regime in Cambodia raised international concern over the plight of refugees across Southeast Asia, and a second group of some 43,000 Hmong arrived in the United States between 1979 and 1981; the largest single group, some 27,000 persons, arrived in 1980. Over the next decade an additional 66,000 Hmong would be admitted to the United States.

Initial resettlement plans sent the Hmong refugees to communities in more than twenty different states. The geographic dispersal of Hmong households is important. While a large number of refugee families in a single city or state might place a heavy burden on social services and local budgets, distributing the costs of these programs more widely would keep expenditures low and would increase opportunities for the economic and social integration of Hmong families; it also would increase pressures on the families to assimilate more rapidly.

The resettlement plans did not give full recognition to the importance of Hmong kinship and political structures. The splintering of kinship networks during the initial resettlement process resulted in family groups being spread across many different communities and states. By the mid-1980s, 85 percent of the Hmong population had become concentrated in just two areas of the United States. The first and largest of these settlements was located in central California, around Fresno; the second concentration involved Minnesota and Wisconsin.

In 1994, the Thai government moved to close the last of the relocation camps, effectively ending the resettlement of Hmong refugees in the United States and other countries. Hmong leaders in the United States maintain strong opposition to the Laotian government, and there has been little return immigration to Laos. This does not seem likely to change, although there has developed a very limited pattern of visiting relatives in Thailand and in Laos by Hmong who have become established in the United States and other countries. While many Hmong elders continue to speak of returning to their Laotian homeland, younger Hmong recognize that their future is in the United States.

Demographics

The first period of resettlement (1976–1978) mainly involved military leaders and their families, followed by a second wave (1978–1982) of other military personnel and their families, who also were political refugees. The third period of resettlement from the refugee camps (1988–1992) involved relatives of the earlier immigrants, but it also increasingly involved groups that the U.N. High Commissioner on Refugees labeled as economic refugees. While the Hmong are sometimes referred to as "new" or "recent" immigrants, these figures demonstrate that most Hmong households date their arrival in the United States to 1982 or earlier.

Birth and death rates, fertility ratios, and the like normally are computed from census data, but this information is notoriously inaccurate for the Hmong population. U.N. and Immigration and Naturalization Service (INS) records indicate that 80,000 Hmong had been admitted to the United States by 1990, yet only some 90,000 Hmong were counted in the 1990 U.S. Census. These figures clearly understate the number of Hmong living in the country; information from one community survey in Wisconsin suggests a census undercount of at least 30 percent.

There has been a very rapid rate of increase in the Hmong population since the 1990 U.S. Census. This is due both to continued resettlement of families from refugee camps and, increasingly, to the natural increase from children born in the United States. The anthropologist William Geddes reported a crude birth rate of 49 to 76 per 1,000 persons for Hmong villages in Thailand in the 1940s, and Peter Kunstadter noted that the Hmong were at "the upper limits of human reproductive capacity." Similar reproductive patterns have been reported in the United States, where a majority of Hmong females are married and begin childbearing during their teenage years. A child-women fertility ratio of 1,750 children per 1,000 women has been reported for the Hmong in San Diego, and a ratio of more than 1,200 children per 1,000 women has been reported in Green Bay. Fertility ratios for the Hmong are consistently reported to be greater than that of other immigrant and refugee groups.

INS figures indicate that 115,000 Hmong refugees were admitted to the United States from 1976 to 1994; given the high rate of natural increase within this population, it can be estimated that the total Hmong population in the United States by 1997 had reached some 200,000 persons. Because of the strong pattern of secondary migration noted above, the Hmong continue to be concentrated in just two areas of the country; central California, around Fresno (estimated at more than 50,000 persons), and the Midwest, where Hmong families are concentrated in St. Paul, Minnesota (estimated at more than 40,000 persons), and in eight smaller

A Hmong textile artisan in Merced, California, concentrates on her needlework. (Eric Crystal)

communities of 4,000 to 6,000 Hmong across central Wisconsin. The recent passage of legislation in California that would restrict benefits to immigrants and refugees reportedly already has led to an out-migration of Hmong families, but similar efforts to restrict benefits through "welfare reform" may prevent a massive movement to Minnesota and Wisconsin.

The Hmong population is highly segmented, a fact that is essential for understanding current developments within the group. First is the adult generation, comprised of persons aged forty and older who were born and brought up in Laos, many of whom were involved in the war as young adults. This group may make up about a quarter of the Hmong population in the United States. Second is the young adult generation, comprised of persons aged twenty-five to forty who were born and spent part of their adolescence or childhood in Laos before fleeing to refugee camps in Thailand. This group may make up another quarter of the Hmong population, and has been labeled as the $1\frac{1}{2}$ generation by some researchers. Finally, there is the younger (second) generation comprised of children and adolescents up to the age of twenty-five who have mostly been born and raised in the United States. This younger group makes up half or more of the Hmong community. These categories do not correspond to generational groupings commonly used in immigration studies, but they more accurately reflect significant groupings within the Hmong community. In some cases, membership in a given age group may not accurately describe the orientation of an individual or family, since some persons in the "young adult" generation may have been born in Laos and lived in a refugee camp for ten years or more before arriving in the United States as a teenager, while others of the same age were born in the United States.

Language

The Hmong are often described as a "preliterate" people who had no written language until their contact with Western missionaries in the 1900s. The Hmong themselves believe that their written language was stolen by the Chinese when the Hmong lost control of their original homeland in the central plains of China. Numerous written scripts have been developed during the twentieth century, including several by Shong Lue Yang, a messianic leader (murdered in 1971) who was known as the "Mother of Writing." The most widely used script, the Romanized Popular Alphabet (RPA), was developed by three Protestant missionaries in the period from 1951 to 1953.

Although language literacy is often thought to be a major problem for the Hmong, about two-thirds of adults report that they are able to speak English; a quarter of this group report that they can speak, read, and write in English. A Wisconsin study indicated that 60 percent of adults could read, write, and speak in Hmong, and 65 percent spoke a second language (usually Laotian). While the rate of English language literacy is probably comparable to that of earlier immigrant populations, it clearly is a hindrance to the full employment and social integration of Hmong adults, many of whom must rely upon their American-born children to translate written documents and to act as intermediaries when shopping or dealing with teachers and others in informal and formal situations.

There are a number of Hmong newspapers in California and Minnesota, the largest of which are bilingual. In some larger cities (such as Seattle) the Hmong press is smaller than that of other Asian American groups, and in other cities (such as Minneapolis–St. Paul) there are Pan-Asian newspapers that offer coverage of the Hmong community (usually in English). In many communities across the United States, Hmong radio shows can be found on local public radio stations, and television shows are found on some public television and local access cable stations.

There is evidence of a significant language shift in the second generation. As a result, relatively fewer Hmong children begin elementary school in ESL (English as a second language) courses, and larger numbers of children participate in mainstream classes by the time they enter middle school. One study in Wisconsin reported that while less than 10 percent of Hmong adults spoke English or mostly English with their children, one-quarter of Hmong children spoke English or mostly English with their siblings, and more than one-third spoke English or mostly English with their friends. The magnitude of this shift from the home language to English in the second generation is comparable to that reported for other recent immigrant groups (such as Mexican immigrants) and probably is greater than that of earlier European immigrants.

The rapid shift from Hmong to English in the second generation is of great concern to Hmong elders. Many traditional Hmong ceremonies require a specialized form of spoken language known as *paj lug* (flowery speech), which children who shift to English in the preteen years may not have an opportunity to learn. In many Hmong community centers classes that emphasize Hmong culture and Hmong language are offered for Hmong children. Some elementary schools also have begun programs that, while not following a bicultural-bilingual model, are designed to encourage learning in both Hmong and in English.

Cultural Characteristics

Economic Patterns. The common view is that the Hmong engaged in primitive swidden agriculture and had little involvement with a modern market economy before arriving in the United States. It is true that in their homeland most Hmong were involved in farming activities and in the military, skills which do not necessarily translate into successful positions in a new country. But new economic activities became available during the war years in Laos and in the Thai refugee centers. Results from studies conducted in refugee camps, as well as interviews with refugees in Minnesota and Wisconsin, show that many adults worked as small-scale entrepreneurs before immigrating to the United States. This may have provided the experience necessary for establishment of the wide range of commercial activities found in the United States, including not only traditional ethnic enterprises such as butcher shops, grocery stores, and craft sales, but also used car dealerships, automotive repair shops, commercial sewing businesses, and more recently travel agencies, insurance companies, and banking and credit associations. Many Hmong have attended vocational and technical institutes and have been employed in legal and medical services, sales and clerical work, and other areas. With large numbers of young adults (both male and female) now going on to college, more Hmong will be prepared for professional careers in education, health, and other fields in the future. Still, census data and information from community studies indicate that most Hmong who are working now are employed in semi-skilled and low-paying service, clerical, and manufacturing jobs that require little knowledge of English. One study in Minnesota found that the most frequently reported service job was that of janitor and that one-third of the employed Hmong were engaged in "bench work," such as sewing machine operators or parts assembly.

Because of language barriers and a lack of formal education, employment has been a significant problem for Hmong adults (those forty-five years of age and older). Some studies indicate that a majority of adult Hmong are unemployed and receive public assistance from one or more sources ten years or longer after their arrival in the United States. This is especially the case for households where the parents may now be in their fifties and sixties, where one or more parent may be missing due to wartime casualties, and where English-language knowledge is lacking. It is clear that many Hmong adults would like to return to farming, as indicated by the secondary migration of Hmong households from states as far away as Tennessee, Pennsylvania, and Connecticut to the Central Valley region of California in the early 1980s. Publicly and privately funded projects sought to train the Hmong how to grow and market crops in the United States. Hmong families pooled resources to rent agricultural land where they raised labor intensive crops such as snow peas and tomatoes, but only a small number of families were able to establish themselves as successful growers. In other areas of the country (including

A customer buys produce at a small farmers' market, run mostly by Hmong, located in Minneapolis, Minnesota. (Owen Franken/Corbis)

Minnesota and Wisconsin), family groups have leased farmland or developed extensive urban gardening to produce a variety of vegetable crops for home consumption and commercial sale through farmers' markets, and Hmong of all ages have begun to replace migrant farm laborers in some areas.

Education. Compared to other refugee groups and minority populations, the Hmong report higher levels of household poverty and unemployment, higher rates of family disruption, and lower levels of parental education. Hmong students have standardized math scores slightly above those of other students, but they have much lower language scores. Despite the prevalence of these "at risk" factors, the majority of Hmong teenagers (90 percent of males and some 80 percent of females) graduate from high school on schedule. Compared to other students, Hmong students spend more hours on homework, earn higher grade points averages, and are less likely to get into trouble or to drop out of school. Hmong high school students and their parents report higher educational aspirations than do Anglo students or other minority students, and Hmong students attend two-year and four-year colleges at rates comparable to that of Anglo students. It is likely that first-generation Hmong have achieved a record of educational success unmatched by earlier ethnic groups.

While many Hmong youths are doing very well in school, others have become involved in youth gang activities to one degree or another. Reports of drive-by shootings and other "gang activities" have become common place in some cities where the Hmong live. The actual number of youths involved in these activities is not known and is often overstated by gang specialists, police officials, and the media. Police officials interviewed for a 1994 study in seven Wisconsin cities stated that Hmong or Asian street gangs were their number one youth crime concern, yet there had been no reported incident involving Asian or Hmong gangs in the previous year. In addition, while police officials expressed strong concern about gang activity by Hmong teenagers, school officials reported no gang problems with Hmong students in their schools. In large and small communities across the United States, Hmong leaders have worked with the public schools, local police departments, and other community organizations to reduce the appeal and influence of gang activity for adolescent Hmong.

Religion and Worldview. Hmong religion is based upon a belief system incorporating an elaborate spirit world. Dangerous spirits that might have the power to possess people, capture souls, or cause illness are associated with mountains and other "wild" domains. Deceased ancestors might aid or punish their living relatives, and other "domestic" spirits associated with the home and garden might also be called upon to protect the family. Shared funeral practices are used to establish and reinforce lineage ties. Hmong shamans perform ceremonies that allow them to enter this spirit world to communicate with spirits causing mental anguish or physical disease. To this basic set of beliefs in a spirit world that transcends the physical world has been added philosophies and practices of other groups and cultures that the Hmong have come into contact with, including Taoism, Confucianism, Buddhism, and Christianity. Many Christian relief organizations were active in the refugee centers in Thailand, and groups such as Catholic Charities and Lutheran Social Services were the primary sponsors for Hmong refugees resettled in the United States in the early 1980s. About half of the Hmong in the United States claim adherence to some form of Christianity. In many cases, however, Hmong have not been integrated into existing congregations. Instead they have tended to elect their own lay leaders and hold their own services separate from that of the larger congregation.

Because traditional Hmong beliefs conflict with Christian teachings, and because sacred rituals

A Hmong immigrant in Merced, California, holds his child, who is dressed for a special ritual to protect the soul from illness. (Eric Crystal)

associated with ancestor worship define the boundaries of the kinship groups and reinforce traditional Hmong values, there is some tension within the community between "traditional" Hmong and Christian Hmong. Some families and lineage groups have split over differences in religious practices, particularly since fundamentalist groups that have recruited converts within Hmong communities insist that traditional Hmong practices and beliefs are incompatible with Christian teachings. Many Christian Hmong continue to make use of a traditional shaman to cure certain illnesses and provide personal guidance; it is not unusual to see Christian Hmong wearing "tie-string" bracelets that have been blessed by a shaman in a traditional Hmong ceremony.

Craft Production and Performing Arts. The Hmong were skilled silversmiths and craftsmen in their homeland, and many traditional crafts have continued, particularly among the adults and the elderly, in the United States. The beautifully embroidered *paj ntaub* (story cloths with elaborate scenes showing life in their homeland) are sold at flea markets and farmers' markets wherever Hmong have settled. In the larger cities, stores selling Hmong crafts have been established and have had some success, although there also is concern that younger Hmong may not want to learn how to perform this handiwork and that the customs may not continue in future generations. A variety of community groups, including informal family groups as well as funded arts organizations, have formed dancing and acting groups that perform traditional Hmong dances and folktales at community events (such as the Hmong New Year celebrations), in public schools, and at other events in the broader community. These groups have the dual purpose of transmitting traditional cultural practices to younger generations, while acting as cultural ambassadors to the general public. The larger and more established of these groups from communities such as St. Paul and Fresno perform in Hmong communities across the United States.

Marriage, Family, and Kinship. The Hmong have been more successful in retaining their traditional form of family and social organization than have other Southeast Asian refugee groups. Hmong society in Laos was organized around a patrilineal clan system, where common descent established obligations among kinship groups but even stronger obligations existed among individuals in family sub-lineages. Marriage occurred only between persons from different clans, resulting in a modified brother-sister sexual taboo. Marriages often were arranged after negotiations among family elders; these typically included a bride price and a written or oral marriage contract. Men married between the ages of eighteen and thirty, women between the ages of fourteen and eighteen. Upon marriage the woman left her father's family, household, and clan and became fully identified with her husband's clan.

As the individual family groups became fragmented during the flight from Laos to Thailand, and then again in the process of resettlement to third countries, the Hmong placed greater reliance on lineage and clan ties as a basis for close cooperation. Lynellen Long's 1980–1982 study of the Ban Vanai refugee camp shows that while the camps structured relationships of dependency between refugees and relief workers, residential areas within the refugee camps reproduced traditional Hmong village and clan structures, and some celebrations, such as the Hmong New Year, were established in new ways to provide meaning to cultural traditions and to daily lives. William Smalley has noted that camp organization allowed Hmong refugees to reclaim their deeper cultural and emotional life, which was lived not simply within the superimposed camp hierarchies, but within traditional families, lineages, subclans, and other social relationships that people brought with them as they migrated.

Hmong community life in the United States continues to be organized around family lineages; for example, marriages occur between individuals from different clans, and clan members sharing specific lineages have Hmong New Year celebrations that differ from those of other lineages. Some aspects of the traditional marriage customs have continued in the United States, including negotiations among clan family elders that result in agreement over the bride price. Arranged marriages are less frequent, particularly among households that have longer residence in the United States. There also is evidence of important changes in family and kinship roles; many traditional male leadership and occupational roles have disappeared, and Hmong women find educational and employment opportunities in the United States that would not have been available to them in Laos. While elder members of the clan retain their important role of resolving internal disputes, increased reliance is placed upon younger adults (both male and female) when dealing with institutions in the host society.

The American fascination with Hmong customs such as arranged marriages and "bride theft" and with the early marriage of Hmong girls probably says more about American culture than it does about Hmong tradition—one monograph used as a title a Hmong proverb about the marriageable age for a girl, "a flower ready for the bee." The sensationalized reporting of these events in local and even national media has distorted the public's understanding of these customs—as well as exaggerated the frequency with which they occur. Interviews with Hmong women in the United States suggest that most women in Laos married between the ages of fourteen and twenty-two, but less than one-fourth of those interviewed said that their marriage had been arranged by parents, and only 10 percent were married as the result of *zij pojniam* (seizing a wife).

Hmong households usually consist of three generations (children, parents, and grandparents) and may include several nuclear families of siblings (usually brothers). This larger household unit provides an important base for resource sharing; family groups will often buy apartment buildings or rent adjacent apartments so that the extended family network can share living space and, along with it, domestic chores such as child care and cooking. Above the household level are larger kin groups consisting of descendants of certain parents or grandparents. The Hmong expression *tsev neeg* (all people) corresponds to this extended lineage group; member households may be located in different neighborhoods within a particular city or across a number of cities and states. While the common view is that Hmong social organization is based upon membership in specific clans, the responsibilities shared among persons in the lineage group may blur the boundaries between clans.

Health and Illness. Refugee status is the consequence of forced or involuntary migration, frequently as the result of military conflict. As a result, refugee groups represent a psychologically at-risk population. Reports from "displaced persons camps" on the Thai-Cambodian border found at least one-third of the inhabitants suffered severe psychiatric disorders, especially anxiety and de-

pression, and nearly half of the persons interviewed in Rubén Rumbaut and Kenji Ima's study of refugee groups in San Diego had experienced the death of one or more family members and had spent more than two years in refugee camps; most feared that they would be killed during their escape; nearly one-third had been assaulted during their escape. Hmong refugees were more likely to have feared that they would be killed, to have fled without immediate family members, and to have spent more than two years in refugee camps than any group except Cambodians. Nearly half of the first group of adult Hmong resettled in Minneapolis–St. Paul achieved depressive scores on various psychological measures and 60 percent experienced a mental or emotional problem after arriving in the United States. Increased symptom level was associated with loss of vocational and social roles, lack of English-language proficiency, and increased dependence on others for financial support. In the 1980s, cases of sudden death syndrome (unexplained death occurring while the person is asleep) were reported for Hmong males in several communities across the country. While adult and elderly Hmong suffered greatly from the trauma of wartime and refugee experience, these symptoms are less common among younger adults and the new generation brought up in the United States, where the results of psychological well-being appear to be comparable to that of non-Hmong youths. The rate of suicide among Hmong adults is not different from that of other groups. In addition, despite the prevalence of early childbearing and the continuation of childbearing into adult years, Hmong women are less likely to have underweight babies or to experience problem pregnancies than are women of other groups.

Social and Political Organization. Political organization in Laos was focused on local villages dominated by family lineages. During the Indochina War, divisions based on kinship, regional loyalty, and dialect were of secondary importance, and the Hmong were united under the direction of General Vang Pao. In the early years after resettlement in the United States the Hmong were once again united under a coalition of leaders headed by

General Vang Pao. Leadership roles within the Hmong community are divided between "traditional" leaders (such as clan elders) and "bureaucratic" leaders (such as persons elected to the board of directors of Hmong community organizations). The establishment of mutual assistance associations (MAAs) is required for participation in a variety of federal and state programs; by law these associations must include representatives of the major Hmong clans in their board of directors. In many cases the MAAs are headed by younger leaders in the community who have completed their college education in the United States. Community groups interested in working with the Hmong community find that they must work through both traditional and bureaucratic leadership structures within the local community. In recent years Hmong leaders have begun to focus attention on the needs of Hmong families in the local community, and some younger leaders no longer support General Vang Pao's continuing fund-raising efforts to overthrow the Laotian government.

As in other areas of community life, family lineages are important in the underlying social organization of the Hmong community. Informal banking associations, based on lineage groupings, exist in most Hmong communities to provide loans and other services for members. In recent years several such associations have become chartered banking institutions, marking again a move from more traditional to bureaucratic forms of social organization within the ethnic community.

Assimilation and Cultural Persistence

A complicated process of cultural change and adaptation is occurring in Hmong communities across the United States—but this process was well under way prior to resettlement. Many persons appear to be unaware of the changes in Hmong life and culture that took place in Laos and in the Thai refugee centers. While teachers say that the Hmong had no written language, Hmong children observe their parents and other adults writing Hmong in three different scripts. Refugee

experiences varied greatly from one relocation camp to another. Smalley notes that while some Hmong were swept along by the quickly changing events in their homeland without learning much more than minimal coping skills, others responded by learning new skills they could apply in the United States. For some, the war and relocation camp experience is a distant childhood memory, and many Hmong high school students were born in the United States and have been through the entire kindergarten-elementary-secondary school system. Even so, many persons continue to view the Hmong through the lenses of anthropological studies that are now more than fifty years old.

Acculturation is not simply a one-way process, and Hmong culture and customs have affected many social institutions. It is common in many hospitals for a Hmong shaman to come to a patient's

A Hmong elementary school dance troupe is dressed in traditional costumes in Sacramento, California. (Eric Crystal)

room to perform ceremonies, and extended family members are often involved in mental health counseling that might ordinarily involve just the patient and counselor. Court cases have established the right of Hmong families and individuals to continue customs from their homeland, perhaps most notably the sacrifice of animals for religious purposes in California.

Hmong culture has confronted unprecedented change since the mid-1970s. The loss of leadership and occupational roles and of status within the family has had a significant effect on Hmong males, while new educational and employment opportunities have greatly expanded the accepted activities and roles for Hmong females. The ambiguity and novelty of the new role of "adolescent" within the Hmong community has led to some degree of confusion for Hmong teenagers, as well as to significant intergenerational conflict with parents and elders. However, as Timothy Dunnigan notes, the issue is not whether Hmong refugees can retain their culture or whether they must accept assimilation to the dominant society; "more to the point are questions regarding the future form and meaning of Hmong identity symbols and the evolving structure of social relations through which these symbols will be expressed." Although certain cultural changes already are under way, such as the loss of the elaborate expression of paj lug used in ritual language contests, other elements of Hmong culture and social organization, particularly the cooperative assistance activities based upon these family lineages will continue. In addition, whereas cultural persistence may be noticeable in areas where there are large concentrations of Hmong, such as in California and Minnesota, acculturation may well be more pronounced in areas where the population base within individual communities is significantly smaller.

See also: LAO; THAI

Bibliography

Chan, S., ed. (1994). *Hmong Means Free: Life in Laos and America.* Philadelphia: Temple University Press.

Dao, Y. (1992). "The Hmong: Enduring Traditions." In *Minority Cultures of Laos: Kammu, Lua', Lahu, Hmong, and Iu-Mein,* edited by J. Lewis. Rancho Cordova, CA: Southeast Asia Community Resource Center.

Donnelly, N. D. (1994). *Changing Lives of Refugee Hmong Women.* Seattle: University of Washington Press.

Dunnigan, T. (1982). "Segmentary Kinship in an Urban Society: The Hmong of St. Paul–Minneapolis." *Anthropological Quarterly* 55:126–134.

Downing, B., and Olney, D. P., eds. (1982). *The Hmong in the West.* Minneapolis: Center for Urban and Regional Affairs, University of Minnesota.

Hein, J. (1995). *From Vietnam, Laos, and Cambodia: A Refugee Experience in the United States.* New York: Twayne.

Hendricks, G. L.; Downing, B. T.; and Deinard, A. S., eds. (1986). *The Hmong in Transition.* New York: Center for Migration Studies.

Hutchison, R. (1992). *Acculturation in the Hmong Community.* Green Bay: Center for Public Affairs, University of Wisconsin.

Hutchinson, R., and McNall, M. (1994). "Early Marriage in a Hmong Cohort." *Journal of Marriage and the Family* 56(3):579–590.

Long, L. D. (1993). *Ban Vanai: The Refugee Camp.* New York: Columbia University Press.

Smalley, W.; Vang, C. K.; and Yang, G. Y. (1990). *Mother of Writing: The Origin and Development of a Hmong Messianic Script.* Chicago: University of Chicago Press.

Trueba, H. T.; Jacobs, L.; and Kirton, E. (1990). *Cultural Conflict and Adaptation: The Case of Hmong Children in American Society.* New York: Falmer Press.

RAY HUTCHISON

HONDURANS

Strikingly, though the Honduran community is defined as a group by national origin, it is ethnically and racially quite diverse, leading to varied experiences of integration, residential patterns, economic participation, and community life in

U.S. society. Honduras's population is 90 percent mestizo or Ladinos, racially and culturally of indigenous and Spanish origin. The other 10 percent consists of eight indigenous groups, the Garifuna, and blacks of West Indian descent, all racially, culturally, and linguistically distinct from mestizos. Black West Indians were brought by the British as slaves to the Bay Islands, off the Atlantic coast of Honduras, in the 1800s; others came as freedmen, mainly from the Cayman Islands. They still speak English and maintain an Anglo-based rather than a Hispanic culture. Another wave of West Indians came to work in the early 1900s on the American-owned United Fruit Company (UFCo) banana plantations on Honduras's Atlantic Coast. The Garifuna and blacks of West Indian descent make up a large percentage of the Honduran immigrant population in the United States despite their minority status within Honduras. These two subgroups are often associated with the Afro-Caribbean diaspora, while mestizos are associated with other Central Americans, especially Salvadorans, through cultural similarity and residential proximity. Despite this linguistic and racial variation, all Honduran immigrants do speak Spanish as a first or second language and are also in the larger category of Hispanic.

Demographic data on Hondurans are difficult to obtain due both to the nature of the community and to the Immigration and Naturalization Service's statistics on Central Americans, which represent only a fraction of the population because they provide no data on undocumented or second- and third-generation Hondurans. Most estimates of undocumented immigrants come from asylum organizations and academics involved in refugee issues in the 1980s; however, because Hondurans have not qualified as political refugees, they are largely ignored in these studies. The U.S. Census is also misleading because the Garifuna and West Indians may be counted as blacks rather than Hispanics. The best estimates are from studies done in the 1980s that placed a total of 15,000 Hondurans in Los Angeles, 30,000 to 60,000 in New Orleans, and 5,000 to 10,000 in Houston in 1985. Considering that New York City had at least as many as New Orleans, and that Boston had at least as many as Los Angeles, this leaves an estimate of 95,000 to 160,000 first-generation Hondurans in those cities alone in the United States in 1985. Considering children of these immigrants as members of the Honduran community would, of course, double or triple these numbers.

Immigration History

The history of Honduran immigration to the United States is intimately connected to the establishment of the American-owned UFCo and Standard Fruit Company on the northern coast of Honduras in the 1880s. The banana companies were given large land grants by the Honduran state, which allowed UFCo to monopolize both the cultivation and transportation of bananas, company stores, railroads, and ports. During World War II Hondurans were hired as merchant marines by UFCo, giving them, as well as housemaids, gardeners, children of Honduran managers, and others connected to the company, entry through New Orleans, New York, New Jersey, and Boston, where many settled and married American citizens. These communities continue to be augmented primarily by immigrants from the northern departments of Honduras (Atlántida, Cortés, Colón, and Yoro).

During the 1960s and 1970s, most Hondurans arrived as students, tourists, or under family reunification quotas. Immigration at this time was mostly middle-class among the mestizos. In the absence of strong Honduran niches within which to settle, more resources were required to get to and survive in the United States. Though most were men, it became more common for both sexes to immigrate on their own, later bringing a spouse from Honduras or marrying in the United States, generating a more even distribution of the sexes. The most common ages of entry are twenty to thirty-four and under fifteen, reflecting the tendency of Hondurans to immigrate at prime working age and, after establishing themselves, to bring over children they left in the care of family in Honduras.

In the 1980s, economic and political crises in Central America generated a dramatic increase in documented and undocumented immigration to the United States. In Honduras, this decade was marked by a national economic modernization plan, based on export agriculture, that displaced many *campesinos* from their land without generating enough job alternatives in industry and the cities to absorb this work force. Regional conflicts prompted the United States to militarize Honduras, compounding an atmosphere of repression, while refugees from neighboring countries poured into Honduras. Meanwhile, the growth of the service sector and subcontracting in U.S. industry created an economic niche that undocumented workers could fill. This new wave of Honduran immigration, which often came through Mexico, was more characteristically undocumented, from poorer sectors of Honduran society. In fact, in 1988, Hondurans were ranked fifth in number of deportees, reflecting this new trend.

Settlement in the United States

Since the 1980s, already established Honduran communities in the United States have grown dramatically, new communities have developed in Houston and Los Angeles, and internal migration and secondary settlement have expanded. These communities have taken on different characteristics depending on the particular ethnic mix of the city and economic niches available. For example, in New York City the Garifuna represent a majority of the Honduran population, living mainly in the South Bronx (in predominantly Dominican and Puerto Rican areas) and in Harlem and Brooklyn (in predominantly African-American areas). They work within a traditionally West Indian and Caribbean economic niche: women in health care and men in building maintenance. Mestizos live dispersed throughout the city in neighborhoods where Salvadorans are numerous, as in Queens, Brooklyn, and elsewhere on Long Island, though many are also in the South Bronx, and generally work in what is considered a Mexican or Central American niche: women as domestics, men in construction, restaurants, and day labor. In Houston and New Orleans, where mestizos are a majority (though the Garifuna still are a sizable percentage), a similar pattern is observed.

Blacks of West Indian descent have settled in West Indian neighborhoods in Brooklyn and were the pioneers of the Honduran community in Boston in the 1950s. In the 1980s, the communities in Boston and New Jersey grew, with many Hondurans seeking greater employment opportunities in factories and domestic work, sectors that were saturated in New York City. Miami, a traditional destination for upper-class Honduran businessmen, also has become an area of secondary settlement, mainly for economically successful Hondurans from the northeastern United States looking for a more tropical climate.

Hondurans immigrate to the United States, as so many other groups do, with the idea of getting an education and/or making enough money to return to their native country and open a business, build a house, and help other family members there. Many Honduran immigrants return to Honduras periodically for vacations and extended stays, eventually reestablishing themselves there (return migration) with a business and/or retirement checks after years of working in the United States. Others find reintegration into Honduran society difficult after many years in the United States and tend to move back and forth between the two countries (circular migration). Still others are never able to save enough to return to live in Honduras, or else they become financially successful in the United States and decide not to return to live in Honduras. While Honduran immigrant communities are more and more rooted in the United States with second and third generations, the steady stream of new immigrants and circular migration keep links to Honduras alive.

The culture and social organization of Hondurans in the United States reflect this transnational system and their relationship to the race/class system of the cities in which they live. Possibilities for class mobility are influenced by the general class position of the community into which they will be integrated because acquisitions of work and housing depend on networks of family and compatriots. For example, many of the earliest immigrants who were not integrated into a large Honduran or Hispanic community and had to learn English (as well as the West Indians who already spoke English and often had had a British-based education in Honduras) have assimilated to more "mainstream" American culture and are now professionals working as teachers, nurses, lawyers, engineers, and so on, representing an emerging middle class. Despite the growth of the Honduran community since the 1980s, class mobility for this generation is more difficult because they tend to live in largely Hispanic neighborhoods where English is less necessary to get by; and they are prevented from studying a profession or at least English by the necessity of working long hours to survive in the United States while also supporting family members in Honduras. What assimilation occurs is most commonly to a "minority" inner-city working class. Concern about this fact has sparked a growth of community organizations (especially among the Garifuna) whose goals are to promote linguistic maintenance and cultural persistence while simultaneously promoting success in U.S. society through education, economic enterprise, and political participation. However, the fractious nature of the community has impeded unity and the creation of a Honduran political and social "bloc."

Employment

Hondurans have not created a strong ethnic economic niche into which new arrivals can be integrated. The few Honduran businesses that exist tend to serve the community's transnational character: restaurants, travel agencies, courier services, shipping agencies. There is an informal ethnic economy of Honduran food vendors at soccer games; bands playing at social events, individuals making videos of weddings, birthdays, and other occasions to be sent to family in Honduras; and people providing intra-community child care. One exception to these small family-run enterprises is a Honduran-owned ice cream factory in New York City that hires many Hondurans to sell *paletas* from street carts in the Hispanic neighborhoods of the city.

Those who entered the United States legally and declared a profession in the 1980s had been concentrated in their homeland in the categories of "service," "operator, fabricator, and laborer," and "precision production, craft, and repair," indicating a mainly blue-collar and low-skilled urban working-class population. Upon arrival in the United States they tended to work in similar sectors of the economy. For both men and women factory work has been a constant source of employment and often is a stepping-stone in the labor market, especially if they are undocumented and speak no English. Yet with the decline of U.S. industry since the 1970s, factories moving to other countries (among them Honduras), and industry's greater reliance on contract labor, this once-stable niche with unions and benefits became highly unstable, relying more on nonunionized labor and undocumented workers. Many more Hondurans are now employed in the growing U.S. service sector, women especially as "home attendants" for the disabled and elderly and as domestics in wealthy suburban homes; men are commonly found in restaurants, construction, and building maintenance.

Though many Honduran professionals immigrate to the United States, those who do not speak English often end up with the same types of jobs as nonprofessionals. Thus for many, immigration means downward class mobility. Yet the immigration stream continues, as lower-class living standards in the United States still allow for greater possibilities for consumption than middle-class status in Honduras, especially if the U.S. consumption is focused on using dollars to invest in property in Honduras.

Housing and Family Structure

Hondurans tend not to dominate any one neighborhood, but may dominate a single apartment building as they either become the superintendent or recommend family and friends as tenants. In more suburban areas groups of households often rent a house together. Most individual households consist of nuclear families, but extended family members also often live together for temporary periods, as with a new arrival from Honduras or in cases of marital separation. Family reunification is a strong ideal among Hondurans. Women work especially hard to make it possible to send for young children they left in Honduras. They also often send for their own parents, who will then take care of the children. Child care is a serious issue within the community as private child care is expensive and government-subsidized child care is hard to get, so the most common solution is to leave children with an unemployed relative or compatriot.

Legal marriage is a desired status; however, the combination of the transnational system and U.S. immigration laws makes this a complicated affair. Many families are separated between the United States and Honduras while waiting for U.S. residency papers to come through; marriages are postponed until legal status can be attained; others are contracted for strictly legal purposes. The result is many common-law unions that produce children, as well as the "ideal type" American nuclear family. Gender relations also are affected by these constraints as both men and women must work to maintain a decent standard of living in the United States while simultaneously supporting family members in Honduras, so it is more common for them to share household and child-care duties. Many women comment that they prefer gender relations in the United States because long work hours and dangerous inner-city street life give men less opportunity to be *callejeando* (in the streets); because spousal and child abuse are more harshly punished in the United States; because women have more opportunity to reduce their dependence on men via government aid; and because of greater educational opportunities. On the other hand, Honduran women in the United States must work long hours away from their children and deal with a state bureaucracy that is complex and often dehumanizing toward non-English-speakers to obtain social services.

Most Hondurans are Catholic, though there are some Evangelicals and Jehovah's Witnesses. Garifuna have their own religion, the practitioners of which are *buyeis* (shamans) who interpret dreams and contact the ancestors in cases of illness or emotional problems. Though most Hondurans go to the hospital for medical care, they also use traditional herbal medicines. AIDS is a serious health problem for Hondurans both in the United States and in their Honduran Atlantic Coast communities, the area with the highest incidence of HIV infection in Central America. Community AIDS workers say it is compounded because those who are known to be infected are reluctant to admit it and take precautions, for fear of being treated as "socially dead" in a culture held together by tightly knit social and family networks.

Family and social gatherings make up for the residential dispersion of the community. Birthday parties, weddings, baptisms, and wakes attract large networks of family members. Often these gatherings are videotaped and sent to family members in Honduras, with the same done from Honduras to the United States. The Garifuna replicate their village life with the patron saint's fiesta, a gala dance, the crowning of the community "queen," and *fedu* and *máscaro* dances at Christmas. Fiestas at social clubs organized by voluntary associations representing each village use profits from admissions and concession stands for development projects in their native Honduran communities, such as the supply of potable water and electricity and the building of schools. In the summer, New York Garifuna also organize day trips to the beach and to Atlantic City.

A few areas of activity attract a wider base of Honduran participation, including national civic events such as Independence Day and the annual Mass for the Virgin of Suyapa, as well as involvement in soccer clubs, social clubs, and cultural associations. Since the 1960s, Honduran soccer clubs have played in city leagues in New York City and New Orleans, drawing large crowds to parks, where they socialize, have barbecues, and eat Honduran food.

Honduran Cultural Contributions

Hondurans, both mestizo and Garifuna, have been particularly active and visible in the arts, especially in New York. For example, the Honduran-American Cultural Association produced a series of major cultural events from the mid-1980s to the mid-1990s, including performances of Honduran popular and contemporary theater, traditional dance troupes both local and based in Honduras, visual arts exhibits, poetry recitals, book sales, and conferences. In the summer of 1995, at an arts festival in the Bronx, a group of Honduran Garifuna and mestizo performers and musicians staged a pioneering outdoor performance representing the arrival of the Garifuna in Honduras. The work of artists in all disciplines has begun to attract media attention and will encourage others. In the mid-1990s, *punta* (drumming music traditionally played at Garifuna wakes) began to achieve acceptance by greater audiences through the Punta Rock movement, with its growing number of Garifuna bands and more sophisticated production, as well as through dance troupes that choreograph traditional Garifuna dances to present to multicultural audiences. Local mestizo dance troupes replicate their Honduran colleagues' research and study of their particular dance forms to help spearhead a movement to enrich and revitalize this long-neglected tradition.

Hondurans are active in the Spanish-language media. Some of Honduras's most respected radio journalists have worked for many years in New York City. In 1995, a core group of Honduran writers founded *Nosotros los Latinos*, a monthly newspaper/magazine with commentary on and analysis of diverse subjects of interest to greater Hispanic audiences and a special focus on the arts. On Bronx local access cable television there are *Abriendo Brechas, Centro América Show* (which sometimes broadcasts in Garifuna), and *Conversando con Antonieta*; these series feature soccer clubs, interviews with members of the community, and coverage of local dance and music performances. The first two are also broadcast in New Orleans, Los Angeles, and Honduras. In Los Angeles a Honduran-run newspaper called *El Sol de Las Américas* covers the entire Hispanic community.

Preference for the Spanish media may be explained by the high degree of bilingualism within the Hispanic community. For most first-generation Hondurans, Spanish still is their primary language. Their children become bilingual through contact with their Hispanic neighborhood and bilingual schools. Garifuna children may also speak Garifuna if their parents reinforce it at home. Though Garifuna is traditionally a nonwritten language, there has been a transnational movement among Garifuna organizations in Los Angeles, New York, Belize, and Honduras to create a standard spelling system for the language so youths can learn to read and write it.

Politics

Despite a growing population and an increase in community organizations, Hondurans' participation in U.S. politics has remained weak. This can be attributed to the lack of a strong ethnic economic niche, residential dispersal, the large number of undocumented immigrants, the ideology of return, community fragmentation, and less of a tradition of large-scale organization around national issues than other Central American groups. Organizational efforts and community identity tend to be strongly focused on Honduras rather than the United States (since most see themselves as only temporary sojourners in the United States), and more specifically on their home communities in Honduras.

Fragmentation and segregation along ethnic, class, and party lines from Honduras carry over to the United States. Additionally, U.S. racial and ethnic politics further divide the community. In the South and Southwest the Garifuna are racialized as black and the mestizos as Hispanic, two often antagonistic and segregated groups. In New York City the presence of Puerto Rican, Dominican, and Cuban blacks has created more leeway for the formation of a middle ground Afro-Latino identity for the Garifuna, yet there still is a marked division between Garifuna and mestizo social and political activities. This means that the Honduran community does not necessarily see itself as a single coherent group with the same needs and goals vis-à-vis U.S. society.

National Awareness and Development

The severe situation of many Honduran immigrants in New York City came to international attention through the March 25, 1990, Happy Land social club fire in the South Bronx, where eighty-seven people, a majority Hondurans, were killed by asphyxiation. Happy Land was, like many other clubs, in blatant violation of city safety regulations, with only one fire exit. Hondurans have gathered in places like this over the years to celebrate family events and listen to punta. The aftermath of the tragedy revealed poor housing conditions, precarious financial situations, a multitude of problems caused by various states of documentation or lack of it, the degree to which many family members in Honduras rely on immigrants for financial support, and the fact that the community had no self-help mechanism or organization to cope with such a large-scale tragedy.

The creation of the Federation of Honduran Organizations of New York in 1991, in response to this tragedy, is an important initiative in the U.S. Honduran community's history. Though it first worked to address the immediate needs of surviving family members, its scope widened to include problems of housing, health care, legalization, financial assistance, English, job training, and small-business development. The federation represents an initial attempt at unity within the community, but many more initiatives are needed for the community to reach a level of development consistent with its numbers.

See also: GARIFUNA

Bibliography

Bromley, R. (1993). "Happy Land: Global Dimensions of a Local Tragedy." Paper presented at the annual fall meeting of the New England Council of Latin American Studies, Brown University.

Chinchilla, N., and Hamilton, N. (1989). *Central American Enterprises in Los Angeles.* Austin: IUP/SSRC Committee for Public Policy Research on Contemporary Hispanic Issues, Center for Mexican-American Studies, University of Texas at Austin.

Chinchilla, N., and Hamilton, N. (1991). "Central American Migration: A Framework for Analysis." *Latin American Research Review* 26(1):75–110.

Davidson, W. (1974). *Historical Geography of the Bay Islands, Honduras: Anglo-Hispanic Conflict in the Western Caribbean.* Birmingham, AL: Southern University Press.

Echeverri-Gent, E. (1992). "Forgotten Workers: British West Indians and the Early Days of the Banana Industry in Costa Rica and Honduras." *Journal of Latin American Studies* 24:275–308.

Gonzalez, J. (1995). *Roll Down Your Window: Stories of a Forgotten America.* London: Verso.

Gonzalez, N. (1987). "Garifuna Settlement in New York: A New Frontier." In *Caribbean Life in New York City: Sociocultural Dimensions*, edited by C. Sutton and E. Chaney. New York: Center for Migration Studies of New York.

Gonzalez, N. (1988). *Sojourners of the Caribbean.* Urbana: University of Illinois Press.

Kerns, V. (1983). *Women and the Ancestors: Black Carib Kinship and Ritual.* Urbana: University of Illinois Press.

New York City Department of City Planning. (1992). *The Newest New Yorkers: An Analysis of Immigration into New York City During the 1980s.* New York: Author.

Rodriguez, N. (1987). "Undocumented Central Americans in Houston: Diverse Populations." *International Migration Review* 21(1):4–26.

Stone, M. C. (1990). "The Afro-Caribbean Presence in Central America." *Belizean Studies* 18(2–3):6–42.

U.S. Immigration and Naturalization Service. (1989). *Statistical Yearbook of the Immigration and Naturalization Service, 1988.* Washington, DC: U.S. Government Printing Office.

Wallace, S. (1986). "Central American and Mexican Immigrant Characteristics and Economic Incorporation in California." *International Migration Review* 20(3):657–671.

Williams, R. (1986). *Export Crops and the Crisis in Central America.* Chapel Hill: University of North Carolina Press.

SARAH ENGLAND
WALTER L. KROCHMAL

HUNGARIANS

Hungarian Americans (or, as they call themselves in Hungarian, Magyar Amerikaiak or Magyar Amerikások, or, as they were called by others, either insultingly or jokingly, Hunkies) are a very diverse group. Beyond the general assertion that Hungarians are those who live in or come from Hungary, or those who identify one or more of their ancestors to be from that country, it is difficult to define who exactly is a Hungarian, and therefore to circumscribe who exactly is a Hungarian American. In part this is because the peoples of east-central Europe constitute an ethnic kaleidoscope as a result of the many wars and revolutions, migrations and return migrations, settlements and resettlements, as well as intermarriages. In part this is also because state and national boundaries were drawn and redrawn in such a way that often people did not cross the borders, but the borders crossed over them. Based primarily on self-ascription in Europe, people who consider themselves Hungarians, speak Hungarian. Yet, while there are self-ascribed Hungarians who speak the language and identify that they hail from German, Romanian, Slavic, Jewish, Roma (Gypsy), or other ancestors, there are also many who identify themselves as descendants of the seven Magyar tribes and therefore are convinced that they are "more" Hungarian than the others.

History

It is believed that the Magyar tribes were an estimated 250,000 individuals who migrated from Asia and in the late ninth century arrived in the Carpathian Basin of east-central Europe. These tribes settled down and, with a blood oath, promised to protect one another from outsiders and to develop and work and stay on the land. In time these tribes shifted from their nomadic and seminomadic pastoralist mode of subsistence to a sedentary and mainly agriculturalist mode. Under their first king, István (who was later canonized and is often referred to St. Stephen, or Szent István), Hungarians accepted Christianity in 1001, a process that sounds much more peaceful than it must have been in reality. The Carpathian Basin is a crossroad between East and West, so not only were the Magyars initially not welcomed, but throughout their history they have continued to struggle with many enemies in and for their land of choice. A millennium after their arrival in central Europe, nineteenth-century Czech historian Frantisek Palacky wrote that the arrival of the Magyars in the Carpathian Basin was the greatest tragedy that had ever befallen the Slavs. Partially because of the strategic location of the Carpathian Basin where they settled, the history of the Magyars was most turbulent, filled with invasions, wars, and occupations, and resulted in a national self-image composed of elements of "being all alone," martyrdom, and suffering as bulwark of Western Christianity and civilization. This image is apt when it is considered that the Tartar invasion and occupation in 1241 killed more than half of the Hungarian population (Germans and others populated the vacated regions) and that a couple of centuries later the very taxing Ottoman occupation lasted 150 years before centuries of Hapsburg rule.

Language

When the Magyars arrived from Asia they had a complex tribal social organization and a distinct linguistic and cultural identity. While in the centuries that followed, hundreds of loanwords entered the Hungarian language, and many of the cultural elements blended with those of their neighbors, the language of the Hungarians remains distinctive. Unlike the languages spoken by the peoples of neighboring countries, Hungarian is not an Indo-European language. It belongs to the Ugric branch of the Finno-Ugric language family. Besides Hungarian, the most important Finno-Ugric languages are Finnish and Estonian. Today Hungarian is spoken by about fourteen million people. Of these, there are about thirteen million indigenous-speakers in the Carpathian Basin: a little over ten million within Hungary, where 98 percent of the population are Hungarian-speakers, about two million in Romania, 600,000 in Slovakia, 300,000 in the former Yugoslavia, 180,000 in Ukraine, and a couple of thousand in Austria. The fact that more than three million ethnic Hungarians live in neighboring countries makes Hungarians one of the largest groups in contemporary Europe that lives outside its own homeland and—until the massive migration in the entire region began, accompanying the demise of state socialism in the late 1980s—gave good reason for some scholars to call Hungarians "exiles of twentieth-century European history." There is a sizable Hungarian-speaking diaspora in Western Europe, North America, Israel, and Australia. Complicating the issue of defining Hungarian Americans is that in the United States language is not necessarily a criterion of national or ethnic belonging. This is clearly illustrated by the major difference between the number of individuals who state that by ancestry they are Hungarian (according to the 1990 U.S. Census, 997,545, and of these, 110,337 are foreign-born immigrants themselves) and those individuals over age five who speak Hungarian at home (147,902). While these data do not necessarily mean that there are fewer than 150,000 Hungarian-speakers in the United States, they clearly show that often those individuals consider themselves Hungarian who themselves or their ancestors came either from present-day Hungary, or anywhere from the areas covered by pre-Trianon Treaty Hungary, when the country was considerably larger and more populous. As a result of the peace treaty at Trianon in 1920, two-thirds of Hungary's land territory and 60 percent of its original population were ceded to Romania and Austria, and to the then newly created Yugoslavia and Czechoslovakia. This further complicates and confuses the definition of who is Hungarian. Since the 1920s, individuals who identify themselves as ethnic Hungarians often arrive in the United States from and as citizens of Austria, Romania, or in the 1990s, the Republics of Slovakia and Ukraine, as well as of the former Yugoslavia; at the time of their arrival they are registered according their country of origin and citizenship, not according to their ethnic and national identity.

Major Waves of Hungarian Immigration

There are intriguing legends about Hungarians among the crew of Leif Erikson in the year 1000, as well as among the first people who greeted Christopher Columbus when he accidently found himself on America's shores, and about Hungarians participating in a sixteenth-century colonizing voyage that was directed by Queen Elizabeth I of England. There are records of a Hungarian colonel in the army of George Washington who was only one of 141 Hungarian soldiers distinguishing themselves in the American Revolution, of many brave Hungarian soldiers who fought in the American Civil War, and of Sándor Bölöni Farkas, who visited North America in 1831 and subsequently published his vivid impressions, which undoubtedly influenced some of his countryfolk to try their fortunes in the United States. However, until the last third of the nineteenth century there was little or no substantial emigration from Hungary, or rather the Austro-Hungarian Empire, as it was known between 1867 and World War I. Six different Hungarian immigrant waves can be distinguished between the late 1800s and the mid-1990s. These immigrations occurred in different social and political contexts, with different push and pull factors, processes, and rates. The immigrants' destinations, their educational levels and social background, as well as their ability and desire to adapt to the ways of the American host society were markedly dissimilar in each of these phases. There also were variations in each group's relationships with and expectations toward their homeland and their natal culture, and in the creation of, adherence to, and strategies with immigrant associations and organizations.

The first and largest wave of Hungarian immigration took place in the period between 1871 and World War I when, based on the U.S. Census, an estimated 1,893,647 immigrants arrived from within Hungary's borders. This was also a period of heavy industrialization in the United States, so the pull factors were particularly powerful. In 1907, the peak year of immigration, 193,460 people arrived from Hungary—an astonishing 15 percent of the year's total of 1,285,439 immigrants. It is difficult to determine, however, how many of these immigrants were ethnic Hungarians and how many were Romanians, Serbians, Slovaks, Ruthenians, Germans, and other nationality groups who lived in Hungary before they immigrated. However, it is known that, while being parts of chain migrations, many arrived alone, there were more men than women, and nearly 70 percent of the immigrants were farmhands or farmers; the remainder were unskilled workers, factory hands, miners, or domestic servants. Most of the immigrants in this first wave were very poor peasants who barely eked out a living in the Austro-Hungarian Empire. These immigrants left their small, remote, rural villages for economic reasons. Their main intentions were to become miners or factory or agrarian workers in the United States, thus making and saving as much money in as short a period of time as possible, and, with their savings,

to return to their villages and resume their rural lifestyles. Therefore, most of these immigrants remained transients (paradoxically this is true even for those who ended up staying in the United States) without much desire to learn English or to leave their various immigrant enclaves other than going to work in their factories or mines among immigrants of various nationalities. The primary associations around which they rallied were boardinghouses, social insurance organizations, and churches that radically changed in function from those of the homeland. Although it is impossible to determine for certain the extent of circular or return migration in this or any of the later waves of immigration, scholars estimate that 16 to 25 percent of this group eventually returned to their homeland, permanently or temporarily. There were "professional immigrants" during this period, individuals who crossed the ocean six or more times in a regular pattern of pendular immigration.

Illustration depicts the reception of Hungarian exiles in Philadelphia in 1850. (Illustrated London News/Corbis)

A Hungarian-American miner's wife brings home a bucket of coal from the slate pile in Chaplin on Scott's Run in West Virginia in 1938. (Library of Congress/ Corbis)

The second major group immigrated between the two world wars, when about thirty thousand individuals arrived from Hungary. It was a much smaller wave than the first because in the early 1920s the new restrictive immigration laws blocked the way of potential newcomers; then the Great Depression further reduced the chances and numbers of immigrants. During this period there were also return migrants, Hungarian Americans who returned from Hungary either directly, if they were American citizens, or indirectly and often clandestinely through Canada to live in the United States along with their family members. A significant percentage of these newcomers, however, came from the urban middle classes and left their homeland for political rather than economic rea-

sons. Many were highly educated professionals; quite a few came from urban Jewish families. A number of these immigrants became internationally known in their various fields. Among these "illustrious immigrants," as Laura Fermi calls them in her 1971 book by that name, were Theodore von Kármán in aeronautics; John von Neumann in the mathematical theory of games and the development of missiles and computers; Leó Szilárd, Edward Teller, and Eugene Wigner in physics, particularly relating to nuclear energy; György von Békésy and Albert Szent-Györgyi in medicine and physiology; Béla Bartók, Eugene Ormándy, Fritz Reiner, József Szigeti, and many others in music; and Ferenc Molnár and Kate Serédy in literature. For many of these immigrants, returning to the homeland was rarely an issue. While some of them joined earlier established associations, many started their own social insurance organizations, churches, burial societies, and particularly political associations, and formal and informal institutions (e.g., the ethnic radio and press began to fluorish, as did amateur plays along with poetry and prose readings, church and cultural center suppers, dances, and such). The lobbying of some of the interwar immigrants, particularly for the return of territories and populations lost under the Trianon treaty, was evident in many of their publications and in the immigrant and national media.

The third phase of Hungarian immigration occurred between the end of World War II and the mid-1950s, when an estimated twenty-five thousand Hungarians became "DPs," since they entered the United States under the Displaced Persons Act. As in the previous wave, most DPs were urban and highly educated who left the homeland mainly for political reasons—to escape from communism and Soviet domination. Some of the DPs were members of the Hungarian Christian middle class. Others hailed from well-known upper, middle, or lesser aristocratic backgrounds. Many were prominent in Hungary's army. Still others were Jews and Roma, who left Europe after they somehow survived the German occupation in which the majority of their relatives and friends perished. Some of the DPs came from Hungary proper, while others arrived from ceded territories in neighboring states. Many DPs experienced tremendous trauma before their arrival in the United States that was often followed, once they settled down, by a sharp socioeconomic fall. Hungarian degrees and professions—particularly in medicine, law, politics, the military, and teaching—were neither accepted nor really appropriate in the United States. High-ranking army officers became unskilled factory workers in automobile and other manufacturing plants. It is not surprising that many of these immigrants, who were already highly politicized and ideologized upon their arrival, became the main actors in creating, articulating, and perpetuating a particular, mostly interwar Hungarian identity and nationalism that, as numerous scholars maintain, are no longer viable or timely, and, understandably, the farthest from their motherland's contemporary reality. In Hungarian-American associations some of these individuals lock themselves into a mirrored labyrinth in which they reinforce each other's Hungarianness, along with each other's real or invented pre–World War II titles and ranks that are no longer recognized by anyone else anywhere. Mostly for political or personal reasons many DPs did not return to Hungary even for visits until the late 1980s or early 1990s, if at all; therefore it is understandable that, after nearly fifty years of immigrant life, their Hungarianness is atavistic, and their reality regarding Hungary has long ceased to be the reality of their homeland. The immigrant associations formed by this wave are perhaps the most complex among all their counterparts. These include the World Federation of Hungarian Veterans and the Hungarian Scout Association Exterris. In the mid-1990s, these organizations were not only still operating—in spite of their aged membership—but also appeared to be functioning well while providing reasons for the very being of their members as well as for not returning permanently to the homeland.

The fourth phase constituted the "'56ers," individuals who left Hungary after the Hungarian Revolution of 1956. Many members of this immigrant wave were young, single, urban, and moderately or well educated. Among all the earlier or later groups of Hungarian immigrants, the '56ers were the most warmly welcomed both by the host society and—at least initially—by members of earlier immigrant groups. The '56ers were also readily helped by the host society, primarily because of their status as actual—or purported—freedom fighters against communism in the atmosphere of Cold War and the overall political and economic situation in the United States at the time of their arrival. Many '56ers were and remain highly politicized and ideologized and active regarding their homeland. Some scholars suggest that this group's politics, lobbying, and other strategies, as well as their relations with the homeland, are somewhat less archaic and a bit more pragmatic than those of some DPs. The reason that '56ers hold a somewhat more realistic image of the homeland than the DPs is that, in general, '56ers have been paying regular visits to Hungary after they received political amnesty there in 1963. Thus they have had an intensive relationship with their homeland. Nevertheless, after a while living away from the homeland, in a sense time stands still for immigrants. The homeland becomes a symbol and an abstraction rather than a concrete place. The lobbying of the '56ers through such organizations as the Hungarian Freedom Fighters Federation, the Hungarian Human Rights Foundation, the World Federation of Hungarians, the Hungarian Lobby, and many others, is evident in the daily national and local media, widely circulated letters and petitions addressed to the president of the United States, and Washington, D.C., circles, as well as on networks of electronic mail.

The fifth wave of immigrants from Hungary could be called the "Kádár orphans." Individuals who were unhappy with the politics and regime of János Kádár that was based on the notion of "those who are not against us are with us," escaped from Hungary during that regime and immigrated to the United States between the early 1960s and the late 1980s. Some of these people left their homeland because they did not like the political regime; others left for a combination of economic, political, and familial reasons, and—as most other groups before them—worked diligently to establish themselves in the United States. Interestingly, some of these individuals appear to be less involved with the larger economic and political issues relating to their homeland than members of the former two waves, the DPs and the '56ers. At the same time the "Kádár orphans" maintain what appears to be considerably more intensive familial and friendship relations, with apparently many more visits to Hungary and with relatives from there than other groups had before.

The sixth phase is comprised of those Hungarians who left after 1989, after the demise of socialism and the beginning of a socioeconomically very difficult period while Hungary shifted from a command economy to the "call of capitalist market," which has been a harsh, costly, and inhumane process for the bulk of Hungary's citizens. The majority of these immigrated for mainly economic and familial reasons. In general, they had considerably higher and more concrete expectations of the West than immigrants before them. As one individual from an earlier wave lamented, "They now know exactly what labels of clothes and other goods they want." Included in the last two waves are those ethnic Hungarians who came from Transylvania and left primarily for political reasons—because they were discriminated against—and who have no desire to return permanently. Many of these individuals are very active in various chapters of the American Transylvanian Federation, in tradition-maintaining circles, and in churches, yet in general they stay away from other Hungarian-American associations. Like most newcomers, these people focus their everyday activities in trying to make an economic go of it in the United States, which in the 1990s, has offered fewer opportunities than these immigrants had initially hoped. The strain in the relationship between the last two groups and the earlier waves of immigrants is particularly evident in contemporary Hungarian-American associational life, which, contrary to earlier expectations of scholars and members of these associations, the newcomers failed to revitalize. Moreover, the political activities of some members of the last two waves, and their intense involvement in the political, social,

and cultural issues of the homeland, are most evident on the Internet, where there are very heated and ongoing political discussions among some newcomers, usually those who comprise the latest wave of the brain drain from their homeland.

Surprisingly few individuals from these more recent immigrant waves permanently returned to Hungary since the end of the socialist regime in the land that even after many decades remains what immigrants often call "our beloved homeland." Why did the DPs, '56er, and some of the "Kádár orphans" not return to Hungary permanently after 1989? These are the very people who still have strong, although different, identifications with Hungary and who left mainly for political reasons; it would appear that the demise of communism also put an end to the commonly held reason for which they initially left their homeland. Many of these individuals have families and other "roots" in the United States, so they remain. Yet DPs and some of the interwar immigrants have a very strong (though romanticized) and, for all practical purposes, archaic political identification with what they consider "all things Hungarian." Many of the '56ers and some of the later immigrants also have as strong an adherence to their own images of Hungary. According to their motivation for leaving Hungary they rationalize why they do not want to return to "the beloved motherland," where, as they repeat during numerous formal occasions, one "must live and die." One DP, a former judge of a military tribunal during the darkest period of World War II and who has never returned for even brief visits to Hungary since December 1944, is still afraid of reprisals from possible survivors, though what he gives as a reason is a convoluted argument about Hungary no longer being his real Hungary but a tragic dominion of the former Soviet Union. Another immigrant, who with his family has been a frequent visitor to Hungary since the late 1960s, says that he would not want to return because of the lack of proper infrastructure there. A '56er, an engineer and a most successful businessman in two states who also has been a frequent visitor to his homeland since 1968, complains that he would return but the "Hungarians do not open up" to him, and they fail to listen to or take his advice, though he could easily turn Hungary into a "tourist paradise." The few individuals who returned permanently to Hungary and were later interviewed were '56ers. They were disappointed in what they found and complained that they got very little respect, much blame, and open disapproval by friends, relatives, and former neighbors in Hungary. The "Kádár orphans" and particularly the "Ceausescu orphans" (those ethnic Hungarians who left Romania during the Ceausescu regime between 1965 and 1989) aim for and are explicit about one primary goal: to make an economic success and a better life for their children in the United States. Among the latter group—the ethnic Hungarians who came from Romania and other neighboring countries—there is a strong conviction that, as ethnic Hungarians, they would be considered an unwanted minority, regardless of the regime. Some of these individuals are confident—as ironical as this may sound—that in the United States they finally have a chance to become "real" Hungarians and maintain their traditions.

Culture

For many—possibly most—of these immigrants, Hungary is no longer where their homeland is geographically located, and not only because they also feel loyalty and gratitude to their chosen host country. Rather, the immigrants continually reconstruct their natal homeland with actual or presumed Hungarian festive and everyday foods, specialty baked goods, and religious and secular customs and rituals, as well as by decorating their homes, churches, restaurants, coffeehouses, cultural centers, and other private and public spheres

Hungarian-American musicians in traditional costume perform for a dance. (Éva Veronika Huseby-Darvas)

with a rich assemblage of material culture. There are specially woven or lavishly embroidered tablecloths and runners, and pillowcases that show typical, and believed to be traditional, flowered or geometrical designs readily identified as from the homeland. In some of these places, there are even specially carved wood furniture, wallpaper, and carvings in the homes that are also filled with Hungarian and Hungarian-American books, dance compositions, and recorded music. Some assemble remarkable memorial parks, like the one in Berkeley Springs, West Virginia. Others—for example, groups of Hungarian Americans in Cleveland and elsewhere—stage annual folkplays, comedies, and parodies about traditional village weddings and the burial of the bass fiddle. Still others tenaciously organise cultural events that focus on recitals of Hungarian poetry and drama, political events such as annual commemorations of revolutions, and social events such as annual dances and fancy-dress balls, pig roasts, grape harvest celebrations, and Hungarian Days. During most of these events and gatherings there are overt manifestations of elements of Hungarian material culture. With the help of these selected symbols, signs, and other cultural elements (which at times are more cherished and recognized by immigrants than by visitors from the natal country) there is an ongoing construction and legitimization of a most variegated Hungarian-American culture and differentiated immigrant identity.

Demographics

While it is difficult to state with certainty how many Hungarian Americans there are and their socioeconomic circumstances, some information can be obtained from the 1990 U.S. Census. The data of the Hungarian-American population mirror not only the equally aging groups but also the very low reproduction rate in Hungary (though during the first couple of decades of the twentieth century the fecundity rate among immigrant women from Hungary was more than twice that of native-born women). Including the "natives," who were born

A Hungarian-American woman prepares special Hungarian noodles. (Éva Veronika Huseby-Darvas)

in the United States but identify themselves as Hungarians by one or more ancestor, as well as the foreign or foreign-born (immigrants who were born in Hungary or in the neighboring countries), there are approximately 997,545 Hungarian Americans, who live in 446,741 households. While there are Hungarian Americans in all fifty states, the ten states they most favor are Ohio (144,002), New York (115,981), California (104,722), Pennsylvania, (92,006), New Jersey, (88,361), Michigan (71,135), Florida (68,049), Illinois (40,232), Connecticut (31,631), and Indiana (26,548).

Small households, with one or two individuals, dominate; 27 percent of the natives and 32.6

percent of the foreign live in single-person households, while 35.2 percent of the natives and 35.6 percent of the foreign live in two-person households. Thus the average household size is small, with 2.34 persons per household among the native population and 1.70 persons among the foreign population. The median age of the native Hungarian Americans is 37.1 years, while of their foreign-born counterparts it is a high 56.6.

Even though marriage data do not tell us who marries whom, it is well known from other sources that, particularly since the 1960s, the role of nationality in the immigrants' and their children's selection of spouses is weakening. The 1990 U.S. Census data illustrate that most adult Hungarian Americans are married, and fertility data show that the rate of fecundity, as in the homeland, is very low. For individuals over age fifteen among the foreign-born, 73 percent of the men and 54.4 percent of the women are married, while of their native cohorts 62.4 percent of the men and 54.8 percent of the women are married. Cohabitation in unmarried partnerships appears to be rare; 1.4 percent of the natives and 0.94 percent of the foreign-born admitted to such an arrangement. The rate of divorce among native men is 6.5 percent, and 9 percent among the women; it is 8.6 percent among the foreign men and 9 percent among the foreign women.

Women of childbearing age are defined by the U.S. Census as between ages fifteen and forty-four, among the natives there are 997 children per 1,000 women in this cohort, while among the foreign there are 1,434 children per 1,000 women. Neither number reaches anywhere near the replacement of the population. The majority of Hungarian-American nuclear families with children under age eighteen appears to be "intact," if the data that among the foreign 86.1 percent and among the native 82.2 percent of children under age eighteen live in a household where both of their parents are present are a reliable indication of that.

Among all Hungarian Americans who are twenty-five years of age or older, 80.8 percent have completed high school (82.9 percent of the natives and 69.7 percent of the foreign), while 26.8 per-

cent have at least a bachelor's degree from a college or university (27.2 of the natives and 24.4 percent of the foreign). The economic status of Hungarian Americans is reflected in per capita and family median incomes. Among the natives the 1989 per capita income was $19,883, while among the foreign this was $25,712; the family median income for the natives was $42,714, and for the foreign this was $43,266. The family mean income for the natives was $54,739; for the foreign, $59,076. While it appears from these figures that the foreign do considerably better financially than the natives, data on individuals who live below the poverty level, particularly those sixty-five or older, seem to contradict this. Among the native families, 4.2 percent live below the poverty line, while among the foreign this figure is 4.9 percent; but among those natives who are sixty-five years old or older, 13.1 percent live below the poverty line, while 25.1 percent of their foreign cohorts do.

Among native individuals over age sixteen, 4.5 percent are unemployed, while among the foreign this is 5.3 percent. It is difficult to determine an occupational pattern; however, the data show that more than one-fourth of Hungarian Americans work as professionals or in service-related industries. It is not easy to interpret what the overwhelmingly large category called "Not in the Labor Force" means exactly — people are retired, in school, working "only" in the household, and so on. But in the population over age sixteen among native Hungarian Americans, 38.8 percent of the total, and 43 percent of the women, while among their foreign cohorts 48.4 percent of the total, and 62.9 percent of the women, are not in the labor force. Obviously this is the work pattern of an aging and aged population, yet it is also possible that in part a traditionally much desired but very seldom realized pattern of husbands working and women staying home to maintain the household is reflected by these data.

See also: AUSTRIANS; CZECHS; ROMANIANS; SLOVAKS

Bibliography

Bognár, D. (1971). *Hungarians in America: A Biographical Directory of Professionals of Hungarian Origin in the Americas,* edited by D. K. Bognár. Mount Vernon, NY: Afi.

Dégh, L. (1968–1969). "Survival and Revival of Folk Cultures in America." *Ethnologia Europeae* II–III:97–107.

Dégh, L. (1980). "The Ethnicity of Hungarian Americans." *Congressus Quintus Internationalis Fenno-Ugristarum* IV:255–290.

Dreisziger, N. F., with Kovács, M. L.; Bôdy, P.; and Kovrig, B. (1982). *Struggle and Hope: The Hungarian-Canadian Experience.* Toronto: McClelland & Stewart.

Fermi, L. (1971). *Illustrious Immigrants: The Intellectual Migration from Europe, 1930–1941.* Chicago: University of Chicago Press.

Fishman, J. A. (1966). *Hungarian Language Maintenance in the United States.* Bloomington: Research Center in Anthropology, Folklore, and Linguistics, University of Indiana.

Grácza. R., and Grácza. M. (1969). *The Hungarians in America.* Minneapolis: Lerner.

Huseby-Darvas, É. V. (1990). " 'Wednesday Hungarians' and Csiga-Noodlemaking in Southeast Michigan." *The Digest: A Review for the Interdisciplinary Study of the Uses of Food* 9(2):4–8.

Huseby-Darvas, É. V. (1994). " 'Coming to America': The Dilemmas of Ethnic Groups Since the 1880s." In *The Development of Arab-American Identity,* edited by E. McCarus. Ann Arbor: University of Michigan Press.

Huseby-Darvas, É. V. (1995). "The Search for Hungarian National Identity." In *Ethnic Identity: Continuities and Change,* 3rd edition, edited by L. Romanucci Ross and G. DeVos. Walnut Creek, CA: AltaMira Press.

Hutchinson, E. P. (1956). *Immigrants and Their Children, 1850–1950.* New York: Wiley.

Kontra, M. (1995). "Changing Names: Onomastic Remarks on Hungarian-Americans." *Journal of English Linguistics* 23:114–122.

Kósa, J. (1956). *Land of Choice.* Toronto: University of Toronto Press.

Lengyel, E. (1948). *Americans from Hungary.* Philadelphia: J. B. Lippincott.

Office of Refugee Resettlement. (1986, 1993). *Report to the Congress: Refugee Resettlement Program.* Washington, DC: U.S. Department of Health and Human Services.

Pulitzer, P. (1990). "The Hungarian Community in North America and the Realities of the 1990s." *Educator: The Newsletter of the American-Hungarian Educators' Association* XI(2):1–4.

Puskás, J. (1983). *From Hungary to the United States, 1880–1914.* Budapest: Akadémiai Kiadó.

Puskás, J., ed. (1990). *Overseas Migration from East-Central and Southeastern Europe, 1880–1940.* Budapest: Akadémiai Kiadó.

Schuchat, M. G. (1971). "Hungarian Refugees in America and Their Counterparts in Hungary (Hungarian Food and The Interrelations Between Cosmopolitanism and Ethnicity)." Ph.D. diss., Catholic University of America.

Széplaki, J. (1975). *The Hungarians in America, 1583–1974: A Chronology and Factbook.* Dobbs Ferry, NY: Oceana.

Várdy, S. B. (1985). *The Hungarian Americans.* Boston: Twayne.

Vázsonyi, A. (1978). "The Cicisbeo and the Magnificent Cuckold: Boardinghouse Life and Lore in Immigrant Communities." *Journal of American Folklore* 91:641–656.

Weinstock, S. A. (1969). *Acculturation and Occupation: A Study of the 1956 Hungarian Refugees in the United States.* The Hague: Nijhoff.

ÉVA VERONIKA HUSEBY-DARVAS

HUTTERITES

The Hutterites, or Hutterian Brethern, are a distinctive Christian denomination that originated in sixteenth-century Europe during the Protestant Reformation. They were part of the Anabaptist movement, which also included the Amish and the Mennonites. The Hutterites believe in adult baptism, pacifism, the collective ownership of property, and communal living. These convictions set them apart from the prevailing beliefs of Catholicism and the new Protestant churches emerging from the Reformation. Additionally, the Hutterites lived in their own distinctive communities, separated from what they considered a sinful world. They suffered periodic and severe persecutions, including the forced baptism of their children, imprisonment of their leader, and death. The Hutterites left their original home in Switzerland for refuge in Moravia, now part of modern Germany. In 1536, their most important early leader, Jacob Hutter, was arrested and burned at the stake. Others also suffered martyrdom in subsequent persecutions, but the Hutterites as pacifists would not retaliate against their tormentors. Instead, they continued to seek refuge in various places.

When the Hutterites found safe locales for establishing new communities, their colonies flourished because the people were skilled farmers and artisans as well as thrifty managers of their collective holdings. Success sometimes brought on the envy of their less prosperous neighbors in addition to the ever-present danger of religious intolerance. Thus a cycle of relative peace and prosperity followed by persecution and martyrdom continued for two hundred years in Austria, Moravia, Slovakia, and Transylvania. By the eighteenth century the small remaining number of Hutterites found safe haven in the Ukraine, where abundant land was available to them. The authorities pledged that the Hutterites could freely practice their religion and way of life, engage in various crafts, and enjoy exemption from military service. That arrangement continued for about a century, at which time the Russian czar canceled earlier guarantees and agreements, particularly regarding military exemption. By the 1870s, the Hutterites faced conscription into the Russian army and once again had to flee if they were to continue the unimpeded practice of their pacifist faith and communal style of living. Throughout this period the Hutterites also continued to speak German, which is a central feature of their identity.

Proliferation of Colonies

Between 1874 and 1877, approximately twelve hundred Hutterites left Russia and settled in South Dakota, where they have enjoyed prosperity and growth, unimpeded by the periodic persecutions so common during three centuries of life in Europe. Yet even in the United States, Hutterites have at times suffered for their beliefs. American entry into World War I stimulated a patriotic fervor resulting in harassment of the Hutterites because of the refusal of their young men to serve in the military. Their use of German also aroused hostility and suspicion.

Some eight hundred of the South Dakota settlers decided to start their new lives on private plots of land, individually owned. Known as the *prairieleut* (prairie people), they thus broke with the Hutterite tradition of collective ownership. Many later affiliated with the Mennonites, related Anabaptists who do not live communally nor hold property in common. The remaining Hutterites belonged to three sections, or *leut* (people), named for their leaders at the time of immigration to South Dakota. They are the Darius Leut, Schmieden Leut, and Lehrer Leut.

The new American Hutterite communities started English schools so their children would learn the language of their adopted country and thus understand their non-Hutterite neighbors. But German has remained the mother tongue. It embodies Hutterite values and serves as the medium of their worship, sermons, sacred texts, and intracolony activity. English, by contrast, is associated with worldliness, and consequently the Hutterites closely scrutinize English-language instruction to ensure that alien influences do not corrupt their children.

Since first forming in South Dakota, Hutterite colonies have proliferated and now number 368 worldwide, with a population of approximately 20,000. The Hutterites have established 113 colonies in the United States and 252 in the Canadian provinces of Alberta, Saskatchewan, and Manitoba. American Hutterite colonies include 51 in South Dakota, 40 in Montana, 6 in North Dakota, 5 each in Minnesota and Washington, 3 in New York, 2 in Pennsylvania, and 1 in Connecticut. Hutterite communities exist once more in Europe, as settlements have started in England and Germany.

Hutterite elders in Miller Colony, Montana, gather around to re-examine their version of the Bible. (Ted Streshinsky/Corbis)

While various social experiments in communal living, such as the Oneida and Amana colonies, have dotted the American landscape since the early nineteenth century, the Hutterites represent the most successful and enduring of these innovative designs for collective living and collective ownership based on religious belief. Indeed, the Hutterites have survived for more than four hundred years, longer than any comparable collectivist community.

Traditions and Values

The Hutterites dress in a distinctive manner that visibly defines who they are and distinguishes them from non-Hutterites. Adult males wear black denim pants with suspenders. Because the Hutterites associate blue jeans with the worldliness of non-Hutterites, they must not wear this color of denim. Coats are black, although shirts of various colors may be worn. Men must wear white shirts for church services. Married men grow beards in accordance with biblical command. Women dress in an equally plain, austere manner, wearing skirts reaching to their ankles; blouses; long aprons; and a long-sleeved jacket, vest, or outer wrap. They also wear head coverings such as small scarves. In the simplicity of their dress and their condemnation of body adornments, the Hutterites indicate their triumph over physical desire and self-indulgence.

Settling in agricultural areas and making their living on the land have helped to protect Hutterite communities from the intrusion of beliefs and practices that might undermine their culture. Hutterite colonies and communalism would hardly be possible in or near cities. Living in rural areas thus helps to insulate the Hutterites from intrusive and corrupting worldly influences. Ideally the Hutterite colony should provide communal self-support without necessitating wage labor away from the settlement. Nevertheless, some colonies are less successful economically than others, and some men must get temporary jobs away from the colony. The rural setting of Hutterite colonies can help check these influences, such as individualism or property accumulation, before they begin to undermine the values on community and self-denial.

The Hutterites recognize the burden of curbing individual appetites, including the desire to gain access to material goods in excess of what the community allows. Still, the Hutterites by and large achieve their ideals through the intense control of individual behavior exerted by church teaching, the daily example of austere living set by other colony members, and managerial control of colony money. Moreover, workers within the community receive no wages. Rather, the manager allocates a monthly stipend to each family. To reach their ideals, the Hutterites depend not only on their religious values but also on specific policies that actively discourage behavior out of keeping with Hutterite principles.

Community Organization

The way of life of the Hutterites is so thoroughly determined by their system of belief that any understanding of their communities must begin with religion. It pervades every feature of the colony, and therefore the church and the community are virtually identical in Hutterite thinking. Almost every dimension of communal life takes on religious significance. The authority of God is unquestioned and encompasses the social and economic arrangements within the colony. The religious foundation of the Hutterites is the Bible, especially the New Testament, accepted literally by the people. They are thus true fundamentalists, for they see in the Bible the revealed word of God.

A Hutterite shoemaker in Bynum, Montana, examines his work. (Dewitt Jones/Corbis)

Their model of appropriate living derives from the earliest days of Christianity, when the church represented a small community of true believers modeling their lives on the holiness and perfection of Christ. Like other Christian denominations, the Hutterites believe that humankind fell from grace through Adam's disobedience. The loss of this blessed state led humankind to selfishness, immodesty, and pleasure-seeking. People can, however, repair their relationship with God by accepting Christ. But beyond this generalized Christian view, the Hutterites are distinctive in believing that salvation depends on more than faith. They must also live communally, thereby establishing the kind of social relationships marked by the early church. These social relationships entail communal solidarity and collective submission to God's command, requiring that one also give up individual desire and choice in favor of the collective will of the church/community. By separating themselves from the world and living in their own colonies with shared property, the Hutterites surrender themselves to God and reestablish the original state of grace.

While some variation occurs among Hutterite communities, a common pattern of organization characterizes them. Like all other aspects of their life, the Hutterites believe that the operation of the group and its leadership derive from God. A general manager assumes responsibility for overseeing the economic life of the colony, now based on diversified commercial farming and mechanized agricultural. Craft production, characteristic of the Hutterites in their early days, has largely disappeared. The general manager supervises the activities of other managers in charge of one or another of the productive activities of the colony, including raising chickens and livestock. In addition, colony members serve as carpenters or specialists in repair and maintenance of equipment. The general manager, production managers, and the preacher constitute the elders and serve as the managing council of the colony.

All baptized people in the community are at the same time members of the church, although men and women assume very different roles. The men may vote on matters brought before them, and male elders assume responsibility for the everyday running of the colony. Before voting the men of the colony pray for guidance, as they believe that the majority carries out the will of God. Therefore, minority voters endorse the majority decision so that they, too, may accede to the divine will. Women, on the other hand, have no role in decisions affecting the entire community. They neither vote nor participate in any policy discussion about the community.

Hutterite colonies require all members to work at tasks the colony assigns them. Work itself takes place for the common good and common need, not for individual benefit, advancement, or monetary profit. A strict division of labor by sex assigns able-bodied men to agricultural work producing colony income. Women's labor centers on family and domestic tasks. With the help of young girls, women tend the kitchen, operate the kindergarten, clean, and sew. Women may neither vote nor hold any office within the colony. Hutterite belief affirms that women are not the equal to men, either in terms of strength or intelligence, and therefore women require male guidance and supervision. Here, too, the Bible provides the rationale for beliefs and practices supporting sexual inequality.

Families and Responsibility

Communal values and sharing extend to residential and eating patterns. Each Hutterite family occupies a meagerly furnished apartment in one of the collective dwelling units of the colony. Considerable amounts of interaction and visiting occur among members of different families residing in neighboring apartments. Privacy is of little concern. Children of different families play throughout the building, and responsibility for their care belongs to the entire colony rather to the parents acting alone. Likewise, families visit freely, not bothering to knock on each other's door or even to hesitate before entering an apartment if the resident family is not home. Colony members eat their meals together three times a day in the communal kitchen, where women not only prepare the food but also do the laundry. An entire colony thus operates as a kind of extended cooperative family, sharing goods, resources, and responsibilities.

Families tend to be large because the Hutterites condemn birth control as a sinful practice. A woman bearing ten children is not unusual. Because of the communal nature of Hutterite society, a mother can immediately depend on the assistance of other women of the colony, particularly her relatives, just after a baby is born. Later, the colony kindergarten and school also ensure that responsibility for children is shared. The youngest children begin learning the values of cooperation and modesty. The colony strongly discourages competition among children, thus ignoring or minimizing the real differences of ability and aptitude that may exist.

By age fifteen, young people begin to assume adult responsibilities in regard to work, although the gradual transition to adult roles begins earlier. Boys as young as ten herd and feed livestock and collect eggs. Girls help the women in communal food preparation and perform domestic tasks within their own families. Teenage boys more fully enter the work world of adults, joining the men as field hands, apprentices to the managers, or operators of the colony's agricultural machinery. Teenage girls continue to work at the domestic routines they began performing as children.

Choosing Baptism

In young adulthood, Hutterites begin thinking about baptism—the single most important ritual in Hutterite society. Baptism represents a critical rite of passage, marking the transition from worldliness to spiritualty, from self-seeking to self-denial, from individual to collective concerns. Interests in material goods and personal ambition give way as young people begin to embrace the common good. Many young men do not opt for baptism until their mid-twenties; young women, more commonly, undergo baptism by age twenty. A group of young people experience baptism together, following their request for the ritual and the community's acceptance. The community will

Two Hutterite women wear polka-dot scarves, floral dresses, and plaid aprons on a Hutterite colony in Sweetgrass, Montana. (Michael S. Yamashita/Corbis)

not grant its approval if anyone expresses disapproval or registers a grievance against a person seeking baptism. The desire for baptism avows Anabaptist faith and represents the considered, conscious choice of people earnestly seeking full membership in the community. Baptism does not occur until the young candidates complete approximately two months of instruction, requiring study of Hutterite religious texts. During this period they must also demonstrate to the satisfaction of the community that they have abandoned willfulness in favor of submission before the collective authority of the colony.

Prior to choosing the Hutterite religion and way of life, some young people may have learned about the outside world as a result of living away from the colony. It is generally expected that during this time away, youths may act like other adolescents in carefree, self-indulgent ways at odds with Hutterite values. Their indulgence in worldly

activities occurs without arousing much concern in the colony, since they are not baptized. But their choice of baptism and commitment to the community effectively ends this period of sowing wild oats. Following the ritual young people become full-fledged members of the church and colony, thus subjecting themselves to the discipline and obligations of Hutterite life. But by then they are ready to assume those responsibilities, since they have consciously chosen the Hutterite way and withdrawal from the world.

Group Conformity

Aside from the expectation that a person will choose a Hutterite spouse, the decision to marry is very much a matter of individual choice. While parents may well express their opinions about their children's prospective mates, they exercise no other influence. Courtship extends over a period of months and affords very little opportunity for the young couple to spend more than a few minutes alone. Once the marriage takes place, the colony establishes the newlyweds in an apartment and provides them with the modest requirements of domestic life.

Although the Hutterite creed identifies the welfare of the individual with the welfare of the group, disharmony and discord erupt from time to time. Pressure to conform to the group is intense and usually sufficient to check antisocial behavior. The ultimate punishment for the most serious breaches of community standards is expulsion, but this sanction rarely occurs. The mere possibility of its use is generally sufficient to ensure conformity. But to clear the air of lingering bad feelings, a yearly church meeting in the spring requires that individuals who have had altercations over the previous months publicly report the resolution of their problems. In this way people can continue to live together interdependently and cooperatively, thus reinforcing the most fundamental Hutterite values.

Still, social mechanisms for resolving discord and ensuring conformity sometimes fail. People occasionally abandon the colony for life in the outside world. Many ultimately return, thus indicating the very strong appeal of the Hutterite way of life to those reared in the tradition. Permanent losses are not so numerous as to threaten the existence of a colony. Nonetheless, defectors cause distress within the community. People leave for various reasons, including unresolved conflicts within the group, the appeal of individualist values that one may have encountered when living away, or the emergence of personal ambitions incapable of satisfaction within a radically communal social order.

Conclusion

Social and physical isolation, collective pressure against individualism and for conformity, and economic communalism sharply distinguish the Hutterites from other ethnic communities in the United States. Most ethnic groups over the course of a few generations have in the main accommodated themselves to American economic and social institutions. They have likewise adopted pervasive American cultural values emphasizing individuality and economic and material accumulation.

While the Hutterites have not remained static, they closely control what elements from the outside can acceptably enter their communities. Hutterite success in commercial agricultural, for example, has depended on the use of modern farm machinery. Hutterite communities remain open to additional technological devices that will solve practical problems. Other, nontechnical innovations that threaten Hutterian religious values and the communal social and economic order will continue to encounter the strongest resistance. That resistance underlies the success of Hutterian communities and is the key to their future.

See also: AMISH; GERMANS; MENNONITES

Bibliography

Bennett, J. W. (1967). *Hutterian Brethern: The Agricultural Economy and Social Organization of a Communal People.* Stanford, CA: Stanford University Press.

Conkin, P. K. (1964). *Two Paths to Utopia: The Hutterites and the Llano Colony.* Lincoln: University of Nebraska Press.

Flint, D. (1975). *The Hutterites: A Study in Prejudice.* Toronto: Oxford University Press.

Hostetler, J. A. (1974). *Hutterite Society.* Baltimore, MD: Johns Hopkins University Press.

Hostetler, J. A., and Huntington, G. E. (1967). *The Hutterites in North America.* New York: Holt, Rinehart and Winston.

Packull, W. O. (1995). *Hutterite Beginnings.* Baltimore, MD: Johns Hopkins University Press.

Peter, K. A. (1987). *The Dynamics of Hutterite Society.* Edmonton: University of Alberta Press.

Satterlee, J. (1993). *The Hutterites: A Study in Cultural Diversity.* Brookings: Agricultural Experiment Station, South Dakota State University.

Stephenson, P. H. (1991). *The Hutterian People: Ritual and Rebirth in the Evolution of Communal Life.* Lanham, MD: University Press of America.

JACK GLAZIER

ICELANDERS

Icelanders emigrated from Iceland, an island in the North Atlantic just below the Arctic Circle. The land area is about the same as that of Ohio or Virginia. In 1994, there were about 262,000 people in Iceland, with almost half living in or near the capital, Reykjavik. On the eve of immigration to America in the 1870s, the population was about 70,000. In 1990, there were 40,529 people in the United States who claimed some Icelandic ancestry. They have never been given a nickname; they are simply Icelanders. They are a part of Scandinavia and consider themselves Europeans.

Immigration History

The first Icelanders to immigrate were Mormons, who arrived in Utah in the 1850s. By 1990, there were 2,970 in Utah who claimed Icelandic ancestry, presumably descendants of the original settlers. They settled around Spanish Fork, where a much larger number of Danish Mormons had put down roots.

The mass emigration from Iceland to America was during the 1870s and 1880s, with the vast majority coming in the 1880s. The first permanent settlement of any size was in Minnesota, centered around the town of Minneota in Lyon County. The first to come took land in Yellow Medicine County, to the north. Others followed and farmed in Lincoln County, west of Lyon County, but Minneota became the focal point. Why did they leave Iceland? Iceland has an active system of volcanoes that, over the past eleven hundred years of settlement, have periodicaly brought wisespread destruction of the land, crops, and livestock. According to the official handbook on Iceland, published in 1986 by the Bank of Iceland, an eruption in 1783 "poured out the largest lava flow on Earth in at least the last thousand years." It was the eruption of another volcano, in the east of Iceland in 1875, and a smallpox epidemic, that prompted a flood of refugees to find a better place to live. Yet it was not simply disaster at home; it was also the availability of land in America. Letters from Norwegians and Danes in America played a role, as did news from a handful of Icelanders who had gone to Wisconsin in 1870. Their letters home were influential after the 1875 eruption. For these reasons, most of the immigrants came from the east, but some also came from the north of Iceland.

Why did Icelanders first go to southwestern Minnesota? In 1873, some fifty immigrants arrived in Wisconsin. An American-educated Icelandic Lutheran pastor, Pall Thorlaksson, persuaded Norwegian farmers in Dane County, Wisconsin, to take the new arrivals on as hired hands to learn farming techniques in the Midwest. In 1875, a Norwegian farmer decided to move to the Minneota area with his Icelandic apprentice and family. The following year a few more Icelandic families followed, and in 1877, fifty more immigrants came directly from Iceland. It was the first settlement of any size in the United States, although a handful of families had settled earlier on Washington Island, off Wisconsin's Green Bay Peninsula.

The second and largest Icelandic settlement in the United States is in Pembina County, in northeast North Dakota. These pioneers were an offshoot of an 1875 group that had taken land at Gimli, on Lake Winnipeg, Manitoba, Canada. While they had escaped the volcanic ash in Iceland, the forested shores of Lake Winnipeg proved a formidable challenge during the first years. The land needed to be cleared and drained, the winters were severe, a smallpox epidemic took many lives, and starvation threatened.

These were the physical conditions that greeted Thorlaksson when he arrived at Gimli during the winter of 1877–1878. A religious controversy also was raging between conservative and liberal Lutherans. Thorlaksson was deemed the more conservative of the two pastors at Gimli. He persuaded more than half the community—some one hundred Icelanders—to follow him to Pembina County, then in Dakota Territory. Great respect and admiration were and still are accorded to Thorlaksson by the North Dakota Icelanders. His untiring efforts to look after both the physical and spiritual needs of his people were heroic. He died in 1882 of tuberculosis at age thirty-two. His motivation in establishing a North Dakota colony was the prospect for a more favorable economy.

A secondary settlement appeared in the mid-1880s in North Dakota. With the influx of arrivals from Iceland, the best land in the Red River Valley and land adjacent to it had been taken. A few young men struck out for McHenry County, in north-central North Dakota. Here they apprenticed themselves to Anglo stock raisers and eventually became cattlemen as well as farmers. This offshoot of the Pembina County settlement was eventually referred to as the Upham settlement, named after a small town that was founded shortly after their arrival. Although much smaller then the Pembina settlement, the Upham group had an active community life. At its peak early in the twentieth century there about sixty families. With the Great Depression and drought of the 1930s, the federal government bought much of their land for a wildlife refuge. While a few remained, most left, some going to the Pembina area. In addition to the three settlements in Minnesota and North Dakota, a handful of Icelanders settled in Roseau County, Minnesota, and Shawano County, Wisconsin, and a few remained elsewhere in Wisconsin.

Demographics

How many came to these settlements from Iceland, and how many claim Icelandic ancestry today? It was not until 1930 that the U.S. Census included Icelanders as a separate group. Prior to 1930, they were counted as Danish immigrants. The only information about Icelanders in the U.S. Census before 1930 appears under "mother tongue," beginning in 1910. Even after 1930, information on Icelanders has remained scant contrasted with that available for other immigrant groups. Consequently the numbers of Icelandic immigrants and their progeny are only estimates. A cautious estimate for the number who came to the United States between 1870 and 1900 is about 5,000. Another 7,000 to 10,000 went to Canada.

The 1990 U.S. Census listing of 40,529 persons claiming Icelandic ancestry represented an infinitesimal percentage—0.0162—of the total U.S. population. The other four Nordic countries (Finland, Denmark, Norway, and Sweden) add up to less than 5 percent (11,520,677). Whether people of Icelandic lineage claim single or mixed ancestry is not given. It can be safely assumed, however, that it is overwhelmingly mixed.

In spite of their very small numbers, the major Icelandic settlements in Minnesota and North Dakota achieved a high profile among their neighbors during the early days of settlement, one that continues to this day. They were invariably surrounded and far outnumbered by Anglos, Irish, Germans, and other Scandinavians. In 1910, the township manuscript rolls for the Pembina and McHenry County settlements, the nearby towns, and the largest cities in North Dakota show 2,784 born in Iceland. This would not include their children born in America. The Minneota settlement in Minnesota had 452 born in Iceland in 1895 and 386 in 1905. On the other hand, the 1910 U.S. Census states that 5,105 persons in the United States had grown up in homes in which the first language was Icelandic.

The tide of Icelandic immigration to the United States clearly peaked in the 1880s, and by 1900, the numbers had fallen off significantly. The reason was better conditions in Iceland. The Minneota community comprising Lyon, Yellow Medicine, and Lincoln counties has experienced a significant decline in numbers. Today few Icelandic farmers are left — perhaps twenty. The others have, over the decades, moved into surrounding towns, but even more to the large cities in Minnesota and elsewhere. As pointed out above, the same can be said for the Icelandic farmers in McHenry County, North Dakota. While there is still an Icelandic presence there, it is small. A 1983 study by William C. Sherman found twenty-nine rural Icelandic households in the McHenry County settlements as of 1965. These people, too, have gone to nearby towns and larger cities such as Minot, North Dakota. In contrast, the rural Pembina County settlement has maintained the boundaries it established by the early 1880s, while at the same time sending even more of its young people off to the cities. Western Pembina County continues to be the largest rural Icelandic settlement in the United States. The Sherman study found 186 rural Icelandic households there as of 1965.

The distribution of the 40,529 people in the 1990 U.S. Census claiming Icelandic ancestry shows no resemblance — with one exception — to the original distribution. First, Icelanders are overwhelmingly urban; second, there are persons of Icelandic ancestry in every state. States with the fewest are Delaware (29), Vermont (44), and Mississippi (84). The Pacific states collectively have the highest number: California (6,512), Washington (5,976), and Oregon (1,200), for a total of 13,688, more than one-third of those claiming Icelandic ancestry in the United States. Some first-generation Icelanders left the Midwest for Seattle, in particular, by 1900. With the exception of Florida (1,348), Icelanders have not settled in any significant numbers in the South. As of 1990, about 40 percent of Icelandic Americans lived in three areas: the Pacific Coast states, Arizona and Colorado, and Florida.

Despite the wide dispersal of Icelanders from Minnesota and North Dakota, these two states of original settlement continue to hold a large and almost identical number of Icelanders — 3,165 and 3,161, respectively. The only states with more in 1990 were California and Washington. Wisconsin, an entry point for some Icelanders, trails with 809, a significant number.

Language

The Icelandic language has changed little during the past nine hundred years, at least in its written form. Schoolchildren today in Iceland can read the prose and poetry of the 1200s. As immigrants they were fortunate in that many knew Danish and could also converse with some Norwegian immigrants from the west coast of Norway. This was helpful in their early years in America. More important, however, was their ability to learn English in a short time. In large part, this was a result of their commitment to education at all levels.

By the mid-twentieth century, use of the Icelandic language was less and less common in America, and by 1990, only the very elderly had any mastery of it. The Ladies' Aid Society in Pembina County kept its record in Icelandic until 1955. Church services and instruction in Icelandic were discontinued by the early 1940s. At the 1978 centennial celebration of the Pembina County settlement, a good deal of Icelandic could still be heard. If the language fails to survive among those of Icelandic ancestry, there are always the university scholars in America who specialize in medieval Icelandic language and literature. This small group of "Old Norse" scholars pass the language on — mostly to students with no Icelandic ancestry!

Employment and Education

The first Icelandic immigrants became farmers. In the early years they raised sheep as they had in Iceland. Grain farming, however, ultimately came to dominate, especially in North Dakota. Beginning with the first and second generations, a fairly high percentage of Icelanders finished high school

K. N. Julius (left) was a farm laborer whose poetry was read in Iceland as well as in America. Jonas Hallgrimson (center) never attended school but studied law and served as Justice of the Peace for his community for fifty years. Stephan G. Stephansson (right), who founded the Icelandic Cultural Society in North Dakota, was a farmer whose poetry was highly regarded in Iceland. (Joe Hall)

and college. These Icelanders became an important feature of the economic pattern of this group, working as attorneys, physicians, teachers, businessmen, and government white-collar employees. In Pembina County, however, the original — and sizable — farming community remained intact. Few became millionaires, but most were successful.

Studies of Icelandic immigrants in America are few, but in all of these there is strong agreement on one thing: Education is important, and the more the better. An old saying in Icelandic culture is "Better shoeless than bookless." The immigrants were almost entirely literate, and this meant more than a grade school knowledge of language. Virtually all literacy came from instruction in the home. There were no more than a couple of small schools in Iceland in the 1870s. Many cut their teeth on medieval Icelandic poetry and prose. This literature, the "sagas" (stories of historical and legendary exploits), and the language are their cultural possessions. To preserve their purity is sacred. The Bible was also a major part of their early education. This strong penchant for language and literature may explain why so many of the young in American chose the professions of teaching, law, and medicine. This was stimulated by a mania among their parents for buying books for adult reading societies. In North Dakota, a study of public schools attended by Icelandic students indicated that Icelandic families donated many more books to their schools than did other immigrant groups in the area. Many of the teachers were men, at least in the early years of settlement. Indeed, the "hero" in Icelandic society is the "man of words," not the warrior! This drive for higher education is surely the most outstanding characteristic of Icelanders in America. It was a tradition from the old country, one that also explains their rapid assimilation into the host society.

Religion

The Icelandic immigrants were Lutheran. It was a moderate and tolerant Lutheranism. Three churches were built in the Minneota settlement; only one remains today. They were moderates and would even tolerate some freethinkers. The Pembina settlement had seven churches in the compact rural colony. Today they are united in one parish, headquartered at Mountain, North Dakota. In the mid-1980s, their pastor, a native of Iceland, estimated that a good 90 percent of his parish was Icelandic. Two towns near the Pembina settlement, Grafton and Pembina, had churches for a few years, but these were shut down.

For a few years in the late nineteenth and early twentieth centuries there were two churches at Gardar, North Dakota, in Pembina County. The congregation had split over the issue of "reason" (or science) versus "revelation." This movement, also strong among Icelandic Canadians in Manitoba, manifested itself as Unitarianism, a liberal religious ideology. It was too liberal for the majority, and they maintained their moderate Lutheranism. Some of the liberals left, such as Stephan G. Stephansson, who went to Alberta to farm. He never joined a Unitarian group but was clearly sympathetic. Stefansson became a poet of exceptional merit among the immigrants, and in Iceland. K. N. Julius, a friend of Stephansson, was also a poet and liberal and is still read in Iceland.

The Upham Icelanders in McHenry County established a church and even hosted the 1928 convention of the Icelandic Evangelical Lutheran Church of America, including the Icelandic Canadians. This church closed down eventually, since many of its members had moved. The Icelandic Synod of America disbanded in 1960, to affiliate with the Evangelical Lutheran Church in America.

Organizations and Publications

Social organizations included bands, cultural societies, literary societies, and choral groups. Several Icelandic halls were built for meetings and socials. Ladies' Aid Societies in the churches were not, properly speaking, social clubs. They were organized to do "the Lord's work" and their contributions to their churches were substantial. The men would donate the land and build the church. Beyond that it was more often the women who would carry on from there, raising money for pews, a finer altar, and whatever else was needed. However, the Ladies' Aid Societies were the primary outlets for the social life of the women.

Icelanders were vitally interested in politics at all levels, although political clubs were never organized. They debated politics, ran for office, and usually were elected as county commissioners, state legislators, attorneys general, and state supreme court justices. If their number was not large in state legislatures or statewide elective offices, they were clearly more prominent than many other — and larger — ethnic groups. A Scandinavian name on a ballot was considered an asset, and Icelandic names generally qualified. The new immigrants were quick to Anglicize their names if it would help others to accept them more readily. Friman became Freeman, Gudmundsson became Goodman, Hallgrimsson became Hall, Jonsson became Johnson, and Benedictsson became Benson. In the early years most voted Republican.

Newspapers in Icelandic have been few. *Lögberg-Heimskringla*, a weekly published in Winnipeg since the 1880s, still has some readers in the United States. It has material in both Icelandic and English. In Minnesota the *Minnesota Mascot*, printed in English, was taken over by an Icelander, Gunnar Bjornson. From 1902 to 1908, he put out a monthly, in Icelandic, with a literary bent. From 1897 to 1905, the *Mascot* printed a quarterly in Icelandic for use in North Dakota Sunday schools. Bjornson's son Valdimar, for many years Minnesota state treasurer, gave Icelandic Americans a high profile. Today, Bill Holm, an Icelandic American and writer-poet, keeps the spirit alive. For the North Dakota settlement, the Arctic explorer and author Vilhjalmur Stefansson remains its most famous son.

Conclusion

There can be no doubt that the offspring of the original five thousand or so Icelandic immigrants to the United States have been fully integrated into American society. They have never been isolated for discrimination. The language is virtually gone, and it is ironic that the most important cultural possession in the old country, the Icelandic language, is the one thing the immigrants have not preserved. On the other hand, they have preserved the love of learning and intellectual curiosity. There has been, of course, a small but steady flow of Icelanders to America since World War II. Today, there is a project afoot in Florida to establish a registry of Icelanders in America, and there are some twenty-four Icelandic societies, mostly in large cities. While few in number, Icelanders in America maintain at least an awareness of their heritage. They show no signs of fading away.

See also: DANES; NORWEGIANS

Bibliography

Holm, B. (1994a). "The Icelanders of Minneota." In *The New Icelanders: A North American Community,* edited by D. Arnason and V. Arnason. Winnipeg, MB: Turnstone Press.

Holm, B. (1994b). "The Icelandic Emigration to Minneota, Minnesota." In *The New Icelanders: A North American Community,* edited by D. Arnason and V. Arnason. Winnipeg, MB: Turnstone Press.

Johnson, S. (1906). "The Icelandic Settlement of Pembina County." In *Collections of the State Historical Society of North Dakota,* Vol. 1, edited by O. G. Libby. Bismarck: State Historical Society of North Dakota.

Kristjanson, W. (1965). *The Icelandic People of Manitoba: A Manitoba Saga.* Winnipeg, MB: Republished by W. A. Kristjanson.

Palmer, H. (1983). "Escape from the Great Plains: The Icelanders in North Dakota and Alberta." In *The Great Plain Quarterly,* Vol. 1. Lincoln, NE: Center for Great Plains Studies.

Regan, A. (1981). "Icelanders." In *They Chose Minnesota: A Survey of the State's Ethnic Groups,* edited by S. Thernstrom. St. Paul: Minnesota Historical Society Press.

Sherman, W. C. (1983). *Prairie Mosaic: An Ethnic Atlas of Rural North Dakota.* Fargo: North Dakota Institute for Regional Studies.

Thorson, P. V. (1986). "Icelanders." In *Plains Folk: North Dakota's Ethnic History,* edited by W. C. Sherman and P. V. Thorson. Fargo: North Dakota Institute for Regional Studies.

Walters, T. J. (1953). *Modern Sagas: The Story of the Icelanders in America.* Fargo: North Dakota Institute for Regional Studies.

PLAYFORD V. THORSON

IGBO

The Igbo (also known as Ibo, or by themselves in the United States as Ndi Igbo), because they speak a distinct African language called Igbo, constitute a distinct language and ethnic group among the immigrant Nigerian, West African, and African communities in the United States.

Origins

All Igbo people have a genealogical link through kinship ties to a geographical homeland known as Ala Igbo or Ani Igbo (Igboland) in southeastern and parts of midwestern Nigeria, where towns, villages, and village groups are generally identified by distinct names of their ancestral founders or by place names. The Igbo numbered about 8.5 million in 1963 and had grown to more than 15 million (some might even claim 30 million or more) by 1993. Presently in Nigeria, they constitute the states of Enugu, Anambra, Abia, and Imo as well as the Ahoada area of Rivers State, while Igbo-speaking people west of the Niger River are in the Asaba, Ika, and Agbo areas of Delta State.

Demography

Igbo immigration can be examined as part of the general patterns of Nigerian immigration to the United States, since figures provided by the Statistical Division of the U.S. Immigration and Naturalization Service give information on ancestry of Africans based on countries of origin, not ethnic origin. There also are no statistics giving places and patterns of settlement, and patterns of circular and return migration. The figures indicate that one

African was admitted into the United States in 1820 and a total of 201,679 Africans gained entry into the United States between 1820 and 1983. Between 1983 and 1993, a total of 238,471 Africans were admitted into the United States, 48,101 of whom were Nigerian by birth. The U.S. Census records 86,875 Nigerians for 1990. The Igbo would constitute well over half of this Nigerian population. Igbo immigration to the United States started well before 1983, including sporadic cases of individual students or professionals who settled after completing their studies. Between 1974 and 1983, a total of 13,366 Nigerians by birth were admitted to the United States. The secessionist Biafran War (1967–1970) stimulated substantial Igbo immigration to and settlement in the United States. The immigration of large numbers of highly qualified Igbo professionals and their families in the 1990s can be attributed to political and economic instability in Nigeria. In the 1980s, a large number of professionals returned to the homeland, but this turned into circular migration in the 1990s. The Igbo are present in most large U.S. cities and their suburbs but have greater concentration in New York, Washington, D.C., Los Angeles, Houston, and Dallas.

Language

The Igbo have their own distinct language, called Igbo, and also speak English as a first language, since English is the official language and the medium of instruction in Nigeria. Of the 86,875 Nigerians in the 1990 U.S. Census, 75,457 were persons over five years of age who spoke English, and 40,105 could speak a language other than English. The Igbo see their language as the umbilical link to the homeland and its culture, and all Igbo ceremonies, prayers, and ethnic association meetings are conducted in Igbo. In some communities Igbo is the first language of a child until age three, when the child is exposed to English and other languages. Through bilingualism at home, ethnic presses, and community language classes, Igbo keep their language alive and try to

pass it on to their children born in the United States. Courses in the Igbo language in some secondary and tertiary educational institutions also contribute to the growth of multilingual education and diversity in the United States.

Cultural Characteristics

For the Igbo, the construction of a single cultural identity or political framework is recent and began with the British colonial administration in 1885. It continues as something necessary for their survival within the Nigerian nation-state and as a diaspora community abroad. To the Igbo, the loss of one's roots is an abomination. A person without roots is an *agafu*, a riffraff or vagabond who does not know his or her origins. In their wider relations with other groups and cultures, the Igbo have been noted as ultrademocratic, highly individualistic in the sense of being independent-minded, insisting on openness, tolerance, and fair play. These are ideals that are thought to carry over from their principles and practice of village democratic confederalism. Both men and women are self-motivated, usually extremely hardworking, and high achievers. They are very philosophical and resilient, a fearless, determined, and proud people. These cultural characteristics enabled them to survive genocide and to reconstruct their society after their crushing defeat by Nigerian federal troops in the Biafran War.

Economic Patterns

A high percentage of Igbo immigrants in the United States are full-fledged professionals making a contribution in every sector of the American economy. They are increasingly in communications, consultancy, engineering, planning, management, transportation, architectural services, law, insurance and finance services, accountancy, computer service, real estate, and medical services. In the 1990 U.S. Census, of 7,245 Nigerians between 18 and 24 years of age, 5,861 were high school or college graduates. Of 52,388 who were 25 years of age or over, only 1,042 had less than a fifth-grade

Children participate in an Igbo Cultural Education Class in Washington, D.C., in 1993. (Ifi Amadiume)

education; 13,948 had a bachelor's degree, of whom 3,650 were female; 10,073 had a master's degree; 1,732 had a professional school degree, of whom 448 were female; and 1,985 had a doctorate, of whom 213 were female. But as immigrants there is no guarantee that these highly qualified professionals will secure the right jobs.

Some Igbo professionals work in restaurants; African craft, garment, and food trade; delivery services; cleaning companies; or utility repair companies. It is not uncommon to discover that a taxi driver in New York or Washington, D.C., is an Igbo with an M.B.A. or a Ph.D. Many Nigerians and other West Africans do extra work to pay their way through college or support relations in the homeland. This remittance economy has been beneficial to all parties, more especially the world economy in stimulating and supporting social change and development initiatives that are not dependent on foreign aid. In this way, immigrants have contributed to local self-initiated social progress and social stability with dignity.

Religion

Igbo immigrants are mostly Christians who attend regular Catholic, Anglican, or Pentecostal/ spiritualist churches. Religious beliefs are, however, syncretic, incorporating prayers to ancestors, who are similar to saints and mediatory spirits, during ceremonial and ritual occasions. Ancestors are invoked as a regulatory and moral force in the lives and conduct of Igbo immigrants. Individuals are reminded that any shame brought on themselves also touches their families at home and the memory of their ancestors. Accordingly, Igbo take death very seriously and treat the dead with reverence, in keeping with ideas and beliefs encoded in traditional Igbo religion. Any Igbo who dies abroad must therefore be returned to be buried in the homeland so that the spirit of the dead will join the world of the ancestors. Consequently Igbo funerals are elaborate and expensive, and ethnic associations come to the aid of their members in providing financial and practical support.

Worldview

The optimistic Igbo worldview symbolized by the links among the living, death, and the afterlife draws its images and metaphors from an ontological world dominated by male ancestors. In this system, the living male, the dead, and the unborn form part of a continuum sharing the mystical power of ancestral blessing. Ontological continuity signified by pride and confidence in the strength and relevance of Igbo culture is more likely to persist with immigrant Igbo males who dominate the ethnic associations than their highly educated and professionally successful female counterparts, who resent this domination. Due to frustration, this class of Igbo women is more likely to accept American concepts of womanhood and use this alien site to challenge male inventions and versions of Igbo culture in the diaspora. This diaspora-produced ontological world is, of course, different from the historical one that gave a prominent place to goddesses and thus supported women's public involvement in village politics in dual-gender Igbo political systems, with women's organizations under the leadership of respected matriarchs who headed village or town women's councils.

The Arts

Igbo aesthetics has given the world much to celebrate in dance, orature, literature, and art. Many Igbo novelists, poets, playwrights, and film and literary critics live in the United States. This includes Africa's foremost novelist, Chinua Achebe, author of the classic novel *Things Fall Apart* (1958). The Igbo are also historically known for their industrial arts, which have produced some of the world's finest ironsmithing, men's wood-carving and fine masks, women's fine pottery and ceramic sculpture, and high-quality patterned woven cloth and mats. Large quantities of these items are imported to and exhibited or sold in the United States. Museums and art galleries in the United States have held successful exhibitions of both traditional and contemporary Igbo art, including an exhibition of Uli art, a traditional Igbo village women's art form that in its contemporary studio form is now very much dominated by men.

Social and Political Oganization

Igbo traditional forms of kinship and kinship ideology of blood relations known as *umunna* and *umunne* provide organizational structures and primary relationships of trust for immigrant families and individuals. Individuals share several levels of collective identities as members of the same descent group, clan, village, village group, or town. Sometimes these organizations, sustained by membership dues and donations, consist of members from different Igbo villages and cultures in a true pan-Igbo ethnic association. New arrivals are welcomed and integrated into the community by long-time resident relatives or by members of Igbo ethnic associations who help with housing, school and college admissions, jobs, or business loans from a bank or one of their numerous savings and loan cooperatives and clubs. In return for social services received, individuals uphold the norms of the Igbo ethnic associations as well as the laws of the host country. If a member gets into serious trouble with the law, the associations provide legal help. In cases of individuals who prove out of control as a result of mental illness or crime, ethnic associations have been known to send such persons back to Nigeria. Successes and failures are shared collectively.

The Nwannedinamba Association was formed in 1985 and is dedicated to the reawakening of Igbo culture in the United States. As such, it has embarked on a $1 million project to build an Igbo cultural center in Washington, D.C. The organization, whose main focus is on educational and civic engagements, sees itself as a pan-Igbo organization for all Ndi Igbo in the United States.

In contrast to the national Igbo membership of the Nwannedinamba Association, the New York metropolitan area harbors closely knit Igbo ethnic organizations and has been described as a miniature Igbo polity. This particular community, with cohesive rituals and ceremonies, is politically or-ganized under an elected leadership. All Igbo na-tionals in this area must also belong to an association called Otu-Ofor. Just as in all other Igbo communities, every year this pan-Igbo civic association organizes the traditional Igbo Ili ji festival, known in the United States as the annual Nigerian New Yam Festival, a grand harvest thanksgiving celebration marked with food con-sumption and cultural display, with dances and drumbeats. During this occasion, friends and neighbors are invited to a feast of boiled yams, goat meat, and spicy chicken. It is a culturally unifying ritual occasion, with distinct ritual officials and ritual procedures for the saying of thanksgiving prayers and the giving of blessings. None of these cultural celebrations ends without the donation of money. Collectively the diaspora group tries to synchronize their own rituals and ceremonies such as birth, marriage, naming, funerals, New Year, and the New Yam celebrations with events in the homeland. Through these cultural performances, the group tries to reproduce itself, as the young and newcomers are socialized into Igbo cultural values. In this way Igbo immigrants resist total loss of identity and assimilation by the hegemonic Judeo-Christian Western European cultures by which they are surrounded.

Marriage and Family

Igbo ideals of marriage as a relationship that extends beyond the married couple to their wider kin have been carried over into the marriage practices of Igbo immigrants in the United States. Many Igbo men, no matter what their level of education, would still return to the homeland or ask their relatives to find a wife. This then sets off the traditional procedure of looking, finding, in-vestigating, and the finalization of marriage. Those who choose a partner in the United States still find it necessary to return home to introduce the

Members of an Igbo family all wear traditional dress. (Ben Igwe)

partner and fulfill customary requirements. Igbo couples usually find themselves going through repeated marriage rituals as they perform the customary wedding, the civil wedding, and the church wedding. Marriage, like all other ceremonies, is an occasion for cultural reaffirmation and gift-giving as a new couple climbs into a more responsible and respectable adult status according to the values of the Igbo community. The community, on its part, keeps an eye on the couple, guiding and supporting them through reproduction, their life together, and death.

Igbo immigrants are family oriented and seek its security and belonging through genuine and fictitious kinship networks that provide informal social welfare systems for immigrants, meeting their social, economic, political, spiritual, and psychological needs. The domestic unit is usually a nuclear family consisting of the mother, the father, and the children. While the husband is generally the breadwinner, the wife can augment his salary with a side jobs, such as running a shop. Sometimes a mother-in-law or other relative is brought over from Nigeria to help new mothers with child care. More professional Igbo women are increasingly heading households as divorced women or single parents.

Relations with Other Groups

Igbo immigrants, like members of other African immigrant communities, have the closest ties with African Americans, with whom there is an intense cultural exchange in the drive for re-Africanization and the Afrocentric movement. For self-help community development, both groups stand to gain culturally and economically from the potential buying power of thirty million African Americans that has been estimated at $270 billion annually. Despite a sometimes difficult relationship with the Africans, African Americans express their admiration for the risk-taking Africans, who often make life from nothing. Igbo immigrants also have a cordial relationship with the wider American public and easily invite neighbors and colleagues to their family and social events. Week-

ends are marked by intense cultural activities, with shopping for Igbo foodstuffs such as *egusi, ogbono, okazi,* palm oil, goat meat, cowfeet, and smoked and dried fish, which are ingredients for a rich Igbo soup. The Igbo also buy gari, yam, and cassava to make their famous foo foo, to be dipped in the soup and skillfully swallowed. The soup, made with *okro* or *ogbono,* slides down the throat much more easily. The Igbo also cherish their fried plantain, jelloff rice, and pepper soup. These dishes are served to guests during various ceremonies. Through these cultural activities, which include pageants and festivals, particularly the annual African Cultural Festival, which the Igbo attend, the Igbo immigrant community promotes intergroup relations and a greater awareness and understanding of African cultural diversity and its rich heritage. Igbo immigrants are usually proud to point out that they have also excelled in sports, naming Christian Okoye, an Igbo who, playing football for the Kansas City Chiefs, led the National Football League in rushing in 1989.

Much as Africans value their ethnic cultures, ethnic organizations of African immigrant communities are far from being ethnically "pure" and involve marriages, in-lawships, and friendships with people of other ethnicities or cultures. Igbo immigrant families and kinships are therefore multicultural and ethnically diverse. The Igbo enjoy situationally invoked multiple identities as pan-Africans, pan-Nigerians, pan-Igbo, and finally their specific Igbo villages or clans.

Discrimination and Cultural Persistence

A great majority of the Igbo as new immigrants lack political rights and usually have to start life anew. Those with lower qualifications find themselves at the bottom of the economic ladder, while some highly qualified professionals have to take low-status jobs to survive. Thus many Igbo immigrants experience rejection and frustration.

In spite of the granting of citizenship, racial polarization in the United States has a direct impact on the survival strategies of immigrant communities. Much as the Igbo treasure openness and democracy, Igbo immigrants have found it necessary to retain and reinvent their traditional values and cultural forms as means of group support and individual survival. This can be seen in the continued use of Igbo names, dress, language, and food. Cultural retention becomes a way to feel at home in an alien environment, and this sometimes is described as spiritual or psychological returning.

See also: AFRICAN AMERICANS; YORUBA

Bibliography

Achebe, C. (1958). *Things Fall Apart*. London: Heinemann.

Anigbo, C. A. (1994). "The African Neo-Diaspora: Dynamics and Prospects for Afrocentrism and Counterpenetration." Ph.D. diss., Howard University.

Herbert, C., and Aniakor, C. (1984). *Igbo Arts: Community and Cosmos*. Los Angeles: Museum of Cultural History, University of California.

Johnson, S. (1993). "Senders and Receivers." *Africa Events* 9(8):19–25.

Mbabuike, M. (1989). "Ethnicity and Ethnoconsciousness in the New York Metropolitan Area: The Case of the Ibos." *Dialectical Anthropology* 14:301–305.

Millman, J. (1994). "Out of Africa—Into America, Immigrant Entrepreneurs Are Remaking Georgia Avenue." *The Washington Post*, October 9.

Mutasa, A. (1993). "Broom Boom." *Africa Events* 9(8):26–28.

Nwabuisi, E. M. (1983). "Investigating How Igbo Socialization Influences the Acquisition of Literacy Among Igbo Children in New York Schools." Ph.D. diss., Teachers College, Columbia University.

Simpson, J. C. (1992). "Buying Black: Mainstream Companies Are Cashing in on African-American Consumers." *Time*, August 31.

Ugwu-Oju, D. (1993). "Pursuit of Happiness." *The New York Times Magazine*, November 14.

U.S. Bureau of the Census. (1990). *1990 Census Population: Ancestry of the Population in the United States*. Washington, DC: U.S. Government Printing Office.

U.S. Immigration and Naturalization Service. (1985). *Statistical Yearbook of the Immigration and Naturalization Service, 1983*. Washington, DC: U.S. Government Printing Office.

U.S. Immigration and Naturalization Service. (1994). *Statistical Yearbook of the Immigration and Naturalization Service, 1993*. Washington, DC: U.S. Government Printing Office.

IFI AMADIUME

INDO-CARIBBEANS

Indo-Caribbeans, as a distinct ethnic group, have emerged in the American cultural mosaic only since the mid-1970s. This emergence has its roots in the subcontinent of India and was transported to the Anglophile Caribbean over the span of 150 years. Through a process of time and socioeconomic and psychological dynamics, the group has increasingly become more cohesive and is gradually evolving into its own sociocultural identity away from the homeland. While still defining and evolving a new character, another leap of the diaspora ensued. In the United States they are in the margin of the mainstream and evolving yet again into a new identity. The second generation, more vibrant, immersed, and adaptable, is resolutely forging ahead in the assimilation process, but not without growing sociopsychological pains.

Definition

"Indo-Caribbean," as a name, was adopted above "Indo-West Indian" at a conference of Indo-Caribbeans in 1984 at the University of the West Indies in Trinidad. Despite Anglophile influences and strong East Indian cultural roots, this group is by no means homogeneous. This cultural amalgam includes Hindus, Muslims, and Christians. There are also rural-urban differences; the urban communities are more educated and upper-middle class. At one time, only the English-speaking countries of the Caribbean saw themselves as Indo-Caribbeans. Now they are joined by the Dutch Hindi-speaking Hindus of Suriname and the French-speaking inhabitants of French Guiana and Martinique.

However, Guyana and Trinidad claim the bulk of the Indo-Caribbean population and are the chief sources of immigration to the United States. The number of individuals of Indian descent in this region is less than one million.

Indo-Caribbeans are likely to remain in the margin of the American mainstream because of their religiocultural practices but especially because of their phenotype. Like the East Indians, they are brown in complexion, with straight black hair and otherwise Caucasian features. A unique linguistic pattern combined with Hindu family surnames also account for ready visibility as a group, albeit small, in a predominantly Anglophile-oriented society. They are often stereotyped with East Indians and derogatorily labeled "curried breath," "Paki," or "dotheads." In cooperation with other minority groups, they socially organize themselves to reduce any and all forms of prejudice and discrimination. This new hegemony has heightened their sense of community and ethnic identity.

History

Historically the Indo-Caribbeans took a rather circuitous route, from India between 1838 and 1917, and from the Caribbean to the United States during the 1960s and 1970s. In 1834, the British Empire abolished slavery, and a labor vacuum was created when the slaves refused to return to work. Experiments with different types of immigrant labor proved the East Indians more suitable, hardy, and adaptable. Thus began the indentureship of East Indians to the Caribbean — to Guyana in 1838 and to Trinidad and Tobago in 1839. Smaller numbers followed to Jamaica, Barbados, and Suriname. Indentureship continued until 1917, when it was discontinued because of abuses in the system. A total of 505,043 immigrants landed in the colonies between 1838 and 1882. During that period 15,727, or 3 percent, returned to India after their indentureship.

The profit motive, initiated and sustained by the British sugar planters of the region, had the blessings of the British government. While they needed cheap labor to continue their profit ventures, the destitute, unemployed East Indians were willing to risk the promises of an unknown land. India was already under British influence and became a Crown Colony in 1857. The overly enthusiastic *arkhati* (recruiters) frequently lied or exaggerated to and even kidnapped prospective recruits. Periods of intensive immigration correlated highly with years of famine in India. The famine of 1860–1861 in the northwest provinces produced 31,493 migrants, but only 6,189 migrated in 1864–1865. The five-year contract gave certified, able-bodied recruits free return passage, earning twenty-four cents per day and free medical care. To encourage reindentureship, they were offered small plots of land for cultivation and/or the raising of livestock. Many took advantage of the offer because it guaranteed an income, and the small acreage was an added incentive. Further incentives for permanent residence in the Caribbean were social stigma and aversive consequences related to crossing the Kalapani (dark waters). In addition, by the end of their indentureship, many had begun their own families and had adapted socially and economically to the new environment. Thus, the sojourners frequently became permanent residents.

Out of necessity, the indentured workers from the initial stage of immigration began a process of assimilation and accommodation in the Caribbean. Caste intermixture at the various holding stations in India and on the ships, as well as shared cooking and eating in cramped living quarters, diminished caste rigidity and communal differences. Religious efficacy of these Hindus and Muslims was reduced because of the lack of priests and social leaders among the early immigrants. The absence of social support or pressure to conform to any previous rigid socioreligious pattern functioned as effective dynamics for radical change and adaptation. There were also language barriers and culture shock. The system emulated the worst practices of slavery; there were frequent physical and social abuses with little personal or legal recourse. In their new and strange environment the new immigrant envied and admired the conspicuous consumption of the Anglo-Saxon culture, although they themselves were perceived merely as economic assets, and their lifestyle was despised. Frequent interactions with Anglicized Afro-Caribbeans, as co-workers or supervisors, slowly but consistently influenced the newcomers. A new social structure was in the making. The exigencies of adaptation for survival and its aftermath were creating a new collective consciousness among the immigrants.

Those who chose to stay, or even to reindenture, had the sociopsychological makeup for successful adaptation. While some continued on the sugar plantations, others acquired land in new settlements and became entrepreneurs. Still others moved to the Afro-Caribbean-dominated urban centers and became more educated, both formally and informally. Many became leaders and spokespersons for the socially inarticulate and the economically disadvantaged. Some became Christian because of the Anglophile identity, social mobility, and job opportunities. The urban settlers emerged as white-collar workers and competitive businessmen. The rural settlers remained sugar workers, farmers, and small businessmen.

The second generation of Indo-Caribbeans have proved relatively successful because of their penny-wise parents and a high level of achievement motivation. The pervasive pattern of successful businessmen and high-level professionals in the second and third generations reliably attests to this adaptation, "for they respect money as only people with a high sense of communal responsibility can" (Lamming, 1966, p. 69). The immigrants were developing a new group identity, distinct from those of India and characterized by more English spoken than Hindi, less caste discrimination, more religious tolerance, greater prosperity, and a more Anglophile outlook. Their self-perception and self-esteem were effecting a new and rapidly changing adaptation process.

After World War II, not unlike many other colonials, Indo-Caribbeans eagerly sought education and job opportunities, first in Europe and then in the United States. Immigration to the United States trickled until the 1960s and 1970s, when it became a plethora. The immigration of Indo-Caribbeans far outweighs that of blacks from the same region.

The motives for this immigration involved the powerful role of the "push-pull" factors. The Caribbean is a typical developing world region with little technology, inadequate technical skills, underdeveloped natural resources, and poor and limited educational opportunities. European imperialism drained colonial resources. Per capita income was relatively low, and living conditions were substandard. In Guyana, racist politics and a black-dominated ruling People's National Congress (PNC) with its policy of "party paramountcy" (1964–1988) were other driving forces. Indo-Caribbean per capita income declined 15 percent between 1976 and 1980, with a 70 percent increase in consumer prices. While many countries were attaining nationhood, such as Trinidad and Tobago in 1962 and Guyana in 1964, Great Britain was restricting colonial immigration. The social and economic unrest in the Caribbean saw outlets in North America. Students seeking a higher level of education but with little preparation found ready admittance in postsecondary and technical schools in New York and Toronto. At this time a new American foreign policy was in place. The Peace Corps of the 1960s created a new developing world awareness. The Immigration Act of 1965 eliminated the quota system of immigration and provided for family reunification. Anglophile sentiments and a common linguistic tradition of English were significant factors in immigration, and they later became quite practical in the assimilation process of Indo-Caribbeans in the United States.

The port of entry for most Indo-Caribbeans to the United States is New York City. From there they have moved to bordering states such as New Jersey and Connecticut, later moving to states such as Florida or Minnesota. On arrival they typically have moved in with friends and/or relatives in overcrowded apartments. Here they are offered moral and financial assistance and are helped to define and understand the mystery of transculturation. Many have experienced the patterns of extended-family living for years. With job security and adequate income and resources, they often relocate, but not far away. Many who have bought homes in these Indo-Caribbean neighborhoods accumulate wealth in the form of savings, home-ownership, and education. Such parsimony and sacrifices have often been at the expense of healthy physiological and social living.

Demography

Demographic patterns are now emerging. Typical is the Richmond Hill area of Queens, New York City, known as "Little Guyana." Within New York are pockets of immigrants, such as in Hollis, Queens, and Cypress Hills, Brooklyn, very often with their own churches, cricket teams, and ethnic shops. Within a mile on Liberty Avenue in Richmond Hill are more than a dozen shops catering to the specific needs of this community, with clothing, ethnic foods, and religious icons. Fifteen Hindu temples exclusively service this community, and another twenty are in the New York City vicinity. Within these areas are Indo-Caribbean doctors, lawyers, teachers, priests, and travel agents who cater to the needs of the community.

Because of the regional concentration and communal life, greater services can be rendered. Inexpensive flights are regularly offered to allow the sojourner an opportunity to return to the homeland. These annual or biannual trips, with gifts and money to friends and families, allow individuals the opportunity to experience old sights and sounds and to reassess their relative accomplishments and self-esteem. In spite of their hopes, the sojourners have little chance of permanently returning. The deterrents in the homeland are the children's local education, family pressures, and inadequate funds for economic independence. Coupled with this are poor jobs opportunities, physiological conditions such as heat and humid-

Members of the Federation of Hindu Mandirs participate in a public celebration. (Parsram Sri Thakur)

ity, and few modern conveniences. However, most first-generation immigrants do not feel psychologically distant from the Caribbean.

In 1995, an official count found 205,200 Indo-Caribbeans spread across the United States. The majority live along the Eastern Seaboard, from New England to Florida. Of these, 130,000 came from Guyana, a country of fewer than 450,000 people of Indian descent. In other parts of the United States, they tend to concentrate in urban areas such as Miami, Chicago, Minneapolis, or Los Angeles. This number, though official, did not consider the large number of undocumented aliens. An estimate by the *Richmond Hill Times* (1995) suggests an approximate population of 270,000. Seventy-six percent live in the New York area, and 7 percent were born in the United States.

Language

Linguistic patterns vary with regional upbringing and education. The uneducated use a form of pidgin English. This unique dialect has been codified in folk songs, poetry, and other literary works. It has accompanied the immigrant. Apart from its academic and aesthetic values, it seems to be of little economic and long-term worth. The diverse intragroup dialects, such as literate-nonliterate, rural-urban, and Guyanese-Trinidadian, however, serve as a psychologically significant cohesive force within each subgroup. The second generation sees less value in a nonstandard dialect and often ignores or speaks disparagingly of it. The literate individuals use a more standard form of English, and their linguistic skills become effective tools for ready employment. Such skills are also crucial for broader socialization and productive adaptation. The Hindi and Sanskrit of the older generation, which is little understood by the younger generations, is used almost exclusively by the priests for religious ceremonies.

Cultural Persistence and Assimilation

Characteristic factors in assimilation, such as employment and recreation, identify both cultural persistence and change. Employment among Indo-Caribbeans has been consistent but often frustrating. They seem eager to be employed at whatever is available. There is a strong drive to seek employment and learning on the job, both formally and informally. For the large number of working women this is first-time employment and a culture shock, yet it is a necessity. For the educated it has been extremely frustrating, as many must take jobs perceived below their academic and/or experiential qualifications.

Cricket has played an important role in understanding recreational Anglophile influences and cultural persistence. More significant, it has become a vital means of socialization for the individual team members, as head of a household, and for the entire family. Many teams are exclusively Indo-Caribbean, or nearly so, making cricket an important source for information-sharing and an opportunity to meet old and new friends.

The information network within the group has long been a concern. As early as 1978, the Indo-Guyanese American League was formed in New York, with a newsletter of the same name. The *Indo-Caribbean World* in Toronto, which began publication in 1983, has a bi-monthly circulation of 30,000. The better-known *Caribbean Daylight* in New York began in March 1991 and has a circulation of approximately 15,000. The *Richmond Hill Times* began in 1991 and has a circulation of 10,000. The *Guyanese-Caribbean Prime News* began in December 1994 and has a circulation of 12,500. The quarterly journal *Indo-Caribbean Review*, based in Ontario, is of high academic excellence. The newsworthy items about politics and economics and the homeland and local news, as well as the notices and advertisements, have served to bind the community economically and sociopsychologically. Frequent academic conferences, especially between 1988 and 1995, were initiated by the rise of a new intellectual elite. Initiated and sustained by the need to define and understand the new and growing identity, numerous books and professional papers have been generated. The business community and government agencies have enthusiastically supported these initiatives.

The younger generation, with family support, is becoming more educated and aspiring to white-collar employment. They are more likely to have friends in the mainstream and do not perceive themselves as sojourners. Many children and some adults have adopted or modified their first names to more typical Anglicized spelling and sounds. Because of more community involvement and a wider interethnic mixture, they have more refined social skills. There are many mixed marriages in spite of parental objections. Members of the younger generation do, however, attend and support ethnic social clubs in their communities. They are not as frugal as their parents and identify less with parental economic and social values. This has become a source of conflict, especially since many teenagers are more independent and control their own money. Male domination in the family has eroded significantly. Wives, who often side with the children, are balking at husbands' control and conservative social outlook.

Indo-Caribbeans in the United States are the products of an experiment in assimilation. There is need, however, especially by the older generation, for greater social awareness and integration (structurally and functionally) into the mainstream. However, this experiment of adaptation can still be considered a relative success. The accumulation of wealth in cash savings, home-ownership, and educational attainment for the past and present generations clearly confirm this observation. However, these accomplishments are not without their sociopsychological cost in mental illness and family disunity. Generational conflicts, divorce, and acculturative stress are dramatically on the rise.

See also: GUYANESE; TRINIDADIANS

Bibliography

Birbalsingh, F., ed. (1988). *Jahaji Bhai: An Anthology of Indo-Caribbean Literature*. Toronto: TSAR.

Dabydeen, D., and Samaroo, B., eds. (1987). *India in the Caribbean*. London: Hansib.

Gonzales, J., Jr. (1990). "The Settlement of Sikh Farmers in the Sacramento Valley of California." In *Dot Headed Americans: The Silent Minority in the United States*, edited by M. Gosine. New York: Windsor Press.

Gosine, M. (1990). *Caribbean East Indians in America*. New York: Windsor Press.

Gosine, M. (1992). *The Coolie Connection: From the Orient to the Occident*. New York: Windsor Press.

"Indo-Caribbean in the USA." (1995). *Richmond Hill Times*, editorial, September 30.

Lamming, G. (1966). "The West Indian People," *New World Quarterly* 2(1):69.

Mangru, B. (1987). *Benevolent Neutrality: Indian Government Policy and Labour Migration to British Guiana, 1854–1884*. London: Hansib.

Mangru, B. (1993). *Indenture and Abolition*. Toronto: TSAR.

Rodney, W. (1979). *Guyanese Sugar Plantations in the Late Nineteenth Century*. Georgetown, Guyana: Release.

Samaroo, B. (1987). "The Indian Connection." In *India in the Caribbean*, edited by D. Debydeen and B. Samaroo. London: Hansib.

Thakur, P. S. (1995). "Discrimination of Indo-Caribbeans by Indians in North America: A New Hegemony." *Indo-Caribbean Review* 2:9–37.

Williams, E. (1964). *British Historians and the West Indies*. Port of Spain, Trinidad: PNM.

PARSRAM SRI THAKUR

INDONESIANS

The Republic of Indonesia is the fourth most populous nation in the world, with a 1993 estimated population of 191 million people. The term "Indonesian" refers to those with citizenship in the republic, and there are two categories: those who are "native" (*pribumi*) and those of "foreign descent" (*keturunan asing*). The former belong to one of the more than two hundred ethnolinguistic groups in Indonesia. The latter descend from groups whose ancestors came in Dutch colonial times and who chose to become citizens after Indonesian independence in 1950, the most numerous and influential being the Chinese. Such citizens still have certain restrictions on their rights to education and employment, so some have gone abroad, either temporarily to study and work or to live permanently, though their proportion among Indonesians in the United States is unknown.

Some native ethnic groups have large populations. The largest, the Javanese, may number more than sixty million, while some groups number only in the tens of thousands. Each has a geographically distinct home region, language, dress, and house style, and cultural traditions and practices that Indonesians call *adat*. Hence the appropriateness of the national motto, "Unity in Diversity" (*Bhinneka Tunggal Ika*). No information is available about the variety of ethnic groups among Indonesians in the United States, but groups that are known for immigration and for seeking education are Minangkabau, Bugis, Batak, and Javanese.

The national language, bahasa Indonesia, is based on Malay, which is the national language of Malaysia and Brunei. For many Indonesians bahasa Indonesia is a second language, but this is not recent. In precolonial and colonial times, Malay was the lingua franca of commerce and statecraft throughout the archipelago. Now bahasa Indonesia is required in schools, the media, and public discourse and government functions, and it is used in communication between people of different ethnic groups. English is a required second language in school, but proficiency in it for most people is limited.

Immigration and Demographics

Indonesians have no tradition of immigration to the United States. Most have arrived after the 1965 changes in the immigration law, and there is little published information about them. What is known comes mainly from the 1990 U.S. Census tables in which Indonesians are mentioned. Their population is given as 30,085. Owing to their small numbers, even among Asian Americans, they are not listed in some census tables (they just appear as "other Asian") or in secondary sources such as almanacs.

Indonesians constituted less than 0.5 percent of the 6,908,638 Asians in the United States in 1990; however, between 1980 and 1990 their numbers more than tripled, from 9,618 to 30,085. There is a small preponderance of males, 15,944 to 14,141 females, which is consistent with two facts. (1) Indonesian men are generally more prone to immigrate and seek education, with immigration for either work or education more likely to be done by single people; for those more than age fifteen in 1990, 45 percent of men and 31 percent of women were single. (2) On the other hand, there is still a strong family orientation among the immigrants, with 50 percent of men and 58 percent of women married.

Indonesian men have long gone to sea, serving on commercial ships, Dutch and others. Some were stranded in American ports during World War II, for example, and others jumped ship, with some staying in the United States. This continues with the growing cruise ship trade since the 1970s. Unlike many Southeast Asians now in the United States, Indonesians have not arrived as political refugees. However, one group from Indonesia, Indo-Europeans (Indos, for short), entered the United States under refugee acts in the decade following Indonesian independence in 1950. In colonial times, race segregated Dutch and other Europeans, foreign Asians (such as Chinese), and native peoples, and the legal, social, and cultural boundaries affected descendents of Europeans who married native Indonesians, the Indos. They were urban, had their own subculture, and held diverse and sometimes influential occupations, but they were looked down upon by many Europeans and by native Indonesians. Consequently, after Independence many Indos, who were Dutch nationals, went to the Netherlands or to the United States. A few Indos immigrated to the United States between 1946 and 1953, but about 30,000 entered under several refugee acts and laws between 1953 and

1962; by 1973 another 30,000 had immigrated, sponsored by relatives and friends.

Beginning in the mid-1950s, Indonesians began arriving in the United States in large numbers to attend graduate school. Most were government employees on scholarships, and most returned to Indonesia, but some chose to remain and become permanent residents or naturalized citizens. Many were married, and their children have become American citizens. As Indonesia's economy grew stronger by the 1980s, more students have gone overseas with private funding, both native Indonesians and particularly Chinese Indonesians.

The children of those first Indonesians in the United States who became citizens have few remaining ties with Indonesia. They are English-speakers, and many have married Americans of other ethnicity, since the Indonesians were geographically widespread and their numbers were few. In some cities and states Indonesian-American associations mainly serve social functions, but these activities may be sporadic. However, this picture of assimilation may be less characteristic for many newer arivals of the 1980s and 1990s. One sign of change was the founding in 1988 of a commercially oriented monthly magazine, *Indonesian Journal*, which is published in the Indonesian language in Upland, California. It has paid subscriptions to homes around the United States and is supplied free of charge to Indonesian consulates, businesses, restaurants, and churches.

Like other Asians, most Indonesians now resident in the United States arrived after passage of the Immigration Law of 1965. By the late 1970s, it was reported that most were twenty to forty years old, and the men were mainly professional, technical, white-collar, or skilled workers. As the 1990 U.S. Census shows, this portrait remains somewhat accurate, but like other Asian immigrants and residents, Indonesians are becoming more diverse.

Where do Indonesians live in the United States? A total of 61 percent live in the West, 16 percent in the South, 13 percent in the Northeast, and 10 percent in the Midwest. The largest population (14,485) was located in California in 1990. Some Indonesians lived in fifty of California's sixty-nine counties; however, twelve counties accounted for 92 percent of them, and seven counties in southern California (Los Angeles, San Bernardino, Orange, San Diego, Riverside, Fresno, and Ventura) accounted for 76 percent. Los Angeles County, with 6,490 Indonesians, alone accounted for 45 percent of the Indonesians in the state. Many live east of central Los Angeles in the area known as the Inland Empire, between Monterey Park (called "the first Chinese American suburb") and San Bernardino. Many Indonesians also live in metropolitan New York and in the Washington, D.C., area (including parts of Virginia and Maryland), but some can be found anywhere from Miami to rural Missouri.

Indonesians in southern California are reported to be mainly students or middle-class business people, though some perform working-class jobs or provide domestic services and some are professionals such as physicians and lawyers. A majority are probably of Chinese-Indonesian origin, many of whom are Christian. In 1995, there were almost four hundred Indonesian-related companies in the area. These companies ranged from computer services to florists, from manufacturers to beauty shops. Transnational ties among the Chinese and other Indonesians of southern California are likely to be quite active. Like other Indonesians, they immigrated to the United States mainly as individuals or nuclear families, but they originate from large families with wide kin networks in Indonesia, and connections between Los Angeles and Jakarta are facilitated by direct flights at reasonable fares on Garuda Indonesian Airways.

Given the recentness of arrival of most Indonesians—85 percent are foreign-born, and 65 percent of those arrived after 1980—it is not surprising that the median age of males in this group is 31.9 and of females 32.4. A quarter of the foreign-born are naturalized American citizens, 89 percent of which immigrated before 1980. Of the noncitizens, only 21 percent came before 1980. These figures may indicate that more naturalization will come as people stay longer, that more of the recent comers are sojourners, or both.

Education

The educational level of Indonesians in the United States is similar to that of other voluntary immigrants from Asia, higher than that of the overall U.S. population, and very high compared to the population in Indonesia, but this is not surprising, since so many immigrated for education purposes. Of those over age twenty-five, half of the men and a third of the women have a bachelor's or postgraduate degree. An additional third of the men and a bit fewer than a third of the women have some university, junior college, or vocational credit, although not a degree. A total of 16 percent of the men and 26 percent of the women have only high school diplomas, while 5 percent of the men and 10 percent of the women have elementary school only. Thus the educational level overall is high (higher for males but not exceptionally so). The fact that more than one-fifth of the males and more than one-third of the females have a high school education or less indicates that Indonesians are diverse in backgrounds and social and occupational levels. Also, in the 1990 U.S. Census one-quarter of the Indonesians reported living in "linguistically isolated" households, and 40 percent of persons over age five reported that they did not speak English very well.

Family and Kinship

Indonesians place emphasis on family and kinship. Traditionally families were large, but government and private efforts in family planning, with a goal of a two-child family, have reduced Indonesian population growth significantly since the 1970s. In 1990, among this group of Indonesians in the United States, women age thirty-five to forty-four had an average of 2.3 children per woman; however, a fifth of those women had no children. Of the remaining women who had children, two-thirds had only one or two children. In Indonesia, large households are common, but in the United States, nearly half of Indonesians reported living alone or in two-person households, which reflects the large number of students and other sojourners in this population.

An Indonesian American prepares to host a gathering in celebration of Indonesia's Independence Day. (Mukul Roy)

Religion

There are more than thirty Indonesian Protestant churches in southern California, representing denominations known in the United States (e.g., Presbyterians, Baptists, Seventh-Day Adventists, Pentecostals, and Full Gospel Fellowship) and ones found only in Indonesia. Some of the latter churches are linked to particular ethnic groups there. Ethnic groups such as the Batak, Menadonese, and Ambonese, who are predominantly Christian in Indonesia, are strongly represented in California and other parts of the United States, as are Christian Javanese and Sundanese who are religious minorities among their mainly Muslim peoples in Indonesia. There are also Roman Catholic churches in five towns near Los Angeles where Indonesian priests hold Indonesian-language services. In California, Indonesians are socially active with fellow churchgoers or fellow members of the same ethnic group (which in some cases may be the same). There are also secular organizations for ethnic groups, such as those for the Batak of Sumatra or the peoples from North Sulawesi. Though Christians are prominent immigrants in California, Indonesian students sojourning in the United States are more likely to be Muslim.

Occupations and Income

The diversity of the Indonesian community is reflected in their range of urban occupations: managerial and professional positions (2,802 men, 1,807 women); technical sales, support, and clerical work (2,156 men, 2,511 women); precision production, craft, repair (1,165 men, 218 women); operators, fabricators, laborers (981 men, 368 women); and service occupations (860 men, 1,152 women). Occupations range from those requiring advanced degrees to those that are manual or service-oriented, and gender differences also exist. Women are only slightly less represented in managerial and professional positions than men (35 percent of men, 30 percent of women), but women are much more involved in sales and clerical or service occupations (32 percent of men, 60 percent

of women). These jobs may complement motherhood and be done by those with less education. Men are more involved also in precision production, craft, and repair and as operators, fabricators, or laborers (26 percent of men, 10 percent of women).

In 1989, the median annual income of the 10,336 Indonesian households was $28,597, but there was considerable variation. Native-born Indonesian Americans earned less, $24,815, but they were younger as a group. The median income of naturalized Indonesian Americans was $27,355, but it differed according to when they first arrived (which also reflects their age). Those who immigrated before 1980 had achieved a median income of $43,438, while those who arrived later reached only $36,818. Those who were not citizens had a lower median income, $28,387, but the difference between earlier and later immigrants was great. Those who arrived before 1980 had a median income of $41,236, while those who arrived between 1980 and 1990 had a median income of $11,694. This group contains many students, and it might also include some of the less-educated newcomers. In this group, 37 percent of the households had incomes of less than $5,000 per year. However, almost one-third of these households had incomes over $25,000, and 98 households (2%) had incomes over $100,000. The distribution of household incomes shows that Indonesians are socioeconomically diverse: In 1989, 32 percent of the households earned less than $15,000; 26 percent earned $15,000 to $35,000; 16 percent earned $35,000 to $50,000; 15 percent earned $50,000 to $75,000; and 11 percent earned more than $75,000.

The Future

One can expect the numbers and diversity of Indonesians in the United States to grow over the coming decades if immigration policy remains similar to that expressed in the 1965 and 1990 laws. Although Indonesia is developing rapidly, it cannot provide the education that many Indonesians want and need, so they will continue to look to the United States. In addition, more and more Indonesians will seek business opportunities abroad even as their own country develops, because the desire for economic self-improvement has been a driving force there since the late 1960s.

See also: INDOS

Bibliography

Brown, S. S. (1994). "Indonesian Culture Takes Root in Hollywood." *Los Angeles Times*, October 2, pp. B1, B4.

Indonesian Business Directory U.S.A. (1994–1995). Upland, CA: Desktop Designs.

Kwik, G. (1989). *The Indos in Southern California.* New York: AMS Press.

U.S. Bureau of the Census. (1980). *1980 Census of Population*, PC80-SI-12, Tables 1, 4. Washington, DC: U.S. Government Printing Office.

U.S. Bureau of the Census. (1990). *1990 Census of Population: Asians and Pacific Islanders in the United States*, CP-3-5. Washington, DC: U.S. Government Printing Office.

U.S. Department of Commerce. (1991). *United States Department of Commerce News.* Release of June 12, 1991 (CB91-215). Washington, DC: U.S. Government Printing Office.

CLARK E. CUNNINGHAM

INDOS

The Indos, also known as "Indo-Europeans," represent a small Eurasian refugee-immigrant group of mostly Dutch-Indonesian descent. The term "Indo" refers to Indonesian and European ancestry and is more specific than the general term "Eurasian." Not every Indo agrees with the term, but the name has stuck.

Orientation

If ever there was a group of people who flashed through American immigrant history seemingly without leaving a trace, it has to be the Indos. They arrived in the late 1950s and early 1960s, barely sixty thousand according to a rough estimate (by the consulate of the Netherlands in Los Angeles in 1971). Many conditions inside and outside the group have contributed to their phenomenal success in entering the mainstream. Very little is known about these refugee-immigrants due to their small numbers, the brevity of time since they first set foot in the United States, and the scarcity of literature on the Indos in English as well as in the Dutch language. Where did this relative handful of people come from? Who were they?

History and Cultural Traditions

Many Indos left their native land, what was then the Dutch East Indies colonies, after these became independent as the Republic of Indonesia in 1949, convinced that there was no future for them in the new republic. They settled in the Netherlands. Those who moved on to the United States arrived during the late 1950s and early 1960s. The number of Indos in the United States could only be estimated, since they were included in the usual Dutch quotas even though the majority of the Indos immigrated under special quotas intended to ease the settlement problems of World War II victims. As such they were also considered refugees.

Indos in the Dutch East Indies evolved into three overlapping socioeconomic categories. The first two gave rise to a dialect and certain art forms that have been associated with the Indo group ever since. During the early period of the East India Company, the language spoken by the Indo was pidgin Portuguese. In the eighteenth century, it evolved into a type of bazaar Malay. With the increasing number of Dutch people in the colonies, more Dutch was spoken by the Indos. The language of the Indos as a group ranged from pure Dutch to pure Indonesian. From the thousands of Indos who lived among the indigenous peoples and who lacked adequate training in Dutch, however, there arose a spoken dialect called *Petjoh*. It

An Indonesian mask dancer performs a traditional dance. (Mukul Roy)

was a lively, dynamic, expressive mode of communication and full of sound imitations, suggestive expressions, and interjections, while exhibiting an economy of words, a specific accent, and a melodious intonation. There is hardly any literature in this dialect, since Indo writers used the Dutch language as their medium.

A type of music inherited from the Portuguese became popular among Indos who modified it to suit their situation and language. The major instrument was the guitar-like *krontjong*, which gave this type of music its name. Malay gradually replaced Portuguese as lyrics for the songs.

A successful art form was created in the late nineteenth century by combining East and West and by making it understandable to all peoples in the Indies. This opera style, called Komedie Stamboel, used the Malay language and represented stories of Western and Eastern origin, such as *Ali Baba and the Forty Thieves, Snow White, Hamlet,* and *Njai Dasima* (a local love drama).

In the area of religion, the majority of the Indos adhered to Protestant denominations or to the Catholic Church. Others were not affiliated with any church, and a minority professed the Islamic faith.

As mentioned, most Indos repatriated to the Netherlands before they immigrated to the United States. "Repatriated" is actually a misnomer, since the overwhelming majority had never set foot in the Netherlands before. For a people born and reared in the tropics, the flatness and smallness of the Netherlands and its northern European climate were great disappointments. The Indos considered their presence in the Netherlands a consequence of political events over which they had no control and for which they blamed the Dutch government. Understanding of the Indo by the Dutch citizenry was minimal. The Dutch were not prepared for the unexpected postwar influx of more than 200,000 individuals from the former colonies, competing for housing and employment. Although familiar with the distinction between European and "Native" (Indonesian), the Dutch were not prepared for the existence of an "in-between," a Eurasian. The Indos objected to being referred to by terms denoting skin color. Indos range from those with blond hair and blue eyes to those with dark skin and black eyes. The active and vocal among them organized. Most were not used to collective action relative to problem solving. However, they were learning about their past and present situations through *Tong-Tong*, a periodical named after the sound of the native alarm system consisting of a hallowed piece of carved wood beaten by a stick. Starting with a handful of subscribers in 1956, its circulation numbered about ten thousand in the early 1960s, while the number of actual readers was estimated at thirty to forty thousand. The enormous popularity of *Tong-Tong* could be attributed to its function as an escape mechanism for those whose loss of the Indies was unbearable and for those who could not cope with the new life. It also provided an outlet for the feeling of those Indos who did not agree with the absorption policy of the Dutch government. Many left the Netherlands for Brazil, Canada, Suriname, and the United States.

The Indos entered the United States under various legislative measures. The major sponsoring organizations were the Church World Service and the Catholic Relief Services. Throughout the years, the problem of obtaining an accurate count of refugee-immigrants remained unsolved. The U.S. Census classified people according to their self-determined ethnic affiliation. Indos could have been included in overlapping categories of "country of origin, other Asians," "total foreign or mixed parentage," "total foreign-born foreign mother tongue," or all three. By 1973, Indos were found in practically all fifty states, with the majority in southern California.

The formation of Indo enclaves was prevented because of a number of factors. First, the refugee-immigrants settled initially with their sponsors or in a location offered to them by the sponsor. When the main provider found a position far from home or when he or she changed employment, the family moved closer to the place of employment. Daily necessities, rather than the wish to establish an ethnic community, dictated the choice of location. Second, the Indos had a wide variety of occupations and in this respect were not limited to certain geographical areas. Third, there were no forces in the host society limiting the choice of location for these refugee-immigrants. Other than minor incidents, very few Indos reported any difficulty in renting or purchasing a home, and they had a rather full choice as to where to settle, with the family income as sole limitation.

Employment

Many Indo refugee-immigrants had completed high school and were not used to manual labor. However, they did not hesitate to accept such labor at the beginning. Practically all of them arrived at an acceptable position only after a number of disparate occupations. For example, one bookkeeper worked as a construction worker, a baker, and finally became a repairman. Another, who had previously worked in metallurgy, took accounting, business administration, and banking courses in a junior college while working as a janitor and ended up as a supervisor for an insurance company. A few Indos returned to the Netherlands.

Although traditionally the Indo woman did not work for wages after marriage, financial necessity was the major motive behind many Indo women seeking employment outside the home. As a whole, the total labor experience and the specific skills the Indos had to offer were useful to the local economy. The fact that the Indos lacked an occupational stereotype further facilitated their absorption into the host society.

Marriage and Divorce

The majority of the refugee-immigrants were married at the time of immigration. Among the unmarried Indos, men preferred Indos as spouses because they considered them more faithful than non-Indos, and the women preferred Indo partners since these were traditionally viewed as dependable providers. The lack of opportunities to meet fellow refugee-immigrants, however, limited the search for suitable partners. Instances of divorce among Indos usually were caused by the real or perceived need for money. Men who worked overtime or attended evening classes endangered satisfactory family lives. Wives, complaining about excessive absence of their husbands, took evening jobs, opening the opportunity to meet men other than their husbands. A combination of continued absenteeism by the men and increased independence by the women appeared to be the major cause of disagreement between married couples. However, the divorce rate was low. This was due to the traditionally strong disapproval of divorce.

Interaction Among Indos

Commercial establishments played a role in the maintenance of an informal network in the 1960s. Indonesian restaurants where Indos met by design or by chance, and ethnic stores that catered to Indos and Indonesians functioned as information centers with announcements on bulletin boards, flyers, or by word of mouth. Indonesian cuisine remained popular among the Indos.

Linguistically the Indos faced the usual difficulties arising from a bilingual environment. Two schools of thought existed among the refugee-immigrants on the subject. One insisted on the use of Dutch at home as a matter of pride and identity. Others believed that since the children, by virtue of birth in the United States, were Americans, the family should speak English so they did not have to deal with two languages simultaneously. In practice, very few families strictly enforced either philosophy. At present most younger Indos use the English language.

De Soos (short for Societeit), an Indo club in southern California, published the periodical *De Indo* in 1964. De Soos itself closed its doors in 1988, but *De Indo* became a popular medium through which the readership is informed about reunions and government regulations, and through which Indos continue to be able to find each other. As of 1995, subscribers numbered more than 2,500, including those in eighteen countries outside the United States, with the majority of subscribers in southern California.

Conclusions

The variables that account for the rapid rate with which the Indos are disappearing as a group are found among the Indos themselves and in the host society.

Those variables inherent among the refugee-immigrants that impeded their unification were (1) the diverse nature of the group, a characteristic inherited from the Dutch colonial period, (2) the lack of a clear concept of and agreement about Indo ethnicity, (3) the unwillingness and/or inability of the Indos to organize, a characteristic inherited from the colonial period, when they suffered from intragroup as well as intergroup competition, (4) the small number of Indos and their geographical dispersion; the group did not increase numerically but was steadily losing members due to factors mentioned below, (5) the lack of a proverbial "old country" for Indos to look back to; World War II and its aftermath had destroyed Indo society in the Dutch East Indies, (6) the lack of continued replacement of the group with new immigrants who could function as reinforcements of traditional behavior, and (7) the familiarity of the Indos with Western culture and behavior, which eased the road to assimilation.

Those variables inherent in the host society that facilitated the absorption of the refugee-immigrants were (1) the multiracial composition of the United States; the physical appearance of the Indos enabled them to blend in with the local population, (2) the lack of overt discrimination toward Indos, enabling the refugee-immigrants to diversify as to occupation and residence and preventing the formation of ethnic enclaves, and (3) the lack of marital discrimination toward Indos; the high rate of marriage outside the group led to the expectation that the Indos as a separately identifiable group would soon disappear.

These conclusions must sadden those Indos who helplessly watch their younger members change. But the older Indos could be strengthened by the fact that there still are a few small Indo clubs, mostly in southern California. There is, however, a strong realization among the Indos that they will be no more as a separate ethnic group.

There might always be Eurasian populations, but never anymore of the Indo type, a combination of one of the many Indonesian peoples and one of the various European peoples who had lived on the Indonesian islands.

See also: INDONESIANS

Bibliography

Koks, J. H. (1932). *De Indo*. Amsterdam: Van Nijgh.

Kwik, G. (1989). *The Indos in Southern California*. New York: AMS Press.

van der Veur, P. W. J. (1955). "Introduction to a Socio-political Study of the Eurasians of Indonesia." Ph.D. thesis, Cornell University.

van der Veur, P. W. J. (1968). "Cultural Aspects of the Eurasian Community in Indonesian Colonial Society." *Indonesie* IV:38–53.

GRETA KWIK

IRANIANS

Iranians are persons who are either born in Iran or who trace their ancestry to that country regardless of their place of birth (e.g., American-born). Iranians are alternatively referred to as Persians, since "Iran" and "Persia" are interchangeably used in the United States. But as a name for this group, "Persian" is not as all-encompassing as "Iranian," since the former excludes non-Persian-speaking minorities from Iran. Outsiders sometimes confuse Iranians with Arabs, but these two groups are ethnically distinct. Based on the fact that Iranian society is predominantly Muslim, outsiders also assume that all Iranian immigrants are Muslim. Despite Iran's relative religious homogeneity, where about 98 percent of its prerevolution population was Muslim, all of Iran's religious minorities are present in the United States. Iranians in the United States consist of a sizable number of religious minorities who fled Iran because the Iranian revolution and the Islamic Republic of Iran threatened the country's non-Muslim minorities.

Historical Background

Direct U.S. influence in Iran dates back at least to the CIA-sponsored coup in 1953, which brought Mohammad Reza Shah back to power and deposed Mohammad Mossadegh, the popular Iranian prime minister who advocated the nationalization of Iranian oil. Thereafter, Iran and the United States established close economic, social, and political ties, which in turn facilitated the movement of Iranians to the United States. The Shah's industrialization drive, which began in the 1960s and took off in the 1970s with rising oil revenues, resulted in a booming Iranian economy. But the educational infrastructure was neither well developed nor sufficiently advanced to prepare Iranian students for the country's expanding technical and managerial tasks. For many students, overseas education was the only alternative as the need for skilled labor grew in Iran, outstripping the supply of universities to educate a burgeoning number of high school graduates. Although Iranian students went to many countries in pursuit of postsecondary education, their favored destination was the United States because of their familiarity with the English language (which was taught in Iranian high schools), the absorptive capacity of the numerous American colleges and universities, and the provision of advanced education in badly needed technical fields in Iran such as engineering.

The Iranian revolution of 1978–1979 took many by surprise because it came at a time when Iran was experiencing an economic boom, though there was a sharp economic downturn prior to the revolution. Therefore, it is possible to say that the

Pro-Islamic Fundamentalists from the Iranian-American community demonstrate in 1980 in Washington, D.C., against the U.S. postrevolutionary support of the Shah of Iran. (Leif Skoogfors/Corbis)

causes of the revolution were more political in nature (e.g., populist opposition to the Shah's autocratic rule) than economic. As the Muslim clergy dominated the revolutionary process and its outcome, fear of religious persecution among the religious minorities and intolerable living conditions for the secular Muslims accounted for their mass flight. This explains why most Iranian Muslims in the United States are secular; indeed, the religious Iranian Muslims have no reason for leaving a strict Muslim society. Early waves of Iranian exiles were drawn from the elite and most modernized segments of Iranian society. The emergence

of a theocratic state in Iran—the only one of its kind in the world at present—and its imposition of a strict code of behavior was particularly intolerable for modernizing Iranian women.

Immigration Patterns

Iranian immigration to the United States has come in two distinctive waves: before and after the Iranian revolution of 1978–1979. Iranians who immigrated before the revolution were mostly students, while those who have left after the revolution are mainly exiles or political refugees—

some Iranians have also immigrated for economic reasons during both waves, especially during the second. The consolidation of the Islamic Republic of Iran on the one hand and the growth of the Iranian community in the United States on the other have sustained the immigration of Iranians to the United States. Data from the Immigration and Naturalization Service (INS) and the U.S. Bureau of the Census show that Iranian immigration to the United States has continued, although not at the high late-1970s levels. From 1950 to 1992, altogether 247,261 Iranians entered the United States as legal immigrants—that is, with a permanent residency visa (illegal immigration from Iran to the United States is negligible, visa overstayers excepted). Although some of these had immigrant status upon arrival, the immigration quotas were not favorable to Iranians, and having no other choice, most were admitted as students or as visitors, and subsequently applied for permanent residency. There was a gradual increase in the number of Iranian immigrants from 2,730 in the 1950s to 8,895 in the 1960s to 23,230 during the period from 1970 to 1977. Starting with the Iranian revolution in 1978–1979, and in spite of the closure of the American embassy in Iran in 1980, there was a sharp increase in the number of immigrants admitted from Iran, reaching an annual average of more than 10,000 in the early 1980s. Almost one-quarter of all Iranian immigrants to the United States first entered as refugees or were classified as asylees after their arrival, and many of those who have arrived with immigrant visas are refugees from outside the United States. For the first thirty years, from 1950 to 1980, there were only 732 Iranian refugees and asylees, but this number increased dramatically to 58,381 in the next twelve years due to the Iranian revolution.

Of the almost 35,000 Iranian immigrants admitted before the revolution (i.e., 1950–1977), fewer than half (almost 14,000) were new arrivals, whereas 30,565 (28%) of the 108,694 Iranian immigrants admitted from 1987 to 1990 were new arrivals. Thus the trend among Iranians is toward obtaining permanent residency and settling in the United States, a trend that has become more pro-

nounced after the revolution. INS data further show that the number of nonimmigrants (students and visitors) from Iran has dropped precipitously from its peak in 1977–1979. By and large, Iranians used to arrive in the United States under student and visitor visas. This pattern has changed as Iranians have increasingly become naturalized citizens of the United States and are able to bring over their immediate relatives under family reunification laws.

It was relatively easy to acquire a U.S. visa before the seizure of the American embassy in Iran and its indefinite closure. It is now impossible to obtain a U.S. visa directly from Iran, since there is no American embassy in that country. Since the closure of the American embassy, Iranians have had to go to a third country to receive a visa to immigrate to the United States. Immigration to the United States is also becoming less feasible economically, since the Iranian currency is weak against the dollar, especially on the black market, thus requiring substantial money to finance the long, arduous trip.

Many Iranians who originally arrived in the United States as temporary immigrants (e.g., students) have become "self-imposed exiles" by changing their mind about returning to Iran. The number of postrevolution exiles who left Iran permanently is greater than the number of prerevolution immigrants, which is reflected in the migration patterns. Iranian immigrants, especially the students, migrated alone. Exiles, many of whom are members of religious minorities from Iran, have migrated to the United States in family units due to their precarious position in Iran. Moving with family members has reduced the probability of return to the country of origin for these minorities.

Economic Adaptation

The 1990 U.S. Census enumerated about 285,000 Iranians in the United States—both foreign- and native-born—of whom 100,000 (35%) were in the Los Angeles metropolitan area (a five-county region), and about 80,000 (28%)

were in Los Angeles County. The vast majority of Iranians in Los Angeles were foreign-born, mainly due to the influx of new exiles and refugees.

Iranians are one of the most educated groups in the United States. According to the 1990 U.S. Census, with half of its population twenty-five years or older holding a bachelor's degree or higher, foreign-born Iranians were the third most highly educated major immigrant group (more than 100,000 persons) in the United States after Asian Indians and Taiwanese. Almost half of Iranians in the United States hold top white-collar professional and managerial specialty occupations. Only 14 percent of Iranians have blue-collar jobs, but even this low rate is misleading, since it includes occupations such as hairdressing (a female-dominated Iranian occupation).

Iranians constitute one of the most entrepreneurial groups in the United States. The rate of self-employment is higher among Iranians in the United States (21%) than it is among many other groups. But unlike other immigrant groups who turn to self-employment because of disadvantages in the labor market (e.g., language barriers), availability of capital and the presence of highly skilled self-employed professionals such as doctors and dentists partly account for the high self-employment rate of Iranians. The rate of Iranian self-employment is even higher in Los Angeles that it is in the United States as a whole due to the greater presence of former commercial minorities (i.e., Armenians and Jews) from Iran. Iranians also have a much higher self-employment rate compared to other groups—33 percent versus 24 percent, 19 percent, and 8 percent for non-Hispanic white, Asian, and Hispanic immigrant males, respectively, in 1990 in Los Angeles.

As in most other immigrant groups, the socioeconomic status of Iranian females is lower than that of males. Still, with 42 percent holding a bachelor's degree or higher, Iranian women in the United States are very highly educated. The most striking feature of the economic adaptation of Iranian females is their very low rate of labor force participation, which is mainly a carryover from Iran. Yet Iranian women have made great strides toward working outside the home in the United States, as reflected in a substantial increase in their labor force participation over time compared to their male counterparts. The Iranian female rate of labor force participation is particularly higher in the United States than it was in Iran, which in 1990 was below 20 percent. But Iran's overall rate is misleading in light of the extreme social class selectivity in Iranian immigrant women in the United States. Nevertheless, Iranian women are increasingly entering the U.S. labor market, a trend that has significant effects for their changing sex roles and family life.

Assimilation and Cultural Persistence

Sociologically speaking, a minority group such as Iranians with high levels of education, occupation, and English-language proficiency is expected to assimilate rapidly into American society. However, Iranians by and large have not assimilated despite their high educational and occupational status and ample financial resources. Some Iranians in the United States are very assimilated, especially those who arrived much earlier as students, subsequently married Americans, and settled down in college towns where there are few Iranians. But most, especially the postrevolution exiles who have congregated in Los Angeles, New York, and Washington, D.C., have tenaciously resisted the pressures of assimilation thus far. Some may argue that the differences between these two groups have less to do with their historical context of migration than with the year of immigration — that is, the earlier arrivals are more assimilated than the later ones. But it is not so much the time of arrival as the pattern of immigration that accounts for the differences in their relative degree of assimilation. Iranian students were well on their way to assimilation because they had immigrated on their own, until they were joined by parents and other relatives, or relocated within the United States to be near them. Conversely, often having migrated with family members, or reunifying with them soon after, the postrevolution exiles have maintained close ties with relatives, thus reenforcing their ethnicity. This is particularly the case among religious minorities from Iran, who have sometimes moved with their entire families.

Discrimination and prejudice are two other key factors that may prevent or delay the assimilation of Iranians, especially Muslims who face more hostility, into American society. Even in multiethnic American metropolitan areas such as Los Angeles and New York, Iranians continue to experience discrimination, although its extent has decreased since the "Iranian hostage crisis" in 1980–1981, when fifty-two Americans were taken hostage for 444 days in Iran. Ironically, this sad event in Iranian-American relations coincided with a massive influx of Iranian exiles into the United States, who soon after arrival faced a presidential decree to deport Iranians who were out of legal status and in violation of their visas. This was an unfair targeting and scapegoating of Iranians in the United States who had been persecuted by a regime they left behind. U.S.-Iranian tensions have continued to the present. Unfortunately, every time these tensions break out as conflicts, Iranians in the United States become scapegoats and suffer the consequences. Not surprisingly, many Iranians still feel that there is prejudice against them in the United States.

All indicators of ethnicity point to its maintenance among Iranians, at least in Los Angeles, where rich data on Iranians are available. Traditionally used as the best indicator of assimilation, the higher the rate of intermarriage, the more assimilated the group. With 90 percent of Iranian females married to Iranian males, Iranians in Los Angeles are very unlikely to have intermarried. Besides marriage in Iran, the sizable presence of endogamous minority groups, notably Jews and Armenians, accounts for the low rate of intermarriage among Iranians.

As another indicator of cultural preservation, the use and maintenance of ethnic language is particularly high among foreign-born Iranians, the majority of whom speak their mother tongue at home despite their English proficiency. Iranians do not come from a country where English is commonly used, yet their level of education, which in

Iranian immigrant children participate in the traditional passing through the flames as part of the celebration of Now Ruz (the Persian New Year). The fire is intended to "burn up" winter paleness and give back a rosy complexion. (Paul Souders/Corbis)

many cases was obtained in the United States, accounts for their fluency in English. Among Los Angeles Iranians who speak a language other than English at home, about 80 percent claim that they speak English well or very well.

Many Iranians in Los Angeles are unassimilated partly because they are members of sizable religioethnic minorities (e.g., Armenians and Jews) with a long and well-defined history of minority experience. Among Iranians subgroups, the Muslims are the most assimilated, but even they are not very assimilated because of their exile status and a strong sense of Iranian nationalism.

In Los Angeles, where all Iranian subgroups are present, including Christian Assyrians, Zoroastrians, and Sunni Muslim Kurds, the extreme diversity of Iranians results in a much more complex pattern of social integration than among most other immigrant groups. This pattern is less complex in New York, where Iranian Muslims and Jews are the two major subgroups, and they tend to live apart. In both Los Angeles and New York, however, Iranians have non-Iranian coreligionists, a factor that partially accounts for their choice of settlement in these two metropolitan regions. Thus, when social integration occurs, the first tendency among Iranian subgroups is toward coreligionists of non-Iranian background (e.g., Jews toward other Jews). This is least likely among Muslims, however, whose secularism and nationalism prevent them from mingling with devout non-Iranian Muslims. Thus the integration of Muslims, which also happens to be the most rapid among all major Iranian subgroups, is very similar to the traditional assimilationist path—that is, into mainstream American society.

In the case of religious minorities from Iran, however, social integration is much more complex than for Muslims. Of particular interest is the extent to which Armenians and Jews, the two largest religious minorities from Iran, have become integrated within the general Armenian and Jewish communities, respectively, in America. At least in Los Angeles, where data on friendship ties and participation in organizations are available, there is no large-scale integration, at least not for the immigrant generation. The close friends of most first-generation Iranian Jews and Armenians are Iranian coreligionists. Furthermore, they are more likely than the Muslims to define their ethnicity in terms of both their nationality and religion, thus setting them apart from other Iranians and also from their coreligionists. Although minorities from Iran might find a congenial coreligionist community, their cultural and class differences are so pronounced as to prevent social integration among the first generation.

These first-generation differences, however, are slowly disappearing among the second generation; fewer than half of Armenian and Jewish Iranian children, both second- and one-and-a-half-generation (i.e., born in Iran and emigrated before age

ten) have exclusively Iranian coreligionists as close friends. These intergenerational differences suggest that as Iranian Jewish and Armenian children grow up they may move away from the Iranian community toward the general Armenian and Jewish American communities, respectively. Of course, the outcome will also depend on whom they marry. Not surprisingly, the first choice of almost all Iranian Jewish and Armenian parents is that their children marry Iranian coreligionists. Surprisingly, however, marrying a non-Iranian Jew or Armenian is the second choice, and marrying an Iranian only a third. Young Iranian Jews in Los Angeles share the same preferences as their parents in terms of mate selection. These data provide preliminary evidence for the absorption of the second-generation minorities from Iran into their broader religioethnic group. If the children of Iranian Armenians and Jews assimilate, they are more likely to do so within the general Armenian and Jewish communities than among Anglos. The assimilationist trajectory of Iranian Muslim children is not clear, but they are likely to move toward the mainstream white American society.

See also: ZOROASTRIANS

Bibliography

Ansari, A. (1988). *Iranian Immigrants in the United States.* New York: Associated Faculty Press.

Bozorgmehr, M. (1995). "Diaspora in the Post-revolutionary Period." *Encyclopedia Iranica* 7:380–383.

Bozorgmehr, M., and Sabagh, G. (1988). "High-Status Immigrants: A Statistical Profile of Iranians in the United States." *Iranian Studies* 21(3–4):4–34.

Dallalfar, A. (1994). "Iranian Women as Immigrant Entrepreneurs. "*Gender and Society* 8(4):541–561.

Fathi, A., ed. (1991). *Iranian Refugees and Exiles Since Khomeini.* Costa Mesa, CA: Mazda.

Hannasab, S. (1991). "Acculturation and Young Iranian Women: Attitudes Toward Sex Roles and Intimate Relationships." *Journal of Multicultural Counseling and Development* 19(1):11–21.

Hoffman, D. (1988). "Cross-Cultural Adaptation and Learning: Iranians and Americans at School." In

School and Society, edited by H. Touba and C. Delgado-Gaitan. New York: Praeger.

Kelley, R., and Friedlander, J., eds. (1993). *Irangeles: Iranians in Los Angeles.* Berkeley: University of California Press.

Light, I.; Sabagh, G.; Bozorgmehr, M.; and Der-Martirosian, C. (1993). "Internal Ethnicity in the Ethnic Economy." *Ethnic and Racial Studies* 16(4):581–597.

Naficy, H. (1993). *The Making of Exile Cultures: Iranian Television in Los Angeles.* Minneapolis: University of Minnesota Press.

Sabagh, G., and Bozorgmehr, M. (1987). "Are the Characteristics of Exiles Different Than the Immigrants? The Case of Iranians in Los Angeles." *Sociology and Social Research* 71(2):77–84.

Sabagh, G., and Bozorgmehr, M. (1994). "Secular Immigrants: Religiosity and Ethnicity Among Iranian Muslims in Los Angeles." In *Muslim Communities in North America,* edited by Y. Y. Haddad and J. I. Smith. Albany: State University of New York Press.

MEHDI BOZORGMEHR

IRAQI CHALDEANS

The largest single group of immigrants from the nation of Iraq are known as Chaldeans, indicating the religious preference observed by members of the group. Chaldeans belong to a specific subgroup, or rite, of the Roman Catholic Church. While they accept all of the major doctrines and rules of the Catholic Church and recognize the pope in Rome as head of the church, Chaldeans use a distinct set of rituals for their masses, which differ from those used by the majority of Roman Catholics. The services follow a different order, the music is oriental in style, and the Aramaic language is used.

Chaldeans are similar to other groups from Middle Eastern countries and often are mistaken for these groups by persons unaware of their distinct origins. Because they are from Iraq, one of the major Arabic-speaking nations, many people think of them as "Arabs," a term the majority of

Chaldeans reject. Because of their Christian religion, they are often associated with other Middle Eastern Christians. In particular, Chaldeans share a cultural heritage with another Christian group from Iraq who follow an early Christian bishop named Nestorius. Until the 1400s, when Chaldeans joined with the pope, their ancestors were part of this religious group, known as Nestorians or Assyrians. All but about 5 percent of Chaldeans in the Detroit area can trace their ancestry to a single town, Telkaif, in the province of Mosul in northern Iraq and near the ruins of the ancient city of Nineveh.

This common ancestry, their common religious heritage, and historical language are the major reasons for their strong sense of identity. Chaldeans tend not to identify with other Iraqis and Arabs, most of whom follow the Muslim faith. Chaldeans also lack a common linguistic tie with other Iraqis and Arabs because the original language of the Chaldeans is Aramaic, not Arabic. However, most Americans fail to distinguish between Chaldeans and immigrants from other Arabic-speaking countries and consider Chaldeans to be Arabs.

Immigration History

Chaldeans began to arrive in the United States around 1910, heading for Detroit, Michigan, the location of the developing automobile industry and target of much immigration at that time. It was also the location of another community of Middle Eastern immigrants: Roman Catholics from Greater Syria. Immigration into the Detroit Chaldean community continued at a slow but regular pace until World War II. At that time, U.S. immigration restrictions limited Iraqi immigrants to one hundred per year. By the end of that war, about one thousand Chaldeans resided in Detroit and the adjacent city of Highland Park.

Following World War II, a student visa was used by many Chaldeans to enter the United States; subsequently they married members of the community and remained in the United States as spouses of citizens. Immigration increased again in the 1970s, following the 1968 implementation of changes in U.S. immigration law that allowed much larger numbers of persons from Iraq to enter the United States.

Over the years, Chaldeans have moved away from the central city to various suburban areas of metropolitan Detroit, primarily southern Oakland County. A major Chaldean settlement remains in the central city, in north-central Detroit, bordering the Oakland County suburban community. This central city settlement continues to serve as the area of first settlement for many recent Chaldean immigrants. The wealthier suburban settlements are populated chiefly by second- and third-generation Chaldeans as well as by those immigrants who have been in the United States for several decades. While some immigrant groups tend to remain in the United States long enough to make some money and return to their homelands, most Chaldeans are permanent immigrants to the United States. Chaldeans usually become U.S. citizens rather soon after their arrival, and few return to Iraq except for occasional visits. In fact, most express a desire to bring their relatives to the United States rather than return to Iraq to join them.

Some Chaldeans have moved to other parts of the United States, primarily San Diego, California, and Phoenix, Arizona. Related communities of persons who identify themselves as "Assyrians" can be found in Chicago, Illinois, and Turlock, California. Census data do not enumerate Chaldeans, but community leaders and researchers estimated the community numbers between 60,000 and 75,000 in 1990. In the past, Chaldeans had fairly large families, averaging six or more children. Recent immigrants are likely to continue the large famly pattern. In second- and third-generation families this size tends to decrease.

Language

When Chaldeans first arrived in the United States they spoke the ancestral language of Telkaif, a dialect of Aramaic. Chaldeans refer to their language as Chaldean or as "Jesus's language," a reference to the fact that Jesus Christ spoke Aramaic during his life on Earth. Chaldeans also take pride in the fact that their church ritual is conducted in the language of Jesus, although changes through the centuries have probably altered this language considerably.

Language patterns in the Chaldean community changed dramatically with the new wave of immigrants who arrived after World War II. By that time Iraq was more highly structured as a nation, and Arabic had become accepted as a national language, largely displacing the village languages. Consequently most immigrants of the last half of the twentieth century speak Arabic, and many know no Aramaic/Chaldean. This creates some problems for the community in that there is no common language. In some Chaldean families the only common language is English. Most community activities now take place in Arabic, since that is the language known by the majority of recent immigrants who do not know English. The community has weathered this language diversity well and remains a single community.

The current language pattern in the community constitutes a mixture of the three languages, all of which may be heard at community gatherings. While recent immigrants know and use primarily Arabic, earlier immigrants prefer to speak the Chaldean language of the village. Persons born and reared in the United States prefer to speak English, although many know one or both of the other languages. The appropriate community language is also a matter of considerable dispute. Many Chaldeans, even those who know only Arabic, would prefer to have their children learn Chaldean/Aramaic, which they consider to be their ancestral language. Others believe that Arabic would be the most useful in international affairs or for return trips to the Middle East to visit.

Chaldean Institutions

There are three major institutions that are absolutely central to the Chaldean community: the Chaldean rite of the Roman Catholic Church; the extended family, which plays a major role in

The Mother of God Church (Our Lady of Chaldeans Cathedral) is located in Southfield, Michigan. (Mary C. Sengstock)

the lives of Chaldeans; and the retail grocery store, which has served as the major means of support for a majority of Chaldean families for more than eighty years.

The first Chaldean parish, called "Mother of God," was established in Detroit in 1948. Since then four additional parishes have been established, one in Detroit and the others in suburbs with large concentrations of Chaldeans. In 1982, the head, or patriarch, of the Chaldean Catholic Church established the first Chaldean diocese outside the Middle East in the Detroit suburb of Southfield, Michigan, one of the major enclaves of the Chaldean community. The bishop of this diocese is responsible for all Chaldean parishes in the United States, including the five parishes in the Detroit area, as well as two parishes in Chicago and four in California.

The importance of the Chaldean Catholic Church in this community cannot be overestimated. The church occupies a central role in all community activities. The church is the focus for the celebration of major life events: marriages, baptisms, first communions, and funerals. These activities usually are the foci of major social events, and the church is intimately involved. The

church also is the focus of routine social activities. Weekly Mass brings extended family and friends together, and the various churches and their social halls are the loci for many community activities, even those that are not religious in nature. Numerous organizations have been established through the Chaldean Church, many of them the usual men's, women's, and youth societies. Less traditional groups, such as the Chaldean Businessmen's Association, illustrate the all-pervasive role of the Chaldean Church in community life.

If any institution rivals the church's importance in Chaldean community life it is the extended family. In Iraq, Chaldean families were very large. Some immigrants report having as many as thirteen or fourteen brothers and sisters. Since the Chaldeans are from an Arabic-speaking country, many Americans assume that the men have multiple wives. However, this custom does not apply to Chaldeans.

Traditional Chaldean families are patriarchal in character, with the male serving as the unquestioned head of the family. Fathers, sons, and brothers maintain close ties throughout life. Property is often held in common by the patriarchal line rather than by the individual or the nuclear family. Originally brothers were responsible for the welfare of each others' wives and children should something happen to one of the brothers. Some remnants of this tradition are still seen in the United States, in that family-owned businesses are common. The importance of the patriarchal tie has diminished somewhat, however, and bilateral family ties are now more common, with Chaldeans maintaining close ties to relatives of both parents.

Chaldean families exert considerable influence over the lives of their members. Even those born in the United States report that they consider the wishes of their parents and other family members in the important decisions of life, such as their choice of an occupation or a spouse. While the influence of the family is decreasing somewhat, young people often forgo their chosen occupation to go into the family business. Many young people still report that they would not marry a non-Chaldean because their family would disapprove.

This extended family has produced an extensive occupational structure in the Detroit Chaldean community. Chaldeans are known throughout the area for their independent grocery stores. It is estimated that approximately twelve hundred independent grocery stores in metropolitan Detroit are owned by Chaldeans, often joint business ventures between or among two or three brothers, father and son, or uncle and nephew. Although many Detroit residents believe that these stores represent the equivalent of a Chaldean grocery store chain, the majority are owned and operated independently.

Community Relations

Recent immigrants who live in the central city tend to exhibit a distinct Arabic culture, with coffeehouses, Arabic signs on the stores, and Arabic spoken on the streets. However, Chaldeans who were born in the United States or have lived in the United States for many years tend to resemble other Americans of similar socioeconomic class. Chaldeans in the suburbs live in similar homes, send their children to the same schools, and enjoy the same kinds of recreational events as other middle-class Americans.

For many years the Chaldean community was divided into three major subgroups: the early immigrants from the village of Telkaif who spoke Chaldean/Aramaic; the more recent immigrants, who spoke Arabic, were from urban areas in Iraq and were often more educated than their predecessors; and those Chaldeans who were born and reared in the United States. This pattern has changed substantially, since few of the earliest immigrants remain. The community is also divided into two groups based on area of residence and economic level, with the wealthier Chaldeans living in suburban areas and exhibiting a middle-class lifestyle and the more recent arrivals living in the Arabic-speaking enclave in the central city. However, extended family ties often cross these divisions and help the members maintain a single community.

Chaldeans have generally believed that they could maintain good relations with other Americans by going about their businesses, raising their families, and generally keeping to themselves. Until the last quarter of the twentieth century they did not believe there was any need to make a special effort to maintain good relations with other ethnic groups. However, numerous antagonistic relationships with other ethnic groups have taught them that some efforts in this area are necessary.

Chaldeans relate to other ethnic groups in neighborhoods in which they live; in contacts with persons from other Arabic-speaking communities; and especially with customers and neighbors near their grocery stores. Chaldeans' large families and late hours often bring them into conflict with their residential neighbors. Many immigrants from Lebanon, Syria, or other Middle Eastern countries are annoyed that Chaldeans do not associate much with persons of other Arabic-speaking backgrounds, including both Muslims and Christians from other sects.

Most Chaldean stores are located in the black neighborhoods of Detroit's central city, and owners have encountered antagonism from their customers similar to that which Jewish or Asian business owners have experienced in other American cities. Chaldeans have been accused of unfair pricing, rudeness, failure to hire local people, and a general lack of sensitivity. However, Chaldean storeowners have established programs with local people to deal more effectively with such difficulties.

Chaldeans maintain strong ties to relatives wherever they live, including other countries. This is more characteristic of immigrants, who still have parents or siblings in Iraq. But even American-born Chaldeans visit Iraq or meet relatives visiting the United States. These kin may include one hundred or more relatives with whom the individual maintains personal contact and for whom he or she feels some responsibility (such as providing a place to live should the individual decide to visit or send a child to school in the United States).

Chaldeans' problems in the United States have increased as a result of the Gulf War between the United States and Iraq. This experience has affected the relations Chaldeans have with Americans of other ethnic groups, ties with their nation of origin, and their identity as Arabs. During the Gulf War, Chaldeans were concerned about their safety in the United States, as many groups targeted Iraqi Americans as the nearest representatives of a foreign enemy. Chaldean stores were targets of vandalism from customers and neighbors; children were harassed in schools; and there even were rumors that Iraqi Americans were to be placed in concentration camps, as were Japanese Americans during World War II.

The already close ties to relatives in Iraq have increased since the Gulf War. Concerned about the safety of these relatives, Chaldeans have conducted numerous projects to provide personal assistance in the form of food, money, and medicine. In most instances these projects have bypassed formal agencies by using family ties to carry aid directly to the Iraqi cities and towns in which relatives and friends lived.

The Gulf War also affected the Chaldeans' view of themselves as a Christian religious community not closely tied with the Arabic-speaking community as a whole. While most Chaldeans still do not identify themselves with Arab Americans, they are more aware that most other Americans do not make this distinction. Since they come from a Middle Eastern nation and speak Arabic, most Americans consider Chaldeans to be Arabs, whatever view the Chaldeans may hold of themselves. This has resulted in many Chaldeans feeling more understanding, if not sympathy, toward their identity as Arab Americans.

See also: IRAQI MUSLIMS

Bibliography

Cook, C., and Schaefer, J. (1991). "Arson Called Evidence of Anti-Arab Feelings." *The Detroit Free Press*, January 31, p. B-1.

Edmonds, P. (1991). "Hate Crimes Grow: Arab Americans Say the Rate Has Jumped Since War Began." *The Detroit Free Press*, February 7, pp. 3, 4A.

Gibbs, N. (1991). "Walking a Tightrope." *Time*, February 4, p. 42.

Goodin, M. (1991). "More Than Party Stores." *Crain's Detroit Business*, December, pp. 17–23.

Sengstock, M. C. (1969). "Differential Rates of Assimilation in an Ethnic Group: In Ritual, Social Interaction, and Normative Culture." *International Migration Review* 3:18–31.

Sengstock, M. C. (1970). "Telkaif, Baghdad, Detroit: Chaldeans Blend Three Cultures." *Michigan History* LIV:293–310.

Sengstock, M. C. (1974a). "Iraqi Christians in Detroit: An Analysis of an Ethnic Occupation." In *Arabic-Speaking Communities in American Cities*, edited by B. C. Aswad. New York: Center for Migration Studies and Association of Arab-American University Graduates.

Sengstock, M. C. (1974b). "Traditional and Nationalist Identity in a Christian Arab Community." *Sociological Analysis* 35:201–210.

Sengstock, M. C. (1975). "Kinship in a Roman Catholic Ethnic Group." *Ethnicity* 2:134–152.

Sengstock, M. C. (1977). "Social Change in the Country of Origin as a Factor in Immigrant Conceptions of Nationality." *Ethnicity* 4:54–70.

Sengstock, M. C. (1978). "Developing an Index of Ethnic Participation." *International Migration Review* 12(Spring):55–69.

Sengstock, M. C. (1982). *Chaldean Americans: Changing Conceptions of Ethnic Identity*. New York: Center for Migration Studies.

MARY C. SENGSTOCK

IRAQI MUSLIMS

Iraqi Muslim immigrants represented the third largest Arab population influx to the United States during the 1980s and 1990s. The 1990 U.S. Census reported a total of 14,359 Iraqi immigrants in the United States. The 1994 Report to Congress by the Office of Refugee Resettlement of the U.S. Department of Health and Human Services listed 18,340 Iraqi applications for refugee status granted by the Immigration and Naturalization Service (INS) between 1980 and 1994, with an additional 489 Iraqis granted asylum status for the same period. Estimates of total population, including first-, second-, and third-generation Iraqis given by Iraqi community members are as high as 300,000. The areas with the largest concentration of Iraqi Muslims are Detroit/Dearborn, Michigan; Chicago; and Los Angeles. States with smaller but significant Iraqi populations include Massachusetts, New York, Virginia, Tennessee, Washington, and Texas. Iraqi Muslims represent approximately 10 percent of Arab Americans, and outsiders would not generally be able to define them as distinct from other ethnic Arab Muslim populations.

Immigration Periods

The first measurable numbers of Iraqi Muslim immigrants entered the United States in the 1950s and 1960s. Most of these immigrants were students from wealthy Iraqi families who were seeking undergraduate or graduate degrees in American universities and remained as residents. Following the 1958 military coup and overthrow of the British-installed monarchy, political instability encouraged many students to remain in the United States.

A larger immigration of Iraqis began in the 1970s and continued through the 1990s. The Ba'ath Party came to power in 1968 with a platform promoting pan-Arab unity. Kurdish Iraqis, demanding an autonomous Kurdistan, were alienated, eventually leading to a failed attempt at revolution in 1975. A great number of Kurdish revolutionaries were forced to flee to Iran, Europe, or the United States as refugees. Proponents of a pan-Arab government were disturbed by the increasing emphasis placed on Iraqi nationalism and territoriality, which coincided with the growing power of Saddam Hussein. The Ba'ath regime is secular, prompting the cry of "godlessness" from Iraqi Shi'as.

In the late 1970s, the government began a program of systematic persecution of all those in opposition to Saddam Hussein's regime, including members of the Communist party, dissident Ba'athists, Kurds, and Shi'as. Approximately 300,000 Shi'as were deported to Iran. Many of those deported to Iran immigrated to the United States. When a cease-fire was agreed upon following the Desert Storm conflict of 1991, many Iraqis who had revolted against Sassam Hussein's regime in support of the international coalition led by the United States fled to Turkey, Iran, and Saudi Arabia. This resulted in a wave of Iraqi refugees arriving in the United States during the 1990s. In 1994 alone, more than 6,000 Iraqis were granted refugee status.

Settlement and Demographics

The Iraqi Muslims who arrived as immigrants settled in large urban areas of Arab concentration such as Detroit/Dearborn, Michigan; Chicago; and Los Angeles. There are several generations of Iraqi-American immigrants in some settlement cities. Refugees were settled in some areas without established Iraqi or other Arab communities; but many relocated, an action called secondary migration, to cities where they had relatives or where there were high concentrations of other Iraqi refugees. Arab Iraqi and Kurdish refugee groups live in the cities where there are established Iraqi communities; but the secondary migration to cities with kin or friends has resulted in additional small communities in Seattle; Dallas; St. Louis; San Diego; and northern Virginia.

The median age for all Iraqi immigrants, as calculated from 1990 U.S. Census data, is 36.6 years for men and 36.3 years for women. More than two-thirds of the adult population are men, and more than two-thirds of the adult men and women are married. Birth rates are approximately 1,500 per 1,000 women between ages 15 and 44.

Early History

Iraqis come from the area of the Middle East that was historically called Mesopotamia. Modern Iraq is bordered by the countries of Iran, Kuwait, Saudi Arabia, Jordan, Syria, and Turkey and by the Persian Gulf. The fertile alluvial plain between the Tigris and Europhrates rivers was the site of one of the earliest centers of civilization. Archaelogical sites such as Shanidar Cave in northern Iraq suggest clues to the way of life of early *Home erectus*. Shanidar is also the site of evidence from the eleventh and tenth millenium B.C.E. of plant and animal domestication as well as larger settlements. The first emergence of cities is found in the excavations of the city of Uruk (dated between 5000 and 4000 B.C.E.), where temples, mass production of pottery, a forerunner of concrete for building, and writing are found. The Babylonian culture contributed much to the beginnings of mathematics, astronomy, and literature. The Code of Hammurabi set out a code of laws for criminal and civil disputes. The *Epic of Gilgamesh* continues to provide an epic poem about the search for eternal life and ideology about creation.

Ethnic and Religious Diversity in Iraq

Iraqi immigrants share a pride in their early cultural beginnings. Their ethnic identification with Iraq is also based on its being a great center for Islamic culture. In fact, more than 90 percent of the population of Iraq is Muslim. There are,

however, small groups that belong to Christian sects, which include Chaldeans (aligned with the Catholic Church), Assyrians, and Eastern Orthodox.

Iraqi Muslims have intragroup ethnic and religious diversity. Approximately 75 percent are Arab. This includes the nomadic, pastoral Bedouins, who inhabit the desert areas of western Iraq. Arabic, which is a Semitic language, is the spoken language. The two major Muslim sects are Sunni and Shi'a. In Iraq Shi'as comprise the majority of the population. The division of Islam into these two sects began with conflict over who should succeed the Prophet Muhammad shortly after the Iraqi population assimilated the culture, language, and religion of the Arab conquerors in 637. Administration of government was through the religious leaders of communities. The Shi'as consider the family of Ali, who was Muhammad's cousin and married to his favorite daughter, to be the hereditary order of succession. Sunnis believe that the caliphate, or successor, should be an elected member of Muhammad's tribe. Since the seventh century, Arab Sunnis have held ruling positions in the government. Shi'as are against secularism and government that is not subject to Islamic law. They believe that religion should be integrated into all social as well as political life. Geographically most Arab Shi'as live in southern Iraq. Linguistically, though most Shi'as speak Arabic, a small percentage of Turkmen Shi'as in northern Iraq speak Turkmen.

The largest ethnic and religious minority in Iraq is the Sunni Kurds in northern Iraq. For many centuries they were tribal nomads who controlled the passage through the mountains from what is today Turkey and Iran into Iraq. They have a separate language, which is of Indo-Aryan origin. The majority of Kurds are Sunni Muslims, although there are Shi'a Kurds (particularly those who have lived as refugees in Iran, or close to the Iranian border). The Kurds sought a separate autonomy several times in the twentieth century and identify themselves as Kurds. There are four to five million Kurds in Iraq, comprising about 23 percent of the Iraqi population.

Iraqi Muslim Diversity in the United States

The ethnic, religious, and class differences of Iraq are also reflected within the Iraqi immigrant population in the United States. The ethnic groups are represented by the Kurds and the Arabs. Religious differences exist in the two different sects within Islam: the Shi'as and the Sunnis. Class differences are found between those immigrants who were raised in wealthy, urban, well-educated families in Iraq and those who were from rural, agricultural villages. There are also class differences between the immigrants who have achieved economic success through long-term residency in the United States and those who have arrived as first-generation refugees. Each difference represents a different worldview for those within the group.

Islamic Religion

Islam is a way of life that is followed by Iraqi Muslim immigrants. Many first-generation Iraqi immigrants are more likely to follow a devout adherence to Islamic practices. This devotion seems particularly common among newly arrived Shi'as. Among other new arrivals, Kurdish Sunnis and more highly educated Iraqis are more likely to ignore orthodox practices and seek rapid integration into American culture. Third-generation Iraqis may find pride in identifying with their Iraqi community, but they also rebel at traditional reli-

Iraqi immigrants march in Washington, D.C., in 1991 to help raise support for Kurdish rebels and other groups in opposition to the Iraqi government. (Reuters/Corbis-Bettmann)

gious customs and dress that mark them as different from their American peers. Despite these acculturation problems, Islam continues to represent an integral part of the culture and social networks of Iraqi Muslims. Cyclical revival movements, new immigrants, and converts through interfaith marriages are all factors that continually reinforce Islam for Iraqi immigrants.

For the followers of Islam, the word of God, as revealed by the angel Gabriel to Muhammad the Prophet, is contained in the holy Koran (or Quran). It cites not only religious practices but also is a guide for the way of life to be practiced by devout Muslims. There are Five Pillars of Islam, which represent the duties that Muslims must perform. They include reciting the *shahada*, which proclaims Allah as the one God and Mohammad as his prophet; praying daily; fasting during the holy month of Ramadan; giving alms to the poor; and a pilgrimage to Mecca at least once in a lifetime.

Shi'as, although a majority of the populations of Iraq and Iran, represent a minority of Muslims worldwide. In the United States, most of the mosques are Sunni structures. Shi'as are not generally active in the religious activities of mosques, although they may support the mosque financially and send their children to Islamic Sunday school. Many times Shi'as form Islamic centers as communal gathering places. For devout Sunnis, however, the mosque is important as a community center for such social activities as gathering for religious holidays, marriages, funerals, and Sunday schools for Islamic instruction for members of the younger generation. The conflict between the sects in Iraq is not as evident in the United States. The feeling in the United States is more that it is important to be a good Muslim.

The two most important holidays of the Muslim year are Id al-Fitr, which celebrates the breaking of the fast at the end of Ramadan, and Id al-Adha, which is a feast of sacrifice held on the tenth of the month of pilgrimage. Shi'as also celebrate Ashura, which is on the tenth of the month of Muharran. Ashura is a day of ritual mourning commemorating the martyrdom of Ali and his son, Hussein. Many Iraqi Muslims in the United States fast during Ramadan and observe the other restrictions against smoking and sexual contact. These obligations begin with dawn each day and end at sunset.

Acculturation and time have effected changes in the practice of Islam in the United States. Acculturation can be interpreted as the accommodations and changes made by individuals when two cultures come into close contact. Employment in the American workplace has dictated changes such as prayers combined into hours before or after work and visiting the mosque after normal work hours on Fridays. The Koranic laws concerning marriage, divorce, inheritance, and child custody are superseded by American civil laws. Although many Iraqi Muslims still prefer to follow dietary laws, it is difficult when smaller communities have no butchers who can provide *halal* (meat or fowl that has been slaughtered and bled in accordance with religious ritual). Many Iraqi immigrants follow the Koranic strictures against eating pork and drinking alcohol.

Language

More than two-thirds of the Iraqi Muslim immigrant population are bilingual in Arabic and English. The Koran is written in Classical Arabic. Modern Standard Arabic is understood across most of the Arab world, even though each country has a dialect. Arabic is now among the languages taught in American universities. Among the third and fourth Iraqi Muslim immigrant generations, Arabic may be replaced by English as the language spoken in the home. Many young people from these later generations, however, are aware of the political conflicts in the Middle East and seek knowledge about their ancestry. Newly arrived refugees from rural areas may not speak any English and may be illiterate in Arabic as well. Wealthier immigrants from urban areas of Iraq learn English in the school system. Many classes in technical schools and universities in Iraq are taught in English. The Kurds speak one of two Kurdish dialects, Kirmanji or Sorani, as well as Arabic, and are fluent in both languages. Many may also speak Turkish or Farsi, according to the location of their home village or town.

There are Iraqi sections within Arabic daily newspapers in the United States, such as the *Arab Times* and *Asharq Al-Awsat*. There is also Iraqi news published in the Islamic paper *Muslims*. More news on Iraq can be found in the weekly magazine *Al Waton Al Arabi*. In San Diego there is a Kurdish-language magazine, *Judi*, for immigrants. There also are a Kurdish radio program and a weekly television program.

Social Structure

Kinship. For centuries in Iraq a tribal social system provided a communal economic subsistence pattern for nomadic groups as well as for sedentary villagers. In the last half of the twentieth century, rapid urbanization eroded the tribal system. Lineage ties have become more important, and they remain important among many Iraqi Muslim immigrants. The Kurds represent a slight difference by placing more emphasis on the individual independence of nuclear families and less on lineage or extended kinship. Lineage is patriarchal, with the name of the family carried through the male line. When a woman marries, she retains her father's family name, but her children will bear her husband's family name.

Extended families of three generations live together in Iraq, with economic wealth pooled for the greater good. The father acts as the patriarch and is consulted for all major life decisions concerning family members. In the United States the nuclear family forms the basic social unit. The father no longer acts as patriarch, with the wife sharing more equally in economic support and major decision making. Larger Iraqi immigrant communities, through a process called chain migration, have sponsored immigration of many extended family members to the United States from Iraq. Secondary migration within the United States also results in the reunion of extended family or clan from other U.S. cities.

Traditionally, nuclear families are large, with five to ten children. Immigrant families in most cases find that the cost of living in the United States prohibits raising a great many children. Large families find reasonable housing difficult to obtain. Those entering the United States with refugee status quickly realize that both spouses must work. The traditional role of the husband as sole supporter and patriarch, with the wife at home running the household and caring for the children, is changed. There is a more egalitarian division of economic responsibilities, with the wife contributing to the family's economic support through employment. This can be difficult for large nuclear families, because without an extended family, child care becomes a major concern. In larger Iraqi communities some families share child-care responsibilities with other nuclear families.

Marriage. Tradition is still a major factor in the institution of marriage for Iraqi Muslim immigrants. Arranged marriages between kin, frequently first cousins, cemented family alliances in Iraq. In the United States, although there are fewer arranged marriages, the couple is obliged to ask for parental approval. Iraqi Muslims prefer endogamy, or marriage within the Iraqi Muslim community. A Kurdish immigrant man often returns to the Kurdish area of Iraq to marry a Kurdish woman and then apply for U.S. residency status for his wife. Personal advertisements are sometimes placed in Arabic newspapers requesting suitable Iraqi Muslim marriage partners. Interethnic marriage with Arab Muslims from countries other than Iraq is generally accepted. The important priority is not so much nationality or ethnicity, but whether the prospective bride or husband is a good Muslim. It is generally unacceptable to parents and the community for a Muslim woman to marry a non-Muslim man. The fear exists that the girl will be lost to the community, and the children will not receive Islamic instruction. It is more easily accepted for an Iraqi Muslim man to marry a non-Muslim woman if there is agreement that children will be raised as Muslims. Many Iraqi men who immigrated to the United States for higher education in the 1960s and 1970s married non-Muslim, American women. In areas of resettlement where there are large communities of

Iraqi Muslims, with new immigrants continually arriving, intrafaith marriages are more common.

The traditional Iraqi bride price, sometimes called a pledge, of gold jewelry paid to the bride to help her through any future economic hardships, has been replaced in the more traditional immigrant Iraqi Muslim culture by a sum of money paid to the bride's parents, or a ring or other gift to the bride, which may include a copy of the Koran. There is a marital contract that is signed and witnessed by several elders. In addition, a civil ceremony is held. Following a marriage, a night is set aside for the families to celebrate. The celebration involves feasting and dancing, with the genders separately performing folk dances.

Education. High value is placed on education among Iraqi immigrants, whether they arrived as students for higher education or as illiterate refugees. English as a second language classes are considered necessary for new arrivals. Graduation from the American public school system for first-generation children is seen as providing a necessary base for future economic success. There is also a strong motivation for education beyond high school, whether vocational school or college. In the 1990 U.S. Census, respondents cited educational attainment at the bachelor's degree or higher at approximately one-third of the population of men twenty-five years or older, and approximately one-fourth of the women twenty-five years or older.

Economic Patterns. There are two different economic classes among Iraqi Muslim immigrants: the successful established community members who are educated professionals, small-business owners, and those employed in other areas; and the newer immigrants, many of whom are refugees who arrive without education, English skills, or transferable occupational skills. Many early immigrants who arrived as students earned doctoral degrees in medicine and are now physicians and scientists. Many others earned engineering degrees, and there are those who became college and university professors. In large, urban Arab communities, some Iraqi Muslim immigrants have opened restaurants, coffee houses, and graphic arts shops.

Following the upward mobility progression of other immigrant groups, many of these successful Iraqi immigrants have moved their residences out of the ethnic enclaves in urban areas to suburban residences.

The refugees and some other immigrants represent a growing community of Iraqi Muslims who are low-income, unskilled workers living in large, urban Arab communities. In cities where there are no large concentrations of Iraqi Muslim or other Arab Muslim communities, they live in inner-city areas where housing is inexpensive but where crime is rampant. Housing and sufficient wages for subsistence are difficult to find for families who have many children and have lead some to dependence on public assistance programs.

When great numbers of refugees began arriving following the Desert Storm conflict in 1991, the established Arab Iraqi Muslim community, as well as other ethnic Arab Muslims, provided material support in the form of food and clothing. Long-term assistance and social integration of these refugees into the community, however, have not generally occurred.

Institutions and Customs. The coffeehouse represents a community institution that exists in all Middle Eastern countries. In large Arab communities in the United States, Iraqi Muslim men meet at coffeehouses to drink thick, dark Turkish coffee, play backgammon, and discuss the hardships of the economy, politics of the United States and Iraq, and other issues of the day. Some of the coffeehouses are owned and frequented only by Iraqis. Business is often conducted in the coffeehouses.

Women do not frequent the male domain of the coffeehouses. Traditional gender roles of women and men call for separation of the sexes in many ways. A devout Arab Muslim woman must pray for the food she has prepared, then eat separately from the men. Some newly arrived immigrant women continue this practice. Kurdish women, however, have more freedom in the community and regularly eat with the whole family. When male visitors are present or a woman is outside the home, she must cover her head with an *asha,* or head scarf. The traditional long, black cloak, *abayah,* worn by Iraqi women in the past, is not usually worn in the United States.

Acculturation and Cultural Persistence

The Iraqi Muslim immigrant families of two and three generations have made many changes in their patterns of cultural behavior over time. They have viewed the advantages of giving up outward displays of ethnicity and religion, such as prayer during the day and wearing head scarves, in return for an easier acculturation and acceptance by the dominant U.S. culture. More subtle changes have included receipt by a number of young women in the community of higher education and then their obtaining jobs that provide economic security, in contrast to the tradition of an early arranged marriage. There has been a change from extended family with communal goals and interests to a nuclear family model with an independent, individual-achievement ideology. There are, however, ethnic community organizations such as the Iraqi Foundation in Washington, D.C., that helps to create a cultural bond.

Most of the refugees are rural people from villages. Some are illiterate in their own language. Their dislocation and resettlement experiences have stripped them of their culture, extended network, and leaders. Some carry memories of interrogation and torture that inhibit their ability to take the risks required for successful adaptation in a new culture. This has made acculturation a slow process, characterized by gathering together in a conservative, adaptive strategy of kinship support, and rejection of outside influences requiring more culture change.

Kurdish refugees and urban Bagdad refugees follow different adaptations to life in the United States. These groups have more resources for coping with the stresses of resettlement. The Kurdish refugees put aside political and tribal differences in the United States to share their traditions. Many experienced forced relocation within Iraq and have a model for learning a new language and new behavioral patterns. There is the nationalistic desire among all to one day have a Kurdish homeland that is autonomous from other countries. In San Diego the Kurdish Muslim Society provides a community center for the large Kurdish refugee population. Many Kurds in California are owners of small businesses, including trucking companies and driver education companies. Urban refugees from Baghdad have a larger worldview from the mixture of lifestyles and cultures offered in Baghdad. Most have some English skills and higher education. They are aware of world and U.S. politics. Many are unafraid of taking risks to improve their social and economic statuses.

There is much diversity among Iraqi Muslim immigrants in the United States. Across this diversity, however, are shared values such as family and community ties and a shared religious ideology for many. Adaptation to the dominant U.S. culture will continue to mean change, but the traditional shared values will continue to make Iraqi Muslim immigrants aware of and open to the culture of their ancestors.

See also: IRAQI CHALDEANS

Bibliography

Abraham, N., and Abraham, S. Y. (1983). *Arabs in the New World: Studies on Arab-American Communities.* Detroit: Center for Urban Studies, Wayne State University.

Baram, A. (1991). *Culture, History, and Ideology in the Formation of Ba'thist Iraq, 1968–89.* New York: St. Martin's Press.

Bulloch, J., and Morris, H. (1991). *Saddam's War: The Origins of the Kuwait Conflict and the International Response.* London: Faber & Faber.

Elkholy, A. A. (1966). *The Arab Moslems in the United States: Religion and Assimilation.* New Haven, CT: College and University Press Services.

Fernea, E. W. (1969). *Guests of the Sheik: An Ethnography of an Iraqi Village.* Garden City, NY: Anchor Books.

Glazer, N., and Moynihan, D. P. (1964). *Beyond the Melting Pot: The Negroes, Puerto Ricans, Jews, Italians, and Irish of New York City.* Cambridge, MA: MIT Press.

Graves, T. D., and Graves, N. B. (1980). "Kinship Ties and the Preferred Adaptive Strategies of Urban Migrants." In *The Versatility of Kinship*, edited by L. S. Cordell and S. J. Beckman. New York: Academic Press.

Harris, G. L. (1958). *Iraq: Its People, Its Society, Its Culture*. New Haven, CT: HRAF Press.

Kreyenbroek, P. G., and Sperl, S., eds. (1992). *The Kurds: A Contemporary Overview*. London: Routledge.

Swan, C. L., and Saba, L. B. (1974). "The Migration of a Minority." In *Arabic-Speaking Communities in American Cities*, edited by B. C. Aswad. New York: Center for Migration Studies of New York.

U.S. Department of Health and Human Services. (1994). *Report to the Congress: Refugee Resettlement Program, FY 1994*. Washington, DC: U.S. Government Printing Office.

Wiley, J. N. (1992). *The Islamic Movement of Iraqi Shi'as*. Boulder, CO: Lynne Reinner.

Zogby, J. (1990). *Arab America Today: A Demographic Profile of Arab Americans*. Washington, DC: Arab American Institute.

WANDA E. CARLILE

IRISH

The Irish experience in America, now almost three centuries long, is sometimes regarded as the stereotypical "immigrant experience." Like other immigrants, they were pulled toward the New World by its chance for individual opportunity and religious freedom, and like others, they have demonstrated intergenerational upward mobility and gradual acceptance into the mainstream. Nonetheless, the experience of the Irish stands apart, shaped by circumstances unique to their homeland and influenced by the environment in America whenever they arrived.

Ireland: The Background

Ireland had a troubled history, long marked by foreign conquest and colonization. When immigration to America began, a majority of the people in Ireland were still descendants of the Celts from northwestern Europe who settled on the island between 350 and 250 B.C.E. And, since the time St. Patrick visited Ireland in the fifth century C.E., most Irish were Roman Catholics. Outsiders had gradually settled in, however, once English kings and armies started asserting control over Ireland in the twelfth century. By the seventeenth century, English kings and Parliaments were newly eager and able to make Ireland serve their own Protestant and colonial purposes. The British government transplanted whole colonies of Scottish and English families to "plantations" on land confiscated from Irish Catholics. Although these re-settled Protestants were concentrated in Northern Ireland, especially in Ulster, and in seaport towns such as Dublin, their power and influence reached all but the most isolated corners of the island. In the early 1700s, Parliament passed the Penal Laws, which limited the religious and civil rights of Catholics and favored the minority among the Protestants — those Anglicans who belonged to the British-imposed Church of Ireland. Even Scotch-Irish and Quakers faced discrimination, but the Irish Catholics suffered the most. A few converted to win British favoritism, but the vast majority insisted on their Catholic faith and persisted in their native Irish language. Still they had little chance but to become tenants on their own former farms, living on tiny allotments that had to be further subdivided when the children reached adulthood. By 1750, only 5 percent of all Irish land remained in Catholic hands, even though about 80 percent of the population was Catholic. This was the Ireland early emigrants left, a land so unequal that the majority could not affort to go even if they wanted to.

Irish Immigration Before 1845

The Irish were among the first immigrants to North America. By the Revolutionary War, there were more Irish in the thirteen colonies than any other white foreign-born group but the English. From the 1600s until the mid-1840s, the immigrants who recorded their place of birth as Ireland overrepresented the Protestants. According to best estimates, only about 20 to 25 percent of the Irish immigrants in this era were Catholic. By contrast, about three-fifths were Scotch-Irish Presbyterians or, less frequently, Quakers. As "dissenters" from the established Church of Ireland, they had suffered periodic religious restrictions, and their ministers began to encourage or even organize emigration among the young in their congregations. The Scotch-Irish — often the artisans, craftsmen, and "middling" farmers in Ulster — also had economic cause to emigrate once industrialization began to alter Northern Ireland's woolen and linen trades and farm conditions. The less advanced American colonies seemed a chance for them to maintain their trades and status. America had an appeal also among the sons of Anglican-Irish landholders, professionals, and businessmen. A fifth of the early Irish immigrants were Church of Ireland members, often young and anxious to take advantage of opportunities available in the colonies to men of their class and religion.

As they left for America, emigrants took their animosities along. Irish Anglicans joined the English colonists in their continuing dislike for Irish Presbyterians and Catholics. Pitted against one another for land and jobs at home, Presbyterian and Catholic Irish hated the English and each other. Conditions in the New World enabled the Irish Anglicans, Presbyterians, and Quakers to settle in more readily than the Irish Catholics. Early in the Colonial era, "the Irish" came to mean the Irish Catholics, a negative image that persisted.

Most of the Irish Catholic immigrants, men and women, could only pay for their passage by agreeing to be indentured servants in America. These poor Irish began to seem so conspicuous that some colonies enacted laws to restrict the importation of "papists" before the end of the seventeenth century. Only a few Irish Catholics arrived in the colonies with wealth. One, Thomas Dongan, served as governor of New York in the 1680s, and New York City as well as Philadelphia had prosperous Irish families. The Carrolls and their descendants, landed aristocrats who first settled in Maryland in the late 1600s, became the most important Irish family in colonial America. Charles Carroll III was the only Catholic to sign the Declaration of Independence, Daniel Carroll was a delegate to the Constitutional Convention, and John Carroll became the first Catholic bishop in the United States.

When the American Revolution began, most Irish Dissenters and Catholics were eager supporters of the cause and fought alongside each other against their common enemy, the English. Their revolutionary participation helped the Irish identify more firmly with the new nation, and an exodus developed once the War of 1812 settled any lingering fears that Britain might retake the former colonies. Between 1815 and 1845, about one million Irish immigrated to the United States; the small island was contributing nearly one-third of all arrivals each year.

It was Protestants, most of them from Northern Ireland, who continued to make up more than their share of the early nineteenth-century emigration. The English generally began to decide that America was a good place for the Irish Catholics, however, and the government lifted restrictions on emigration in 1827. Lower ship fares also began to enable more Irish to afford passage. By the 1840s, about nine out of ten Irish emigrants were Catholics, and they were coming now from poor as well as rich counties.

By their actions, the Irish Catholics contributed to their visibility as an identifiable group in the United States. They spoke English, but often imperfectly and with a "brogue" that invited caricature. They usually arrived young and single; a self-protective preference to marry and associate with each other led to charges of "clannish" behavior. The Irish also displeased British sympathizers by starting clubs to support homeland causes of Catholic emancipation. American temperance advocates despised the Irish neighborhood saloons, and established interests objected to Irish involvement in American politics. If Irish individuals or groups insisted on standing up to "their betters," became too vocal in political contests, or got involved in brawls, it convinced their detractors

Irish clam diggers gather on a wharf in nineteenth-century Boston. (The National Archives/Corbis)

that Irish Catholics were an aggressive, hot-tempered, and "uncivilized" lot.

Above all, their religion set Irish Catholics apart and fueled prejudice against them from the outset. Wherever they settled, Irish families organized Irish churches and insisted on priests of their own nationality, a habit that resulted in the separate ethnic parishes that soon came to characterize the American Catholic Church. Meanwhile, Irish priests and bishops gained permanent dominance within the Church hierarchy. Irish Catholic nuns arrived to care for children in orphanages and to teach; the children of immigrants began to learn precepts of the faith their parents and grandparents had followed in Ireland out of habit and defensive hatred for the English.

When evangelical revivals reinvigorated American Protestantism in the 1820s and 1830s, religious enthusiasts turned their holy wrath on the "papist" Catholics who had been their adversaries since the days of the Protestant Reformation. Catholic foes maintained that foreign despots were using immigrants in America to undermine democracy. These "nativists" began to justify their attacks on Catholics in the name of loyalty to the nation. A mob struck out the "enemy" Roman pope by burning a convent in Charlestown, Massachusetts, in 1834, and another mob vandalized a Catholic Church in Philadelphia in 1844. Anti-Catholics enthusiastically exploited fabricated tales about sexual misconduct between priests and nuns. A few Irish Catholics converted to eliminate the religious problem while, on their part, Irish Protestants deliberately became less "Irish" and more Protestant to distance themselves from any taint.

Like the children's nursery rhyme, the Irish had their "rich man, poor man, beggar man, and thief," but most of the generation who came into Jacksonian America busied themselves carving out opportunities somewhere amid the American "middling" classes. Irish lawyers, architects, teachers, and accountants contributed to the ranks of the professional classes. Irish businessmen catered to their countrymen in saloons, boarding-houses, and groceries. Immigrant craftsmen found jobs as carpenters or blacksmiths, and Irish laborers found work on the docks and on street, railroad, and canal-building crews. A small but significant share of the Irish merged with Yankee Protestant migrants heading to farmland in the Old Northwest (the area of Ohio, Indiana, Illinois, Michigan, and Wisconsin) or to towns on the urban frontier.

Despite prejudice and enemies they could not appease, Irish Catholics had established a foothold in America by the mid-1840s. They were beginning to experience upward occupational mobility, and they were establishing themselves in neighborhoods proudly centered around their churches. They might have consolidated their gains and conciliated their critics more smoothly in the following years but for the potato famine that struck Ireland in 1845.

The Famine Irish Immigrants, 1845–1870

When the potato crop turned out to be rotten in 1845, it was just the beginning of the Great Famine that lasted until the early 1850s. Nearly every year, if the recurring fungus did not destroy the crop, discouraged peasants had planted so few potatoes that the yield was not enough to feed them. Most Irish peasants had been living entirely on a diet of boiled potatoes, eating an average of ten or twelve pounds a day. The famine was so severe and relief efforts were so inadequate that, out of a population of fewer than nine million, more than one million Irish died of malnutrition, scurvy, or fever. Irish Catholic peasants had often vowed to live and die in their homeland, but now their attitude toward emigration reversed and they tumbled out. The most destitute made it only as far as Britain, but Canada or the United States became the destination for 1.8 million. These were the "famine Irish," a generation especially desperate to

leave Ireland and particularly disadvantaged in America because they arrived in such a huge wave.

They came, unsettling Protestant-dominated America, just at a time when urbanization, industrialization, and mass political participation were taking hold. All classes of Irish continued to arrive, but for the first time, immigration mirrored the mass of people who lived in Ireland. The famine Irish were generally poor, unskilled, anti-British, and defensively religious. Now, too, most of the immigrants came as families rather as single individuals, as had been the previous habit. Their financial and psychological resources exhausted by the ocean trip on "coffin ships," they stayed in the cities where their boats landed. Sudden Irish ghettos swelled Boston, New York, Philadelphia, and New Orleans. Landlords profited by cramming the new immigrants into dismal corners, attics, and basements. Such situations bred cholera, tuberculosis, mental illness, alcoholism, and vice. Even Catholic bishops and priests misunderstood how few alternatives poverty-stricken immigrants had; the chorus swelled, decrying Irish indifference to morality and a lack of self-help.

The only work these famine immigrants could get was at the bottom of the economic ladder. By their numbers they helped advance industrialization, holding the low-paying, unskilled, and dangerous jobs in the cities or joining railroad, canal, and road-building crews. Husbands wandered off in search of work or just away from agonizing responsibilities. Deserted mothers joined unmarried Irish women and widows to swell the ranks of domestic servants and sweatshop workers. "No Irish Need Apply" notices appeared in East Coast advertisements and in store windows, but other employers took advantage of the thousands of desperate Irish. They fired any troublesome employees or those who threatened to strike for better wages, and they hired Irish replacements who would take whatever wage was offered. Displaced workers turned their anger on the Irish. Pitched street fights regularly resulted in permanent injuries and deaths. A stereotyped notion of Irish Catholic immigrants took permanent form now, based on the poor who were so visible.

The lot of the immigrants was not so gloomy away from the crowded milltowns and city slums, however. From the 1820s, Irish immigrants had filtered westward, and they encouraged friends and relatives to join them. Bishops in Dubuque, Iowa, and St. Paul, Minnesota, urged the famine immigrants to go inland. New York's Irish Emigration Society made efforts to propel newcomers from ocean steamer to inland-bound ship. Some studies calculate that 25 out of every 100 immigrants left East Coast cities for points farther west. By 1850, 15 percent of the Irish-born immigrants in the United States lived in the Midwest, most in towns along the Great Lakes and inland rivers.

The plentiful mass of job-seeking Irish workers helped change the American landscape; they cleared Michigan forests as lumberjacks, dug coal in Pennsylvania, went down into copper or iron ore mines, headed for the California gold fields, and laid railroad tracks along the way. States such as Kansas were dotted with rural churches named after St. Bridget or St. Patrick, centers for the Irish farm communities that plowed the Midwest.

The economic and social opportunities of the booming frontier helped the Irish find a wider range of jobs and greater acceptance once they were away from the East Coast. Also, there were differences between those who could manage to go west and those who stayed behind. Young single Irish males and females and family heads with skills or education were better able to move than the older or unskilled famine Irish. At midcentury in Detroit, half of the Irish males were laborers, but half were skilled tradesmen, businessmen, or professionals. This contrasted sharply with the situation of Irish in places such as New York and Boston, where to be Irish was almost synonymous with being among the poor laboring class. Critics who blamed Irish poverty on a "weak character" failed to appreciate that in this "land of opportunity" it was important to be in the right place at the right time and that advantages of background, youth, and good health often fostered success.

Irish stereotypes based on the highly visible urban poor and on the long-standing Protestant animosities toward Catholics were reinforced by the role the Irish played in politics. The sudden famine influx of Irish Catholics occurred at a time when mass political participation was taking hold. In most states, residence rather than citizenship was enough to qualify men to vote. From almost the minute they stepped off the boat, the urban Irish were courted, usually by Democratic political machines such as New York's Tammany Hall, which offered low-level political positions, jobs, relief, and drinks in return for loyalty at the polls. But the Irish became Democrats not only because of such organized efforts; the party appealed to them because of its emphasis on the rights of the "common man."

The Irish mingled interests of the Democrats with particular interests of their own and, in so

An Irish Catholic wedding in the 1950s is held at St. Bridget's in Axtell, Kansas. (JoEllen McNergney Vinyard)

doing, became especially obnoxious to old-stock Protestant Americans who were championing reforms such as temperance, abolition, women's rights, and public education. Many Irish and Catholic leaders were urging voluntary temperance, but Irish, like German immigrants, opposed temperance laws that would outlaw saloons and breweries, eliminating not only neighborhood centers but also jobs. The Irish were uninterested in the abolitionists' antislavery crusades and sometimes were even hostile, worrying that freed slaves would present more job competition. Moreover, the Irish also opposed Sabbath laws, and their priests declared that women's rights advocates were threats to the home.

It was the religious education of their children that proved to be the most divisive and lasting issue separating Catholics and Protestants. In the 1850s, the "school wars" erupted between them. Public, tax-supported schools were just organizing in many communities at midcentury; Catholics protested, however, because the Protestants' King James Bible and Protestant teachers usually dominated the curriculum. Unable to achieve any acceptable accommodation with local public school boards, Catholics demanded a share of tax money to provide their own separate parochial schools. In some communities, the controversy split Protestant Democrats from Catholic Democrats and fractured the party. When one state legislature after another rejected the Catholics' request, Irish, German, French, and Belgian Catholic parishes proceeded to build parochial schools alongside their churches at their own expense.

Meanwhile, the controversy had added fuel to the wave of nativism and bigotry sweeping the country. The new party commonly termed the "Know-Nothings" maintained that the Catholics' position on education was convincing evidence that "papists" posed a dangerous threat to the very foundations of democracy in America. The party's supporters wanted to limit or eliminate the influence of Catholic immigrants as voters and candidates for office, maintaining they would take direction from the foreign pope. Know-Nothing adherents merged their cause with the hodgepodge

of diverse political interests that created the Republican party by the late 1850s. Their presence amid the otherwise reform-minded temperance and abolitionist Republicans gave the Irish Catholics even more reason to find permanent shelter as staunch Democrats.

As Democrats, Irish Catholics joined in issues broader than their own. Dating from the late 1850s, Irish in the North and Irish in the South adopted their particular section's position on slavery and war. Once the Civil War erupted, there were Irish-born officers and Irish regiments on each side. Since most Irish lived in the North, however, the great majority of Irish soldiers fought on that side. While they believed in saving the

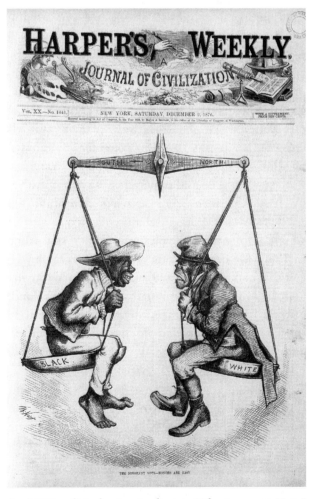

An 1876 political cartoon depicts "The Ignorant Vote" of the Irish and the African Americans balancing one another out. (Library of Congress/Corbis)

Union, the Emancipation Proclamation made it a war to free the slaves and, at about the same time, the draft started in the North. It seemed, with some accuracy in places such as New York City, that Irishmen were drawn for the draft more often than was their share. Further, few Irish could afford the option of paying substitutes. They sent letters home warning countrymen not to be fooled by recruiters from America who might promise them jobs but would, in fact, be signing them up for the army. Scapegoated, blacks became victims of draft riots in cities across the North. The most serious occurred in New York City, where, during four days of mob violence in 1863, blacks were beaten, hanged, and their orphan asylum was burned. For years after, critics and history books emphasized the part the Irish played in the draft riots, failing to acknowledge the heavy death toll among Irish soldiers and the decisive role Irish regiments played on Civil War battlefields.

For a generation, the massive famine emigration helped focus public attention on the poor and the "troublemakers" who seemed to confirm previous notions that the Irish were a dangerous element. Irish gamblers and prizefighters dominated headlines and scandalized the genteel Yankees. Protestant middle and upper classes were outraged by Irish-American labor activists and imported "radical" causes. Young Ireland collected money in America to support revolutionaries across Europe in 1848; the Fenians launched efforts from American soil in 1866 and 1870, aiming to seize Canada and then offer it to the British in trade for Ireland; a secret Irish society, the Molly Maguires, horrified the establishment by employing bombs, murder, and intimidation on behalf of Pennsylvania coal miners in the 1860s and 1870s.

Although they drew less notice, Irish immigrants established dozens of mutual aid societies for insurance, burial, and poor funds to take care of their own. As early as the 1840s, Irish women in New York City became the first to establish institutionalized care for orphans. The famine Irish grew old, still disproportionately concentrated in unskilled jobs, but thousands of Irish families had pooled their hard-earned salaries to fashion respectable lives centered around the neighborhoods, churches, schools, and institutions their children inherited.

The Postfamine Irish, 1870–1921

The famine had initiated a habit of mass emigration, and by the late nineteenth century, there were nearly as many Irish-born in the United States as there were in Ireland. By 1920, more than one million people in the United States had been born in Ireland; more than three million were the American-born children of Irish immigrants.

Ever after the famine, most Irish in America were Catholics, with origins in the twenty-six counties of southern Ireland. Entire families continued to arrive together, but about four out of five Irish immigrants in the last decades of the nineteenth century were young and single. In many years, young single females outnumbered males among the immigrants. Since Irish Americans put off marriage, sometimes into their thirties, single women now became a significant part of the work force. Coming from the poorer counties of Ireland, they had little to offer but a willingness to work and so moved into domestic service, printing, meat packing, garmentmaking, and textile factories. Irish women were active in the labor movement; organizers such as Mary Harris Jones — "Mother Jones" — defied "polite society's" notions about acceptable female behavior. Young Irish men, fluent in English and with friends and relatives already here, found it easier to advance by the end of the nineteenth century; employers chose them over the newest wave of Polish and southeastern European immigrants.

Irish families often gave their daughters more education than their sons; accordingly, second-generation Irish women were able to take advantage of opportunities becoming available to females. They were religious sisters, store clerks, secretaries, and nurses. Catholic women, most of them Irish, made up a fifth to a quarter of the teachers in public schools in nearly all American cities by about 1910. Catholic religious orders of men initiated colleges that filled with Irish sons.

Notre Dame athletic teams captured widespread headlines for the "Fighting Irish," but of greater permanent significance, Catholic college graduates were moving into the ranks of middle-class professionals.

Their successful intrusion into new jobs, their continued insistence on having Catholic parochial schools, and the swelling of Catholic ranks with new immigrants such as the Poles led to waves of nativism in the 1890s and again in the 1920s. In the 1890s, the American Protective Association (APA) attacked Catholicism as "alien" and wanted to restrict the flow of immigration. In the 1920s, tensions in society helped revive a new version of the Ku Klux Klan, which targeted Catholic, Jewish, and black Americans as dangers to democracy. Both the APA and the Klan capitalized on long-standing prejudices, but thanks to their efforts to prove respectability and patriotism, Catholics won broad-based support. Protestants rallied to the defense of Catholics in several states where nativists tried to outlaw parochial schools by constitutional amendments. The 1920s marked the end of the last organized nativist movements.

Irish Immigration After 1921

The number of foreign-born Irish in the United States began to diminish after World War I. The old immigrants died, the creation of the Irish Free State in 1921 gave the young more reason to stay at home, and the Great Depression of the 1930s choked off job opportunities in the United States. Emigration did not soar again until the 1950s, a period when the American economy was strong and the Irish economy was stagnant.

It was the children, grandchildren, and great-granchildren of immigrants who gave shape to the Irish-American experience for most of the twentieth century. As from the time of the famine, the Irish Catholics still represented "the Irish" in the popular imagination. Auto industrialist Henry Ford, the son of Irish Protestant immigrants, became an American folk hero. Yet the press generally hailed him as an "American" success story.

Most Irish Americans began blending the heritage of their ancestors with their experiences in the United States, sometimes railing against Irish Catholicism as a disability and sometimes embracing it as a strength. The plays of Eugene O'Neill and the novels of James T. Farrell and Edwin O'Connor were just part of a literary outpouring that told of lives familiar to many Irish Americans; yet such portrayals captivated Americans who had grown up in families not Irish. Reflecting other interests, novels by the third-generation and Princeton-educated F. Scott Fitzgerald revealed the American upper-class Protestant society he knew.

In one arena after another from the 1920s onward, Irish Americans moved between the immigrant world of their parents or grandparents and their own more plural, class-based society. Screen stars such as Spencer Tracy and Bing Crosby took on both stereotypical Irish roles and roles without any "ethnic" character. Labor leaders Philip Murray and George Meany, whose ancestors were Irish immigrant laborers, presided over powerful unions and spoke for working-class interests that crossed lines of ethnicity and religion.

Certain Irish Catholics were embarrassed by the famous 1930s "radio priest" Father Charles Coughlin, who blamed the Depression and its lingering effects on an "international Jewish conspiracy." And in the early 1950s, when Wisconsin's Republican senator Joseph R. McCarthy launched the national "Red Scare" and a witch-hunt for Communists, many critics attributed his cause and tactics to his Irish Catholicism. Each man did gain important support from among Irish Catholics, but their wider appeal reflected bigotry, fear, and an enthusiasm for easy answers shared by many Americans in times of political tension.

Whereas earlier immigrant politicians gained power in urban politics based on a bloc of Irish votes, the second and third generation moved into positions of national influence because they managed to have broader appeal, albeit often among Catholic and working-class voters. In 1928, Governor Alfred E. Smith of New York became the first Irish Catholic nominated for president. Throughout his presidency, Franklin D. Roosevelt

Police officers wearing "Emerald Society" sashes march in Chicago's 1996 St. Patrick's Day Parade. (Sandy Felsenthal/Corbis)

rewarded Irish Democratic loyalty by appointing an unprecedented number of Irish Catholics to judgeships and important New Deal posts. In many states Irish Americans were winning election to the Senate and House of Representatives. Nonetheless, old-style Irish bosses such as Boston's James Michael Curley reinforced prevailing stereotypes of manipulative Irish politicians, an image still perpetuated by Chicago's mayor, Richard J. Daley, in the 1960s.

In 1960, John F. Kennedy became the first Catholic president. Kennedy's great-grandfather was a famine emigrant, but his maternal grandfather was mayor of Boston in the classic tradition of urban Irish politicians, and his wealthy father was ambassador to Great Britain from 1937 to 1940. Harvard-educated and already a U.S. senator, Kennedy was hardly typical. To win, moreover, he made it clear that he was more a loyal

"American" than a Catholic. Nonetheless, Irish Catholics felt they had cleared the last hurdle to full acceptance. Indeed, after Kennedy died and other Irish Catholics sought the office, including Robert Kennedy and Eugene McCarthy in 1968, opponents no longer made Catholicism an issue.

Their identity had begun to wane when Irish Catholics celebrated having "arrived" with Kennedy. Immigrant legislation in the 1960s reversed previous favoritism to northwestern Europeans, and admission became more difficult for the Irish. Fewer than 40,000 Irish entered the United States between 1971 and 1989. Meanwhile, decades of intermarriage meant many second-, third-, and fourth-generation families were only partially Irish and Catholic. Uncritical religious attachments were weakened, variously, by changes in the old Latin Mass after Vatican II, by papal pronouncements against birth control, and by the continuing subordination of religious sisters and laywomen. Upward mobility brought an end to old Irish neighborhoods; families settled in class-based suburbs, and their children attended public schools. Social and economic changes added up, even, to an "Irish Catholic vote" that was no longer predictably Democratic.

Paradoxically, the third, fourth, and fifth generations show interest in rediscovering their heritage, part of American society's growing appreciation for diverse cultures that emerged in the 1960s. They search genealogical records for Irish ancestors and travel to Ireland. They register for Irish history courses and listen to Irish musical groups. A few study the Irish language, and a few donate to the Irish Republican Army's ongoing battle against the "Brits" in Northern Ireland. They sometimes create new romanticized stereotypes.

If the old Irish Catholics are a "vanishing breed," as some among them fear, gone, too, are the "No Irish Need Apply" signs, the nativists' anti-Catholic campaigns, and the informal agreements to keep Irish Catholics out of upper-class neighborhoods, elite clubs, and prestigious corporate boardrooms. Current generations enjoy wider opportunity and greater freedom than their Irish immigrant ancestors ever anticipated when they set sail for America. There can be only a measured lament for a past that was, in fact, often frightening, hard, and unfair.

See also: SCOTCH-IRISH; TRAVELERS

Bibliograhy

Adams, W. F. (1960). *Ireland and the Irish Emigration to the New World from 1815 to the Famine.* New York: Russell & Russell.

Clarke, D. (1973). *The Irish in Philadelphia: Ten Generations of Urban Experience.* Philadelphia: Temple University Press.

Conzen, K. N. (1976). *Immigrant Milwaukee, 1836–1860: Accommodation and Community in a Frontier City.* Cambridge, MA: Harvard University Press.

Diner, H. R. (1983). *Erin's Daughters in America: Irish Immigrant Women in the Nineteenth Century.* Baltimore, MD: Johns Hopkins University Press.

Dolan, J. P. (1975). *The Immigrant Church: New York's Irish and German Catholics, 1815–1865.* Notre Dame, IN: University of Notre Dame Press.

Greeley, A. M. (1981). *The Irish Americans: The Rise to Money and Power.* New York: Harper & Row.

Handlin, O. (1979). *Boston's Immigrants: A Study in Acculturation,* revised edition. Cambridge, MA: Harvard University Press.

Kennedy, R. E. (1973). *The Irish: Emigration, Marriage, and Fertility.* Berkeley: University of California Press.

McCaffrey, L. J. (1976). *The Irish Diaspora in America.* Bloomington: Indiana University Press.

McCaffrey, L. J. (1987). *The Irish in Chicago.* Champaign: University of Illinois Press.

Miller, K. A. (1985). *Emigrants and Exiles: Ireland and the Irish Exodus to North America.* New York: Oxford University Press.

Schrier, A. (1958). *Ireland and the American Emigration, 1850–1900.* Minneapolis: University of Minnesota Press.

Shannon, W. V. (1963). *The American Irish.* London: Macmillan.

Vinyard, J. M. (1974). *The Irish on the Urban Frontier: Detroit, 1850–1880.* New York: Arno Press.

JoEllen McNergney Vinyard

ISMAILIS

The Shi'a Imami Ismaili Muslims are generally known as the Ismailis. They belong to the Shi'a branch of Islam; the other, larger branch being the Sunni. During its long history, from the seventh century C.E., the Ismaili community has included people from many different cultures, and cultural diversity continues to characterize the community.

In 1995, the Ismailis lived in more than twenty-five different countries, mainly in Central and South Asia, East Africa, the Middle East, Western Europe, Australia, New Zealand, Canada, and the United States. The Ismailis in America are predominantly of Indo-Pakistani origin. They are also known as Nizari Ismailis, Khojas, Aga Khanis, and Batinis.

In common with other Shi'a Muslims, the Ismailis affirm that after the death of Prophet Muhammad, his cousin and son-in-law, Ali, became the first Imam (spiritual leader) of the Muslim community. They believe that this spiritual leadership, known as Imamat, continues through the hereditary line of Ali and his wife Fatima, the Prophet's daughter. According to Shi'a doctrine and tradition, succession to the Imamat is by designation (nass). It is the absolute prerogative of the Imam to appoint his successor from amongst any of his male descendants, whether they be sons or remoter issue.

Prince Karim Aga Khan IV is the forty-ninth hereditary Imam of the Ismailis, having succeeded his grandfather Sir Sultan Mohammed Shah Aga Khan III on July 11, 1957. Spiritual allegiance to the Imam of the Time (Hazar Imam) supersedes ethnic, cultural, geographic, and linguistic diversity within the global Ismaili community. The Ismaili identity is a religious one.

Throughout the centuries, the Ismailis have made major contributions to Islamic civilization. The University of al-Azhar, the Academy of Science, and the city of Cairo were founded by Ismaili imams, who also ruled as Fatimid caliphs from 934 to 1095.

Immigration Patterns

The Ismaili presence in America began in the early 1960s, with students mainly from the newly independent East African countries of Kenya, Tanzania, and Uganda. They were later followed by coreligionists from the South Asian countries of India and Pakistan. Significantly, Karim Aga Khan had graduated with a B.A. (honors) degree in Islamic history from Harvard in 1959. His grandfather had strongly encouraged Ismaili students to seek higher education at Western universities. Aga Khan scholarships and several American governmental programs enabled many Ismailis to enroll at universities throughout America.

The postindependence political, economic, and racial situations, especially the "Africanization" policies in East Africa, dimmed prospects for all minorities of Indian origin, which included Ismailis. Consequently some Ismaili students accepted professional positions in America, while others returned to America, having become disillusioned about their future in their countries of birth. In the late 1960s a majority of the eight hundred to one thousand Ismailis in America were unmarried students, professionals, and entrepreneurs residing around college towns mostly in the eastern United States.

In 1972, the mass expulsion of Asians from Uganda by its military dictator, Idi Amin, swelled the Ismaili population of America to about two thousand. Coincidentally, Karim Aga Khan's uncle, Prince Sadruddin Aga Khan, was then U.N. High Commissioner for Refugees. His personal efforts helped admit more Ugandan Asian refugees to America. During 1972–1973 seven Christian and Jewish voluntary agencies resettled some two thousand refugees, of whom approximately one thousand were Ismailis, the rest being other Muslims and Hindus. Their sponsors either created small Ugandan clusters (as in Spartanburg, South Carolina; Tampa Bay, Florida; New York–New Jersey; Milwaukee; and Harrisburg-Lancaster, Pennsylvania) or scattered them across the country. This was the agencies' first experience of resettling non-Christian and non-Jewish refugees, yet the operation was remarkably successful.

However, as the Ismailis made contact with other Ismailis or friends and relatives in America—often through their sponsors—some of them immigrated to one of the clusters or to a different but economically attractive destination. Some families left Florida because they experienced the same types of discrimination as the Hispanics in housing, employment, pay, and promotions.

In 1976, there were about 2,500 Ismailis in America. The 1985 estimate was 25,000 to 30,000, and the 1995 figure was 55,000 to 60,000. The vast majority had come from South Asia under a liberal U.S. immigration policy.

When Karim Aga Khan celebrated his Imamat's silver jubilee with his followers in America in November 1982, the majority of them lived in Houston, Chicago, Dallas, Los Angeles, Miami,

New York–New Jersey, Atlanta, and in smaller numbers in more than fifty other cities across America. The majority were from Pakistan. The rest came from Tanzania, Uganda, Canada, Kenya, India, the United Kingdom, and Bangladesh.

Thirteen years later, in 1995, 40 percent of America's Ismailis were of Pakistani origin, the others being from India (30%); East Africa (15%); Bangladesh and Burma (5%); and the Middle East and Central Asia (2%). Eight percent were born in the West—the United States, Canada, and the United Kingdom. Geographically they were concentrated in the same cities listed earlier, though many smaller congregations (*jamats*) had grown substantially, especially in booming cities such as Albuquerque; Atlanta; Austin; Memphis; Orlando; Phoenix; Portland, Oregon; Raleigh-Durham; San Antonio; and Seattle. This relatively highly educated community's emphasis on education, especially of girls, has resulted in smaller families compared to the countries of origin. Two-parent, two-children households were common, although some households had grandparents. During the 1980s, 60 percent of the Ismailis were male.

Language

Almost all East African Ismailis spoke English, Gujarati, and Swahili. Many also spoke Hindi. Ismailis from Pakistan spoke English, Urdu, and Gujarati. Those from India spoke English, Hindi, and Gujarati. However, many lacked fluency in English. By the late 1980s, the community began English classes at most multipurpose community centers (*jamatkhanas*). Television was and still is an important medium for teaching American English to such newcomers.

There is only one official Ismaili periodical, *The Ismaili, USA,* published three times a year by the Ismaili National Council in New York. It covers the activities of national and local community institutions and features articles on various aspects of community life. Imamat activities are highlighted. As the emphasis is on proficiency in English, the community has no native-language

maintenance program. Instead, students are encouraged to learn new languages such as Spanish, French, and Arabic.

Assimilation

A majority of the Ismailis were merchants, professionals, and clerical-technical workers in their countries of origin. Many who immigrated to the United States with capital immediately ventured into business, while many more chose to gain experience working for others before doing so. Others aspired to become business owners during their lifetime. Ismailis preponderated in convenience stores/gas stations; franchised fast food restaurants; dry cleaning plants and pickup stations; jewelry and gift shops; franchised hotels and motels; laundromats; printing and office supply stores, and Asian Indian grocery stores and restaurants.

Some of these businesses had multiple locations locally, regionally, nationally, and even internationally. One Houston family boasted fifty franchised hotels and motels, while another owned fewer hotels, but these had more than twenty thousand rooms. An Atlanta family ran a network of thirty-one convenience stores, all in the metropolitan Atlanta area. At least fifty Atlanta Ismaili businesses had multiple locations.

Ismaili entrepreneurs were also found in manufacturing, distribution, export-import, wholesale, construction, land development, assembling, and communications. Surprisingly, a large number of these enterprises were owned and operated by former accountants, engineers, lawyers, or other professionals who either did not get American accreditation, chose to abandon their fields, or were squeezed out by corporate downsizing. This gave rise to a new breed of Ismaili degreed *dukawallahs* (shopkeepers).

Ismaili students and professionals who entered America in the 1960s and the 1970s were pioneers. They held leadership positions disproportionately in community institutions as honorary workers. Outside the community, they and the newer generation were well represented in diverse professions. Ismaili accountants, dentists, doctors, lawyers, consultants, professors, pharmacists, corporate executives, computer programmers, and systems analysts were quite common. The only Ismaili college president (Hahnemann University, Philadelphia) had the further distinction of being the sixth-highest-paid private college president in 1994. Ismailis also held senior posts at the World Bank and the United Nations.

Ismailis have been a minority for the greater part of their history, so discrimination is a familiar experience for them. It has surfaced in employment, promotion, remuneration, purchasing houses in certain areas, and renting space in some business centers. However, legal remedies are available, and some Ismailis have successfully used them. The 1990s witnessed a noticeable return migration to East Africa and South Asia. This was sparked not by discrimination in America but by irresistible economic opportunities in their original homelands. This is a temporary absence from America, which is their permanent home. In September 1995, there were eighty-five jamatkhanas in America to reflect the community's permanence.

Once they were financially secure, Ismailis turned their attention to home ownership. Back home, they were highly urbanized. Aga Khan Housing Boards had built apartment complexes for less prosperous Ismailis whereby renters could eventually become owners. In 1995, about 60 percent of the Ismailis in America were homeowners. Based on the Atlanta example, Ismailis tended to live in apartment complexes near the three local jamatkhanas. A majority bought homes in close proximity to the jamatkhanas and superior schools. Prices ranged between $90,000 and $600,000, with the majority in the $100,000 to $200,000 bracket.

Religious Life

Religion, guided by the Imam of the Time, is central to Ismaili life. Prayers and ethics are among the pillars of the faith. Daily jamatkhana attendance is common. The multipurpose jamatkhana facility features a prayer hall, social hall, library, religious education classrooms, and administrative offices. Ismaili hereditary Imams, being considered infallible in spiritual matters, have guided their followers to have a progressive, practical, multicultural outlook on Islam, emphasizing the use of intellect in the practice of the faith.

America's Ismailis are part of an international community linked by their Imam and the Imamat's Aga Khan Development Network (AKDN), which is concerned with three main areas: social development, economic development, and culture. In social development, most AKDN activities take place in East Africa and South Asia. The key institutions are the Aga Khan Foundation, established in 1967 in Geneva; Aga Khan University, founded in 1985 in Pakistan; Aga Khan Health Services; Aga Khan Education Services; and Aga Khan Housing Boards.

The AKDN's economic activities are executed by the Aga Khan Fund for Economic Development and its affiliates—Tourism Promotion Services, Industrial Promotion Services, and financial institutions located in Africa and Asia.

The Aga Khan Trust for Culture coordinates the activities of the Aga Khan Award for Architecture; the Aga Khan Program for Islamic Architecture, created in 1979 at Harvard University and the Massachusetts Institute of Technology; and the Historic Cities Support Program.

The AKDN has seventy-four governmental and nongovernmental partners throughout the world, such as the World Bank, USAID, and the Rockefeller Foundation. This list reads like a "Who's Who" in philanthropy, education, health, economic development, architecture, appropriate technology, agriculture, child development, and women's welfare. The Aga Khan oversees these myriad activities from his secretariat at Aiglemont, France.

The global outlook comes, additionally, from a tradition of international service in Karim Aga Khan's family. His grandfather Sultan Mohammed Shah Aga Khan was president of the League of Nations from 1937 to 1939. His father, Prince Aly Khan, was Pakistan's ambassador to the United Nations. His brother, Prince Amyn Aga Khan, joined the U.N. Secretariat upon graduating from

THE AGA KHAN DEVELOPMENT NETWORK

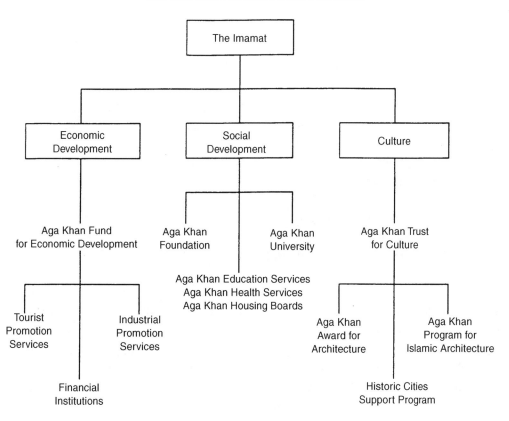

Harvard in 1965, later moving to the Aga Khan's secretariat in 1968. His uncle, Prince Sadruddin Aga Khan, was the U.N. High Commissioner for Refugees from 1965 to 1977.

The Aga Khan's position as the Imam of some fifteen million Ismaili Muslims worldwide, his enlightened leadership, his philanthropy, and his personal contacts with leaders around the world have made him a global leader and a bridge between Muslims and non-Muslims and between industrial and developing countries. American Ismailis share their Imam's vision of "a frontierless brotherhood of mankind" and are seen as "the jamat of destiny" by the Imam. This privileged position places responsibility to share their wealth and talent with all less fortunate peoples, particularly in the developing world.

Marriages are monogamous and almost entirely endogamous (between Ismailis), and divorce is rare. Family is extremely important, and kinship is valued. Interpersonal relations have revealed strains particularly as youths try to balance their Ismaili and American identities, and some adults are in a transitional period of adjustment to all aspects of life in America. Hitherto generally dominant male heads of households have had their authority challenged or diluted by their children's greater Westernization and wives' financial independence, wherein they are both breadmakers and breadwinners.

Health, housing, education, and economic matters have had priority over the arts since 1965, and as a community, the Ismailis are apolitical. However, their community institutions are elaborate and are generally the same in all countries.

Under the Aga Khan Council for the United States, headquartered in New York City, are seven local councils. The Executive Committee of the National Council includes the chairpersons of the Aga Khan Economic Planning Board, the Aga Khan Education Board, and the Aga Khan Health Board. These three national boards in turn have local boards in each region. All local boards must implement the authorized objectives and current policies of their respective national boards.

The Aga Khan wants the Ismailis to obtain the best secular education available and to succeed in a meritocratic society. Good health and economic prosperity are repeatedly stressed by the Imam. To achieve these objectives, the various boards and portfolios such as cultural and women's affairs, youth and sports development, and social welfare committees organize seminars, workshops, lectures, exhibitions, clinics, and personal consultations.

The Tariqah and Religious Education Board is entrusted with the vitally important task of imparting religious education to school-age children and organizing programs for adults.

Disputes within the community are settled through the Conciliation and Arbitration Board. Finally, overseeing all these institutions' compliance with budgets and proper standards of financial discipline is the Grants and Review Board.

All the community institutions at the international, national, regional, and local levels are staffed by volunteers. As volunteerism is critical for the continued progress of the jamat, the Imam wants to "professionalize" the volunteers and "volunteerize" the professionals in the community. Karim Aga Khan's daughter Princess Zahra Aga Khan, a 1994 Harvard graduate, immediately joined the Aga Khan's secretariat to implement this mission and head its social welfare department.

The American Ismailis, whose identity is a religious one, are a resilient, progressive group with a worldwide perspective. They desire to integrate with the dominant American culture and make a meaningful contribution toward making America a better place for everyone. In accordance with the guidance of their Imam, they seek good relations with all people of their adopted homeland.

The Aga Khan constantly reminds his followers to model their lives on that of Prophet Muhammad, whose life was characterized by integrity; honesty; humility; generosity; solicitude for the weak, sick, and poor; and wisdom in conceiving new solutions for problems that could not be solved by traditional methods without compromising the fundamentals of the faith.

Bibliography

Aga Khan. (1954). *The Memoirs of Aga Khan: World Enough and Time.* New York: Simon & Schuster.

Aga Khan Foundation. (1994). *The Aga Khan Development Network. Washington, DC: Author.*

Daftary, F. (1990). *The Ismailis: Their History and Doctrines.* Cambridge, Eng.: Cambridge University Press.

Daftary, F. (1994). *The Assassin Legends: Myths of the Ismailis.* London: I. B. Tarius.

McCarry, J. (1994). "High Road to Hunza." *National Geographic* 185(3):114–134.

Makerem, S. N., ed. and tr. (1977). *The Political Doctrine of the Ismailis.* Delmar, NY: Caravan Books.

Motani, N. A. (1975a). "The Ugandan Civil Service and the Asian Problem, 1894–1972." In *Expulsion of a Minority: Essays on Ugandan Asians,* edited by M. Twaddle. London: Athlone Press.

Motani, N. A. (1975b). "Uganda's Asian Refugees: Their Historical Background and Resettlement in Canada and the USA." *Kenya Historical Review* 4:27–46.

Motani, N. A. (1978). "Uganda's Asians Refugees in North America." In *World Minorities: A Second Volume,* edited by G. Ashworth. London: Quartermaine House.

Nanji, A. (1983). "The Nizari Ismaili Muslim Community in North America: Background and Development." In *The Muslim Community in North America,* edited by E. Waugh. Edmonton: University of Alberta Press.

Thobhani, A. (1993). *Islam's Quiet Revolutionary: The Story of Aga Khan IV.* New York: Vantage Press.

Williams, R. B. (1988). *Religions of Immigrants from India and Pakistan: New Threads in the American Tapestry.* (1988). Cambridge, Eng.: Cambridge University Press.

NIZAR A. MOTANI

ISRAELI JEWS

See JEWS, ISRAELI

ITALIANS

Between 1880 and 1920, the period of large-scale emigration from Italy to the United States, some four million Italians entered America. Before the 1880s, Italians had been arriving in America in small numbers as far back as the seventeenth century. Indeed, in 1610, only a few short years after the first English settlement at Jamestown, several Italian craftsmen immigrated to Virginia. They were followed in 1622 by a group of Venetian glassmakers, who took up their trade in the colony. With unsettled conditions in sixteenth- and seventeenth-century Italy, many Italians left for political and religious reasons. A group of Italian Protestants known as Waldensians fled persecution in northern Italy and sought refuge in America. Many Italian intellectuals and revolutionaries immigrated to the United States for the same reason. One of the most prominent was the political philosopher Filippo Mazzei, a friend of Thomas Jefferson. Mazzei wrote a series of articles in which he espoused the idea of the equality of all men and of a true democratic government. Denouncing the British government as tyrannical, Mazzei's arguments had a significant influence on America's revolutionary leaders. Another famous Italian-American revolutionary leader was William Paca, a signer of the Declaration of Independence. In 1782, Paca became the governor of Maryland, the first governor of Italian heritage in the nation.

In the years preceding the Civil War, Italian immigrants arrived chiefly from the northern and economically more advanced areas of Genoa, Tuscany, Venetia, Lombardy, and Piedmont. Many were farmers from rich Piedmont and Liguria and were attracted to California, where they developed rich citrus and wine enterprises. Several hundred Italians were attracted by the 1849 Gold Rush in California, while others settled in Louisiana, where they worked as seamen at the port of New Orleans. In Milwaukee, many Italian artisans worked for Casper Hennecke, a nationally known statuary maker.

The turning point in the history of Italian immigration to the United States was 1880. Of the nearly four million Italians who entered America between 1880 and 1920, the vast majority emigrated from the poor agricultural regions of the South, the provinces of Abruzzi, Campania, Apulia, Basilicata (Lucania), Calabria, and the island of Sicily. A combination of "push-pull" factors caused this massive emigration from southern Italy. The "push" factors were conditions in Italy that undermined opportunities for economic improvement and social mobility. The "pull" factors were those conditions in the receiving society that attracted emigrants by offering them opportunities for employment and social and economic mobility.

The "push" factors causing the great post-1880 emigration included extremely low wages; infertility of the soil and primitive agricultural methods; overpopulation and poor health conditions; slow industrial growth; a system of heavy, indirect taxation; an unresponsive and distant national government; corruption in local government; and the exploitation of landless peasants by wealthy landowners. The problems associated with southern agriculture were the most severe. Almost all property was owned by a landed elite, who left management of their estates to hired foremen. Most Italian peasants did not work their own land but labored for the benefit of others. Creating further pressure on the land was the Italian population, which doubled between 1861 and 1901, reaching twelve million, and increasing to eighteen million by 1916.

In the late 1880s, the Italian economy experienced three major setbacks that triggered emigration. Italians were faced with a ruined economy when the United States cut its imports of Italian citrus fruits due to improved production in California and Florida. At the same time, plant lice invaded Italian vineyards, leaving thousands of acres destroyed. In addition, France set up high tariffs, which cut off a major market for the grape growers of Apulia, Calabria, and Sicily.

Emigration offered an important means of upward mobility for Italians. Industry in the United States was burgeoning, and the promise of jobs beckoned many Italians. While America was the major destination for most Italians who left their homeland, it was not the only one. Italians went to South America, especially Brazil and Argentina, where they had been arriving in fairly large numbers since the early nineteenth century.

A large number of Italians who left southern Italy after 1880 were men between sixteen and forty-five whose goals were to work in America for a short time, save as much money as possible, and return to their native country to buy their own land. Italian patterns show that emigration and return migration were much more frequent when land was for sale than when it was not. Between 1899 and 1924, a total of 3.8 million Italians landed in the United States, but some 2.1 million departed in the same period. These people were labeled "birds of passage" by Americans who looked disapprovingly at this practice. Immigration gradually became more stable after the turn of the twentieth century as women and children joined men and families began to form.

Settlement Patterns

The majority of Italians settled on the East Coast, in New York, Rhode Island, Connecticut, Massachusetts, and New Jersey. Other Italian communities grew in Detroit, Pittsburgh, San Francisco, Milwaukee, and Chicago. During the decades of large-scale immigration, 97 percent of Italian immigrants landed in New York City, making it the city with the largest number of Italian immigrants.

According to census figures, there were nearly fifteen million Italian Americans in the United States in 1990. More than 50 percent (7,517,801) of all persons of Italian ancestry lived in the

"We no work now — stop and have picture took!"

Italian immigrant laborers pose for a portrait during construction of the New Troy, Rensselaer, and Pittsfield Electric Railway through the Lebanon Valley in New York. The caption under the picture seems to make fun of their English: "We no work now — stop and have picture took!" (H. M. Gillet/Corbis)

Northeast. Fewer than 20 percent lived in any of the other three regions — the Midwest (2,443,004), South (2,482,645), and West (2,271,489). Continuing the trend that began earlier in the century, 92 percent (11,450,322) lived in urban areas, about 36 percent (4,102,207) lived in central cities, while 64 percent (7,348,115) lived in the urban fringes of cities.

In 1990, Italian Americans comprised the fourth-largest immigrant group in America. (This count does not include African Americans or Hispanics.) In New Jersey, New York, Rhode Island, and Connecticut, Italians remain the largest ethnic group.

The data on family structure from the 1980 U.S. Census provides support for the hypothesis that family relationships are very strong among the Italian population. In New York as well as in New Jersey and Pennsylvania, the proportion of families in 1980 who were married couples (both husband and wife present) were higher among the Italians than among the total population. The proportion of persons under eighteen years living with both parents was higher for Italians than for the total state population. Also, the proportion of older persons living in families was higher among Italians than the total population sixty years or over of the states in this study.

A 1974 study found that Italian-American Catholics had the second lowest divorce rate (2%) of the ethnic groups reviewed. However, the Italians' rate of divorce in 1979 was not significantly different from that among the total U.S. population. In 1980, married Italian women age thirty-five to forty-five in New York, New Jersey, and Pennsylvania had approximately 2.5 children, which was slightly below the U.S. average of 2.8 children.

Family

In Italy the social structure of the rural village was founded on the family (*la famiglia*), whose interests and needs determined individuals' attitudes toward church, state, and school. Each mem-

A 1914 passport photo for an Italian immigrant and her son. (Italo "Ethan" Pace)

ber was expected to uphold family honor and to fulfill his or her particular duties and responsibilities. In America as in Italy, the family was a tightly knit unit, encompassing a wide range of relationships and retaining close ties even after the marriage of the children.

The obligation to support the aged is very important in Italian-American families. In the early days of immigration the father was recognized as head of the household. However, while Italian women were quick to acknowledge their husbands as the family head, they almost invariably had a strong hand in the important decisions of the family. They were particularly influential in the social and religious lives of their children.

Families discouraged marriage with non-Italians, while divorce, at least among the first generation, was almost unknown.

Religion

While the family has traditionally been the most important institution of Italian society, the church also has exerted profound influence on Italian life. When Italians arrived in America they found a church organization and culture that was totally outside their experience. Dominated by the Irish, American Catholicism appeared cold, stern, and disciplined, unlike the casual attitude of worship practiced by Italians.

In his article "Prelates and Peasants" (1969), Rudolph Vecoli describes Italians as nominally Roman Catholics but explains that theirs was a folk religion, a fusion of Christian and pre-Christian elements such as animism, polytheism, and sorcery with the sacraments of the church. Southern Italians transplanted their religious practices to America. Religious lucky charms, especially in the shape of horns (*corne*), were worn by Italian women in America to ward off evil spirits. The "evil eye" (*il mal occhio*) was greatly feared, for many Italians believed that certain people had powers to give the "evil eye" to others, resulting in ill health or other misfortune.

Southern Italians, especially, attributed special powers to individual saints. These local saints were believed to be significant personages whose favors were valuable to the peasants. One of the most significant aspects of religion for Italians was the feast day (*festa*) of the Madonna or a patron saint. This was the high point in the life of the village and the most authentic expression of Italian culture transplanted to the New World. With processions, bands, and fireworks, these celebrations exalted the miraculous powers of the patron saint and invoked his or her protection on the village. In every Italian community the feast day continues to be an important expression of Italian-American Catholicism.

Economics

Although the majority of Italians did not travel to America motivated by a desire to pursue agriculture, there were a significant number who desired to work the land. Some emigrations from Italy were undertaken for the express purpose of agricultural colonization. In Independence, Louisiana, nearly three hundred Italian immigrants from Palermo bought the land at low prices from native farmers because it was considered too wet to be productive. The Italians constructed ditches and drainage canals, converting the swampy land into fruitful soil. In another, much smaller, colony in Genoa, Wisconsin, several Italian families settled in 1863 and started dairy farming. Eventually more families joined the colony.

Italian colonies were especially successful in market and truck gardening. As early as 1844, Italians were engaged in market gardening near Providence, Rhode Island, and later in upstate New York and on Long Island. In California Italians grew oranges, lemons, and other fruits, while grape growing and wine manufacturing were undertaken on a large scale.

Even before the end of the nineteenth century the fruit trade in New York City was controlled by Italian entrepreneurs. The same was true for Milwaukee, Wisconsin, where Italians gained prominence in supplying fruits and vegetables to the city. In every city of significant Italian population their role as suppliers of fruits and vegetables became part of the business establishment.

Most Italians who were skilled workers practiced their trades and crafts in the ethnic neighborhoods and cities in which they lived. Italians worked as masons and stonecutters, mechanics, shoemakers, barbers, tailors, and musicians. Most immigrants at the turn of the twentieth century, however, were not skilled workers and were forced to take jobs as common laborers or as unskilled factory workers. Many single men, in particular, were itinerant workers, following jobs from one state to another. Many newcomers worked as common laborers on railroads, in shipyards, as ditch diggers and hod carriers. They worked in the coal mines of Pennsylvania, Illinois, and West Virginia; in the iron ore mines of Michigan, Wisconsin, and Minnesota; in the precious-metal mines of the Far West; in the phosphate mines of the South; and in the stone quarries of New England. In New York

City, Italians help build the subways and entered the garment trades.

Many southern Italian immigrants knew little about American life and had no way of contacting potential employers for work. The Italian *padrone* (labor boss) played an important role in securing work for Italian immigrants. Some padrones recruited men in Italy, paid for their passage, and arranged work for them in the United States. In return, the padrone was paid a fee. The padrone also wrote letters and acted as banker and translator for Italian immigrants. Although he often played an important role helping immigrants bridge the Old World with the New, the padrone was viewed as one who exploits his own people for monetary gain.

Italian immigrants received less pay than the native worker, and since Italians usually had larger families, their standard of living was necessarily lower. Since fathers alone could rarely maintain the family, Italians had to depend on other sources of income. Wives and children contributed to the economic well-being of the family. Italian women took in boarders and worked at home in the finishing trades. They also entered the work force. In New York City the majority of workers in the garment trade were Italian women. In Endicott, New York, they were employed in the shoe factories; in Paterson, New Jersey, they worked in the silk mills; in Ybor City (Tampa, Florida), they worked in the cigar factories. Italian women also operated their own grocery stores, dry goods stores, restaurants, and saloons. Italian children often worked as soon as the law permitted. This pattern was part of the tradition brought from Italy, where everyone worked for the well-being of the family.

Ethnic Community Development

Immigrants seldom left their homelands without knowing exactly where they wanted to go and how to get there. Relatives and friends constantly sent information back regarding locations to live and potential places of employment. Italian immigration has always been a "chain" phenomenon. The first to leave from a particular village attracted others to the New World. From the very beginning the Italians settled in what have been termed "Little Italys." In these ethnic enclaves immigrants spoke and heard a familiar language, built their own churches, and operated grocery stores that specialized in imported food items.

Neighborhoods often were settled by Italian immigrants according to their native province, town, or village of origin. In New York City, for example, Calabrians lived on Mott Street, Sicilians lived on Prince and Elizabeth streets, Neapolitans lived on Mulberry Street, and the Genovesi on Baxter Street. These immigrants were called Italians, but they identified themselves as belonging to a particular province or village in Italy. They were Siciliani, Barese, or Ferrazzani. They possessed a fierce pride and loyalty to their provincial customs and dialects. Most were not able to under-

Italian-American female clothing workers sew Women's Army Auxiliary Corps (WAAC) uniforms in 1943 in New York City. (Library of Congress/Corbis)

stand immigrants from other regions of Italy. Even though the standard language of Italy is expressed in the Tuscan dialect, most immigrants arriving in America after 1880 had little education and arrived knowing only the dialect of their region. Consequently they were reduced to speaking a mixture of standard Italian with regional dialect combined with newly learned English words.

Ethnic Press

In 1849, the first newspaper printed entirely in Italian in America was founded: *L'Eco d'Italia* in New York City. Italian newspapers would not flourish until after the 1880s, when an expanding Italian population was substantial enough to sustain an immigrant press. Between 1880 and 1921, twenty Italian language newspapers appeared in Chicago. The country's leading Italian newspaper was *Il Progresso Italo-Americano* (first published in 1880) of New York, which became the most important in the community and, still in print, the most long-lived among foreign-language newspapers in the country. The immigrant press promoted Italian national pride and helped strengthen ties with Italy. It also assisted with the assimilation of immigrants to American society and served as an intermediary between the immigrants and their new homeland.

Home Ownership

When Italians settled in ethnic neighborhoods in large cities such as New York or Chicago, they were often restricted to tenement living. Later, second- and third-generation inner-city Italian Americans moved to suburban areas and purchased their own homes. Italians who migrated to smaller cities and towns, however, were more likely to achieve home ownership in their own lifetime. Studies of social mobility in communities throughout the United States reveal that home ownership represented a major marker of success among immigrants. Italians have had one of the highest percentages of home ownership of all immigrant groups in America. In addition to provid-

ing a sense of status, it has given them greater control over their environment, offered a form of enforced savings with a resultant equity, and offered the potential of providing a source of income. For Italian Americans home ownership has been the cornerstone of their conception of stability, respectability, and independence.

Mutual Aid Societies

Italians transplanted many Old World traditions to America. One tradition that took on even greater importance in America was the mutual aid society. John Briggs discovered that mutual aid societies existed in southern Italy soon after Italian unification. In *An Italian Passage* (1978), he noted that southern Italians maintained voluntary associations and recognized the possibilities for promoting individual goals through their associative endeavors. Among these were health, life, and unemployment insurance; education; support of the economic and trade interests of members; advancement of local communal interests; and maintenance of social centers. Italians met the realities of unemployment, widowhood, burial, and even social activities through their membership in mutual aid societies. The largest and most influential Italian organization in the country, the Order of the Sons of Italy in America, originated in New York City in 1905. By the 1920s, its membership had soared to 300,000.

More recently, Italian-American organizations have moved into underwriting programs, supporting the creation and dissemination of publications, films, and exhibits about the history and contemporary status of Italian Americans. Other organizations, such as UNICO (Unity, Neighborliness, Integrity, Charity, Opportunity) and the National Italian-American Foundation, support education by offering scholarships and research awards for Italian-American students.

Discrimination

Perhaps more than other European ethnic groups, Italians faced considerable prejudice in

America. They were hired for low wages and, along with other southern Europeans of dark skin, labeled as "swarthy." Italians became a significant factor in the growth of American nativism. In the 1880s and 1890s, Italians played a role in American life that lent itself to nativist interpretation. They were to symbolize the social and economic ills with which the nativists generally identified the immigrants. Italian immigrants in the post-1880 period had the distinction of having all three nativist impulses directed against them: anti-radicalism, anti-Catholicism, and racial nativism.

The wave of Italian immigration came during an era of intense social and economic upheavals that "native" Americans did not understand. The development of slums and a variety of social problems coincided with an increasingly urbanized America. Increasingly, industrialization led to millions of skilled and unskilled workers crowding into the cities. At the turn of the twentieth century more than 50 percent of Italian immigrants lived in cities. Thus reformers fixed on the immigrants in general, and the Italians in particular, as the major source of social disorders in the city. Nativism reemerged when the movement to redeem the cities became an organized crusade. To nativist reformers the Italian immigrants were the source of the squalor and corruption of the cities. To workmen they were a threat to their livelihood, while militant Protestants saw them as tools of Rome. Thomas Nixon Carver, a conservative economist, blamed them for causing the widening gulf between capital and labor. The major strikes of the period evoked references to dangerous foreign radicals who menaced orderly freedom. This was reinforced by the Haymarket riot in 1886, which convinced Americans that immigration, radicalism, and lawlessness were parts of the same whole.

During the 1880s, the American press often associated southern Italians with criminality and a lowering of the standard of living. Antiforeign sentiment filtered through a specific ethnic stereotype when Italians were involved. They suggested the Mafia and deeds of impassioned violence.

As the 1880s closed, an initial distrust born of contact with different cultures swelled into hatred and violence. Italians were viewed as a class hostile to the nation's institutions or to its best interests. The rapid increase in their numbers raised fear among nativists. In addition, Italians were perceived by many as a dangerous people. The press accounts and descriptions added that Italians were lazy, cruel, ferocious, and bloodthirsty. But cruel and ferocious behavior was more often experienced by the immigrants themselves, who were often victims of rabid discrimination.

Italians were victims of violence, as evidenced in 1891 when the leading citizens of New Orleans led a lynching party into a prison and systematically slaughtered eleven Italians who had just been found not guilty of murder. During the years of the "Red scare" in America, two Italian anarchists, Nicola Sacco and Bartolomeo Vanzetti, were arrested for a murder committed in connection with a payroll robbery in Massachusetts. They were found guilty and sentenced to death. The actual evidence against them was not conclusive, and the suspicion grew that they had been convicted not because they had committed the crime but because of their political beliefs. The judge's conduct of the trial, in which he made little secret of his feelings about anarchists, only deepened suspicion of the verdict. When Sacco and Vanzetti were sent to the electric chair in 1927, in the midst of worldwide protest, millions were convinced that guilty or innocent, they had not been given a fair trial.

The negative images that have plagued Italian Americans are most pointedly expressed in the word "Mafia." Since 1890, Italians have been connected in the public's imagination with criminality and violence. The very small percentage of Italian Americans who have been involved with organized crime have colored public perceptions of law-abiding Italian Americans, who comprise the vast majority of the group.

Italians in Public Life

Italian Americans have made notable contributions to American public life in music, theater, sports, entertainment, science, and politics. Several have had an especially significant impact on

Italian men play bocci ball at the courts in Aquatic Park in San Francisco. (Ted Streshinsky/Corbis)

American culture, such as Frank Capra, acknowledged master of American filmmakers and producers. In music the dean of Italian-American composers is Giancarlo Menotti, founder of the Festival of Two Worlds at Spoleto, Italy, and its American counterpart in Charleston, South Carolina.

Italian-American writers have poignantly depicted the Italian-American experience. Among them, the 1938 novel *Christ in Concrete* by Pietro di Donato is a classic. This critically acclaimed work portrays hardworking Italian immigrants on the Lower East Side of New York before the Great Depression. Mario Puzo, best known for *The Godfather,* achieved great success as a novelist from writings molded by his experience growing up during the Depression in New York's "Hell's

Kitchen," which resulted in his second novel, *The Fortunate Pilgrim.*

In science, Italian Americans have played a significant role from the nineteenth century, when Antonio Meucci perfected a workable telephone (prior to the work of Alexander Graham Bell), to the twentieth century, with the construction of the first atomic bomb. Enrico Fermi was the first person to achieve a nuclear chain reaction and was one of the top scientists engaged in the construction of the atomic bomb at Los Alamos.

Italians faced great challenges breaking into politics. Fiorello LaGuardia, the mayor of New York City from 1934 to 1945, was the first to win a highly visible public office. Representative Geraldine Ferraro was the first woman to run for vice president of the United States, while Associate

Justice Antonin Scalia was the first Italian American appointed to the U.S. Supreme Court.

For Italian Americans the immigrant era has long since passed. It has been more than a century since southern Italians began to arrive in the United States in large numbers. The period of large-scale immigration lasted until the early 1920s, when federal legislation severely restricted entry into America.

Italian Americans have been responsible for extensive accomplishments and have achieved significant economic success. Italians are attending college in ever-increasing numbers. Typically, the children of Italian storekeepers and small-businessmen went to college and became professionals. By the 1970s, Italian Americans comprised approximately one-third of students enrolled in the City University of New York and half of the student body at Fordham University. As a result of their strong qualifications and better educational background, the children and grandchildren of Italian immigrants moved into the white collar fields.

Italians remain loyal to the Catholic Church, although they do not exert leadership within it in America proportionate to their numbers. Intermarriage, once discouraged by first-generation immigrants, is now commonplace. Today's Italian Americans are not only more likely than members of earlier generations to marry outside the ethnic group, they also are more likely to divorce. The Italian-American family tends to resemble the smaller, more egalitarian, child-centered family typical of the American middle class with fertility rates among Italian-American women lower than those for other American women.

Of all the contributions of Italians to American life, perhaps the most influential has been Italian cuisine. Pizza, introduced by Neapolitans, is as popular as the all-American hamburger. Spaghetti and meatballs have been replaced by the healthier pasta dishes, using fresh tomatoes and fresh herbs. Cooking with olive oil and drinking a glass of wine a day (which Italians have been doing for centuries) are now heralded as good for one's health.

See also: SARDINIANS; SICILIANS

Bibliography

Briggs, J. (1978). *An Italian Passage: Immigrants to Three American Cities, 1890–1930*. New Haven, CT: Yale University Press.

Campisi, P. (1948). "Ethnic Family Patterns: The Italian Family in the United States." *American Journal of Sociology* 53:443–449.

Gallo, P. (1981). *Old Bread, New Wine: A Portrait of the Italian Americans*. Chicago: Nelson-Hall.

Iorizzo, L., and Mondello, S. (1980). *The Italian Americans*, revised edition. New York: Twayne.

Kessner, T. (1977). *The Golden Door: Italians and Jewish Immigrant Mobility in New York City, 1880–1915*. New York: Oxford University Press.

Lopreato, J. (1970). *Italian Americans*. New York: Random House.

Mormino, G., and Pozzetta, G. (1987). *The Immigrant World of Ybor City*. Urbana: University of Illinois Press.

Nelli, H. S. (1975). *Italians in Chicago, 1880–1930*. New York: Oxford University Press.

Pisani, L. (1957). *The Italian in America*. New York: Exposition Press.

Vecoli, R. (1969). "Prelates and Peasants: Italian Immigrants and the Catholic Church." *Journal of Social History* 2:217–286.

Yans-McLaughlin, V. (1982). *Family and Community: Italian Immigrants in Buffalo, 1880–1930*. Urbana: University of Illinois Press.

DIANE C. VECCHIO

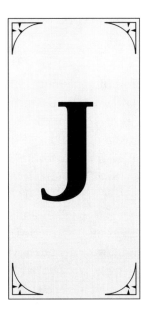

JAINS

Jains in America are immigrants from various parts in India who follow the Jain religious tradition. Most come from the northwestern Indian states of Gujarat and Rajasthan and from the central state of Maharashtra. They are included in the category "Asian Indian" by the U.S. government, along with those from Muslim, Hindu, Sikh, or other religious communities on the Indian subcontinent. This designation of a special minority category is new, having been created by the U.S. Census Bureau in 1980 at the urging of several Asian Indian groups in America. It places immigrants from India within the "Asian or Pacific Islander" classification as an ethnic minority, replacing their previous classification as simply Caucasian. It is not precise, however, since India is composed of numerous culturally divergent regions, fifteen official languages as well as innumerable local dialects, and many different religious traditions. The Asian Indians in America are therefore an extremely diverse group, even though they share a national and general cultural identity. The term "Jain" refers to religious affiliation and means literally, "follower of a Jina" or spiritual victor, a perfected human being who teaches others the way to liberation from the suffering of life in the world. According to the tradition, teachers are born at regular intervals, and the most recent teacher, called Mahavira, "great hero," lived in the sixth century B.C.E. He is credited with formulating the beliefs and practices of the tradition as it is known today, so the Jains are followers of the teachings of Mahavira, the last Jina of this era.

Demography and Economic Patterns

Because Jains are not enumerated separately from other Asian Indian groups by the U.S. Bureau of the Census, precise information on population size and places of settlement in the United States is not available. Leaders of the community estimate that there are 55,000 to 60,000 Jains in North America, of whom 40,000 to 50,000 are in the United States. A 1993 community directory based on information from questionnaires finds that 80 percent of the Jain families in North America have settled in ten states and the Canadian province of Ontario. Most settlement has occurred on the coasts: 35 percent on the East Coast, predominantly in New Jersey and New York, and 15 percent on the West Coast, in California. In India, Jains live in urban centers, where they engage in business or a profession. This is the dominant pattern because their religion has a strong ethical component of noninjury to any living creature, which prohibits certain occupations, including agriculture. Jain immigrants arrived in the United States as professionals or as students pursuing a higher degree and so joined the upper middle class and settled in affluent suburban communities. Jains in the United States have not isolated themselves from the surrounding population, as Indians and Jains in East Africa and to some extent in the United Kingdom have tended to do, but are scattered around metropolitan areas among other professionals. The reason for this may be the ease with which they have identified with and blended economically with the American professional class. According to the Jain directory, 32 percent are employed as engineers; 16 percent are in business; 14 percent are in the medical profession; and 14 percent are involved in finance, management, or computers.

Immigration History

Until Indian independence in 1947, Indian and Jain immigration was primarily directed toward the United Kingdom and British colonies. In the early 1900s, when British colonial rule was interested in providing laborers for the development of East Africa, Indians became well established there, and a number of Gujarati Jains immigrated to coastal towns and later inland, particularly to Kenya, to open businesses. A widespread exodus occurred, however, during the trauma of the independence of African nations (particularly in Uganda in the 1970s), and many Indians fled to the United Kingdom. Few Jains, or Asian Indians, entered the United States before 1965, since until that time the immigration laws in effect set an annual quota for each country, and reserved 90 percent of those quotas for persons from northern or western Europe. Only students were easily allowed entry, so most of the first Indian, including Jain, immigrants were among the students who arrived in the United States seeking higher education.

The Immigration Act of 1965 changed the situation drastically, and opened the way for the first wave of Indian immigration to the United States. The Jain community in America came into existence during the decade following the passage of this act. The Immigration Act of 1965 repealed the old national-origins quota system, replacing it with an annual maximum quota for *all* countries outside the Western Hemisphere (at the time 170,000 immigrants), and, of significance to the Jain and other Indian students already present in America, the act allowed persons entering on a student visa to change their status to resident alien. The act also established an allocation system of preferences for the permitted number of immigrants, and this system worked to the benefit of Jains. Of the six preference categories it established, the third, under which most Indians immigrated (since the first two involved bringing family members, and few Indians were yet in residence), designated members of professions of exceptional ability in fields identified by the Department of Labor as ones with shortages, such as chemistry, engineering, mathematics, and physics. Jains were professionals in India and easily moved into professional positions in the United States.

During the decade after the change in immigration laws, the majority of Asian Indian immigrants were of high educational and professional status. In 1975, 93 percent of Indian immigrants were classified as either professional/technical workers or as the spouses or children of such workers. The Indian community as a whole commonly spoke of having two occupational groups: doctors and engineers. After the first decade, the shortages perceived by the Department of Labor shifted, and it became difficult for physicians, engineers, and other technical workers to get immigration status. Immigration continued after that under the first two preference categories, which allowed relatives into the United States. The growing Jain, and Indian, community was educated and successful, with nine out of ten individuals being high school graduates and two out of three being college graduates. In the mid-1990s, the immigration of relatives of resident families declined sharply, with the requirement of a lengthy waiting period of ten years or more; young relatives by

Gujarati Jains prepare to participate in a religious ceremony. (Mukul Roy)

then are often too established in their lives to leave India. Asian Indians still frequently enter the United States on a student visa and then immigrate permanently through either marriage or employment.

Marriage and Family

Indians settling in the United States experience radical changes in family structure. The multigenerational, extended-family system of India cannot be transplanted to America, and the young adults who immigrated after 1965 settled into nuclear family units, in single-family homes. While many sponsored the immigration of brothers, sisters, or cousins, these individuals moved into their own homes and established their own families.

Parents and older relatives, well rooted in the Indian environment and culture, have not chosen to leave India. Jains who arrived in the wave of immigration after the 1965 act was passed are now in their mid-fifties. Since they have not yet reached retirement age, there are no figures on how many will choose to return to India in their retirement, but community leaders speculate that a very small percentage will choose to do so, since their children are settled in America. The common family pattern has been a yearly trip to India if possible, to visit parents and other relatives and to allow children some familiarity with the home culture. The "arranged" marriage system of India, in which the parents choose a partner for their child, has been replaced by a system of "facilitated" marriages in America, in which the young people play the primary part in the decision-making process. Family connections remain strong, however, and young people generally see marriage as a tie between two families, not just two individuals. Marriage for Jains is almost exclusively within the Asian Indian community, either between two Jains or between a Jain and a Hindu, which is also a common occurrence in India.

Jain families try to transmit Indian culture to their children. Formally, this is done through classes in Indian dance or music and in the home language, often in conjunction with Hindu groups. Informally, home videos bring the aesthetic tastes, dance and music styles, and traditional epic stories to the children in a way that is enthusiastically received. The videos also contribute to familiarity with the language heard at home. Jain immigrants arrived fluent in Gujarati and/or Hindi as well as English. Either Gujarati or Hindi is spoken in the home, and the children are familiar at a conversational level with one or the other. Since their education takes place only in English, however, as do all social interactions outside the home, their acquisition of the Indian languages rarely goes beyond the conversational and never reaches the level of skill their parents have. Education of the children is a primary concern in Jain families, and constant attention is given to both exposing them to as much Indian culture as possible and preparing them for a secure and successful future in the United States.

Social and Religious Organizations

Most Jain organizations have a religious component, since that is what defines Jains as a distinct group among Asian Indians. Jains may share national, regional, and linguistic aspects of their identity with other Indian immigrants, but religious beliefs and practices set them apart from Hindus, Sikhs, Muslims, and all other religious groups. As Jain families became settled around metropolitan areas, they began to establish centers for social and religious gatherings. At first, meetings were held in individual homes; then, as numbers and support increased, buildings, such as vacated Christian churches, were purchased and converted, or built specifically to meet the needs of the community. These centers have multiplied considerably since the early 1970s, when they began to appear; the Jain directory lists nine in 1979, thirty-four in 1987, and sixty-eight in 1992.

The centers offer a place for visiting teachers to lecture and for educational activities to be held, which may include study meetings for adults and classes in the Jain religion and in the home language for children. They also organize celebrations of the principal festivals throughout the year, particularly Mahavir Jayanti, which commemorates the birth of the teacher Mahavira, and Paryushan Parva, a holy time for fasting and turning attention toward the spiritual, during what is in India the rainy season. On a weekly basis they provide a place for devotional rituals. In these last capacities, they serve as temples, and various centers set aside space for religious activities in different ways. Some have one large meeting room that serves both social and religious purposes and has a raised platform at one end with images for religious functions; the platform can be partitioned off for social gatherings. Others, particularly those that have been designed and built by the community, have a large room set aside to serve specifically as a temple, a place for devotional practices. Such spaces can be quite elaborate. The Jain Center of Southern California, which is located in Buena Park and is one of the largest, brought Indian craftsmen to carve an intricate enclosure of marble arches that houses five marble statues in a huge, bright temple room.

Some centers share religious space with Hindu worshipers, and in these cases an image of Mahavira has been added to those that were chosen for worship by Hindu members. Sometimes these images appear together on one platform, as in the Hindu-Jain Temple in San Jose, California, and sometimes a separate platform is established for Jain images in addition to those that hold Hindu deities, as in the Hindu-Jain Temple in Pittsburgh. This is possible because ritual practices are similar in that both Hindus and Jains perform *puja*, the devotional act of offering flowers and food to an image that represents what is held to be sacred. The similarity ends there, however, because, in addition to the fact that Jain and Hindu history, holy days, and descriptions of spiritual progress are different, their conceptions of the divine differ radically. Hindu images represent forms of the divine available to the devotee to grant requests, listen to prayers, and offer comfort. Jain images represent Mahavira and the twenty-three other great teachers, the Tirthankaras or ford-crossers, human beings who have reached perfection. Their wisdom is embodied in the teachings of the Jain tradition, and images of them stand as examples of what a human being can become and of the qualities to be cultivated on the path to perfection. The Jains locate divinity only in the perfected soul and have no separate god to worship. Images of Tirthankaras are reminders of the teachings and the perfect qualities, not beings who are available for aid and comfort through devotion. From the Jain perspective, the gods hold a position between that of ordinary human beings and that of perfected, liberated souls. In many Jain temples, images of divine guardians or deities appear beside the Tirthankaras, as beings who have helped the great teachers and are available to help their devotees also. Hindu and Jain images seem to be able to stand comfortably together in the temples, carrying different meanings for the worshipers of the two communities.

The numerous Jain centers are connected through the umbrella organization of JAINA, the

Jains participate in the groundbreaking ceremony for a new temple in the Chicago area. (Mukul Roy)

Federation of Jain Associations in North America. The federation representatives met for the first time in Los Angeles in 1981 and have continued to hold a convention every two years in an effort to facilitate communication among the centers and to unite the community, in spite of its present widely scattered distribution and its original differences in regional customs, language, and sectarian beliefs. A primary concern of the leaders of the federation is transmitting the tradition to the American Jain children, and they devote attention to youth activities, have a national youth organization, and operate a marriage information service to help young people find partners within the community. They invite scholars from India to lecture at centers, publish a journal, and have set up libraries in Lubbock, Texas, and Toronto to collect and make available books from India on Jainism. The Jain Academic Foundation of North America sponsors seminars, provides scholarships to students, and is generally concerned with encouraging public awareness of the Jain tradition. Another organization, Mahavir World Vision, Inc., was created to produce videos and multimedia materials related to Jain principles. The Jains have no separate, specifically political organizations. They do have particular ethical issues, most notably that of *ahimsa,* noninjury to all living beings, which is a tenet so central to the teachings of the tradition that it is referred to as their defining characteristic. Leaders have said that while they do not enter into politics as a group, they would support any candidate who was clearly committed to the ethical principles of their tradition.

Religious Institutions in Transformation

What is visible in the Jain community is the creation of the first generation of immigrants, those who arrived in the first wave in the decade after 1965. Their children are now of college age, and some generational differences are apparent. Most obviously, the language emphasis is changing toward English, and proficiency in the original home language is lost, just as it has been among second- and third-generation European immi-

grants. At a more subtle level, religious orientations are shifting. Attitudes toward sectarian differences have undergone several changes. As soon as the community began to organize, leaders placed a strong emphasis on its unity, on the principles all Jains have in common, and downplayed sectarian differences. In India there are two main sects, the Svetambara (white-clad), who are settled predominantly in the northeast, and the Digambara (sky-clad), who are settled predominantly in the south. The sects differ on rules for the monks, most obviously concerning clothing: Svetambara monks wear white robes, while Digambara monks must not wear clothing at all. The sects also differ on some lay rituals, festival dates, and points of doctrine. Individual Jain centers have quietly tried to accommodate the different needs of Svetambara and Digambara members while maintaining a unified front. At this point, adult members are beginning to assert the preferences of their own sect in the rituals, so there is some dissent. However, since the sectarian differences primarily involve the rituals and grow originally out of differences in the opinions of the monks, they are not of any real concern to the young people. Therefore, there should be little resistance to the future realization of the ideal of the unified community. What will happen to the devotional rituals is questionable, since unless some of the young people are interested enough to learn them, they will not be passed to later generations.

The most fundamental change faced by the community in its move to the American environment is the loss of the presence of the mendicants, the peripatetic monks and nuns. In India, interaction between the mendicants and the laypeople is a constant part of the life of the community. Wandering monks and nuns are the teachers of the tradition, the center of holy days, and offer the opportunity for earning merit, since giving to a monk or nun is one of the most auspicious of good deeds. There is a kind of checks-and-balance system within the interaction. Laypeople give food, clothing, medicine, and other basic needs to the mendicants in the knowledge that they are following the stringent ascetic rules of the tradition by living a simple, careful, restrained, and homeless life. In return for the gifts, which allow for survival without participation in the world, mendicants teach, offer counsel, officiate at the inauguration of temples, participate in holy days, and uphold daily the ideal of living the Jain path to liberation.

The laypeople in America are faced with a very different situation, in which the Indian pattern is unworkable. Since monks and nuns are not allowed to ride in vehicles, traveling to the United States at all is breaking the rules of the tradition. More crucially, the lifestyle of the Indian mendicant is impossible in the United States, with the community spread out in various suburban settings that hardly lend themselves to daily alms rounds. Monks and nuns that immigrate to America teach, inaugurate temples, and preside over holy days. However, they also travel constantly, handle money themselves, and request it for causes at home in India. Laypeople in America want to believe that the mendicants who visit are sincere practitioners upholding the ideals of the tradition, yet they see authority being claimed by individuals who have broken with the traditional rules in some obvious ways and whose daily practices, whose actual lifestyle, cannot be observed. The Indian checks-and-balance system, in which gifts are given in accordance with purity of conduct, does not work in America, where the lay population has only occasional contact with a few visiting mendicants. The dilemma is that to question the sincerity of the mendicants is to question the fundamental ideal of the tradition and so undermine its survival in the United States, yet to allow individuals to claim the title of monk or nun who do not fully live the role also undermines the ideal and so the existence of the tradition. Because Jains are not only new to America but also new to the experience of immigration, there is no ready-made answer to the mendicant problem. Lay leaders are increasingly aware of it, and it is likely that the Jain tradition in America, which is held by essentially a lay community, will take a very different form from that in India.

See also: GUJARATIS; MAHARASHTRIANS

Bibliography

Dundas, P. (1992). *The Jains.* London: Routledge.

Folkert, K. (1993). *Scripture and Community: Collected Essays on the Jains,* edited by J. Cort. Atlanta: Scholars Press.

Jaini, P. S. (1979). *The Jaina Path of Purification.* Berkeley: University of California Press.

Williams, R. B. (1988). *Religions of Immigrants from India and Pakistan: New Threads in the American Tapestry.* Cambridge, Eng.: Cambridge University Press.

HOLLY A. SEELING

JAMAICANS

People from the West Indian island of Jamaica comprise one of the largest new immigrant groups in the United States. During the 1980s, Jamaica, with a population of about 2.5 million, was one of the top ten source countries for immigrants to the United States. By 1990, the U.S. Census counted some 334,000 foreign-born Jamaicans in the United States.

Causes of Jamaican Immigration

The root causes of Jamaican immigration to the United States are the underdeveloped state of the Jamaican economy, as structured by the distorting effects of slavery, British colonial rule (Jamaica became independent in 1962), and the domination of the island's economy by plantation agriculture for so many years.

In Jamaica, there have long been too many people with too few opportunities to earn a decent living. Unequal land distribution patterns, for example, mean that small farmers do not have enough land. When Jamaicans look to other, or additional, ways to make a living (and increasing numbers of young people are leaving the rural parishes for Kingston), they are very often disappointed. The big growth industries of the post–World War II decades in the nonagricultural sector—bauxite, manufacturing, and tourism—have not created many new jobs. In the 1980s and 1990s, economic conditions worsened with, among other things, a fall in prices for exports and increasing foreign debt. Inflation rates have soared—the rate was 80 percent in 1991—and prices for basic foodstuffs and consumer goods have escalated.

Unemployment and underemployment are very high, with unemployment at more than 20 percent throughout the 1980s. Even for those with jobs—and most immigrants to the United States had jobs before they left—employment was often not steady or only part-time. And all too frequently, the earnings were low and prospects for advancement dim.

This is compounded by rising aspirations as people at all levels of the society want to achieve a standard of living like that of the North American middle classes. These aspirations have been fueled by reports and visits from immigrants as well as by such changes as improved communications, promises by new political elites, and expansion of educational opportunities.

Moving to the United States has come to be seen as part of the normal life course in Jamaica. Despite close bonds with kin, Jamaicans think it is natural—and from a financial point of view, desirable—to spend much of one's life, perhaps the rest of one's life, abroad. One survey showed that 60 percent of the population of the island would move to the United States if given the chance. The United States offers the promise of jobs, higher wages, higher levels of living, and more consumer goods. The prospect of more widely available higher education is an additional attraction, especially for middle-class Jamaicans.

Once the movement to the United States got under way in the 1960s, it had a kind of snowball effect. People in Jamaica learned of the benefits to be had abroad not only through the mass media but also from letters and visits from friends and relatives in the United States. Many Jamaicans visited the United States before moving there. In addition to spreading encouraging news to relatives and friends, immigrants sometimes exert pressure on spouses or dependents to join them. They frequently send back the funds to finance the trip, serve as sponsors, help prospective newcomers meet requirements for entry or immigration, offer accommodation, and familiarize the new arrivals with the United States.

Settlement Patterns and Demographics

Jamaicans are not newcomers to the United States. The first large wave of Jamaican immigrants arrived early in the twentieth century. The movement started shortly after 1900 and peaked in the late 1910s and early 1920s, before being sharply cut by restrictive U.S. legislation in 1924. Estimates indicate that about fifty thousand Jamaicans

A Jamaican laborer begins to burn a field of sugar cane prior to a 1983 harvest. (Tony Arruza/Corbis)

immigrated to the United States during this period, with most settling in New York City.

Jamaicans were an important presence in Harlem in the 1920s. One of the best known was Marcus Garvey, leader of the mass black nationalist movement, the Universal Negro Improvement Association. The Jamaican poet-novelist Claude McKay was a major figure among black writers and scholars in the "Harlem Renaissance."

The second, larger wave of Jamaican immigration was ushered in by the Immigration Act of 1965, which eliminated the tiny quota Jamaica had been subject to under earlier legislation. As soon as the new law went into effect, Jamaican immigration skyrocketed, going from 2,743 in 1966 to 10,483 in 1967. In the ten years after the immigration reform, Jamaican immigration exceeded that of the previous seventy years, and the numbers continued to grow after that.

Given the large immigration in the 1980s—in some years more than twenty thousand—it is not surprising that close to half of the Jamaicans counted in the 1990 U.S. Census arrived in the 1980s. (Only 5 percent came before 1960.) Between 1982 and 1989 alone, 162,691 Jamaicans legally settled in the United States. These figures do not include the enormous number of undocumented immigrants, who are estimated to be 25 to 100 percent of the size of the legal flow. Nor do the figures include the large number of second-generation Jamaicans also living in the United States. Estimating conservatively, there are more than half a million first- and second-generation Jamaicans in the United States.

In terms of Jamaican immigrants' age profile, the median age in 1990 was thirty-six, and 12 percent were sixty years or older. The immigrant stream to the United States has included a high percentage of professionals and other highly trained Jamaicans. There also are more women than men; in 1990, 55 percent of the Jamaican-born population in the United States was female. Jamaican women frequently arrive in the United States on their own, later followed by their children and spouses. The proportion of women was particularly high in the late 1960s. It was easier for women that men to get labor certification, largely due to the demand for domestic labor in American cities. Not surprisingly, the percentage of total immigrant workers who were classified as private household workers peaked in the same years that the percentage of women immigrants was so high. Women also could obtain immigrant visas as nurses. As the immigration progressed, and as a larger percentage of Jamaicans qualified for immigrant status on the basis of family ties rather than occupation, women were probably as likely as men to have relatives in the United States to sponsor them—a reason why the sex ratios began to even out after the first three years of the post-1965 immigration. Women make up a high proportion of the illegal stream as well, partly because they can readily find jobs in private households as domestics, attendants to the elderly, and child-care workers.

Jamaicans are heavily concentrated in a few places in the United States; nearly three-quarters live in three states: New York, New Jersey, and Florida. The largest number—about a third—live in New York City, although there are also sizable Jamaican communities in Miami, Hartford, and Washington, D.C. Within each city, Jamaicans, along with English-speaking West Indians from other countries, cluster in certain neighborhoods. In New York, central Brooklyn is the main area of settlement. Businesses, churches, schools, and health-care institutions in the Crown Heights, Flatbush, and East Flatbush sections of Brooklyn have taken on a decidedly West Indian flavor. Even shops that are owned by non-West Indians often display some Caribbean referent such as a flag, a country's name, or a painted palm tree. Elsewhere in New York City, neighborhoods in the northeastern Bronx and southeastern Queens have also become home to large numbers of Jamaicans.

Jamaicans also cluster in certain occupations, mainly in low-level service sector and clerical jobs. In the New York City area, Jamaican women are overwhelmingly concentrated in the lower ranks of the nursing and health-care occupations and in private households as child-care workers and attendants to the elderly. In addition, they are in clerical, key punch, and data enty jobs. Men are found in a wide range of occupations. Many work in construction, mostly in the nonunionized, small-scale strata of that industry. Some drive cabs, trucks, or vans; others work in factories or hospitals; still others work as clerks, security guards, or janitors.

Race and Ethnicity

As Jamaicans come to terms with and adjust to life in the United States, new meanings, ideologies, and patterns of behavior emerge in response to the social arrangements and dominant cultural patterns they encounter. Most harsh is the racial hierarchy in American society, something that touches virtually every aspect of Jamaican immigrants' lives and leads to new conceptions of themselves and others.

As part of the larger black population in a racially divided America, Jamaicans find that they are subject to prejudice and discrimination of a sort they had not encountered in their home country. Granted, the slavery legacy lingers in Jamaica; white skin still is associated with wealth, privilege, and power, and people are still conscious of shade distinctions (which imply the lighter, the better). Yet in Jamaica, blackness was not itself—and has not been since the 1950s—a barrier to upward social mobility or to social acceptance "at the top." Black and colored Jamaicans dominate public affairs and fill the prestigious, lucrative, and professional positions on the island. Indeed, blacks are an overwhelming majority in Jamaica.

In the United States, however, even high levels of education or income do not automatically enable people to transcend the prejudices inherent in American life. Nor are whites sensitive to shade differences among Jamaican immigrants, as people are in Jamaica. Whites tend to lump Jamaicans with American blacks and ignore shade and ethnic distinctions. Whatever their achievements or shade, Jamaicans in the United States, as blacks, are victims of racial discrimination in housing, employment, and education. Thus, many Jamaicans in the United States become, for the first time, acutely aware of black skin as a significant status marker.

Among the various disabilities Jamaicans face as blacks in America are informal limitations on where they can rent or buy housing. Many prefer to live in black neighborhoods to avoid the likelihood of encountering racial discrimination in other areas. In the world of work, Jamaicans in high-level white-collar positions or skilled construction trades are most likely to compete with whites for jobs—and to be bitter about racial barriers in getting and keeping employment, and advancing on the job.

The new racial awareness among Jamaicans in the United States provides a potential bond with native and other immigrant blacks in political and social movements and, at the individual level, in interpersonal relations on the job, in the neighborhood, and at school. In the world of politics, Jamaicans (and other West Indians) are especially likely to join together with African Americans when "black" and "white" interests are seen as being in conflict. At the same time, though, Jamaicans have an expanded consciousness of their separateness as Jamaicans. The movement from a society where being Jamaican was taken for granted to one where they are not only a minority, but also lumped together with American blacks in the hostile eyes of much of the white majority, has heightened Jamaicans' ethnic identity.

Jamaican immigrants' sense of ethnic distinctiveness is expressed and reinforced by their social networks. Outside of work they move in a largely Jamaican social world. Contact with Jamaicans back home also fortifies immigrants' identity as Jamaicans. Even while living in the United States, Jamaicans typically maintain close connections with the island. They phone relatives and friends on the island, send letters, and visit back and forth. Many leave children behind to be reared and educated, send substantial amounts of money back in remittances, and build houses and buy land that they supervise from abroad. While Jamaicans read American newspapers and keep up with local news in the United States, many also receive *The Jamaican Weekly Gleaner,* the North American edition of Jamaica's largest newspaper, which has a paid circulation of about twenty-one thousand in the United States and Canada.

Jamaicans also emphasize their ethnic identity as a way to differentiate themselves from African Americans and to show, to the white majority, that they deserve to be viewed and treated as superior and deserving of respect. Setting themselves apart from black Americans, many Jamaicans believe, brings greater acceptance from whites. Their distinct Jamaican or West Indian character also is a matter of ethnic pride. Jamaicans generally feel that they are different from—indeed, superior to—black Americans, that they are more ambitious, harder workers, and greater achievers. They say they save more and are less likely to go on welfare or live off of government benefits. (In fact, only 8 percent of Jamaican households in the United States in 1990 received public assistance, as compared to 20 percent of native-born black households.)

If ethnicity divides Jamaicans from American blacks, it draws them together with other English-speaking West Indian immigrants. A generalized West Indian identity has become important in the United States, fostered by a shared cultural and linguistic background with immigrants from the Commonwealth Caribbean. Informally, bonds develop with other West Indians in the neighborhood and workplace. Rather than forming congregations on their own, Jamaicans attend churches that generally cater to a broad spectrum of West Indians. (Most are Protestant churches in a variety of denominations, including Baptist, Seventh-Day Adventist, and various Pentecostal churches.) Jamaicans also regularly join with other West Indians in work-related and neighborhood associations and, in New York, once a year, in Brooklyn's West Indian Labor Day Carnival, which draws crowds of well over a million people. Along with other West Indians in New York, Jamaicans support the weekly *New York Carib News,* which boasted a circulation of sixty-two thousand in 1986.

Cultural Continuities

The West Indian Labor Day Carnival is a New York invention and something entirely new for Jamaicans. There was no Carnival in Jamaica, and the New York celebration is modeled after Trinidad's carnival. Yet as Jamaicans change and adapt to life in the United States, they also bring with them cultural patterns and social practices from Jamaica that continue to have force in their new home. There is pressure in the United States to speak standard English more of the time, but, as in Jamaica, Jamaicans still often speak patois among themselves. Jamaicans now eat many "American" foods, such as hamburgers and Kentucky Fried Chicken, yet most prefer Jamaican food and continue to cook curried goat, rice and peas, ackee (canned) and saltfish, and other Jamaican dishes at home as often as possible. Jamaican restaurants have sprung up in West Indian neighborhoods; there are bakeries that sell Jamaican-style bread; and several companies make and market Jamaican meat patties. Jamaicans in the United States join together in informal rotating credit associations like those they belonged to on the island. Known as "partners" in Jamaica, these associations offer a way to save money, usually for large purchases. Typically they consist of ten to fifteen members who make weekly or biweekly contributions of anywhere from $10 to more than $100 to a fund that is given, in its entirety, to each contributor in rotation. Finally, there is Jamaican music. Many Jamaicans continue to be devoted to reggae and dance hall music and, in the process, have had a strong influence on the American popular music scene.

See also: AFRICAN AMERICANS

Bibliography

Bonnett, A. (1982). *Institutional Adaptations of West Indian Immigrants to America: An Analysis of Rotating Credit Associations.* Washington, DC: University Press of America.

Bryce-Laporte, R. S. (1972). "Black Immigrants: The

Experience of Invisibility and Inequality." *Journal of Black Studies* 3:29–56.

Colen, S. (1990). "Housekeeping for the Green Card: West Indian Household Workers, the State, and Stratified Reproduction in New York." In *At Work in Homes: Household Workers in World Perspective,* edited by R. Sanjek and S. Colen. Washington, DC: American Anthropological Association.

Foner, N. (1986). "Sex Roles and Sensibilities: Jamaican Women in New York and London." In *International Migration: The Female Experience,* edited by R. Simon and C. Brettell. Totowa, NJ: Rowman & Allanheld.

Foner, N. (1987). "The Jamaicans: Race and Ethnicity Among Jamaicans in New York." In *New Immigrants in New York,* edited by N. Foner. New York: Columbia University Press.

Kasinitz, P. (1992). *Caribbean New York: Black Immigrants and the Politics of Race.* Ithaca, NY: Cornell University Press.

Reid, I. de. (1939). *The Negro Immigrant in New York: His Background, Characteristics, and Social Adjustment, 1899–1937.* New York: AMS Press.

Sutton, C., and Makiesky, S. (1987). "Migration and West Indian Racial and Ethnic Consciousness." In *Caribbean Life in New York City,* edited by C. Sutton and E. Chaney. New York: Center for Migration Studies.

NANCY FONER

JAPANESE

The experience of Japanese in America is marked by exclusion, discrimination, perseverance, and success. In 1853, Commodore Matthew G. Perry sailed American ships to Japan, seeking to establish trade agreements. His arrival initiated the dismantling of Japan's isolationist stance. Within the following five decades, the United States began to receive its first immigrants from Japan.

Japanese immigration to the United States was preceded by the immigration of Chinese laborers, who arrived in significant numbers during the California Gold Rush of 1849. Like the Chinese, the Japanese were viewed as unassimilable and belonging to an inferior race.

The need for laborers in the independent monarchy of Hawaii led to the arrival of Japanese contract laborers. Approximately 150 Japanese males from Tokyo and Yokohama were recruited in 1868, but they were ill suited to work in the Hawaiian sugar plantations.

Recruitment then centered around attracting hardworking laborers from agricultural prefectures such as Hiroshima, Yamaguchi, and Kumamoto. Initially the Japanese immigrants, like the other immigrant laborers, were segregated on the Hawaiian plantations. This isolation led to a reproduction of Japanese village life and the establishment of a strong ethnic community.

The majority of the early Japanese immigrants were young males from agricultural backgrounds. They began to arrive in the United States during the late 1800s. By 1890, a total of twelve thousand Japanese had settled in Hawaii and two thousand in the continental United States. The earliest settlement, The Lost Colony of Wakamatsu, was founded in 1869 but collapsed as a result of crop failure. Throughout this stage of their immigration, all Japanese immigrants were legally considered to be "aliens ineligible to citizenship."

Diplomatic correspondence in late 1907 and early 1908 resulted in a "Gentlemen's Agreement" between the United States and Japan. Japan agreed not to issue any further passports for laborers immigrating to the United States. The United States, in return, promised not to prohibit immigration of Japanese, and most Japanese students in the United States were integrated into the public school systems. It was also agreed that laborers who had been in the United States could return and that family members could join laborers already in the United States. When the California legislature passed the Alien Land Law of 1913 (the Webb-Heney Act), aliens who were "ineligible to citizenship" also were made ineligible for ownership of agricultural property. A California Alien Land Law of 1920 provided further restrictions. Despite such exclusionary laws, between 1890 and 1924 a total of 295,820 Japanese entered the

United States. Not all remained. The U.S. Census reported 111,010 Japanese Americans in 1920 and 138,834 in 1930.

Japanese Americans have distinct terms for different generational cohorts. The immigrating generation is referred to as the first generation, or Issei. The children of the Issei (the first American-born generation) are the Nisei, the second generation. The Sansei are the third generation. The Yonsei are the fourth generation. This method of counting generations differs from that some Western immigrant groups use, referring to the first generation born in America as the first generation.

The Issei developed their own communities, such as "Little Tokyo" in Los Angeles. Health and legal services, employment, recreation, and other resources were available in these communities. In urban settings many Japanese were employed in domestic service, or ran small businesses such as laundries, rooming houses, grocery stores, or barbershops. They developed an interdependent ethnic network in which services and goods were provided by the Japanese in America for the Japanese in America.

The Issei started their own local protective, educational, religious (Christian and Buddhist), and banking (*tanomoshi*) organizations. The leadership was primarily male, and activities included sponsoring picnics, providing interpreters, participating in parades, and developing cemetery

Immigration officials examine Japanese immigrants aboard the ship Shimyo Maru off Angel Island, California, in 1931. (The National Archives/Corbis)

space. A basic purpose of the community organizations was to uphold the reputation of the Japanese in America. Although they were excluded from the mainstream, they wished to be recognized as good and loyal citizens.

The Issei brought with them the values and beliefs of Meiji-period Japan. These values were deeply rooted in the Confucian prescriptions of hierarchical social relationships, group cohesiveness, and a blend of Buddhism and Shintoism. These beliefs were reflected in a vertical, male-dominated family and community structure that stressed the values of hard work, loyalty, and obedience.

The mainstream society was often hostile to Japanese in America. Newspapers such as William Randolph Hearst's press revived fears that the Japanese represented a "yellow peril." Specific Asian-exclusion organizations were formed, while established groups such as the Native Sons and Daughters of the Golden West, the American Legion, and labor organizations promulgated anti-Japanese sentiments.

Even though persons of Japanese ancestry never comprised more than 1 percent of the California population, self-proclaimed nativists continued to be alarmed about being overrun by Asian immigrants. As a result, Japanese immigrants faced restrictions in all facets of their lives. There were laws that forbade Japanese in America from owning or inheriting land, marrying white persons, employing white females, or owning power engines. Japanese in America had limited employment opportunities and were forced to live in segregated ghettos.

On the federal level, the 1922 U.S. Supreme Court case of *Ozawa v. United States* reinforced that the Issei were considered "aliens ineligible to citizenship" and could not apply for naturalization. In reaction to the general public's fear that uncontrolled immigration was a danger to social and economic stability, the Immigration Act of 1924 was passed, establishing fixed quotas by national origin for all immigrants. Japanese, and other aliens "ineligible to citizenship," were completely barred from legal entry into the United States. The prohibition of Japanese immigration remained until well after World War II.

The Nisei

Initially, the vast majority of Issei immigrated as single males. They quickly established family life in America by marrying women from Japan. Marriage was often arranged through an exchange of pictures between women in Japan and male Issei. These women were called "picture brides." The decision to marry picture brides was not based solely on cultural preference or practice. Antimiscegenation legislation and cultural differences presented insurmountable barriers.

The most important outcome of these marriages was the birth of the second generation, the Nisei. Through the Nisei, the Japanese population now included an American-born generation, citizens by birthright. The Issei were now able to register their holdings under the names of these Nisei children.

The Nisei were expected to adjust readily to the new society on a more equitable basis. They had citizenship, knew the language, and were educated in the American system. Although many Nisei children were forced to attend Japanese-language schools after their regular schools, very few became fluent in the Japanese language. The term *kodomo no tame ni* (for the sake of the children) reflected the common parental value of making sacrifices for the children.

Most of the Nisei were born between 1910 and the 1940s and faced difficult times. The Great Depression of the 1930s, coupled with high expectations, racism, and discrimination, meant a future full of challenge for the Nisei. Even college-educated Nisei could find only limited employment outside their community and were forced into low-paying jobs in the Japanese-American community. There were not accepted by the American society, even though most had become acculturated to American life. The Nisei were not accepted by the Issei community because they had become too American.

An important event in the early years of the Japanese-American community was the organization of the Japanese-American Citizens League (JACL), which was founded in the late 1920s to increase Nisei involvment in politics. It was to become the largest national Japanese-American organization. In addition to the development of political organizations was the establishment of social and community-oriented groups (e.g., Japanese-American Boy and Girl Scout troops, churches, social clubs). Japanese-American athletic leagues were also created, and they have continued to be very popular well into the 1990s.

Wartime Incarceration, 1942–1945

For Japanese Americans, the wartime evacuation and incarceration stands out as a distinct defining experience. When meeting for the first time, conversations between people who were interned will often include questions about each other's camp experiences. Nisei and older Sansei will describe time periods as "before camp" or "after camp."

During World War II, individuals of Japanese ancestry on the West Coast of the continental United States, regardless of citizenship or legal residency, were evacuated and interned. On February 19, 1942, President Franklin D. Roosevelt signed Executive Order 9066, which designated areas from which military commanders could exclude persons. The executive order also authorized the building of "relocation camps." It led to the exclusion and incarceration of more than 110,000 Japanese in America, both citizens and aliens, residing along the Pacific Coast. Additionally, selected individuals from Hawaii were also sent to these camps. The vast majority of these individuals were never formally charged with any crime and never given a trial or hearing.

There was a strong consensus among the American public in support of the evacuation. Congress, the executive branch, the mass media, and influential community leaders all voiced their concerns about the loyalty of the Japanese in America. Despite information from the Federal

Young evacuees of Japanese ancestry await their turn for baggage inspection upon arrival at a World War II assembly center in Turlock, California, before being transported to a relocation camp. (The National Archives/Corbis)

Bureau of Investigation, the Federal Communications Commission, and the office of Naval Intelligence (the three main agencies concerned with Japanese espionage) that there was no military need to evacuate and detain Japanese Americans on the West Coast, government officials proceeded with the policy. Only some Quaker groups and individual members of the American Civil Liberties Union voiced any opposition to the policy.

Despite governmental proclamations that there was a military necessity, Japanese Americans in the territory of Hawaii (the site of the recent attack on Pearl Harbor) were not evacuated as a group. Logistical problems such as not having enough ships to transport this large amount of people, and that Japanese Americans represented one-third of the work force in Hawaii, discouraged any mass evacuation program. In addition, the ethnic diversity of Hawaii produced a more tolerant view of Japanese Americans.

The evacuation notices typically provided individuals with only a few days of notice. Individuals were instructed to gather just those belongings they could carry and to report for mass transport to the temporary assembly centers. Personal property and belongings were often hastily sold at great loss, given away to friends and neighbors, or simply left behind.

By August 1942, the U.S. Army had placed the Japanese Americans and resident aliens into temporary assembly centers, such as the Tanforan and Santa Anita racetracks in California. Many families were housed in stables that only weeks earlier had accommodated horses. Later they were moved into more permanent camps under the War Relocation Authority (WRA). These camps were located in desolate areas and surrounded by barbed wire and armed guards. Ten such camps existed in Manzanar and Tule Lake, California; Poston and Gila River, Arizona; Heart Mountain, Wyoming; Granada (Amache), Colorado; Topaz, Utah; Minidoka, Idaho; and Rowher and Jerome, Arkansas. In addition, there were two other types of camps: internment and citizen isolation.

The camps were not fully closed. There was a policy that encouraged individuals to apply for leave. After obtaining government clearance, they could move to the Midwest or the East Coast. Nearly thirty-five thousand individuals, primarily college students and young adults, were able to take advantage of this policy.

The concentration camp experience had a long-lasting effect on the Japanese-American community. Many Japanese families were ruined economically. The structure of the community and of individual families was reordered, while individuals experienced the physical and psychological pain and torment of undue incarceration.

The exclusion and incarceration orders were legally challenged by four individuals: Minoru Yasui, Gordon K. Hirabayashi, Fred T. Korematsu, and Mitsuye Endo. All four cases eventually were heard by the U.S. Supreme Court.

Yasui, Hirabayashi, and Korematsu were all tried and convicted of violating the curfew and evacuation orders. In June 1943, the Supreme Court upheld the convictions of Hirabayashi and Yasui based on the claimed military necessity for the curfew and evacuation orders. In December 1944 the Court concluded in a split decision in the Korematsu case that the identification and exclusion of a single racial group was permissible through the war powers of Congress and the president. The Court ruled that Korematsu was excluded not because of his race but because of the war with the Japanese Empire and the military urgency of the situation. The Court's decisions addressed only the constitutionality of the exclusion orders and remained silent on the incarceration directives.

Endo pursued a different legal challenge. Endo filed a habeas corpus petition (*Endo v. Eisenhower*) on July 12, 1942. The Supreme Court heard the case and issued a unanimous ruling on December 18, 1944. The Court ruled that the WRA did not have the authority to subject loyal citizens to its regulations. By this time, however, the war was nearing an end and the camps had been directed to close.

Japanese Americans in the Military

Throughout the internment experience, the Japanese Americans dealt with the issue of how best to demonstrate their loyalty. From out of this oppressive experience emerged one of the most amazing stories of loyalty and patriotism. Despite the racism, discrimination, and wholesale violation of constitutional rights to which they were subjected, the Japanese-American community produced three of the most decorated military units in American military history: the 442nd Regimental Combat Team, the 100th Battalion, and the Military Intelligence Service.

The Military Intelligence Service Language School (MISLS) was formed in early 1941 to train personnel to become language interpreters and translators. The linguistic skills of Japanese Americans were used in the Pacific theater to translate

A veteran who fought with the 442nd Infantry Regiment shows the Bronze Star he earned in World War II. (Dean Wong/Corbis)

captured enemy documents and determine the enemy's battle plans.

The 100th Battalion originally was part of the Hawaii National Guard. Its commander, Lieutenant General Delos Emmons, recommended the formation of a Nisei battalion to be sent to the European theater. They were sent to North Africa and Italy and suffered heavy casualties. By the time they were finally pulled from battle, they had earned nine hundred Purple Hearts and were appropriately nicknamed the "Purple Heart Battalion." In Italy they were joined by the other Nisei unit, the 442nd Regimental Combat Team.

On January 28, 1943, the creation of a segregated Japanese-American combat team was announced. Nearly 10,000 Nisei from Hawaii volunteered immediately, of whom nearly 2,700 were inducted. From behind barbed wire in the continental United States, 1,256 Nisei volunteered, of whom approximately 800 were inducted.

The military draft had been suspended for Japanese Americans but was reinstated on January 14, 1944. Some Japanese Americans, however, recognized the hypocrisy of asking men to go to war while their families were interned. As a matter of principle, 315 Japanese Americans interned in the concentration camps resisted the draft.

The 442nd Regimental Combat Team and the 100th Battalion enthusiastically adopted the motto "Go for Broke," a Hawaiian pidgin gambling phrase that meant to "shoot the works." They bravely entered into battle and became the most decorated unit of its size and length of service in American military history. Many of the decorations were for the more than seven hundred men killed. Additionally, the total number of wounded was more than three times the operating size of the regiment.

After World War II

Following World War II and their release from the concentration camps, the prevailing focus for the majority of Japanese Americans was to reestablish their lives. Everyday concerns such as making a living, finding decent housing, and getting an education were high priorities.

Initially, acts of terrorism against Japanese Americans hindered their return home to the West Coast. By May 1945, twenty-four such incidents were reported. An incident in Hood River, Oregon, demonstrated the common inability to differentiate between Japanese from Japan and Japanese Americans. The names of sixteen Japanese-American veterans were removed from the town's honor roll. Four of these American veterans had been killed in battle and ten had received the Purple Heart. The local paper ran a column indicating that Japanese were not welcome in Hood River.

By the end of the 1940s, however, approximately 85,000 of the original 168,000 Japanese Americans on the West Coast returned. The mood

Japanese-American children dress in traditional kimonos for the Cherry Blossom Festival in San Francisco. (Nik Wheeler/Corbis)

of the country and the West Coast were becoming more accepting of Japanese Americans. In November 1946, California voters rejected Proposition 15, which would have incorporated the alien land laws into the California Constitution. It was the first time in the state's history that an anti–Asian American ballot was defeated.

In the late 1940s, different courts began to rule that the alien land laws were unconstitutional. In 1948, the U.S. Supreme Court handed down a decision (*Oyama v. California*), which stated that the alien land laws violated the equal protection clause of the Fourteenth Amendment to the U.S. Constitution. The U.S. Congress also demonstrated a slightly more sympathetic position by passing the Japanese-American Evacuation Claims Act of 1948, which provided compensation for documented physical losses from the evacuation (although very inadequate in the amount of claims paid).

In the early 1950s, Congress passed the Immigration and Nationality Act of 1952 (the McCarran-Walter Act), overriding President Harry Truman's veto. This act was the first general immigration act since 1924 and had a mixed effect on the Japanese-American community. The act allowed individuals of all races to become eligible for naturalization. For the first time, the Issei were given the opportunity to become American citizens. The act also provided family reunification as a legitimate reason for immigration on a nonquota basis. However, the act restricted immigration based on race and included a national-origins quota system. Japan was given a yearly quota of 185 immigrants. However, between 1952 and 1964, nearly sixty-three thousand Japanese immigrated to the United States.

The Korean War reinforced the importance of Japan in the anti-Communist struggle. Since the image of Japanese Americans was still closely tied to the image of the Japanese in Japan, the Japanese-American community experienced a slightly better reception from the general American public.

In 1954, the Democratic party vaulted into political leadership in the territory of Hawaii. Daniel K. Inouye, a World War II decorated veteran, led a generation of young Nisei politicians in taking over both houses of the territorial legislature. In 1959, when Hawaii became the fiftieth state, Inouye was elected to the U.S. Congress. Subsequently he was elected to the U.S. Senate, in 1962. Inouye was soon to be followed by other Japanese Americans, such as Spark M. Matsunaga (D-HI) in the U.S. Senate and Patsy Takemoto Mink (D-HI) and Patricia F. Saiki (R-HI) in the U.S. House of Representatives. California eventually elected two U.S. representatives in the 1970s, Norman Y. Mineta (D-CA) and Robert T. Matsui (D-CA), and Samuel I. Hayakawa (R-CA) served one term as a U.S. senator from California. Hayakawa, however, was considered not representative of and received little support from the Japanese-American community.

By the mid-1960s, the American media's portrayal of Japanese Americans was becoming more positive but no less stereotypic. *The New York Times* published an article titled "Success Story: Japanese-American Style," which described Japanese Americans as a "model minority" (Petersen, 1966).

The 1960s brought the civil rights movement, which sought to overthrow the system of racial discrimination and oppression of minorities by the dominant power structure. Many younger Nisei saw a clear relationship between the concentration camp experience and the assault on civil rights of all ethnic minorities.

Japanese Americans participated in the 1963 March on Washington. The JACL had seats reserved for its representatives on the platform of the Lincoln Memorial where Martin Luther King Jr. delivered his famous "I have a dream" speech. Other Japanese Americans supported the more militant ideology of Malcolm X. Yuri Kochiyama, a Nisei political activist who had been interned, established a close and ongoing relationship with Malcolm X. She was by Malcolm X's side when he was assassinated and after his death continued to carry on his internationalist concept of human rights. The participation by Japanese Americans in the civil rights movement, while not highly publicized, was instrumental in gaining the community a legitimate place among civil rights supporters.

The Civil Liberties Act of 1988

The treatment of Japanese Americans during World War II is now considered an egregious constitutional error. The struggle to obtain this acknowledgment began in 1970, when the JACL started a redress campaign. Over the next twenty years other Japanese-American organizations (the National Coalition for Redress and Reparations, the National Council for Japanese-American Redress) and civil rights groups joined the redress battle, which incorporated legislative, judicial, and grassroots strategies.

On August 10, 1988, President Ronald Reagan signed the Civil Liberties Act of 1988. This act provided Japanese Americans who had been incarcerated with monetary redress compensation of $20,000 and a presidential apology for the violation of their constitutional and human rights. Despite setting a historic precedent, this legislation was limited in scope. Only individuals alive at the time of the legislation's passage were considered eligible. Individuals who had been excluded and incarcerated during World War II but who had died prior to 1988 were not included. Ironically, it was these people who suffered the most economic and psychological losses.

Japanese-American Values

There are several Japanese values that remain a part of the Japanese-American culture. These values include *enryo, amae,* filial piety, *gaman,* and fatalism.

Enryo is a concept that originally involved the way in which inferiors were to behave toward superiors but now includes how to behave in ambiguous situations and avoid embarrassment, confusion, and anxiety. The norm includes deference, obsequiousness, modesty, and a keen awareness and avoidance of behavior that may be ridiculed.

Amae is the term used to refer to the need to be loved and cherished. It is a way of interacting that asks for love, attention, and recognition. It is not easily translated into English and oftentimes is confused with dependency. However, it is an acceptable cultural way of coping with the enryo norm.

Filial piety is the value of having an obligation to one's family. In its original form, individuals were expected to comply with familial and societal authority. It was originally a reciprocal obligation, but the Issei, and subsequently the Nisei, practiced it in a unilateral fashion from parent to child.

Gaman is a major value that many Japanese Americans still adhere to, even though the term may be unfamiliar to them. Gaman is best described as emotional restraint. It is an internalization and suppression of anger, which has served Japanese Americans as a major defense mechanism against racism.

The value of fatalism is best exemplified by the phrase *shikata ga nai* (it cannot be helped). This acceptance of one's situation was a value that was further developed by Japanese Americans as a defense against racism.

These five Japanese values reflect a cultural prescription based on the value system of Meiji-period Japan. Not all Japanese Americans equally hold and practice each of these values. Generational, acculturational, and geograhical differences determine the degree to which one has been exposed to and maintains these values.

Geographical Differences

There are differences between Japanese Americans from the continental United States and those from Hawaii. Japanese Americans from the continental United States are referred to as "Kotonks." The term reflects the facetious belief that mainland Japanese Americans have hard and hollow heads. "Kotonk" is the sound made when a hollow head hits the floor. "Kotonks" are generally viewed by the Japanese in Hawaii as being standoffish and uptight, too acculturated, and too haolefied (i.e., white).

The Japanese in Hawaii are occasionally referred to as "pineapples" by their mainland counterparts. Japanese Americans in Hawaii constitute a powerful group with a number of social and economic alternatives; they have not been a political, social, economic, or even numerical minority. They exhibit greater ease with their ethnicity, and their acculturation process has taken place within an ethnically more tolerant environment. Many Japanese Americans from Hawaii indicate little experience with racial discrimination. It is the amalgamation of these experiences that facilitated a different development between Japanese Americans in Hawaii and Japanese Americans from the continental United States.

The Current State of Japanese Americans

The 1990 U.S. Census indicated that there are 847,562 Japanese Americans in the United States.

The vast majority of Japanese Americans live in the Pacific Census Division (608,703). The five states with the largest population of Japanese Americans are Hawaii (247,486), California (312,989), New York (35,281), Washington (34,366), and Illinois (21,831).

According to the 1990 U.S. Census, Japanese Americans have an average family income of $60,305.00. A total of 34.5 percent of adults over age twenty-five have obtained a bachelor's degree or higher, and only 7 percent (59,127) of the population is below the federal poverty line. The mean age of Japanese Americans is 36.5 years, and 76 percent of the population are citizens by birth or naturalization. Although the 104th U.S. Congress had only one Japanese-American senator and two representatives, Japanese Americans are becoming more visible in federally appointed positions, especially as judges and administrators. Additionally, Japanese Americans are becoming more visible at the state, county, and city government levels of primarily the western states. Professionally, Japanese Americans are well represented as physicians, attorneys, educators, and in related professions.

Despite such gains, Japanese Americans still must battle obstacles such as institutionalized racism, hate crimes against Asians, stereotypic media images, and the lessening but still present inability to differentiate between Japanese nationals and Japanese Americans.

A significant internal challenge before the Japanese American community is its evolving ethnic makeup. The Japanese-American community has a very high percentage of individuals who marry outside their ethnicity. In Los Angeles County in 1989, the percentage for females was 58.3 percent; for males, 41.7 percent. With the high degree of intermarriage with other ethnicities, the definition of what it means to be Japanese American will evolve in the coming generations. Additionally, the Japanese American community is gaining recently arrived first-generation immigrants. These immigrants are referred to as shin-Issei, or new Issei. They are generally well educated, employed, and have a more contemporary set of Japanese values.

The Japanese-American community has influential organizations and publications that maintain the Japanese-American identity and experience. Examples of national organizations are the JACL and the Japanese-American National Museum. Several national Japanese-American professional groups, such as the Japanese-American Medical Association and the Japanese-American Bar Association, are also active. At the local level there are numerous church, political, athletic, and social organizations that are primarily Japanese American. The largest Japanese-American newspapers include the *Rafu Shimpo* (Los Angeles), the *Hawaii Herald* (Honolulu), and the *Hokubei Mainichi* (San Francisco). The JACL's publication, *The Pacific Citizen,* is also well read by the community.

Conclusion

As a community, Japanese Americans have persevered and overcome policies of exclusion and discrimination. While Japanese Americans have attained success in some areas, they continue to struggle for equitable representation in others. As the Japanese-American community continues to change, the dynamics of a strong identity, acculturation, new immigration, and interethnic marriages will challenge and shape the evolving culture and definition of the community.

See also: OKINAWANS

Bibliography

Daniels, R. (1993). *Prisoners Without Trial: Japanese Americans in World War II.* New York: Hill & Wang.

Daniels, R.; Taylor, S.; and Kitano, H. H. L., eds. (1986). *Japanese Americans: From Relocation to Redress.* Seattle: University of Washington Press.

Fugita, S., and O'Brien, D. (1991). *Japanese American Ethnicity: The Persistence of a Community.* Seattle: University of Washington Press.

Hatamiya, L. (1993). *Righting a Wrong: Japanese Americans and the Passage of the Civil Liberties Act of 1988.* Stanford, CA: Stanford University Press.

Hosokawa, B. (1969). *Nisei: The Quiet Americans.* New York: William Morrow.

Iritani, F., and Iritani, J. (1994). *Ten Visits: Accounts of Visits to All the Japanese American Relocation Centers.* San Mateo, CA: Japanese American Curriculum Project.

Irons, P., ed. (1989). *Justice Delayed: The Record of the Japanese American Internment Cases.* Middletown, CT: Wesleyan University Press.

Kitano, H. H. L. (1976). *Japanese Americans: The Evolution of a Subculture.* Englewood Cliffs, NJ: Prentice Hall.

Kitano, H. H. L. (1993). *Generations and Identity.* Boston: Ginn.

Niiya, B., ed. (1993). *Japanese American History: An A-to-Z Reference from 1868 to the Present.* Los Angeles: Japanese American National Museum.

Petersen, W. (1966). "Success Story, Japanese-American Style." *New York Times,* January 9, p. 21.

Petersen, W. (1971). *Japanese Americans: Oppression and Success.* New York: Random House.

Tamura, E. (1994). *Americanization, Acculturation, and Ethnic Identity: The Nisei Generation in Hawaii.* Urbana: University of Illinois Press.

Weglyn, M. (1976). *Years of Infamy: The Untold Story of America's Concentration Camps.* New York: William Morrow.

MITCHELL T. MAKI

JEWS, EUROPEAN

Jewish life in North America begins before the founding of the United States. A few Jewish crew members served on Christopher Columbus's ships, and during the colonial period a small Jewish population had established itself. Most of the Jews settling in colonial America were Sephardim—descendants of the Jews of Spain. The latter had suffered expulsion from their homeland beginning in the year of Columbus's first westward voyage. After 1492, the Spanish Jewish refugees managed to find safe haven in a few places, including the Ottoman Empire, Holland, and the settlements of the Americas. Although the Jewish population of colonial America was not large, the individuals fit into their new homeland and easily adjusted to the majority Christian population. In Spain, the Sephardic Jews had lived as a generally prosperous, cosmopolitan minority, respected by their neighbors and unconfined to ghettos or other restricted areas. They mingled easily with the Christian majority, establishing a pattern that would continue in the American colonies. By the early nineteenth century, many Sephardic Jews had converted to Christianity or else married Christians in such large proportions that their children soon assimilated into the majority population.

During the eighteenth century, other European Jews joined their Sephardic coreligionists in America and soon outnumbered the latter. Known collectively as Ashkenazic Jews, the newcomers came from central Europe and the German states, where their forebears had lived since Roman times. Outside of Spain, the lot of Europe's Jews began to decline sharply after the First Crusade, when anti-Jewish sentiment proliferated. The Jews soon fell victim to centuries of severe, official restrictions, including an enforced ghetto existence. As speakers of Yiddish and generally very strict in their observance of Orthodox Jewish belief and practice, the Ashkenazim were distinct from the Sephardic Jews.

By the early nineteenth century, the civil status of Jews in the German states and in parts of western Europe had improved dramatically after the granting of citizenship rights. They gained many of the social and political rights enjoyed by non-Jewish citizens, thus enabling them to participate in mainstream life. In this way a process of linguistic and cultural assimilation began, as Jewish communities became German-speaking and other differences between Jews and their neighbors eroded. At the same time, currents of religious change brought about a liberalization of Jewish belief and practice in some communities.

Nonetheless, by the 1820s, economic decline and periodic outbreaks of anti-Semitism spurred many Jews in central Europe, including the German states and Austria-Hungary, to seek refuge and commercial opportunities in the United States.

This process continued over the next thirty years, increasing the Jewish population of the United States from roughly fifteen hundred at the turn of the nineteenth century to approximately fifty thousand in 1850. Predominantly traders and merchants, the newcomers were eager to make a new life where their Jewishness would not severely restrict their opportunities. They settled in American towns and cities as well as on the frontier, establishing shops or becoming itinerant peddlers. Many contemporary American Jewish communities thus trace their origins to the early settlers from central Europe, often referred to simply as "German Jews." Until the 1880s they established the character of American Jewish life.

Having left European homes where the spirit of religious liberalization of old Orthodox practice was under way, the new immigrants founded communities based on the innovative practices of Jewish religious reformers. At the same time, the pragmatic character of American society and the demands of small-town or frontier existence encouraged a flexible style of living, even in religious matters. Accordingly, the newcomers accommodated themselves to their adopted country with relative ease. Old European Jewish patterns of strict adherence to the dietary laws, the rigorous observance of the Sabbath and other religious holy days, and social separation from their non-Jewish neighbors quickly attenuated. The newcomers avidly participated in community affairs, where their religious beliefs and practices did not dramatically set them apart from their non-Jewish neighbors. Assimilation of the cultural styles of the new country and the adaptation of Jewish religious and social patterns to American communities defined the American Jewish population throughout most of the nineteenth century. Indeed, by the 1880s, the United States had become a major center of Reform Judaism, marked most clearly by the founding in Cincinnati of Hebrew Union College for the training of Reform Jewish rabbis. But the distinctive features of American Jewish life shaped by the German and central European immigrants was to change fundamentally as a result of events unfolding in eastern Europe.

The Changing Population

In 1881, revolutionaries assassinated the Russian czar, Alexander II, in the expectation that the inevitable political repression and retaliation of his successor would spark an uprising among the Russian peasantry. Instead, popular and officially sanctioned violence was directed against the Jews, who suffered a series of pogroms, or persecutions, following the assassination. For months after the czar's murder, hundreds of Jewish communities across Russia endured murder, rape, and property destruction. The government also enacted the notorious May Laws of 1882, severely curtailing the rights of Jews to gain an education, to live in particular places, to earn a living, or, in short, to eke out even the most meager existence. The bleakness of the Jewish future in Russia was apparent as periodic violence and official repression continued into the twentieth century.

Jewish peddlers line up along the curb at Rivington Street on the Lower East Side of New York City during the early twentieth century. (Library of Congress/ Corbis)

After some six hundred years in eastern Europe, the Ashkenazic Jewish communities of imperial Russia were in turmoil. They had over the centuries withstood periodic violence and other state-sponsored repressions, but the catastrophic events of 1881 and 1882 immediately stimulated immigration to the United States that continued for four decades. Russian Jews joined other eastern and southern Europeans in a great exodus that continued until severe immigration restrictions based on numerical quotas were instituted by Congress in 1924. On the eve of this momentous movement of people, the American Jewish population numbered approximately 250,000. In 1900, one million Jews lived in the United States, and by 1920, the American Jewish population had reached four million. This massive transference of Russian Jews—the largest Jewish migration in history—effectively shifted the center of Jewish life from Europe to America. Relatedly, since Russian Jews differed significantly in terms of culture and religion from the American Jewish population of German background, the mass immigration redefined American Jewish life. Of the approximately 5.5 million Jews in the United States today, the overwhelming majority are descendants of immigrants from Russia and eastern Europe.

The new Jewish immigrants were a diverse lot, but all shared the Yiddish language and the experience of official political repression, religious intolerance, and periodic violence at the hands of the peasantry. They had enjoyed none of the civil rights that the Jews of central and Western Europe had been granted, beginning in the closing years of the eighteenth century. In America they hoped to escape the physical threats inspired by popular and official anti-Semitism, to earn a living unimpeded by government edicts, and to live on much the same terms as other American citizens. Some newcomers were Orthodox adherents to Jewish law and custom, while others were secular critics of Jewish practice and belief, animated by socialist ideals and a general skepticism about all religion. But whether in religious, political, or cultural terms, the Russian Jews were ethnically distinct from the established American Jewish population.

A Jewish family in Washington, D.C., works together to bake challah bread. (Richard Nowitz/Corbis)

They even dressed and acted differently, in strange and unattractive ways in the view of many American Jews.

Because American Jews of German background emphasized cultural assimilation and took enormous pride in their own remarkable economic and social success, they grew anxious at the rapidly increasing numbers of eastern European Jews in their midst. They believed that the new immigrants, so unlike themselves in language, values, and culture, might jeopardize the position and security of the established Jewish population. Accordingly, American Jews urged the newcomers to cast off, as rapidly as possible and with American Jewish guidance, the behaviors marking their peculiar, immigrant status—whether it was radical politics or stubborn adherence to ancient and medieval religious practices that did not seem to fit well into the new country. The immigrants, for their part, regarded such efforts to make them over

as the arrogant paternalism of Jews who differed little from Christians, either in religious or cultural terms. Inevitably, frictions and resentments over the course of two generations marked the relationship between the American Jews of German background and the Russian Jewish immigrants and their children.

Ironically, the apprehension of American Jews about the capacity of the Russian Jewish immigrants to adjust to their new country was misplaced. The newcomers accommodated themselves rapidly to American life. Many of the Russian Jews, like the previous Jewish immigrants, went into business. In addition, the children of the Russian Jews attended college and university in steadily increasing numbers, thus enabling many to enter the professions. Consequently a very large proportion of immigrant families achieved an extraordinary economic and social mobility in a relatively short period of time.

Between 1900 and 1924, another European Jewish immigration was also under way. Much smaller than the mass movement of Russian Jews to America, approximately twenty-five thousand Sephardic Jews left the Ottoman territories for the United States. These immigrants were descendants of the Jews who had found safe haven under Ottoman rule following their expulsion from Spain at the end of the fifteenth century. They settled in modern-day Turkey, Greece, Rhodes, and other Balkan territories under the rule of the sultan and generally flourished for four hundred years. Anti-Semitism was not a significant factor in motivating their move to America early in the twentieth century. Rather, war and political instability in the Balkans had severely disrupted economic life, thus prompting the immigration of the Sephardim. Although they shared many liturgical and religious practices, including the use of Hebrew in worship, with the Ashkenazic Jews of Russia, prominent ethnic differences distinguished the two groups. They were, in other words, culturally and linguistically distinct. The Sephardim were not Yiddish-speakers but rather used Ladino as their first language. Ladino was based on fifteenth-century Spanish and also incorporated elements from Hebrew, Turkish, and other languages spoken in the Balkans. Much smaller in number than the Russian Jewish immigrants who settled throughout the United States, the Sephardim established only a few communities in such cities as New York, Los Angeles, Atlanta, and Seattle as well as smaller settlements in Indianapolis; Portland, Oregon; and Rochester, New York.

Unlike the immigration of many other European ethnic groups, such as Italians during the same era, 1881–1924, Jewish immigration from both Russia and the Balkans tended to be permanent. Moreover, the Jewish immigration was characterized by the movement of families, although it may have occurred in stages, further pointing up the permanent nature of the immigration. By contrast, Italian immigrants were predominantly men, many of whom worked in the United States before returning home with wages far in excess of what they could earn in Europe.

Other European Jewish immigrants arrived following the rise to power of the Nazis in Germany in 1933. A number of German Jews sought refuge in America from anti-Semitic violence and persecution. During World War II the Nazis murdered many millions of German and eastern European Jews, especially in Poland and Russia. The Sephardic Jewish communities of Greece and Yugoslavia also fell victim to the Nazis. For several years after the war, Jewish survivors of the Holocaust resettled in several countries, including the United States and Israel.

Acculturation

Like all immigrants starting anew in America, European Jews faced the competing and often contradictory demands of their religion and tradition on the one hand and American values and practices on the other. Faced with the necessity of earning a living in their adopted country, immigrant Jews often had to compromise religious observances when they interfered with the rhythms of economic life. For example, it was often impossible for immigrant Jews to maintain Saturday, the Jewish Sabbath, as a day of rest because Saturday was a workday in America. At the same time, immigrants accustomed to the official and popular hostility toward Jews in Russia found in the openness of American society freedom and opportunity unprecedented in Jewish experience. Yet participation in an open society—in education, business, the arts, entertainment, sports, leisure, civic life, and the like—usually proved incompatible with the maintenance of customary styles of living. Active engagement in a wide range of American institutions drew the immigrants and, particularly, their children and grandchildren away from time-honored traditional practices.

Language provides a very clear example of the process of acculturation, or culture change brought on by contact between the Jews and their non-Jewish neighbors. Yiddish- and Ladino-speaking communities flourished for hundreds of years in Europe, encoding Ashkenazic and Sephardic

Jewish culture and providing continuity through the centuries. In the United States, over the course of a single generation, speaking competence in Yiddish and Ladino fell off dramatically. The children of the immigrants, socialized into the new country through public schools and other American institutions, learned English and valued it far above their parents' native tongues. Upward social and economic mobility as well as entrance into the professions depended on English mastery and on the adoption of generally accepted values and behavior. The grandchildren and great-grandchildren of the immigrants are further estranged from the native languages of their forebears as they have no direct experience with communities of European Jewish immigrants. Efforts to revive Yiddish and Ladino in America have proven negligible, and a once-flourishing Yiddish and Ladino press has become moribund.

An additional consequence of language loss and other acculturative processes is that the descendants of the various European Jewish immigrants (Russian and German Ashkenazic Jews and Sephardic Jews) have converged around their incorporation into middle-class American life. Set apart neither by language nor by salient cultural practices linked to Europe, they are achieving the ideals of accommodation and adaptation originally articulated by the reform-minded Jewish immigrants of the early to mid-nineteenth century.

As the descendants of each Jewish immigrant group come to resemble each other in social, economic, and cultural terms, the old antagonisms between American Jews of German origin and the Russian Jewish immigrants have faded. Likewise, the uneasy encounter between the Russian Jewish immigrants and the Sephardic Jewish immigrants, differing from each other culturally and linguistically, has no bearing on the relationships between their descendants. Among the latter, their shared American Jewish identity counts for a good deal more than the European-formed experiences of their immigrant forebears.

In a similar vein, Jewish cultural continuity has proven problematic owing to the frequency of intermarriage between Jews and non-Jews. In Europe and among the generation of immigrants, endogamy (the highly valued practice of marriage within the group) contributed to the perpetuation of traditional cultural and religious observances, reflecting as well a deeply ingrained Jewish consciousness. Steadily, each generation following the immigration era has experienced increasing acceptance and tolerance, marked above all by the possibility of marriage with non-Jews. A clear emblem of the open society, marriage between people of various ethnic, religious, or racial groups erodes the social boundaries between them. As a result, groups tend to become more alike as their differences diminish. Marriage between Jews and non-Jews in the immigrant generation was a very unusual event, at odds with Jewish values and the cohesion of Jewish communities. At the same time, prejudice toward Jews also inhibited the possibility of intermarriage. As the descendants of the immigrants have entered every sphere of American life, intermarriage has become commonplace three generations after the end of the European immigration era. By some estimates, the intermarriage rate is approaching 50 percent.

Religion and Identity

American Jewish religious practice runs the gamut from highly observant Orthodoxy to liberal and modernist Reform Judaism. Among Orthodox Jews, one should strictly follow Jewish law as codified in the Torah, regarded as the divine word. The Torah prescribes ancient rules of proper behavior in every domain of life, even in the contemporary world. The Reform movement, on the other hand, adapted Judaism to modern ways of living by rejecting many of the ancient rules and beliefs, such as the dietary laws, that seemed irrational or incompatible with scientific understanding. At the end of the nineteenth century, a number of American Jews found the efforts of the German Jewish reformers too extreme. As a result, Conservative Judaism emerged as a distinctly American branch of the religion. Conservative Jews believe that some adaptations of Orthodoxy to contemporary life are necessary but that such changes require

A Jewish boy in Brooklyn, New York, puts on a phylactery for his morning prayers. (Richard Nowitz/Corbis)

moderation. Reconstructionism, a small offshoot of Conservative Judaism, emphasizes Jewish peoplehood and how it has evolved as a civilization. Its conceptions of divinity are diffuse.

In addition to the religious and ethnic elements within Judaism, American Jewish identity is closely bound to support for Israel. Many American Jews, whether or not they actively practice their religion, define their Jewishness in terms of a historic connection to the restored Jewish homeland. Israel represents the realization of an old tradition (two thousand years) of prayer and longing for the restoration of a Jewish state and the revival of the Hebrew language following the Roman conquest of Palestine during the first century of the Christian era. Furthermore, Israel resonates deeply in Jewish consciousness as a reborn Jewish nation following the destruction of most of Europe's Jews during World War II. It is regarded as a permanent haven where any threatened Diaspora community can find certain refuge unavailable to the Jewish victims of the Nazis. Thus, in Jewish consciousness, both in America and abroad, the rebirth of Israel and the Holocaust are inextricably linked as the two most significant events of modern Jewish history. While the number of American Jews settling in Israel remains small, American Jewish communities provide Israel with critical moral and financial support. Many American Jews visit Israel each year, and their children often take advantage of opportunities to study or work there. For American Jews interested in learning a Jewish language, modern Hebrew has supplanted Yiddish and Ladino.

Despite the powerful symbolism of Israel and the Holocaust in Jewish self-definition as well as a return to Orthodoxy by a small number of people, American Jewish communities now express greater concern about the perpetuation of Jewish life in the United States than at any time in the past. With much anxiety about the future, these communities are actively promoting cultural and religious renewal, innovations in religious worship to meet the perceived needs of younger generations, and efforts to incorporate fully intermarried couples and their children. The question of how American Jews and other cultural and religious groups can maintain their distinctiveness in an open society thus endures.

See also: JEWS, HASIDIC; JEWS, ISRAELI; JEWS, MIDDLE EASTERN; JEWS, SOVIET

Bibliography

Cohen, S. M. (1983). *American Modernity and Jewish Identity*. New York: Tavistock.

Cowan, N. M., and Cowan, R. S. (1989). *Our Parents' Lives: The Americanization of Eastern European Jews*. New York: Basic Books.

Dawidowicz, L. S. (1982). *On Equal Terms*. New York: Holt, Rinehart and Winston.

Glazer, N. (1974). *American Judaism*. Chicago: University of Chicago Press.

Meyer, M. (1988). *Response to Modernity: A History of the Reform Movement in Judaism*. New York: Oxford University Press.

Sachar, H. (1992). *A History of Jews in America*. New York: Alfred A. Knopf.

Sanders, R. (1988). *Shores of Refuge*. New York: Henry Holt.

Silberman, C. E. (1985). *A Certain People: American Jews and Their Lives Today*. New York: Summit Books.

Sklare, M., and Greenblum, J. (1979). *Jewish Identity on the Suburban Frontier: A Study of Group Survival in the Open Society.* Chicago: University of Chicago Press.

Wertheimer, J. (1993). *A People Divided.* New York: Basic Books.

Zenner, W. P., ed. (1988). *Persistence and Flexibility: Anthropological Perspectives on the American Jewish Experience.* Albany: State University of New York Press.

JACK GLAZIER

JEWS, HASIDIC

The term "Hasid" stems from the Hebrew root *hesed*, meaning piety, mercy, and loving kindness, and is commonly translated as "pious one." The Bible refers to a Hasid as an exceptionally pious and virtuous man—in essence, one who practices hesed. Beginning with the Hellenistic period (323 B.C.E), "Hasid" signified a man of refined sanctity and holiness who was noted for his scrupulous ritual observance.

Over time, a number of social movements adopted the mantle "Hasidim." Among the best known are the Hasidim ha-Rishonim (Pious Men of Old), described in the Talmud (the authoritative body of Jewish tradition) as delaying prayer for an hour to better apprehend the Almighty, and the Hasidei Ashkenaz, medieval German pietists who dedicated themselves to ascetic forms of purification rituals. Contemporary Hasidic Jews are adherents of a movement that originated in mid- to late eighteenth-century eastern Europe in response to the political anarchy, financial impoverishment, and spiritual malaise that afflicted Ashkenazic Jewry.

Hasidic Jews are also known by the following ethnonyms: Hasid (pl., Hasidim), Chassid (pl., Chassidim), Hassid (pl., Hassidim), Lubavitcher Hasidim, Chabad, Bobover Hasidim, Satmarer Hasidim, Gerer Hasidim, Belzer Hasidim, Skverer Hasidim, Vishnitzer Hasidim, Bostoner Hasidim, and Munkaczer Hasidim.

History and Ideology

The modern-era Hasidic movement was established in the eighteenth century by Israel ben Eliezer, known as the Baal Shem Tov (Master of the Good Name). An itinerant healer and storyteller, he championed the joyous worship of God through ecstatic prayer, aesthetic practice, and emotionally charged pieties. Key to the Baal Shem Tov's teachings is the mystical concept of *devekuth*—the cleaving to God. This spiritual domain, the Baal Shem Tov taught, can be mastered and performed by every individual who worships the Almighty with humility (*shipluth*), joy (*simhkab*), and enthusiasm (*hithlahabuth*).

From its base in the Podolia and Volhynia regions of Poland, the Hasidic movement rapidly spread northward into Belarus and Lithuania and westward into Galicia and the heartland of Poland. Under the Baal Shem Tov's successors, Hasidism evolved from an elite community of God-seekers to a popular, egalitarian movement that espoused "practical mysticism" for the people.

The Hasidic movement revised old ritual practices and pioneered new religious institutions, the most important being that of the Hasidic *rebbe* (rabbi). A rebbe's authority derived from his piety and charisma, from his perceived ability to bring his followers closer to God, and God's grace to his flock. In time the rebbe's leadership became dynastic; with a few exceptions, the mantle was passed from father to son, who took up residence in courts throughout the towns and cities of eastern Europe. These rebbes reflected a multiplicity of worldviews and ritual practices that all too often spawned bitter disputes among them.

The Hasidic movement reached its apogee in the 1830s. Hasidism became the dominant way of life in many communities, despite the enmity it encountered from "normative Jews" who called themselves Mitnaggedim or "opponents" of the Hasidim. By the second half of the nineteenth century, however, Hasidism closed ranks with its detractors to combat a common foe: secularism. In the twentieth century, those Hasidim who withstood assimilation became victims of Europe's world wars. The Holocaust dealt a fatal blow to remaining Hasidic centers. Survivors resettled elsewhere, pioneering new communities in the Old and New worlds.

Emigration

Postwar Hasidism is a global religious phenomenon. Although sizable Hasidic communities exist throughout Europe (particularly in England, Belgium, and France), South America, and Australia, the centers of Hasidic life are in Israel and North America, particularly metropolitan New York City.

The history of Hasidim in North America hails back to the late nineteenth century. The historical record chronicles a number of Hasidic rabbis ministering to congregations of Hasidic Jews. Perhaps the first of these individuals was Rabbi Joshua Segal, who arrived in New York City in 1875 and became the spiritual leader to some twenty Hasidic congregations there. It was not until the beginning of the twentieth century, however, that *shtikl rebbes* (minor rebbes) and their emissaries began to immigrate. In 1912, a descendant of the Talner Rebbe settled in New York City. A year later, Rabbi Yudel Rosenberg, the Tarler Rebbe, arrived in Toronto. In 1916 the nephew of the Lelover Rebbe, Rabbi Pinchas David Horowitz, established the first "American" Hasidic court in Boston, identifying himself as the Bostoner Rebbe. In the following decades such prominent rebbes as the Radutzer (Rabbi Israel Hager) and the Lubavitcher (Rabbi Joseph Isaac Schneersohn) would make extensive tours of North America in 1914 and 1929, respectively.

In the wake of the Holocaust, Hasidim and their rebbes arrived in the New World in great numbers. In Brooklyn, New York, the revered Satmarer and Kausenberger Rebbes were among those who built courts in Williamsburgh; the Lubavitcher Rebbe sunk roots in Crown Heights; the Stoliner Rebbe and others took up residence in Boro Park; and the Bobover Rebbe settled on Manhattan's Upper West Side.

Demographics

By the mid-1960s, the Hasidic population in New York was estimated to be 40,000 to 50,000 persons with Satmar at 1,300 families and the communities of Stolin, Bobov, Klausenberg, and Lubavitch with some 100 to 500 families among them. By the mid-1990s, the Hasidic population had soared. Figures are not always reliable, as the Hasidim tend to inflate their numbers, but it is estimated that by the early 1990s there were as many as 250,000 Hasidim in the world, of whom 190,000 live in the United States, with 160,000 residing in New York State alone. These figures reflect the Hasidic community's high birthrate (in Boro Park, the birthrate averages five to six children per household; in Willamsburg, seven to nine children), and also, though to a much lesser degree, the number of Jews who become Hasidim by choice.

Settlements

The heart of American Hasidim rests in Brooklyn—specifically in the neighborhoods of Crown Heights, Williamsburgh, and Boro Park.

With a population of twenty-five thousand Hasidim, Crown Heights is headquarters to the Lubavitcher Hasidim. Lubavitch is perhaps the best-known Hasidic group, largely on account of their aggressive outreach campaign and their world-renowned rebbe, the late Menachem Mendel Schneerson. Outside New York City, Lubavitch is known for its Chabad houses (community centers–synagogues), whose mission is to rekindle the spark of *Yiddishkeit* (Jewishness) in unobservant Jews.

Williamsburg is home to most of the city's forty-five thousand or so Hungarian Hasidim. It is dominated by the Satmarer Hasidim, the largest Hasidic community in the world. Satmar is well known for its virulent anti-Zionism and uncompromising attitudes toward law and custom. Satmar is also distinguished by its insular lifestyle. Until 1979, the community was lead by the late Rabbi Joel Teitelbaum, who dedicated himself to preserving the laws and customs of his forefathers.

Of these Brooklyn neighborhoods, Boro Park is the most recent, middle class, and diverse. In the early 1990s, the Boro Park Hasidic population was estimated at forty-five thousand; it is home to more than three hundred synagogues and *shteiblekh* (Hasidic prayer rooms) as well as scores of yeshivas and day schools. Among the rebbes who have built courts there are the Bobover, Stoliner, Stuchiner, Blueshover, Bostoner (of New York), Munkaczer, Kapishnitzer, Novominsker, and Skolyer. No one community dominates the neighborhood, though Bobov, believed to be the third-largest Hasidic dynasty in the United States, has achieved considerable influence because of its congenital and respected rebbe, Rabbi Solomon Halberstam, and his traditional, centrist brand of Hasidism.

Outside New York City, in Rockland and Orange counties, are the Hasidic communities of New Square, Kiryas Joel, and Monsey. Each was pioneered by Hasidim who desired a safe haven from America's modern influences. In 1954, Rabbi Yaakov Yosef Twersky, the Skverer Rebbe, purchased land near Spring Valley as the site of the Village of New Square. After decades of struggle, more than 450 families settled there in the 1990s. In the early 1970s, Satmar established a satellite community in the township of Monroe and named it "Kiryas Joel" after their revered rebbe. Kiryas Joel is a thriving village with a population of well over eight thousand people. In nearby Rockland County is located the community of Monsey, founded in 1972 when Rabbi Mordechai Hager, the Vishnitzer rebbe, settled there. Monsey is the most diverse of these communities. Although the majority of Hasidim are Vishnitzer, Hasidim from Ger, Belz, Lubavitch, Satmar, and other dynasties reside there as well.

The most prominent Hasidic communities outside New York flourish in Boston, Montreal,

Hasidic Jews pray at a Crown Heights synagogue in Brooklyn, New York. (Earl Kowall/Corbis)

Chicago, and Los Angeles. The New England Chassidic Center, established by the Bostoner Rebbe, Rabbi Levi Yetzhak Horowitz, is based in Boston. Like Lubavitch, Boston is well known for its accessibility to outsiders. It is distinguished, however, by its medical service program, ROFEH, which provides referrals to visiting patients and accommodations for their families. Montreal has Canada's largest Hasidic community, with an estimated four thousand Hasidim and some ten dynasties. Lubavitch is the largest community, of about 225 families. In Chicago, most Hasidim are Lubavitchers or affiliated with Satmar. The city is also home to a number of shtikl rebbes. A burgeoning Hasidic population resides in Los Angeles. Lubavitch is the largest community, with more than twenty institutions: Chabad houses; schools; synagogues; a drug rehabilitation center; and Iranian, Russian, and Israeli outreach programs. Along with Lubavitch, there are Gerer and Satmarer communities, each including some thirty families, and assorted shtikl rebbes.

Hasidim and shtikl rebbes are scattered throughout the United States. For example, Detroit is the residence of the Vienner Rebbe; Rabbi Mickel Twersky, son of the late Hornistaypler rebbe, maintains a synagogue in Milwaukee; and his late brother, Rabbi Shlomo Twersky, presided over a court in Denver until his early death in 1981. Lubavitch is by far the most wide-ranging Hasidic community, with at least one Chabad house in virtually all fifty states.

Economic Life

Hasidic economic life is molded by ultra-Orthodox belief and observance: The Hasidim's insular lifestyle eschews college education; it is forbidden to work on a holiday or on the Sabbath; a frequent lack of English-language fluency combined with the decidedly nonmodern appearance of Hasidic men make it difficult for Hasidim to find jobs outside the Jewish community.

Typically, Hasidic men work as employees of Hasidic firms (as bookkeepers, salesmen, or managers), small business owners (insurance and real estate agents, jewelers, brokers, proprietors of electronics and computer concerns), skilled and semiskilled craftsmen (plumbers, carpenters, precious-stone cutters and polishers, electricians, mechanics, locksmiths), teachers at yeshivas, or as religious functionaires. Women often work as teachers, entrepreneurs, secretaries, bookkeepers, computer programmers, and in sales. They are customarily the managers of home-based wholesale stores that specialize in clothing, jewelry, linen, china, and crystal.

The Hasidim's entrepreneurial success has been facilitated by community leadership. The Council of Jewish Organizations of Boro Park, the United Jewish Organizations of Williamsburg, the Opportunity Development Association in Williamsburg, and Chevra Machazikei Hashcunah, Inc., of Crown Heights are examples of grassroots efforts that provide economic assistance to the Hasidic community. Programs such as job training, employment services, and loan assistance programs for small businesses are facilitated by the millions of dollars in government grants (e.g., Comprehensive Employment Training Act [CETA] funding, HUD money, and Section 8 housing assistance) that are awarded to these organizations.

In 1984, the Hasidim were designated as a disadvantaged minority by the federal government. This status allowed them to apply for a wider range of federal funding and to apply for contracts designated for minority businesses.

Political Organization

Hasidim vigorously exercise their political rights through the ballot and the legal system. They vote in high numbers, and at the behest of their rebbes, vote in blocks. Because of their electoral influence, Hasidic Jews are courted by all candidates running for office, from president to councilman.

The Hasidim have tried to redraw the legislative map to consolidate their voting strength. Their success has been mixed: In December 1976, the Lubavitcher Hasidim succeeded in creating their own community district to enhance their influence in local affairs. By contrast, in May 1974, the Satmarer community was divided into two Senate and Assembly districts in which Hasidic Jews were the minority. Claiming that their fourteenth and fifteenth Amendment rights were violated, Satmar brought the case before the U.S. Supreme Court. On March 1, 1977, the Court ruled against the Hasidim by a seven to one margin.

Hasidim do not shy away from using the courts to advance their causes. On July 3, 1989, the U.S. Supreme Court upheld the legality of displaying menorahs and Christmas trees on government property. This decision enabled the Lubavitcher Hasidim to display a Chanukah menorah on public grounds. After much litigation, the Kiryas Joel Village Union Free School District was established on July 25, 1989, by New York State to educate disabled Satmar youth. The decision was overturned by the U.S. Supreme Court five years later.

The deaths of the two most revered Hasidic rebbes of the twentieth century—the Lubavitcher Rebbe Menachem Mendel Schneerson (in 1994) and the Satmarer Rebbe Joel Teitelbaum (in 1979)—left a power vacuum that pitted factions in the Lubavitcher leadership against one another for administrative control and fueled the bitter acrimony between the old Satmarer Rebbe's widow, Feiga Teitelbaum, and the new rebbe, Rebbe Moshe Teitelbaum, the former rebbe's nephew.

Feuds between Hasidic communities are not uncommon. Since the 1950s, there has been a great deal of animosity between Satmar and the dynasties of Belz and Lubavitch on account of the former's virulent anti-Zionism and the latter's support of the State of Israel. Tensions were further aggravated in the late 1970s when Belz challenged Satmar's control of religious courts and *kashrut* (kosher) standards in Israel, and when Lubavitch proselytized in Williamsburg among the Satmarer youths.

Language

Hasidic Jews are multilingual: they pray in *loshn koydesh* (an amalgam of rabbinic Hebrew and

Two boys look through books in a Hasidic bookstore. (Janet S. Belcove-Shalin)

Aramaic); speak, with various degrees of fluency, their national tongue; and communicate among themselves in Yiddish.

Yiddish, like English, is a fusion language. Yiddish originated in the fifteenth century kingdom of Lotharingia (Lorraine) as a medieval German language spoken by Jews. Yiddish was distinguished from other German tongues by the presence of words from local Romance dialects, which linguists label Old French and Old Italian, as well as from the Jews' own sacred language, loshn koydesh. As Jews migrated eastward, Slavic vocabulary and grammatical constructions were assimilated into Yiddish. The Yiddish spoken by modern Hasidic Americans is marked by extensive borrowing of English vocabulary words.

Hasidim in America speak Yiddish dialects that reflect their European origins: Belz and Bobov, for example, speak Galicianer Yiddish; Lubavitcher Hasidim are exemplars of Russian Yiddish. The Hungarian community is known for speaking their native tongue in addition to Yiddish. Although the men prefer Yiddish, the women, usually the European-born, speak Hungarian, particularly when they are gossiping.

Yiddish is valued by the Hasidic community as a mechanism for maintaining communal solidarity and as a bulwark against assimilation. It is spoken in and outside the home and is the medium of instruction in school. Hasidim do not read Yiddish literature, though they publish Yiddish-language community papers, of which the *Algemeiner Journal* and *Der Yid* have the greatest circulation. While a rebbe speaks to his Hasidim in Yiddish, formal correspondence and discourse on law and ceremonial issues are written in loshn koydesh.

Marriage and Family

Hasidic life is structured by the observance of the 613 mitzvot (divine commandments–good deeds) that are found in the Old Testament. Among the most salient for family life are the laws of kashrut, regulating preparation and consumption of ritually sanctified food, and the laws of family purity, which govern sexual contact between husband and wife. The home is the focal point of ritual celebration for Jews, although celebrations at the rebbe's *tish* (table) are a hallmark of Hasidic life.

Acculturation begins early in a child's life, with the recitation of simple blessings and prayers. At age three, boys commence their formal religious education, with girls following suit a few years later. The key rite of passage for a youth is marriage, which typically occurs in a youngster's late teens or possibly early twenties. Dating is unknown among Hasidim. Meetings between potential spouses are arranged by family members, friends, or professional matchmakers. The rebbe is generally sought after for his advice and/or blessing. Hasidic weddings are lavish, joyous events, culminating in a week of celebration.

The newlywed husband will often continue his studies while supported by his wife or her family. A woman works until she has children. Bearing children is a cultural imperative: While Jewish law requires that each man bear a son and a daughter, in point of fact, birth control is forbidden unless a serious health issue arises. Marital fidelity is a key value among Hasidim. Divorce is uncommon, although the rate is increasing.

Assimilation and Cultural Persistence

The Hasidic community is an insular one that labors to separate itself from secular values and customs. Still, Hasidic Jews embrace modern technology and work hard to reap the benefits of the American political and economic systems. Although Hasidim zealously guard themselves from the religious values of non-Orthodox Jews, some communities, notably Chabad and the Bostoner Hasidim's New England Chassidic Center, have active outreach programs geared to foster observance among nonreligious Jews.

Among a sizable number of secular Jews, Hasidism has come to symbolize "authentic" Judaism. Hasidic lore and music are admired, while the community's commitment to Orthodoxy is respected, even if grudgingly. And in an attempt to lead a more meaningful life, thousands of Jews, called Ba'alei Teshuvah, have turned their backs on secularism and affiliated themselves with Hasidism.

American culture in the late twentieth century has exhibited a fascination with Hasidic life. Hasidic characters appear in movies and on television and serve as protagonists in the short stories and novels of Nobel Prize winners Isaac Bashevis Singer and Elie Wiesel. Hasidic Jewry has even been the inspiration for a line of *haute couture* men's clothing by the Italian fashion designer Fabio Inghirami.

See also: JEWS, EUROPEAN; JEWS, ISRAELI; JEWS, MIDDLE EASTERN; JEWS, SOVIET

Bibliography

Alpert, Z. (1980). "A Guide to the World of Hasidism." In *The Third Jewish Catalog,* edited by S. and M. Strassfeld. Philadelphia: Jewish Publication Society of America.

Belcove-Shalin, J. S. (1988). "Becoming More of an Eskimo: Fieldwork Among the Hasidim of Boro Park." In *Between Two Worlds: Essays on the Ethnography of American Jewry,* edited by J. Kugelmass. Ithaca, NY: Cornell University Press.

Belcove-Shalin, J. S. (1994). *New World Hasidism: Ethnographic Studies of Hasidic Jews in America,* edited by J. S. Belcove-Shalin. Albany: State University of New York Press.

Idel, M. (1994). *Hasidism: Between Ecstasy and Magic.* Albany: State University of New York Press.

Kaufman, D. R. (1991). *Rachel's Daughters: Newly Orthodox Jewish Women.* New Brunswick, NJ: Rutgers University Press.

Kranzler, G. (1961). *Williamsburg: A Jewish Community in Transition.* New York: Philipp Feldheim.

Levy, S. (1972). "Shifting Patterns of Ethnic Identification Among the Hassidim." In *The New Ethnicity: Perspectives from Ethnology,* edited by J. W. Bennett. St. Paul, MN: West Publishing.

Mintz, J. R. (1968). *Legends of the Hasidim.* Chicago: University of Chicago Press.

Mintz, J. R. (1992). *Hasidic People.* Cambridge, MA: Harvard University Press.

Poll, S. (1962). *The Hasidic Community of Williamsburg.* New York: Free Press.

Poll, S. (1965). "The Role of Yiddish in American Ultra-Orthodox and Hasidic Communities." YIVO Annual of *Jewish Social Science* 13:125–152.

Robinson, I. (1992). "The First Hasidic Rabbis in North America." *American Jewish Archives* 44:502–515.

Rubinstein, A. (1975). *Hasidism.* New York: Leon Amiel.

Schatz-Uffenheimer, R. (1971–1972). "Hasidism." In *Encyclopaedia Judaica,* 16 vols., edited by C. Roth and G. Wigoder. New York: Macmillan.

Shaffir, W. (1974). *Life in a Religious Community: The Lubavitcher Chassidim in Montreal.* Toronto: Holt, Rinehart and Winston.

JANET S. BELCOVE-SHALIN

JEWS, ISRAELI

According to the 1990 U.S. Census, approximately ninety thousand Israeli-born persons reside in the United States. While this accounts for a relatively small community in comparison to many other foreign-born nationalities, the proportion of the entire Israeli population who now live in the United States (close to 1 percent) is similar to that of other major sources of immigration, including Taiwan, the Philippines, Korea, and Vietnam.

As a nation of immigrants, Israel encompasses persons with various national origins ranging, from eastern and western Europe to the Americas, North Africa, and the Middle East. All these nationality groups are represented within the Israeli-American population. While the official language of Israel is Hebrew, many other languages are spoken among immigrants, including Arabic, Russian, Yiddish, and English. Although other ethno-religious groups have also emigrated from Israel to the United States, including Armenians, Palestinians, and Lebanese representing both Christian and Muslim faiths, this entry deals only with Jewish Israelis.

Israelis in the United States have a complex ethnic identity. While all are Jews, they vary greatly in their degree of religious involvement and the ways in which they practice their religion, which diverge considerably according to their denominational affiliation and philosophy of life. A small fraction of Israelis are devoutly Orthodox and painstakingly conform to an extensive code of ritual requirements. The vast majority, however, are secular and follow a pattern of life typical of Western industrialized nations.

Founded in 1948, the nation of Israel has worked to develop a common culture, emphasizing the shared experiences as Israelis rather than as Jews per se. Nevertheless, many of its citizens remain attached to the habits of their countries of origin, be they Morocco, Poland, Yemen, or Russia.

During the 1970s and 1980s, emigrants from Israel were sometimes viewed by American Jews and Israelis alike as violators of Zionist ideology and a potential threat to the survival of the Jewish state. Consequently they were referred to as *yordim*—a stigmatizing Hebrew term that describes those who "descend" from the "higher" place of Israel to the Diaspora, as opposed to immigrants, *olim*, who "ascend" from the Diaspora to Israel. However, since that time both Israel and the American Jewish community have taken a more conciliatory approach toward Israeli expatriates. American coethnics provide them with communal assistance, while Israel offers its overseas citizens a package of services and benefits, including reduced import duties and airfares, job placement services, and financial incentives to return home.

When asked why they immigrated to the United States, most Israelis refer to enhanced economic opportunities (including education), family unification, and a need for broader horizons. Other link their U.S. presence to an extended stopover made during the protracted travel that is an informal rite of passage for Israelis who have completed their compulsory military service. Israelis who are from low-status minority backgrounds sometimes claim they left because of discrimination. Finally, Israelis occasionally describe their exit as an effort to escape the ever-present violence and military duty associated with life in the Middle East.

Demographic Data

The number of Israelis in the United States has been the subject of controversy since the early 1980s. In the 1970s and 1980s, various Jewish publications and officials provided estimates of the Israeli émigré population in the United States ranging up to half a million. Further, during the 1980s, the "common wisdom" of Jewish community officials in New York and Los Angeles—the two largest settlements of Israelis in the United States—confidently assumed that each city had well in excess of 100,000 Israeli residents. However, estimates based on both the 1990 U.S. Census and the 1990 National Jewish Population Survey, and backed up by data from the U.S. Immigration and Naturalization Service and the Israeli Census, suggest that between 90,000 and 170,000 Jewish Israelis live in the United States, with about 30,000 in the metropolitan New York area and fewer than 15,000 living in Los Angeles.

Emigrants from Israel tend to be young and Israeli-born. For example, in 1990, 79 percent of Israelis in New York and 70 percent of Israelis in Los Angeles were below age forty-four. In both communities there were more males than females. The marriage rate of Israelis living in New York is quite high, about 80 percent in 1980. At the same time, New York Israelis' divorce rate—2 to 5 percent—is lower that for other New York Jews, whose rate of divorce is 10 percent. Israelis also tend to have more children per family than American-born Jews. In 1986, more than one-third of the Israelis in the United States received immigrant status through marriage to a U.S. citizen, indicating the importance of family unification as a cause of Israeli emigration.

Period of Immigration. Since 1948, the flow of legal immigration to the United States from Israel has slowly increased, from about 1,000 per year in 1948 to almost 6,000 a year by 1990. Israeli government sources report that the number of Israelis returning home has increased substantially since 1992—the year that marked the election of the peace-oriented Labor party in Israel, the start of an official outreach policy toward expatriates, and a major U.S. economic recession.

According to the 1990 U.S. Census, Israelis in the United States are relatively well educated; 54 percent in New York and 58 percent in Los Angeles have at least some college, while less than 15 percent in either city are not high school graduates. In both New York and Los Angeles, almost half of those age twenty-four to sixty-five are employed as managers, administrators, professionals, or technical specialists. Another quarter in either city are employed in sales. Their rates of self-employment are the second highest of all nationality groups in the United States, exceeded only by Koreans. High rates of self-employment are achieved by extensive economic cooperation, involving coethnic hiring, subcontracting, and by the concentration of Israelis in a number of areas of economic specialization. Israelis are notably active in the real estate, construction, jewelry and diamond, retail sales, security, garment, engineering, and media industries.

Finally, a small but highly visible fraction of the Israeli immigrant community have made impressive achievements as leading entrepreneurs, academics, scientists, and musicians. Members of this group include major figures in the fashion industry, the principal conductor of the Civic Orchestra of Chicago, and a president of the American Sociological Association.

As their generally prestigious occupations might indicate, the earnings of Israelis in the United States are considerable. In fact, persons tracing their ancestry to Israel rank fifth in family income out of ninety-nine ancestry groups tabulated in the 1990 U.S. Census. Employed Israeli men residing in New York City were making approximately $35,000 annually in 1990, while their counterparts in Los Angeles were making almost $49,000. These figures exceed those of all foreign-born men in either city by nearly $10,000 annually, and best the earnings of even native-born whites in Los Angeles. Employed Israeli women in New York and Los Angeles also earn about $6,000 a year more than the average for all foreign-born women, but make about $4,000 less annually than native-born white women in these cities. As native speakers of Hebrew who are often trained as educators, Israeli women frequently find employment as instructors in American Jewish synagogues and schools.

While men have very high rates of labor force participation, a fairly large fraction of Israeli women are not in the labor market, which can be considered an indicator of Israelis' economic advancement over their status in Israel. A survey of naturalized Israelis in New York found that only 4 percent of the women indicated that "housewife" had been their occupation in Israel, while 36 percent indicated that it was now their occupation in the United States. This makes Israelis distinct from many other contemporary immigrant groups

that maintain higher labor force participation rates for women in the United States than in the countries of origin.

Ethnicity. Jews are generally classified into two ethnic groups: Ashkenazic, who trace their ancestry to eastern and northern Europe and the Americas, and Sephardic Jews from southern Europe, North Africa, and the Middle East. Various estimates indicate that while more than 50 percent of Israelis in the United States are of Ashkenazic origin, a sizable fraction—slightly less than 40 percent—are Sephardic. The remainder are of mixed or unknown ancestry. While Israelis of diverse ethnic origins interact in the United States, several studies suggest that patterns of social interaction, religious practice, social activities, and economic specialization often take place within the boundaries of these subethnic groups. Further, a number of Israelis in the United States follow communal patterns based on their countries of origin prior to Israel. Among these are networks of Yemeni Israelis and Iranian Israelis. Members of various nationality groups also develop relations

An Israeli garment manufacturer at work in Los Angeles. (Steven J. Gold)

with Jews from their pre-Israel country of origin. For example, Israelis who trace their origins to Iran, Morocco, or the former Soviet Union often associate with Iranian, Moroccan, and Soviet Jews in the United States. Finally, other kinds of Israel-based social ties, such as membership in the kibbutz (rural cooperative) movement, specific military units, religious communities, or political groups often serve as bases for organizing networks within the Israeli-American community.

Communal Patterns

Nearly all the Jews who have entered the United States during the past three hundred years have been de jure or de facto refugees, with few possibilities of returning to their countries of origin. By contrast, Israelis have a real possibility of going back to Israel, and American Jews, the Jewish state, and even the immigrants themselves generally agree that they should return. This distinguishes Israelis from nearly all other Jewish entrants in U.S. history. While most American Jews have been staunchly nationalistic soon after their arrival, Israelis in the United States often discuss their desire to return home, and many make frequent trips back to the Jewish state, sometimes culminating in permanent resettlement. In the words of one community leader in Los Angeles:

> Israelis would always suffer a certain touch of nostalgia because they are missing the things that they grew up with. Psychologically, most Israelis did not come here to be Americans. They did not come here to swear to the flag, to sing the national anthem, and to go to Dodgers games. They came here to have the house and the swimming pool and the two cars and the job and the money.

However, despite their ambivalence about being in the United States, Israelis have been active in building a life for themselves. In fact, Israeli immigrants in Los Angeles, New York, Chicago, and other locations have developed many activities and organizations to resolve their misgivings about being in the United States. Community activities include socializing with other Israelis; living near coethnics (and within Jewish communities); consuming Hebrew-language media (originating in both the United States and Israel); attending Israeli restaurants, nightclubs, social events, and celebrations; joining Israeli associations; working in jobs with other Israelis; consuming goods and services provided by Israeli professionals and entrepreneurs; keeping funds in Israeli banks; sending children to Israeli-oriented religious, language, recreational, day-care, and cultural/national activities; raising money for Israeli causes; calling relatives in Israel on the phone; and hosting Israeli visitors.

In the course of fieldwork in Los Angeles, one research team identified some twenty-seven Israeli organizations, ranging from synagogues, Hebrew schools, and political groups to scouting programs, sports teams, business associations, and even a recreational flying club. These organizations allow émigrés to maintain various Israeli practices and outlooks in an American setting.

Economic and Domestic Life. In reflecting on their experience in the United States, Israelis frequently contrast the nation's positive economic and occupational environment to its communal and cultural liabilities. Immigrants almost universally regard Israel as a better place for children. While admitting that higher education is more accessible in the United States, Israelis generally feel that their country of origin is safer, has fewer social problems, and does not impose the manifold generational conflicts Israelis confront when raising children in the United States. Further, in Israel, Jews are culturally and religiously the dominant group. The institutions of the larger society teach children Hebrew and instruct them in basic national, ethnic, and religious identity as well as in Jewish history. However, in immigrating to the United States, Israelis become a minority group and lose communal networks based on family, friendship, and neighborhood, which provided a social life and assistance in raising children.

Jewish Identity and Participation. Israeli and American Jewish notions of group membership contrast because the basic group identities associated

Israeli-American children learn Israeli folk dancing in North Hollywood, California. (Steven J. Gold)

with being Israeli, on the one hand, and American Jewish, on the other, are rooted in particular cultural/national contexts. For many Israelis, ethnic identity is secular and nationalistic. While they know Jewish holidays and speak Hebrew, they connect these behaviors to "Israeliness" rather than Jewishness. The majority do not actively participate in organized religious activities—as is the case among most American Jews—and depend on the larger society and public institutions to socialize their children. For example, the western denominations of Reform and Conservative Judaism, with which the great majority of American Jews affiliate, are all but unknown in the Jewish state, and marriages performed by Reform rabbis in Israel have no legal standing there. Finally, while American Jews are accustomed to life as a subcommunity in a religiously pluralistic society, Israelis grew up in a environment where religion and nationality were one and the same.

Because of Israelis' lack of familiarity with American forms of Jewish involvement, some pun-dits decry a trend of their assimilation to non-Jewish cultural patterns. They assert that Israelis' very exit from the Holy Land signifies a move away from the Jewish ideal, and that their participation in and contribution to Jewish activities is limited and oriented toward secular pursuits with little religious content—meals, parties, Israeli folk dancing, and sports.

In contrast, other observers argue that Israelis actively participate in American Jewish life while simultaneously maintaining their links to Israel, noting that the Israelis speak Hebrew, live in Jewish neighborhoods, are involved in a variety of Jewish institutions, and visit Israel frequently. While survey data on Israeli behaviors are relatively scarce, those that do exist indicate that established émigrés engage in many Jewish behaviors at higher rates than is the case among native-born Jews. For example, Israeli immigrants' synagogue membership (27%) is above that of Jewish Americans (25%). Further, 80 percent of Israeli parents provide their children with some form of Jewish education, and 50 percent of Israeli children in Los Angeles and 35 percent in New York attend Jewish day schools. Their rate of intermarriage to non-Jews, at only 8 percent, is 40 percent less than the recent average for American Jews. Finally, when comparing Israeli immigrants' observance of Jewish religious practices—lighting candles on Shabbat (the Jewish Sabbath) and Chanukah, attending synagogue on the High Holy Days and Shabbat, and fasting on Yom Kippur—with their patterns in Israel, it is found that ritual behaviors actually increase among naturalized Israelis in New York and Los Angeles.

Finally, a growing number of Israeli-American parents are taking actions to reestablish connections with Israeli and/or Jewish behaviors through special family activities of their own creation or involvement in various Israeli-American programs such as after-school Israeli Hebrew courses and Hebrew-language scouting activities.

Conclusion

Jews have been immigrating to the United States since the 1600s, under a variety of circumstances and in possession of a broad range of outlooks and resources. Israelis are among the most recent of these groups. American Jews' support of the State of Israel, along with Israel's own antiemigration outlook, have sometimes resulted in a less-than-welcoming reception for these arrivals. Further, because Israelis and American Jews are party to distinct cultural and linguistic traditions and express their identities in different ways, Israelis have encountered some difficulties in joining the religious and communal activities of their American coethnics. However, in terms of skills, education, and Jewish knowledge, Israelis have much to offer both to American society in general and the American Jewish community in particular. Since the mid-1980s, the potential benefits provided by Israeli immigrants has become more apparent to American Jewish organizations, and efforts to facilitate either their merger into the American Jewish community or their return home have been undertaken with some success.

See also: JEWS, EUROPEAN; JEWS, HASIDIC; JEWS, MIDDLE EASTERN; JEWS, SOVIET

Bibliography

Gold, S. J. (1994a). "Israeli Immigrants in the United States: The Question of Community." *Qualitative Sociology* 17:325–363.

Gold, S. J. (1994b). "Patterns of Economic Cooperation Among Israeli Immigrants in Los Angeles." *International Migration Review* 28 (105):114–135.

Gold, S. J., and Phillips, B. A. (1996). "Israelis in the United States." *American Jewish Yearbook* 96:51–101.

Greenberg, H. (1979). *Israel: Social Problems.* Tel Aviv: Dekel.

Kass, D., and Lipset, S. M. (1982). "Jewish Immigration to the United States from 1967 to the Present: Israelis and Others." In *Understanding American Jewry,* edited by Marshall Sklare. New Brunswick, NJ: Transaction.

Mittelberg, D., and Waters, M. C. (1992). "The Process of Ethnogenesis Among Haitian and Israeli Immigrants in the United States." *Ethnic and Racial Studies* 15:412–435.

Ritterband, P. (1986). "Israelis in New York." *Contemporary Jewry* 7:113–126.

Rosenthal, M., and Auerbach, C. (1992). "Cultural and Social Assimilation of Israeli Immigrants in the United States." *International Migration Review* 99 (26):982–991.

Shokeid, M. (1988). *Children of Circumstances: Israeli Immigrants in New York.* Ithaca, NY: Cornell University Press.

Sobel, Z. (1986). *Migrants from the Promised Land.* New Brunswick, NJ: Transaction.

Uriely, N. (1994). "Rhetorical Ethnicity of Permanent Sojourners: The Case of Israeli Immigrants in the Chicago Area." *International Sociology* 9:431–445.

Uriely, N. (1995). "Patterns of Identification and Integration with Jewish Americans Among Israeli Immigrants in Chicago: Variations Across Status and Generation." *Contemporary Jewry* 16:27–49.

STEVEN J. GOLD

JEWS, MIDDLE EASTERN

Middle Eastern Jews are generally understood to be those whose backgrounds stem from Muslim lands of the Mediterranean littoral and somewhat beyond. Significant groups of Jews of Middle Eastern background in the United States come from Turkey, Syria, Iraq, Iran, Israel, Yemen, Egypt, and Morocco. Others come from Lebanon, Libya, Algeria, and Tunisia.

In the United States, members of this group are often called Sephardim, the Hebrew word referring to descendants of the Jews of medieval Spain and Portugal. This distinguishes them from the majority group of American Jews known as Ashkenazim, Jews of central and eastern European background. Although many Middle Eastern Jews descend from medieval Iberian Jewry, many others do not. Nevertheless, almost all Middle Eastern Jews in the United States tend to be identified with the Sephardic community, since they share basic religious and cultural characteristics.

Although they are called Sephardim in relationship to the outside world, among themselves they make distinctions based on lands of origin, such as Iraqi Jews (Bavlim), Iranian Jews (Persians), Syrian Jews, and Yemenite Jews (Temanim). Although most Middle Eastern Jews are culturally part of the Sephardic community, this does not include thousands of Ashkenazim from Israel who have immigrated to the United States. Israeli Ashkenazim identify with mainstream Ashkenazic institutions or with immigrant Israeli communities.

During the early twentieth century, Middle Eastern (and Balkan) Jewish arrivals in America were sometimes called Oriental Jews. This term was popularized by those who wished to distinguish between the existing Spanish and Portuguese communities of the United States and the immigrant newcomers. By referring to the newcomers as Orientals the term "Sephardic" could be reserved for the historic and Americanized Sephardic community. In 1912, the Sephardic immigrants themselves adopted the term when they established the Federation of Oriental Jews. However, community leaders within the immigrant group rejected the term "Oriental" by 1915. The Federation of Oriental Jews soon faded away, and all new organizations had the word "Sephardic" in their names—for example, the Sephardic Jewish Community (established 1924), the Union of Sephardic Congregations (founded 1928), and the Central Sephardic Jewish Community of America (founded 1941). The terms "Oriental" and "Levantine" continued to be used—primarily among non-Sephardim and academics—through the 1950s, 1960s, and early 1970s. By the mid-1970s, though, these appellations had largely been dropped.

Immigration History

Between 1899 and 1925, a total of 25,000 to 35,000 Sephardim arrived in the United States, primarily from Turkey and Syria. This number also included Sephardim who had come from Greece and the Balkan countries. By 1926, it was estimated that 50,000 to 60,000 Sephardim lived in the United States, with at least 40,000 in New York City. The others were scattered in cities throughout the country, with large groupings in Seattle, Los Angeles, and Atlanta.

The largest group within the Sephardic population during the first quarter of the twentieth century was from Turkey and the Balkan countries. Descendants of medieval Spanish Jewry, they continued to speak a uniquely Jewish form of medieval Spanish, known variously as Judeo-Spanish, Ladino, or Judeo-Espanyol. The Jews from Syria spoke Judeo-Arabic, forming a distinct group within the Sephardic community.

The primary point of settlement for most Sephardim was the Lower East Side in New York City. By the 1920s, when increasing affluence allowed them to move away, Sephardim established themselves in other neighborhoods throughout New York. The Judeo-Spanish-speaking Sephardim moved to such neighborhoods as Harlem, New Lots (Brooklyn), and the West Bronx. Syrians moved to Bay Parkway and Flatbush in Brooklyn.

Second- and third-generation Syrian Sephardim tended to remain in Flatbush. During the

1970s and 1980s, a significant Syrian-Jewish community emerged in Deal, New Jersey. Syrian Jews have tended to live in the same neighborhoods, marry within their own group, and work in family-owned businesses. They also have been successful in retaining their traditional religious practices and customs. This is certainly true in Syrian synagogues, which reflect the liturgical and musical traditions that have been brought to America from Aleppo and Damascus. Most families continue to celebrate Sabbath, religious festivals, and life-cycle events according to their own distinctive traditions.

On the other hand, the Turkish Jews (and Judeo-Spanish-speaking Sephardim in general) experienced a loosening of traditional sociological bonds. Although members of the immigrant generation and their children tended to live in neighborhoods with high concentrations of Sephardim, by the 1950s second- and third-generation American-born Judeo-Spanish Sephardim were moving to the suburbs like other Americans. As more of them were receiving university education, they felt less need to live among their own group. Whereas in the 1940s and early 1950s a huge percentage of Sephardim of Judeo-Spanish background lived within walking distance of their synagogues, this situation changed dramatically by the late 1950s and through the 1960s. By the 1970s and 1980s, most Sephardim of Judeo-Spanish background did not live within easy walking distance of a Sephardic synagogue of their own tradition.

During the 1950s and 1960s, a new wave of Middle Eastern Jews arrived in the United States, primarily from Israel and the Arab countries. Many chose to live in New York. A large center also

A Jewish family poses with their neighbors shortly before immigrating to the United States during the early twentieth century. (Marc D. Angel)

developed in Los Angeles. Many members of this wave of immigration spoke Hebrew, Arabic, and/or French. During the 1970s and 1980s, thousands of Iranian Jews settled in the United States, with major centers in New York City, Long Island, and Los Angeles.

The largest concentration of Middle Eastern Jews is in New York City and environs. Other large concentrations are in Los Angeles, Miami, and Seattle, with many other communities throughout the United States, including Chicago, Atlanta, San Francisco, and Washington, D.C.

Estimates of the number of Middle Eastern Jews in the United States in 1995 vary from 200,000 to 300,000, or approximately 15 to 20 percent of the Jewish population of the country. By comparison, nearly all American Jews were of Ashkenazic or European-Sephardic background in 1900.

Languages

Middle Eastern Jews arrived in the United States with a variety of languages. Aside from their mother tongues, many also had mastery of other languages, mainly Hebrew and French.

The first Judeo-Spanish newspaper published in the United States was *La America*, edited by Moise Gadol, originally of Bulgaria. This weekly, which appeared from 1910 to 1924, was a lively cultural organ that reached Sephardic readers throughout the United States and beyond. It included news items, essays, poetry, and a variety of feature articles. *La Vara*, also a weekly Judeo-Spanish newspaper, appeared from 1922 until February 1948. In 1926, it had a circulation of 9,000, which rose to 16,500 in 1928. This was the heyday of Judeo-Spanish culture in the United States. As the American-born generation used English as its mother tongue, the need for the Judeo-Spanish press declined.

La America, La Vara, and other Judeo-Spanish newspapers often reported on Sephardic cultural activities in the various communities throughout the country. Judeo-Spanish dramatic productions attracted large crowds wherever the Sephardim lived. In the days before television, oratory was a popular form of entertainment and enlightenment. Sephardic orators could be heard in the various synagogues and organizations frequented by Jews of Judeo-Spanish background in 1900.

By the 1950s, Judeo-Spanish was hardly spoken as a mother tongue except by the old-timers who had originally come from Turkey and the Balkan countries. Their children still spoke the language fluently, but seldom used it in their conversations with their own children. By the third and fourth generations, the language ceased to be a medium of communication, but Judeo-Spanish survives in songs and proverbs. A number of synagogues include prayers sung in Judeo-Spanish. The Spanish and Portuguese synagogue in New York City has offered classes in Judeo-Spanish language and culture since 1973 and also has sponsored dramatic productions in Judeo-Spanish.

Among the Syrian Jews, Judeo-Arabic has given way to English as the main language of communication. But Judeo-Arabic proverbs and phrases have continued to be part of the daily vocabulary of the Syrian Jews.

The more recent immigrant groups learn English but prefer speaking their mother tongues among themselves. When members of the various subgroups of Middle Eastern Jews meet, the proceedings usually are in English or Hebrew, depending on the composition of the group.

Sociological Characteristics

As indicated earlier, Middle Eastern Jews generally identify with the Sephardic Jewish religious traditions. The synagogues use the Sephardic liturgy, and religious practice is generally governed by Sephardic rabbinic authority. The synagogue music often has a Middle Eastern flavor and is clearly distinguishable from the synagogue music of Ashkenazim and Western Sephardim.

Turkish Jews who arrived early in the twentieth century were generally unskilled laborers, finding employment in the textile industry, as merchants of small enterprises such as grocery or shoe repair stores, and in various trades. By the second American-born generation, most Jews of Turkish background have had a college education and engage in a wide variety of economic enterprises and professions. Jews of Turkish background do not live in tightly knit neighborhoods, nor do they generally marry among themselves. This, of course, has major cultural ramifications, since it is far more difficult to maintain Sephardic patterns of life in "mixed" marriages.

Syrian Jews have tended to maintain their own neighborhoods and also have a high rate of marriage within the group. While the community has produced a number of professionals, the large majority are proprietors of stores, such as for clothing, electronics, or antiques. The Syrian Jewish community has established its own schools, community centers, and social service institutions. During the 1990s, the Syrian community mobilized to absorb several thousand Jews who were allowed to immigrate to the United States from Syria.

The more recent immigrant groups have tended to live in neighborhoods with concentrations of other Middle Eastern Jews. They prefer to marry among themselves, work together in business, and support communal institutions that serve their needs.

Among Jews of Turkish background, the role of women has evolved along with general trends in America. While during the first generation, virtually no Turkish women attended college and very few worked in the marketplace, by the second American-born generation almost all of them received at least a high school education and most also attended college. They have entered the workplace in a wide variety of occupations. Syrian-Jewish women have tended to receive less education, with only a minority receiving formal education beyond high school. It is not uncommon among Syrian Jews for women to be married at a relatively young age, with brides of eighteen or nineteen years old not being unusual. Among the more recent immigrants, the educational and economic opportunities of women vary.

Cultural Continuity

When Middle Eastern Jews began arriving in the United States in significant numbers early in the twentieth century, the existing Jewish community—almost exclusively Ashkenazic—did not relate well to the newcomers. Ashkenazic Jews questioned the Jewishness of Sephardic immigrants who did not speak Yiddish, whose names sounded Spanish or Arabic, and whose religious and folk customs were very different from those common among Ashkenazim. Since Jewish communal organizations and schools were dominated by Ashkenazim, Sephardim often felt ignored. Schools seldom taught Sephardic history and culture. This situation continued through the 1950s and 1960s, although 1963 marked the establishment of a Sephardic studies program at Yeshiva University.

In 1972, a convention of the American Sephardi Federation was held at the historic Spanish and Portuguese Synagogue of New York, Congregation Shearith Israel, to revitalize the Sephardic community. The American Sephardi Federation became the umbrella group for Jews of Middle Eastern background and has sponsored annual conventions bringing together hundreds of delegates.

In 1973, Sephardic House, a national organization dedicated to fostering Sephardic history and culture, was established at Shearith Israel. Sephardic House has sponsored numerous classes, concerts, photographic exhibitions, film festivals, and other programs relating to all aspects of Sephardic history and culture. It also has published books and pamphlets, and it has distributed many thousands of books on a national level.

Sephardic individuals have become involved in the various organizations and institutions of American Jewry and gradually have been integrating themselves into the establishment. From 1990 to 1992, Rabbi Marc Angel served as president of the Rabbinical Council of America, the largest Orthodox rabbinical organization in the world, and was the first Sephardic rabbi elected to the presidency of this organization. In 1995, Leon Levy, president of the American Sephardi Federation, became chairman of the Conference of Presidents of Major Jewish Organizations, the first Sephardic Jew to reach this high position.

The interior of the Congregation Shearith Israel in New York City. The building was consecrated in May 1897. (Marc D. Angel)

The Syrian Jews in Brooklyn and Deal, New Jersey, have become a dominant element in Jewish community life in these areas, and Ashkenazim sometimes feel that the Syrians have taken over too much responsibility and power.

Middle Eastern Jewish arrivals during the 1970s, 1980s, and 1990s are still generally steeped in their own cultural traditions. However, assimilation tendencies are clearly evident: diminished religious observance among some of the more Americanized members of the group, an increase in interfaith marriages, and a growing desire by young people to adopt the lifestyle patterns of acculturated Americans. On the other hand, many Middle Eastern Jews are traditional-minded and are quite committed to their religious traditions.

As of the mid-1990s, different sociological currents were evident among the groupings of Middle Eastern Jews in the United States. Some were becoming more assimilated into American society, abandoning many cultural traditions. Others were keenly interested in maintaining at least some elements of their historical traditions, even while leaving others behind (e.g., singing Judeo-Spanish songs but giving up traditional observance of the Sabbath). Middle Eastern Jews generally see themselves as being traditional and tolerant. On the other hand, a growing number of Middle Eastern Jews have been attracted to right-wing Orthodoxy.

In spite of the many variations among Jews of Middle Eastern background, as a group they maintain a sense of kinship with each other. They have been persistent—and largely successful—in maintaining a distinctive religious and cultural identity. To foster their own distinctiveness, they have established numerous synagogues. They also have established a number of Sephardic day schools and have worked to incorporate Middle Eastern curricular elements in the mainstream Jewish schools. National organizations such as the American Sephardi Federation and Sephardic House, as well as local community committees, have sponsored numerous programs and events to highlight the intellectual, spiritual, musical, and ethnic traditions of the various Jews of Middle Eastern background.

See also: JEWS, EUROPEAN; JEWS, HASIDIC; JEWS, ISRAELI; JEWS, SOVIET

Bibliography

Angel, M. D. (1973). "The Sephardim of the United States: An Exploratory Study." In *American Jewish Yearbook*, edited by M. Fine and M. Himmelfarb. New York and Philadelphia: American Jewish Committee and Jewish Publication Society of America.

Angel, M. D. (1982). *La America: The Sephardic Experience in the United States.* Philadelphia: Jewish Publication Society of America.

Angel, M. D. (1987). "The American Experience of a Sephardic Synagogue." In *The American Synagogue: A Sanctuary Transformed*, edited by J. Wertheimer. Cambridge, Eng.: Cambridge University Press.

Angel, M. D. (1992). "Aspects of the Sephardic Spirit." In *The Sephardic Journey 1492–1992.* New York: Yeshiva University Museum.

Angel, M. D. (1994). *Seeking Good, Speaking Peace.* Hoboken, NJ: Ktav Publishing House.

Benardete, M. J. (1982). *Hispanic Culture and Character of the Sephardic Jews.* New York: Sephardic House.

Sutton, J. (1979). *Magic Carpet: Aleppo-in-Flatbush.* New York: Thayer-Jacoby.

Sutton, J. (1988). *Aleppo Chronicles.* New York: Thayer-Jacoby.

MARC D. ANGEL

JEWS, SOVIET

Soviet Jews are those persons of Jewish ancestry or religion who entered the United States from the former Soviet Union after the 1960s. Also known as Russian Jews, or simply as Russians, most resided in major European cities of the former USSR, especially the Ukrainian or Russian republics. Members of this group, which includes more than 325,000 persons, generally speak Russian as their native language, but also may know Ukrainian or Yiddish. In addition to the members of this group who have immigrated to the United States, almost 800,000 have moved to Israel, while several thousand reside in Canada and Germany. Jews from the former Soviet Union constitute the largest single group of Jewish immigrants to enter the United States since the 1920s.

Members of this population are notable for their high levels of skill and education, the extensive resettlement services they receive from both Jewish and government agencies, and their minimal preimmigration exposure to formalized Jewish training. Despite their experience with anti-Semitism and their status as a religiously defined ethnic minority group in the former Soviet Union, most have little knowledge about Jewish religion or history.

Motives for Exit

Jews have long had a significant presence in Russia and eastern Europe, but they have suffered from considerable discrimination there. In the mid-nineteenth century, they were restricted to particular geographical regions known as "the pale of settlement," excluded from all but a few fields of economic endeavor, and subjected to violent attacks and lifelong conscription. Such conditions caused millions of Jews—including the ancestors of most American Jews—to leave Russia and eastern Europe.

In an attempt to improve their chances for survival, many of those who stayed supported movements for social reform, including the Russian Revolution. Despite their contributions, Jews soon found their support of communism betrayed. By the 1920s, the Communists banned Jewish religious study and practice, prevented Jews from maintaining links with relatives and religious communities abroad, and encouraged Jews' resettlement from the European republics where most lived to Birobidzhan—a desolate "Jewish home-

An elderly Russian Jewish immigrant, wearing heavy clothing and surrounded by all his luggage, stands outside a building on Ellis Island in 1900. (Library of Congress/Corbis)

land" on the Manchurian border. In addition to blocking formal religious activities and training, after the 1960s the Soviet government also restricted educational and occupational opportunities for Jews. Finally, personal harassment has been a fact of daily life for Russian Jews, from the era of the czars to the present.

While denying Jews the right to practice their religious traditions, the Soviet system nevertheless institutionalized outsider status by recording Jewish citizens' nationality as "Jewish" on passports regardless of their place of residency or birth. Further, despite the Soviet system's dislike of Jews, the group's ability to emigrate or even travel abroad was strongly limited for political reasons until the late 1980s.

At present the new openness of the former USSR has permitted Russian Jews to freely engage in a variety of religious and cultural activities for the first time in seventy years. However, as Communist party control of ideology has been replaced by freedom of expression, anti-Semites have also become increasingly open, active, and virulent. The current climate in the former USSR—one characterized by economic distress, social disorder, a revival of intolerant churches, and the rise of ultranationalism—appears to be a textbook example of a setting ripe for anti-Semitic outbreaks. Accordingly, many Russian Jews still hope to leave for the United States, Israel, or other Western nations.

Demographics

Prior to the 1970s, little Jewish emigration was permitted from the USSR. However, during the late 1970s, and then a decade later in the late 1980s and early 1990s, thousands of Jews were able to leave. Peak years of entry into the United States were 1979, when 28,794 arrived, and 1992, when 45,888 Jews from the former Soviet Union entered the States. Nearly all Soviet Jews have received resettlement assistance from the Hebrew Immigration Aid Service (HIAS), a nonprofit Jewish agency.

The greatest number of Soviet Jews came from the Russian and Ukrainian republics of the Soviet Union, which also had the greatest Jewish populations. However, while the Russian Republic had the largest number of Jews, the Ukraine was the major source of émigrés. Of the 194,047 Soviet Jews who entered the United States between 1980 and May 1993, 42 percent (81,421) were Ukrainians, and 24 percent (46,391) were from the Russian Republic.

State-level data from the 1990 U.S. Census reveal that 30 percent of USSR-born American Jews live in New York, 23 percent in California, 6 percent each in New Jersey and Illinois, and 5 percent each in Florida, Pennsylvania, and Massachusetts. Hence, 80 percent of those born in the Soviet Union reside in seven states. In general they live in cities and neighborhoods with an established Jewish presence. While their largest settlement is in Brooklyn, New York, other communities of note are in West Hollywood, California; Chicago; and Boston.

Soviet Jewish families tend to be intact, multigenerational, and have few children. Their small size, both parents' familiarity with working outside of the home, and the high priority placed on children's education are typical of the urban middle class of the former Soviet Union. Transferred to the United States, these patterns generally facilitate social and economic adjustment to American society. At the same time, several authors suggest that the extreme closeness of Soviet Jewish families provokes generational conflict and hinders émigré children's efforts to develop the degree of personal autonomy considered appropriate among American young people.

The average age for Soviet Jews is consistently reported as being the highest of all refugee groups entering the United States. Of those entering the United States during 1991, 34 percent were over age fifty and 15 percent were over sixty-five. The significant number of elderly among the Soviet Jewish population yields distinct patterns of adjustment. Unlike most immigrant and refugee groups who are characterized by a youthful population, many Russian Jewish families contain elderly individuals. Refugee families experience problems because the elderly have difficulties learning English, finding employment, and making their way in the United States. At the same time, elderly émigrés help with child care and provide a strong sense of community as they congregate on streets, in parks, and at community centers in the neighborhoods where they settle.

Employment and Economic Factors

Soviet Jews are highly educated and experienced in technical and professional fields. Their average educational level, at about 13.5 years, is among the highest of all immigrant groups entering the country and exceeds that of the U.S. population by a year. A unique economic asset of the Soviet Jews over natives and most other immigrant groups is the unusually high number of women with professional and technical skills; 67 percent of Soviet Jewish women in the United States were engineers, technicians, or other kinds of professionals prior to immigration. In contrast, only 16.5 percent of American women work in these occupations. According to the 1990 U.S. Census, 29 percent of post-1965 Soviet émigré women in New York City and 26 percent of émigré women in Los Angeles County work as professionals in the United States.

Due to their high levels of training and skill, after an initial adjustment period Soviet Jews in the United States appear to be finding jobs and are earning a good living. One problem they confront, however, is an inability to reach their previous level of occupational prestige. For example, a study of New York's Soviet Jewish community found that while 66 percent had professional, technical, or managerial occupations in the USSR, only half of these, 33 percent, found similar jobs in the United States. Problems in finding appropriate American jobs for highly skilled Soviet Jews are related to their lacking job-related licenses and certification, their limited English-language skills, and the incompatibility between certain Soviet and American occupations. Data reveal that a large fraction of recent Soviet Jews are able to adapt to the U.S. economy by finding jobs in the skilled trades, bookkeeping and accounting, computer programming, and engineering.

Data from the 1990 U.S. Census suggest that a sizable fraction of Soviets are self-employed, including 15 percent in New York and 25 percent in Los Angeles. When compared to 1990 U.S. Census data for all groups, Soviet Jews are among those with the highest rates of self-employment. Former Soviets gravitate toward several enterprises, including engineering companies, restaurants, grocery stores, retail trade, construction, and real estate. In the 1980s, taxi companies in New York and Los Angeles included many Soviets, but émigrés often leave this risky enterprise after only a few years. While many Soviets are becoming self-employed, others are entering white-collar and professional occupations. This pattern is consistent with that revealed by other highly skilled, educated, and English-speaking migrant groups, such as Asian Indians and Filipinos. Finally, most of the elderly members of the Soviet Jewish émigré population do not share in the rapid economic adjustment experienced by the younger immigrants.

Resettlement and School Adjustment

Soviet Jews in the United States enjoy perhaps the most well-funded and professionally staffed resettlement system ever devoted to recent immigrants and refugees. Benefits provided by both government and religious agencies include housing, cash assistance, health care, job training and placement, language training, and recreational and religious programming. Nevertheless, émigrés still confront difficulties adjusting to the United States. Their major problems are learning English, finding jobs, earning enough money, and missing family and friends. Soviet émigrés (with the exception of the elderly) tend to make excellent progress with language. While about 50 percent spoke no English on arrival, within a few years upwards of two-thirds or more rate themselves as "good" (or better) in the English language, and a large proportion, 50 to 70 percent, have taken English classes.

School-age émigrés are generally well educated and tend to excel in U.S. schools. For example, in a 1991 comparison of the twelve largest immigrant groups in the New York City public schools in grades three to twelve and who had been in the country three years or less, students from the former USSR ranked first in reading scores, second in math, and fifth in English. Their reading and math scores were much higher than the average for all students in the New York schools, including the American-born students. In addition, the mean

Russian Jews participate in a religious service in North Hollywood, California. (Steven J. Gold)

increase in score over the previous year for the Soviet students was the highest of all groups in both reading and English and among the highest in math.

Social Organization

Soviet Jews have much informal and social interaction with each other. Their communities are often geographically concentrated, allowing the many aged émigrés to interact easily. Many ethnic businesses direct their goods and services to émigrés. Various Russian publications are available as well as Russian-language television and radio. While their communities are marked by divisions based on ideology, region of origin, occupation, and other factors, Jews from the former Soviet Union, especially the great majority from the European republics, bear many social similarities. They tend to be educated, urbanized, Russian-speaking, and share many common values. In contrast to generally liberal American Jews, former Soviets are politically conservative, and when naturalized join the Republican party. Émigrés rely on frequent interaction for both a social life and obtaining important information and resources. In contrast, because of the rather broad cultural and linguistic gap between émigrés and American Jews, Soviet Jews do not form a great number of close relations with American Jews or Gentiles.

In addition, Soviet Jewish émigrés generally avoid formal organizations, even among themselves, because they lack experience in creating voluntary associations and because in the USSR such entities were imposed by government bureaucrats rather than created voluntarily by members. According to reports on Soviet Jewish émigré organizations, the figure of the social activist acquired a permanent negative classification in the minds of many new immigrants. Reflecting this trend, studies on both coasts describe émigrés' difficulties in creating viable associations. Nevertheless, several associations organized on the basis of occupations, religion, cultural and leisure pursuits, political concerns, and veterans' interests have been created.

Jewish Identity and Behavior

Jewish identity is a complex issue for Soviet émigrés. While they have little formal Jewish education (only 4 percent had one year prior to immigration), many appear to have deep feelings of connectedness and strong ethnic identification as Jews. A major question involves the ways through which such sentiments are manifested in behavior. Perhaps due to their origins in the anti-Semitic USSR, Soviet émigrés maintain a private and personal approach to Judaism that does not lend itself to participation in organized Jewish activities. In general, Jewish identification among Soviet émigrés is secular rather than religious. In a national survey, sociologist Barry Kosmin found that more than 60 percent felt that the meaning of being Jewish in America was "cultural," while less than 30 percent felt it was "religious."

Despite their low levels of Jewish education, émigrés from the former Soviet Union are in various ways more "ethnic" (in terms of their involvement with coethnic persons, networks, and outlooks) than many American Jews. Soviet émigrés' strong ethnic ties are suggested by the responses to several questions in the 1990–1991 New York Jewish Population Study. For example, Jews from the former Soviet Union have higher rates of Yiddish competence, membership in Jewish community centers, and reading Jewish publications than all New York Jews and are much more likely to have close friends or immediate family living in Israel than all New York Jews, exceed all New York Jews by 30 percent in terms of the fraction asserting that most or all of their closest friends are Jewish, and much more strongly believe that when it comes to a crisis, Jews can only depend on other Jews. These measures suggest that despite Russian émigrés' lower rates of Jewish education and religiosity than American Jews, they are involved with other Jews in certain ways that exceed those of the general community.

While Soviet Jews generally dislike communism, many retain a feeling of attachment to the culture, language, cuisine, literature, landscape, and ways of life of their homeland and are unwill-

Soviet Jewish children sing at Chabad Day Camp in West Hollywood, California. (Steven J. Gold)

ing to abandon these traditions in favor of Americanisms. When Americans approach former Soviets with strident criticisms of Russia and clear expectations that they should forsake their background, émigrés are alienated. Consequently, just as many Russian Jews resisted American Jews' assimilation programs early in the twentieth century, so too do today's former Soviets often dislike Americanization activities intended for them.

Conclusion

The patterns of economic and social adaptation of Soviet Jewish émigrés appear to be fairly clear. Skilled, educated, and availed excellent services, émigrés have achieved an enviable economic record. While they learn English quickly, most prefer to interact among themselves in an informal context that emphasizes their Russian language and culture. Identifying as Jews, most are not highly religious but maintain certain forms of ethnic attachment to their community that exceed those of American Jews.

Accordingly, what remains to be seen is the degree to which these émigrés will become involved with Jewish life in the future, either on their own terms or in consort with the American Jewish community. While the general consensus regarding former Soviet Jews' communal and religious lives suggests that they are neither highly organized nor religiously involved, that image is beginning to be challenged as a number of reports reveal that groups of émigrés in various communities throughout the United States are creating organizations and becoming involved in Jewish life.

See also: JEWS, EUROPEAN; JEWS, HASIDIC; JEWS, ISRAELI; JEWS, MIDDLE EASTERN

Bibliography

Chiswick, B. (1993). "Soviet Jews in the United States: An Analysis of Their Linguistic and Economic Adjustment." *International Migration Review* 27(102): 260–285.

Gold, S. J. (1992). *Refugee Communities: A Comparative Field Study*. Newbury Park, CA: Sage Publications.

Gold, S. J. (1994). "Soviet Jews in the United States." *American Jewish Yearbook* 94:3–57.

Kochan, L., ed. (1978). *The Jews in Soviet Russia Since 1917*. London: Oxford University Press.

Kosmin, B. (1990). *The Class of 1979: The "Acculturation" of Jewish Immigrants from the Soviet Union*. New York: Council of Jewish Federations.

Markowitz, F. (1993). *A Community in Spite of Itself: Soviet Jewish Émigrés in New York*. Washington, DC: Smithsonian Institution Press.

Office of Refugee Resettlement. (1994). *Report to Congress: Refugee Resettlement Program*. Washington, DC: Author.

Orleck, A. (1987). "The Soviet Jews: Life in Brighton Beach, Brooklyn." In *New Immigrants in New York*, edited by N. Foner. New York: Columbia University Press.

Simon, R. J., ed. (1985). *New Lives: The Adjustment of Soviet Jewish Immigrants in the United States and Israel*. Lexington, MA: Lexington Books.

STEVEN J. GOLD

JORDANIANS

The Jordanian-American community is a subgroup of the Arab-American ethnic group. They share with each other a common culture and heritage. The Jordanian-American ethnic group in the United States is relatively small, estimated at fewer than 100,000 people. However, from a demographic point of view, it is difficult to give an accurate number of Jordanian Americans for the following reasons:

1. The 1990 U.S. Census did not create a separate ethnic/demographic identity for Jordanian Americans as a subgroup under the Arab Americans. Subidentities were created for Egyptians, Iraqis, Syrians, and Lebanese. The rest of the Arab-American groups were identified as "other Arab groups."

2. Many Palestinians entered the United States on a Jordanian passport, and demographers classified Jordanians and Palestinians under one category, "Palestinian/Jordanian." Therefore, it is difficult to estimate the number of immigrants from the East Bank of the Jordan (Jordanians) and those from the West Bank of the Jordan (Palestinians).

Jordanian immigrants are considered to be recent immigrants to the United States in comparison to other Arab-American groups such as Syrian Americans and Lebanese Americans (who began immigrating to the United States during the second half of the nineteenth century). The influx of the Jordanians, first in small number, began in the late 1940s and early 1950s. The trend to immigrate to the United States was accelerated during the 1960s as a result of wars that led to political and economic unrest in the region. Another factor that encouraged immigration was the pursuit of higher education.

The vast majority of Jordanian immigrants were better educated than other Arab immigrants who preceded them. In addition, the Jordanians were urban dwellers, whereas the earlier Arab immigrants had been rural dwellers.

Family and Kinship Network

The Jordanian-American family is a tightly knit social unit that defines roles and performs certain functions for its members. The norms and values the members of the Jordanian-American family acquire, through the process of socialization, define the relationships and obligations. Socialization as well as respect and support for parents are emphasized as part of the process of acculturation. Fathers head the households and hold authority. Such norms and values are reflected in the children's behavior toward their parents, grandparents, uncles, and aunts. This feeling is also reflected by the love and affection adults demonstrate toward their children. Younger siblings play subordinate roles to their elder brothers and sisters.

In most cases, elderly parents are incorporated into the family of one of their offspring. Putting an elderly parent in a nursing home is not acceptable. There are elderly parents who live alone, but in most cases they are in close proximity to their children and/or other relatives. Moreover, age does not present a barrier or discourage elderly people from participating in social and cultural events.

The Jordanian-American family stresses close contact with its members. This strength is reflected in the maintenance of ties and the frequency of social interaction between parents and their children, especially when they are not living together. The ethic of filial piety in Arab culture requires children not only to show respect but also to assume their duty toward their parents regardless of the burden. The Jordanian-American family places emphasis on the extended family and kinship network. Such emphasis affects the individual socialization, or self-identity, the feeling of belonging, and social interaction beyond the nuclear family and ethnic social network.

Children are taught to respect and care for parents, siblings, grandparents, uncles, and aunts and also to include others who are members of the extended family and social network. Such relationships are evident in the use of terms to address elderly people as "Uncle" or "Aunt," even sometimes if the person is not related by blood. This traditional pattern of behavior also reflects the sense of belonging among the members of the kin groups.

Marriage

Jordanian Americans are encouraged to marry within their ethnic and religious group, but there is less emphasis on this among educated and professional young people. However, even among the educated, families on both sides still provide the couple with advice, but they cannot enforce it. Similarities between groom and bride in the area of educational and socioeconomic backgrounds are major concerns for the family of the bride-to-be. They want to make sure that the man who will marry their daughter is economically capable of taking care of her. This concern surpasses the personal feeling that the couple might have for each other. The traditional cultural interpretation is that love develops and blossoms after marriage, not before.

In general, a Jordanian American tends to select a marriage partner from within the ethnic community. Sometimes the selection will extend to other Arab-American groups with the community. It is not unusual, however, for a young Jordanian-American man to travel to Jordan in search of a bride. Hence, marriage outside the Jordanian ethnic group is an exception to the rule. However, when such a marriage occurs, it usually is accepted by the two families, and typically the couple is integrated within both families.

Religious affiliation plays an important factor in mate selection among Jordanian Americans as well as among other Arab-American groups. It is not considered acceptable for a Christian to marry a Muslim unless the Christian converts to Islam. The conversion of a Muslim to Christianity to marry a Christian is unacceptable socially, culturally, and especially religiously. This applies to both men and women. Therefore, marriage across religious boundaries is not common, and whenever such marriage occurs it would be an exception to the rule. In most cases interreligious marriages, whenever they take place, would be based on civil contracts.

Free dating among Jordanian Americans, especially for young girls, is not usually permitted. Young girls may go out with other young people of both sexes and participate in various social, religious, and cultural activities as a group, but not as part of a single couple. Many parents believe that young people do not behave rationally while on a date. They maintain that the possibility of the young couple having sexual intercourse, when alone, is not uncommon. Jordanian Americans as well as Arab Americans in general proscribe premarital sexual intercourse, especially in the case of young girls.

The concept of single parenthood is disallowed among Jordanian Americans. Single parenthood resulting from an illicit relationship would bring dishonor and shame to the woman and her family. Young men, however, are not subject to the same social rules. Men have the freedom to go out and date girls who are not ethnically affiliated with the Jordanian community.

The responsibility of planning and arranging for a wedding is shared by the couple and by both their families. However, the wedding expense is solely the responsibility of the groom and his family. This is the usual custom in the Arab world and has been carried over by the different Arab-American groups who have immigrated to the United States.

Divorce among Jordanian Americans is rare. It is not acceptable socially, culturally, or religiously. Marriage is viewed as a lifelong contract. When conflicts and problems occur between a married couple, parents and relatives on both sides of the family intervene to reconcile the couple, especially if the couple has children. It is believed that the couple should resolve their problems for the sake of the children.

Religious Beliefs

In the United States the majority of Arab Americans, including the Jordanian-American community, adhere to the Christian faith. This reflects the opposite demographic composition in the Arab world, where 90 percent of the population adheres to the Islamic faith.

The majority of the early Arabs immigrating to the United States were from Lebanon and Syria and were Christians. In the second half of the twentieth century the number of Arab-American immigrants adhering to Islam began to rise. However, despite their increase in numbers, Muslim Arab Americans are still a minority. The same rationale is reflected within the Jordanian-American community, where the majority are Christians. Approximately 8 percent of Jordanian Americans are Muslims.

The Jordanian-American Christians belong to different interdenominational churches. The ma-jority belong to the Greek Orthodox Church. Those in the second-largest group belong to the Roman Catholic Church. The remainder belong to various Protestant and evangelical churches.

The Jordanian-American Christians and Muslims share their places of worship with other Arab-American groups of the same religious denomination. They participate with other Arab Americans in the celebration of religious festivities, and in social and cultural events. Religious institutions such as churches and mosques play an important role in the life of Arab Americans in general and Jordanian Americans in particular. These institutions provide group identity and serve as mechanisms to maintain traditional culture.

Education and Occupation

Education is a principal focus of Jordanian-American families. They inculcate their children with the value and importance of succeeding in education. Parents usually are deeply involved in their children's education. They maintain close links with schools to reinforce the importance of education to their children. This is found among parents who are educated as well as those who are illiterate or semiliterate. It is seen that success in education would not only reflect the children's achievements but also would bring prestige to the parents and kin groups.

The number of Jordanians with college degrees, in various academic fields, is relatively high in comparison to other Arab-American groups in the United States. Among other factors that have contributed to a high percentage of college graduates among Jordanian Americans is the fact that many Jordanians who entered the United States to pursue higher education have decided to settle in the United States.

Jordanian Americans occupy various professional fields: academia, medicine, engineering, and business. A large number of Jordanian Americans are engaged in different types of business activities and many are self-employed.

There is no marked difference between genders in terms of education and employment, especially among the younger generation. However, it is not uncommon for young women to quit working after having children in order to take care of the children. If the mother or mother-in-law is living with the couple, she will assume the role of caring for the young. In such cases the young mother will continue to work.

Residential Location

Jordanian Americans, like other Arab Americans, live in communities and neighborhoods where there are other members of their ethnic group. This trend is very important among newcomers. The new immigrants locate near relatives and friends they knew from their country of origin and who will help them in their initial adjustment. Within such neighborhoods there are various social, cultural, and religious institutions and business outlets designed to provide ethnic food and services. Each of these neighborhoods reflects the socioeconomic status of the people who live there.

Highly educated and successful businesspeople usually are dispersed in suburban neighborhoods in metropolitan areas of the United States. Even in such locations, one sees a cluster of families and friends residing not too far from each other. The proximity of the residential location is important because it enhances the frequency of social interaction among relatives and friends. The regularity and frequency of social interaction among Jordanian Americans and Arab Americans in general is very important and in many respects reflects traditional cultural continuity.

Language Use and Affiliation

Arabic is the national language of all Arab Americans who emigrated from the Arab world. However, various Arab-American groups have different dialects, such as the Jordanian, Egyptian, and Lebanese dialects. Jordanian Americans, like other Arab-American groups, continue to preserve at least the spoken version of the language during the process of socialization.

Since the 1960s, the number of people in the United States who speak fluent Arabic has increased, and there is a larger social context within which it is appropriate to speak Arabic. This is leading to a revival of Arab-American identity, which is reflected in the increasing use of the Arabic language. Other social and political factors also have contributed to the maintenance and continuity of the Arabic language in the United States. The impact of the civil rights movement led to the introduction of new federal legislation prohibiting racial and ethnic discrimination. This same movement led to the understanding that American society is a pluralistic one, reflecting the diversity of its cultural composition. It enhanced the rise of ethnic identity, which in turn is reflected in the maintenance of the Arabic language. The emphasis on maintaining the language increases when the parents are well educated and especially when the mother speaks Arabic. Recently there has been an increase in the teaching of Arabic within the Jordanian-American community and other Arab communities. This reflects a growing interest in the preservation of Arabic and its use as an intragroup and intergroup language with first-language status.

Death and Rites of Passage

For both Christians and Muslims within the Jordanian-American community, there is belief in an afterlife, where the deceased persons will be judged by God and will be either rewarded or punished according to their deeds and actions while they were living.

Funeral rites in the United States reflect basic changes when compared to the traditional funeral ritual in the Arab world, where the deceased person is usually buried within twenty-four hours. An Arabic common saying is, "Quick burial bestows honor and dignity on the deceased person." Burial rituals among the Christian and Muslim Jordanian Americans in the United States reflect an adaptation to the American rite of passage. The deceased person is sent to a funeral home instead of being kept at home to be prepared for burial.

Jordanians participate in the performance of a traditional dance at an Arab-American social gathering. (Hani Fakhouri)

The body of the deceased is put on display for a number of days for friends and relatives to pay their last respects and extend their condolences to the deceased person's family. Muslims, however, do not display the body of the deceased.

Friends and relatives send food to the home of the dead person's family every day while the deceased is still in the funeral home. This might last from two to four days. On burial day, participants in the funeral rituals are invited by the family of the deceased to share a meal in the person's memory. After the burial, friends and relatives go to the home of the deceased to express their condolences again and to extend their moral support to the family. Such rituals will continue for several days; the duration depends on the social status of the deceased and his or her family. The rite of passage among Jordanian Americans reflects group or community collective effort.

Assimilation and Cultural Adaptation

Since Jordanian Americans are recent immigrants to the United States in comparison to the Syrian and Lebanese Americans, the Jordanians are considered the least assimilated group. The majority of Jordanian Americans are of the first or second generation. Therefore, the process of acculturation is not deeply rooted but is progressing at a slow pace and at different rates with different people.

A number of factors have affected the process of acculturation. Since many newcomers from Jordan are sponsored by a kin member or friend, the newcomers usually are met and assisted in locating in a neighborhood close to their relatives. Such neighborhoods usually are close to the various social, religious, and commercial outlets that provide a broad range of services to the newcomers. Initially such neighborhoods serve as a traditional zone for newcomers as well as a primary-group social network. In such settings people interact and communicate in their own dialect with other Jordanians and/or other Arab Americans. This type of arrangement minimizes physical and social disruption to the traditional lives of the newcomers; it also supports the continuity of Jordanian cultural traditions and minimizes the impact of acculturation.

The ability of the newcomer to speak and communicate in English has a bearing on the process of acculturation. Those who are fluent in English are better able to interact with members of the dominant group at work or in social settings. Therefore, the ability to communicate expediates acculturation.

The educational and economic background of the individual Jordanian immigrant also has a bearing on acculturation. The higher the educational attainment of the immigrant, the faster the process of adaptation to American life. This also will affect the children, who usually are influenced by the process of acculturation at a more rapid rate than their parents. The nature of the individual immigrant's occupation is important in assimilation. Daily contact with members of the dominant group facilitates acculturation. In addition, the environmental background of the Jordanian immigrant is a pivotal role in acculturation. For example, those who came from an urban background and were already exposed to many features of Western life adjust much more quickly than those who came from a rural background.

The impact of participating in expressive social, religious, and cultural events contributes to the continuity of the traditional culture. These events are organized and sponsored by churches, mosques, and cultural organizations. Musical performances, singing and dancing, and a variety of art performances take place regularly within the Arab-American community. Jordanian Americans participate in such cultural events. Quite frequently singers, dancers, and musicians who are well known in the Arab world perform in the United States for Arab-American groups. Such events contribute to the continuity of Arab traditional culture in the United States.

The mass media also have a role in the life of Jordanian and Arab Americans. Several national Arabic newspapers are published in the United States and are available to readers in the Arab-American community. Arabic radio and television programs, especially the latter, are available through cable networks in many metropolitan communities in the United States. A variety of Arabic programs and Arabic movies are shown daily. All these events foster continuity of the traditional culture, especially among first-generation immigrants.

The rise of political consciousness and awareness of ethnic rights and identity have played a role in the maintenance and continuity of the traditional culture. Most Jordanian immigrants arrived in the United States at a time of drastic changes in the area of human rights. The Jordanian-American political and cultural environment was greatly influenced by the U.S. civil rights movement during the latter 1950s and 1960s. The passage of sweeping federal laws prohibiting discrimination against minorities reflected the fact that American society is a "pluralistic one with multiculturalism."

The emphasis on cultural diversity has created a new political and social atmosphere for all minority groups in the United States. The traditional approach, to assimilate, has begun to evaporate. In addition, new immigrants are urged to be proud of their ethnicity, culture, and traditions as well as their contributions to American life. The recognition of ethnic subcultures as part of the American national culture has contributed to the rise of ethnic identity and political consciousness among Jordanian-American as well as other Arab-American groups, who have joined various political, social, and cultural organizations and have begun to participate in politics at both the state and national levels. This participation reflects the acculturation of Jordanian Americans into the wider social and political system of the United States.

See also: PALESTINIANS

Bibliography

Abraham, S. Y., and Abraham, N., eds. (1983). *Arabs in the New World.* Detroit: Center for Urban Studies, Wayne State University.

Alldredge, E. (1984). "Child-Rearing Practices in the Homes of Arab Immigrants: A Study of Ethnic Persistence." Ph.D. diss., Michigan State University.

Aswad, B. (1988). "The Lebanese Community in Dearborn, Michigan." In *A Century of Lebanese Emigration,* edited by N. Shahadi. London: Taurus Press.

Aswad, B., ed. (1974). *Arabic-Speaking Communities in American Cities.* New York: Center for Migration Studies.

Elkholy, A. (1981). "The Arab-American Family." In *Ethnic Families in America: Patterns and Variations,* 2nd edition, edited by C. H. Mindel and R. W. Habensten. Amsterdam: Elsevier, North-Holland.

Hooglund, E. J., ed. (1987). *Crossing the Waters.* Washington, DC: Smithsonian Institution Press.

Jaafari, L. I. (1973). "The Brain Drain to the United States: The Migration of Jordanian and Palestinian Professionals and Students." *Journal of Palestine Studies* 3:119–131.

Naff, A. (1985). *Becoming American: The Early Arab Immigrant Experience.* Carbondale: Southern Illinois University Press.

Nigem, E. T. (1986). "Arab Americans: Migration, Socioeconomic and Demographic Characteristics." *International Migration Review* 20:629–645.

Sawaie, M., and Fishman, J. A. (1985–1986). "Arabic-Language Maintenance Efforts in the United States." *Journal of Ethnic Studies* 13:33–49.

Scott, W. A., and Scott, R. (1989). *Adaptation of Immigrants.* New York: Pergamon.

Sinai, A., and Pollack, A. (1977). *The Hashemite Kingdom of Jordan and the West Bank.* New York: American Academic Association for Peace in the Middle East.

HANI FAKHOURI

BLOOMINGTON PUBLIC LIBRARY

A11904 962024

DISCARD